Writing Women in
Late Imperial China

Writing Women in
Late Imperial China

Ellen Widmer

Kang-i Sun Chang

Editors

Stanford University Press
Stanford, California

Stanford University Press
Stanford, California
© 1997 by the Board of Trustees of the
Leland Stanford Junior University

Printed in the United States of America

CIP data appear at the end of the book

Publication of this book was underwritten in
part by a grant from the Chiang Ching-kuo
Foundation for International Scholarly Exchange (USA).

To the writing women of China, past and present

Acknowledgments

The genesis of this volume is best described in terms of the conference for which the papers were written. Entitled "Women and Literature in Ming-Qing China," it was generously funded through several stages of development by the American Council of Learned Societies, the National Endowment for the Humanities, the Chiang Ching-kuo Foundation, and the Wu Foundation. It owes much as well to the hospitality of Yale University, whose staff, faculty, library, and students expended considerable energy and extended many kindnesses before, during, and after five days of meetings in June 1993. In particular, we would like to thank Sharon Sanderson, Senior Administrative Assistant to the Department of East Asian Languages and Literatures, Dr. Wen-k'ai Kung of the East Asian Collection, Sterling Memorial Library, Associate Provost Arline McCord, the Office of Grants and Contracts, and Conference Services. We also owe much to the graduate students who tended to local arrangements and translation: Mark Borer, Tek-wah King, Mary Ellen Friends, Ch'iu-ti Judy Liu, Xinmin Liu, and Chi-hung Yim; and we give special thanks to Mary Ellen Friends for designing the conference poster. As the Chair of the Council on East Asian Studies at the time the conference took place, Jonathan Spence, too, deserves our special gratitude.

The editors of the current volume were the principal organizers of the conference. The conference planning committee consisted, in addition, of Pei-kai Cheng, Charlotte Furth, Perry Link, Susan Mann, and Pauline Yu, who gave very generously of their time. Perry Link was replaced by Maureen Robertson on a second committee that oversaw the planning of the volume. None of these scholars should be blamed for the shape of its final version, however, which is the responsibility of the two editors.

In addition to those whose contributions are included in this volume, the conference benefited significantly from the other participants in the program. These included Chang Ching-erh, Pei-kai Cheng, Patricia Ebrey, Charlotte Furth, Valerie Hansen, Hsiung Ping-chen, Kang Zhengguo, Lin Mei-yi, Shuen-fu Lin, Susan Mann, Susan Naquin, Jonathan Spence, Su Zhecong, Catherine Swatek, Yenna Wu, Xu Shuofang, Ye Changhai, Yeh Chia-ying, Chun-fang Yu, Anthony Yu, Pauline Yu, and Yue Daiyun. Mention should also be made of the many others who sat in on our meetings, some coming from as far away as France, China, Japan, and New Zealand to join us. As expected, there was a strong and enthusiastic representation from New York and New England and vicinity, and from elsewhere in the United States and Canada. The liveliness of the conference derived in large measure from this wide and varied audience, which enhanced the exchange of views.

A selection of some papers presented in Chinese at the conference may be found in the Summer 1994 issue of *Jiuzhou xuekan* (Chinese culture quarterly; 6, no. 2), under the editorship of Pei-kai Cheng. The editors are most grateful for the sensitive and knowledgeable guidance of the editorial staff of Stanford University Press, John Ziemer in particular.

E.W.
K.S.C.

Contents

Contributors

Nancy Armstrong is Nancy Duke Lewis Professor of Comparative Literature, English, and Modern Culture and Media at Brown University. Books to her credit include *Desire and Domestic Fiction: A Political History of the Novel* (Oxford, 1987), with Leonard Tennenhouse, *The Imaginary Puritan: Literature, Intellectual Labor and the Origins of Personal Life* (University of California Press, 1992), and *Things Seen and Obscene: The Visuality of Victorian Culture* (Harvard, forthcoming). She has also edited two collections with Leonard Tennenhouse: *The Ideology of Conduct: Literature and the History of Sexuality* (Routledge, 1986) and *The Ideology of Violence: Literature and the History of Violence* (Routledge, 1989).

Katherine Carlitz is adjunct faculty in the Asian Studies Program at the University of Pittsburgh. She is the author of *The Rhetoric of "Chin p'ing mei"* (Indiana, 1986) and has published articles on Ming dynasty vernacular literature and on the late imperial Chinese cult of women's virtue.

Kang-i Sun Chang received her Ph.D. degree from Princeton University and is now Professor of Chinese Literature at Yale University. Her scholarly publications include *The Evolution of Chinese Tz'u Poetry* (Princeton, 1980), *Six Dynasties Poetry* (Princeton, 1986), and *The Late Ming Poet Ch'en Tzu-lung: Crises of Love and Loyalism* (Yale, 1991). She is also the compiler and co-editor (with Haun Saussy) of *Chinese Women*

Poets: An Anthology of Poetry and Criticism from Ancient Times to 1911 (Stanford, forthcoming).

Grace S. Fong is Associate Professor of Chinese at McGill University. She is the author of *Wu Wenying and the Art of Southern Song Ci Poetry* (Princeton,1987), and her recent publications include "Inscribing Desire: Zhu Yizun's Love Lyrics in *Jingzhi ju qinqu,*" in the *Harvard Journal of Asiatic Studies* (54, no. 2, 1994). Her current research focuses on critical issues in the interaction between gender and genre in classical Chinese poetry and in women's writings in late imperial China.

Dorothy Ko is working on a history of Chinese costumes and the concept of fashion, part of her quest for the meanings of footbinding in premodern Chinese eyes. Her earlier book, *Teachers of the Inner Chambers* (Stanford, 1994), is a study of women and the written word in the seventeenth century. She is Associate Professor of History and Women's Studies at Rutgers University.

Wai-yee Li is Associate Professor of Chinese Literature at Princeton University. She is the author of *Enchantment and Disenchantment: Love and Illusion in Chinese Literature* (Princeton, 1993). She is writing a book entitled *The Readability of the Past in Classical Chinese Literature* (Stanford, forthcoming).

Yasushi Ōki is an Associate Professor at the University of Tokyo. His specialty is Chinese Literature. He is the author of "A Study of Printing Culture in the Jiangnan District in Late Ming China" ("Minmatsu Kōnan ni okeru shuppan bunka no kenkyū") in *Hiroshima daigaku bungakubu kiyō* (50, special issue 1, 1991), and *Feng Menglong and Suzhou Culture: A Unique Intellectual in Late Ming China* (*Minmatsu no hagure chishikijin: Fū Muryū to Soshū bunka*, Kōdansha, 1995).

Maureen Robertson is Associate Professor in the Department of Asian Languages and Literature and in the Program in Comparative Literature at the University of Iowa. She has published articles on Chinese poetry and Chinese literary theory and criticism, as well as translations from Chinese, French, and Spanish. She is completing a book on Chinese poetry written by women before the twentieth century.

Paul S. Ropp is Professor of History at Clark University. Author of *Dissent in Early Modern China* (Michigan, 1981) and editor of *Heritage of China* (California, 1990), he is currently at work on a study of the eighteenth-century literatus Shi Zhenlin and the peasant woman poet Shuangqing.

Haun Saussy is Associate Professor in the Departments of Asian Languages and of Comparative Literature at Stanford. He is the author of *The Problem of a Chinese Aesthetic* (Stanford, 1993) and co-editor, with Kang-i Sun Chang, of *Chinese Women Poets: An Anthology of Poetry and Criticism from Ancient Times to 1911* (Stanford, forthcoming).

Ann Waltner is Associate Professor of History at the University of Minnesota. She is one of the editors, along with Mary Jo Maynes, Brigitte Soland, and Ulrike Strasser, of *Gender, Kinship, Power: A Comparative and Interdisciplinary History* (Routledge, 1996); with Edward Farmer and Romeyn Taylor, of *Ming History: An Introductory Guide to Research* (Ming Studies Monograph Series, 1994); and the author of *Getting an Heir: Adoption and the Construction of Kinship in Late Imperial China* (Hawaii, 1990). She is the author of numerous articles on gender, kinship, and religion in Chinese society.

Ellen Widmer is Professor of Asian Languages and Literatures at Wesleyan University. She is the author of *The Margins of Utopia: "Shui-hu hou-chuan" and the Literature of Ming Loyalism* (Harvard, 1987) and co-editor, with David Wang, of *From May Fourth to June Fourth: Fiction and Film in Twentieth-Century China* (Harvard, 1993). She is currently at work on a book about women and fiction in late imperial China.

Wu Hung is Harrie Vanderstappen Distinguished Service Professor in Chinese Art at the University of Chicago. His book *The Wu Liang Shrine: The Ideology of Early Chinese Pictorial Art* (Stanford, 1989), won the 1990 Joseph Levenson Prize for the best book in Chinese studies (traditional). His most recent publications include *Monumentality in Early Chinese Art and Architecture* (Stanford, 1995) and *The Double Screen: Medium and Representation in Chinese Painting* (Reaktion and Chicago, 1996).

Judith T. Zeitlin is Associate Professor of Chinese Literature at the University of Chicago. The author of *Historian of the Strange: Pu Songling and the Chinese Classical Tale* (Stanford, 1993), she is currently at work on a book-length study of ghosts, writing, and representation in late imperial China.

Introduction

ELLEN WIDMER

This volume is the fruit of an international conference that took place at Yale University in June 1993.[1] Gender studies were a major incentive for this meeting, which was further motivated by research in the rich archives of little or never-studied materials that this methodology brings into view. Whether the authors in this volume came to their subjects through history, literature, or art history, their work testifies to the powerful impact of this combination of new methods and fresh materials on studies of China around the world.

The title *Writing Women in Late Imperial China* leads us into the vagaries of historical accounting. The term "late imperial China" is a fairly recent one in the study of China. It harks back to, yet supplants, an earlier vision — of a China mired in stagnation, one that only began to modernize in response to Western invasion. Now widely used, it refers broadly to the last two dynasties, the Ming (1368–1644), when Chinese ruled themselves, and the Qing (1644–1911), when the country was conquered by Manchus, the "barbarian" neighbors to the north, who continued most of the institutions of Ming rule. In its narrower application, the term implies "a more organic periodization than a dynastic framework easily allows."[2] Here it encompasses an era that began in the late Ming, perhaps around 1550, when a combination of economic stimuli prompted an expansion of commerce and an increase in urbanization, publishing, courtesan culture, and other luxury trades. Although scholars have yet to agree on the relationship between these developments and Euro-American capitalism, their influence continued in fits and starts until the last days of the Qing. "Late imperial China," then, demarcates a highly dynamic period in Chinese history. It is one of the most actively researched areas in the China field.

As for "writing women," scholarship of the past ten years has only just begun to document their role in this lively period. Interest has focused on two groups of women—the high-level courtesans, whose wit and style enlivened urban culture during the late Ming in particular; and the cloistered women of established families, who had begun to read and write at home. Both groups included some women whose literacy went well beyond an elementary ability to read. The great courtesans could match wits with highly literate male patrons, and the cloistered gentry woman might find herself striving for a new cultural ideal, the "companionate marriage," one that involved intellectual sharing, although their companionate husbands would still have been free to bring concubines into their households and to form liaisons outside the home.

Both types of women, moreover, participated in poetry exchanges with their peers, probably the most important stimulus to the many collections of women's poetry that survive. Only rarely did courtesans exchange poetry with gentry women; the exceptions were the few that had married into gentry families as concubines. Poetry societies were an important form of recreation and intellectual development for gentry women from the late Ming. Such societies might consist only of family members, but they could cover a large area, for in parts of China (especially the Yangtze delta area, known as Jiangnan), transportation was highly developed and literary ties between close companions could be continued after a woman married and left home. Moreover, the rapid development of the publishing industry from the mid-sixteenth century became a forcing ground for new cultural models. One immediate consequence was that women who had never met might see one another's poems and so become friends. In other words, women could now aspire to a literary reputation. Painting became a similar avenue of communication. It was a means of expressing affection, and—unlike music, chess, and other arts and pastimes practiced by women— it created artifacts that could be circulated and exchanged. Indeed poems and paintings were often composed together, as parts of a single whole. The emphasis on writing in the present volume is explained in part by the greater survival rate of written records, as well as by the training of most of the contributors, but it should be remembered that the "writing women" of the title represents only one talent of the women concerned.

From what we know of the publication of women's writing in this era, it was largely paid for and hence controlled by their families. Only occasionally did commercial publishers bring out the works of women. Sometimes, too, women had to sell their poems and paintings in exchange for bare necessities. Whether a poem was sold, sent to a friend, or produced only for the amusement of the author, unless it was written on a painting or preserved in some collection, it was unlikely to survive.

A typical collection consists of poetry in several genres and sometimes letters and other writings in classical prose. The collected works of individuals constitute the largest category of surviving titles. Some women published their work together with family members or groups of friends. There are also anthologies in various forms. In addition, a handful of plays and long narrative tales in verse (known as *tanci*) written by women survive.

Equally germane to this volume are the works by men *about* the new "writing woman." These began appearing in the second half of the sixteenth century. Some of them take the lives of actual women as their subjects, some build on fantasies common among writing women, some use the conceit of feminine authorship, and some even crib from writings by the author's female relatives and friends. As males, the authors were classically educated and had prepared for the series of examinations leading to official careers. When they write on women, however, they tend to present themselves as alienated from such ambitions and to emphasize feeling as opposed to erudition. Even so, their works often became vehicles to fame, if not fortune. Past scholarship focused largely on these works *on* women. By contrast, works by Chinese women of the period are only now beginning to be taken seriously in the academic world. The delayed reaction is not simply a matter of changing literary tastes. It reflects a shift in the ways this material and the women who produced it have been viewed over the past century.

"Late imperial China" formally ended with the fall of the Qing dynasty in 1911, although signs of impending disaster had been manifest long before. To China's earliest literary "modernizers" — from the late Qing reformer Liang Qichao to those of the May Fourth era (approximately 1915–27) in particular — the rich corpus of writings by

Ming-Qing women was largely irrelevant. Predominantly young, male, and educated under a new system, they were intent on their nation's future. They offered a picture of a benighted past from which China and Chinese culture were about to be rescued through their efforts. Although they might hail certain traditional works that exposed the ills of the old order, especially novels like *Hong lou meng* (Dream of the red chamber, first published in 1792), the writings of traditional women held little interest for them. They vowed to do away with prostitution, concubinage, and cloistered wifehood, the very context from which late imperial poetry by women had emerged. In addition, their view of fiction as the essential modern genre disposed them to ignore the writings of women, which were mainly in other genres. In addition, women's writings tended to be dismissed as vanity publishing, and the May Fourth movement prided itself on liberating womanhood and bringing women writers to the fore for the first time.

To another, less dominant group of early twentieth-century writers, however, the literature of Ming and Qing women represented an important cultural heritage. They acknowledged that this writing was being supplanted by more modern types of expression, but they sought to collect, edit, and republish it. Mostly women, occasionally the descendants of famous women, they viewed it as a precious relic of past times. They updated some of the great Qing anthologies to incorporate newer writings, brought out new collections published by family presses, and reissued earlier anthologies and sets of individual writings. Meanwhile, women's writings in the old styles continued to be produced until 1949. Their efforts were complemented by more mainstream undertakings, some by leading male scholars, such as the historian Chen Yinke, who devoted much of his talent to sustained studies of a few individual women, and the literary historian Hu Wenkai, whose bibliography of traditional women's writings was begun in the 1940's and first published in 1957.

Building on these efforts, late twentieth-century scholars — the authors represented in this volume, but many others as well — have begun to approach Ming-Qing women with a third set of attitudes. Their emphasis is on recovering the works and lives of women under the old order from the oblivion into which they lapsed during the May Fourth movement. Of equal interest have been the circumstances that led male writers to use feminine voices in certain of their writings during the Ming and Qing.

The study of women, and gender studies in general, is provoking a major rethinking in other fields covering the same period. This is due partly to gender studies unconnected to China and partly to the conviction that China has particular significance, because of the large, well catalogued fund of source materials. Especially since the publication of a widely available revised edition of Hu Wenkai's catalogue in 1985, the possibility of a considerable expansion of these studies has existed. The present volume is an early witness to this possibility.[3]

One result of these studies has been the exposure of contrasts and contradictions among the primary materials from this period. This is not simply because the application of contemporary methods of analysis to a static traditional field inevitably leads to new insights. It is also because the "writing woman" herself has been controversial since her own time and subject to myriad reinterpretations. The consideration of such conflicts combined with a new analysis offers hope for more sophisticated conclusions.

Feminine virtue is one avenue of approach. A number of traditional anthologists subjected women to evaluation on the basis of virtue rather than literary talent, relegating courtesans to the back of their books, demoting wives who had married more than once, and so forth. The late Ming poet Wu Qi is a case in point. In her day, she was ranked among the top female poets in anthologies by male writers and became a celebrity among other women, to the extent that she was called upon to write prefaces to poetry collections. However, in Wang Duanshu's *Mingyuan shiwei* (Classics of poetry by famous women) of 1667, one of the first major anthologies edited by a woman, she was assigned to the category of the less than completely virtuous, possibly because she remarried after her first husband's death.[4] This meant that she ranked artistically toward the middle. Under the different ethical system of the twentieth century, Hu Wenkai called attention to Wu Qi's former prominence and issued a new collection of her writings.[5]

Promotion as well as demotion was possible in the rankings of virtue. The late Ming courtesan-poet Li Yin (1616–85) is an example of promotion. In her early days, her name was linked with those of Liu Rushi and Wang Wei, as one of a trio of exceptionally famous courtesans. All three eventually married into gentry families; in Li's case she became the concubine of Ge Zhengqi. Like many other Ming loyalists, Ge committed suicide in 1645. Li lived out many years of celibacy as a widow, seeking solace in art, literature, and religion and leaving behind a group of loyalist poems. By doing so, she came to symbolize moral purity to later generations as well as her own. Eventually her reputation transcended her earlier association with courtesans. She began to take part in the poetry and painting societies of gentry wives, and contemporary anthologies, including at least one edited by a gentry woman, ranked her as a virtuous wife.[6] Even by the standards of Yun Zhu's rather starchy *Guochao guixiu zhengshi ji* (Collected correct beginnings of gentlewomen of the dynasty) of 1831, Li takes her place as a virtuous wife near the beginning of the book, whereas Liu Rushi and Wang Wei (both of whom also married into gentry families) appear in a section devoted to courtesans at the end.[7] But for a biography of Li by Huang Zongxi (1610–95), an outstanding scholar in a society that venerated scholars, her past might have faded from view altogether.[8]

Li's changing fortunes point to another major tendency in the historiography of late Ming and early Qing women writers, the high premium placed on those who remained loyal to the Ming. Given the widespread ambivalence about the Manchu conquest among Ming supporters, it is unlikely that every woman writer of the period was a Ming loyalist. Today, however, following a sifting process that began under the Qing, all the major women figures of this era appear to be associated with the loyalist cause. This is true whether they are gentry wives (such as Shang Jinglan, whose husband was another loyalist suicide) or former courtesans like Liu Rushi, who was linked to various loyalists. In this calculus of loyalty, courtesans often outshone their gentry counterparts, not because they tended to live more colorful lives, but because, as public women, they were in a better position to represent the nation as a whole. It is no accident that the fortunes of the late Ming courtesan Li Xiangjun are immortalized in *Peach Blossom Fan*, Kong Shangren's famous drama about Ming loyalism and accommodation, which appeared in 1699.

The upheavals of the early twentieth century have left few if any adherents of wifely seclusion and other traditional virtues, but they have had a more complicated effect on the reputation of loyalist women, especially loyalist courtesans like Li Xiangjun and Liu Rushi. To the May Fourth modernizers, the word "courtesan" was equated with prostitution and denounced as a national shame. Yet from another angle, the loyalist courtesans of the mid-seventeenth century were inspiring because of their principled last stand against the invaders or their untrammeled pursuit of love. Evidence of such views is already visible in the early nineteenth-century wave of nostalgia for the late Ming, and they seem not to have died out since that time. For much of the twentieth century, admirers of courtesans reversed the negative judgment of May Fourth modernizers. They looked back to a China free of Western influence, one in which loyalist women (and their male companions) took a forthright stand. The strength of the urge to extol loyalist womanhood makes it difficult to debunk the exaggerations in this picture or to gain a nuanced sense of how women negotiated the moral straits of their time.

Not every chapter in this volume is concerned with historical accounting, nor is every one engaged with loyalism, chastity, and other traditional measures of right and wrong. With a rich arsenal of contemporary methods at their disposal, the authors in this volume present new readings of traditionally acclaimed masterpieces and formulate questions that break new ground. Issues of voice and representation are among the most central questions to this series of studies, and not only because long dead late imperial women have been reborn in such a variety of interpretive contexts. Questions about their various interpreters, male and female, also demand attention. For example, the issue of what "woman" meant to a specific male interpreter can be phrased in terms of his historical circumstances, but it also takes shape on a more artistic plane. These include the devices and conventions by which a woman is called up narratively — séances, dream,s and lapidary narrators being some of the possibilities in China — and the source of the illusion that she then steps out of the printed page. The other side of this coin is the struggle of women to "produce themselves" in poetry and painting, using language and symbolism originally designed for other ends. There is no doubt that the questions posed in this volume are shaped by, and can be couched in terms of, contemporary literary discourse; yet they would not have been altogether alien to late imperial writers themselves. *The Dream of the Red Chamber* turns on its own version of such questions, although it phrases them differently. Moreover, poetry by Ming and Qing women shows that self-invention could be a conscious process and that female authors adjusted their self-portraits when they moved from genre to genre.

Part I of this volume, "Writing the Courtesan," has two subjects: the courtesan herself and the men who wrote about courtesans. It begins with Paul Ropp's historical overview of the different types of courtesan imagery found in Ming and Qing writings and his effort to account for ambiguities in this imagery, as well as variations over time. He calls attention to the symbiosis linking courtesans to their chroniclers, the "male voyeurs," whose self-images are linked to those of the courtesans they describe.

Wai-yee Li addresses similar questions but focuses on the paradox that seemingly marginal courtesans could have performed the role of "cultural ideal" from the early Qing dynasty. She shows a link between idealization and self-invention, suggesting that the appeal of these women to their male admirers lay in their ability to rise above humiliation and create new destinies for themselves. Self-invention is also linked to the "invention of another" through which literati created images of courtesans throughout the Qing.

Dorothy Ko, in contrast, begins with the courtesan's "aura" but goes on to explore the "vulgarization," or degeneration, of this aura, starting in the nineteenth century and demonstrated by commentary about bound feet in guides to the courtesans' quarters and other literature about them. She links the courtesan's fate to other variables: the shabbier her appearance in literary descriptions, the less elegant her male chronicler and the closer the dynasty to its final decline. Her chapter also explores the range of relationships between gentry women and courtesans, which included friendship, mutual imitation, and enforced separation.

Katherine Carlitz's analysis of a late Ming drama, Chen Yujiao's *Parrot Island*, presents a close-up picture of relations among courtesan, faithful wife, and literatus at this time. Carlitz is interested in how wife (or wife-like concubine) and courtesan are perceived by male observers and the threats to a man's reputation that arise when he focuses too much attention on women of either kind. To an extent, her chapter is about symbols, particularly the way in which the courtesan/wife dichotomy translates into a system of checks and balances between expressions of romantic feeling and their control. In addition, she calls attention to the way gentry women readers might have responded to images of the less conventionally respectable women in this play. The ostensible lessons of *Parrot Island* do not force the gentry woman to reject the figure of the courtesan outright, although it was clear that gentry women and courtesans were supposed to inhabit separate worlds.

Yasushi Ōki, similarly, focuses on a single work of late Ming literature, in this case a collection of poems known as *Mountain Songs*, edited during the early seventeenth century by the famed (though unconventional) man of letters, Feng Menglong (1574–1646). Ōki organizes his paper as a problem: how to account for the surprising sexual frankness of the poems, which put them at odds with the standard Confucian literature of Feng's day. After tracing the evolution of the "mountain song" from its origins in folk literature, through a phase in which such songs were sung by courtesan-entertainers in the city, to its final stage as a model for literati authors, Ōki accounts for Feng's interest in these fresh materials as a way of escaping tired clichés.

Part II, "Norms and Selves," juxtaposes a pair of essays, one on Ming-Qing anthologies of women's poetry, whose editors included both literati and gentry women, and one on the gentry women poets whose work was the mainstay of those anthologies. From this perspective the courtesan figures as an outsider, who was rarely if ever allowed to set standards for other women and who did not lead poetry societies within the home.

Kang-i Sun Chang writes about the anthologies of the Ming and Qing. Her principal interest is in introducing these works and in describing and contrasting their authorship, emphases, and points of view. She argues that categorization by virtue is more prevalent among female than male anthologists; the former were more anxious to show how their somewhat egregious act of editing worked to support Confucian norms. Chang also offers insight into the lack of attention these materials have received up to now. In her view, this oversight is not completely explained by the fact that women's literature is perforce a marginal category. It also reflects canonical neglect of all Ming and Qing poetry, on the grounds that it is inferior to the poetry of other dynasties and that the best writing of the Ming and Qing is found in other genres. In Chang's view, this prejudice needs to be overturned.

Unlike Chang's chapter, Maureen Robertson's confines itself to gentry women. It concerns a "double discourse" found in their prefaces to their own work, which apologize for the very act of self-display. In contrast, the "self" is somewhat less vigorously effaced in their lyric poetry. Even there, however, one can isolate ongoing tensions—between "performing masculine conventions," "reinscribing" them as feminine, and inventing new vocabularies for feminine literary expression, all of which continue throughout the Ming and Qing.

With Part III, "Poems in Contexts," attention bifurcates to encompass both poet or poem and narrative framework, and the materials studied become predominantly prose. For the most part, the women presented in this section come from outside the social center, being

ghosts, maidens, or members of the lower classes. This arrangement
has the effect of accentuating the illusion of dependence: on the man
who writes their story or with whom they fall in love.

Ann Waltner's subject is the much anthologized and rewritten
tale of Li Yuying, who lived in the sixteenth century. She explores conflicting versions of her subject's story, which revolves around the
troubles set in motion when a young woman's seemingly innocent
poems lend themselves to an erotic reading. When Li's pen becomes
the means through which she extricates herself from these same troubles (she writes a memorial protesting her innocence to the throne),
her story points to the controversy women's writings could arouse.
Eventually, the balance is tipped in favor of the literate female, as the
emperor comes to Li's rescue after reading her works correctly. Most
versions of this complex of stories go on to demonize the men who are
threatened by writers like Li.

Judith Zeitlin's chapter on ghosts introduces a new category of
writing, ghost poetry, that has never received scholarly scrutiny before. Granting that the ghosts called up in séances and elsewhere
could be male as well as female, Zeitlin nevertheless explores evidence of a special affinity between femininity and ghostliness. The
link lies in the trope of the emaciated though beautiful maiden-poet,
that — as Chinese literary convention would have it — is doomed to die
at an early age. This figure is paired with a masculine redeemer, usually somewhat effete and sensitive in nature. Through its connection
with frustrated, unfulfilled, and ethereal beauty, spectral poetry
gained special currency during the Ming and Qing. Especially after
the Ming-Qing transition, ghosts and their poems built on all too familiar memories of slaughter and suicide, the hallmarks of those tran-
sitional years.

Grace Fong's study of an eighteenth-century work introduces another ethereal figure, the poet He Shuangqing. Like Zeitlin's ghosts,
Fong's heroine poses questions about real and unreal, because the
historical subject is so heavily filtered through the dreams and purposes of her chronicler, the scholar Shi Zhenlin. However, Shuangqing's corporeality is not at issue in Shi's account, which chronicles
the physical and mental abuses suffered at the hands of her mother-
in-law. After considering the pedestal of Confucian filiality on which
Shi sets her, Fong seeks a new basis on which to ascribe "genuineness"

to Shuangqing as a person and as a poet. She concludes with the thought that the historical Shuangqing to be retrieved from all the verbiage, if that is possible, can best be located in the poems, which fit poorly within Shi's narrative frame.

Part IV, "*Hong lou meng*" (Dream of the red chamber), is entirely devoted to one eighteenth-century novel. However, the divergent methodologies used and problems considered make it the most eclectic of the four.

Haun Saussy's chapter is close in spirit to those of the previous section, for it ponders the meaning talented women held for their male observers, and it measures its answers alongside the manifest rhetoric of the novel as a whole. Its subject matter is the conflicting interpretations of the "lantern riddles" of chapter 22 of the novel. In establishing the family patriarch, Jia Zheng, as a better reader than the poems' female authors, Saussy comes close to putting himself at odds with those who would see this novel as a celebration of female talent, by showing women's continuing dependence on Jia Zheng's "male gaze." However, he offers some redress from this judgment in his exploration of another female character, Bao Qin, whose poems on history align her voice with that of the narrator-author. They also set her apart from other female talents in the novel, in that Bao Qin grasps the import of her own poetic words.

Wu Hung applies a gender-based analysis to architecture, space, and narrative order as set forth in *Dream of the Red Chamber*. His juxtaposition of the stereotypical series of twelve beauties presented in the opening section of the novel with series of twelve beauties in earlier literature and in painting leads to the conclusion that the space inhabited by these figures is feminized by them, even when, as in the novel, they evolve from stereotype to fully realized characters. By definition, feminized space contrasts with its masculine opposite. In the novel, this contrast points to the superiority of the feminine world and those who inhabit it. In Qing court art, on the other hand, feminine space is marked as vulnerable and alluring, but not as superior to its masculine counterpart. Wu's inquiry complements historicist readings of the novel, which explore characterization in terms of the author's life and circle of acquaintances, but it also challenges such approaches, by demonstrating the stereotypical underpinnings to some of what the novel has to say.

Ellen Widmer's chapter takes an altogether different tack in its inquiry into the factors that led women writers to incorporate new genres into their repertories and the reasons they held back from writing fiction. She shows that *Hong lou meng* did elicit new interest in fiction among women readers, as witnessed in their poetry about this and another novel, *Jinghua yuan* (Flowers in the mirror, of about 1828), which they regarded as a sequel to *Hong lou meng*. Yet the versified *tanci* used in oral storytelling provided a far more comfortable model for women who wanted to write narrative. In a postscript she identifies one long work of prose fiction by a woman — perhaps significantly a Manchu woman. This is Gu Taiqing's *Hong lou meng ying* (Shadows of *Hong lou meng*), whose preface was written in 1860, but which was not published until 1877.

The volume's four parts are followed by a Postface by Nancy Armstrong that reflects her role as "outside expert" for the project as a whole. In no way a summary or conclusion, the Postface brings comparative insight to questions raised in discussions at the conference and elsewhere in the volume. Its intensity of focus on the Widmer paper, to which it responds more fully than to any other, results from Widmer's sustained look at issues raised in Armstrong's *Desire and Domestic Fiction*. Thus, Widmer frames her question about women and novel writing as an analogy to Armstrong's description of the emergence of women novelists in response to Richardson's *Pamela*, published in England in 1740. Readers of the Widmer and Armstrong chapters, or of both against the background of Armstrong's 1987 study, may find that they talk past each other in certain ways. In this sense they are emblematic of the distance separate academic discourses can impose on contemporaries, even when those contemporaries speak the same language and come from the same school. These dissonances are reminders of the still greater distance separating the scholar of today from the Ming-Qing woman, a point with which Armstrong's chapter begins.

Yet even amid such dissonances, Armstrong's "answer" to the volume produces striking formulations. Her look at Rey Chow's *Woman and Chinese Modernity* in conjunction with the Widmer chapter, via Foucault's theory of "remainders," prompts speculation about what is unarticulated, both by Ming and Qing women and by a new type of sentimental writing in early modern China, of the so-called Mandarin Duck and Butterfly school. Nowhere else in this volume are such links between late imperial China and modern literature proposed. Armstrong's discussion of the "feminine authority that could not reveal itself for what it was without losing that authority" in nineteenth-century England, further, may prove richly suggestive when transplanted to a Chinese setting. It invites comparison to the "meekness and gentleness" promoted by Yun Zhu and other Ming-Qing women anthologists, even as they exercised stern control over the organization of their anthologies and attempted to set standards for gentlewomankind. Finally, Armstrong is the only author in this set of papers to use the term "intellectual" to refer to Chinese women, whether gentry or courtesan, and to draw conclusions about the power of all literate women based on her understanding of this term. If upon further reflection one were to conclude that the term does not work well for China's writing women, the effort to say why could add something of value to the field.

Collectively, these chapters address the tensions in the paintings and poems they describe. In the case of poems by women, tensions arise when traditional categorizations of feminine worth and virtue give way to other measures of literary value. In the case of narratives about women, they emerge when subjects are pried from contexts and readings take place across the grain. Such tensions call attention to the "gaze" of female anthologists and male chroniclers, who had their own reasons for losing themselves in the "writing woman" and their own rhetorical axes to grind. They call attention, further, to the rhetoric of Chinese modernism, whose construction of traditional Chinese womanhood was largely antithetical to the types of inquiry found in this volume and whose deepest orthodoxies still hold sway. On another level, tensions result from the ordering of these essays, whose various chapters enter into dialogues across categories and show other signs of resisting the rubric under which they have been assigned. For example, the issue of language that is central to Ōki's chapter on what makes *Mountain Songs* so fresh, could have been a major heading, in which case the Fong and Robertson chapters might have made appropriate neighbors. This arrangement would have focused attention on what takes place linguistically when one person writes on behalf of another or struggles to put old symbols to new ends. At times such stresses and strains can be formulated as clear-cut questions. At other times they are more unfocused, as when the variety of approaches and topics merely implies a field of inquiry in its early stages, not one whose central questions have been resolved. Yet in concert with one another, and given the rich archive of little-touched materials, these essays demonstrate the promise of gender studies at this juncture and their power to identify new paths of inquiry, subvert the canon, and rewrite the history of the Ming and Qing.

Part I

Writing the Courtesan

1

Ambiguous Images of Courtesan Culture in Late Imperial China

PAUL S. ROPP

Courtesan culture in late Ming China was centered in the major cities of Jiangnan, the southern lower Yangzi River valley, yet it was not confined only to that region, and the personalities, deeds, and accomplishments of prominent late Ming courtesans were famous throughout the empire from the early seventeenth century through the entire Qing period. Courtesan life thus assumed an importance in late imperial culture far beyond the geographical and temporal confines of late Ming Jiangnan. In this chapter, I explore a small sampling of writings, with an emphasis on poetry, by and/or about Chinese courtesans, to illustrate the various meanings and images associated with courtesanship in late imperial times. Although poetry is by no means the only source of reliable information about courtesan culture and its place in late imperial China, it is the most direct testimony we have from courtesans themselves.[1]

Particularly striking in writings by and about courtesans in late imperial times are the variety, ambiguity, and even contradictory nature of the images associated with courtesan life. I focus on seven images in particular, arranged in three groups: (1) love and talent, the predominant themes in poetry that courtesans wrote for their most favored clients; (2) glamour and nostalgia, popular themes in male literati writings about the courtesan quarters, particularly in relation to urban centers of the late Ming; (3) sex, bondage, and shame, themes associated particularly (though not exclusively) with the lower ranks of courtesan life as described in popular songs and the writings of Confucian moralists. In my view, some of these contrasting images reflect class differences (between lower-class prostitutes and upper-class courtesans) or a combination of gender and class differences (between female courtesans and male literati clients); others attest to a shift in attitudes over time (from late Ming to mid-Qing, for example); still others result from differences in literary genres (as seen in the contrasting concerns of romantic poems, nostalgic memoirs, and satirical novels); and some represent conflicting views within elite culture or between elite critics and popular attitudes.

While noting gender and class differences in accounting for the wide range of images associated with courtesanship, I pay special attention to two lines of analysis. First, I argue that most of these conflicting images reflect the profoundly ambiguous position of courtesan culture in the larger culture of late imperial China. Second, I believe that many of the positive images associated with elite courtesans date from the late Ming and the era of the Ming-Qing transition (from the early sixteenth century to the middle of the seventeenth century); by the early eighteenth century, after the passing of the Ming survivor generation, those positive images of courtesanship appear in the record less frequently, and courtesanship is more often associated with somber and negative images.

With regard to the ambivalent position of courtesan culture, the terms *jinü* and *changji* are highly ambiguous; they may refer to women entertainers of any social rank, from the lowliest prostitute to the most celebrated and expensive courtesan. As Dorothy Ko rightly notes, the most appropriate Chinese term for courtesan is *mingji* (or famous prostitute).[2] In this chapter, I use the term "courtesan" rather than "prostitute," even for those who were not necessarily famous, because the *jinü* I discuss were literate and skilled in a variety of entertainment arts, and their services were not confined to the sale of sex.

As will become clear from the following discussion, even the upper ranks of the courtesan world occupied a profoundly ambiguous place in Ming/Qing culture. In one sense courtesans were honorary literati; they occupied the only place in the culture where women could openly socialize with men who were not their husbands. The most prominent among them enjoyed a level of renown unattainable by any other type of woman. At the upper levels of the profession, courtesans in China could and often enough did become powerful symbols of morality and virtue. But such was the Janus-face of Confucian culture that courtesans could not escape the taint of notoriety. Even the most famous of courtesans aspired above all to leave the "flower lanes," to be purchased and thereby "redeemed" into "respectability," and taken as a concubine by a wealthy, talented, and sensitive lover-client.

In her chapter in this volume (see pp. 46–73) on the late Ming courtesan as a cultural ideal, Li Wai-yee amply demonstrates the powerful sense of identification between Chinese literati and elite courtesans in the sixteenth and seventeenth centuries. In the eyes of Ming loyalists, a number of famous courtesans came to symbolize freedom, self-creation, the possibility of heroic action, and the embodiment of elite cultural ideals. In the first section of this chapter, which deals with positive images of courtesan culture, I present a few poems by one famous late Ming courtesan, Jing Pianpian, to illustrate the themes of flirtation, love, and talent in courtesan writings.

The Manchu conquest, in my view, fundamentally altered the position of courtesan culture in late imperial China by making courtesans symbolic of the loss of those ideals of freedom, self-creation, and the possibility of heroic action. In the early Qing, late Ming courtesans came to represent in many minds a lost world of elegance, destroyed by the brutal Manchu conquest. Thus, increasingly after 1644, courtesan culture is more eulogized than celebrated. In the early Qing period, discussed in the second section of this chapter, literati nostalgia for the now-lost glamour associated with late Ming courtesans is an indirect (and therefore politically safe) way to express nostalgia for the fallen Ming dynasty and to mourn its demise.

By the eighteenth century, many Chinese literati still visited the courtesan quarters of Nanjing's Qinhuai district, but the most prominent literati seldom published poems or essays celebrating their liaisons with well-known courtesans, and in contrast with the most famous literati in the late Ming, they seldom took courtesans into their homes as companionate concubines. From being symbols of freedom and self-creation and objects of admiration in the late Ming and early Qing, courtesans in the eighteenth and nineteenth centuries were more often seen as objects of pity. There was still a strong element of literati identification with courtesans, however, and part of the decline in the courtesan image in the mid-Qing period probably reflects a corresponding decline in the self-image of male literati (especially those literati who still wrote about courtesans). As courtesans, held in bondage, hoped against high odds for redemption in marriage, so

Han literati, lowly subjects of exalted Manchu emperors, hoped against high odds for examination success and political prominence. Courtesans were subject to the whims and demands of their customers, and literati were subject to the whims and demands of their sovereign. Thus, as seen in the final section of this chapter, literati and courtesan poems from the eighteenth and nineteenth centuries place less emphasis on love, talent, glamour, or nostalgia and more on the sufferings of courtesans from sexual exploitation, bondage, and shame.

I emphasize that the change from relatively positive to relatively negative images of courtesanship (and the correspondences between these changing images and social change from the sixteenth to the nineteenth century) is a matter of degree: one can find negative images of courtesanship in the late Ming, and positive images in the late Qing. The predominant images associated with courtesans, however, definitely changed after the Ming collapse in 1644. Needless to say, the divisions in this chapter are somewhat arbitrary and artificial, and the boundaries between them are porous; few works fit neatly into any one category. Love and talent are not always closely related, sexual connotations may suggest love rather than bondage or shame, and nostalgia may at times have little to do with glamour. The subheadings below are intended merely to suggest the wide range of images attached to courtesanship, the direction of change in these images over several centuries, and the ways some of these images are intertwined.

Love and Talent

> I am touched by your letter on Wu Paper,
> With two magpies drawn in full flight.
> May our bond match the flying pair of birds
> Rather than the thinness of the paper.
>
> — Zhao Yanru (Ming courtesan)

I have argued elsewhere that the courtesan culture of the late Ming was important in helping to make literacy and skill in poetry, painting, calligraphy, and music desirable qualities in a woman.[3] In contrast to the rigid segregation of men and women in gentry society, courtesan culture provided an environment in which men and women of comparable talents could socialize freely and openly and develop ties of affection based on physical attraction as well as shared intellectual interests and artistic talents. Given the uniqueness of the courtesan world as a meeting ground for men and women, it is not surprising that love and talent were prominent twin themes in poetry by and about courtesans. A courtesan who wanted to win a client's heart and to become his concubine had to rely first on her physical allure and entertainment skills to attract a client's attention and favor. If more than a superficial relationship developed, her personality, talent, sensitivity, strength of character, and declared devotion to a particular man could be decisive in winning him over. Alternatively, she might frighten a man away with an open avowal of love if he did not have the means or the will to take her as a concubine. Poetry was a primary means of written communication between courtesans and their clients, and they frequently wrote letters to each other in the form of poems. Poetic talent was an important part of a courtesan's allure.

Jing Pianpian (*ming* Yao; *zi* Sanmei, fl. 1570's), a famous late Ming courtesan from Ganjiang in eastern Jiangxi, wrote a number of mildly flirtatious poems that illustrate the importance of love, and talent, in courtesan poetry. Because she frequently traveled to Jian'an in Fujian, she is identified in some works as a Fujian courtesan. Famous for her erudition, she was on good terms with many well-known Fujian literati and was widely praised as one of the best courtesan poets of the Ming period. According to Jing Pianpian's biography, she was eventually redeemed from the courtesan quarters by marriage. After at least one broken engagement, to Mei Zisou, she eventually married a man named Ding Changfa. But her life ended tragically just the same, for when her husband was charged with a crime, arrested, and taken away to a magistrate's yamen, she committed suicide.[4]

The following poem by Jing Pianpian reads like a celebration of the upper-class courtesan's lifestyle; it refers to an unidentified lover and was probably intended to impress and attract a particular male client.

> Every day fancy carriages arrive,
> Intimate words with upper-class friends.
> But no one here is from Suzhou,
> And I miss those Suzhou soft sounds.
>
> Together we feast deep into the night.
> After I've softly tuned the lute,
> We sit and tie a lover's knot,
> Inviting the moon into the room.[5]

With an emphasis on the wealth of her clients and the intimacy of her setting, the images here are entirely positive. Her declared fondness for the soft sounds of a Suzhou accent may have been intended as an enticement for a Suzhou man. The last verse highlights the pleasures her paramour may enjoy if he calls on her. There will be lavish feasting deep into the night, soft music performed by the courtesan who, with her guest and the moon, will form a ménage à trois. The lover's knot (tongxinjie) in the last couplet is a knot uniting two hearts, often hung from a man's or woman's belt as a pendant. Of course, in such a setting, the connotation of a lover's knot goes well beyond the tying of a pendant.

Many of Jing Pianpian's poems are addressed more directly to a particular man, and in some of these she adopts a scolding and even mocking tone toward a fickle lover, at least hinting that a sharp-witted courtesan might hope to shame a man into treating her with more respect. In the following "Poem of Resentment" ("Yuan ci"), she chides a would-be lover for his long absences and lame excuses and contrasts her own anxiety and her steadfast loyalty to him with his apparent lack of serious commitment to her.

> Why do you complain that the distance is great
> When it is your hesitation that keeps you away?
> My heart, like the wheel of a cart,
> Travels miles and miles each day,
> Though I, like the water in a mountain stream,
> Never flow far from the streambed stones.
> A tiny blossom from a poplar tree,
> You drift in the breeze, going nowhere.[6]

Of course, it is possible that these poems were simply examples of a genre of flirtatious poems intended to be circulated and to impress a wider audience than the "man" addressed in the poem. We might legitimately ask whether a man as fickle as Jing Pianpian describes would be likely to be moved either by her declarations of love or her hints of anger over his infidelities.[7] But whether intended for one man or a larger readership, clever courtesan poems of flirtation served as lures or advertisements for courtesan culture, where flirtation was, after all, institutionalized as one of the main attractions of the pleasure quarters. When such poems were anthologized and read by a wider audience including gentry women, they may well have served to inspire similar arts beyond the pleasure district.[8]

In addition to a flirtatious wit, a courtesan might also win a man's attention with more serious displays of emotion and poetic talent. If a relationship was to move beyond infatuation (or if one's lover had a weak sense of humor!), earnest declarations of love and reminders of a courtesan's vulnerability might be more effective than ironic scolding. In a much more somber and poignant poem on nature, beauty, and love, Jing Pianpian demonstrated her vulnerability and her talent in a serious and elaborate way. "Boudoir Thoughts" ("Guisi," labeled "a composition sent to Master Chen") is a word portrait of her lonely self reflecting on the beauties of nature but feeling sad even in the glorious springtime. The poem is also a quietly flamboyant demonstration of the poet's cleverness and skill, for it is a palindrome (*huiwenshi*) that makes sense and rhymes when read in reverse (see Fig. 1.1). Palindromes probably originated in works of embroidery, and they were particularly popular among women writers as a way to demonstrate their literary talent.[9]

> Flute sounds in this quiet room fill the morning
>   with feeling;
> Piece by piece, floating blossoms brightly shimmer
>   in the sun.
> A sprinkling of lonely tears has stained the pair
>   of pillows;
> For short songs and long ones, I tune and retune
>   the *zheng*.
>
> Drooping by the bridge, willows look thinner than
>   painted eyebrows;
> On the couch with a flick of my sleeve I disperse
>   a swirl of red clouds.
> In the distance, dark green mountains, as far as
>   the eye can see;
> From hidden spots, orioles burst forth in a
>   breath-taking chorus.[10]

Quite apart from the tour de force of the palindrome, Jing Pianpian here portrays herself in lonely solitude amid a glorious springtime. Music and flowers pervade the scene, but because her lover is absent, her tears stain the pair of pillows where they once made love. She tunes and retunes the *zheng*, as if anticipating his arrival, but he makes no appearance. In the second stanza, the woman appears only in the second line, listless on her couch, dispersing a swirl of red clouds, presumably incense, with a flick of her sleeve. Willows, symbolic of spring, of parting lovers, and of courtesans and sexual liai-

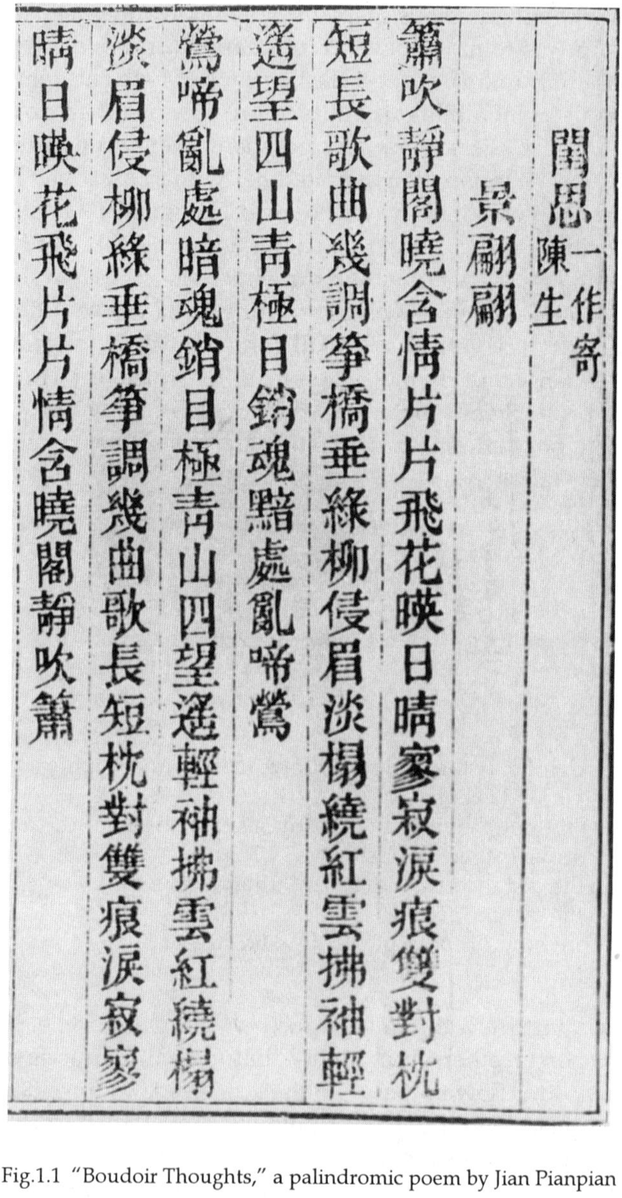

閨思 一作寄陳生

景翩翩

簫吹靜閣曉含情片片飛花映日晴寥寂淚痕雙對枕
短長歌曲幾調箏橋垂絲柳侵眉淡楊繞紅雲拂袖輕
遙望四山青極目銷魂黯處亂啼鶯
鶯啼亂處暗魂銷目極青山四望遙輕袖拂雲紅繞楊
淡眉侵柳絲垂橋箏調幾曲歌長短枕對雙痕淚寂寥
晴日映花飛片片情含曉閣靜吹簫

Fig.1.1 "Boudoir Thoughts," a palindromic poem by Jian Pianpian sons, sadly droop, and the dark green mountains filling the horizon as far as she can see intensify the courtesan's sense of isolation. Known for their beautiful songs, orioles are especially associated with joy, friendship, and courtesans. Their sudden burst of song in a breath-taking chorus may be suggestive of beautiful courtesan songs, or it may simply startle the otherwise lonely poet and remind her anew that this is the season when she should, but cannot, enjoy a reunion with her lover.

Courtesan poetry was widely published in the late Ming and was important in establishing many of the popular images of courtesan culture. The flirtatious poems above, the clever evocations of seductive scenes, and the carefully crafted displays of poetic talent are representative, even stereotypical, of courtesan writings, but they present only part of the cultural record. Many male literati also wrote about courtesans and courtesan culture, and their writings were at least as influential in creating popular images of the courtesan world. The following section deals primarily with literati reactions to courtesan culture.

Glamour and Nostalgia

> Alas! The years and months pass by in a flash. All the gentlemen have their bones buried in the green mountains, and the beauties too now dwell in the yellow earth. The rivers and mountains are far away. How can one fail to grieve?   – Yu Huai

In a culture as conscious of history as China's, nostalgia for the past carries many meanings. For literati clients of courtesans, glamour and nostalgia were perhaps the main qualities they associated with courtesan culture. Literati nostalgia for courtesan culture can be seen in many guises in the late Ming and early Qing period. In her studies of Chen Zilong (1608–47) and Wu Weiye (1609–71), Kang-i Sun Chang has demonstrated the importance of the courtesan's image to the cult of *qing* (feelings or love) and to the development of the Ming loyalist poetic tradition.[11] In his celebrated play, *The Peach Blossom Fan* (*Taohua shan*), Kong Shangren (1648–1718) immortalized the romantic liaison of Hou Fangyu (1618–55) and his courtesan mistress Li Xiangjun (fl. 1640's), their doomed love, and their equally doomed efforts to defend the collapsing Ming dynasty. Elegant and luxurious courtesan quarters conjured up for Ming literati memories of the glories of the

Six Dynasties and the bustling capitals of Chang'an and Kaifeng in their halcyon days. Qing literati were reminded in addition of the thriving pleasure quarters of such cities as Nanjing and Yangzhou in the late Ming. They associated courtesans with artistic talent and material splendor, with high aspirations and disappointed hopes, with sensitive souls held in bondage; courtesans reminded literati of themselves and their own circumstances. As Kang-i Sun Chang writes, "After the fall of the Ming, the courtesan became a metaphor for the loyalist poets' vision of themselves."[12]

Courtesan culture reached the peak of its popularity in the late Ming when a number of prominent scholars and poets, including Chen Zilong (1608–47), Wu Weiye, Mao Xiang (1611–93), Hou Fangyu, and Qian Qianyi (1582–1664), enjoyed celebrated liaisons with famous and talented courtesans. Willard Peterson has aptly summarized the cultural importance of courtesanship during this period.

> The tendency in many writings was to romanticize the liaisons between prostitutes and literati. The marvelous talent and beauty of this or that woman, together with her sensitivity to higher moral values and to her paramour's dilemmas, were the subject matter of prose and poetry that played *tristesse* off against glamour, and lessons on fidelity off against titillation. In the 1630s entertainment by "singing girls" was well established for literati, especially in the cities, although it all seems more elegant than debauched.[13]

Courtesan culture was so much a part of late Ming literati life that in the late sixteenth and early seventeenth centuries, even a respectable gentry wife could write a poem describing it. Lu Qingzi (*ming* Fuchang, fl. 1590's) was the daughter of Lu Shidao, a Suzhou painter and disciple of Wen Zhengming (1489–1573). At age 15 *sui*, she married a literatus, Zhao Yiguang (*zi* Fanfu, 1559–1625) with whom she lived in seclusion in Hanshan. Lu Qingzi's poetry was said to follow that of the Six Dynasties, and her reputation far surpassed that of her husband.[14] Dorothy Ko has documented Lu Qingzi's friendship with many courtesans;[15] in the following "Song of White Linen" ("Baizhuci"), Lu celebrates the beauty of courtesans as if she herself were one of their literati-clients.

> They begin to sing,
> To move their red lips.
> Hair fixed high, eyebrows just painted,
> Beauties of Handan, worth whole cities,
> Their glamour outshines springtime itself.

> For gentlemen, sleeves twirl to the song of white linen,
> Fine and delicate fabrics float in the breeze.
> As the sun sets behind blue hills, sadness intensifies.[16]

This celebration of the beauty, glamour, and economic value of courtesans raises the possibility that a gentry wife might even envy such
elegant and talented entertainers twirling their fine linen sleeves for
their audience of gentlemen. However, the sadness intensifying as the
night comes on seems to qualify the earlier images of beauty, luxury,
and glamour, suggesting that the courtesan's life was also one of suffering. In any case, this combination of beauty and sadness was to
typify the nostalgic writings of many literati descriptions of courtesan
culture.

Wai-yee Li, in her chapter on the late Ming courtesan in this volume, rightly emphasizes the profound identification that many seventeenth-century literati felt with courtesans. The association of courtesan culture with glamour and nostalgia may be seen most clearly in
such famous tributes to Ming courtesan life as the memoirs of two
male literati, Mei Dingzuo (1549–1618) and Yu Huai (1616–96). In
Qingni lianhua ji (A record of lotus flowers in dark mud), Mei recalled
the lives and writings of famous courtesans, emphasizing their embodiment of various talents and virtues. The title of Mei's work suggests respect for the purity of beautiful courtesans and pity for their
having to endure the degradations of their profession. Yu Huai, in
Banqiao zaji (Miscellaneous records of the Wooden Bridge), reminisced
about the famous courtesans of the Qinhuai River district in the final
days of the Ming dynasty. Literati in the early Qing could identify
strongly with both types of images: purity defiled and greatness lost.
In their own view of themselves, the greater the purity of their love for
the Ming, the greater their defilement by forced servitude to the new
Manchu conquerors. The glamorous days of the late Ming (when
courtesans and literati clients flourished together in Nanjing, and
when Ming sovereignty was secure) were now irrecoverably lost.

Nostalgic celebrations of the glamour of Nanjing's Qinhuai River
district were not confined to such marginal aesthetes as Yu Huai.
Wang Shizhen (1634–1711), one of the most prominent officials and
influential literary critics of the early Qing period, wrote a famous series of erudite poems on the Qinhuai district, recalling many incidents
in its glorious history. Daniel Bryant, who has expertly translated and
analyzed these poems, notes Wang Shizhen's fascination with two periods of particular elegance, the Six Dynasties and the Ming: "That the

elegance often, and increasingly, tended toward decadence only made it the more interesting to later ages. Cluck as they might, later writers found in this spectacle of splendor and then decay a source of continual fascination."[17]

One can find nostalgic tributes to the courtesan quarters even in *Guochao shiduo*, a nineteenth-century Confucian anthology of Qing dynasty poetry compiled by Zhang Yingchang (1790–1874) for the moral edification of officials. Zhang was a conscientious scholar-official who worked in the Grand Secretariat, edited commentaries on the *Spring and Autumn Annals*, and wrote a study of the *Nanbeishi* (History of the Northern and Southern Dynasties [420–589 A.D.]). He published his anthology of about 2,000 poems in 1869 and proclaimed it to be in the Music Bureau (*yuefu*) tradition of compiling popular songs and poetry to sensitize rulers to the lives and concerns of the common people. In his preface he assured the reader that he had eliminated all vulgar works and chosen only the best and most moral poems produced in the dynasty.[18] The first poem in Zhang's brief section on prostitutes and actors (*changyou*) is the "Song of the Qinhuai River" ("Qinhuaihe ge") by Yan Weixu (fl. 1690's) from Xinyu county in Jiangxi. Written in the late seventeenth or early eighteenth century, Yan's poem is devoted precisely to descriptions of the glamour of the Qinhuai district and to nostalgia for the district's now-faded glories. Its inclusion in a nineteenth-century Confucian anthology suggests that the glamour and nostalgia associated with courtesanship continued to appeal to the literati imagination several centuries after the Ming collapse.

> Through Jinling City runs the Qinhuai River,
> It matches the Qu River's banks in old Chang'an.
> In spring the Qu's banks were filled with young
>   beauties;
> The Qinhuai's banks are also graced with silk gowns.
> For ten *li* pearl inlaid curtains hang on jade hooks;
> Dances, gowns, fans, and songs compete in
>   extravagance.
> Along the water grow green willows and red
>   pomegranates
> Partly shading the elegant red curtains of wealthy
>   homes.
> Newly made-up beauties show off from their
>   balconies;

> With their captivating smiles they look like
>   immortals.
> Boats line up, banquets and dandelion wine
>   fill the air;
> The music never stops in the realm of mist and
>   flowers.
> Commoners and scholars, the girls welcome one
>   and all;
> In this urban domain all these amusements reign
>   supreme.
> Alas!
> The Qinhuai River is very nearby to Swallow Lane;
> But the era of Wang Tanzhi and Xie An is long past.
> Swallow Lane was the Six Dynasties' liveliest place;
> But now it is gone as if having flowed down the
>   river to the east.[19]

With images of wealth, luxury, and glamour of the courtesan quarters along the Qu River in Chang'an and on Swallow Lane in Nanjing, Yan Weixu conjured up glorious times that had by the Qing period faded into the distant past. The beauties were dazzling and the entertainments endless in these urban utopias where pleasure was available to commoner and scholar alike. The famous Jin dynasty scholar-officials Wang Tanzhi and Xie An (both fourth c. A.D.) were known for their devotion to cultured leisure and elegant refinement. But now all that is gone. The courtesan has become a representation of the literati's own "lost world."

As important as glamour was to the image of late Ming courtesan culture, we seldom find glamorous self-portraits in the writings of courtesans themselves. The daily grind of entertaining, even in upper-class brothels, was not glamorous to the entertainers who *had* to be there. Nostalgia can be found in courtesan poetry, but if nostalgia is a bittersweet longing for the past, courtesan longing was generally more bitter than sweet. For courtesans as for literati, longing for the past meant longing for their own lost youth, lost innocence, lost aspirations, and lost illusions. And for courtesans who survived the Manchu conquest, the sense of loss was compounded in many cases by abduction and forced servitude under new and alien masters.

Some of the many women kidnapped in the 1640's by bandits or soldiers during the dislocations of the conquest responded by writing laments and recounting their experiences on the walls of inns and temples.[20] A typical example of a "song lyric written on a wall" (*tibici*) is the following by Gao Zhixian (dates unknown), a Qing woman coerced into prostitution after being kidnapped by bandits.

> The moon is old, my sorrow is new,
>   The night is long, my rest is short,
>   How can I fall asleep tonight?
> The lamp appears haloed through tears;
>   The wine is bitter as my sadness;
>   Both give a taste of my broken heart.
> Alone with my back to the window
>   I count the hours all the cold night long,
>   Not even caring to seek out the double quilt.
> And now horses chomp at their empty troughs;
>   The remote post stirs with voices;
>   The din soon fills your ears.
>
> I sigh in vain,
>   Falling willow catkins soak in the mud
>   And floating flowers sink into the pigsty,
>   But I cannot bear to rehash the past.
> The beautiful maiden Hongfu,
>   And the yellow-robed knight-errant;
>   I doubt it ever happened that way.
> But I would like to ask Heaven so vast:
>   Could it happen this year
>   That a knight-errant with a precious sword
>   Might call on me in the flower lane?[21]

For one supposedly kidnapped and forced into prostitution, Gao Zhixian seems remarkably quick to assume the guise of the tenderhearted courtesan who still holds to the unlikely hope of finding "a man of true feeling." But whatever our doubts about its author, this kind of poem was quite typical of published laments by courtesans torn between despair and hope (however slight or unrealistic) for genuine love and/or marriage.[22] Gao Zhixian seems devastated by disappointment on finding herself alone, perhaps abandoned by one she took to be a lover, in a bustling roadside inn. She laments the past more than she dares hope for the future, yet she also shows here a determination to endure despite strong odds against her. Hongfu is a female warrior in several Ming short stories, and the yellow-robed knight-errant is a character who intervenes to help reunite separated lovers in the Tang story "Huo Xiaoyu zhuan" (Biography of Huo Xiaoyu) and in Tang Xianzu's play *Zichai ji* (The purple jade hairpins).[23] In light of her bitter doubts about maidens rescued by gallant men, Gao's final four lines become a mocking and ironic commentary on the courtesan's hopes for romance and/or security.

One reason that many Qing literati found this kind of lament so appealing was that it resonated powerfully with their own fading hopes for examination success and official appointment in an increasingly competitive world. In the later chapters of his satirical novel, *The Scholars* (*Rulin waishi*), Wu Jingzi (1701–54), who had spent many of his youthful days and nights in the Qinhuai district, turned his ironic eye toward the parallels between courtesans and literati in their shared (and often unrealistic) hopes for wealth, rank, and fame. In chapters 53 and 54, Wu describes Pinniang, an attractive and literate but low-ranking courtesan, who dreams only of becoming the wife of an official. She becomes so obsessed with officials that she offends all her other clients and fights fiercely with the husband and wife who manage the brothel and try to reprimand her. When she threatens suicide, they decide to cut their losses and release her to join a nunnery. Wu Jingzi's portrait is deliberately comical, but it illuminates close parallels between literati and courtesans in their hopes for wealth, rank, fame, and security in an era of intense competition, rising social fluidity, and, as a consequence, insecurity.

Writing in the mid-eighteenth century, Wu Jingzi exhibited some nostalgia for the glories of the late Ming and for his own lost youth, but he portrayed both courtesans and literati (himself included) in a far more ironic and less glamorous light than had an earlier generation of late Ming and early Qing writers such as Mei Dingzuo, Yu Huai, Mao Xiang, Kong Shangren, and Wang Shizhen. In the following section, poems from the eighteenth and nineteenth centuries, not coincidentally in my view, focus almost entirely on negative images associated with courtesanship.

Sex, Bondage, and Shame

> A tiny piece of worthless bone
> Cast over and over again.
> Since falling into disgrace
> I go tumbling without end.
> — "Song of the Dice"
> anonymous Ming courtesan

The shame attached to the courtesan's profession was associated more often with the bondage or forced service of the courtesan than with the selling of sex per se. As will become clear below, courtesans sometimes described the selling of sex as disgusting and distasteful, but literati writings seldom portrayed courtesans as morally culpable for the pleasures they were forced to provide. Critics of courtesan culture attributed the shame not to the courtesans themselves or to their clients but rather to those who sold girls or women into prostitution and those who profited from the business of training such woman, holding them in bondage, and exploiting their talents and vulnerabilities. Several poems on courtesans in Zhang Yingchang's *Guochao shiduo* illustrate the point.

In the mid-nineteenth century, Zou Zaiheng (fl. 1850's), a *shengyuan* (or lowest-level civil-service degree holder) from Qiantang, who once served as an assistant magistrate in Jiangsu, wrote a short but chillingly graphic description of the transport of young girls on the Huai River for sale as prostitutes. He describes a virtual form of slavery, as young girls are brought in large boats from Yancheng, a poor area north of Nantong, down the Grand Canal and the Yangtze River for eventual sale to the managers of the brothels in Shanghai.

> "Tie her up!
> Tie her up!"
> People are haggling over the price of young girls;
> These innocent young orioles, thirteen or fourteen *sui*.
> The large boats sail in from Yancheng;
> The Yancheng girls arrive at Qingjiangpu.
> Changing their attire, learning to primp and prettify,
> They perfect the art of selling themselves for money.
> How they suffer in miserable houses of prostitution!
> How their parents love cash more than their young ones!
> With chilling calculation they cast delicate daughters
>   into the mire.
> How can they help but shed tears while playing the lute?
> What a slim chance to escape the mud before it's too late![24]

Zou Zaiheng is distressed at the corruption of innocent girls being taught the arts of elegant dressing and makeup as forms of seduction, and he holds the parents of such girls responsible for selling their daughters into virtual slavery for the sake of money. In one sense, Zou's condemnation may be seen as an upper-class view of lower-class survival strategies. From the perspective of a poor family with ten children, the sale of a daughter to be trained as a courtesan might in fact represent the girl's best chance for survival and even upward social mobility. Zou Zaiheng seems dimly aware of the social inequities that foster such behavior, but he simply calls upon the lower classes to behave more like the wealthy, without recognizing the economic pressures they face.

Although most of the poems on courtesans in Zhang's anthology say little about the clients who frequent brothels, the "Song of the Gusu Boatwomen," by Zhu Peng (fl. late eighteenth c.), from Qiantang, refers pointedly to "young wastrels who lounge with glasses raised," at least implying that the demand for such entertainment services helps to keep innocent young women in bondage and hardship. Zhu describes young girls who work on a pleasure boat on a river in Gusu, an area named after Mount Gusu in Wu county in Jiangsu.

> Green plant-filled mountain pond swollen with
>   spring rains;
> A large boat lightly floats with fancy curtained
>   windows.
> This boat will not set sail for merchants and their
>   goods;
> But rather for young wastrels who lounge with
>   glasses raised.
> Inside are dazzling girls in fine, thin, fluttering
>   sleeves;
> Floating like the waves with stunning grace and
>   beauty.
> Like shadows of swallows, they lean askew on the
>   anchor ropes;
> At the lavish banquet, their soft singing echoes the
>   orioles.
> Plaintive sounds of flutes and strings go on all day
>   and night;
> From the sorrow and sadness of lovers parting,
>   there is no escape.
> Have you ever, on the river, seen these women burn
>   reeds to cook?
> Young girls are tossed about by waves the whole night
>   through.
> With hair straggling in disarray from too much wind
>   and mist,
> They rise long before the sun to tend the boat and
>   take the helm.[25]

Zhu is not oblivious to the glamorous side of the entertainments these girls offer, but he portrays them quite rightly as merchandise, exploited for the pleasure of some and the wealth of others. These young girls sing plaintive songs of love, but for them love means the sorrow and sadness of lovers parting rather than the fulfillment and security of love that endures. Their lives are precarious, "tossed about by waves," and full of hardships. These are not pampered prima donnas who only perfect the arts of entertainment. After performing the whole night through, they spend long days cooking and tending the boat before facing another endless night of work. Interestingly, Zhu's poem is included not in the section of Zhang's anthology on courtesans, but rather in the section on women (*funü*) wherein many types of women's hardships are described and condemned.

Another poem in Zhang's anthology makes an explicit comparison between prostitutes and poor women who eke out a meager living as tailors. In a northern-style *yuefu* entitled "The Pipa Girl," Chen Shenghe (fl. late eighteenth c.), from Zhaowen (in Suzhou prefecture, Jiangsu), describes and quotes a young pipa (a type of lute) player as an example of the hardships suffered by poor women.

> The girl pipa player,
> Has barely reached the age of twelve.
> Carrying her pipa to the front of the banquet hall,
> Her eyes shine brightly, full of expression.
> Her fingers bring the pipa to life;
> Elegant hands on the strings, after tuning, she begins.
> She has never known the love of man and woman,
> But the songs she sings are all about love;
> And with genuine feeling she sings of love's sorrow;
> Images of water dance like flying flowers, plains of grass.
> "Last year my mistress began teaching me beautiful songs;
> Having learned them I was taught to sing them for money.
> The customers are free to ignore my songs if they wish,
> But then when I return she will scold me and beat me.
> My fate is a bad one, like a lotus deep in the mud,
>   hardly able to maintain its pure nature;
> Like a willow catkin, I am still fortunate that the
>   wind is light, so I have not lost my virtue."
> Have you not seen the women who are prostitutes?
> They are truly to be pitied;
> On earthen beds they must sleep with donkey-like men.
> Or have you not seen poor women who are tailors?
> Bitterly waiting, baskets in hands by other people's doors?[26]

Although this girl is fortunate in that she has not yet been compelled to sleep with customers, her self-description as a lotus in the mud or the fragile willow catkin suggests the fate that is surely in store for her: to be blown by inevitable winds and eventually soiled by the mire and the mud. Chen Shenghe's last two lines suggest that poverty-stricken women who work as tailors are just as unfortunate as prostitutes forced to sleep with donkey-like men. It is, he implies, not the prostitutes' selling of sex per se, but their poverty, insecurity, and subjection to the whims of strangers, that is most to be pitied.

More graphic descriptions of courtesan suffering may be seen in a collection of popular songs compiled by Hua Guangsheng (exact dates unknown) in the early nineteenth century. From Licheng in Shandong, Hua collected contemporary popular songs from urban areas. Hua's *Baixue yiyin* (preface dated 1804) was published in 1828. Arranged by tunes, Hua's collection includes several stirring laments attributed to anonymous courtesans. In the following translation of "The Sorrows of a Courtesan" ("Jinü beishang"), I have omitted musical notations but included parenthetical comments, padding syllables (*chenci* or *chen ju*), that often serve to lengthen a line, as a kind of refrain, and as a more personal commentary on the action described.[27]

> With all the sorrows of a prostitute,
> > I detest my parents:
> > Your greatest wrong
> > Was to sell me to the mist and flower lane;
> > Propriety, righteousness, honesty, and shame
> > All mean nothing to you.
> At twelve and thirteen, I learned to play and sing;
> > Gradually growing up,
> > Groomed and displayed amidst the din of customers.[28]
> I've a few dresses and a number of quilts,
> > Not to mention hairpins and makeup.
> When evening arrives,
> > In shame and misery,
> > I climb into the ivory bed;
> I steal a glance at the heartless cad:
> > Look at him!
> > In his whole being, not a trace of elegance.
> With no way to escape,
> > I am forced with him to enter the golden canopy;
> > Tossing and turning, he takes control of me.
> With no end of difficulty;
> > I bear all this 'til dawn lights the east.

With the guest departing,
    I hardly have a chance to feel relief.
As soon as the manager spies me,
    He too wants to sleep with me!
    He too wants to sleep with me!
    How can I ever rest in peace?
Every day and every night—
    What can I do?
    What can I do?
    How sad I am! (Aiya!)
    How sad I am!
A musician now enters my room; (Aiya!)
    Reeking of dried urine;
    He wants, wants to have his way with me;
    I can only beg, (Aiya!)
    I can only plead.
Pretending warmth, I offer him soup and tea; (Aiya!)
    When he has eaten and gone,
    Only then can I feel at ease.
When a client comes
    I fill his pipe,
    Offer warm greetings,
    Sit off to the side,
    Order the table set
    With wine and dishes aplenty;
    I fill his cup, play drinking games;
    How merrily he laughs.
Passing me the pipa,
    He bids, orders, commands, me to sing.
I look carefully all around;
    My ears attuned to every sound;
    If I fail to meet any expectation,
    Disaster will come crashing down.
I am so pitiful,
    From the corner of my eye I look flirtatiously
    At him, him, him.
Thinking over the past,
    Tears roll down my cheeks.
The manager is a ruthless man
    Who cares only for the money I make.
    When I bring in silver and gold, he is delighted;
    But when I do not, disaster is sure to strike.
He turns fierce and angry,
    Cursing and waving his whip;
    He beats me until I am bruised all over;

My heart breaks with the pain.

When will such a life ever end?
>   Welcoming the new and sending off the old,
>   The days are endless as the sky.

I can never again
>   See my father and mother;
Never again
>   Invite my own sisters into my room;
I can never
>   Bear sons and raise daughters to keep the incense burning;
I can never
>   Be famous as the elegant wife of a wealthy gentleman.
I have today
>   Neither a surname nor a husband;
>   My heart is empty, gloomy, and sad.
I have only
>   A pair of jade-like arms to pillow a thousand men;
>   And a pair of red lips to kiss ten thousand guests.
Whenever I think of this,
>   Tears well up in my eyes;
>   This is worse than a life in Hell.
Filled with anxiety, I wonder,
>   To whom will I belong in the future?
My cries must startle Heaven itself;
>   Perhaps a former life has determined my present fate.
The only way out is this:
>   To wait until one day there comes a man of feeling
>   To rescue me with a decent marriage.[29]

Beginning with the sale of a daughter into bondage by shame-
lessly greedy parents, this song candidly portrays the dark side of
courtesan life. The clients in this woman's experience have neither
grace, charm, nor talent. Rather, they have only demands to make
upon her. After sending the last guest off, she is seen as a potential
sexual partner and harassed even by the musicians and the manager
of her brothel. Her true role, she well understands, is financial; if she
fails to bring in money, "disaster is sure to strike." As with many courtesan laments, this woman bemoans her insecurity and her lack of
family ties, and declares her longing to be rescued by a "man of feeling," however unlikely that may seem in the dismal setting she has
described.

The language of this popular song is coarser and more colloquial
than most of the other works I have quoted. I cannot say whether it

originated in an oral tradition, was written by a courtesan performer, or was written by a literatus or male musician in a courtesan's voice. The life portrayed seems to be at the lower levels of the courtesan world; there is no attempt to romanticize or glorify either the courtesan or her clients. The song begins with hints that this is an upper-class view of lower-class courtesan life. The woman's condemnation of her parents, with references to propriety, righteousness, honesty, and shame, ignores the often harsh economic alternatives faced by truly impoverished families. Having detested her parents in the opening lines, she later laments that she will never see them or her sisters again, nor bear sons to keep the incense burning. Of course, a popular song is meant to create a feeling, not to construct a logical argument. Nevertheless, insofar as we can read a logic here, it is a logic intelligible in elite Confucian terms: only sinful parents would sell a daughter into bondage, but even sinful parents should be served by filial son-bearing daughters.

"Sighing Through the Night's Five Watches" ("Tan wugeng"), another of Hua Guangsheng's courtesan songs, gives a brief biography of a young courtesan and a detailed description of one long night in her brothel.

> An ailing beautiful maiden
>> Sits in lonely silence
>> Languid and listless.
> Closing the embroidered doors,
>> She enters her curtained bed;
>> Leans against the pillow,
>> And cradles her fragrant cheeks in her hands.
> Deep in thought,
>> She recalls the past:
> Who has invented this world of mist and flowers?
>> (The suffering of girls used as prostitutes)
>> I lost my virginity in disgrace;
>> I detest my parents
>> (they made the mistake to begin with);
>> Who have no sense of right or wrong,
>> But cast me "under the balcony."[30]
>> (I am immersed in mist and rain.)
> In the past few years
>> I have welcomed guests and sent them off,
>> Suffering endless shocks and scares.
>> (My tears now cascade out.)

How pitiful I am;
    Hardly have I closed my weary almond eyes
    When the clatter of approaching horses wakes me up again.
I hear the drum in the tower
    starting to mark the night.
    (My thoughts all confused.)
The night drum sounds the first watch;
    The moon shines brightly in the window;
    I sigh at my terrible fate.
Destroying the bloom of my youth,[31]
    I suffered the fall into prostitution;
    Forsaking my home, traveling afar,
    And leaving my parents behind.
Regrettably at that time,
    I was mistakenly "married to a husband";
    To welcome guests and see them off;
    These duties were all forced on me.
If my attentiveness fell short;
    I was immediately beaten. (My God!)
With sly flirtatious glances
    I had to encourage the guests to stay.

When the night drum sounds the second watch,
    The moon casts a cold shadow on the window.
How pitiful, entertaining guests is so difficult;
    How annoying
    To have to talk with every guest who comes and goes.
Tobacco and tea I serve with my own hands;
    Maintaining friendly smiles all the while.
What is truly frightening:
    To encounter drunken guests at the banquet table;
    "Ill-fated beauty" does not begin to capture the shame.
How many days until I can escape this mire? (My God!)
    Yet for the sake of money I have to endure it all.

When the drum sounds the third watch,
    The moon shines brightly on the window;
    Sadly sighing, I enter the curtained bed
    Accompanying my guest;
    No matter whether young or old, he becomes my partner;
    No passion for me in this lover's tryst;
    Clouds and rain are all his doing;
    He wants to crush my flower's heart to pieces;
    We toss and turn, my agony is endless.
If I fail in the slightest way,
    I quickly put on a smile to make amends. (My God!)

What did I do in a previous life
    To bring down such retribution?

When the drum sounds the fourth watch,
    Moonlight comes slanting through the window;
    I sigh beside the sleeping guest.
Startled by fleeting dreams;
    What is worse, this is our first time together;
    I cannot be sure of his temperament;
    I want to doze off but dare not sleep.
I can only
    Muster all my strength to seem warm and compliant;
    Pressing my cheeks against his;
    Whispering sweet and flattering words;
    Exhausting every bit of my cunning;
    To swindle him out of his money. (My God!)
Even with the most disgusting of men,
    I dare show no sign of resistance.

The drum sounds the fifth watch;
    The moonlight lingers by the window;
    I sigh, whether winter or summer,
    Who can know my sufferings?
Through hunger and cold, plenty and warmth,
    I've only myself for commiseration.
Most fearful in winter is the chilling cold
    When I send off friends, my coat pulled around tight.
Most fearful in summer is doing "that thing" in the heat;
Welcoming the new, sending off the old
    Down to the day I am an old woman.
Thinking about my bitter plight,
    What I have endured, I alone know; (My God!)
    After death I will ask the King of Hades
    To see what the next life will bring.
One whole night without sleep;
    When the golden cock announces the dawn,
    I scramble down from the ivory bed;
    Fix my hair, apply makeup;
    To prepare to receive new guests.
If I am the slightest bit late,
    The damned old madam will be along
    To beat and scold once more.
(I am dying of misery in this brothel.)[32]

This hour-by-hour narrative of one courtesan's night vividly depicts the difficulty of forced flirtation and dalliance with strangers who are often drunk and even violent. The courtesan has to be attuned to every nuance of every interaction, lest she offend a customer and suffer further punishment from the manager. In the third watch, she describes a violently aroused customer who "wants to crush my flower's heart to pieces." The phrase here, *ba nude huaxin lai rousui*, is literally, "to take my flower's heart and twist it into pieces." Given the sexual connotation of *huaxin*, implying clitoris or vagina, this is a strikingly vivid description of what amounts to a sexual assault.[33] The parenthetical comments of the singer serve to fill out or extend some lines, and they provide a more personal response to the horrors being described. The phrase "My God!" (*Wode tian Yao hai!*) periodically signifies the singer's disgust at having to engage in such humiliating activities as feigning interest in flirting and making love with loathsome customers for the sake of a meager livelihood.

Whether these songs from *Baixue yiyin* were composed by courtesans, male musicians, or literati, the image of courtesanship they present is at the opposite end of the spectrum from the love poems of courtesans, or the nostalgic tributes of literati cited earlier. Clearly, in these popular songs, romanticism has given way to hard economics. Such songs may stir pity in their audience, but they hardly seem designed to flatter or to win customers for the courtesans in whose voices they are written.

Conclusion

How might we account for the contrast among the three sections in this chapter? And what should we conclude from that contrast? Part of it, no doubt, is one of class. "Sleeping with donkey-like men" is not a phrase Yu Huai would have used for the Qinhuai courtesans who entertained prominent literati and ambitious examination candidates in Nanjing. The popular songs compiled by Hua Guangsheng describe a much lower class of brothel than those portrayed by Lu Qingzi or Wang Shizhen. The contrast also reflects the differing purposes of anthologists or genres. Within the broad range of poetry, Zhang Yingchang's nineteenth-century anthology reflects his concerns as a Confucian social reformer, whereas *Gonggui wenxuan*, a collection of women's poetry from Zhou through Ming times, is much more likely to include poems that highlight the talent and physical allure of elite courtesans. The early Qing memoir of Yu Huai identifies elite courtesan culture nostalgically with the lost world of late Ming loyalism and romance, and the nineteenth-century popular songs of Hua Guangsheng emphasize the suffering of women in cheap brothels.

In addition to contrasting genres, temporal change, as I have tried to argue, also plays a role in the contrasting images of courtesan culture. As the glorious Ming dynasty faded from personal memory, so too did the appeal of nostalgia for its lost glories. Certainly by the eighteenth century, for many the dominant image of the late Ming was one of decadence and irresponsibility. By that time, the Qinhuai district of Nanjing flourished again as it had in the late Ming, but the most prominent literati in the empire were far less likely to celebrate in their published writings their own participation in the pleasure quarters.[34]

Kang-i Sun Chang has described the changes in attitudes toward courtesans and courtesan writings that followed the passing of the generation of Ming loyalists, namely, the revulsion against late Ming romanticism, and the revival of neo-Confucianism in the middle Qing period.

> Most scholars and poets of the early Qing still, of course, shared the late Ming idealization of *qing* and believed that romantic love was a crucial part of the character of a great man. However, from the Middle Qing on, a rather different, much more Confucian and "moralistic" attitude toward love and women is reflected in poetry — partly owing to the revival of orthodox neo-Confucianism during the period. With this change came a completely different view of courtesans. Whereas courtesan-poets of the seventeenth century had enjoyed a position as important as that of the gentry women poets (if not more so), by the eighteenth century courtesans were virtually excluded from the world of refined letters and seldom published their poems. (Even if they did, it was rare for their works to be preserved and respected.) As a result, the eminent female writers of poetry whose names have come down to us from the Middle Qing on were almost invariably born into "literary and official families" (*shuxiang shihuan*).[35]

Yet there are similarities that tie together these seemingly disparate worlds, of late Ming romanticism and mid-Qing sobriety, and of upper-class courtesans and lower-class prostitutes. Throughout both the Ming and Qing, the courtesan world encompassed talented, expensive, and prominent courtesans on the one hand and lower-class "cheap sex" prostitutes on the other. The most elite courtesans were still held in bondage by their brothels, and lower-class courtesans, or prostitutes, might cultivate their artistic talents and hope for redemption by marriage. Both the nostalgic odes to famous beauties and the critical descriptions of poor prostitutes were designed in part to show the sensitivity of the poet to the sufferings of others. Whether rich and famous or poor and obscure, courtesans at all levels sold their services and their bodies in exchange for money. Being in most cases forced to do so, they were not seen as sinful or guilty so much as oppressed and unfortunate. An air of misfortune was attached even to the stars of the profession.

Courtesan voices in the cultural record sometimes parallel literati voices, and sometimes contradict them. Courtesan culture helped inspire romantic love as a theme in poetry and as a reality for some couples. Poems of sad farewell echo literati poems of friendship, and from the late Ming through the Qing period, such farewell poems came to be written by husbands and wives as well. Courtesans also wrote poems to display their talent, their strength of character, or their sensitivity. Similarly, literati, through many centuries, composed poems to impress a superior, win a client, or secure an official appointment.[36]

As for contrasts between courtesan and literati voices, courtesans were much more clear-eyed in seeing through the "glamour" of their profession. Jing Pianpian might paint an alluring image to attract a client, but glamour was not the dominant trait she associated with her business. Whether serving gentlemen or "donkey-like men," the courtesan always knew whose pleasure was being served. Whereas literati often expressed pity at the courtesan's plight, the courtesan was more likely to express anger, whether in the form of wit and sarcasm as with Jing Pianpian or in the anguished cries of anonymous courtesans against the drudgery and oppression they were forced to endure. Literati pity for the oppressed courtesan was more fatalistic than reformist; few even conceived, much less proposed, the abolition of courtesanship's bonded servitude.

I believe the ambiguity of these images ultimately reflects the ambiguous position of courtesanship in Ming and Qing society. Courtesanship stood entirely outside the kinship foundation blocks of Chinese society; yet courtesan quarters flourished because demand for their services was high, and they posed little real threat to kinship structures. They were, moreover, built securely into the structure of a society that was steeply hierarchical yet surprisingly fluid. Lower-class families sold daughters for cash, but their daughters thereby survived and received training in a competitive atmosphere where beauty, talent, and accomplishment were valued, and where upward social mobility through marriage or concubinage was a possibility. The Confucian condemnation of lower-class families for selling their daughters should not distract us from the fact that upper-class families frequently bought such women, as concubines and servants, in a commodity market that flourished through most of the late imperial period. "It could even be argued," Craig Clunas writes,

> that women in Ming [and I would add, Qing] society, particularly those whose status was that of secondary wives or concubines, were in effect commodities, exchanged between families for very large sums of ready cash. . . . When in the early 1640s the scholar Gong Dingzi exchanged 1,000 ounces of silver for the celebrated courtesan Gu Mei, he was not simply living out one manifestation of Ming romanticism, where affairs between men of the elite class and women who lived on the sale of sexual and cultural services were generally acceptable to the former. The fact that the woman's price should survive as a matter of record is powerfully suggestive of the kind of relationship of which it was just a particularly spectacular example.[37]

The prices of commodities being exchanged are seldom recorded in poetry, and in a variety of ways poetry may soften and romanticize the harsh realities of bonded entertainers (and even upper-class courtesans were still held in bondage). Literati nostalgia for lost youth and lost glory might easily distort their, and our, perceptions of the past. Yet some of the poetic images presented above may also exaggerate the negative side of courtesanship. By virtue of our dependence on written sources, we tend to see courtesanship as filtered through the perceptions of upper-class literati who were schooled in Confucian values and held a paternalistic and condescending view of poor and illiterate commoners. Many courtesans undoubtedly longed for redemption from the pleasure quarters, but the popularity of that image in anthologies must owe something to the flattering literati self-image as potential saviors of talented, sensitive women in desperate search of "men of true feeling." Some courtesans must surely have seen their profession and their slim chances for escape clearly enough not to live on false hopes regarding their clients and customers. And it is probably not coincidental that the literati condemnations of the traffic in women tend to attack the supply, rather than the demand, side of the commodity market.

A number of important themes besides economics are missing from this survey. Further research is needed, for example, to explore such questions as religion and its importance to courtesans. To what degree did popular religion (or for the highly literate, elite religion) provide solace to courtesans without families to support them in old age and care for their souls after death? To what degree did the fictive kinship terms used in brothels reflect more than a terminology of convenience or convention? Were there strong ties of sisterhood among courtesans to substitute for the family support systems that permeated the rest of society? Did courtesans see themselves in potential competition with one another for suitors, or did they emphasize their common interests, feel united in their bondage, and turn to each other for companionship in nonexploitive relationships?

The lack of attention to these questions in this chapter reflects in part the tastes, interests, and concerns of the literati who, in collecting, compiling, and publishing poetry by and about courtesans, also determined what has and has not survived. In prizing talent, beauty, and love, in expressing nostalgia for their loss, and in commiserating with women in bondage, Chinese literati were, after all, defining themselves and promoting their own values as they wrote, sifted, collected, and preserved the cultural record of their time.

Even in this necessarily small and selective sampling of writings by and about courtesans, what is striking to me, from these few sources and from the distance of several centuries, is how varied and contradictory are the images associated with courtesan life. The variations and contradictions often reflect class and gender differences in the origins of the sources, but, even more clearly, they reflect the sharp cultural and psychological changes produced by the Ming collapse and the Manchu conquest in the seventeenth century. They also reflect the profoundly ambiguous position of courtesanship, and the complex role of courtesan life, in the culture and society of late imperial China.

2

The Late Ming Courtesan:
Invention of a Cultural Ideal

WAI-YEE LI

The late Ming courtesan is often presented as the epitome of elite culture and sometimes credited with a significant role in the public realm and, more specifically, in the cataclysmic political turmoil of the mid-seventeenth century. This may be traced both in contemporary writings and in later literary or historical reconstructions. Prominent examples include Chen Huan (*zi* [courtesy name] Yuanyuan), Bian Sai (Daoist name: Yujing daoren), and Dong Bai (*zi* Xiaowan) in the poems of Wu Weiye (1609–71); Li Xiang (or Xiangjun) in Kong Shangren's (1648–1718) *The Peach Blossom Fan* (*Taohua shan*);[1] Dong Bai and Chen Yuanyuan in Mao Xiang's (1611–93) *Memories of the Plum Shadows Studio* (*Yingmei an yiyu*);[2] the courtesans of Qinhuai in Yu Huai's (1616–96) *Miscellaneous Records of the Wooden Bridge* (*Banqiao zaji*);[3] Liu Rushi (1618?–64) in the poems by Qian Qianyi (1582–1664) and Chen Zilong (1608–47); and, most recently, Liu Rushi in her biography by Chen Yinke[4] (1890–1969), one of the greatest Chinese historians of the twentieth century. Accidents of character and circumstance probably account in part for this abiding fascination. Even genius or force of personality must, however, have worked within a receptive, perhaps formative, context. It is this context that I propose to examine here. Drawing from the literature on and by these women, I consider questions of how and why the late Ming courtesan became fashioned as a cultural ideal. I focus on two overlapping issues: (1) the connection between the marginality and dubious social station of the late Ming courtesan and her elevation as the symbol of refinement, high culture, freedom, and the possibility of action; (2) the role of male self-representation in creating this image. These issues are in turn related to the idea of the courtesan's self-invention and her invention, including the notion of her self-invention, by the male literati. To provide a context for these questions, I first consider the cultural nostalgia that motivated the interest of contemporaries and later generations in late Ming courtesans.

Cultural Nostalgia

By the early twentieth century, collections of writings on the pleasure quarters of Qinhuai,[5] such as *Encyclopaedia of Qinhuai (Qinhuai guangji,* 1912) or *A Collection of Books on the Allure of Qinhuai (Qinhuai xiangyan congshu,* 1928), could look back to a pattern of splendor and decline over the preceding three hundred years. The periods of decline were apparently occasioned by decrees prohibiting prostitution in the early fifteenth century, late seventeenth to early eighteenth century, and intermittently in the nineteenth century.[6] Far more traumatic for the fortunes of Qinhuai, however, were the wars and political turmoil of the mid-seventeenth, mid-nineteenth, and early twentieth centuries. Records of Qinhuai are almost invariably nostalgic and melancholic: from *Sequel to the Miscellaneous Records of the Wooden Bridge (Xu banqiao zaji,* 1785) to *Remembrances of Qinhuai (Qinhuai ganjiu,* 1906), chronicles of the Qinhuai pleasure quarters hark back to Yu Huai's *Miscellaneous Records of the Wooden Bridge* and evoke its pathos of ephemeral splendor. For later writers, the courtesan culture of their time usually pales beside its late Ming counterpart, as described in Yu Huai's work. But more compelling in the constant references to Yu Huai may be the pathos of linking courtesan culture to personal loss, the end of a dynasty, and the destruction of a culture: the pain of remembrance retroactively legitimizes pleasure. From the mid-nineteenth century on, the sense of an ending associated with the late Ming courtesan is echoed in the looming crisis facing China. Perhaps this explains why late Ming courtesans, first celebrated in the seventeenth century, should encounter a second wave of intense interest in another era of cataclysmic transition and cultural nostalgia, the late-nineteenth and twentieth century.

We shall first explore the intensely elegiac mood of seventeenth-century writings on late Ming courtesans, especially those works written after the fall of the Ming dynasty. It is as representatives of a lost world that the famous courtesans of the period are remembered and imagined. Since the courtesan culture of the lower Yangtze area declined after the collapse of the Ming dynasty, to mourn this lost world implies, at least potentially, a political statement. The best literary example of this mood and its political implications is probably the song of Su Kunsheng, pleasure-quarter music teacher turned woodcutter, in the last act of *The Peach Blossom Fan*. In this song in the last scene, "Lament for the South of the River" ("Ai Jiangnan"), Su describes his vision of devastated Jinling (sequel to scene 40, *THS*, 217–18): the ravaged palace and imperial tombs are starkly juxtaposed with the ruins of the Qinhuai pleasure quarters.[7] Su's song distinguishes itself from its antecedents by fusing historical past and personal past with the immediacy of passionate grief. Instead of offering a sustained meditation on mutability, Su fastens on his experience of the destruction of the pleasure quarters:

> With my own eyes I saw the vermilion mansions
>   being erected;
> With my own eyes I saw feasts being spread;
> With my own eyes I saw the mansions fallen.
> This pile of green moss and blue tiles
> Is where I have slept my wanton sleep,
> And have seen my fill of fifty years of glory
>   and destruction.[8]

A nostalgic tone may evince loyalist sentiments toward the fallen dynasty or, more generally, broad philosophical reflections on the mutability and vicissitudes of history. Sometimes such ruminations became the justification for writing about courtesans. Thus Yu Huai wrote in proleptic defense of his *Miscellaneous Records of the Wooden Bridge*:

> My words are precisely what sum up the prosperity and decline of an era, the feelings for, and reflections over, events of a thousand years. This is not merely an account of pleasure-seeking adventures, or a record of beautiful and glamorous personalities. (*BQ*, 1)

Rather, he claims a moral intention:

> But to linger and forget to return, and to be intoxicated and satiated at all hours — even if a lover should love his beloved, how can one mistake allow another? As a result, to lose the moral fortitude of a

lifetime and to incur the condemnation of those defending the rites and rules of conduct, is that not [like] dark winds that drift and sink and the blue seas' ford of delusion? My compilation of these records, although transmitting the fragrant names [of remarkable women], actually [also] hands down warnings. As Wang Youjun [Wang Xizhi (312–79), famous calligrapher and man of letters] said, "The readers to come will yet be moved by this composition." (*BQ*, 21)

There are inherent tensions here between "transmitting fragrant names" (*chuanfang*) and "handing down warnings" (*chuijie*). On one level, nostalgia over the cultural heritage of Jinling may purport to be an indirect tribute to Ming rule, because the Jinling pleasure quarters may be traced to the "sixteen mansions" (*shiliu lou*), sites of institutionalized entertainment and prostitution established by the first Ming emperor.[9] However, the claims of philosophical reflection and moral vigilance notwithstanding, Yu Huai's book is filled with personal memories too nostalgic to admit of much critical distance. He recalled with pride his role as scribe in this world (*ping'an Du shuji*) and recorded the poems he wrote for various courtesans, although in the postscript he claimed to have burned all the poems and essays he wrote before 1644. He described past associations and love that might have been (with one Li Mei promised to him; *BQ*, 9).[10] As is often the case with this kind of writing, in Yu Huai's book nostalgia for the courtesans' world is bound up with nostalgia for one's youth or another image of oneself.

In a similar vein, but with greater visual force, Mao Xiang described, with typical late Ming self-observation and self-appreciation, how in 1642 he and Dong Bai caused quite a commotion as they climbed Mount Jin. Dong Bai was wearing, at Mao's initiative, a gown "thin as cicada wings, pure as driven snow" made from European gauze over a red dress.

> At that time four or five dragon boats came up against the waves. There were several thousand travelers on the mountain who followed us, pointing to us as immortals. As we went around the mountain, wherever the two of us stopped, dragon boats vied with each other to meet us, making several rounds and not leaving. . . . The splendor of rivers, mountains, and personalities was the highlight of the time. To this day people still speak about the occasion with immense admiration. (*YMA*, 7).[11]

Memories of association with courtesans often involve perception of oneself as a character in a scholar-beauty romance. Mao Xiang writes about attending a new performance of *The Swallow's Letter*[12] with Dong Bai, when Dong and other ladies present were moved to tears: "At that time, talented scholars and beauties, mansions and pavilions, mist and water, new music and bright moon, were all worthy of the ages to come. To this day, when I think about it, it is no different from roaming with immortals or dreams and illusions sought on the pillow" (*YMA*, 7).

Late Ming courtesans continue to fascinate later generations. By the twentieth century, they also come to represent a lost world destroyed by modernity, wars, and revolution. The cultural nostalgia of twentieth-century writers is expressed by the very art form with which they pay tribute to these courtesans. Mao Guangsheng (1873–1959), distantly related to Mao Xiang, wrote *Bian Yujing Remembers Meicun in Death* (*Bian Yujing siyi Meicun*; Meicun is Wu Weiye's *zi*), *Zheng Tuoniang*[13] (*Zheng Tuoniang zaju*), *Ma Xianglan Celebrates Bogu's Birthday* (*Ma Xianglan shengshou Bogu*: Bogu is Wang Zhideng's [1535–1612] *zi*), all included in *Eight Zaju Plays by Regrets Studio* (*Jiuzhai zaju bazhong*; "Jiuzhai" is Mao Guangsheng's *hao*).[14] Wu Mei (1884–1939) celebrates the courtesan Li Shiniang, described in Yu Huai's *Miscellaneous Records*, in a *zaju* play, *Xiangzhen Pavilion* (*Xiangzhen ge*, preface dated 1933). The presumed pivotal role of Chen Yuanyuan in the fall of the Ming—Wu Sangui invited Manchu troops into Beijing upon discovering that his beloved concubine, the former courtesan Chen Yuanyuan, had been abducted by the rebels—revived interest in her as the collapse of the Qing dynasty became first imminent future, then recent past. Chen Yuanyuan emerges as an increasingly heroic figure in plays such as Ding Chuanjing's *Beauty in the Turmoils of History* (*Cangsang yan*, preface dated 1908), Zhang Hongbin's *Headgear-Raising Anger*[15] (*Chongguan nu*, preface dated 1920), and Jieyu Sheng's *Regrets of Yu'an*[16] (*Yu'an hen chuanqi*, preface dated 1938). The defiant anachronism of writing *zaju* and *chuanqi* in the twentieth century and, in the case of *chuanqi*, in evoking the musical world of *kunqu*, the proper domain of late Ming courtesans, is rooted in nostalgia for a lost culture.

The fusion of personal and cultural nostalgia acquires a totally new dimension in Chen Yinke's biography of the courtesan-poet Liu Rushi. Chen's immense admiration for, and empathic identification with, Liu Rushi are evident in his choice of the names Gold Brightness Studio (Jinming guan) and Cold Willow Hall (Hanliu tang) to entitle collections of his writings, for both refer to Liu Rushi's song lyric

"Gold Brightness Pond, on Cold Willows" ("Jinming chi yung hanliu ci," in *LRS*, 336–37).[17] In Chen's biography nostalgia extends to the entirety of traditional Chinese culture. His empathy with Ming loyalism and Liu Rushi's involvement in it can be understood only in terms of his own attachment to a cultural tradition that had suffered drastic ruptures with the onset of modernity and, more specifically, with the policies of the Communist regime.[18] Yu Yingshi's term, "remnant of a culture" (*wenhua yimin*),[19] amply captures Chen's sense of displacement and anguish.

There are moving autobiographical echoes to the biography of Liu Rushi. At the beginning, Chen describes how as a youth he had read the poetry of Qian Qianyi without, he modestly claims, any adequate understanding. During the war with Japan (around 1937) he bought from a seller of old books a red bean supposedly from Qian and Liu's garden at Changshu.[20] "Since I acquired this bean, twenty years have passed in a trice. Although the bean is still kept hidden away in boxes, it is as if it exists yet does not. I no longer look at it. But since then I have reread the writings of Qian, not merely to relive old dreams and to express my longing, but also to test the extent of my learning" (*LRS*, 3). Qian was an immensely learned man whose knowledge extended to esoteric Buddhist and Daoist texts, and Chen was also interested in, and wrote extensively on, Buddhism and Central Asia.

Despite Chen Yinke's protestations of inadequacy, he must have realized that he was one of the few scholars equipped with the necessary literary and cultural competence to explain the works of late imperial poets such as Qian Qianyi and Liu Rushi. In his biography, after unraveling a complex allusion to older literature and to contemporary events,[21] Chen sometimes exclaims: "This would not be understood by many" (see, e.g., *LRS*, 564). The purpose of his enterprise is to show how Liu Rushi, often misunderstood and sometimes maligned, embodies "the independence of spirit and freedom of thought of our people" (*LRS*, 4). To the extent that Chen understands his appreciation of Liu Rushi as a function of his being "the condensation and realization of the spirit of Chinese culture" (the phrase he uses to describe Wang Guowei),[22] one may even say that he is nostalgic about his own nostalgia.

Personal and cultural nostalgia fuse in the poem Chen Yinke composed upon completion of his book. I quote the last two lines: "Through kalpa ashes, the red bean of Kunming is still here, / The longing of twenty years had waited till now to be fulfilled" (*LRS*, 1).

"Red bean" (*hongdou*), also called "seeds of longing" (*xiangsi zi*), here represents a tenuous continuity between past and present. (The motif is also used in Chen's poems on Liu Rushi; see *LRS*, 447.) Kunming, the city where Chen acquired the red bean, is a convenient pun on the Pond of Kunming, which Emperor Wu of the Han dynasty built for naval exercises, and which in classical poetry serves as a standard allusion to vanished glory and power. Kalpa ashes, found when the pond was dug, are ashes that remain from the periodic destruction of the world.[23] The kalpa ashes of Kunming thus symbolize cataclysmic changes that threaten all attempts to recuperate meaning from history. Yet, defying forces of obliteration is the image of the red bean, which establishes the continuity between Chen's experience of twentieth-century Chinese history and his perception of previous periods of turmoil, in this case the seventeenth century. In order to reconstruct the life and writings of Liu Rushi, Chen had to battle two and a half centuries of neglect, misunderstanding, destruction, and suppression. Many of Liu's writings are lost, and their existence or meaning can be inferred only indirectly from the works of her friends and lovers.[24] Chen Yinke is implying that his relationship to the literary and cultural heritage of China is similarly "archaeological," as fragments are retrieved and reconstituted. But the very possibility of overcoming absence and lacunae confirms the faith in cultural continuity.

Chen Yinke sums up his attitude toward the *Biography of Liu Rushi* by quoting Xiang Hongzuo's (1798–1835) preface to his lyrics (*Yiyunci binggao xu*): "Yet if I do not do that which is useless, how can I take pleasure in this life that does have a limit."[25] There is self-conscious irony in the epithet "useless" (*wuyi*). Only the category of the useless can establish the individual's freedom to define a private realm of significance, which is in turn a response to mortality. Chen was doubtful that the book would ever be published, given the circumstances of his final years. (He died in 1969, and his collected works, with the exception of manuscripts destroyed during the Cultural Revolution, were published in 1980.) "Uselessness" is also a proleptic reply to the possible charge that this monumental biography is somehow not the appropriate crowning achievement of a great historian who devoted most of his life to political and institutional history and the history of ideas. The courtesan-poet Liu Rushi was, arguably, not a major figure in seventeenth-century history. However, by showing how Liu inspires as a cultural ideal, Chen Yinke redefined categories of significance in history.

Self-invention

The late Ming was an age of self-conscious passion, dramatic gestures, and deep concern with the meaning of creating a self or a persona. The appeal of the late Ming courtesan stems in part from the idea of self-invention. Most of these courtesans had humble and obscure beginnings. Yet some of them managed to raise themselves by sheer force of will and became accomplished poets, painters, musicians, and persons noted for their refined taste. Liu Rushi, for instance, apparently spent her early years as a maid-servant-concubine in the household of Prime Minister Zhou Daodeng, and eventually achieved renown in poetry, painting, and calligraphy.

Although such accomplishments may have been part of a courtesan's education, many courtesans often took artistic self-definition seriously, probably going well beyond consideration of how their artistic accomplishments might enhance their market value. Liu Rushi, for instance, seems to have self-consciously evolved different poetic styles, partly through association with different literary groups. Chen Yinke shows how Liu moved away from the influence of the Jishe,[26] the literary-political society founded by, among others, her lover Chen Zilong, and thereafter became freer in her allusions to Song poetry, which was held in low regard by Jishe members. Her subsequent association with the older poets from Jiading was in part an attempt to explore new artistic possibilities (*LRS*, 439).

The marginality and dubious social station of the courtesan in a rigidly hierarchical society sometimes became the basis of their freedom of self-definition. Perhaps the best symbols of this freedom are Gu Mei's house and Liu Rushi's boat. Gu Mei's house, famous for its refinement, sumptuousness, excellent cuisine, and endless feasts and gatherings, was dubbed "House of Labyrinths" (*Milou*, a pun on *Meilou*, Mei's mansion) by Yu Huai (*BQ*, 11–12), an allusion to the Palace of Labyrinths supposedly built by the last emperor of the Sui dynasty, who sought therein to indulge in the most extravagant desires and fantasies. The palace was such a maze that, "even were immortals to enter, they would not be able to find their way out."[27] Gu Mei's house is thus portrayed as an ideal space unabashedly devoted to the pursuit of pleasure, in contrast to the more subdued atmosphere of other courtesans' quarters (see, for example, Yu Huai's description of Li Shiniang's compound [*BQ*, 8]). With her marriage to the minister-poet Gong Dingzi and a title conferred by the new Qing emperor (a title Gong's principal wife refused to accept), Gu Mei was among the courtesans who rose most conspicuously on the social ladder.

Whereas Gu Mei's house represents pleasure, select company, and upward social mobility, Liu Rushi's boat symbolizes freedom and independence of spirit. Liu took great pride in the smallness of her bound feet, which probably accounted for her hesitation to travel in mountains (see Liu's letter to Wang Ranming, in *LRS*, 309). Yet this restriction was recompensed by her boat excursions, which she undertook to visit friends and lovers. Qian Zhao'ao describes how "on her leaf-like boat she roamed among lakes and mountains, consorting with great talents and famous artists" (*Zhizhi tan'er, Liu Ruzhi yishi*).[28] The image of the boat figures prominently in Liu's correspondence with Wang Ranming[29] and in the poetic exchange between Liu Rushi and Qian Qianyi.[30] The boat is used, for instance, as the symbol of detachment and freedom (with an implicit reference to Fan Li[ca. 6th c. B.C.] who set his boat adrift on the Five Lakes after his retirement from office): "Over ten thousand miles — why then should you travel in this narrow boat? / The Five Lakes have already allowed a small vessel to be distinguished" (Qian Qianyi, "Adrift on a Boat in a Winter Day with Rushi: Written as a Gift [to Her]"; "Dongri tong Rushi fanzhou youzeng").[31] Using similar motifs, Liu Rushi writes about her life with Qian Qianyi:

> *Following the Same Rhyme, a Respectful Harmonizing*
> ("Yiyun fenghe"), first poem
>
> Under moon-lit curtains, as the songs subside,
>   I search for the duster,
> On the wind-swept bed, with books in disorder,
>   I look for the hair-ornament.
> The mist and water of the Five Lakes will always
>   be like this,
> I wish to follow Zhiyi[32] and drift along the swift
>   stream.

The duster (*zhuwei*) is the inevitable paraphernalia of philosophical discussions (the so-called pure conversations [*qingtan*]) during the Wei-Jin period. The juxtapositions of the duster with songs and of the hair ornament with books suggest a sensuous appreciation for the life of the mind. Defying conventional separation of spheres of experience, Liu celebrates freedom from social constraints in the image of the boat.

The image of the boat also symbolizes mutual understanding: "How dare I give the jade pendant of River Han in the manner of the goddess, / The Prince of E is already moved by the song of Yue" (Liu Rushi, "Following the Same Rhyme, a Respectful Reply" ["Ciyun fengda," the poem is written in the same rhyme as Qian's poem quoted above]," *MZ*, 1284). In the first line Liu disavows any connection with the inconstant goddesses of or by the river.[33] In the second line she alludes to a well-known story from Liu Xiang's (77–6 B.C.) *Shuoyuan*: the Prince of E, as he is being ferried across a river, hears the boatman sing a song in the Yue dialect, which expresses his gladness over sharing the boat with the prince. At first uncomprehending, the prince is so moved when the song is translated into the Chu dialect that he embraces the boatman and gives him sumptuous gifts. The allusion thus conveys the joy of mutual appreciation that overcomes all social barriers.

In the poems exchanged between Qian and Liu, the image of the boat is reminiscent of the quest of the shaman-poet of the *Chuci* for the river goddess, who, in this instance, happens to reciprocate: "Putting both oars in place I welcome you" (Qian, "There Is a Beauty, One Hundred Rhymes" ["Youmei shi yibai yun"], *MZ*, 1300); "My Lord is already expecting me, the oars are in place, / How dare I[34] decline to learn to set my boat adrift" (Liu, "Following the Same Tune, a Respectful Harmonizing," *MZ*, 1400). Qian and Liu were married in a boat and seemed to have stayed there until the completion of the I Have Heard Chamber (Wowen shi),[35] which must have been a rather small enclosed space reminiscent of a cabin on a boat: "The green windows are like those of the magnolia boat" (Qian, "For a Literary Gathering in a Cold Evening, I Composed Another Poem to the Previous Rhyme. That Day the Building of the I Have Heard Chamber Was Completed" ["Hanxi wenyan zaidie qianyun shiri Wowen shi luocheng"], *MZ*, 1284–85). The boat thus combines movement and repose, longing and fulfillment, and suggests freedom and independence in Liu Rushi's exchanges with her friends and lovers.

The idea of self-invention implies a range of possibilities and an aura of mystery. Thus Chen Yinke devotes the first section of his biography of Liu Rushi to deciphering her various names (*LRS*, 17–37). Naming is defining: it is as if different personas or aspects of personality are disclosed through these names. Two of Liu's names are Yun (clouds) and Yin (recluse, hidden). Chen points out that both names were popular among courtesans and unconventional ladies of the period. For example, Xu Fo's *zi* was Yunxuan (Flying clouds); Yang Huilin's, Yunyou (Cloud-friend; *LRS*, 588); Huang Yuanjie's, Liyin (Separate reclusion; *LRS*, 473); and Zhang Wanxian's, Xiangyin (Fragrant reclusion; *LRS*, 34–35, 100).

Among Liu Rushi's earlier names are Zhao (Morning), Zhaoyun (Morning cloud), and Yunjuan (Cloud-beauty). The word *yun* refers to Morning Cloud, the all too willing yet unpredictable goddess of "*Fu on Gaotang*" ("Gaotang fu") and "*Fu on the Goddess*" ("Shennü fu") attributed to Song Yu.[36] Morning Cloud was also the name of Su Shi's devoted concubine. Chen adduces the latter as the probable source of the name Yun (*LRS*, 588), but he is obviously also tempted to compare Liu, and perhaps by extension other courtesans, with the ambivalent divine women from the Chinese literary tradition, such as Du Lanxiang and E Lühua (*LRS*, 502, 621–22), who "came not to any fixed abode" and "left not at any appointed time" (Chen is alluding to lines from Li Shangyin's [812–58] "Passing Again the Temple of the Goddess" ["Chongguo Shengnü ci"], *LRS*, 196, 200). He also quotes "Wandering clouds, without fixed abode," a line from Yuan Zhen's (779–831) "Sequel to the Meeting with the Immortal" ("Xu huizhen shi") in "Story of Yingying" ("Yingying zhuan"), to describe Liu Rushi's peregrinations in the Wu-Yue area (*LRS*, 56–57). (According to Chen Yinke, these associations recur in the poems Liu's admirers and lovers addressed to her. Cheng Mengyang's poems on "Morning Clouds" ["Zhaoyun"] and "Swift Clouds" ["Gengyun," *LRS*, 169–88, 193–225] are good examples.)[37] The late Ming cult of *qing* depends in part on an obscure object of desire, for the obverse side of the infinitude of desire is the multiple possibilities implied by mystery and uncertainty: hence the echoes of the ambivalent divine women, a recurrent topos in Chinese literature, in the courtesan's invention of a persona. At one point in the biography, Chen Yinke suggests that the host of goddesses, ghosts, and fox-spirits in Pu Songling's (1640–1715) *Strange Records from the Liaozhai Studio* (*Liaozhai zhiyi*) had their real-life counterparts in late Ming courtesans from the lower Yangtze area. According to Chen, such is the difference in sensibility between late Ming and early Qing, and between north and south, that Pu can only recreate in his imagination a figure that existed in another time and place.[38]

Although the word *yin*, like *yun*, suggests the elusive and the inaccessible, it has more serious implications of a gap between self and world and a sense of ironic distance from the glamour and splendor of a courtesan's existence. Thus when Liu Rushi styled herself Yin or Yinwen (Hidden cloud-colors),[39] compared herself to the hermit Xu Xuan (active mid-4th c.) disheartened by the crowd (*Wuyin cao*, third poem in a series of eight poems on "Early autumn" ["Chuqiu"]; *LRS*, 306, 312), or wrote about the urgency of "hiding her traces" (*biji*, fifth letter to Wang Ranming; *LRS*, 312, 383–84), there seems to be a genuine preoccupation with escape from her milieu. We can understand this inward distance better if we examine the context of Liu's words: the allusion to Xu Xuan appears in a poem expressing Liu's sense of foreboding about the love between herself and Chen Zilong, and Liu wished to "hide her traces" because of the unwelcome attention of one of her suitors, Xie Xiangsan. In works such as "Written on the Ninth Day" ("Jiuri zuo"), "Evening Views at the End of Autumn" ("Qiujin wantiao"), or "On Late Chrysanthemums" ("Yong wanju"), Liu Rushi uses the image of chrysanthemums to evoke echoes of reclusion and longing through associations with Tao Qian (372–427) and Li Qingzhao (1081–1141) (*LRS*, 352–53). Taken together, her name Liu Yin may mean "being a recluse among the willows of Zhangtai" (*yinyu Zhangtai liu*), that is, hiding her true aspirations behind the facade of her existence in the pleasure quarters. In one of the ten "Xiling" poems from *Wuyin cao*, Liu concludes with an image of concealment: "One tree of red pear blossoms is especially melancholy, / With deliberation it has turned toward the painted pavilion." She thus sets herself apart from other famous courtesans of the West Lake (*LRS*, 451–53).

The creation of a persona often involves dramatic gestures or self-dramatization. Most courtesans were singers and musicians, although Yu Huai remarks that some considered it beneath their dignity to perform (*BQ*, 4). Recall that in *The Peach Blossom Fan*, Li Xiangjun expresses both romantic longing and heroic political action through the language of the theater. In scene 2, she is introduced as learning from the pleasure-quarter musician Su Kunsheng arias from scene 10 of *The Peony Pavilion* (*Mudan ting*). The music lesson is presented as symbolic initiation into love, for in the same scene her union with Hou Fangyu is proposed by Yang Wencong. For Li Xiangjun heroic action is no less mediated and theatrical. When she is forced to perform in front of the evil ministers of the Southern Ming court, she denounces Ruan Dacheng and Ma Shiying (1591–1646) as reincarnation of the villains Yan Song (1480–1565) and Zhao Wenhua (Yan's adopted son), "performing the real *Singing Phoenix*"[40] (scene 24, *THS*, 124). She expresses her disdain in the manner of Mi Heng (ca. 2nd c.), who is celebrated in *The Mad Drummer Played the Yuyang Tune Three Times* (*Kuang guli yuyang sanlong*), the first of four *zaju* plays in *Four Cries of the Gibbon* (*Sisheng yuan*) by Xu Wei (1521–93). (Xu Wei's play depicts a re-enactment in the underworld of Mi Heng's historical denunciation of Cao Cao [155–220], that is, it is itself staged as a performance vindicating a performance that was historically ineffective and cost Mi Heng his life.) As in Xu Wei's play, gestures are turned into cogent political action in *The Peach Blossom Fan*: Li Xiangjun's condemnation of the Southern Ming court is presented as the only mode of action available to her.

Although such meta-theatrical references in *The Peach Blossom Fan* may be explained as a concern specific to the genre, episodes from the lives of courtesans often suggest a sensibility formed through drama or a penchant for dramatizing emotions. We may turn, for instance, to the relationship between Liu Rushi and Song Zhengyu.

> In the beginning, before Yuanwen [Song Zhengyu's *zi*] ever met Liu, Ruzhi [Rushi] arranged for a meeting when they stopped their boats at the White Dragon Pond. Yuanwen came earlier than the appointed time, and Ruzhi had not risen. She passed on a message: "Songlang should not yet board the boat. If he is indeed one of deep feelings, he should jump into the water and wait there." Song immediately got into the water. The weather was cold then. Ruzhi hastily asked the boatman to bring him up, took him to bed, and embraced him to keep him warm. That was how their love began and deepened. . . . Not long afterward, when she was expelled [as a "wandering prostitute," *liuji*] by the provincial governor, Ruzhi consulted Yuanwen for advice. She had put an ancient lute and a Japanese knife on a low table. She asked Yuanwen, "As for our plans now, what is to be done?" Yuanwen answered slowly, "Just try for the time being to dodge the danger." Ruzhi said in great anger, "If others talk like this, it is not surprising. But you should not be like this. From now on I break off all connection with you!" She hewed the lute with the knife and all seven strings broke. Yuanwen left in shock and dismay. (Qian Zhao'ao, *Liu Ruzhi yishi*, in *LRS*, 69)

Life imitates art in these dramatic gestures. Song Yuanwen's ordeal in water is reminiscent of Weisheng, the stubborn lover in the *Zhuangzi*, who clings to a pillar of a bridge waiting for his beloved, as he is swept away by the floods. When Song failed the second test of love and Liu broke the strings of the lute, we are reminded of yet other literary allusions: "How much regret and sorrow can my dark hair bear, / Yet I refuse to be unfeeling like the broken strings" (Yan Jidao [ca. 11th c.], to the tune "Po zhenzi").[41]

In the second test of love Liu Rushi set for Song Yuanwen, she was in effect proposing to him. Liu was not alone in thus taking matters into her own hands and departing from the stereotype of female passivity. Bian Yujing proposed to Wu Weiye at their first meeting, but was too proud to speak about it again when Wu pretended not to understand (Wu Weiye, "Passing by the Grave of the Daoist Priestess Yujing at Brocade Forest, with Appended Biography" ["Guo Jinshulin Yujing daoren mu bing zhuan"], in *WMC*, 250). Dong Bai, described as otherwise withdrawn, frail, long-suffering, though resourceful in *Memories of Plum Shadows Studio*, actively pursued a union with Mao Xiang (*YMA*, 3–5). The same is true of Chen Yuanyuan, who also proposed to Mao Xiang (*YMA*, 2–3), although in Wu Weiye's famous poem, the "Song of Yuanyuan" (*WMC*, 78–79), she is presented as a passive victim.

Metaphors of maleness are sometimes employed in accounts of such active and determined behavior. One is reminded of the androgynous ideal in drama and fiction from this period. In the play *Ideal Love Match* (*Yizhong yuan*) by Li Yu (1611–ca.1680), for example, the courtesan-painter Lin Tiansu disguises herself as a man and "marries" the other painter-heroine Yang Yunyou, as part of a ruse to bring about the union between Yang and the famous painter Dong Qichang (1555–1635). In the play Lin herself marries another famous man of letters, Chen Jiru (1558–1639). (These matches have no historical basis, but both Lin Tiansu and Yang Yunyu were famous seventeenth-century courtesan-painters.)[42] There is every suggestion that Lin is a more impressive "hero" than the other two—male—protagonists of the play. The androgynous ideal is often fashioned around the figure of a beautiful woman endowed with supposedly male talents and virtues, who dresses as a man and assumes male roles, and who nevertheless happily reverts to female roles (as in *The Female Prize Candidate Refused One Offer of Marriage and Received Another* [*Nü zhuangyuan cifeng dehuang*] and *Hua Mulan Joined the Army in Her Father's Name* [*Ci Mulan daifu congjun*] by Xu Wei). Sometimes male talent and female charm reinforce each other, as in Wu Weiye's *Facing Spring Pavilion* (*Linchun ge*), which overturns traditional injunctions against women assuming power in the body politic and presents as the only saving grace of the failing Chen dynasty (557–89) Zhang Lihua, the favored imperial concubine, and Lady Chaoguo, leaders in the civil and military spheres, respectively. Representation of this fusion of gender roles is often playful in tone, for it is not perceived as a threat to sociopolitical order. The woman assuming male attire and male roles in fiction and drama combines complementary opposites and is therefore all the more desirable.[43]

As is well known, Liu Rushi first visited Qian Qianyi dressed as a man. I quote from Gu Ling's *Hedong jun zhuan*: "In the winter of the *gengchen* year of the Chongzhen era [1641], Liu took her boat and visited Qian. She had put on a square scarf (of a scholar), bow shoes (for bound feet), and men's clothes. She was eloquent, free and spirited in expression, with the air of one from the bamboo groves [i.e., one of the seven sages]." The disguise was incomplete, for Liu took care to display her small feet. Liu's male attire was thus a token of the combination of feminine charms with eloquence and intellectuality, supposedly male attributes. According to another, less reliable account of this meeting, from *Muzhai yishi*, at first Qian drove Liu away under the impression that she was one of his ordinary visitors. "But Liu had already revealed her feminine side in some of her poems. When Qian received them, he was greatly surprised. He asked the gatekeeper, 'Was the person who left the visiting card a literatus or a woman?' The gatekeeper said, 'A literatus.' Muzhai became ever more suspicious. He hastily climbed into his carriage and went to look for Liu in her boat and found therein a beautiful woman" (*LRS*, 519–20). We have here two interpretations of Liu's male attire. In the latter version, Liu's disguise was simply a means to cultivate an aura of mystery and was thus part of the game of seduction. She was man and then woman, and it was only as woman that she and her writings could attract Qian's attention. Here she also reverted to being passive, sought after, and even named (in this account Qian concluded by giving her the name Liu Shi and the *zi* Rushi). By contrast, in Gu Ling's account Liu's male aspect is an integral part of her role as friend and intellectual companion. It must have been in this spirit of claiming to be an equal in intellectual exchange that Liu Rushi styled herself "younger brother" (*di*) in her correspondence with Wang Ranming. Her lovers and male friends respected this claim and sometimes addressed her, half in jest, as a man. Qian Qianyi, for instance, referred to her as his "gifted younger brother" (*gaodi*) and punned on her name, calling her "Literatus Liu" ("Liu Rushi").

There are also implications of male attributes and transcendence of gender boundaries in the appellation *nüxia* or *xianü*, often translated "female knight-errant," to courtesans such as Liu Rushi, Li Zhenli, Li Xiang, Ma Shouzhen (*zi* Xianglan, "Orchids of River Xiang," because of her talent as painter of orchids), Kou Mei (*zi* Baimen), Yang Wan (*zi* Wanshu), or Xue Susu.[44] Although the figure of *nüxia* in fiction and drama evokes the image of one adept in martial arts and feats of vengeance, the meaning of the term here is less precise and connotes unconventional behavior, courage, generosity, resoluteness, and independence of spirit. Thus Kou Baimen, concubine of one Zhu Baoguo gong (lord-protector of the state), convinced her husband that it was more profitable to release her when he decided to sell her upon losing everything with the collapse of the Ming dynasty. Kou returned to Qinhuai, set herself up in her old business, and sent Zhu ten thousand pieces of gold within a month.[45] Yu Huai gives a slightly different version in *Miscellaneous Records of the Wooden Bridge*: "In the third month of *jiashen* [1644], the capital fell. Baoguo gong's property and household were confiscated. Baimen gave Baoguo a thousand pieces of gold to redeem herself. Wearing a short jacket, followed by a maid, she returned on horseback [to Qinhuai]. Upon her return she became a *nüxia*, built gardens, entertained friends, consorting daily with poets and artists. Warm and intoxicated with wine, she might sing or cry, mourning the declining years of a beautiful woman—a veritable red bean adrift and homeless" (*BQ*, 50–51). For thus taking her destiny into her own hands and freely expressing her independence of spirit, Qian Qianyi also described her as *nüxia* ("Who knows Baimen for a female knight-errant?"; "Miscellaneous Titles on Jinling" ["Jinling zati"], *MZ*, 2245).

In other cases the term *nüxia* indicates appreciation of unconventional, or even by traditional standards immoral, behavior. Yang Wan, another famous Jinling courtesan, had various lovers after her marriage with the scholar-poet Mao Yuanyi. "Mao prided himself on his generous and unconventional spirit, knew about this and did not interfere."[46] In a poem addressed to Yang Wan on her fortieth birthday, Yang Wencong praised her as "female hero" (*nü yingxiong*) and "knight-errant of Mount E-mei" (*E'mei jianxia*), referring to her association with Mao's military exploits and experience at the frontier (*LRS*, 767–73), perhaps also in tacit acceptance of the more defiant aspects of her personality.

The appellation *nüxia* may also imply the delicate balance between intimacy and restraint, erotic attachment and friendship, in the relationship between a courtesan and her male friends. A good example is the friendship between Wang Zhideng and the famous Qinhuai courtesan-painter Ma Xianglan. According to Wang's biography of Ma, Ma wanted to marry him after he had helped her out of a lawsuit, but he declined. "And yet deep inside us there was a solid bond that could not be undone. As Chan practitioners say, 'For the fish drinking water will know whether it's cold or warm.' Between Ma Xianglan and myself, our hearts were in perfect accord."[47] Wang went on to describe, as one token of Ma's knight-errant temperament, how at 50 she had a lover half her age. Ma's cavalier attitude toward money and her liberal gifts to young men also earned her the reputation of a knight-errant. Wang wrote in the preface to a collection of Ma's poems: "She set little store by money, treating it as mere dust and earth—a veritable Zhu Jia with green sleeves. She took promises seriously, as if they were unalterable as mountains—no less than a Ji Bu wearing rouge and powder"[48] (Zhu Jia and Ji Bu were famous knights-errant from the Han dynasty).[49] On Wang's seventieth birthday, Ma came from Jinling and feted him for a month to fulfill a promise made 30 years earlier. Wang described the event with obvious pride and relish. Shortly thereafter Ma Xianglan died, at the age of 57. "Like a lotus in the house of fire," Wang wrote, Ma had duly prepared for her death with Buddhist ceremony. "As for the Luo Goddess riding on mist, or the Wu goddess turned into clouds,[50] they had not left the realm of desire in the four heavens. How can they be compared to Ma Xianglan!"[51] Ma's serene death and Buddhist detachment are thus presented as a fitting close to her defiant, unconventional life.

In the case of Liu Rushi, the term *nüxia* refers specifically to her military interests and commitment to the Ming loyalist cause. In many ways the hints of an androgynous ideal are most interesting in the case of Liu. In Chen Yinke's biography, she is described as conforming to stereotypes of what passes for the most feminine and most masculine traits. Chen compares her to Lin Daiyu, the heroine of the *Hong lou meng*, "full of sorrow and sickness" (*duoqiu duobing; LRS,* 572), frail and sometimes whimsical; at the same time she was most courageous, engaged, and determined. Liu was famous for her calligraphy in "wild grass script" (*kuangcao*) filled with a "daring, awe-inspiring spirit" (*qiqi; LRS,* 67), which suggests an independent and nonconformist character. Liu's early poems are distinguished by a rugged syntax and a heroic mode.[52] One is tempted to attribute autobiographical echoes to her song lyric on the kite: "To seek in the bright sky a place for freedom and unrestraint" ("On the Kite," to the tune "Shengsheng ling"; quoted in *LRS*, 272–73). Chen Yinke describes her as "literatus and knight-errant in one" (*rushi er jian xianü; LRS*, 144). Liu also implicitly compared herself to Liang Hongyu (*LRS*, 166, 751), another courtesan turned heroic woman of action from the Song dynasty (she assisted her husband, Han Shizhong, in military campaigns against the Jurchens), a comparison often echoed in Qian Qianyi's poems to her (*LRS*, 1025; *MZ*, 1416). Qian Qianyi wrote about recalling in Liu's company memories of military discussions in "Autumn Evening in Yanyu Hall, Moved by Conversations on the Past" ("Qiuxi Yanyu tang huajiu shi yougan"; *MZ*, 1398, and *LRS*, 1, 651–52, 664). I quote the last four lines:

> Heroes buried in the land of fragrant grass,
> Years worn away in the sky with setting sun,
> In the nuptial chamber, with the light of the autumn
>   lamp in the pure night,
> Together we studied the chapter "Discoursing on
>   Swords" in *Zhuangzi*.

In a poem addressed to Qian Qianyi, Du Rangshui refers to Liu Rushi as "a true knight-errant, flower-like, enclosed within the curtains" (*LRS*, 3, 1141).

The fusion of male and female perspectives is amply demonstrated in Liu's prose-poem "Male Spirit of the River Luo" ("Nan Luoshen fu") addressed to the poet Chen Zilong (*LRS*, 133–41).[53] In her preface Liu grounds the prose-poem in her empathy with her friend (*youren*, an unconventional way to refer to a lover, it suggests that Liu consorted with men as their intellectual equal): "It thus occurred to me that the ancients who sought the beginnings [of literary composition] in what is nonexistent and empty, may yet not [produce something] as genuine as this work" (*LRS*, 133). Here we have a gender reversal with a twist. Herself often described as the "goddess of the River Luo" (*LRS*, 135), Liu now writes as a woman addressing a male spirit. However, instead of transferring to the male spirit the skepticism and fears attending the mystique of the feminine in prose-poems on the divine woman, Liu writes in simple praise of the male spirit of the River Luo, undertakes a determined quest of the beloved spirit on her boat, and gives a direct, trustful avowal of love. Traditionally, the quest for the goddess in Chinese literature, especially in the genre of *fu*, is fraught with hesitation, because the goddess is often ambivalent, unpredictable, and ultimately inaccessible.[54] Here we have fervent praise of the spiritual and physical beauty of the male spirit, and the *fu* concludes with the affirmation of love and longing for union:

> Harmonizing with the mysterious music of the goddess
>   of the River Xiang,[55]
> Matching the Gourd with the Weaver Maid [both are
>   names of constellations].
> . . . .
>
> This [love] is not exhausted by those who seek mere
>   resemblance,
> How can it be fathomed by undiscerning communication?
>
> *LRS,* 134

Paradoxically, although the idea of self-invention suggests doubleness and self-dramatization, it has as its core a longing for genuineness.

Inventing Another

Self-invention and inventing another are in some ways two sides of the same coin, especially since the writings, paintings, and calligraphy of these courtesans are in many cases no longer extant, and we often know them only as presented by their male contemporaries or later male authors. In other words, the idea of the courtesan's self-invention is also in part an invention of male literati. The courtesan's self-conscious development of her talent or the mystique of her persona was often aided by a coterie of complicit admirers, who were sometimes also self-appointed mentors. Thus Chen Zilong welcomes Liu as a like-minded soul in his preface to a collection of Liu's poems, *Wuyin cao* (1638):

> And now Liuzi's poetry, how did it come to be so inspired, pure, penetrating, expansive, subtle, and free? . . . For what she sees is no more than the glory of grass and trees, and her gaze does not extend beyond a hundred *li*. . . . Liuzi thus emerged from the blue chamber, and without her conferring or consorting with us, her poetry yet displays a profound affinity with ours. Is this not hard to come by? Is this not hard to come by?" (*LRS,* 112).[56]

The use of the term *Liuzi* here is rather unusual, and suggests a gender-neutral honorific. Although women's poetry was often praised for subtle and nuanced observations and emotions, here Chen praised Liu's poems for their boldness of vision and execution, despite her small world and limited experience as one coming from the "blue chamber" (*qingsuo*, an allusion to *Shishuo xinyu*, meaning "inner chamber," and a skillful avoidance of the term "blue tower" [*qinglou*],[57] a euphemism for the pleasure quarters). Chen Zilong pays tribute to Liu Rushi's independence of spirit, and the motif of "standing alone" (*duli*) recurs in poems addressed to Liu. Early sympathy ("Thinking how difficult it is for you to stand alone"; "Early Plum" ["Zaomei"],[58] *LRS*, 563) merges with increasing respect: "At time standing alone in front of the autumn wind" ("Poem on a Painting of Picking Lotus, Written a Day After the Beginning of Autumn," *CZL*, 246–47; *LRS*, 300); "The weeping willow [a pun on Liu's name] at the ancient waterfront where there is no one: / In all its beauty standing alone on the Hantang Road" ("Shangyi xing," *CZL*, 263; *LRS*, 334).

Earlier I referred to Liu Rushi's various names. In "There Is a Beauty, One Hundred Rhymes" (*MZ*, 1300), possibly the most impressive tribute to a courtesan written in this period, Qian Qianyi set out to establish a distinguished genealogy for Liu Rushi. Although Liu may be an assumed name and Liu's provenance is not certain, Qian treated Liu as her real surname and enlarged on Liu's connection to poets such as Liu Yun (ca. early 6th c.), Liu Zongyuan, and Liu Yong (ca. mid-11th c.). Qian also made a series of allusions to poems and lyrics on willows (*liu*), especially those by Li Shangyin.[59] The poem refers with regret and sympathy to Liu's status as a courtesan: "The willow branch mourns being broken off; / The *miwu* grass unfortunately marks abandonment." ("Miwu" is another of Liu's names: it is an allusion to an ancient style poem [*gushi*, ca. 3rd c.] that describes an encounter between an abandoned woman and her former husband as she goes up the mountain to gather *miwu* grass.)[60] There is, however, also a keen appreciation of how her milieu makes her unique:

> In spirit she was exceptionally free and unrestrained,
> For her education had been different from that of
>   other ladies.
> . . . .
>
> Pure as jade in fire,
> Fragrant as lotus in mud,
> Closing the door she seems to enter the Dao,
> In deep intoxication she wants to escape from Chan
>   teachings.[61]

In other words, by the logic of this poem, the courtesan's life creates for Liu a new freedom, a lack of restraints, detachment, and a sense of irony. Liu Rushi's unconventional character apparently encouraged Qian Qianyi to act in a similarly defiant fashion. Braving social censure, he treated Liu as principal wife (*LRS*, 642).

The courtesan's independence of spirit sometimes has as its corollary the literati's self-representation as a knight-errant defending her rights in a disinterested fashion. Thus Yu Huai defended Gu Mei in a libel suit and proudly recorded his indictment of her accuser (*BQ*, 12). Wang Ranming styled himself "the person in the yellow cloak" (*huangshan*, an allusion to the "knight in a yellow cloak" who brings the unwilling Li Yi to the bedside of the dying Huo Xiaoyu in the Tang tale "Huo Xiaoyu zhuan")[62] as he devoted himself to the interest of his courtesan friends (*LRS*, 367).[63] He was probably responsible for bringing about the meeting of Qian Qianyi and Liu Rushi. Mao Xiang lamented his inability to play the role of "the knight-errant in yellow cloak" vis-à-vis Dong Bai, and his friend Liu Luding offered several *hu* of ginseng to help Dong Bai pay off her debt (*YMA*, 6). Qian Qianyi was considered General Overseer of Romantic Affairs (*guangda fengliu jiaozhu*; *LRS*, 642, 701)[64] and personally escorted Dong Bai to Mao Xiang's home at Rugao (*YMA*, 8). He also tried to arrange a meeting between Wu Weiye and Bian Yujing after they presumably had broken off their relationship (*WMC*, 159–61, 1139–40; *LRS*, 497). The courtesans' independent choices were made possible by the help and appreciation of their literati friends. As mentioned above, these relationships often combine disinterested friendship with nuances of intimacy.

The image of the courtesan's freedom and independence of spirit stands in flagrant contrast to the pathos of bondage and humiliation in the lives of some courtesans, especially during the chaotic years of dynastic transition. Yu Huai's *Miscellaneous Records* contains many such accounts. However, the courtesan's victimhood or helplessness also captured the imagination of the cultural elite. This happened, first, by way of identification. Thus the eighteenth-century scholar-essayist Wang Zhong (1745–94) expressed his empathy with the courtesan-painter Ma Xianglan in his "Elegy for Ma Shouzhen, upon Passing by the Former Compound" ("Jing jiuyuan diao Ma Shouzhen wen").[65] Wang Zhong congratulated himself on being born a man and thus spared the pain and humiliation of being a woman and a courtesan, but he could certainly identify with the burden of "showing different faces upon raising and lowering one's head, and having one's joys and sorrows controlled by others," and the frustration of talent unrecognized, the parallel between the unloved beauty and the unappreciated scholar being a standard conceit in classical poetry. (As mentioned above, Ma was rejected by Wang Zhideng, the man of her choice, although he did write a laudatory preface for a collection of her poems.)

Second, victimhood captured the imagination because it dramatizes the disjunction between individual experience and momentous historical events. Such disjunctions are intrinsic to our experience and understanding of history. The famous "Song of Yuanyuan" by Wu Weiye (*WMC*, 78–79) is a case in point. The poem in effect contains two stories, that of the courtesan Chen Yuanyuan and that of the fall of the Ming dynasty. Wu Weiye described how Chen Yuanyuan realizes the cliché of "toppling the city and toppling the country" (*qingguo qingcheng*) merely by being "the object of desire." Chen Yuanyuan has no control over her drastic changes of fortune. She is not even credited with understanding the implications of her lover Wu Sangui's actions. From Chen's point of view (which dominates the whole middle section of the poem), she is just a hapless victim who happens to be vindicated by circumstances (in the sense that she achieved reunion with Wu Sangui):

> Then she was burdened by her fame,
> Noble and powerful houses vied with each other for
>   her possession.
> "One *hu* of pearls" was sung with ten thousand *hu* of
>   sorrow,
> She wasted away as she drifted through the land.
> But she was wrong to blame the ruthless wind for
>   scattering the fallen blossoms,
> For boundless spring has returned to heaven and earth.

The real agent of action in the poem, the main culprit as it were, is Wu Sangui. The pathos of Chen Yuanyuan's story lies in her role in bringing about the collapse of the Ming dynasty in her uncomprehending passivity.

In later accounts of Chen Yuanyuan's life, she takes her destiny in her own hands. In Lu Yunshi's biography, Chen actively pursues union with Wu Sangui. She urges Tian Wan, her master, to seek the protection of Wu. In the course of a banquet for Wu, she makes it clear to Wu that she was another Red Duster seeking a more worthy master.[66] Later, when she is abducted by the rebels, she makes the most of the situation and in the end achieves reunion with Wu. Together with Wu, she plots rebellion against the Qing dynasty. Chen emerges as an ambitious, resourceful, and ruthless character in this account. By contrast, Niu Yuqiao vindicates Chen Yuanyuan in his biography and removes all suggestions of ambition and opportunism. Niu emphasizes her self-abnegation, loyalty, and inward detachment. She refuses to be Wu Sangui's principal wife after Wu gains great honor for the key role he plays in the Ming-Qing transition. When she finds out about Wu's plot to rebel, she asks to become a Daoist nun to atone for the sins of Wu. After the failure of the rebellion and the death of Wu, she mysteriously disappears. In Niu's account, Chen comes to symbolize the attempt to preserve integrity in troubled times, an attempt dignified by the aura of mystery and religious renunciation.

Ding Chuanjing's play *Beauty in the Turmoils of History* draws from both Lu's and Niu's accounts and adds a final "expiatory" act to Chen's life. After Wu Sangui's rebellion fails, she commits suicide by throwing herself into a lotus pond, out of personal loyalty to Wu. The last three acts of the play are devoted to the remembrance and interpretation of Chen's life. In scene 18, "The Spirit Wanders" ("Hunyou"), Chen's ghost comes back and visit sites of personal and historical significance: Wu's palaces in Yunnan, Suzhou, and Beijing. In scene 19, "The Spirit Descends" ("Jiangluan"), her spirit comes forth in an invocation ritual to tell her life story in eight song-lyrics. The last scene, "Visiting the Grave" ("Fangmu"), shows a scholar retracing the memories and legends of Chen Yuanyuan at her grave. The various overviews of Chen's life in the last three scenes of the play turn Chen's perception and experience into a symbol of the dilemmas of the individual caught in the upheavals of history.

Published in 1908, Ding's play still adheres to the official version of the Manchu conquest as just and necessary. It follows, therefore, that Chen Yuanyuan is the key agent of a necessary historical process, and it is as such that Ding Chuanjing pays her tribute. Zhang Hongbin's *Headgear-Raising Anger*, fragments of which were published in 1920, presents a more heroic and loyalist Chen Yuanyuan. Here Chen's avowed model is Liang Hongyu. When she urges Wu Sangui to leave for military duty shortly after their marriage, Wu's father calls her "a man among women." Acting as a Ming loyalist, she agrees to marry the rebel leader Li Zicheng, in the hope of provoking Wu San-gui to turn against Li. (Zhang describes Wu as being ready to surrender to Li.) Lamenting her fate and the fate of her country, she borrows the language of an abandoned courtesan from the Tang *chuanqi* story "Huo Xiaoyu zhuan." "I, a woman, am yet ever so unshaken in my will, while you, a man, betray your intention in this manner. What hope can there still be for the country!"[67]

The later developments of Chen Yuanyuan's story combine two dominant themes in the romanticized image of the courtesan caught in a historical crisis: heroic action and religious renunciation. In *The Peach Blossom Fan*, the heroine Li Xiangjun also embodies these two alternatives. Although not represented as being engaged in political action, Li Xiangjun becomes a symbol of heroic resistance against the corrupt forces of the Southern Ming court. According to Hou Fang-yu's (1618–55) biography, the historical Li Xiang "could discern the integrity or lack thereof among scholar-officials." Her dramatic rejection of the trousseau supplied by Ruan Dacheng (*THS*, scene 7) is based on her advice to Hou to refuse the role of mediator in the bitter recriminations of the Fushe scholars against Ruan Dacheng. Hou also tells of her refusal to marry the powerful minister Tian Yang (*THS*, scene 22).[68] In other words, Li Xiang's heroic image is first celebrated by her lover Hou Fangyu. As Kang-i Sun Chang has shown in *The Late Ming Poet Ch'en Tzu-lung*, the cult of romantic love and the pathos of heroic action in the public realm are closely intertwined in the Ming-Qing literary tradition. The blood-spattered peach-blossom fan shows how self-representation, artistic pursuit, and the preoccupation with romantic love have to be by definition also a political statement after the upheavals of the mid-seventeenth century. At the end of the play, Li Xiangjun realizes the futility of passion in the midst of general chaos and collapse and becomes a Daoist nun, taking Bian Yujing as her teacher.

There are correspondences to these literary examples in the life of Liu Rushi. In Liu's case, reclusion and withdrawal were apparently consequent upon the acceptance that heroic action was no longer possible. As Chen Yinke so well documented, Liu Rushi was actively engaged in attempts to restore the Ming and perceived herself as a latter-day Liang Hongyu. When all hopes for the Ming cause were lost, Liu chose religious renunciation and reclusion.

The loyalist activities of Liu Rushi were, of course, a tabooed subject during the Qing dynasty. But the martyrdom of another courtesan, Ge Nen, is described in *Miscellaneous Records of the Wooden Bridge*. Ge Nen's lover, Sun Lin (*zi* Kexian, 1611–46), was involved in the resistance against the Manchus. When Ge was arrested with Sun, she defended her honor and conviction with a gruesome death (*BQ*, 10). Here the juxtaposition of the accounts of how Sun Lin quickly became enamored of Ge Nen and how he was inspired by Ge's martyrdom to die a heroic death suggests that the same intensity of feeling can inspire both romantic passion and courageous action (*BQ*, 10). Ge Nen's martyrdom is celebrated in a *chuanqi* play, *Flowers of Blood* (*Bixue hua*) by Wang Yunzhang (1884–1942).[69] Accounts of the late Ming courtesan as heroic loyalist, whether historical or fictional, were mostly written in the twentieth century. Qing literature often enlarged upon another image of the courtesan: the recluse who embraces religious renunciation.

The best-known examples are probably Wu Weiye's poems on Bian Yujing. The "Song on Hearing the Daoist Nun Bian Yujing Play the Zither" ("Ting nüdaoshi Yujing tanqin ge") was probably written in the same year as "Song of Yuanyuan" (1652). Both Bian and Chen at one point lived in Lindun Lane (Lindun li). Both suffered the most drastic reversals in the chaotic Ming-Qing transition. Bian, however, escaped the suspicion of being a beneficiary of political turmoil by becoming a Daoist nun, singing of the misfortune of women dislocated like herself. Bian acquired a privileged position as commentator on the vicissitudes of history and may in this sense function as another persona of the poet.[70] With the consolidation of the new dynasty, the choice of withdrawal and reclusion was one of the more honorable alternatives, but not one that many members of the literati were at liberty to take. Many had to take the civil service examination and serve in the Qing government against their will. Refusal to participate in the examinations was sometimes considered tantamount to resistance against the new regime (*LRS*, 715–16). Perhaps this explains the tendency to romanticize the pathos of the courtesan's choice of renunciation, the rationale being that they could withdraw from the public realm in which they were marginal to begin with.

In reality, of course, withdrawal was not necessarily a happy choice — Bian Yujing, for example, became a Daoist nun because of an unhappy marriage. In the "Song on Hearing the Daoist Nun Bian Yujing Play the Zither," however, Bian acquires the aura of one acting with resolution and judicious judgment and telling her own story with understanding. She escapes the fate of abduction by the northern troops by a timely decision:

> I secretly changed my garb and came to the river,
> And by chance encountered the boats from Danyang
>   at the sandbank.
> I cut a robe of yellow cloth and with relish became a Daoist,
> Carrying a green patterned lute to tell of [the woes of]
>   beautiful women.
>
> WMC, 63–64

Courtesans are sometimes presented as being those most capable of detaching themselves from sensuous existence precisely because they have lived it to the full. The notable example of Ma Xianglan has already been mentioned. According to Qian Qianyi, other courtesan-poets that became interested in Buddhism include Wang Wei (the Grass-cloth Daoist [Caoyi daoren]),[71] Zheng Ruying, Zhu Wuxia, Ma Ruyu, and Xue Susu.[72] With varying degrees of historical veracity, the choice of religious renunciation in the cases of Liu Rushi, Bian Yujing, Li Xiangjun, and Chen Yuanyuan (the latter two examples probably have no historical basis) is represented as a political statement.

The heroines in traditional drama and fiction are often more passionate and interesting than the heroes. Li Xiangjun is much more appealing than Hou Fangyu in *The Peach Blossom Fan*: whereas Li is single-mindedly devoted to heroic and romantic ideals, Hou is inclined to compromise (*THS*, scene 7) and intermittently forgetful of his association with Li.[73] This disparity persists in historical accounts such as Chen Yinke's portrayal of Qian Qianyi and Liu Rushi.[74] Although Chen Yinke takes pains to vindicate Qian Qianyi and traces his involvement in attempts to restore the Ming, he concedes that although Liu modeled herself on Liang Hongyu, Qian was not one to play Han Shizhong (*LRS*, 1025). Chen also commends the Hongguang emperor for not granting Qian's request for military command, "for had his wish been granted, Hedong jun would, of course, have been another Ge Nen, but Muzhai might not have been able to act like Sun Third [Sun Lin]" (*LRS*, 668). The question remains why such images of heroic action, moving testimony, or authoritative commentary are celebrated in literature and history. I conclude by speculating on the possible connection among these images and the self-perception of the authors producing them.

72   WAI-YEE LI

As is well known, Bian Yujing was a former lover of Wu Weiye. Is there possibly a bad conscience at work as Wu concedes to Bian a superior vision and merges his voice with hers? Wu Weiye was not alone in betraying the love or expectations of a courtesan. Other examples are Chen Zilong and Song Zhengyu with Liu Rushi, Mao Xiang with Chen Yuanyuan and possibly Dong Bai (although Mao seems quite unaware of it),[75] and even Yu Huai with Li Mei. In addition, there is often a suggestion that these courtesans set standards of honorable action during the dynastic transition that male literati were unable to meet. According to Gu Ling, Liu Rushi tried to convince Qian Qianyi to die a martyr to the fallen Ming, but he could not follow her advice. Liu then tried to drown herself but was held back. A similar story, probably with less basis in fact, is told about Gu Mei and Gong Dingzi.[76] Wu Weiye's poems on Bian Yujing also reveal a sense of unease about his own compromise with the new regime, which compares unfavorably with Bian's choice of reclusion and religious renunciation. Perhaps in some cases faint echoes of the preface to *Hong lou meng* retroactively apply — in other words, the sense of being unfulfilled and unjustified in one's existence is combined with the idealization of women who to some extent escape social and political constraints. The sensuous existence of the courtesan is thus perceived as the embodiment of *qing*, variously expressed as freedom and independence of spirit, courage and heroic action, detachment and understanding, and the overcoming of the boundaries between private and public spheres.

If the idealization of the late Ming courtesan by her literati associates is often a function of their own sense of inadequacy and failure, then the abiding fascination with these figures in later periods is based on the power of these romanticized images and sometimes related to the perception of contemporary historical crisis. Thus with Chen Yinke, for instance, the burden of negativity is both personal and historical. The distortion and suppression of the "truth" of Liu Rushi's life and writings are explained by the traditional and, even more so, contemporary repressive forces of Chinese culture and society. As my conclusion, I quote Chen's poem (third in a group of three) on a painting of Liu Rushi:

> Buddhaland and Bodhisattva Mansjuri all turned
>   into dust.
> Why then should I still write about the person
>   scattering flowers?[77]

White poplars in front of the grave have changed
    many times,
Only the red bean, left behind forever, preserves the
    spring.
Limitless heaven and earth have betrayed you.
Seas and mulberry fields[78] only deepen the sorrow.
Declining and decrepit, how dare I discuss events of
    a thousand years?
I can only write poems on the reality of Cui Hui in
    the painting.[79]

3

The Written Word and
the Bound Foot: A History
of the Courtesan's Aura

DOROTHY KO

Once the national hub of sensuous pleasures, the courtesan quarter in Nanjing was reduced to ruins in 1645. Jiangnan gentry society, which had lavished money in the late Ming period (ca. 1550–1644) and lent the courtesans its own cultural aura, was dealt a severe blow by the Manchu monarchs. By 1673, the Qing court had formally ended the centuries-long tradition of maintaining official prostitutes in the capital and the provinces. Although the pleasure industry continued to operate in the private sector under the nominal supervision of civilian authorities, it had lost its luster.[1]

It took a very long time, almost 150 years, before pleasure seekers trickled back to Nanjing with their writing brushes in the late eighteenth century. One connoisseur, who called himself the Flower-Extolling Scholar, made the rounds with two friends. Stopping by a courtesan house, they visited a pair of sisters. While exchanging niceties, the Scholar casually inquired: "Are you both well versed in literature?" The elder sister replied that "my younger sister knows everything." The Scholar teased her: "You don't mean that she knows even the word 'one'?" Written in a horizontal stroke, the word "one" is the easiest in the entire Chinese language. This simple fact, however, eluded the courtesan, who let out a solemn and triumphant "For sure."[2] She was utterly illiterate.

The Scholar's lament over the courtesan's sorry decline was packaged for profit: a guide he had published in the previous year had fared so well that within months pirated editions appeared. He hoped that the hastily produced sequel could cash in on the success.[3] The vulgarization of courtesan culture in the nineteenth century is thus evident in both the goods purveyed and their buyers: the women's illiteracy and the lower social position of their clients. Not only did the courtesan turn out to be a shadow of her glamorous past, the Scholar himself was at best an impersonator of a literatus. Merchants and semi-literate vendors had replaced aspirant and high-ranking scholar-officials as the financiers and chroniclers of pleasure. Announcement of profit and instant gratification, not deferment and concealment of desires, became the mark of the trade.

The Written Word and the Bound Foot: Two Faces of Civility

Ironically, this vulgarization offers the historian an unprecedented opportunity to look directly at the courtesan, unbedazzled by her blinding aura. With perfect hindsight, the historian may begin to understand and reconstruct the courtesan's aura as an integral part of a bygone universe — an ambience, a textual tradition, a culture, a civilization. The courtesan was a popular yet elusive figure in Chinese cultural history. Like a quantum wave-particle in physics, she was everywhere and nowhere at the same time. Social and gender ambiguities lie at the heart of her personal mystique and social function. Born in the lowest ranks of society, she mingled with the most exalted men in the empire. Her abode was fashioned after the gentleman's studio, a private retreat in the domestic realm, yet it was there public men networked over the wine and food she served. To her male suitors, she was the embodiment of feminine charm; in the eyes of domestic women, she rivaled men in boldness and mobility. Throughout the dynasties, vernacular stories, poetry anthologies, jottings, and memoirs constructed and transmitted her multiple literary personae: the powerful femme fatale, the pitiful old maid, the sagacious lover, the virtuous heroine.

This chapter seeks to illuminate the centrality of the courtesan's aura in Chinese literati culture while trying to locate her in historical time and place. We begin with a brief review of the historical forces that brought on the decline of courtesan culture and some remarks on the generic characteristics of "blue-building [brothel] literature." The bulk of the chapter explores the tension between two of the courtesan's defining attributes: her membership in the scholar-official's world, one signified by his monopoly over the written word as gateway to political power and cultural authority, and her embodiment of sensuous femininity in the form of footbinding. In part, this tension is expressed in terms of a gender ambiguity between the courtesan who wrote and the courtesan who had her feet bound. We will see that this tension between the public nature of her name and the concealed mystique of her bound feet constituted the aura of courtesan culture at its height.

Equally salient to the courtesan's elusiveness are her ambiguous positions in class and kinship hierarchies. This ambiguity manifested itself most clearly in the courtesan's ambivalent relationship with the gentry wife. At their zenith in the late Ming, highly erudite courtesans commanded an artistic respect that, in the eyes of some editors, put them on a par with the equally erudite gentry wives. Their poetry was published between the same covers, and courtesan and wife occasionally befriended each other. In the eighteenth and nineteenth centuries, however, the gentry wife continued to publish her poetry on the condition that she chastise and exclude the entertainer, and the ranks of pleasure women swelled as illiterate daughters flocked to the trade. The nineteenth-century courtesan's illiteracy thus signaled a hardening of boundary separating the wife from the entertainer and an ideological purge that sought to sanctify domesticity as the seat of feminine virtue and purity. A degree of interpenetration between the domestic and courtesan's worlds gave way to mutual exclusion, as elite women celebrated their public monopoly over the female poetic word.

During the twilight of imperial China, the practice and status of both writing and footbinding changed radically. The advent of popular education, lithography, and tabloid journalism fashioned the written word as an instrument of a new politics of inclusion instead of exclusion.[4] Writing became a means to mass entertainment, social engineering, and even national salvation. What transpired sounds dangerously close to a tautology: the written word was vulgarized when more than a chosen few could lay claims to its utility and authority. Footbinding met the same fate when mothers from the lower classes and peripheral areas began to emulate the gentry wife by binding their daughters' feet. Once footbinding ceased to be a marker of refinement and class distinction, its downward spiral mirrored that of courtesan culture: both had become a measure of a civility that was irrevocably lost. The history of the courtesan's aura, in the final analysis, is an integral chapter in the history of the Chinese imperium and the power of *wen* (literature, civility, culture) on which the imperium rested its cultural and political authority.

By the nineteenth century, the social and economic foundations of courtesan culture were so shaken to the core that the courtesan's demise was inevitable. Not only had the caliber of the women plummeted, but the economic basis of courtesan culture had dissipated. The political decline of the gentry class, the subsequent destruction of Jiangnan during the protracted Taiping Rebellion (1850–64), and the shifting of the empire's economic locus to such coastal ports as Shanghai had further robbed the Nanjing quarters of worthwhile patrons. Wealthy examination candidates and sons from the upper strata of literati society — the mainstay of late Ming opulence — had ceased to exist as a social class.[5] The abolition of the civil-service examination in 1905 signaled not only the imminent end of a dynasty but also the demise of the culture-power nexus that lent the imperium its legitimacy. Although prostitutes at the top of their trade continued to fashion themselves "courtesans" in twentieth-century Shanghai, they were as far removed from the imperial courtesans as the dejected examination candidates were from the literati.

The vulgarization of courtesan culture did not simply coincide in time with the decline of the Chinese imperium, nor is it enough to state that the two were propelled by the same economic and demographic dynamics. This chapter will argue that the worlds of imperial elites and courtesans were in fact conjoined, that the former was reflected and magnified in the latter. The waning of one spelled the demise of the other. To the extent that the Scholar's encounter with the illiterate courtesan signified a historical denouement, his lament has to be distinguished from the cultural nostalgia that constituted the aura of the courtesan world at its heyday, a theme that Wai-yee Li explores in this volume (see Chapter 2). That literate courtesan-turned-concubines continued to appear in nineteenth-century domestic memoirs does not detract from the general erosion of the cultural positions of the courtesan and her patron.[6]

Yet the Flower-Extolling Scholar's broaching of the subject of literature is significant. The cultural ideal of the literate courtesan endured, however remote it may have been from nineteenth-century realities. The impossible distance, in fact, only served to enhance the allure of the ideal. This special connection between the Chinese courtesan and the written word—and, by extension, the civil world of *wen*—constitutes one of the twin concerns of this chapter. A courtesan (*mingji*, literally "famous prostitute"), in fact, distinguished herself from a mere prostitute (*ji*) by being well known: a courtesan was one who was being written about. At the same time, a courtesan worthy of her name was also expected to be well versed in literature, always ready to compose a lyric. The writing courtesan was engaging in a male activity, often in the presence of men. In the late Ming times, she was the harbinger of a new womanhood that gentry wives found attractive. The relationship between this attraction and writing will also be explored in this chapter.

The second of the chapter's concerns is the courtesan's special connection with footbinding. Palace dancers and courtesans in the tenth to twelfth centuries were believed to be the first to bind their feet.[7] In imperial China, the tiny-footed entertainer was the ultimate arbiter of female sensuality. There is, however, a curious paucity of overt praise of the courtesan's bound foot in the genre of blue-building literature produced in the seventeenth century. It was not until the courtesan's vulgarization had become a fact that explicit references to her feet became common in nineteenth-century accounts. The paucity of mentions of footbinding in the late Ming accounts, when it clearly was a valorized practice in the entertainment quarters, bespeaks a gap between social practice and textual expressions. This gap, in itself, constituted the enchantment of the world of illusory pleasure.

This disjuncture stems in part from the particular nature of blue-building literature. Although the genre was instrumental in defining and transmitting a literary tradition of the courtesan's aura through the dynasties, its goal was never simply realistic depiction. As a literary genre, blue-building literature is as multifarious and ever-changing as the courtesan herself. In late imperial times, it borrowed from, and in turn inspired, the genre of "reminiscence" (*yiyu*), highly expressive memoirs by bereaved husbands of the domestic bliss shared with a concubine procured from the entertainment quarters.[8] Furthermore, Andrea Goldman has shown that authors of "flower registers" (*huapu*), a genre that flourished among patrons of the Beijing theater in the late eighteenth and nineteenth centuries, depicted the sensuality of male actors in terms that were self-consciously modeled after those of courtesans in the blue-building literature.[9]

The prototype of the genre is Sun Qi's *Records of the Northern Quar-*

ters (Beili zhi), a personal description of the pleasure quarters in Chang'an, the Tang capital city, during the waning decades (ca. 847–88) of the once-glorious dynasty.[10] In four respects, the *Records* sets the tone for subsequent works in the genre: authorship by an elite male; portrayal of courtesans as individuals in a biographical format; definitions of the courtesan's allure in terms of her beauty, living quarters, music, and poetry; and in the end a moral warning against indulgence. In spite of, or perhaps because of, the uniformity and detached tone of the biographical treatment, the courtesans often appear to be akin more to a prototype than to genuine individuals. The courtesan's quarters, in turn, are remembered less as the site of private pleasures than as a stage for national and existential dramas, permeated by deceit, illusion, enchantment, regret, and mourning.

The Courtesan's Name: Being Written About

Whereas courtesans featured only in works of blue-building literature often appear as a prototype, The Courtesan as it were, those who were being written about in multiple genres emerge as willful and memorable individuals. This may explain the apparent profusion of courtesans and their striking textual visibility in late Ming scholar-official culture. The names and deeds of courtesans turned up in the most unlikely sources — unlikely because of the author's or the genre's respectability — collected essays of leading members of the literati; poetry anthologies compiled by men of letters; collected verse of gentry wives.[11] The terms in which courtesans were described in these accounts bespeak the high artistic and social standing that the most distinguished public women enjoyed.

The Fujian courtesan Lin Tiansu, for example, received praise from her friend, Dong Qichang (1555–1636), the foremost painter and critic of his times. Art historian Marsha Weidner has described Lin as primarily a landscape painter who "was well-versed in the styles of the 'orthodox' lineage of Dong Qichang's Southern School."[12] Few painters could have hoped for a kinder word from the illustrious Dong: "For thirty years as I diddled in the mountains, I have been hearing about many ladies who can paint, all working around the West Lake in Wulin [Hangzhou]. First there was Lin Tiansu, then came Wang Youyun. Tiansu's paintings are elegant to the extreme, while Youyun's are diffuse and remote."[13]

Dong's reference to Lin as "lady" (*guixiu*) is curious. The term *gui-xiu* (short for *guifang zhixiu*), literally "elegance from the inner quarters," was commonly used in the late Ming to denote a gentry woman with artistic talent. The idealized separation between the gentry woman's secluded world and the courtesan's public world is emphasized by a common contrast of *guixiu* with "airs from the forest" (*linxia zhifeng*), which conjures up an image of the unrestrained courtesan or Daoist woman. Dong Qichang's reference to Lin Tiansu as *guixiu*, then, is an annulment of the idealized separation between the female chambers and entertainment quarters on the one hand, and between the domestic and public women on the other.[14]

The same interpenetration of the two previously disjointed categories of women is evident in the address of Lin to another courtesan who thrived in the same patronage circles, Wang Wei (ca. 1600–ca. 1647). In a preface to the collected letters of a mutual courtesan friend, Liu Rushi (1618?–64), Lin referred to Wang Wei as "lady-scholar" (*nü-shi*). Similar to *guixiu*, the honorary title *nüshi* had been a prerogative of the respectable domestic woman before it was appropriated for the courtesan.[15] In late Ming Jiangnan, as the numbers, visibility, and respectability of the educated women grew, *nüshi* became a marker not of a woman's social location but of her learning. The prefix *nü* was a nagging reminder of the gender ideal that assumed scholarship to be a male vocation. A courtesan who was called *guixiu* was honored as a gentry wife, whereas the wife or courtesan who was called *nüshi* was crowned an honorary man.

Being an honorary man is not what the courtesan was about. The vocation of the courtesan was to be a woman in a man's world, to be the man's companion if she was mediocre and his alter ego if she was outstanding. Famed as an avid traveler, Daoist, and poet-editor, Wang Wei was superb. Her longtime friend and fellow traveler Tan Youxia (1583–1637) highlighted her femininity while trying to capture her multiple identities in a preface he contributed to a poetry volume of Wang's:

> In the autumn of 1619, I met Wang Wei on the West Lake and took her to be a man [*ren*] on the lake. After a while she longed to retire to the waters, and I took her to be a man from the lofty distance. She forsook her fragrant powder, but her hair was still piled up as clouds; I took her to be a lady. Everyday she wandered in and out of the autumn waters and fallen leaves with people in the likes of me, as if she had no worries to attend to. I took her to be a man of leisure.

In her outings she behaved like a man yet looked like a woman. As such, Wang Wei was a perfect companion.

Tan appreciated the same shifting qualities in Wang's poetry: "In her verse there are words from the streets, words from the female chambers, and words from the Dao." Yet to Tan, her poetic talent and male-like nonchalance were the true markers of her womanhood: "[A third-century man] Xun Fengqian once said, 'Neither talent or virtue is relevant to a woman. She should be signified primarily by her beauty [*se*].' These are uninformed words. For a person like her with poetry like hers, what does beauty matter? Yet the world does not know it, and still takes her to be a mere woman."[16] A courtesan who was called a female alter ego of a man, Wang Wei occupied a gender-ambivalent space of her own. Tan boasted no high office, but he belonged to a select literati group, the Return [to Antiquity] Society, that was at the forefront of late Ming political and literary reforms.

Wang kept more illustrious company. On one occasion, she had a tomb built for herself, emulating the Tang official and poetry critic Sikong Tu (837–908). The gesture of staring death in its eyes was a willful celebration of life, and the party that gathered at the opening festivities responded in kind. Dong Qichang, whose calligraphy was worth its weight in gold, dedicated a colophon: "'Tis the Chamber of the Future." Chen Jiru (1558–1639), another arbiter of literati taste, wrote a commemorative essay. Chen's address to Wang Wei in his essay is the epitome of the exalted location of the late Ming courtesan: Chen simply referred to her as "Wei the Daoist Adept" (Wei Daoren). He did not use a prefixal female marker, nor did he allude to her entertainer identity by attaching the usual *mingji* or *ji* (a different word in Chinese than prostitute: maiden, concubine). A courtesan who was not called one: this lack of a name is the ultimate marker of a woman who was at the pinnacle of her trade.

Chen Jiru further complimented Wang Wei in the preamble of his essay: "To commemorate the completion of the tomb, Mei the Daoist Adept [Mei Daoren] offered this record."[17] "Mei the Daoist Adept" derived from Chen's courtesy name, Meigong. In fashioning his own sobriquet in a rhymed pairing with Wang's, Chen gave a name to the self-identification that the late Ming literati forged with the courtesan, a theme to be expanded on below.

The courtesan's world being what it was—a world of inflated compliments and exaggerated claims—it is hard to convey how truly famous Dong and Chen were without further abusing the adjective.

Suffice it to say that in the genteel circles of late Ming Jiangnan they belonged to a privileged few who needed no introduction nor appendages to their names.[18] Lin Tiansu and Wang Wei kept significant company. Being written to and about by Dong Qichang and Chen Jiru is an achievement in itself, an announcement that the courtesan in question had risen to the top of her trade. It is also a testimony to how the courtesan culture as a whole derived its aura from the *wen* culture of the scholar-official class, ideally the only people who were destined to write and to rule.

The Courtesan's Game: Playing the Examination Candidate

The scholar-official's identification with the courtesan was rooted in a larger process: the late Ming courtesan was integral to the operation of the civil-service examination, the process that reproduced the empire's political and cultural elites. The connection between examination and whoring is ancient. Successful candidates in the Tang dynasty, the Presented Scholars, brought their entourage to celebrations in the pleasure quarters in the capital city. The National University students of the Song dynasty, too, were not unfamiliar with ways of the trade.[19] Yet in the early Tang, when the bureaucratic state was weak and aristocratic clan ties remained a principal criterion of recruitment, the examination did not play as central a role in the political life of the empire as in the Ming dynasty. The consolidation of the examination as the sole channel to a bureaucratic career and hence formal political power in the Southern Song engendered a symbiotic relationship between the literati and courtesan cultures. The candidate's political dominance elevated the social standing of the courtesan, an integral part of the candidate's rites of passage to elite manhood and his eventual prize to claim.

In the late Ming, when candidates converged in Nanjing for the triennial provincial examination, they forged patronage and friendship ties in the city's entertainment district along the Qinhuai River crucial to their future careers. The future scholar-official's coming of age, in political and sometimes sexual terms, took place in the courtesan's house. In a passage translated by Willard Peterson, Fang Yizhi (1611–71), one of the successful candidates who journeyed onto intellectual prominence, captured the dual functions of the courtesan in a word play: "Playing on the word *ye*, meaning to melt or fuse metal as well as to seduce, and also used to refer to Nanjing, Fang wrote,

'Nanjing being a place where sexual passion (*ye*) is indulged [or, where one goes and smelting (*ye*) occurs], literati from all over often form inseparable associations [i.e., are bonded] with other literati there.'"[20] The courtesan functioned as a facilitator for male bonding.

The failed aspirant to power could thus be doubly humiliated. Ma Xianglan (1548–1604), a courtesan painter so gifted that even envoys from Siam sought to buy her fans, developed a reputation for rejecting unworthy candidates. One reject, a man by the name of Zheng Yingni (Baoxian), was said to be so vengeful that he cast Ma in a southern-style drama, *The White Silk Skirt* (*Bailian qun*), and summoned her to watch the taunting performance. It is not known how he acquired the power to summon Ma; the account is part of an enduring legend of Ma's snobbish treatment of failed examination candidates.[21] The story of the courtesan Ma as both audience and subject of drama could not have but enhanced her allure. Being written about by Dong Qichang and Chen Jiru was surely a sign of achievement, but being made game of by a dejected aspirant was no less flattering.

Competition was thus the ultimate game in the courtesan's quarters, as it was in the examination. Its attendant themes of fairness–foul play or winning–losing were played out by the candidate and the entertainer in counterpoint. The two worlds did not merely mirror each other; they were in fact ruled by the same logic and arbitrated by the same successful men. The failed candidate could seek no reprieve from the courtesan's quarters, for winners in the political game became the arbiters of taste in the world of enchantment as well. It is no accident that the most popular late Ming game was Name the Candidate: the courtesan was ranked and named according to degree titles on the examination roster.

The popularizer of the game, Cao Dazhang (1521–75), was a venerable Hanlin academician when he was forced out of office in 1560. He retired to the Nanjing quarters on the banks of Qinhuai and passed the time with a group of friends. They became known for a game they devised by the name of Immortals on a Lotus Pedestal, whereby they gathered fourteen courtesans around a table, with an ample supply of wine. Each woman was dealt a card face down. On the face was a fancy design featuring a flower, each representing a step on the examination ladder. Of the fourteen, two were successful bureaucrats: Hanlin Chancellor and Hanlin Compiler; two were unproved aspirants: Talents-in-waiting; the other ten were the top-scorers in the local, provincial, and metropolitan examinations: Principal Graduate,

Metropolitan Graduate, and so on.[22] The three groups constituted an entire political history: those who have made it, those whose feet are in the door, and those who hope to be so lucky.

The two courtesans who were dealt the Hanlin Chancellor and Hanlin Compiler cards played the examiners, the ultimate arbiters of talent. Their ostensive goal was to guess the Principal Graduate. The real purpose for everyone was to create noise and generate excuses for drinking and merriment. Yet the game's resemblance to the bureaucratic life that the merrymakers tried to leave behind was uncanny. First, the game was rigged against the aspirants. The two Talents-in-waiting could not respond to the examiners; they could only sit passively by and be picked on. Five strikes and they were out, to be made fun of by the top three candidates. Nor were the examiners secure in their superior position. If they failed to pick the top candidates in ten tries, they were kicked out, which presumably led to more drinking and feasting, before the cards were dealt again.

Such insecurity and the sense of vulnerability had clearly crept in from the world at large. Minor adjustments in the number of degrees awarded failed to keep up with the steady population growth after the late fifteenth century, resulting in an increasingly competitive examination system. It was estimated that as many as 600,000 candidates sat for the Qing metropolitan examination every three years, of whom an average of 200 would pass and capture the highest degree, the ticket to officialdom.[23] The pressure did not ease afterward. Factional strife and scandal-mongering were so rampant in the late Ming court that bureaucratic careers were marked by sudden changes of fortune, banishment, confiscation of property, imprisonment, and sometimes even death. As one connoisseur of the Nanjing quarters watched the courtesans play the Name the Candidate game, the lines between game and life became so blurred that he began to address his fellow scholars as if he were still talking about the courtesans: "A scholar is frustrated only because he hasn't met an examiner [who appreciated him], how could it be that his talent is at fault? Those talents-in-waiting who struck gold, it's written in their destiny; the examiner should claim no credit."[24] Behind the contradictory logic between the two arguments, both winner and loser could equally take comfort in their own talent and the randomness of the game.

The drinking game that fashioned the courtesans as scholars inspired another pastime, the ranking of courtesans according to the examination title but by an entirely different set of standards. The academician Cao Dazhang recalled the famous discussion between the Song poets Su Shi and Qin Guan as his guide: sentiment and temperament (*qingxing*) constitute the foremost criterion in ranking a courtesan, second is talent and craft, last comes appearance and deportment.[25] Instead of leaving it to the cards, pleasure seekers appropriated the authority of the examiner in ranking women, an authority that few would dispute because it was exercised only on paper. Hence a patron could dub his favorite courtesan the Female Hanlin Chancellor and justify his choice in verse, or claim to discover the truly worthwhile young aspirant and crown her "Talent-in-waiting," and so on.

These gaming pageantries, popular in the Xining reign period (1068–77) of the Northern Song, gained poignancy in the late Ming. Probably due to roving examination candidates, the game spread from the Nanjing pleasure quarters to Beijing, the political center of the empire. When recorded in the blue-building literature, these festivities often assumed the solemnity of significant historical events, with tallies of the year of occurrence, names of the instigators, and magnificent details. Not unlike epical events, the winners of some flower contests turned out to be predetermined. Yu Huai (1616–96), the foremost chronicler of the late Ming Nanjing quarters, recalled one such occasion when a doting suitor orchestrated a gala so that his favorite, Wang Weibo, could claim her laurel in style:

> One bright evening, the night when the Weaving Mind traverses the Milky Way, [Sun Wugong of Tongcheng] called a massive gathering of the girls in a pavilion above water, the sojourning quarters of Fang Mi. The vehicles of notables from four corners filled the roads and alleys; actors from three theatrical troupes put on shows side-by-side. Spectator boats encircled the pavilion like an impenetrable wall. The flower table was rated and ranked, and a terraced stage was erected to showcase the Principal Graduate. Of twenty-some candidates who passed, Weibo was deemed number one. She ascended the stage; the orchestra struck up tunes; golden ingots were presented; wine cups were raised. Looking dejected, the other women gradually receded. We did not stop drinking until day broke and spent the following day composing poems to commemorate the occasion.[26]

The game of ranking women by the examination roster was so in vogue in the late Ming pleasure quarters that the dramatist Li Yu (1611–ca. 1680) used it for an episode in one of his plays, but one with less lofty criteria than Su Shi's. A scholar, disenchanted by his well-endowed but ugly wife, joins a crowd on a Hangzhou bridge peering over the railings at a horde of women returning from a pleasure boat ride. Two of the beauties are about sixteen of age. "With the several layers of bedraggled garments sticking to their naked bodies, even the succulent chest and jade breasts are half-concealed and half-revealed. The crowd saw them and exclaimed in unison: 'Here's the Principal Graduate, followed by Second Graduate. What a pity that there is no Third Graduate in sight.'"[27] The women and the candidate were coupled in their desire for upward mobility and in its attendant vulnerability.

The crowning of prostitutes as degree-holders epitomizes the proximity between the brothel and political culture, as well as the blurred lines between pleasure seeking and power seeking. Called "flower registers" (*huabang*) or "flower adjudications" (*hua'an*, also "flower table"), the very term for the late Ming pageantries recalls the bureaucratic life and legal power of the *successful* candidate who, soon after his name was entered on the register of degree-holders, embarked on an official career, most likely as a local magistrate-cum-judge. Coincidentally, so enduring was this identification between the courtesan and the political process that as late as 1928, tax-farmers in the Canton government organized a similar contest in the brothels to enrich the municipal coffers. In step with the reformist politics and democratic rhetoric of the modern times, these contests were renamed "flower-register *elections*" (*huabang xuanju*).[28]

The identification of the courtesan with the public political man was more than a game. Kang-i Sun Chang has argued that "after the fall of the Ming, the courtesan became a metaphor for the loyalist poets' vision of themselves." Their predicaments were similar, locked in the futility of recalling a world that had collapsed and of resuscitating meaning in their shattered public and private lives.[29] This identification, in fact, had been the most salient truth about the world that was annihilated by the southward march of the Manchu army in 1645. For a hundred years before the fall, the auras of the courtesan and the scholar-official had constructed and reinforced each other. As such, the late Ming courtesan was a key figure of the Han Chinese imperium, a luminous politico-cultural world of *wen* signified by literature and civility. The resultant visibility and respectability of courtesan culture was a historical fact particular to the late Ming moment. Below, we examine yet another aspect of this respectability, the courtesan's literary fame, and its implications for the domestic women.

The Courtesan's Fame: Intrusion into Domesticity

Poetic finesse was a generic courtesan trait. So strong was the identification of courtesan with poetry that the name of the famous Tang courtesan poet Xue Tao (ca. 768–ca. 831) and her sobriquet, "Female Collator," became euphemisms for the courtesan in the late Ming period. Maureen Robertson has characterized the tradition of courtesan poetry in these terms: "The feminine voices of entertainers and courtesans were more expressive of forms of feminine subjectivity, but their thematic range and their self-presentation remained linked to the identification of women with the body and sexuality, consistent with their address to the expectations of a male audience and readership."[30] Our purpose here is not to probe the modes of feminine subjectivity in the poetry of late Ming courtesans, but to examine the manner in which courtesan poetry was published and anthologized in the late Ming.

The prominence of courtesan authors in late Ming poetic anthologies is further testimony to the proximity of the courtesan's world to literati society and the visibility of courtesans as cultural producers. However, the inclusion of courtesans in late Ming anthologies was by no means unproblematic. Gentry women editors seem particularly keen on delineating a boundary between the boudoir and the brothel. As Kang-i Sun Chang has shown, the gentry writer Wang Duanshu (1621–ca. 1706) opted to "arrange her anthology of about one thousand women poets in descending order of social status. Gentry women are grouped in the category of 'the proper' (*zheng*), courtesans in the category of 'the erotic' (*yin*)."[31] In an anthology that is no longer extant, a virtuous widow, Fang Weiyi (1584–1668), also grouped women writers into "correct" (*zheng*) and "licentious" (*xie*) categories. Another gentry editor, Shen Yixiu (1590–1635), failed to include the works of courtesans in her short anthology, *Her Meditations* (*Yirensi*; preface dated 1636).[32]

This tendency of late Ming gentry women to separate the verse of courtesans from that of domestic women has to be assessed in the context of two historical considerations. First, it should be remembered that other gentry women did not uphold such rigid boundaries; preserved in their oeuvres were poems they exchanged with courtesans and singing girls, as we will see later. Second, the very fact of the courtesan's inclusion under the same anthology cover, albeit in a separate and inferior space, is a significant late Ming development. In the nineteenth century, as courtesan culture suffered vulgarization, editor Yun Zhu (1771–1833) opted for outright exclusion.

Yun's moral purpose was stated in the "Guide to Selection" of her anthology, *Correct Beginnings* (*Guochao guixiu zhengshi ji*): "Women from the blue buildings — those who have transgressed their virtues — have produced works on the wind, clouds, moon, and dewdrops. Previous editors delighted in selecting and circulating them. They will not be found in this volume." However, Yun made a minor concession by including the works of Wang Wei, Liu Rushi, and eleven other ex-courtesans in the appendix. "Their later integrity [i.e., marriage] covered up their early transgressions," Yun explained.[33]

Late Ming male editors seem more likely to use the poet's perceived literary merit instead of her social location as the criterion of inclusion and placement in their anthologies. A most glaring example was Zhong Xing (1574–1624), editor of *Poetic Retrospective of Famous Ladies* (*Mingyuan shigui*), who interspersed the poems of courtesans with those of elite daughters throughout the chapters. The courtesan Wang Wei, whose works Zhong admired, was one of the five poets given an entire chapter. In fact, Zhong seemed intent on blurring the usual moral and ethnic boundaries: another poet so favored was Xu Jingfan, a Korean woman whose work was popular in Ming China.[34] The verse she composed in classical Chinese was taken to be a shining testimony to the far-reaching brilliance of the Han Chinese imperium, as exemplified by the *wen* culture of the scholar-official class.

In short, the anthologies of women's verse constituted a field in which the symbolic boundaries between the courtesan and the virtuous wife were being articulated. We have noted a trend from the courtesan's inclusion to exclusion that separated the late Ming from the nineteenth century, a trend that was part of the vulgarization of courtesan culture alluded to above. We have also noted a gender gap, with women editors in the Ming and the Qing being more insistent on drawing boundaries between voices from the domestic realm and those of the pleasure quarters. However, it is important to emphasize that in the late Ming, the boundaries being articulated on the printed page were sometimes transgressed in real life, as the friendship between gentry wives and famed courtesans attests.

These incidences of intimacy represent an intrusion of courtesan culture into the domestic sanctuary and are yet another manifestation of the power of courtesan culture in its late Ming heyday. Having bonded with entertainers in the examination circuit, late Ming scholar-officials began routinely to invite public women into their households to entertain guests during parties and to perform plays.[35] This shift in the location of interaction between gentleman and courtesan is significant, for it brought the domestic women into personal contact with entertainers without any transgressive movements on the parts of the former.

The various expressive modes of courtesan-wife friendship can be placed on a *qing-wen* (emotional-literary) continuum: some were more platonic in tone, built as they were on a shared devotion to poetry; others were more expressive of emotional and physical intimacies. An example of the former was Wang Wei's friendship with a gentry wife, Xiang Lanzhen, to whom Wang referred by her husband's name, as Madame Huang Mengwan. Xiang, a native of Jiaxing, was a prolific poet with two published poetry collections and one posthumous volume. Wife of a Provincial Candidate, Xiang married into a literati family. She was also remembered as a stern mother who supervised the studies of her son, an imperial student.[36] In other words, Xiang Lanzhen was a respectable gentry woman who fulfilled her duties as wife and mother irreproachably. She was, at the same time, extremely serious about her poetic pursuits. In her last words to her husband, she declared: "I have no regrets in this world but this wish: may my name be appended to those of other lady-poets [*guixiu*] by virtue of my insignificant scribbles."[37]

Although the circumstances of their meeting are not known, Xiang and Wang Wei became friends while they were living in an unidentified site amid lakes and mountains. Impressed by Xiang's erudition, Wang sought her company in drinking parties and outings to temples, as attested by a poem she crafted in response to one that Xiang sent. Her fondness for Xiang was later expressed in a eulogistic poem replete with Chan Buddhist overtones:

> A pebble in an autumn dike,
> Who sees through it as our previous, present, and
>   future lives?
> Her perceptive mind is not fated to live as long as
>   the pine,
> But her plum soul will shine as bright as the moon.
> Words on bamboo leaves and white silk fill her toiletry
>   chest,
> Even casual scribbles turned into sounds of pure jade.

The last two lines establish Xiang's poetic legacy, in contrast to the earlier allusion to the impermanence of life. In the final two lines of this poem, Wang paid tribute to the conjugal love that Xiang enjoyed: "I think your husband, now in mourning like Xun Fengqian before, / Can never deny the true love he feels for you."[38]

The emotional contours of the friendship between Wang and Xiang have been lost. Yet what does remain and what we do know are in themselves significant. An exemplary gentry wife and a courtesan befriended each other. Poems by the courtesan documenting their shared love of literature were preserved in anthologies. As far as I know, this happened only in the late Ming.

Wife and Entertainer: Writing Expressive Communities

Whereas the friendship between Wang Wei and Xiang Lanzhen was apparently built on a shared dedication to literature, other liaisons between the domestic woman and entertainer were more physical and sensuous in their poetic expressions. The poems for entertainers by a gentry wife, Xu Yuan (1560–1620), are one such example. Daughter of a Suzhou scholar family, Xu received a literary and moral education from a female instructor and was said to be conversant with didactic works for women. Her husband, Fan Yunlin (1558–1641), served as secretary of the Ministry of War, a job that took him to the riotous border regions of the empire. When not serving in the government, however, Fan was a core member of Suzhou literati society, entertaining leading scholar-officials of the day, viewing drama performances, and financing printing projects.[39] Xu and Fan apparently enjoyed a cordial relationship, exchanging verse frequently.

Despite her conventional education, Xu Yuan was not a conventional gentry wife. Her voluminous poetic works are eclectic and ironic, dotted with such incongruities as the use of vulgar colloquial expressions to convey lofty moral ideals or the placement of poems she wrote for prostitutes and Daoist adepts immediately following a traditional lament for her deceased parents. It is clear that Xu thrived on contradictions. On the one hand, she seemed to have accepted the ideal norms for women taught in the didactic literature. The title of her twelve-chapter poetry collection, *Shuttling Chants* (*Luowei yin*, which can also be rendered *Cricket Chants*), refers to the repetitious sound of the spool carrying the woof thread back and forth between the warp threads. Not only did she compare herself to a weaving maid, vocation of the ideal housewife, but she also included exhortations to Confucian virtues in many of her poems.

On the other hand, Xu Yuan seems to have flaunted her defiance of norms of decency not only by composing a number of provocative verses for courtesans and singing girls but also by including them in her published collection. Most notable was a series of five regulated verses for the famous Suzhou courtesan-painter Xue Susu (fl. 1565–1635), in which she compared the talented Xue to the fifth-century courtesan Su Xiaoxiao and three other historic figures surnamed Xue: the Tang courtesan-poet Xue Tao; a Wei court lady from the Three Kingdoms period, Xue Lingyun (fl. 220–26); a certain Commander Xue, which most probably referred to the famous Tang general Xue Rengui (614–83), who was remembered in history and popular legends as an expert archer.[40] Each of these three Xues stood for aspects of Xue Susu's extraordinary life: Xue Tao, for Susu's courtesan background and erudition; Xue Lingyun, a woman who could sew in the dark and was revered as "god of the needle," for Susu's magical fingers and wrists as a painter; and General Xue, for Susu's renowned skills as a horseback archer and her interest in military affairs. Similar to the Daoist courtesan Wang Wei, Xue Susu also combined the most masculine traits with ultimate expressions of femininity.

Highlighting Xue Susu's exquisite feminine charms, Xu Yuan utilized two legends of palace women to allude to Xue's bound feet: "Lotus blossoms as you move your pair of arches, / Your tiny waist, just a handful, is light enough to dance on a palm."[41] The "lotus blossom" line refers to the indulgence of Xiao Baojuan, emperor of the Southern Qi (r. 499–501). According to legend, he built golden lotus pedestals in his garden and had his favorite, Consort Pan, trod on them. Although it is not known if Pan had her feet bound, "lotus footprints" became an expression describing the graceful walk of a woman with bound feet. The "dance on a palm" line alludes to another legend that traces the origins of footbinding to palace dancers. It is noteworthy that both of Xu's poetic allusions highlight the agility and elegance of a woman with bound feet, not her crippled immobility. I will expand on this below.

The poems of friendship between Xu and entertainers bespoke not only an intrusion of courtesan culture into the domestic realm but also the actual presence of entertainers in the boudoir. Xu Yuan came into contact with Xue Susu most probably through her husband, Fan

Yunlin. Fan had admired Xue when she was a famed courtesan, as evinced by a colophon he attached to a painting, "Flowers," that Xue crafted in 1615.[42] Although it is not clear if Xu befriended Xue only after the latter had left the trade, nor do we know how intimate they were, we do have evidence of Xu's frequent visits with less renowned singing girls. In a poem dedicated to one "Anqing the Singing Girl," for example, Xu wrote: "I was sojourning on a lake one day in spring when Anqing came by and presented me with a gift of 'Spring Songs.' Her pure voice echoes like the whistle of light breeze in a flute; all those present were delighted."[43] Since it was customary for late Ming literati to invite courtesans to parties at their homes, the wives of these men evidently found it proper to follow suit.

The presence of singing girls in Xu's quarters was quite common. In another series of five poems, "Written in Jest for Sanli the Singing Girl," Xu Yuan focused entirely on the girl's body. One of them reads:

> The tender and bewitching girl, skin smoother
>   than jade,
> Fragrance wafts from every step the lotus makes.
> Slender waist can hardly withstand the morning
>   breeze;
> Why not build a jade terrace and hide her in
>   mansions of gold?[44]

Both the jade terrace and golden mansion are abodes of goddesses. In her reference to the slender beauty's feet ("every step the lotus makes"), Xu again emphasized the agility of the girl as she walked and the perfume of her bound feet.

The appeal of the feminine body to Xu was collaborated by other poems. Once she was so taken by the charms of a woman who sat in a boat moored next to hers that she composed three poems. Whereas in classical poetry composed by male scholar-officials, the word *meiren* (literally, "beauty") was a symbol for the upright gentleman, in Xu Yuan's hands the literal meaning of the word was restored. Its frequent appearance in her poetry clearly referred to the beautiful women she encountered.[45]

Although Xu Yuan was not without her critics, her works were widely read in her native Suzhou and elsewhere, since many major seventeenth-century anthologies devoted space to her verse and prose.[46] Her name and the titles of her two poetry collections were enshrined in successive editions of local gazetteers. It was, in fact, scholar-officials from the Suzhou establishment who first vied to admire and circulate her works. Commercial publishers followed suit to capitalize on this explosion of interest.[47] Xu Yuan's popularity in late Ming genteel circles testifies to a degree of tolerance for her liaisons and her bold expressions. In her chapter in this volume, Katherine Carlitz has written of the "feminization of late Ming literati culture," whereby Confucian men redefined the meaning of being Confucian by tapping into the rich courtesan tradition of sensuality.[48] Xu Yuan's popularity was but one manifestation of this larger development.

The presence of this tradition of sensuality in late Ming domestic chambers was most evident in the works of Lu Qingzi, a close friend of Xu Yuan. Like Xu, Lu was a gentry wife who delighted in composing verse for singing girls and whose works were laden with references to the feminine body. Lu, too, hailed from the moneyed and cultured society of Suzhou. Her father served briefly as secretary of the Ministry of Rites, but spent most of his life as an amateur painter. Lu Qingzi married a man who led an equally idyllic life, Zhao Yiguang (1559–1625), a descendant of the Song imperial family. Zhao fancied himself a recluse but often busied himself entertaining powerful and learned friends.[49]

Xu and Lu were widely known as close friends who exchanged poetry. Lu's social net was cast wider than Xu's, however; recipients of her poetry included a prostitute-turned-nun, lay Buddhist devotees, maids, a large number of concubines and singing girls, together with the usual circle of gentry wives and chaste widows. Lu, like Xu, kept company with singing girls, as her poems for "prostitutes" (*ji*) testify.[50] In addition, Lu called a number of women who frequented her parties by their surnames followed by the term "beauty" (*meiren*) instead of the usual "madame" or "sister," an uncommon usage also adopted by Xu Yuan. Lu's poems to these women, who were probably singing girls or concubines, are fixated on their bodily charms: slender waists, rosy cheeks, trembling steps, flowing hair.

The enchantment of the female body was a recurring theme in Lu's verse. Even poems she composed for several filial and chaste women were dotted with descriptions of their fair appearance or tender age.[51] The same is true for those dedicated to Xu Yuan and other respectable wives who frequented Lu's quarters. In particular, Lu expressed her fondness for Xu in highly emotional terms. When Xu went on a long distance trip, Lu sighed:

> Fragrance swirls around my gate,
> Inanimate objects stir up my deep
>   longing.
> I love and adore that tender beauty,
> Her jade face as fair as raw white silk."[52]

Such expressions as "to love and adore" (*wanlian*) are not part of the repertoire of language used in farewells between casual friends.

The same intensity of longing is evident in the ten farewell poems written on the eve of Xu's travel to faraway Yunnan. In one, Lu lamented:

> Your face is a dazzling crimson,
> My hair, a desolate white.
> I want to pursue the pleasure of my lifetime,
> But the vehicles crowding the road cannot
>   bring me there.[53]

Although Lu's exact dates are unknown, judging from her husband's years she was about the same age as Xu. Hence her contrast of Xu's youthfulness with her own fatigued looks is more likely to signify her emotional distress at parting than a gap in biological age. Lu's explicit use of such expressions as "to love and adore" and "pleasure of a lifetime" suggests an intimacy between the two women that would be described as sensuous if not outright erotic in modern terminology.

Taken together, the expressive poems composed by Xu Yuan and Lu Qingzi are suggestive of the emotional contours of a women's culture created by gentry ladies in the boudoir, although we do not know enough about the poetic codes women used to ascertain the nature of their liaisons in practice. Maureen Robertson has suggested that late Ming gentry women poets borrowed tropes from male heterosexual poetry in their friendship poetry because they had yet to develop their own tropes. Yet the female desire in women's friendship poetry did not derive from male desire in the heterosexual model but instead was a desire that placed a premium on companionship and sensuality.[54]

The poems composed by Xu and Lu evoke a world of female intimacies in which emotions are mediated by and expressed in corporeal terms. Slender waist, beautiful face, and, above all, the graceful movement of a pair of bound feet recur as sites of feminine charm. Whatever its relations to practices in the female chambers, this sensuousness of poetic language is itself significant. Although solid proof is hard to obtain, one can surmise that the respectability of courtesan culture in literati society changed the tone of domestic life for some gentry wives. The presence of entertainers in the house emboldened some domestic women to compose lyrics with a more sensuous voice. In the eighteenth and nineteenth centuries, it was gentry women themselves who were outraged by this intrusion of the courtesan into the late Ming gentry household. They thus sought to reaffirm the boundaries between the domestic world and the brothel by expunging the courtesan's voice from poetry anthologies.

The Enigma of the Courtesan's Bound Feet

Although the title of this chapter advertises footbinding, thus far the discussion has focused on the derivation of the courtesan's aura from the written word and the intrusion of this aura into the domestic realm. To summarize the arguments advanced thus far, the courtesan who wrote and was being written about partook in the aura of the *wen* culture of the literati, hence her respectability in the late Ming world. The cultural visibility of the courtesan found its most stunning expression in the way courtesans became guests in gentry households and occasional friends of gentry wives. The presence of courtesans in the house, in turn, may have emboldened gentry wives to adopt a more sensuous poetic language. The portrait of the courtesan that emerged is that of a visible woman with shifting identities who occupied multiple locations: she was at once a private and public figure, at home both in the political world of scholar-officials and in the women's boudoir.

This emphasis on the visibility of the courtesan as a cultural producer is not a digression, but is the crux of the problem of the courtesan's bound foot. Since we think of the courtesan as the embodiment of female sensuality, and footbinding as the ultimate expression of that sensuality in imperial China, the scarcity of references in the blue-building literature to the courtesan's feet at the peak of her cultural presence is surprising and puzzling. In this section, I argue that in the enigma itself lies part of the solution: only in the context of the heightened textual visibility, domestic presence, and artistic respectability of the late Ming courtesan can the paucity of descriptions of her bound feet be understood.

Early examples of blue-building literature make only cursory remarks about the entertainer's feet, but what was being revealed was as significant as what could have been concealed. Written before the spread of footbinding, the *Records of the Northern Quarters* did not refer to the custom. Its Yuan dynasty successor, *The Blue Building* (*Qinglou ji*), contains a most revealing description of an actress, Tian Xixiu: "Her feet are extremely small, but her stride is militant and forceful. Her heavenly endowed beauty is slightly below par, but the result of her *own efforts* is impressive" (my italics).[55] Similar to the poetic allusions made by gentry woman Xu Yuan, which emphasize the grace and agility of the bound feet, footbinding is construed here as a desirable trait for an entertainer because it enhances her movement. More important, the actress's small feet were testimony to her tenacity in improving herself. Diametrically opposed to modern perceptions, footbinding was seen in this light as a willful act that proclaimed the triumph of culture — a result of human efforts — over her natural body.

In this formulation of footbinding-as-culture, the practice of concealing raw flesh with cloth can be interpreted as a female expression of *wen* culture, a form of female bodily inscription or "writing." Indeed, in the blue-building accounts, footbinding was presented as one of the many cultural achievements of the courtesan, on par with her command of lyrics and painting. One example is the portrait of Gu Mei in Yu Huai's *Miscellaneous Records of the Wooden Bridge* (*Banqiao zaji*), reminiscences of the courtesan district in late Ming Nanjing. Of the over twenty courtesans from the elite Old Quarters that Yu mentioned, only Gu's feet received special attention. Yu's often-quoted account presents her as: "poised and elegantly beautiful, with incomparable demeanor and grace. Her hair was piled up in cloud-like buns, and her face was colored in a peach blossom hue. Her bent arches were slender and small, and her body was light and airy from the waist down." A pair of bound feet was merely one constituent of Gu's beauty, and appearance itself was but one of the many attributes of her fame. Yu continued: "She was educated in literature and history, and skilled in orchid paintings. Her orchids were almost as good as Ma Shouzhen's [Xianglan], but Gu's demeanor and face surpassed Ma's. People at the time considered her the first in the Old Quarters."[56] In other words, it was a combination of beauty and artistic talent that accounted for Gu's appeal.

This accent on cultural refinement and artistic talent recalls the cultural respectability enjoyed by such courtesans as Lin Tiansu and Wang Wei, who appeared as alter egos of the literati. At the peak of courtesan culture in the late Ming, the ultimate compliment was to present the courtesan as skilled in the arts of the male scholar-official. Even when footbinding was mentioned, it functioned as a contrast, a reminder that the accomplished artist was, after all, female. The infrequent remarks on the courtesan's bound feet, then, served to highlight the very gender ambiguity on which the courtesan's aura rested. In other words, in de-emphasizing the bound feet, the quintessential female marker, chroniclers accentuated the courtesan's male-like qualities and facilitated the scholar-official's personal identification with her.

Most suggestive of this identification is the decor of Gu Mei's private room, decorated with brocaded curtains and nicknamed by Yu, the Building of Enchantment.[57] Implements found in the literati studio were displayed in the room: desks were piled with scrolls, stationery, and musical instruments, and swirls of tasteful incense permeated the atmosphere. Gu Mei's persona as a distinguished courtesan was in part marked by the decor and surroundings of her abode, a reproduction of the scholar's studio. Real scholars vied to hold banquets at Gu's quarters, for the exquisite cuisine from her kitchen was legendary.[58] This combination of masculine and feminine traits constituted the magic of the illusory world that Gu presided over: she was at once the master of the scholar's studio and provider at the kitchen; the painter of beauty and the beauty herself. Her pair of bound feet was but one component of this exercise in contradictions.

Although Yu Huai did not highlight footbinding as the exquisite marker of the courtesan, he gave indirect evidence of the prevalence of the practice in his description of two lesser entertainers than Gu Mei. One, by the name of Gu Xi, "had a forthright personality. Her body was voluptuous; her feet were neither slender nor refined. People nicknamed her 'Big Feet Gu' [Gu Dajiao]; also 'Screen of Flesh' [Rou Pingfeng]." Another, Zhang Yuan, was said to "have a slender waist and she moved about with an exaggerated sway. Her coyness is attractive in its own way. People called her 'Tiny Feet Zhang' [Zhang Xiaojiao]." In face-to-face encounters, seekers of pleasure did not hesitate to call attention to the entertainer's feet, to the point of signifying her by their size. Yet even Big Feet Gu had no lack of admirers. Yu Huai recognized her outstanding qualities in "her abandoned and scornful air, and her haughty and out-of-the-ordinary looks. She was not a creature to be confined by fences and walls."[59]

The paucity of explicit descriptions of footbinding in blue-building literature contrasts sharply with its visibility in other seventeenth- and eighteenth-century texts by men, primarily erotic fiction. In his study of eighteenth-century erotic romances, Keith McMahon has identified the usual trope of a man squeezing his lover's bound foot as "fetishistic displacement of naked, genital contact." Instead of describing a sex scene in full, authors of Qing erotic fiction used hints of virginal blood and a shoe slipping off the bound foot as synecdoches. Attention to the bound foot in its various guises thus signifies a heightened erotic interest in women's bodies. Significantly, even with this profusion of footbinding as the erotic sign, the binders were rarely loosened for the reader's eyes.[60] The concealment of raw flesh, or footbinding-as-culture, continued to signify the practice.

In the *Carnal Prayer Mat* (*Rouputuan*), the best-known late imperial erotic fiction, the centrality of footbinding to definitions of female beauty, sensuality, and sexual intercourse is unmistakable. The effectiveness of footbinding as erotic trope hinges on the tension it engenders between concealment and visibility. In a telling scene, the wife of a silk vendor who is tending her husband's shop passes the initial test of beauty when the protagonist, Weiyangsheng, sees everything he can: "Her ten fingers look as tender as buds of the lotus root; her pair of small feet is less than three inches long." He then plots to check a more hidden feature, the fairness of her skin, before he launches his seduction.[61]

In this scene, the pair of bound feet constitutes a visible sign of a woman's beauty. But this visibility is limited to its external shape and size, not physical texture and smell. The aura of footbinding lay in the concealment of its physicality, as the author explained: "When a female binds her feet, she is most concerned with keeping the bottom of the foot smooth; the ten toes cannot help but be a little uneven. Hence there is not a whole lot of merit [in baring the covers]. Moreover, as far as the three-inch golden lotus goes, it is interesting only if hidden under leggings. Otherwise, it is like a flower unadorned by leaves—too plain to hold my interest."[62] Weiyangsheng thus taught his inexperienced bride to keep her leggings on, while he disrobed her and then stripped himself naked.

Footbinding served as foreplay to sexual intercourse in two ways, as object to be played with and as image to be viewed. Besides the fondling so often portrayed in erotic paintings, the viewing of bound foot in these paintings itself was supposed to constitute foreplay. Although women were never depicted as fondling their own feet, they partook in the construction of desires as viewers of erotic paintings.

Their excitement, in turn, excited the male partner. Hence Weiyang-sheng prepared his new wife for intercourse by showing her a set of paintings, two featuring postures of elevating the pair of small feet, while reading her the colophons describing the scene.[63]

To summarize, the lack of overt descriptions of the courtesan's feet in blue-building literature does not reflect the unimportance of footbinding in the sexual discourses in the seventeenth and eighteenth centuries. In fact, the averted eyes and the covertness of textual expressions constituted the attraction of footbinding. In altering and concealing the raw physicality of the natural body, footbinding can be read as an expression of female culture. As advertisement for a woman's efforts at self-improvement, footbinding represents the ultimate women's handiwork. As culture and work, footbinding bears a striking resemblance to the Confucian ideal of *wen*, the most salient impulses of which were the creation of order out of the chaos of nature and the draping of that order in the trimmings of civility.

The textual and physical concealment of the bound foot began to unravel on the pages of blue-building literature from the late eighteenth and nineteenth centuries, which are splattered with descriptions of courtesans' feet. For the right price, the insistent pleasure seeker might even persuade a courtesan to unwrap her binders. Significantly, at a time when the courtesan's feet could be bared, it was just as likely for one to encounter a pair of poorly bound feet as a pair of good ones. Two late Qing chroniclers of the pleasure quarters of Yangzhou, a center that rivaled Nanjing at the time, voiced similar complaints.

Daoist Adept of Pearly Spring, one of the Yangzhou chroniclers, described a famed courtesan called Min De'er, who claimed to be a native of Suzhou, the home of southern beauties: "Her eyebrows are slender and her eyes sparkle; her face is extremely pretty. But she has a heavy and tainted accent between her throat and tongue that does not resemble the Wu dialect [of Suzhou]. Moreover, the problem with her looks is her pair of feet. She was stumbling in front of the pavilion [where I first met her] — her feet are way too narrow."[64] Having run its course, the practice was being carried to a ridiculous extreme. A pair of feet so small and narrow that the owner could only stumble had never been the allure of footbinding. In an age of decline, smallness was no longer a sign of gentility and distinction but its exact opposite: vulgar imitation.[65]

Another chronicler lamented that the problem of badly bound feet was pervasive among Yangzhou courtesans: "Walking in lotus steps is a must for beauties. A [foot shaped like a] hook covered with soft silk socks and hidden underneath her dress is sure to enchant one's soul. But upon surveying all the ladies here, I found that although there are no lowly big feet, most suffer from the Xianglan disease [slightly too big]. No reborn Yang Tieya will ever want to use their shoes as wine cups." Yang was a Yuan dynasty connoisseur who filled the shoes of courtesans with wine for drinking games.[66] There is no more fitting sign of the vulgarization of courtesan culture than a pair of ill-shaped or putrid feet.

The history of the aura of courtesan culture is thus inversely related to the overtness of textual expressions of her bound foot. When courtesan culture was at its zenith in artistic and political influence in the late Ming, the courtesan's bound foot was rarely mentioned in writing by its admirers; when that culture was in irrevocable decline in the nineteenth century, it became possible to depict the courtesan's foot in graphic detail. The logic of this inverse relationship is simple: the aura of footbinding hinged on concealment, as explained by the protagonist of the *Carnal Prayer Mat*. The very moment the binders could be unwrapped for a customer, when details of the erotic rituals could be disclosed in writing, when the bare flesh could be photographed and x-rayed by curious foreigners, footbinding ceased to be a marker of exclusiveness. Although it was still being practiced by millions of women, it had lost its raison d'être. No longer a female expression of *wen* culture, footbinding had become as vulgar as the courtesan culture chronicled by petty commercial writers and featuring illiterate women with foul feet.

Anthropologist Laurel Bossen has reported that women in Yunnan, among the last to practice footbinding, were forced to unbind in 1957 when the government erected roadblocks and checkpoints.[67] Yet long before its eradication in the 1950's, footbinding had died a natural death. The end was already foreshadowed in the nineteenth century—not simply the end of a custom, but the end of an imperium built on the examination system and the hegemony of the scholar-official class, the very imperium from which the courtesan derived her aura.

4

Desire and Writing
in the Late Ming Play
"Parrot Island"

KATHERINE CARLITZ

The fiction, drama, and poetry of the late Ming dynasty assumed
the literacy of women. In these genres a courtesan might spread her
glittering aura, a faithful wife might scratch a poem on a temple wall
for her absent husband, a clever daughter might set her suitor literary
tests. Even the heroines of the didactic tales on which girls were supposed to be raised were literate: illustrations show them seated at their
writing tables, little maids handing them scrolls and books.

The relationship of these images to the actual lives of women was
complex. The chapters in this volume chart the rise of a self-conscious
literary culture among both courtesans and governing-class women, a
culture with its own networks and nuances. All the images mentioned
above, however, are typical Ming male descriptions of the writing
woman. Women wrote in a world where they, too, were consumers of
these images, and they had to draw on a heritage of male-created
voices to express their own literary subjectivity. But the Ming literati
who created that courtesan, wife, or daughter did not operate from a
position of static dominance: they were also continually renegotiating
their subject position with regard to power, prestige, and authenticity
of expression.

The play *Parrot Island* (*Ying wu zhou*), by the literati playwright
Chen Yujiao (1544–1611), exemplifies how depictions of women, writing, and the slippery, multivalent idea of *qing* (passion) could be used
in these governing-class renegotiations. This *chuanqi* drama, pub-

lished sometime around 1600, has been little studied by literary historians.[1] Its very obscurity, however, suggests its value for us: if we want to understand the social effects of powerful new concepts — who accepted them, who transformed them, whose lives were transformed by them — it often helps to look below the first rank. (And Chen Yujiao himself, as we will see, was anything but obscure; he was a connoisseur and editor of drama well known in the literary circles of his day.) Enjoying only minor fame, *Parrot Island* takes on major themes that animated the late Ming stage: the power of qing, the limits of qing, the relation of qing to official Confucian morality. Chen Yujiao was far less daring in his treatment of qing than were the racy classical-language novellas of the early Ming, with their ardent gentry heroines.[2] He was less daring than the giant of late Ming drama, Tang Xianzu (1550–1616), whose celebrated play *Peony Pavilion* (*Mudan ting*) made just such a heroine his instrument for testing the limits of passion in society.[3] But in his more cautious enjoyment of the emotional freedom of his age, he may be a far more representative figure than Tang. And when we ask, later, how the women in Chen Yujiao's family or families like his might have responded to *Parrot Island*, we will be able at least to speculate about the way images of women and writing affected actual late Ming women who wrote.

Parrot Island expands the tale of the Tang dynasty military hero Wei Gao and his faithful concubine Yuxiao, who pines away after he fails to return from what was supposed to be a temporary absence. In a trope beloved in the Ming (it is at the center of Tang Xianzu's *Peony Pavilion*), their mutual passion is powerful enough to bring her back to life. Chen also introduced a parallel plot about the meetings and partings of the male poet Yuan Zhen and the courtesan Xue Tao, perhaps the most celebrated courtesan-poet in Chinese history (a vast amount of Xue Tao lore was in circulation at the end of the Ming). By interweaving the two plots, Chen Yujiao reframed Wei Gao and Yuxiao's story to ask questions about the nature and appropriate objects of fidelity, the worth of different kinds of qing, and the seductiveness of poetry. Although Xue Tao's presence is everywhere in the play, Chen Yujiao did not permit her to triumph: Yuan Zhen is unfaithful to her, whereas the concubine Yuxiao, cleaving to the fidelity prescribed by normative texts for women, is brought back to life to be united with Wei Gao. But to complicate matters, Wei Gao woos, wins, and is ultimately reunited with Yuxiao in a setting evocative of the courtesan world. Chen Yujiao's Wei Gao and Yuxiao do not act out the standard plot typically reserved for gentry heroines in scholar-beauty romances. Chen seemed to want to explore issues of qing, sensuality, writing, and fidelity—even the fidelity of normative Confucian texts—*outside* the realm of the conventional family. Why did he do so?

Answering this question will take us to the heart of the late Ming literati struggle for self-definition. Chen Yujiao and men like him wanted to animate convention with emotion, but they wondered anxiously whether passion would destabilize the hierarchies they had been educated to uphold. The conventional family was the seedbed of Ming Confucian hierarchy—but the courtesan world was the idealized realm in which all that was *oppressive* in that hierarchy could be transcended. We will see, however, that Chen Yujiao was not willing to give up the conventional hierarchies altogether.

Women were often the emblems chosen by Ming literati to dramatize issues of fidelity and freedom. In *Parrot Island*, the courtesan Xue Tao bestows the ring that unites Yuxiao and Wei Gao, Yuxiao's pathetic death is performed at far greater length than the battles that make Wei Gao a hero, and Wei Gao, bereaved for much of the play, is to all intents and purposes a faithful widow! The fact that women were relegated to the inner quarters made woman-as-icon a valuable emblem for the inner dimensions of the literati self. The containment of women could be an emblem for the tempering of *male* desire.

We will start by examining some of the tensions and contradictions that Chen Yujiao may have been trying to resolve. How was the literatus, whose self-definition depended in part on the seclusion of women, to deal with the fact that women's writing was being collected and published? And how did he valorize the courtesan, whose world depended on the money, power, and sex to which he was supposed to be indifferent? A look at these issues will give us a sense of Chen Yujiao's world, and a brief examination of his biography will show where he fit into that world. We will examine *Parrot Island* in detail, comparing it with other versions of the Yuxiao story circulating in the late sixteenth and early seventeenth centuries. Finally we will ask how *Parrot Island* (either as spectacle or as luxury reading material) might have looked to the women of Chen Yujiao's family. The resources for answering this last question are more than one might imagine, and range from letters to epitaphs, collections of women's poetry, and some surprisingly nondidactic moments in Ming commentaries on the didactic classics.

Women, Writing, and Literati Ideals

In Scene 19 of *Parrot Island*, Wei Gao's constancy is tested when a Daoist recluse feasts him and invites Xue Tao to "help serve the wine." As Wei Gao sees the other guests off, Xue Tao murmurs in an aside that Wei, by having designs on her, has treated Yuan Zhen with disrespect. The stage directions at this point read like a sentence from the late Ming novels: "[Wei Gao] enters and listens surreptitiously, with an ironic smile." He speaks up and makes his true feelings clear: "It is not at all as you think; I would never presume to insult you in that fashion. Nothing could be farther from my thoughts. When I bade farewell to my wife [Yuxiao], I gave her the jade ring [that you had bestowed on me]. Now she and I are parted by rivers and mountains, and I dream alone in an empty bed. Why, but a few days ago . . . ," and he launches into an aria about the pain of separation. Later, in Scene 27, Wei Gao is incensed at his friend Jiang Jingbao's assumption that he has found consolation with Xue Tao. What these scenes underscore is that Wei Gao is *choosing* between two radically different kinds of woman: Xue Tao, free of all constraints, and Yuxiao, constant in the manner of Confucian exemplars. Writing is at the center of the scene that distinguishes Xue Tao from Yuxiao most clearly: when Xue Tao is engaged as tutor to the reincarnated Yuxiao in Scene 29, Yuxiao refuses to learn the sensuous poetic arts that have made Xue Tao famous. "Teach me only the poetry of calm and repose, give me only the *Instructions for Women* to read!" Xue Tao has just sung of traveling the empire with her zither; Yuxiao wants to stay home with her embroidery.

As the chapters in this volume make clear, the wives, concubines, and courtesans of late Ming literati did not, in real life, fall neatly into the separate categories that Xue Tao and Yuxiao suggest here. Centuries of male writing about lonely wives adorning themselves in solitude had created an erotically charged language that could be used to depict both gentry women *and* courtesans. As Dorothy Ko notes, the gentry woman poet Shen Yixiu even used this erotically charged language to describe her daughter Ye Xiaoluan![4]

And except in the plaintive dreams of certain moralists, the literary cultivation of governing-class women was not radically different from that of celebrated courtesans. As Dorothy Ko's research on the education of girls in seventeenth-century Jiangnan makes clear, in the late Ming cultivated courtesans and cultivated governing-class wives were members of the same literary culture.[5] The educated wife might be the better scholar, and the educated courtesan the better performer, but both were in varying degrees adept at poetry, chess, calligraphy, painting, and music. (The "scholar and beauty" stories that were already flourishing in the fifteenth century lent the gentry daughter's accomplishments an almost courtesan-like allure.) Financial transactions were involved in taking a wife *or* beginning a liaison with a courtesan. Ming prosperity and commercial growth produced the surplus necessary both for the courtesans' luxury establishments and for the education of governing-class daughters. The examination culture that perpetuated the late Ming status hierarchy affected the content of governing-class daughters' education, even as it fostered courtesan culture. (The richest courtesan culture was in the Jiangnan region, whose output of degreeholders was enough to provoke anxiety and quotas from the court in Beijing.) This was clearly an age of interpenetration between courtesan culture and literati domestic culture.

But this interpenetration was occurring in a world whose dominant new mode of thinking about women was the Confucian cult of women's virtue, the Five Relationships that made a wife's fidelity to her husband's patriline the domestic analogue of her husband's loyalty to empire.[6] Arches and shrines to faithful widows and glorious suicides were being constructed everywhere, in increasing numbers. And the Confucian cult of women's virtue posited the existence of two radically different kinds of women, the *liang* ("good" women, whose ritually complete marriages were supposed to be concluded without financial considerations, and who would live secluded within the family compound) and the *jian* ("mean" women, who could be bought and sold, and were visible / sexually available in public). In this schema, the liang and the jian were "different paths" (*yi tu*) or the "traces of different wheels" (*yi gui*), in the quite representative words of one 1620's didactic writer: "If a woman wants to preserve her purity [*zhen*], she must follow her husband and cleave to the liang, [whereas] if she unleashes her desires [*yin*], then she cannot but drift into the realms of jian." The liang and the jian worlds were to be understood as completely separate, although since the two notions had developed in tandem, they depended on each other for definition by contrast. (The 1620's writer is exploiting this interdependence to its fullest, since he is commenting on a young singing-girl who wants to go straight.)[7]

The distinction between liang and jian (the aspiration to the one, the fear of contamination by the other) was at the heart of conventional statements about the education of women. In constructing Yuxiao's literary preferences, Chen Yujiao was following more or less the curriculum laid down by the reformer Lü Kun (1536–1618), whose aim was to rehabilitate canonical hierarchies and make them function properly in his own society. Yuxiao's was just the sort of literary taste Lü considered appropriate for women. In his *Female Exemplars* (*Guifan*), an expansion of the Han dynasty classic *Biographies of Notable Women* (*Lienü zhuan*), he lays out a curriculum that would restrict a girl's education to the *Classic of Filial Piety* (*Xiao jing*), the Confucian *Analects* (women's versions of both were widely used in the Ming), and the second-century *Precepts for Women* (*Nüjie*) — all of which she should be able to expound for her mother.[8] Eight of the 88 accounts in *Female Exemplars* concern women who write, but all of Lü Kun's literate heroines either write from moral necessity, as, for example, the Tang dynasty daughters whose poetry gained their release from the courtesan rolls before their chastity was lost, or are so old that they are no longer vulnerable to temptation, like the 80-year-old Madame Song, so famous for instructing her son Wei Cheng that she was made a teacher to the local examination candidates (she taught them from behind a screen).[9]

To this vision of containment the idealized Ming courtesan stood in complete contrast. She might be the "immortal" with whom literati men wandered in the mountains or exchanged poetry. She was no longer the devouring succubus of earlier traditions, who brought down kingdoms: on the contrary, literati men who saw themselves as the avant-garde wrote that union with such a courtesan might be just what was needed for great deeds.[10] In her society, a man of the appropriate attainments would produce his best poetry, find literary models independent of the hated examination curriculum, and achieve true literary cultivation untainted by ambition.

This image was not, of course, associated with all the vast numbers of women sold into the service of male pleasure. It was the image of the courtesan elite, and this was important to the way literati understood their liaisons with courtesans. As early as the mid-fifteenth century, the courtesan world was perceived as stratified, with only the most accomplished and cultivated courtesans entering into the liaisons with prominent literati that fueled the imagination of the age. A Xue Tao story from the early fifteenth-century classical-language collection *Further Tales While Trimming the Lamp* (*Jian deng yu hua*) shows how a liaison with such a courtesan could be seen as part of the literary and sentimental education of the sort of young man who would become a pillar of state. In "Tianshu Composes Linked Verse with Xue Tao," the young protagonist spends a year of clandestine nights with a young woman of extraordinary refinement, from whom he learns not only the craft but also the essential spirit of Tang poetry. At one of their meetings the young woman gently sharpens his powers of discernment by refusing to let him label Xue Tao a "prostitute" (*ji nü*), reminding him that Xue Tao was, rather, an arbiter of elegance and the worthy confidante of the foremost poets of the Tang. When the young woman and her dwelling disappear, she is, of course, found to have been a visitation of Xue Tao herself. The young man (thunderstruck, along with his father and his father's friend) goes on to pass the *jinshi*, or highest-level civil-service examination.[11]

What this stratification produced was the image of a rarefied being at the top, a near-immortal who could simultaneously be eroticized and serve as a vehicle for metaphysical musings. Lines from a poem by Zhong Xing (1574–1625) depict a courtesan at her toilette, a winter-blooming plum reflected with her in the mirror, and turn the conventional comparison of woman to flower into a meditation on image and reality: "The flower on its stem does not feel for Man—" (she has been talking to the unresponsive flower); "—but sometimes the reflection of love is better than the reality." The musing courtesan imagines a way out of earthly difficulties altogether: "Perhaps I should just put my self into the mirror's realm, and forget the flower and self of the world outside!"[12]

In a companion poem, a courtesan who is planting a flower meditates on the consequences of her action:

> Time and place may give things their allotted span,
> But only the heart's devotion can make them thrive.[13]

The poems Ming literati wrote for courtesans express erotic connoisseurship of a being so refined and free of earthly constraints that in writing of her, the poet imagines himself free to escape those constraints himself.

Scene 29 of *Parrot Island*, in which Xue Tao is engaged as Yuxiao's tutor, simultaneously acknowledges and denies the interpenetration of courtesan and literati-domestic culture. Invited into the inner chambers Xue Tao is rebuffed by an assertion of the distinction between the liang and jian worlds. It is precisely this tension that shows how ideological were the impulses that motivated Chen Yujiao. Going against reality by constructing two classes of women (and their writing) as polar opposites, Chen is able to structure Wei Gao's choice in terms of the polarities late Ming literati used when they struggled with their own existential dilemmas: authenticity versus hypocrisy, sensuality versus restraint. If literati like Chen Yujiao were to take on questions about women, qing, and literary cultivation, they had to find answers that would construct the literati self in a positive way.

With regard to the courtesan, this involved issues of luxury, power, and sexual attraction. Paul Ropp quotes in this volume a verse by the late Ming courtesan Jing Pianpian that suggests the luxury typical of the most elegant and expensive courtesan establishments.[14] The banquets at private houses where courtesans entertained were intended to reproduce that luxury in the domestic setting. These banquets, and the web of favors and obligations that men created by bestowing visits to the "immortals" on each other, allowed elite men of the late Ming to reproduce their power relationships by initiating young colleagues into the manners and customs of their elders, in a sensuous analogue to the socialization by examination described by Benjamin Elman.[15]

But if the literati attraction to the courtesan world involved only luxury, power, and sex, it could not have been valorized by these men of Confucian education, who would then have had to understand themselves as slaves to sensuous desire. From the mid-sixteenth century on (that is to say, as their prosperity increased), we find literati marking themselves off from "small men" precisely by asserting that they are *not* slaves to desire. The wealthy Jiangnan essayist and connoisseur of drama He Liangjun (1506–73), for example, compiled a long anthology of exemplary accounts praising the true literatus or *shi* as a man impervious to financial and sexual temptation.[16] In the tales of shi virtue that were paired with tales of virtuous women, a shi would refuse to debauch his servants, arranging legitimate marriages for them instead.[17] (These shi stories always functioned as a kind of class marker, implicitly stigmatizing those who had not been educated and socialized as shi.) A relationship founded only on luxury, power, and sex would have connotations of *yin* or license, a term whose etymology suggests excess (water overflowing its banks), but which for millennia had often connoted *sexual* excess. For a moralist like Lü Kun, those human desires for which the sage rulers of antiquity had made provision through law and ritual were natural and acceptable, whereas all others (particularly sexual desire outside of marriage — or even *within* marriage, if not carefully regulated) were yin. And Lü Kun's comments on "the establishments of actors and singing-girls" (no immortals for him!) made such places yin or licentious indeed: "In the entertainment district" (where desire flourished unrestrained) "every man is a husband."[18]

The late Ming intellectuals who patronized courtesans did not, of course, want to understand their behavior in Lü Kun's terms. What they did, instead, was to construct their visits to the immortals as an ascent from the world of vulgar opportunism and ambition. Chafing under the constraints of the examination system, they needed a discourse that distinguished genuine literary cultivation from the rote learning needed to pass the examinations. Famous literati like Gui Youguang (1507–71), who may never have visited courtesans himself, provided them with language by revalorizing the word "yin," applying it to the artificial and excessive rhetoric of the examination candidate eager for a job.[19] Men like Gui Youguang and his friends were after *zhen*, or "the genuine," which they often claimed to find in the songs of the people, understood as the precise opposite to the showy rhetoric they rejected.[20]

In this complex of slogans, yin or excessive rhetoric was identified not with licentiousness but with hateful ambition; since the courtesan stood outside *all* the normative hierarchies of family and officialdom, a liaison with her (never mind all the deals made at those convivial banquets) could be represented not as indulging in licentious behavior but as transcending ambition.[21] Poetry shared with her could be represented as a repudiation of pernicious yin rhetoric. The stratification of the courtesan world helped the literatus understand himself in a positive way, since a liaison with a cultivated courtesan associated him with someone he understood as a superior being. And even if the shi subscribed to models of heroic virtue that made him reject the courtesan in her "negative" aspects (as the personification of unchanneled desire), still she could elevate his moral stature by offering temptation that he could, in Wai-yee Li's phrase, "relish and resist."[22]

In this and other similar ways, many late Ming literati identified the courtesan and her poetry with an acceptably Confucian version (namely, safeguarding true principle from ambition and opportunism) of the genuine. But what of other writing women? How did late Ming literati understand the active literary lives of their own mothers, wives, and daughters? And how did they use that understanding to construct their image of themselves?

Literati who valued the literary achievements of the women in their families could put a safe, normative Confucian frame around those achievements, as we see in this epitaph by the official-turned-playwright Li Kaixian (1502–68):

> A guest bearing a copy of "The Collected Records of the Xiang Household" visited me at my rustic abode, and as I perused the volumes I reached the section entitled "Records of a Loving Mother." All the elegant poems and essays therein were composed by Xiang's mother Zhou *an ren* [a title bestowed on her in honor of her son's achievements]. I put the book down and sighed deeply. Women's responsibility is to manage the inner affairs of the household; their words thus never go beyond their own walls, unlike men whose affairs take them to the four quarters of the empire. If not for virtuous descendants, filial sons, and men of letters to make them known, [events in the] inner quarters would never be heard of, and what would the dynastic historians compiling biographies of notable women find to record?[23]

Li closed his essay by noting the pride Ming gentry fathers could take in their talented daughters: Zhou's father called her a "female 'man of spirit' [*nü zhangfu*], in no way inferior to her brothers, Wei and Can." But Li framed her achievements by telling the reader how diligently Zhou served her husband's family and by praising the *men* of the family for circulating her achievements abroad. Li Kaixian's strategy of containment makes men the custodians of a woman's writing as well as of her person.

Central to the literati construction of wife and courtesan was the association of women with the "inner quarters" — on the literal level, the inner quarters of the gentry household, but in larger metaphorical terms, the inner domains that could be contrasted with the public world of male striving and self-assertion. The association of women and the inner quarters was Confucian-canonical for gentry wives and daughters, but as any cursory reading of Chinese poetry will reveal, the idea of a secluded inner realm penetrated by the eye of the voyeur was also central to the erotic appeal of the courtesan.

And the late Ming was an era when the notion of inner realms was central to the self-construction of literati men as well. Wang Yang-ming's (1472–1529) seminal teachings about looking inward to one's own heart-and-mind for Confucian enlightenment gave form to this inward-looking tendency and gave it the language that would affect everyone from quietists, who might be accused of Buddhist tendencies, to the vigorous reformer Lü Kun, who looked for true knowledge to a "tacit connection" (*mo qi*) between Heaven (*tian*) and the individual heart-and-mind (*xin*).[24] Moreover, many late Ming literati were convinced that canonical loyalty and fidelity needed to be animated by qing to be authentic. Although this can be seen as a way of channeling the discourse on qing when it threatened to get out of hand, still the very perception that qing needed to be channeled shows the power associated with emotions arising spontaneously within one's inner being. Destiny itself, as we see in the lines of Zhong Xing quoted above, could be affected by the heart-and-mind within.

Talking about women, then — women the *inner*, women the *secluded* — could be a coded way of talking about the inner dimension of the literati self, understood as the genuine dimension, capable of passion, especially given the male eroticization of women's secluded sphere. But where to situate this discourse? Within the literati household, as Tang Xianzu shocked his contemporaries by doing in *Peony Pavilion*?[25] Or in the courtesans' quarters, where qing was conventionally expected to reign supreme? As we will see, Chen Yujiao opted for a solution in between.

Chen Yujiao

At first glance it seems almost misguided to look for tensions and ambiguities in Chen Yujiao's career as a playwright. He lived in luxurious retirement, he was part of an active literati community devoted to vernacular fiction and drama, and like other members of this community, he published his own plays, four long chuanqi dramas and five four-act *zaju*, in elegant illustrated editions.[26] The stresses of the examination system were long behind him, and until the imprisonment of his son in 1605, he cannot have experienced practical difficulties. And yet, in their writings, Chen Yujiao and men like him often characterize their way of life as a gesture of refusal, a solution to a problem, a principled withdrawal from the world of opportunism and faction. Much of their drama is implicitly organized around the question of how to characterize that world and respond to it. Theirs was an exceedingly comfortable counterculture, but we will not understand how it articulated with the society around them unless we remember that Chen Yujiao and his friends had a repertoire of ways to understand themselves so different from ours that what to us looks like a life of opportunity could be understood by them as (or at any rate, comfortably presented as) a refusal of opportunism.

Chen Yujiao's family, based in Haining county, Zhejiang, was part of the "oligopoly" that controlled the government salt monopoly.[27] We know from the illustrious career and writings of Chen's contemporary Wang Daokun (1525–93) that such salt merchant families could rise to high literati status, marked by unexceptionable adherence to literati gender conventions.[28] Chen Yujiao himself passed unimpeded through the examinations: *xiucai*, or local qualifying examination, at fifteen (this was also the year he was married), *juren*, or provincial examination, at 23, and the jinshi, or highest civil-service degree, at 30. He rose steadily into the upper half of court bureaucracy until 1592, when his faction (who would have resisted that description of themselves) lost power and he was dismissed on an insignificant charge. He retired to the life described above, writing not only literati drama but also the guides to cultural literacy that became a staple of commercial booksellers during the late Ming printing boom: annotated editions of the Tang poet Du Fu and of the classic sixth-century anthology *Selections from Refined Literature* (*Wen xuan*), and a handbook on literary style.

We know from the example of another Wanli era (1573–1620) playwright, Wang Tingna, how fabulously pleasant such a life could be.[29] Wang, whose fortune may also have come from salt (he had purchased a post in the salt bureaucracy and vigorously defended it against the opprobrium that Ray Huang says was the order of the day),[30] has left us in his *Chess Manual* (*Qi pu*) a record of refined recreation and conversation with a stream of high-literati visitors who came to visit and forget the world outside. The exquisite calligraphy of the prefaces that he attributed (probably falsely) to famous literati is followed by three exceptionally beautiful and detailed woodcut illustrations of preparation for a chess game, in one of the fantastic grottoes with which such men decorated their estates.[31]

Chen Yujiao seems to have defined himself as a playwright largely with reference to the literati drama community. Both he and Wang Tingna wrote *zaju* plays about the "wolf of Zhong shan," whose philosopher-hero is menaced by the very wolf he has saved from the huntsman (this story was a standard vehicle for criticism of tyrannical officials during the Ming). Two of Chen's chuanqi dramas revise the work of earlier literati playwrights (one of them, *The Efficacious Sword* [*Ling bao dao*], is a revision of Li Kaixian's *Jeweled Sword* [*Bao jian ji*]), and the two others take on themes treated by the giant of the community, Tang Xianzu: illusion and reality expressed as "waking from a dream" in Tang's *The Story of Nan Ke* (*Nan Ke ji*) and Chen's *A Dream of Cherries* (*Ying tao meng*), and the relation of qing to "virtue" (*de*) in Tang's *Peony Pavilion* and Chen's *Parrot Island*.[32] Chen was writing, then, for an intended audience of his peers, and this must be kept in mind as we analyze his subject position below. Moreover, the fact that Chen published his plays in high-quality illustrated editions suggests that they were meant for reading as well as performance, and this, too, will guide our discussion.

"Parrot Island"

Parrot Island retells the story of the Tang military hero Wei Gao (745–805) and his concubine Yuxiao, closely following an account in the tenth-century anthology *Taiping guangji*.[33] The play opens with Wei Gao's announcement that he wants to be released from the official duties to which he has been assigned. (As in the Tang sources for Wei Gao's life, this is a time of trouble and corruption.) He visits the Jiang family, friends of his father's, and falls in love with their adopted daughter Yuxiao. (She is a nursemaid's orphaned child, whom the late Madam Jiang has instructed the family to raise as their own.) When Wei Gao leaves for his post, he promises to return within seven years and gives Yuxiao a jade ring as a token of fidelity. But the military exploits on which his fame rests keep him away past the appointed time, and Yuxiao retreats to Parrot Island, where she prays, pines away, and dies, having copied one of Wei Gao's poems onto her sash. Wei Gao, distraught when he learns of her death, repairs temples and has sutras copied in order to repay her karmic debt and bring her back to life; a seer summons her soul, who tells him that he has succeeded. She is reborn as an adopted daughter in the home of another prominent official, available once again as a young, desirable concubine. On the finger of the reincarnated Yuxiao is a raised ring of flesh.

What *Parrot Island* adds to the *Taiping guangji* account is a parallel story of the Tang courtesan-poet Xue Tao (770–832) and her celebrated romantic adventures with Wei Gao and the poet Yuan Zhen (779–831). (The liaisons of the historical Xue Tao with these two men were the stuff of legend by Ming times.)[34] As the parallel stories are interwoven, Xue Tao and Yuan Zhen act out separation, fidelity, and infidelity in ways that are contrasted with Wei Gao and Yuxiao. The stories intersect as Wei Gao, traveling to the Jiang household, meets Xue Tao on her way to join Yuan Zhen; she recognizes Wei Gao's incipient greatness and gives him the jade ring that he will later give to Yuxiao. Yuan Zhen suffers pangs of jealousy over Xue Tao's interest in Wei Gao (he confides his fears to their mutual friend, the celebrated Tang dynasty poet Bo Juyi). Xue Tao's and Yuan Zhen's poems are quoted and woven into song throughout the play. At the end of *Parrot Island*, Xue Tao is engaged to tutor the reincarnated Yuxiao in the literary arts. But by this time Xue Tao has become a Daoist nun, as the only way to extirpate the jealousy *she* feels when she learns that Yuan Zhen has been exchanging poems with the courtesan Liu Caichun.[35] (She also wants to shake off the unwelcome attentions of a boorish merchant.)

In the last five scenes, the play's competing models of life and writing confront each other explicitly. Xue Tao sings of the joys of the courtesan's untrammeled life, traveling the empire with only her zither and a copy of the *Odes* ("Don't you get bored here?" she asks the reincarnated Yuxiao, who is happy praying, embroidering, and tending her parrot). But Yuxiao begs to be taught to read only didactic texts like the *Instructions for Women* (*Nü xun*), a conduct book from the hand of the Ming Zhengde empress (r. 1506–22),[36] and says she does not want to learn to write anything that would trouble her spirit with improper longings. (Chen Yujiao has no compunctions about giving his Tang dynasty heroine a Ming dynasty book to read; he was, of course, using this Tang tale as a vehicle for his Ming concerns.) Xue Tao has had to overcome Yuxiao's resistance to learning anything of literature at all: Yuxiao points out that her embroidery will still be beautiful twenty years hence, whereas she is likely to forget everything she learns about reading and writing. Xue Tao counters that Yuxiao needs to study if she is to be an appropriate companion for a learned husband. Yuxiao grounds her resistance in the observation that girls who wrote, like Zhuo Wenjun (who eloped with the poet Sima Xiangru at the beginning of the Han), were thrown over by their lovers: she thus effectively identifies writing — the illicit public voice — with illicit sexuality.

But Yuxiao's desire to retreat into the world of private women's work is not so much a rigid moral stance as a defense against the forces of passion. In a long scene in the garden, Yuxiao's maid teases her into confessing a dream of sexual desire, a dream startlingly similar to that of Tang Xianzu's heroine Du Liniang in *Peony Pavilion*. Yuxiao, however, represses her dream, rather than embracing it as did Du Liniang.[37] Yuxiao's response to Xue Tao is to set the didactic classics up as a bulwark against desire, if that desire is not ritually sanctioned. Chen Yujiao seemed to want to make clear that the revivifying force of qing can operate properly only within the bounds of Confucian fidelity and propriety: Wei Gao, for all his spiritual and aesthetic affinity with Xue Tao, rejects her sexual advances, bending all his efforts instead to bringing Yuxiao back. The notion that qing for a courtesan can be revivifying in the same way is made huge sport of in the scene following Yuxiao's spirit-appearance. Wei Gao's friend Jiang Jingbao, besotted after Xue Tao's appearance to him in a dream, becomes distraught over false rumors of her death—and Wei Gao tricks him into believing that an aging prostitute hired for the occasion is actually Xue Tao, brought back to life by Jiang's desire.

Other scenes in the play are paired to keep this distinction between two kinds of qing before us. Wei Gao's devotion to Yuxiao and Yuan Zhen's to Xue Tao are juxtaposed so often that we cannot help comparing the two couples: Wei Gao's affecting separation from Yuxiao in Scene 11 is followed by Yuan Zhen's songs of the pain of parting in Scene 12; Wei Gao sends a letter to Yuxiao in Scene 16, and Yuan Zhen to Xue Tao in Scene 17. But by Scene 22, Bo Juyi's teasing tells us that Yuan Zhen has a new courtesan-paramour—whereas Scene 23 shows us Wei Gao embracing the spirit of his departed love, who promises him their future happiness together.

Parrot Island draws on traditions noted above to code Wei Gao's and Yuxiao's fidelity and restraint not just as correct *moral* behavior, but as correct *class or status* behavior, idealized in the language Chen Yujiao and his friends used to idealize themselves. This coding requires the containment of women (one mark of a literati family was that its women were secluded)—but as noted above, Chen's deepest concern was with tempering Wei Gao's passions. This is first made clear by negative example, as Chen Yujiao shows us the tendencies Wei Gao must learn to suppress. In the early scenes of *Parrot Island*, Wei Gao is as impulsive as his friend Jiang and makes suggestive advances to Yuxiao the first time he is alone with her (Scene 7). But Yuxiao repulses him with Confucian indignation: outraged and mortified, she refuses to be compared to famous icons of licentiousness who want love outside marriage. And by the time her supposed protector Jiang Jingbao decides to make a grand gesture by bestowing her on Wei Gao in Scene 9, Wei Gao himself has come to his Confucian senses: "I fear that this would harm my *shidafu* [Confucian scholar-gentry] reputation!" (The idealized shidafu does *not* debauch innocent girls left in his care.) Yuxiao's arias at this point maintain a culturally correct counterpoint to his anxiety, as she sings that she always thought she was being brought up for legitimate marriage. The matter is speedily resolved when Jiang Jingbao performs the ritually required role of matchmaker, red candles are lit, and enough ceremony is performed to convince all present that Yuxiao will receive the honors due a wife when Wei Gao rises to high rank. What Chen Yujiao has done with the tenth-century tale, even by this early point in the play, is to set it up as a Confucian quest story, in which Wei Gao's qing must be educated, trained, and chastened before he can realize its erotic possibilities. Yuxiao and his own belated conscience set the terms, and his fidelity during the years of separation earns him his reward.

This was, however, a Confucian quest story by a late Ming literatus who knew the courtesan world well—too well to want to repudiate it! In Scene 22, when Yuan Zhen drinks wine and trades stories with the poet Bo Juyi, Chen Yujiao adumbrates the canon of Tang courtesans celebrated by late Ming literati. They range from Xue Tao to the circumspect Guan Panpan, whose moral delicacy in delaying her suicide after her patron died (she did not want to call their relationship to the world's attention) was threatened by the very poems Bo Juyi wrote in her praise. We have seen above in the fifteenth-century tale "Tianshu Composes Linked Verse" how Xue Tao, the epitome of the courtesan elite, could be presented not only as the quintessential fusion of talent and elegance but also as a teacher of judgment and refinement. Chen Yujiao was heir to a line of literary men like the official-turned-poet Yang Shen (1488–1559), whose claim to knowledge of Xue Tao poems that others considered lost was meant to communicate his *own* powers of discernment to his peers.[38] Chen did not want to deprive his hero of all that lent glamour to his own milieu: Xue Tao may be curbed and her aura channeled in *Parrot Island*, but still it is *her* perceptions that first signal Wei Gao's greatness, as she confers on Wei Gao her poetry and her perspicacity.

Scene 6 shows in a small compass the strategy that Chen Yujiao used in the play as a whole, giving permission for the experience of qing but suggesting the limitations within which he allowed it to operate. Yuan Zhen opens the scene by giving Xue Tao the manuscript of his newly completed "Golden Oriole" ("Ying ying zhuan"), the seminal tale that would be transformed over the following centuries into a series of hugely popular plays. Xue Tao praises "Golden Oriole" as "the ancestor to all chuanqi [tales of the marvelous]," noting that he shows in it a perfect mastery of the depiction of qing. Yuan Zhen demurs: Will not this "mere love affair" disgrace the "four friends of the studio" (the scholar's brush and ink, paper and inkstone)? Xue Tao assures him that he is too modest and seals her approval with a colophon. Xue Tao has been coded as a hero herself from the moment she appears in Scene 3 (her literary talents would "top the lists" if only she were a man), and her approval here is a signal that qing is to be taken seriously. The Ming audience knew "Golden Oriole" well: in Yuan Zhen's tale, the young hero and heroine (both of good family) exchange poetry and secretly consummate their love but are ultimately parted forever. In the Yuan and Ming plays that transformed the tale, they marry. In either version, the story was viewed in Ming times as a triumph of qing (the delicate renunciations of the Tang tale perhaps even surpassing the happy ending of the plays), and the tenth-century tale of Wei Gao and Yuxiao owes much to Yuan Zhen.

Chen Yujiao's next authorial move imbues Scene 6 still further with the aura of qing, as a troupe of actors performs for Yuan Zhen and Xue Tao the story of Song Yu the poet composing his "Rhyme-prose About Gao tang" ("Gao tang fu") for the third-century B.C. King of Chu. (Song Yu explains to the king—in language the audience knew by heart—how a mythical ruler of old achieved sensual union with a goddess, who then vanished as "clouds and rain.")[39] By Ming times, this allusion was a standard evocation of the courtesan world, and it functioned in Chinese culture as the sensual equivalent of culture-hero stories about the invention of paper or the taming of floods. Chen Yujiao has the master of the troupe issue the standard disclaimer that Song Yu's real aim was to awaken the ruler to the perils of passion and the danger of misusing his authority. But the Ming audience, whose repeated inoculation had rendered them relatively immune to this disclaimer, would have seen the allusion for what it was, namely, the introduction of the courtesan aura into the world of the play. Chen Yujiao reined the allusion in, however, by having Xue Tao sigh that our life of qing, of meetings and partings, is thus no more than a dream—and by having Yuan Zhen concur.

This is Chen Yujiao setting limits and granting permission at the

same time. Yuan Zhen's attachment to Xue Tao will indeed be as evanescent as a dream, but Xue Tao's air of glamour and qing will be
evoked whenever she appears in the play, which is to say in almost
half the scenes. Chen Yujiao caps Scene 6 with Scene 7, in which
Yuxiao puts the allusion in its place by turning on her heel when Wei
Gao suggests they turn the temple where he is staying into a "pavilion
of Chu" — but still it is Xue Tao, the goddess of sensuality, who blesses
their union by giving Wei Gao the ring that will bind him to Yuxiao.
Xue Tao even gives him the possibility of achieving the companionate
marriage that many of Chen's own contemporaries enjoyed, by insisting that Yuxiao take the trouble to learn something! And one of
Xue Tao's most celebrated poems is evoked when the reincarnated
Yuxiao is bestowed again on Wei Gao.[40] Yuxiao's dream of passion,
which she now feels free to realize (she whispers to her maid that Wei
Gao matches the husband of her dreams), promises him that his fidelity will be rewarded in the bedchamber as well as in the spirit.

Yuxiao, neither quite courtesan nor quite gentry woman, is an appropriately ambivalent instrument for Chen Yujiao's expression of his
own ambivalence about passion and containment. In order to let his
hero have the full experience of qing, Chen Yujiao feels the need to
eroticize, valorize, and sentimentalize a heroine who cleaves to the
liang values that were a marker for his own status group. But, as we
have already noted, he chooses to affirm these liang values *outside* the
idealized family unit, the hierarchized structure conventionally exalted as the seedbed for those values. Wei Gao apparently does marry
after he leaves Yuxiao in *Parrot Island*, since he is referred to in Scene
16 as the son-in-law of Military Commissioner (*jie du shi*) Zhang. Here
Chen Yujiao was bowing to convention: the historical Zhang was Wei
Gao's predecessor in office, and we will note below a series of plays
that put Wei Gao's marriage to Zhang's daughter at the center. Chen
Yujiao chose to downplay that bit of standard Wei Gao lore and emphasize another sort of relationship altogether. In the scenes where
Wei Gao meets Yuxiao, is united with her, and is parted from her,
there are no grownups! Jiang Jingbao's father is off at the front and his
mother has died, and the three young people, two male peers and
their lovely protegée, are shaping their own destiny. Not only is this a
daring departure from normal family hierarchy — it is, in essence, the
courtesan situation, where a man was free to bestow the rich potential
of qing (that is to say, a lovely woman) on friend or sworn brother.

Chen's literati readers and playwright peers doubtless caught these courtesan resonances, because of all the elements of plot and literary context that coded Yuxiao as a type of courtesan herself. Introducing her to Wei Gao in Scene 5, Jiang Jingbao says that in accordance with his mother's wishes, she is being brought up "like a sister" to him. The accomplishments he cites, however, are skills at playing music and serving wine. Although music might indeed be an accomplishment of the gentry daughter, the mere fact that Yuxiao emerges from the women's quarters to serve wine to visitors marks her as subordinate and sexually available.

The mid-seventeenth century commentary edition of the vernacular novel *Romance of the Three Kingdoms* (*San guo yanyi*) gives a name to the cultural slot Yuxiao seems to occupy. Like the famous Diao Chan, used in *Three Kingdoms* as "bait" to trap a notorious villain, Yuxiao is both an "adopted daughter" and a "*jia ji*" or household entertainer.[41] The Yuxiao of the tenth-century *Taiping guangji* tale was similarly rich in ambiguity, a household favorite who could nevertheless be exposed to public view, and by Chen Yujiao's time, Qiao Ji's (d. 1435) *Two Lives of Love* (*Liang shi yin yuan*), a fourteenth-century Yuan dynasty zaju version of the Yuxiao story, had taken the obvious step of making Yuxiao into that cultural favorite, the constant singing-girl. This Yuan play was a favorite of Ming connoisseurs of drama, and even though *Parrot Island* ignores the zaju and returns instead to the tenth-century tale for its plot outline, still Yuxiao-as-singing-girl would have been hovering in the wings of every performance (or reading experience). The reincarnated Yuxiao introduced in Scene 28 of *Parrot Island* is even more unambiguously a household entertainer than was her avatar at the beginning of the play; although here, too, she is an "adopted daughter," still her peers are the other *maids*, who complain that Yuxiao is the favorite—but then sigh and admit that she has always outsung and outdanced them all.

The constant singing-girl, a cautionary trope in Tang tales (where she rescues the hero from his own debauchery) and a charming rhetorical surprise in Yuan drama, was already a martyr to loyalty in the fourteenth-century plays of the prince Zhu Youdun (1379–1439), whose singing-girl heroines hang or drown themselves to escape from their life.[42] The Yuxiao of *Parrot Island* preserves all these resonances but adds something new: not only does she cleave to shidafu values, but she insists on her rightful place in the shidafu world! When she is to be reborn as an adopted daughter at the end of the play, she protests to the heavenly court that she deserves to be a real one. (The judges explain that since it is her destiny to become a concubine once again, she must be reborn in the appropriate status.) Her repeated demands to be treated as a full daughter or wife evince a shidafu consciousness that validates Wei Gao's constancy to her.

By coding Yuxiao as a courtesan who claims shidafu respectability, Chen Yujiao is able to have it both ways: shidafu constancy with the rich sensual aura of the courtesan world. (Even as he curbs Xue Tao, he reserves her rich sensuality for men of his class; she will have nothing to do with the importunate merchant.) And by having his hero cleave to Yuxiao-as-courtesan rather than to Xue Tao, he keeps the courtesan aura from threatening shidafu hierarchy. Yuxiao may demand the place of wife, but the fact that her demand is not granted reinscribes her as subordinate. Chen Yujiao puts her death at the climactic midpoint of his well-made play, pulling out all the rhetorical stops[43] — but it is a *pathetic* death, deriving its rhetorical effect from the heroine's powerlessness. Chen operated similarly in his revision of Li Kaixian's *Jeweled Sword*, putting the death of a concubine (who sacrifices herself for her mistress) at the midpoint of the play. And in his zaju *The Righteous Dog of the Yuan Family* (*Yuan shi yi quan*), whose villain kills the hero's infant son, it is the nursemaid's arias as the baby meets the knife that are used to convey the full pathos of the situation. In all these plays, Chen Yujiao derived rhetorical power from having a subordinate embody dominant cultural values (by exalting the powerless, he gave himself the power to criticize misguided authority) — but he effectively reinscribed the shidafu hierarchy by strongly coding the subordinate *as subordinate*. It is Wei Gao, his male shidafu hero, who realizes the full heroism of the chaste widow ideal.

This would not be everyone's solution to questions of status and passion. The vernacular retelling of the Yuxiao story in the 1620's collection *The Rocks Nod Their Heads* (*Shi dian tou*) would naturalize the Tang tale by showing how frightened an actual Yuxiao might have been.[44] (The vernacular story thus suggests a jaundiced view of the men who feel free to bestow Yuxiao on each other.) Or the courtesan might be valorized far more unambiguously than Chen Yujiao was willing to do: by the 1640's, as Kang-i Sun Chang has brilliantly shown, the poet Chen Zilong (1608–47) would write of his shidafu loyalty in the ardent language publicly identified with his feelings for the courtesan Liu Rushi.[45] And staying strictly within the shidafu compass, Tang Xianzu had created the gentry daughter Du Liniang, who assented happily to the sort of dream that Chen Yujiao's Yuxiao held at arm's length. Other literati writers fused poetry and passion in an unproblematic way: the protagonists of the fifteenth-century classical-language novella *A Graceful Account of Profound Love* (*Zhong qing li ji*), contemporary with the story "Tianshu Composes Linked Verse with Xue Tao," are a girl and a boy of good family who exchange poetry, secretly consummate their love, and then marry once the boy passes the examinations.[46] (As in *Parrot Island*, the hero's courtesan friends bless his union—but in contrast to *Parrot Island*, the gentry heroine of *A Graceful Account* feels no need to repudiate them.) The comedic ending to such stories served to justify the life of feeling within the *liang* community, and Chen Zilong's older contemporary Feng Menglong (1574–1646) anthologized many such stories in his *Classified Compendium of the History of Love* (*Qing shi lei lüe*).

Another solution was simply to transfer the Yuxiao story to the *liang* world. The fourteenth-century Yuan *zaju* version of the Yuxiao story, Qiao Ji's *Two Lives of Love*, was expanded during the sixteenth and early seventeenth centuries as the *chuanqi* drama *Tale of the Jade Ring* (*Yu huan ji*).[47] Here the parallel plot to the tale of Wei Gao and Yuxiao is not the story of Xue Tao, but rather of Wei Gao's marriage to the daughter of Military Commissioner Zhang. In typical *chuanqi* fashion, both extant editions of *Jade Ring* feature the separation and eventual reunion of husband and wife, as he fights for empire and she undergoes ordeals of fidelity and filial piety. Wei Gao's reunion with Yuxiao (a Yuxiao who, as in *Two Lives of Love*, is a constant singing-girl) occurs only at the end of *Jade Ring*, where it seems something of an afterthought. In their stress on the virtues associated with the Three Bonds and Five Relationships, *Jade Ring* and its revisions are more *conventionally liang* than *Parrot Island*, and they may have had even wider literati currency. *Jade Ring* was the version of the Yuxiao story chosen for the mid-seventeenth-century compendium *Sixty Plays* (*Liu shi zhong qu*), and in the novel *Golden Lotus* (*Jin ping mei*), allusions to the heroes of *Jade Ring* serve to point up by contrast the villainy of corrupt officials (even as the expansive complexity of the novel pokes subtle fun at the one-dimensional heroes of the play).[48] *Jade Ring* does not create the same sort of tension as *Parrot Island*: the Yuxiao of *Jade Ring* may be a virtuous singing-girl (in one edition she asks Wei Gao to teach her the *Mencius*), but the true courtesan milieu is never evoked in the play, and Yuxiao herself drops out after the first few scenes.

Chen Yujiao's solution, more daring than the *Jade Ring* plays but far more cautious than Chen Zilong's poetry, lets him justify his life of comfortable retirement. Like Wang Tingna, Chen Yujiao's Wei Gao considers himself an "old rustic" who has withdrawn from the official corruption he sees around him. Wei Gao's attachment to Yuxiao effectively sets up the life of qing as a counterweight to the life of ambition. Chen can prove his moral stature by subduing (relishing and resisting) Xue Tao, but he simultaneously signals his powers of discernment by making Xue Tao and her poetry central to his play. By putting Xue Tao's aura in the service of the values he was taught to uphold, Chen Yujiao permits himself to practice the sensuous writing she represents. But what, in the meantime, were women writers thinking?

Men, Women, and "Parrot Island"

As we will see below, Xue Tao and Yuxiao were familiar figures to the educated wives and daughters of men like Chen Yujiao. But did their stories mean the same things to women and to men? Ellen Widmer has shown how differently men and women responded to the story of Xiaoqing, a concubine-poet said to have pined away and died (rather like our Yuxiao) on the shores of West Lake in the 1620's. For her male admirers, Xiaoqing's death epitomized the tragic fate of beauty fused with talent, whereas for women, the very title of Xiaoqing's posthumous collection, "Manuscripts Saved from Burning," stimulated efforts to collect and preserve women's poetry.[49] In trying to reconstruct a female audience for *Parrot Island* (an audience of governing-class women, Chen Yujiao's female peers), we will be aiming for a similar bifocal view of the way the play was integrated into late Ming culture.

Imagine a governing-class woman in a literary household with the supportive father, husband, and son evoked by Li Kaixian's account of Zhou *an ren*. Such a woman had the confidence to write, and her male relatives published her work — as men would increasingly do during the seventeenth century. But recent research has shown that much of her pleasure in writing might well have come from the way it connected her with other women. Sources dated shortly after *Parrot Island* show us convivial poetry parties late at night in the women's quarters, with letters and the exchange of poems over long distances widening women's literary communities beyond the compass of their own relatives.[50] And in families like the one Li Kaixian evokes, cultivated wives were often close literary companions to their husbands. Paul Ropp notes the rise of the companionate marriage ideal during the Qing, when it displaced the idealized companionship of shi and courtesan,[51] but we need to remember that such companionate literati marriages were already highly valued by the mid-sixteenth century. Here is the famous essayist and teacher Gui Youguang in his epitaph for Mao *ru ren* (another honorific title), the wife of his countryman Zhou Ruheng:

> When Mao *ru ren* was a child, she had had female teachers, and she thoroughly penetrated the great affairs of past and present. . . . Ruheng sat for the jinshi degree, but returned home when he failed to pass the examination at the Ministry of Rites. Together they read books and delved into history, unmoved by questions of success or failure.[52]

By the 1620's or so, even the didactic literature preferred by the reincarnated Yuxiao could encourage girls and women to write. In *Illustrated Biographies of Notable Women* (*Hui tu Lienü zhuan*), one of the longest and most frequently reprinted late Ming expansions of the Han classic *Biographies of Notable Women* (*Lienü zhuan*),[53] nearly 10 percent of the illustrations have books in the picture — sometimes (in this bibliophilic age) even for stories that are not about reading and writing at all. The filial daughter of the Wang family, for instance, venerating the bones of her father, mother, and stepmother in a graveside hut, is shown reading at her table.[54] And even more significantly, the illustrations create the image of a literate woman in a pose of magisterial authority, as when the Ming literary prodigy Zou Saizhen is shown seated in a chamber filled with books. Although the commentator issues the conventional warning that "brush and ink do not belong in the women's quarters" (and admonishes the ordinary run of women against imagining that *they* can achieve literary greatness), still he praises Zou Saizhen solely on the merits of her poetry, with no reference to the conventional Confucian virtues that *Biographies of Notable Women* was supposed to teach.[55] Several of the Ming poets in *Illustrated Biographies* are also included in the seventeenth-century anthologies of women's poetry analyzed by Kang-i Sun Chang in this volume.[56] This movement back and forth between genres shows that the woman as writing subject had achieved an identity with a certain degree of autonomy.

Would such a writing woman, in Chen Yujiao's day and the decades immediately following, have had access to *Parrot Island*? And if so, how would it have fit into her literary world?

Literary governing-class women of the early seventeenth century certainly saw and read drama; the talented middle daughter of Shen Yixiu (Shen was a poet herself and an anthologist of women's poetry) completed a play of her own in 1636.[57] Performances of drama were a conventional element in family or lineage-based celebrations among the Jiangsu elite, and Tanaka Issei has provided a summary of the kinds of plays said to be performed at such celebrations around 1600. These plays, taken together, "reflect a highly conventional view of life: children are admonished to be virtuous and hard-working; wives and mothers exhort their husbands and sons to strive for success, and wait patiently at home while they are away; men leave their homes to make their way in the world, and eventually send letters reporting success back to their anxious families; filial children and loyal friends are held up as models of virtue; the successful man secures his position by cultivating patrons and friends, and does not neglect to enlist Heaven on his side."[58] *Parrot Island* ethicizes the Yuxiao story in a somewhat *un*conventional way, but still it could perhaps have fit into this compass—especially since Tanaka's data show that the compass could be stretched to include *The Romance of the Western Chamber* (*Xi xiang ji*), the dramatic version of Yuan Zhen's "Golden Oriole" that Xue Tao admires in Scene 6 of *Parrot Island*. Whether or not *Parrot Island* ever achieved wide performance, we can imagine the performance of at least selected scenes within the author's own cultivated household.

But from the lore of women's responses to *Peony Pavilion* (describing this response became a significant seventeenth-century way of talking about women's sensibilities), we can see that *reading* was the conventional image of the governing-class woman's access to drama. (In a trope that swept the literary world, Xiaoqing is said to have pined away after reading *Peony Pavilion*.)[59] And as noted above, *Parrot Island* was also produced in an edition obviously intended for reading. The waves of women's commentary to *Peony Pavilion* (and of drama composed *by* women) gathered strength after the fall of the Ming, but poems and commentary do exist to show that women were already reading *Peony Pavilion* by the early decades of the seventeenth century.[60] Given Chen Yujiao's prominence in Jiangnan drama circles, his beautiful editions may have circulated to other gentry-playwright households as well — and some of the women who were reading *Peony Pavilion* may have read *Parrot Island*.

What would *Parrot Island* have looked like to them? Here we must consider both the story and the physical book in which women would have encountered it. In both aspects *Parrot Island* would have awakened a sense of familiarity. As I have noted elsewhere, books like *Illustrated Biographies* and the early seventeenth-century edition of Lü Kun's *Female Exemplars* shared a pool of illustrators (mostly from Shexian in Huizhou) with the publications of dramatists like Chen Yujiao and Wang Tingna.[61] *Parrot Island* would thus have *looked* quite similar to the sort of material that girls in good families were supposed to read — or at least have on display.

I have also noted that the passionate dedication infusing Ming stories of faithful fiancées, wives, and widows blurred the boundary between stories of virtue and stories of love.[62] We should not be surprised to learn that didactic commentators, by the 1620's at least, were capable of assuming that liang women would know the stuff-material of *Parrot Island*. The selfless courtesan Guan Panpan, relatively easy for the didactic commentator to assimilate to his design, turns up everywhere: in his *Spring and Autumn Mirror for Humanity* (*Ren jing yang qiu*), a compendium of accounts of virtue, Wang Tingna wraps a faithful self-sacrificing concubine in Panpan's mantle,[63] and Panpan joins another similarly self-effacing Tang courtesan in *Illustrated Biographies*.[64] The commentator to *Illustrated Biographies* also assumes that his women readers will know Xue Tao, Wei Gao, and Yuxiao! Although he warns us that "the poetry of prostitutes [*ji nü*] is not to be taken seriously," still his sympathetic entry on Guan Panpan compares Panpan and her patron to Yuxiao and Wei Gao and offers the connoisseur's comment that in terms of qing even Xue Tao ranked below Guan Panpan, whereas Yuxiao was not "worth counting on my little finger."

The audience of governing-class women that we are constructing for *Parrot Island* thus apparently shared a good deal of sensuous late Ming culture with their fathers, husbands, and brothers. How would they respond to the plot that unfolded on the pages of Chen Yujiao's elegant book? Would they, too, tailor the qing they claimed for themselves, by curbing a Xue Tao while valorizing the virtuous innocence of a Yuxiao? A survey of recent research suggests that not all of them would have done so.

First, we need to remind ourselves how powerfully the demands of shidafu male subjectivity affected the self-construction of both wives and courtesans in the shidafu orbit. Even the courtesan must have been profoundly affected by the shidafu male construction of her role: the remarkable Liu Rushi launched herself from a platform prepared for her by the poetry of men like Zhong Xing. The writer of beautiful poetry was expected to be beautiful herself, a trope so ingrained that gentry women poets used it to address each other.[65] The dominance of literati male paradigms could move both the high-ranking courtesan *and* the governing-class wife to imitate the male persona in her own way: Liu Rushi was famous for dressing as a man and calling herself the "younger brother" of her male mentors, whereas a few governing-class wives, as Dorothy Ko shows in this volume, turned a connoisseur's eye on the courtesan world and wrote poetry to courtesans using what Maureen Robertson calls the "literati-masculine" voice.[66]

These "literati-masculine" poems, in which women adopt the male "gaze" to describe other women, suggest the complexities involved as governing-class women negotiated their own subjectivity in a world where the image of the courtesan was so powerfully present. On the one hand, the texts supposed to separate the liang and jian worlds were actually opening these worlds to each other here and there: *Illustrated Biographies* reflects the interpenetration of the gentry and courtesan worlds by mixing in courtesans (albeit the most high-minded of courtesans) with its liang women and praising liang women poets in the language typical of the connoisseurship of courtesans. (The young widow Yu *shi*, revived by her relatives after a suicide try, went on to express her fidelity in two poems about chrysanthemums—and as we saw Zhong Xing do above for his unnamed courtesan, the *Illustrated Biographies* compiler compares her to the flower, here willing to sacrifice her "pure and fragrant flesh" for the sake of fidelity. He condemns those who fail to recognize her talent and exalt her fidelity as being "deficient in qing.")[67] Moreover, the male culture that invented and deified the courtesan opened up roles and avenues of expression for governing-class women. Paul Ropp quotes the poetry of desire that gentry women wrote to their absent husbands,[68] and a Shen Yixiu might lead her household poetry society up into the hills to respond to the beauties of nature just like the men and their courtesan-companions.[69]

But on the other hand, the "literati-masculine" voice in which governing-class women echoed the male connoisseurship of courtesans reminds us that, for the most part, the way wife and courtesan met socially was as patron and entertainer. There were no courtesans in the kin-based poetry societies of governing-class women, and governing-class women did not ask courtesans for prefaces to their collections of poetry.[70] Paul Ropp's chapter in this volume reminds us that even at the height of courtesan glamour, the courtesan could still be presented as someone *bound* in her situation and hence to be pitied. *Illustrated Biographies* contains not just accounts of the elite courtesan-consorts of powerful men but also the affecting stories (typologically very similar to stories of young widows resisting remarriage) of young singing-girls who want to reform.

Few of the literary women discussed here turned to drama (more would do so in the Qing), and even fewer of their works have survived, but three extant plays by late Ming women hint that status distinctions between wives and courtesans were expressed in women's literary subjectivity. From the research of Ye Changhai we learn that the one extant woman-authored Ming play *about* a courtesan is *by* a courtesan; of the other two, both by women from literati families, one is a "daring" depiction of a love match between the Herd-Boy and Weaving-Maid of star lore (inspired, perhaps, by all those love matches between literary young people?). The other is the play that Ye Xiaowan, Shen Yixiu's middle daughter, wrote to express her grief after the death of her two talented sisters. Ye Xiaowan consoles herself with the conventions of the deliverance play (a favorite of literati authors for centuries), placing her sisters among the immortals surrounding the Queen Mother of the West.[71] Xiaowan's play reminds us how important to governing-class writing women was the society of their peers (Xiaowan's sisters in a more general sense). This sample of plays by women, tiny though it is, suggests that late Ming governing-class women writers developed a different range of themes from those of courtesans.

But would these factors have compelled governing-class women writers to renounce the cultural power of a figure like Xue Tao? No, because just as Ming literati trimmed the image of the courtesan to meet their own (not always uniform) needs, so late Ming governing-class women poets could create a usable Xue Tao for themselves. Xue Tao was a courtesan—but even though governing-class women were patrons rather than peers of courtesans, still the visits of courtesans to the women's quarters of gentry homes meant that ties of friendship might develop.[72] And Chen Yujiao himself endowed his Xue Tao with some of the attributes that Ming governing-class women might find attractive: as literary tutor to a high-ranking family, the Xue Tao of *Parrot Island* plays a social role newly open to *respectable* women in late Ming society.[73] Xue Tao, for governing-class women, could be an agent of their writing community, valued for her literary achievement and independence of spirit. These were the qualities that led the gentry woman poet Shang Jinglan to praise Huang Yuanjie, one of the most self-sufficient of seventeenth-century gentry women poets and painters, as a Xue Tao.[74] And Huang Yuanjie, not a courtesan but a gentry woman whose life came closest to the freedom achieved by some of the courtesan elite (indeed she was befriended by Liu Rushi *after* Liu married), *was* in demand as a writer of prefaces,[75] suggesting that whatever they thought of actual courtesan status, the image of courtesan-like freedom was attractive to gentry women as well as to gentry men. Chen Yujiao's Xue Tao is a courtesan (beautiful, jealous, torn between two men), but for poets like Shang Jinglan, who brings her into the gentry orbit, she is more of a teacher, a model, a culture hero.

What then of Yuxiao? Governing-class women readers may well have applauded the spirit with which she demands to be made a wife; they would recognize the trope from books directed at them, like the Ming expansions of *Biographies of Notable Women*, and it was a favorite refrain in the songs that courtesans may have sung when entertaining wives in their homes.[76] But such readers may have been impatient with the way Chen Yujiao packaged Yuxiao's desire. What late Ming and early Qing women writers did value, apparently, was *zhi qing*, which could mean both the *experience* of the extremity of qing and the *realization* of qing to its fullest. The phrase had a long history in Chinese literature: the hero of Yuan Zhen's ninth-century story "Golden Oriole," for example, is overcome by the need to "zhi qing" when he first catches sight of the heroine. "Zhi qing" did not have to connote sexual desire; the poet Gong Xu (1382–1469) praised the "extremity of [moral] passion" of a young woman whose admiring husband allowed her to commit suicide, once she explained that she had to remain faithful to the family of her dead fiancé.[77] By the time the mid-seventeenth-century gentry woman poet Wu Qi wrote of Du Liniang that "only in death could she prove her undying passion,"[78] the phrase fused love and moral passion into an assertion of personal integrity, a heroic willingness to give one's all.

But Chen Yujiao's Yuxiao is no Du Liniang, and her death is more pathetic (a male-imagined Xiaoqing-like death) than heroic. Moreover, the passion with which women read *Peony Pavilion* suggests that Yuxiao's sexual caution might have bored at least some of her governing-class women readers. Yuxiao, repulsing Wei Gao's initial advances, refuses to have her name associated with the shocking tale of Sima Xiangru (recall that she brings up Sima Xiangru and Zhuo Wenjun again in Scene 29, when she is being pestered to learn poetry). Shang Jinglan, however, praised Huang Yuanjie not just as a Xue Tao but as a Sima Xiangru.[79] Charges of impropriety apparently paled beside the admiration Shang Jinglan felt for Sima Xiangru's ability to rise above convention.

Nevertheless, the fact that Shang Jinglan calls Huang Yuanjie a Sima Xiangru (the poet) rather than a Zhuo Wenjun (his daring lover) reminds us of the limits within which she and women like her would have read *Parrot Island*. A gentry wife might admire or even mirror the fantasy of freedom that the courtesan seemed to embody, but she had to do so in a way that preserved a *liang* exterior for the world to see. Zhuo Wenjun, famous both for her sexual daring and for the song of sorrow she wrote after Sima Xiangru abandoned her, could serve as an emblem for Chen Yujiao's Xue Tao in *Parrot Island* (Yuan Zhen makes the comparison in Scene 17, and Xue Tao laughs at the scandalized response of her maid), but not for a gentry wife, however many the delightful stories in circulation about *liang* boys and girls hiding their love from their parents. Sima Xiangru was in any case the more *empowering* model—a poet with an oeuvre, not a woman abandoned, with a single poem to her name. Governing-class women were writing with increasing confidence in the early seventeenth century, and a Shang Jinglan would not agree with Yuxiao that writing made her a Zhuo Wenjun.

The late Ming fantasy of freedom affected all subject positions— or at any rate all the subjects with enough social power to act out aspects of the fantasy. Tang Xianzu situated it within the gentry household (although even he marries off his reincarnated heroine in a perfectly respectable fashion); Chen Yujiao created a carefully tailored version for his hero Wei Gao; the courtesan elite could embody apparent freedom from *shidafu* gender constraints (although in reality they

operated withi   poets
and playwrigh   d access to the surr

    Parrot Isla   ecord
show how rea   r and
status. Like C]   have
imagined read   se late
Ming freedom. ____   le and
status. But the record suggests that some of these women may have
experienced a more heady freedom than the fathers, brothers, and
sons who had to make a living from literacy: whereas Chen Yujiao
held his Xue Tao back, to keep her from destabilizing his world, Shang
Jinglan's Xue Tao and Sima Xiangru open a new world of teachers,
writers, and disciples.

5

Women in Feng Menglong's "Mountain Songs"

YASUSHI ŌKI

Mountain Songs (*Shan'ge*), a remarkable 10-*juan* collection of Suzhou folk songs compiled by the late Ming writer Feng Menglong
(1574–1646),[1] merits attention for both linguistic and literary reasons.
Although people in the Suzhou area had been singing folk songs
since antiquity, these songs—for example, the Wu songs of the Six
Dynasties period—had been transcribed in the literary language. In
sharp contrast to most verse in Chinese classical literature, however,
Feng used the contemporary local dialect of late Ming Suzhou to
write down the verses in *Mountain Songs*.[2] As he pointed out, the
rhymes of the words *sheng*, *sheng*, and *zheng* are incorrect in terms of
standard prosody; he defended his compilation on the grounds that
it was not necessary that these songs follow the rules as if they were
"imperial orders." Although Feng never explicitly stated that *Mountain Songs* marks the birth of a dialectical literature, in effect it is.

By using the local dialect, Feng could express what had previously never been expressed. Most of the songs deal with love, and
not a few could be considered lewd. The women who appear in
them, especially in the four-line songs about secret love in the first
four *juan*, are remarkably bold and active, traits not seen in other
works.[3]

The anthology contains nine *juan* of songs from Suzhou and a
tenth *juan* of songs from Tongcheng in Anhui province. The songs
from Suzhou in *juan* 1–9 are arranged first by length and then by

subject matter. *Juan* 1–4 present quatrains dealing with intimate feelings; *juan* 5 consists of quatrains on miscellaneous themes, *juan* 6 of quatrains about articles (*yongwu*), *juan* 7 of medium-length songs about intimate feelings, *juan* 8 of long songs about intimate feelings, and *juan* 9 of long songs on miscellaneous themes. The verses in the anthology have diverse origins. Most songs in *juan* 1–4 originated among the common people; those in the other *juan* are for the most part literati imitations.

(handwritten note in margin: How did he determine this?)

Songs of the Common People

I begin by introducing a few songs from *juan* 1–4, translated here in their entirety.

Midnight

If you call on me at midnight, don't knock at the
   back door.
Better to pluck a feather off a bird and make it
   call out
As if it had been caught by a weasel.
I will put on my single-layered skirt and go
   out to drive the weasel off.   (*juan* 1)

Here a girl who fears that her boyfriend's nocturnal visit will awaken her parents suggests how he can give her an excuse to meet him. The song expresses the girl's strong desire for a rendezvous, even though it entails deceiving her parents. Note that the singer (or editor) refrained from censuring what would normally be considered immoral.

Clever

Mother is clever, but her daughter is clever too.
Mother has strewn the floor with lime.
So I carry my boyfriend to the bed on my back.
We leave one person's footprints on the floor.   (*juan* 1)

Stratagem

My boyfriend came in a snowstorm.
Someone may find footprints on the ground.
I paid three copper coins for straw sandals and
   had him wear them front to back.
Now people will think he has left, not that he came in.
                                        (*juan* 1)

(handwritten note in margin: same image from the shijing)

Both verses portray a young woman concealing her boyfriend's visit as she boldly pursues her very human desires.

Gazing at the Stars

As soon as I opened the window and gazed at the
    stars in the sky,
My mother immediately said, "I suppose it's a man."
Even stomach worms could not sense such a thing
    so quickly.
That's what comes from mother's having experienced
    this too.   (*juan* 1)

Here the young girl, faced with her mother's discovery of her hidden love, realizes the reason for the mother's insight.

Another song describes a girl of startling independence.

Mother Hit Me

Although mother has hit and humiliated me,
I do not mind inviting my boyfriend every night.
If you and I can leave a legend of love like that
    of ancient lovers,
I would willingly be killed by my mother.   (*juan* 1)

Young girls prove very vigorous in another pair of songs.

Seduction

She dresses her hair until it shines like a lacquer bowl,
And in the presence of others seduces a man with
    her small feet.
Usually the man seduces the girl,
But recently in this new age girls are bold enough to
    entice a man.   (*juan* 2)

Seduction

Don't be timid when you seduce a man.
If we are caught, I will take the responsibility.
I will fall on my knees before the Judge and tell him
    the truth—
That it was I who seduced the man.   (*juan* 2)

In the first poem the young girl's active pursuit of love is tolerated as a new custom of contemporary society, and in the second the girl would risk punishment rather than give up her love affair. Feng finds her praiseworthy: "This girl has a chivalrous spirit."

Beginning Sexual Relations

When the wind begins to blow south by east, I
    feel lonely.
I cannot entice that pretty sixteen-year-old maiden —
Just as I cannot put my hand into boiling water.
Just as I cannot thread a needle.

Hearing that, the girl replies, "Don't worry.
You may entice me while I am young.
You can ladle the boiling water.
You can twist the loose thread and put it through."

                                                    (*juan* 2)

Such dialogues between two lovers are not uncommon in folk literature in China and elsewhere. The boy sees problems, the girl does not.

These examples of songs from the first two *juan* dealing with intimacy have in common not only bold women but a sympathy for these women's expression of desire. All these women are unmarried, and in a society such as traditional China where marriage arrangements rested with the parents and the matchmaker, these bold daughters were violating a major social principle.

Similar daring is evident in verses about married women.

Gazing

That young man is very bold.
Why do you gaze back at me after passing my gate?
My husband is not blind.
Why not come to the back gate if you wish to see me?

                                                    (*juan* 1)

Adultery was, of course, a serious violation of morality. Chinese families, concerned with the purity and verifiability of the paternal line, treasured female chastity. An adulteress would have suffered not only familial punishment but possibly that of the state as well. It would have been extremely dangerous for a family to tolerate such a woman in its ranks.[4]

Mountain Songs was, I suspect, the first work in the history of Chinese poetry to describe, without condemnation, women actively pursuing extramarital relations. How can we account for this unique treatment of women and their sexual desires? Part of the explanation lies in the origins of these songs.

In the preface to *Mountain Songs*, Feng Menglong says of these songs, "They are echoes of the people's feelings"; "they are the way farmers and village children air and express their feelings"; and "the only songs in fashion today are all accounts of immoral intimacy." As is evident from their content, the *Mountain Songs* derived from a rural rather than an urban milieu. What kinds of songs were sung in villages? *why ?*

First, villagers sang when working together. Lu Shiyi, a contemporary of Feng and a resident of nearby Suzhou, left a revealing description of peasants' planting songs.

> The songs sung at planting are extremely charming. The fields are numerous, the farmers gather together, their numbers are considerable, and their voices rough. If they are not chattering, then they tease one another. Even if you prohibit such goings-on, they cannot be stopped. But as soon as a song is begun, the crowd falls silent and sings in harmony as they get on with their work. They work together, and the work proceeds quickly, but the lewdness of their verses does particular damage to mores. (*Lu Futing xiansheng Sibian lu jiyao, juan* 10)

Lu may have appreciated the positive impact on productivity of these songs, but he still criticized them for their immorality. Lu is not calling for a return to the tastes and interests of peasants. Rather, in a context shaped by religion and folklore, the group singing of lewd songs by men and women performing agricultural work is an example of what James Frazer called "homeopathic magic." By singing of ties between human beings, these men and women were praying for a good harvest. These songs were sung not only during work but also during festivals at which song competitions provided young men and women a chance to find a spouse. This custom can still be observed among minority peoples in southeast China. A particularly famous example is the climbing festival of the Miao in Guizhou province.

> The Climbing Festival is one of the fixed events in the calendar of minority peoples in Guizhou. Virtually all the peoples there have annual activities related to mountain climbing. *The Schedule of Annual Events of Minority Peoples of Guizhou* records more than a hundred mountain-climbing festivals. . . . The biggest such festivals . . . attract more than 30,000 participants.
>
> Also, the "Bull Horn Festival" is held every year at Wangfeng xiang in Leishan county. . . . Stretching over three consecutive days, it peaks on the second day. During the festival people gather, the

He is making a connection here between Rural people and minority people —

sounds of their music reach to the heavens, and there is no end to
their raucous calling out and searching for one another. All sorts of
songs are sung—flying songs, love songs, and mountain songs. The
young seek out their mate through love songs, the middle-aged
show their strength in the horse races, and the elderly delight in the
beauty and intelligence of their young offspring.[5]

The site of these festivals is often a small hill or a nearby mountain.
The most basic meaning of the generic term *mountain song* may lie
precisely in the types of song sung during such festivals. Many extant sources from the Lower Yangtze area mention festivals that
combine singing and dancing.[6] In songs from contemporary festivals
in Guizhou, we find examples of women expressing feelings of love
with the same frankness encountered in Feng's *Mountain Songs*. For
centuries, village songs have contained wishes for a good harvest.
They also often have a bawdy side, with women presented as exceptionally forward and active. This tradition lies behind the inclusion
of so many songs with these themes in *Mountain Songs*.

Not all the songs in Feng's anthology, however, originated in
village festivals. Many refer to life in the city of Suzhou, Feng's
birthplace, which by the seventeenth century was the commercial
center of south China and one of China's largest cities.

Imitation

The girls next door and across the street are all carrying
    on with men.
I too am influenced by them.
I have seen how fine the peach blossoms are.
If one washes in an indigo pond, one's whole body will
    be blue. How will one get it clean again?   (*juan* 1)

The burgeoning textile industry of late Ming Suzhou gave rise to
many dyehouses and pools full of indigo dye. It also offered employment to peasants anxious to leave their villages. In Shengze, a
famous textile center and market town near Suzhou, these workers
held a large mountain-song festival. "On the night of the last day of
the Lantern Festival, about ten thousand clothworkers, male and female alike, assemble at East Temple, West Temple, and Sheng-ming
Bridge in order to compete with one another till dawn in the singing
of mountain songs."[7] Although rural in origin, mountain songs began to express urban themes and to describe urban situations. They
also began to include city girls. Feng Menglong had ample opportu-

nity to hear and collect such songs. The development of this literary genre is an overlooked feature of the complex process of urbanization in the Lower Yangtze region during the late Ming.

Literati Participation

What was Feng Menglong's motive for compiling 380 songs to form *Mountain Songs*? This act was not only unprecedented but would not be repeated until the twentieth century. The Wanli era (1573–1620) stands out in the history of Chinese literature in many ways. Such masterpieces of popular fiction as *Romance of the Three Kingdoms, Water Margin, Journey to the West,* and *Jin Ping Mei* were completed and published during this period. In drama, there was a revival of the Yuan dynasty *Record of the Western Chamber,* as well as the creation of Tang Xianzu's remarkable *Peony Pavilion.* In poetry, Yuan Hongdao's (1568–1610) Gong'an school decried the imitation of archaic styles. In philosophy, intellectual circles were shaken by the iconoclasm of Li Zhi (1527–1602). Feng's *Mountain Songs,* with their daring freshness and realism, were not an isolated phenomenon.

Feng's preface explains his view that songs and poetry developed from both the rustic airs (*feng*) and the elegant poems (*ya*) in the *Book of Odes* (*Shijing*). The rustic airs, Feng argued, are the ancestors of the mountain songs, whereas the elegant poems became *The Songs of the South* (*Chuci*), Tang poetry, and the recent verse of poetry circles. In closing, Feng made the following assessment.

> Even though the present is a time of decline and the classical-style poetry and prose [*shiwen*] written today are shams, there are no sham mountain songs. Because mountain songs do not vie for fame with the classical-style poetry and prose of today, they pay no heed to falsity. Since they pay no heed to falsity, it is appropriate that they survive through my book. Now, if we find that the former [the falsity of contemporary classical-style writings] resembles what is related in the ancient chronicles [*taishi*] and that the latter [mountain songs] is what remains among the people in recent times, this insight will merely provide a focus for discussion of current affairs. But if by means of the true feelings of men and women we produce the medicines to counteract the school of names [*mingjiao*, i.e., Confucianism], the accomplishments [of this book] will equal those of the *Guazhier* [another collection of popular songs]. Therefore after recording the *Guazhier*, I have moved onto the mountain songs.

Feng's aim was clearly to inject new life into the artificial world of late Ming poetry. The authenticity of the mountain songs would, he hoped, help revive a literary form in decline. This view had already received eloquent expression in Yuan Hongdao's preface to his brother Yuan Zhongdao's (1570–1624) poetry collection.

> If there is just one copy of something in the world, it is not invariably the case that it will disappear. Thus, even if I want it to disappear, there is nothing I can do. If, however, it is indiscriminately like everything else in the world, then it is possible it will disappear. Thus, even if I want it not to disappear, there is nothing I can do. Therefore, I say that recent poetry and prose written in the classical style will not be handed down to posterity. If by chance something is handed down, it will probably be the likes of [popular songs such as] "Pipoyu" and "Dacaogan," which are sung by women and children in villages. These songs come from authentic persons [zhenren], without learning, and hence they have many true sounds. They do not knit their brows learning from the Han and Wei, and they have not learned how to walk from the High Tang. They emerge, relying on their own nature. They are still capable of penetrating to the joys and sorrows of men, their likes and feelings. This is something to give one pleasure. . . . In general, emotionally powerful words can of their own accord move people. They are what I call "true poetry," and they should be handed down.

The two songs mentioned here, though not mountain songs, were folk songs, and hence for Yuan were authentic and valuable. We can assume that Feng was influenced by Yuan. The Gong'an school had criticized the Ancient Writing school's view that the best way for contemporary writers to produce great literature was to imitate the prose of the Qin and the Han and the poetry of the High Tang. The Gong'an school opposed imitation as not expressing true feelings, a matter of great importance for the Gong'an school. But even Li Mengyang (1473–1529), an adherent of the Ancient Writing school, made a similar judgment: "Poems [shi] are the sounds of the universe and of nature. Those sung in the streets, during work or rest, or in harmonious chorus are true. They are the 'airs' [feng] in the Book of Odes. Confucius said, 'If rites are lost, search for them in the fields.' Although the true poems are now among the people, the literati often make rhymed verses and call them poems." Li also asserted that true poetry remains alive among the common people, and he was said to value a popular love songs known as "Suonanzhi."

Although Li and Yuan differed about writing methods, they

agreed that true poetry survived among the common people and that popular love poetry should be appreciated. Like many other late Ming intellectuals, they felt an antipathy toward the restrictions of Confucianism and were interested in and sympathetic toward the apparent openness and freedom of the common people. This sympathy lies behind the warm reception of such popular genres as drama, fiction, and song in the late Ming. Feng's appreciation for bold women would be unthinkable outside the world of late Ming intellectuals. His statement that "by means of the true feelings of men and women we produce the medicines to counteract the school of names" reveals the feelings of these intellectuals. Feng's willingness to give literary form to these feelings in *Mountain Songs* derives to some extent from this awareness within late Ming literati circles.

By the late Ming, intellectuals who had once despised popular literature began to be interested in folk songs.[8] Mountain songs began to be sung at literati banquets. In a comment on the song "Du" in *juan* 7 of *Mountain Songs*, Feng observed: "I learned of this song from Fu Si of Songjiang. Fu was a famous courtesan." Feng inserted such songs as well into his anthology.[9] Most songs sung in the entertainment quarters were popular songs such as "Guazhier," which Feng used as the title for an earlier anthology. The following example is from *juan* 6 of that collection.

Curse

I have been patient and have had a hard time because
    of you.
But now I have gotten angry.
I have been thinking of my past and future.
When will you give me a good answer?
Following you, I never listened to other people's
    criticism.
I am always currying favor with you, but you hate me.
I am always worrying about you, but you never take
    note of me.
If you are so unfaithful to me,
I will put a curse on you and kill you.

Although the language seems strong, such songs of bitter longing are not uncommon in traditional Chinese poetry. In contrast to the verses in *Mountain Songs*, those in *Guazhier*, which also deal with love, were produced in an urban milieu and reflect the influence of earlier written poetry and lyrics.

In the entertainment quarters, mountain songs were sung alongside urban popular songs such as "Guazhier." *Hundred Beauties*, a
ranking of courtesans in Nanjing, mentions both types of verse. Some
themes in *juan* 6 of *Mountain Songs* are similar to those in *Guazhier*. I
think the literati may have vied with each other to produce imitations of popular songs. For example:

An Inking Line

A girl is just like an inking line.
A man held her down and seized her.
She said to him, "I go and come back on a straight line.
That I have never gone awry angered you."

Mountain Song, juan 6

An Inking Line

He is an able man, like an inking line.
He can stretch out and lie down, long or short, as he
    likes.
He comes straight and goes straight, not awry.
He is an honest man.
Don't think that he has a blackness in his heart.
Even if he had a blackness in his heart, he could not
    conceal it.   *Guazhier, juan* 8

Mountain songs changed from village songs to urban songs to
songs of the entertainment quarters and finally to literati songs. Beginning with *juan* 6, most of the verses in *Mountain Songs* are imitations by literati.[10] The following example shows how the character of
the songs changed.

The Gate God

Philandering is just like dealing with the gate god.
It's going after the new and discarding the old —
    how heartless!
(speech)
"I have not forgotten that last year on New Year's eve, he
    printed me, he printed me, he printed me thousands
    of times.
Pleased to the full by his printing,
Thousands of requests, tens of thousands of requests
    came in,
And I did my best for you.
I helped you make a living,
And you respected me like a god.

I hoped for nothing more than to set up a real home
   and to live with you day and night in the same house.
Whenever a rash young man stroked my hand and foot,
I did not change my countenance.
I did not allow spirits and ghosts into the big gate
   of your house.
I suffered the wind and the dew for you, being out
   under the moon and stars.
How many times did I see through the malice of burglars
   trying to sneak into the house,
And how many times did I pick up gossip through the
   cracks in the wall?
At first you saw my bright colors and cheered me on.
Seeing my pretty clothes, you treated me as important.
But once pasted on the gate, my skin and muscles
   grew flabby.
Being rubbed, my hair became dried up and dusty.
A year had not yet passed,
And you could only think fondly of the new one.
You do not consider me a lady.
I knew you were not a good man, and you were trying
   to drive me away.
However, you had a bit of poison in your heart.
When December came,
You gave me not a moment of your time.
Sprinkling cold water on my body,
First I thought, it is only a joke.
You brought a broom and picked at me.
But I did not raise my voice.
You tore at my clothes, and I put up with it.
It was only when you ripped up my face that I first
   understood what you were about.
I was gouged at, I was gouged at to your liking.
No! That charge is false.
I ended up being completely scraped away by you.
Heartless, that is what you are.
I have made these lyrics, so listen to me!"

(Song of Yupaodu)
Your heart is really cruel,
Forgetting how you go after the new girl and discard
   the old.
Even so, just think about it—The old one was once the
   new girl,
And the new girl will not always be the new girl.
The day will come when your feeling will change,

Table 5.1
Feng Menglong's Rankings of the Verses in *Mountain Songs*

| | Number of songs ranked | | | | | |
Juan	Excellent	Great	Good	Fair	Average	Poor
1	6	8	32	9	3	1
2	4	6	25	9	13	1
3	2	6	13	3	5	1
4	6	2	20	2	1	0
5	2	8	14	5	4	0
6	1	10	30	17	8	1
7	1	1	10	7	2	0
8	0	2	5	5	0	1
9	0	3	4	0	0	1
10	1	5	9	6	2	1

And you will regret having discarded the old one.

(Song)
She told the man, "I say to you and the new one on
    the front of the big gate:
'The ship up front is a mirror for the ship
    that follows.
Let me calculate: You will be new for at most a year.'"

This is, of course, much more than a poem about an object. The gate god, considered a talisman against evil, is a metaphor for a woman, but a woman who is a far cry from those found in popular songs. A picture of the gate god is pasted up anew each New Year's Day. Gradually over the course of the year, it becomes tattered and dirty until it is ripped off and a new one affixed. The woman is figured similarly. From *juan* 6 on, many such pieces can be found in *Mountain Songs*, and their character is quite different from those songs rooted in village mountain songs.

In collecting such songs and in presenting an image of women as sexually adventurous, late Ming literati gave evidence of their openness. But in songs written in imitation of mountain songs, they tended to depict abused and tormented women who acted much more passively. This contrast allows us to discern a split in late Ming literati's perception of women.

In editing this anthology, did Feng attach more importance to the songs of the common people or to those of the literati? Despite Feng's claims in his preface, the issue is not easy to judge because he presented both types and ultimately each of his selections reflects a man's view of women. His taste is visible, however, in his comments and in a ranking system he devised. Feng ranked each song into one of six categories (see Table 5.1). Most of those with the highest ranking fall in *juan* 1–4.

Part II

Norms and Selves

6

Ming and Qing Anthologies
of Women's Poetry and
Their Selection Strategies

KANG-I SUN CHANG

No nation has produced more anthologies or collections of women's poetry than late imperial China. Especially from the seventeenth century on (that is, during the late Ming and early Qing dynasties), there was a sudden increase of such publications, partly attributable to a dramatic rise of women's literacy and the widespread development of printing. The proliferation of women's anthologies and collections during the Ming and Qing eras, altogether more than 3,000 titles, is simply stunning.[1] This is especially impressive, if compared to the situation before the late Ming: few collections of pre-Ming poetry by women have survived.

Why this sudden increase? First, it was not until the late Ming that scholar-poets, male and female alike, began to notice that writings by women, whatever their quality, were simply not being preserved. Many of these scholars and poets therefore assumed the role of editors and anthologists, comparing their efforts in collecting women's works to Confucius' compilation of the *Shijing* (Canon of poetry), a collection that, as the new anthologists were quick to remind their public, many scholars thought contained a large percentage of songs written by women. Tian Yiheng, editor of the anthology *Shi nüshi* (published sometime during the Jiajing reign, 1522–66), was perhaps the first male scholar in the Ming to dwell so much on the importance of transmitting women's works.[2] He observed that the literary achievements of numerous women poets from ancient times were equal to men's. But, as he explained in his preface, it was the lack of "collecting or anthologizing" (*caiguan*) that had kept women's names so obscure in literary history (Hu Wenkai, 876). In a similar way, the woman poet Shen Yixiu (1590–1635), mother of the legendary female genius Ye Xiaoluan (1616–32), stepped into the gap and assumed responsibility for the transmission of women's poems and their poetic reputation. She stressed the importance of collecting *contemporary* works, claiming that her anthology *Yiren si* (published posthumously in 1636) departed from the conventional way of "following the old" (*yangu*).[3] Whatever their approaches, it is obvious that all these scholars and poets were inspired by the curatorial function of anthology making.

Unfortunately, until recently, scholars of Chinese literature (men and women alike) have failed to consider the numerous anthologies and collections of women's poetry produced in the Ming and Qing, and hence many valuable texts have been lost. As a result, histories of Chinese literature have consistently provided a misleading picture of women's literary position in this period. As was noted by Maureen Robertson, "In the 1,355 page edition of his history of premodern Chinese literature, a history that spans over 2,500 years, Liu Dajie mentions only five women who produced literary texts, none of them from periods later than the Song Dynasty."[4]

This brings us to an interesting question: Why have modern scholars failed to take note of the existing anthologies and collections of female poetry, which would have revised our general perceptions of women's literature, or for that matter Chinese literature? My own study of Ming and Qing women poets has inspired me to contemplate the many implications of this broad question, leading me to seek further information in a host of available anthologies and collections; this search has gradually shaped the framework of my research. In this paper, I would like to share my own thoughts and experience concerning the use of some of these sources for Ming and Qing women poets, which I believe are extremely relevant to our study of Chinese literature in general.

First, my past failures in locating the right poems and other source materials have more to do with a blind spot in my general conception and methodology than with the availability of texts. For a long time, I had primarily been using anthologies such as Zhu Yizun's *Mingshi zong* (1701), Shen Deqian's *Mingshi biecai ji* (1739) and *Qingshi biecai ji* (1760), Zhang Yingchang's *Qingshiduo* (1869), Ding Shaoyi's *Qingci zong bu* (1894), and Xu Shichang's *Qing shi hui* (1929) — texts available in convenient modern reprints. These are indeed important sources, for all of them are first-rate anthologies that aim at preserving what the anthologists deem to be the "best works" in the designated periods. But the problem with these "standard" anthologies is that although they generally include an impressive number of women poets, the selections from each poet number only two or three poems each. Moreover, these anthologies have explicitly assigned a marginal position to women by putting their works at the end, alongside those by monks — a procedure of selection first adopted by the Five Dynasties poet Wei Zhuang (836–910) in his *Youxuan ji*.[5] Such a policy of selection — reflecting what the modern scholar Shi Zhicun calls "a regressive view of literature"[6] — makes for a misleading profile of women's place in Ming and Qing literature. In fact, not only was the number of women poets recorded in late imperial China unprecedented, but many learned women during the period shared a world with men. They acted not as auxiliary attachments to a male sphere or as denizens of a parallel female world, but often as full-fledged participants in the poetic traditions and expressions that defined the larger cultural and social context.

It took me quite some time to realize that the best available source materials on Ming and Qing female poetry are those anthologies that record women's works exclusively. Ironically, it is through reading and using these *separate* — that is, separate from male authors — anthologies that we can view the "total history" and fully appreciate the close relations and interdependence between male and female literary activities. This is because the published products of Ming and Qing women poets were simply too numerous for the traditional form of anthology, recording male and female poets, to do them justice. (For example, the publisher who printed Lu Chang's highly acclaimed *Collected Poems and Song Lyrics of Famous Women of Past Ages* [*Lichao mingyuan shi ci*] in 1773 explained that Lu Chang's anthology had to omit works of Ming and Qing women altogether simply because "there were too many of them.")[7] But given the existing underrepresentation of female poets in conventional anthologies and the severe lack of preservation mechanisms for women's works, it is not surprising that forward-looking Ming and Qing women and their male friends and patrons pursued new and different selection strategies for their anthologies. There is enough pluralism in the arenas of women's writings during the Ming and Qing — similar to the diversity of male literary works — to necessitate the creation of separate anthologies. I

am not, however, denying the existence of a male-dominated principle in the conventional anthologies such as those by Shen Deqian. My
purpose is simply to call attention to the importance of a new "female" approach in anthology making in this period—an approach
that provided the right kind of preservation mechanism necessary for
women poets to thrive. In other words, what we need is a "bifocal
view" of Ming and Qing scholarship, one that takes into account both
male- and female-oriented source materials.[8]

Indeed, when I started to explore the many women's anthologies
and collections of poetry, I found the experience immensely gratify-
ing. Overwhelmed by the number of texts and amount of information
available to me, I began to wonder why I had once complained about
the lack of source materials on women poets. Indeed, as Dorothy Ko
says, "The source materials do exist, if we look for them in the right
places."[9]

What these sources "in the right places" told me is a story about
Ming and Qing men and women working *together* to revalue and
promote women's writings. Indeed, male scholars, rather than female
writers themselves, served as the major editorial brain behind most of
the earlier women's anthologies. These editors and compilers tried to
"canonize" women's writings by repeatedly associating their anthologies with the classical canon, the *Shijing*, or with the other classical
source of poetry, the *Li sao*. An example of the latter is the *Female Sao*
(*Nüsao*) published in 1618, obviously named after the *Li sao*. In his
foreword, Zhao Shiyong wrote that the purpose of the anthology was
to ensure that poems by women "be remembered forever by posterity," just like "classics and edicts" (Hu Wenkai, 885). Also of great interest is the growing tendency of Ming and Qing scholars to give their
anthologies titles that reveal their respect for women—titles that include words like "female talents" (*nüzhong caizi*), "gentry women poets" (*shiyuan*), "female scribes" (*nüshi*), "famous masters" (*mingjia*),
and the like.

It is not surprising that, encouraged by these liberal-minded male
literati, many Ming and Qing women began to compile poetry anthologies in which they confidently stated their principles of inclusion
and exclusion. Indeed, there finally emerged a kind of "contextual poetics"[10] for women's poetry whereby anthologies became a crucial
means of literary promotion and critical evaluation. Most important,
various sources have proved that, as Ellen Widmer says, "contemporary women writers strove to be included in women's poetical an-

thologies."[11] Apparently for them, anthologies were selective canons that provided "models, ideals, and inspiration."[12] And through the anthologies and private collections, these women wished to become known to future generations.[13]

A Basic List of Anthologies

The following is a preliminary attempt to provide a basic, or minimum, list of women's anthologies produced in late imperial China; I hope this endeavor will illustrate particular acts of selection by anthologists, male or female. In selecting this short list, I had to rely on my own experience and judgment in deciding what is central and what secondary. I make no claim of definitiveness, but I believe the list will provide a standard of "cultural literacy" in researching Ming and Qing women's poetry and its literary status.

Mingyuan shigui (ca. after 1626), 36 *juan*, comp. attributed to Zhong Xing

The *Mingyuan shigui* is an essential item for studying women's *shi* poetry from ancient times to the late Ming. It contains useful biographical notes and short commentaries on individual poems and covers works by all kinds of women — gentry women, courtesans, Daoist nuns, painters, women officials, Korean ladies who wrote in Chinese. The selection of Ming writers is extremely extensive (*juan* 25–*juan* 36). The anthology has been dated loosely from 1573 to 1620 (the Wanli reign), simply because the man traditionally considered the editor, Zhong Xing (1574–1624), lived during that period. But the fact that *juan* 34 of the anthology contains 81 poems by Bo Shaojun (?-1625) that were not written and published until 1625 and 1626, respectively, makes me inclined to date the anthology to some time after 1626. In fact, we do not know exactly when the anthology was compiled and published.[14]

Some Qing scholars, chief among them Wang Shizhen (1634–1711), seriously doubted that Zhong Xing was the editor,[15] but for the wrong reason — that the anthology contains works whose authorship is in question. Interestingly, the Qing scholar Ji Yun (1724–1805) used precisely such arguments to raise doubts about Tian Yiheng's editorship of *Shi nüshi*, an anthology printed almost a century before *Mingyuan shigui*. It is indeed true that, as Ji Yun pointed out, Ming anthologists often seem to be rather lax in their selection policies, as compared to those of the Qing.[16] But at a time when the tradition of women's anthologies was in its infancy, editorial inexactitude is understandable. It is possible that Zhong Xing did edit *Mingyuan shigui* but bookdealers later added more material to it before publishing it. Or the collection may have been put together by bookdealers who did not understand much about scholarship. For our purpose, however, it is enough to remember that *Mingyuan shigui*, whether edited by Zhong Xing himself or not, is an ambitious and important Ming anthology that offers more primary source materials than do other similar poetry collections published at the time.

Most important, Zhong Xing's preface to *Mingyuan shigui* is an excellent example of the way late Ming male scholars assigned value to women's writings. Zhong Xing relied on an alleged female "purity" (*qing*) to make his argument—claiming that ideal poetry must come from this quality of *qing* with which women are innately endowed. Since poetic "purity" is a "female" attribute, he further suggested, women's poetry was an ideal remedy for the problem of artificiality (*qiao*) in contemporary male poetry. This faith in the corrective function of women's poetry no doubt encouraged more women to take on poetry writing as their vocation.

> *Gujin nüshi* (1628), comp. Zhao Shijie. Modern reprint in
> two volumes: *Lidai nüzi shiji*, 8 *juan*; and *Lidai nüzi wenji*,
> 12 *juan* (Shanghai: Saoye sanfang, 1928).

Unlike Zhong Xing's anthology, in which Ming works figure most prominently, *Gujin nüshi* devotes most of its space to women's poetry before the Ming. (Its small selection of Ming works focuses merely on major poets such as Lu Qingzi, Xu Yuan, and Duan Shuqing.) In his preface Zhao Shijie dwelled at length on the curatorial function of anthologies, for he obviously recognized the ultimately tenuous nature of the transmission process:

> In the days of the Seven Warring States (475 B.C.–221 A.D.), with battles going on day and night, no time was left for literary composition, but Lady Fan and Zheng Xiu must not have lacked wit and conversational skill. Han E sang but once, yet her sorrows clung to the beams of the inn. Nonetheless, these women's compositions have all vanished without a trace—and not only on account of wars or as a result of the fires in the palace of Qin, but also because bamboo codices and lacquered books, while hard to make, were not easy to keep. (Hu Wenkai, 888)[17]

Thus in his role as preserver and editor of women's poetry, Zhao Shijie found a precedent in the example of the editor-sage Confucius.

> Confucius surveyed the *Airs of the States* and said: "Poetry can stimulate; it teaches observation, sociability, and the expression of grievances." In collecting those rhymed sayings, he did not reject the songs of the "wandering girls" of the Han and Yangtze rivers. Who will say that the Three Hundred Odes [of the *Shijing*], the *Elegantiae* and the rest, can only have been composed by upright scholars and sages. (Hu Wenkai, 888)[18]

This preface proves that Yuan Mei (1716–97) was not the first, as is often assumed, to point out that the speakers in many of the poems in the *Shijing* were women. And Zhao Shijie was only one of the many late Ming literati who used this argument in the attempt to place women's poetic works in the literary "canon." Such a claim may sound problematic to modern scholars, for it seems dependent on a conflation of two separable notions, that of the "author" and that of the "persona." But the stratagem not only was convincing to contemporary editors and readers alike but also remained compelling for subsequent collectors of female poetry.

Juan 4 of "Runji," ed. Liu Shi and Qian Qianyi. In *Liechao shiji*, ed. Qian Qianyi, completed 1649; printed 1652?

It is common knowledge that the compiler and editor of *Liechao shiji*, an extensive anthology of Ming poetry with about 2,000 biographies appended to it, was the poet and bibliophile Qian Qianyi (1582–1664). But few knew, until very recently, that its section on women poets (*juan* 4 of "Runji") was mainly edited by the famous courtesan-poet Liu Shi (also known as Liu Rushi, 1618?–64). According to Hu Wenkai (who based his research partly on the *Gonggui shiji yiwen kaolüe*), Liu Shi not only edited the poems but also was responsible for the extensive annotations on women poets in this section (Hu Wenkai, 433). I have been unable to verify Hu Wenkai's theory, but find his views extremely plausible on the basis of what I know of Liu Shi's particular preferences in poetry — although I believe that the annotations on the poets were done jointly by Liu and Qian.[19] In this paper, I shall simply assume that Liu Shi was the main editor of this section.

The story goes that in winter 1640 Liu Shi went to visit Qian, then almost sixty years old, at his private residence, which was called Banye tang. By then, Liu Shi was already a recognized author, having published her two collections of poems, the *Wuyin cao* (1638) and *Hushang cao* (1639).[20] Qian and Liu exchanged many poems (later to be collected in *Dongshan chouhe ji*), and Qian was immensely struck by Liu's talent and beauty. The couple married the following year, and in 1643 Qian built for Liu a studio, the famous Jiangyun lou, where they together compiled the *Liechao shiji*[21] and where their great collection of rare books was housed. (Unfortunately in 1650 a fire destroyed the studio and most of their collections.)

In her role as literary editor, Liu Shi distinguished herself as one who understood the power of editorial selection in an anthology. A courtesan-poet who had struggled to establish a literary position, Liu Shi seemed to be concerned primarily with elevating the status of courtesan poetry. As I have shown elsewhere, courtesans played a crucial place in the development of early seventeenth-century literature and arts.[22] In particular, the famous anthologist Zhou Zhibiao listed the courtesan Wang Wei as one of the Seven Female Talents in his collection *Nüzhong qi caizi lanke ji*, and devoted two *juan* to her (Hu Wenkai, 844). Other major anthologies and studies such as Zhong Xing's *Mingyuan shigui* and Chen Weisong's *Furen ji* gave a prominent place to contemporary courtesan-poets — not to mention the numerous anthologies exclusively devoted to courtesan poetry, such as the famous *Qinhuai siji shi* celebrating the literary status of four famous courtesans of the Qinhuai quarters of Nanjing (Hu Wenkai, 844). It should also be mentioned that in his *Gujin nüshi* Zhao Shijie emphasized the distinction of the Tang courtesan-poets Xue Tao (ca. 768–ca. 831) and Yu Xuanji (845–68) by including an unusually large selection of their works. Most important, in all these collections courtesans and gentry women poets are treated as equals and placed in the same category.

In her section on women poets in the *Liechao shiji*, Liu Shi not only put courtesans in the same category as gentry women poets, she predominantly selected poems by major courtesans. For example, she includes 61 poems from Wang Wei (ca. 1600–ca. 1647), 52 poems from Jing Pianpian (fl. late 16th c.), and 19 poems from Yang Wan (fl. early 17th c.). Such generous and representative selections from courtesan-poets was unprecedented. Although the anthology also includes works of many gentry women poets of the Ming, the selections from such major poets as Xu Yuan (fl. 1596) are surprisingly few, in Xu's case only two poems. Generally, among gentry women poets, Liu seemed to favor those who dwelled on images of romantic love in their poetry — a style resembling that of courtesan poetry, where personal meaning seems to be determined by the male-female relationship. In any case, Liu's generous selections from such "romantic" gentry poets as Zhang Hongqiao (fl. 14th c.; 12 poems), Ye Xiaoluan (14 poems), and Dong Shaoyu (fl. 1544; 17 poems) seems to confirm my speculation.

As a commentator, Liu Shi was forthright in her criticism (and her praise) of individual poets. A case in point is her comment on the Korean poet Xu Jingfan (Ho Nansorhon), whom she accuses of plagiarism (Hu Wenkai, 433).[23] In passing judgment on Xu Yuan and Lu Qingzi, the "two great poets of Wumen [Suzhou],"[24] Liu adopts the traditional male critical method of *pin*, a procedure of ranking first made popular by the Six Dynasties critic Zhong Rong (459–518). Liu ranked Lu Qingzi above Xu Yuan—adding that in her view, Lu Qingzi was even superior to most literati men.[25] As for Xu Yuan, Liu could not agree with the extreme views of Lady Fang of Tongcheng, who accused Xu Yuan of "fishing for fame and lacking in learning" (*haoming er wuxue*), but she nonetheless thought that there might be some justification for such severe criticism.[26] This might be why Liu's anthology includes only two poems by Xu Yuan.

Liu Shi's Ming loyalist concerns are revealed in her comments on the courtesan Wang Wei, the poet with the most poems (66) in Liu's anthology. Unlike Zhong Xing, who wrote a brief biographical note on Wang Wei in his *Mingyuan shigui* (naturally enough, given that Wang Wei was still quite young then), Liu Shi provided detailed notes on Wang Wei's life—especially on her role as a Ming loyalist participating in various resistance activities against the Manchu invaders. So far as I know, Liu Shi was the first person to report that Wang Wei died "three years" after the "political crisis" (*luan*), which I take to mean the Ming-Qing transition.[27] It is because of Liu Shi's research that I feel confident in assigning the approximate dates 1600–1647 for Wang Wei.

Liu's loyalist approach was in keeping with Qian Qianyi's general method of commentary in the *Liechao shiji*, which was the main reason the anthology was banned by the Qing government during the Qianlong emperor's reign (1736–95). Although Qian Qianyi had submitted to the Manchus in 1645, it was felt that his true loyalty was still to the Ming; his commentary seems to confirm this suspicion. (I accept the view of the modern scholar Chen Yinke who claimed that it was Liu Shi who turned Qian into a true Ming loyalist, albeit one involved only in underground resistance activities.)[28] In any case, Qian's *Liechao shiji* was harshly criticized by the Qing scholar-official and apologist Ji

Yun, who accused Qian of "twisting the facts and confusing right and wrong."[29] According to Ji Yun, Zhu Yizun's (1629–1709) anthology of Ming poetry, *Ming shi zong* (1705), had been compiled to correct the "factual errors" found in Qian Qianyi's *Liechao shiji*.[30] Whether Ji's theory is right or wrong, it is true that in his anthology, Zhu Yizun took a different tack from Qian Qianyi (and Liu Shi). With regard to women poets, for instance, Zhu clearly distinguished gentry women poets from courtesan-poets, putting the former under the category of "guimen" (*juan* 86) and assigning the latter the unflattering classification of "jinü," literally "prostitutes" (*juan* 98). In his biographical notes on the courtesan Wang Wei, his description is again different from the one given by Liu Shi. In particular, Wang Wei's loyalist activities are left unmentioned in Zhu's anthology.[31]

From the perspective of Ming studies, it is indeed regrettable that Qian's *Liechao shiji* and Liu's section on women in the "Runji" were banned in the eighteenth century. This no doubt led to the Qing scholars' "misreading" of many Ming poets, including major women poets such as Wang Wei.

> *Shiyuan ba mingjia ji* (preface dated 1655), comp. Zou
> Siyi. Original in the Chinese Academy of Sciences
> Library, Beijing.

The *Shiyuan ba mingjia ji* , whose title literally means "Collected works of eight famous women poets," is a rare item. The anthology includes works by the following poets, arranged in this order:

1. Wang Duanshu
2. Wu Qi (poet-painter)
3. Wu Xiao (poet-painter and sister of Wu Qi)
4. Liu Shi
5. Huang Yuanjie (poet-painter)
6. Ji Xian
7. Wu Shan (poet-painter)
8. Bian Mengjue (daughter of Wu Shan)

Like Wang Shilu (elder brother of the famous poet Wang Shizhen), Zou Siyi was one of those "male-feminists" of the mid-seventeenth century who seemed to devote their life to the promotion of contemporary women's writings. But unlike Wang's anthology, *Ranzhi ji* (preface dated 1658), which appears all-inclusive in its approach,[32] Zou's is selective and dwells on the evaluation of a few female talents. Zou's detailed comments on the eight poets' lives and works are meant to provide a frame of reference and explanatory basis for assigning value. For example, his preface to the section on Liu Shi begins with this statement based on the principle of *pin*: "After evaluating works of the many contemporary famous women poets, I will have to say that Hedong [Liu Shi] ranks first." Then he continues by citing examples to show Liu Shi's poetry is more gentle and more beautiful than the works of Bo Juyi (772–846) and many other male poets of ancient times.

Zou's anthology of eight famous women poets was later expanded to an anthology of ten poets in his *Shiyuan shi mingjia ji*, which supposedly includes works by two other poets, Gu Wenwan and Pu Yinglu (Hu Wenkai, 849). The Beijing Library has an incomplete copy of the *Shiyuan shi mingjia ji*; the parts on Qu Wenwan and Pu Yinglu are unfortunately missing.

> *Mingyuan shiwei* (completed 1664; printed 1667),
> comp. Wang Duanshu. Originals in the Beijing
> Library and the Central Library of Taibei.

Like Liu Shi, Wang Duanshu (1621–ca. 1706) was one of the most prominent women poets and scholars of the seventeenth century. But whereas Liu Shi's origins were obscure, Wang was born and raised in a respectable gentry family. Daughter of the famous scholar Wang Siren (1575–1646), Wang Duanshu was taught to read the classics from an early age. She was one of those literate women who enjoyed the respect and friendship of contemporary male scholars.[33] The number of male friends who called themselves "sworn brothers" (*mengdi*) and signed their names as sponsors of Wang's own collected works, *Yinhong ji*, is astonishing.[34] And most important, Qian Qianyi was among those who wrote prefaces to Wang's anthology of women's poetry, the *Mingyuan shiwei*.[35] Wang Duanshu also compiled a comparable anthology of prose works by women (*Mingyuan wenwei*) and was the author of a collection of biographies of imperial princes and consorts, entitled *Lidai diwang houfei kao* (Hu Wenkai, 248).

Compared to Liu Shi's anthology in the "Runji" of *Liechao shiji*, Wang Duanshu's *Mingyuan shiwei* is more ambitious in scope. It contains 42 *juan*, covering works of about 1,000 women poets. Almost all these are Ming and Qing poets, although the anthology also includes some newly found poems by earlier authors. The project took Wang 25 years to complete, from 1639 to 1664. Liu's anthology is selective in nature; Wang's comprehensive. Wang even urged contemporary poets and readers to send her more selections they might have (see "Fanli," 3a). Indeed, in Wang Duanshu, we see for the first time a female editor working conscientiously to perform her proper curatorial duties in passing along a great volume of poetic works to contemporary and future readers. Wang believed that the problem of transmitting women's works resulted chiefly from their conservative notion that "words are not to pass from the women's quarters to the outside world" (neiyan buchu).[36] Thus, it was up to her (Wang Duanshu) to preserve women's works for later generations and to make sure that she herself was not guilty of failing to rescue poems from obscurity (3a–3b). Her husband, Ding Shengzhao, explained this idea most clearly in his foreword to the anthology: "Why did my wife Yuying [Duanshu] compile this Mingyuan shiwei? It is because she cannot bear to see the excellent poems of women of our times vanishing like mist and grass" (1a).

Wang Duanshu attempted to give her anthology of women poets canonical status by naming it Classic Poetry by Famous Women (Mingyuan shiwei), a direct reference, or challenge, to the arch-canonical text of the Shijing. The key word for "classics" is wei (parallel to jing in the Shijing), which literally means "woof" — an exact complement to "weft" (jing). By saying that "without the woof threads, there would be no warp threads" (buwei ze bujing), she was in fact arguing for the necessity of a new pluralism that expressed a new female point of view regarding the classics, or even the concept of classics.[37] In a sense, by compiling such an anthology, Wang Duanshu wrote a new literary history; as Qian Qianyi put it, "[Her work] is both a history and a classic" (yi shi yi jing).[38]

Notable also is Wang Duanshu's attempt to establish proper literary credentials for gentry women poets, as opposed to courtesan-poets. As I have shown elsewhere, by the early seventeenth century, courtesans had become the prototype of the "talented woman" (cainü) in both real life and contemporary fiction.[39] Indeed, the popular image of courtesans as "talented women" symbolizing the ultimate ideal in literature and the arts in effect slighted such gentry women poets as Wang Duanshu. In any case, she arranged her anthology of about 1,000 women poets in descending order of social status. Gentry women are grouped in the category of "the proper" (zheng), and courtesans in the category of "the erotic" (yan). The only exceptions are people like Liu Shi, Li Yin, and Wang Wei — these onetime courtesans managed to become "gentry women" by marrying prominent male literati. Therefore, their works are included in the section of "*zheng*" rather than "*yan*." However, it is clear that Wang Duanshu was still prejudiced against these courtesans turned gentry women, for the anthology includes only six poems by Liu Shi,[40] and three by Li Yin—in sharp contrast to the great number of poems by such gentry women poets as Xu Yuan (28 poems),[41] Fang Weiyi (20 poems), and Huang Yuanjie (16 poems).

Most important, and most interesting, Wang Duanshu includes 63 of her own poems, which are printed in the last section (*juan* 42) of the anthology. Needless to say, she was attempting to enter the canon herself by "logrolling"—a method Wendell Harris defines as the "active espousal" by writers "of texts or criteria congenial to their own aims" and also by the power of their writing and influence. As Harris demonstrates, Western writers such as Wordsworth, Arnold, Emerson, and Longfellow all used similar methods to canonize themselves.[42]

Tianxia mingjia shiguan chuji (preface dated 1672),
comp. Deng Hanyi.[43] Original in Naikaku bunko, Japan.

Although only *juan* 12 of this anthology is devoted to female authors, *Tianxia mingjia shiguan chuji* is an extremely important source for studying poetry of the Jiangnan area during the mid-seventeenth century. It includes works by 45 major women poets. The fact that Deng Hanyi put female authors in the general category of "Famous Poets" (*mingjia*)—for the title of his anthology literally means "A look at the famous poets in the whole nation"—is significant in itself. In reading through the poems (along with Deng's comments), one gets the impression that women poets are judged independently of gender—or, rather, they seem to be evaluated largely as if they were male poets. Their status as "famous poets" is attested through the many detailed biographical notes prepared by Deng Hanyi, which often contain interesting anecdotes concerning their involvement with other literary figures, male or female. The anthology is especially useful for tracing the literary association between women poets. For example, in the section on Shang Jinglan and her daughters (and daughters-in-law), all the poems selected are their farewell poems to the famous poet-painter Huang Yuanjie (22.24a–25b). Deng Hanyi's comments especially call attention to the fact that Li Yin was an admiring friend of Liu Shi. It was Li Yin who provided Teng (supposedly after Liu Shi's death) with the remarkable story of Liu's life.

Cuilou ji (1673), comp. Liu Yunfen. Modern punctuated
edition by Shi Zhicun (Shanghai: Zazhi gongsi, 1936).

Cuilou ji is divided into three parts (*chuji, erji,* and *xinji*), altogether
covering about 700 poems by 200 women poets. Perhaps as a reaction
against contemporary anthologies of works by women, which had begun to dwell on Qing rather than Ming writers, Liu Yunfen claimed
that his anthology was devoted exclusively to the female poetry produced "in the 300 years of the Ming." He was impressed by the "sheer
bulk" of Ming women's verses (which he likened to "an expansive
sea") and was extremely "taken" (*xindong*) by the fine quality of the
poems.[44] Since most of his selections were newly discovered poems
not available in other current anthologies, *Cuilou ji* is an important
source for studying Ming women's poetry. The selections from the
following poets are especially useful: Wang Wei (26 poems), Lu Qingzi (23 poems), Shen Yixiu (40 poems), Ye Xiaoluan (36 poems), and Xu
Jingfan (25 poems).

Liu, who remarked that research on women's works was his life-
long ambition (*zhi*),[45] apparently devoted much of his time to literary
archaeology, judging from his many interesting discoveries. In his
foreword to the anthology, Zong Yuanding summed up the two main
obstacles encountered in anthologizing earlier women's works: (1) it
was extremely difficult to search for unpublished sources, and (2)
even published materials listed in major bibliographic catalogs were
often lost. Zong further complimented Liu Yunfen for producing such
a carefully researched anthology under these difficult circumstances.

Cuilou ji is unusual also for a section called "*zuli,*" which highlights the regional origins of women poets. It is an immensely helpful
guide for those interested in studying the geographic distribution of
female talent in the Ming.

Zhongxiang ci (1690), comp. Xu Shumin and Qian Yue

Zhongxiang ci is one of the three major anthologies of "song lyrics"
(*ci*) of women poets—the other two being *Linxia cixuan* (1671) and *Gujin mingyuan baihua shiyu* (1685)—published in the last decades of the
seventeenth century. The anthology focuses on more than 400 women
ci poets during the Ming-Qing transition, and the scope of its coverage
testifies to the important role women played in the movement to revive the song-lyric genre in the early seventeenth century.[46] As I have
shown elsewhere, by the late Ming the *ci* genre had been viewed as a

"dying genre" for over three centuries. It was Liu Shi, the courtesan-poet, who helped her lover Chen Zilong (1608–47) establish the important Yunjian School of *Ci* Revival.[47] Both men and women were strongly affected by this revival, but especially for women *ci* suddenly became the main expressive vehicle. The number of women *ci* poets during the Ming-Qing transition is simply unprecedented.

In his foreword to *Zhongxiang ci* (literally, "Song-lyrics of numerous fragrances"), Wu Qi dwelled on the conception of "femininity" as a generic trait of *ci*. He suggested that women, being female, are able to produce better song-lyrics. Wu's argument, right or wrong, reflects a convergence between biological femaleness and stylistic femininity common to the thinking of many Ming and Qing critics that no doubt encouraged women to embark upon *ci* writing as the vehicle for their poetic ambitions.

In fact, the two other near-contemporary anthologies of women *ci* poets also took this same theory of "femininity" as their basic premise. In his foreword to *Linxia cixuan* (1671) compiled by Zhou Ming,[48] the famous scholar You Tong (1618–1704) claimed that *ci* writing, rooted in the feminine style of "delicate restraint" during the Song, is particularly suitable for women poets (Hu Wenkai, 896). In a similar fashion, Sun Huiyuan—one of the four female compilers of *Gujin mingyuan baihua shiyu* (1685)—argued in her preface that that compilation is a truly female and feminine anthology; indeed the works in it are more convincing than those in the "feminine mode" written by men that seem to fill the earlier *ci* anthologies such as *Huajian ji* and *Caotang shiyu* (Hu Wenkai, 900). In passing, I should mention that *Gujin mingyuan baihua shiyu* was an unusual anthology not only because it was edited and compiled by four women poets, but also because it was organized by a special symbolic device. In it 93 women *ci* poets dating from the eleventh to the seventeenth centuries were arranged according to the sequence of the four seasons—a device that emphasized "femininity" as the unique quality of song lyrics (Hu Wenkai, 900). Sun Huiyuan's preface is noted for its "spring metaphors":

> Let its beauty surprise you, since, like the rain, it is always the same and always new. The spring colors of the Shanglin garden do not need to be adorned with ribbons; must the plant branches of the Jingu garden wait for the East Wind's imperial breath? Truly, the flower-historians are female historians, and the rhyming of words is a rhyming of minds.[49]

In general, *Zhongxiang ci* differs from both *Gujin mingyuan baihua shiyu* and *Linxia cixuan* in its arrangement of poets. Most noticeable is the fact that its six parts are named after the six arts that ancient Confucian scholars were required to master: *li* (rites); *yue* (music); *she* (archery); *yu* (chariot driving); *shū* (learning); *shù* (mathematics). Although there seems no real correlation between the names of the six sections and the poets included in them, these Confucian designations reflect the anthologists' value judgment. The anthology arranges its over 400 female authors in a descending order of social status, with courtesans at the end (in the sixth part). Courtesans such as Liu Shi, Dong Bai, and Gu Mei who later married famed scholar-officials, however, belong to the fifth part. This organizing principle recalls that of Wang Duanshu's *Mingyuan shiwei*, although it is far more rigid and elaborate.

Through this particular method of arrangement, or classification, the compilers of *Zhongxiang ci* had in mind a certain interpretive strategy that would help them canonize and judge the writings of certain distinguished gentry women. At the very beginning of the anthology, for instance, Xu Can (ca. 1610–after 1677) is hailed as "the greatest poet of the present dynasty" because her song lyrics were imbued with "the style of the Northern Song dynasty, devoid of the ornate and frivolous qualities" (pt. I, 1a). In a similar way, her great-aunt Xu Yuan—who incidentally was one of those criticized by Liu Shi—also received high marks from the compilers: "Poems by Luowei [Xu Yuan] can be compared to the opening songs in the *Shijing*, 'Guanju' and 'Juaner'"(preface, pt. I). Thus, by referring to the canonical text, the *Shijing*, the compilers were again able to claim for themselves a moral power that supported the canonical status they claimed for women in literature. This strategy certainly worked in the case of Xu Can, who has been recognized (even up to this day) as the best of the Ming and Qing women *ci* poets.[50]

All things considered, *Zhongxiang ci* seems to have satisfied the changing needs and tastes of *ci* critics during the last decades of the seventeenth century. By then the romantic Southern Tang–style *ci* promoted by Chen Zilong and Liu Shi in the 1630's had gone out of fashion. In its place, the Song dynasty–style *ci* became the favored mode, as attested by the elevated position of Xu Can in *Zhongxiang ci*. This shift in poetic taste can also be seen in contemporary anthologies of male *ci* poets. For example, the male anthology *Qingping cixuan* (1678) was compiled and edited by two scholars from Songjiang, Chen

Zilong's home town, in an attempt to propagate Southern Tang–style *ci*, no doubt as a reaction to the Song dynasty style championed by the poets Chen Weisong and Zhu Yizun, which was gradually gaining in importance.[51] A decade later, the famous anthology *Yaohua ji* (1687) was almost entirely given over to Song dynasty–style *ci*—it presents 148 poems by Chen Weisong and 111 by Zhu Yizun, in sharp contrast to the 29 by Chen Zilong.[52] Although *Yaohua ji* also includes some poems by women poets such as Xu Can (10 poems) and Xu Yuan (5 poems), there are no selections from Liu Shi.

Thus, in many ways, *Zhongxiang ci* could be seen as an exact parallel to *Yaohua ji*—with the former focusing on female poets and the latter on male poets. Although their works might be preserved in two different anthologies, however, these male and female poets were the products of the same literary milieu.

Suiyuan nüdizi shixuan (1796), comp. Yuan Mei

Suiyuan nüdizi shixuan, in six *juan*, is an anthology of poems by Yuan Mei's female disciples, compiled by Yuan Mei himself. Yuan Mei was the first person in Chinese history to collect an entourage of women students, but few realize that he did not actively seek to teach women until he was in his seventies. When he published this anthology at the age of 80, he had already acquired as many as 28 female disciples. According to the table of contents, the anthology includes poems by all 28 disciples. But for some reason, works by nine students—including such famous ones as Qu Bingyun, Gui Maoyi, and Wang Yuzhen—are missing from the extant version. Xi Peilan (Yuan Mei's prize student) appears at the beginning of the anthology, with two congratulatory verses for the anthology, written at the request of Yuan Mei.

Perhaps it was to forestall criticism of his female disciples from people such as Zhang Xuecheng that Yuan Mei asked Wang Gu (the publisher) to write a foreword to the *Suiyuan nüdizi shixuan*,[53] defending the close relationship between women's poetry writing and the ancient classics. Wang Gu based his promotion of women poets entirely on Yuan Mei's interpretation of the *Book of Changes* (*Yijing*). He reminded the reader (as Yuan Mei did elsewhere) that according to the commentary in the *Book of Changes*, the *dui* trigram (lake), which symbolizes "the third daughter" (*shaonü*), provides the principle by which the sage "joins with his friends for discussion and practice."[54] And similarly, the *li* trigram (fire), which symbolizes "the second daughter" (*zhongnü*), is the source from which the sage built civilization "by perpetuating this brightness."[55] He also repeated the (by then) common argument that odes written by women (e.g., "Getan" and "Juaner") had been placed at the beginning of the canonical *Shijing*, a view to which, as we know, Zhang Xuecheng strongly objected.[56]

In promoting his female students, Yuan was at the same time corroborating his own poetic theory, which was centered around the idea of "innate sensibility" (*xingling*).[57] Central to the concept of *xingling* is the basic assumption that anyone, male or female, when poetically inspired, could create a true voice in poetry. It was a theory that Yuan Mei's female disciples learned well.

Guochao guixiu zhengshi ji (1831), comp. Yun Zhu;
Xuji (1863), ed. Miao Lianbao

Guochao guixiu zhengshi ji is an ambitious anthology of more than 1,500 Qing women poets, with over 3,000 *shi* poems. A Han Chinese who married into a Manchu family, Yun Zhu adopted the Confucian attribute of "meekness and gentleness" (*wenrou dunhou*) as the criterion of selection for her anthology. *Wenrou dunhou* was a typical quality of emotional restraint long celebrated in the Confucian hermeneutic tradition and specifically in the appreciation of the *Shijing*. It was also the principle of selection invoked by Shen Deqian (1673–1769) in his *Qingshi biecai ji* (1760), an anthology that Yun Zhu acknowledged as her model ("Liyan," 5b). As I have said elsewhere, Yun Zhu's anthology (which she called *The Correct Beginnings: Collected Women's Poetry of Our Dynasty*) is a perfect example of how orthodox Confucianism influenced some literati women after the mid-Qing.[58]

As an anthology of Qing gentry women poets, Yun Zhu's *Guochao guixiu zhengshi ji* is indispensable. It is much more ambitious in scope than Shen Deqian's *Qingshi biecai ji*, and unlike Shen's anthology, which contained only the works of authors no longer living at the time of compilation, Yun Zhu included extensive selections from contemporary authors.

Gonggui wenxuan (1843), comp. Zhou Shouchang (1814–84)

Gonggui wenxuan, as its title clearly indicates, is a "female *Wenxuan*," deliberately modeled on Xiao Tong's (501–31) prestigious anthology, *Selections of Refined Literature*.[59] Like Xiao Tong, Zhou Shouchang arranged the work by genre—*fu* poetry, prose (*wen*), *yuefu* songs, *shi* poetry, and so on. Again, like Xiao Tong's collection, Zhou's *Gonggui wenxuan* is a comprehensive, representative anthology. It selects works of women writers from ancient times to the end of the Ming—with *juan* 1–10 covering works in *fu* and *wen*, and *juan* 11–26 covering *yuefu* and all forms of *shi* poetry.

In other ways, however, *Gonggui wenxuan* recalls Xu Ling's (503–83) anthology, the *New Songs from the Jade Terrace* (*Yutai xinyong*),[60] which was compiled under the patronage of Xiao Gang (503–51) in an attempt to challenge the basic selection policy of the *Wenxuan*. First, Zhou's preface, written in a flowery parallel prose (*pianwen*) style, is reminiscent of Xu Ling's preface to *Yutai xinyong*, which focuses on the description of languishing beauties indulging in editing and reading verses. The fact that *Yutai xinyong* included numerous poems by women—and the fact that it was intended for female readers[61]—made it a wonderful precedent for Ming and Qing women's anthologies, although these later anthologies never made women readers their sole audience. Still, as an anthology *Gonggui wenxuan* departs from *Yutai xinyong* in one significant way: it does not claim, as *Yutai xinyong* did, to be a "contemporary" collection comprising mostly "new" poems by living authors. Instead, Zhou Shouchang deliberately took an "archaic" approach, excluding all Qing works from his anthology, making the end of the Ming (200 years before his time!) the cutoff date of his selection. Was Zhou a Ming loyalist? Or was he simply presenting pre-Qing women's literature as a kind of model literature—the kind that in his view preserved the best of women's writings? I do not have immediate answers to these questions. But Zhou's way of mixing together a large number of courtesans' poems with the gentry women's verses does lead us to suspect that his open-minded approach might be a direct reaction to the orthodox Confucian approach adopted by Yun Zhu's anthology, published 12 years before Zhou's.

Guochao guige shichao (1844), 10 vols.; *xubian* (1874),
2 vols. Comp. Cai Dianqi.

Beginning with the late eighteenth century, one witnesses a growing interest on the part of editors and publishers in producing composite compilations (*heke*) of the collected works of individual poets. These compilations were apparently created as a convenient way of promoting, or canonizing, particular groups of prominent women poets who shared a similar background or interests. For example,

Yuan shi san mei shigao heke, 1759) joins the poetic works of Yuan Mei's three talented sisters, Yuan Ji, Yuan Zhu, and Yuan Tang — which obviously inspired the publication of *Jingjiang Baoshi san nüshi shichao heke* (1882), a composite compilation of the works of the three legendary Bao sisters, Bao Zhilan, Bao Zhihui, and Bao Zhifen. Some *heke* compilations are primarily defined by their "local" nature, among them the *Wuzhong shi zi shichao* (1789) edited by Zhang Zilan, which brings together the collected poems of ten major women poets (*shi zi*, or "ten masters") from the Wu area.[62] Some *heke*, however, were created in order to honor talented women also known for their great virtue — a case in point is the *Wujiang san jiefu ji* (1857), which collects works of three women from Wujiang (in the Suzhou district) who died protecting their chastity.[63] Again, some *heke* were published for the purpose of providing literary models for contemporary women poets and readers — of which the most famous might be the *Linxia yayin ji* (1854), compiled and annotated by the learned woman scholar Mao Jun (1828–81). This collection presents four women poets Wang Caiwei, Wang Duan (1793–1838), Wu Zao (ca. 1800–55), and Zhuang Panzhu as foremost model poets. Most *heke* were relatively small in size, attempting to single out a few individual poets for one reason or another.

Cai Dianqi's *Guochao guige shichao* (1844), however, departs from the conventional *heke* practice by aiming to be inclusive. It comprises exclusively women of the Qing dynasty, as "guochao" indicates. The anthology brings together works of 100 poets (or 120, if we include the sequel [*xubian*] published in 1874), convincingly supporting its editor's claim to have given the finest female poets of the Qing a most exhaustive presentation.[64] Indeed, Cai Dianqi's *heke* is by far the most valuable source for the study of Qing women poetry writing *shi*.

Xiaotanluanshi huike baijia guixiu ci (1896), 10 *ji*;
Guixiu cichao (1906), 16 *juan*, comp. Xu Naichang

Xiaotanluanshi huike baijia guixiu ci, an anthology — or more precisely a *heke* compilation — of the collected works of 100 poets writing in *ci* was apparently modeled on Cai Dianqi's *Guochao guige shichao*. Like Cai Dianqi's collection, Xu Naichang's *Xiaotanluanshi huike baijia guixiu ci* is primarily a Qing anthology, although it also includes four late Ming authors, Shen Yixiu, Ye Wanwan, Ye Xiaoluan, and Shang Jinglan. With a preface by Wang Pengyun (1849–1904), a renowned poet and scholar largely responsible for the late Qing revival of song lyrics, Xu Naichang's anthology reveals how female poets were deeply involved in the *ci* revival movement. As William Schultz has pointed out, this late renaissance of the *ci* is "in part traceable to the emergence of the so-called Changzhou school in the late eighteenth century, and its insistence on the use of allegory and allusion in commenting on contemporary realities."[65] That late Qing women poets writing in the *ci* style became deeply interested (like their male contemporaries) in current affairs, and hence in writing topical allegories, no doubt helped *ci* become an elevated form of poetry.

Again like Cai Dianqi, Xu Naichang later compiled a sequel to his anthology in order to bring his research up to date. But, unlike Cai Dianqi's *xubian* (1874), which is merely a composite collection of published works by twenty poets, Xu Naichang's sequel *Guixiu cichao* (1906) is an extremely ambitious and well-edited anthology that collects some 1,500 newly discovered *ci* poems by 521 poets. Most important, it also provides a useful index for poets, indicating their birthplace and titles of *ci* collections. Thus, the *Guixiu cichao*, in 16 *juan*, is an indispensable source material for the study of late imperial women's *ci* poetry. In comparison, Ding Shaoyi's famous *Qingci zong bu* (ca. 1894), which also contains works by female *ci* poets, seems almost inconsequential.

Other Relevant Anthologies and Source Materials

Many other female anthologies deserve to be examined as well—such as those devoted to poetry criticism, among them the *Minchuan guixiu shihua* (1849) and *Guixiu shi ping* (1877). In addition, the importance of the recently discovered "women's script" (*nüshu*) in Hunan should also be weighed.[66] The women's script reveals the existence, according to some reports, since early times of a long-standing female oral tradition supported by a written tradition unique to country women in one small region of southern China. The numerous folksongs and ballads set down in the women's script are especially worth noting, for their styles resemble the traditional *yuefu* and other popular songs.[67] The mere presence of these folksongs could have been used to refute Zhang Xuecheng's argument that "women of ancient times" could not have possibly "opened their mouths and poured out complete verses."[68] But Zhang Xuecheng obviously did not know of the women's script, which, however limited in time and space its use may prove to have been, transmitted a genuine "women's voice" among those who used it.

Finally, an anthology of male poets (entitled *Ming sanshi jia shixuan*) compiled by the woman poet Wang Duan (1793–1838) deserves special attention. This anthology reveals how broad and thorough the education of gentry women was; it was not restricted to the so-called female tradition. Wang Duan's *Ming sanshi jia shixuan* (printed 1822, reprinted 1873) was unusual not only because it was compiled by a woman, but also because it was judged by many to be the finest anthology of Ming poetry. According to *Ranzhi yuyun*, for example, Wang Duan's anthology is far superior to those compiled by Qian Qianyi, Zhu Yizun, and Shen Deqian.[69] Wang Duan's anthology was especially distinguished for her insightful views on Chinese poetry, expressed through extremely thoughtful introductions to each of the 30 male poets she included. Her "Fanli" (Editorial principles) departs from the conventional pattern of dwelling on the technical points involved in the anthologist's policy of selection. Instead, it is a superb essay of literary criticism, demonstrating Wang Duan's brilliant exploration into the 300-year history of Ming poetry. Deeply concerned with the qualities of "purity" (*qing*) and "sincerity" (*zhen*) in poetry, Wang Duan especially praised the poet Gao Qi (1336–1374). Wang Duan was apparently influenced by her famous father-in-law, Chen Wenshu, who was deeply interested in Ming loyalism, for she devoted a whole *juan* to the loyalist poets Chen Zilong and Gu Yanwu (1613–82; see *juan* 7). But as Ellen Widmer has pointed out in another context, this interest in loyalism on the part of Chen Wenshu's circle (which included many women poets) was meaningful "perhaps more for its romantic than its political side."[70] As a critic, Wang Duan had an enthusiasm for ideas, especially those concerning originality and poetic traditions, as her able recounting of the history of poetic trends and individual creativity shows. Indeed, Wang Duan wrote with a self-assurance and authority that she seemed to have inherited from the Song dynasty poet Li Qingzhao, the first female critic to write confidently about male poets. In many ways, however, Wang Duan was the exact opposite of Li Qingzhao. Whereas Li Qingzhao was always finding fault with male poets, Wang Duan affirmed the artistic achievement of many male poets who suffered undeserved obscurity. Most important, as the first female anthologist of male poetry in the Chinese tradition, Wang Duan demonstrated how compiling an anthology gave power and prestige to one's critical vocation. Clearly her goal was not to celebrate the "female" tradition in poetry. She seemed to prefer instead to erase the boundaries between the male and the female.

But as a woman, Wang Duan was clearly an exceptional anthologist. In passing, I would mention that in my study of the Ming and Qing anthologies of women poets, I have noticed a common (though by no means absolute) difference between those put together by women and those put together by men. Women anthologists, and in fact women critics in general,[71] often ranked women poets according to their virtue, although this was not automatically done in anthologies organized by male scholars, such as Zhong Xing, Zhao Shijie, Zou Siyi, Deng Hanyi, and Yuan Mei. Whereas female editors like Wang Duanshu and Yun Zhu felt compelled to regard virtue as an essential component in their anthologies, there had been a long tradition for literal-minded male anthologists, indeed from the time of Xu Ling's *Yutai xinyong*, to promote women's talent. Such a striking difference between male and female attitudes explains why more women than men during the Ming and Qing believed that "a woman without talent is a woman of virtue" (*nüzi wucai bianshi de*). Perhaps it is also in this connection that the impulse to compile an anthology often interacts with the conflict women experienced over whether to publish their own work or burn it.[72] As I have said elsewhere, "faced with the 'danger' of publishing, many literate Qing women simply burned, or attempted to burn, their poems."[73] Viewed in this context, it is entirely possible that the early Qing female poet Wang Duanshu compiled the anthology *Mingyuan shiwei* partly as an excuse to publish her own poems — as indicated by the fact that Wang included 63 of her own poems, the largest selection from a single author in the anthology.

No doubt the complex issue of virtue and talent reflects just another cultural concern that affected women's anthology making in the Ming and Qing. As Pauline Yu says, "Anthologies put poems in their place metaphorically and historically, addressing directly or indirectly the values of the time."[74] The very variety of selection strategies and criteria evident in Ming and Qing anthologies of women poets reveals a rather pluralistic and evolving literary scene — a picture that other kinds of sources might not have offered. Indeed, Shi Shuyi shows an understanding of the value of anthology making when she acknowledges that the selection of significant figures to be treated in her *Biographies of Qing Women Poets* (1922) was based largely on their inclusion in previous anthologies.[75] Unfortunately, modern scholars of Chinese literary history have heretofore failed to take advantage of the numerous anthologies of female poetry produced in the Ming and Qing. Their neglect is regrettable, for these important anthologies would have constituted perhaps the strongest argument against the modern view of literary history that claims traditional women were largely excluded from the literary establishment.

Behind this problem lies another. Not only the women poets but also the male poets of the Ming and Qing periods, together with their anthologies, have been neglected by modern scholars and critics. As I have observed elsewhere, the problem is partly caused by many Chinese scholars' stubborn adherence to a rigid scheme of historical evolution, one that labels the Tang dynasty (618–907) the golden age of *shi*, the Song dynasty (960–1279) that of *ci*, the Yuan (1234–1368) that of *qu* and drama, and the Ming and Qing dynasties the period of vernacular fiction.[76] Indeed, such a biased view seriously distorts the real nature of literary development in traditional China. When the *shi* and *ci* poetry of the Ming and Qing is judged by how well it emulates (or, more often, fails to emulate) the works of the great Tang and Song predecessors, it can only be rejected as lacking dynamic originality. But such a view of literary history need no longer hold us in thrall. "Belatedness," to use Harold Bloom's term in a way counter to Bloom's own theory,[77] does not have to connote derivativeness. There are ways of inheriting and revising a tradition that are themselves dynamic and creative. I think the most effective remedy for the prejudice against the poetry of China's last two dynasties is to call attention to the numerous poetry anthologies produced in the Ming and Qing.

7

Changing the Subject: Gender and Self-inscription in Authors' Prefaces and "Shi" Poetry

MAUREEN ROBERTSON

In the Treasure Room of the Harvard-Yenching Library, there is a rare 1789 edition of a work titled *Wuzhong nüshi shichao* (Poems by women scholars of Wu; alternative title, *Linwu yinxie*, Poetry kiosk by the house in the grove). This work comprises, in the editor's words, the "combined collections" (*heji*) of poems by the members of a literary coterie, the Clear Creek Poetry Club (Qingxi yinshe), ten Suzhou women, all of whom were close relatives or friends. The anthology was compiled primarily by Zhang Yunzi (b. 1756; known by her *zi*, Zilan), with final editing (*yueding*, "examined and approved") by Zhang's husband, Ren Zhaolin (*zi*, Wentian; *hao*, Linwu shanren).[1] The women's poems are accompanied by a diverse array of supporting texts — dedicatory inscriptions in poetry and prose, prefaces, biographies, colophons, a letter, a prose commendation — by the writers themselves, by relatives and family friends, and even by the magistrate of Wujiang district, Long Shi. This multi-voiced, multi-genred, collaboratively produced text vividly displays the communal context within which women's poetry was written and given printed form in late imperial China. Such a text reminds us how little access we now have to the many individually published collections of Ming and Qing dynasty women's writings, whose titles are recorded in bibliographies, anthologies, gazetteers, and writings by other family members. Access to collections now lost would contextualize, far better than the selected poems available in anthologies, contemporary representa-

tions of Ming and Qing women as writers; authors' prefaces attached
to the collections would provide a better understanding of the circumstances under which women's poetry was written, and give further
insight into strategies of self-presentation practiced by literary women
of the Ming and Qing.[2]

The celebratory nature of supporting texts to *Poems by Women
Scholars of Wu*, the links with poetic tradition and family traditions of
learning that they establish, and the warmth with which the coterie
writers acknowledged their colleagues' literary achievements are accompanied by evidence that customary role practices within the gender hierarchy were maintained: although as leader among the women
of the club Zhang selected most of the poems included, the final editing was performed by her husband. As the club's acknowledged literary instructor and mentor, it was Ren Zhaolin who authorized the
quality and suitability of items included, in view of the possibility of
some form of public circulation once the work was printed, and it was
he who sponsored the printing of the collection. Further, the district
magistrate, in commending this text as worthy of publication, attributed its merits to the influence of Ren Zhaolin and to a family lineage
that had "promoted literature for nine generations," making the literary talent, *cai*, of its women possible (Zhang Zilan and Ren Zhaolin,
2b). This rather sublimated representation of the woman writer reflects one kind of contemporary evaluation of her, characterizing her
achievement as due to the "trickle-down" effect of a family heritage, a
devotion to literature by educated ancestors and family elders. It is a
representation that tends to reflect credit primarily upon men of the
family, past and present.[3]

A rather different representation of the woman writer emerges
from a poem in four stanzas written by another Clear Creek Poetry
Club member, Jiang Zhu, as a dedicatory inscription for Zhang Zilan's
poetry. The poem, "Respectfully Presented After Reading Lady Ren
[Zhang] of Songling's poem 'A Spring Day Spent Quietly at Home,'
Matching the Original Rhymes" begins with the following lines:

Flowering trees deeply shade the "three paths"
When one's spirit is reclusive, the place is empty too.
Studying classics, you pursue ultimate principles;
Researching antiquities, you love the rarest books.
(Zhang Zilan and Ren Zhaolin, 3a)

The poem, in four stanzas, describes Zhang as a scholar and a writer who merits representation through its several allusions to Jin dynasty poet Tao Qian. Prompted by Zhang's own use of a motif from Tao's poetry, the implicit claim of Jiang's representation of her is that, regardless of sexual difference, Zhang is comparable to Tao, one of the greatest poets of tradition, by virtue of a private lifestyle, a devotion to classical values, and a remarkable gift for poetry.[4]

These two samples from among the materials framing the poems of the Clear Creek group offer a glimpse of the diverse but complementary representations of the woman writer to be found in a single text. Fathers, husbands, brothers, children, other women as literary friends and relatives, family friends, a local official, and the author/ editor herself contribute their perspectives on the women and their work. Taken together, they provide an orchestrated portrait that defines the writing woman as writer, reader, and addressee in a community of same-sex writers; as a wife, daughter, or mother whose literariness and learning come into play in her relationships with other family members (where she may be literary companion to a husband, a teacher of children, a mentor for younger women, and a literary friend and critic of women both inside and outside the immediate family); and as a representative of her lineage and her household. The author's preface represents the writer as a textual subjectivity, attempting to compose a self-image defined in terms of both literary and domestic values.

The variety of representations of the writer embedded in the framing of such a collection suggests the range and circumstances of address that the published work must accommodate. It is this larger context that must be inferred by modern readers when our only access to the works of the majority of Ming and Qing women writers is through anthologized poems, which at best are introduced with brief biographical notes. Further erosion of our ability to contextualize the work of these authors can be reckoned when we consider the highly selected character of the poetry transmitted in anthologies. The careful selection process that must have preceded the limited circulation of women's collected works (cautious selection by the writer herself and possibly further editing by family members) is followed by the selection of a relatively small number of the published poems by the anthologist, poems now stripped of the intimate context and rich relational resonances with which they were first presented to readers.[5]

Yet, for most modern readers, it is precisely the single voice of the woman in the text, speaking for the author herself, that is of compelling interest. "Spoken for" by men for so many centuries, the experiences, interests, and perspectives of premodern Chinese women, at least those relatively few who were literate, at last seem to find substantially more direct expression in the expanded volume of women's texts during the Ming and Qing. Under these circumstances, curiosity and a desire for insight into women's lives may lead one to read a text as a transparent and unproblematic revelation of a historical woman's thoughts and feelings and to overlook the multiply-mediated nature of feminine voices in literary texts. Without context, the reader can misunderstand the demands of address, misinterpret textual irony, or fail to identify subtexts. Similar problems arise, of course, in the reading of literati poetry when there is insufficient context; however, the potentially transgressive character of gentry women's writing, their confinement to the household and reliance on male family members for publication, and their use of an already masculinized literary medium give the context of their writing an especially complex specificity.

Whether women's texts are read as documentary sources for social history or as literary sources for literary history and critical analysis, the modern reader may approach them with unconscious assumptions about the autonomy of poems, the independent "creative" process, and the intimacy of text-reader relations that are alien not only to the context of women's writing but also to that of traditional poetry generally. The highly selective format of the anthology, like that of the academic study, presents poems in a way that encourages these assumptions for modern readers. Because the present study of forms of feminine self-inscription in literary texts uses illustrative prefaces and poems, removing them from their communal context of family, coterie, and network, it may allow the reader to forget that these poems are always variously mediated forms of self-representation, whether from the constraints of literary convention, from restrictions imposed by the gender system, or from the local politics of family life. Therefore, this chapter begins with a cautionary preamble intended to install a vision of the populous, family- and community-based scene of women's authorship, a reminder of the complexity of self-representation and address.

Elsewhere, I have discussed the problematic relationship of women and their representation in literature where gender ideology allocated the production of written texts to men and where conventions of genre, voice, topic, and image-coding in literature evolved to

articulate the concerns and experiences of men.[6] This essay will further pursue the questions surrounding efforts of governing-class
women in the late Ming and the Qing dynasties to establish discursive
space and subject positions in texts, making claims upon and changes
in both the conventional literati representations of the feminine and
the explicitly masculine models of self-inscription that they encountered in the writings of men. As authors, they invented speaking
selves in the textual subjects of their poems; as readers of women's
writings, they found new subject positions for themselves to occupy.
Both processes were rich with the potential for an increase in women's
critical self-awareness and a more objective understanding of what
they shared with other women.

This study begins with a discussion of self-representation by
women in their authors' prefaces to collected writings. Valuable
sources of information about women's education and their family-
based literary and intellectual activities, authors' prefaces also illustrate how women's self-representations could be complicated by a
lack of fit between the demands of the preface as a genre and those of
their gendered roles.

The author's preface written by a woman is the site of a potentially contradictory representation of self, one that the writers themselves were aware of and that they often attempted either to cover
over or to reconcile. Since women, through interpellation into the
gendered roles society offered them, internalized the rules of a gender
system that inhibited their participation in literary culture, their prefaces often manifested a need to assure family members that their
writing was not a violation of propriety; at the same time the writers
addressed their own ambivalence about writing.[7] Prefaces thus may
offer insight into a process of negotiation where the writer attempts to
reconcile a contradiction affecting her self-representation and, in so
doing, explores ways of rationalizing an adjustment taking place in
the Confucian gender system, which taught that women's words did
not circulate.

The second half of the chapter, under the headings of performance, reinscription, and invention, provides some answers to the
question: how did women "change the subject" in the lyric poetry
(*shi*) and ballad (*yuefu*) of the literati tradition, in order to represent
themselves speaking in texts? With the change of genre from preface
to poetry, self-representation undergoes changes. Not only do textual
voices appear less guarded or conflicted, but authors undertake a

broad and innovative engagement with and reinscription of literati *shi* voices, images, and concerns. In the genre of lyric poetry, the writer has far more freedom to assume, through authorial strategies, a variety of subject positions, to perform masculine voices, or to use the scenarios of literati poetry in new ways that feature feminine subjectivity. The performative character of poetry and the relative freedom permitted them upon entry into the symbolic space of art allow writers to explore the presentation of self in ways impossible in the preface.

Before proceeding further, I will define certain terms used in the following discussion. The term "self" (like its more ideologically colored alternative, "individual") refers to the commonly experienced sense, at any given moment, of a unitary presence and identity, an "unconsciously structured illusion of plentitude."[8] "Self" can be understood as a figment or reification of consciousness present to itself, an overarching idea that consciousness has about consciousness. When the word is used here to refer either to the seeming coherence of the historical person's sense of identity or to the perceived expressive coherence of the subject speaking in a poem, one might imagine the word as permanently enclosed within quotation marks as a sign of the illusory stability of its referent. The actual complex mutability and fluidity of consciousness and mental dispositions in our interactions with "the world" through time are, however, displayed in the varied positions we occupy as *subjects*, beings shaped by socialization and interpellated into a variety of social roles and discursive systems. The subject is not univocal or unitary; as the object of the determining forces of history, culture, and language, it is capable of occupying multiple positions in relationships with "others," positions that may even contradict each other. Moreover, although it may be conceptualized in a less "inner-determined" way than "self," neither is the subject wholly determined by external forces; the subject is also the site of negotiation between the shaping and constructing forces of society and language on the one hand and conscious or unconscious desire on the other, at moments when these are not congruent. Likewise, the subjects that are created to speak in texts may do so from many different discursive or ideological positions, most of which are codified as conventions in traditional literatures. However, here too, the language of a literary text is a dynamic field where desire, self, and voice may not be univocal.

Since this chapter centers upon the ways in which a gendered self is inscribed in literary languages and forms by subjects who were women entering a tradition devoted to the representation of masculine "selves," it may be useful to distinguish, merely for the purposes of this analysis, between three different kinds of "subject" (or three functional roles indicated by the word "subject"), each with its own status and function, and each with the potential for assuming a gendered position of its own. To distinguish them, I shall use the terms *existential* (or historical) *subject, authorial* (or writing) *subject*, and *textual* (or speaking) *subject*.

The existential subject is the historical man or woman who, when moved to do so, has chosen to "speak" through the medium of a literary text. The reader of the text has no direct access to the existential subject; however, a traditional, shared belief in "self"-expression through texts in which the "I" who speaks is in some sense autobiographical or non-fictional may generate in the reader a sense of direct communion with an absent existential subject.[9] The authorial subject is the existential subject in the role of author. The author, mediating between existential subjectivity and text, takes up a position from which to negotiate with language and literary convention to produce a textual subject that "speaks for" and represents the existential subject/self. The author selects from among options so that aspects of a given existential subject position are fitted to appropriate elements from the repertory of signifying voices, scenarios, and forms provided by the literary tradition. In doing so, the author has a guarantee of being able to communicate with an educated readership that demands observance of established generic and rhetorical conventions as a condition for recognition of the text as, say, a poem or a memorial. As the poem is a conventionally less "self"-effacing genre than the memorial, reader expectations will vary accordingly; the poem should, its reliance on convention notwithstanding, offer a "sincere," persuasively inscribed speaker, voicing a "self" that is an amalgam of convention and the authorial attempt to represent the existential subjectivity in a distinctive way.

Inevitably, the particularity of the existential subject's desire or experience will be shaped and normatized to varying degrees in its encounter with literary language and convention (although an acquaintance with poetry of tradition teaches us how to "experience" poetically, too, and the production of a textual subject may have a reflexive effect upon the subjectivity or self-conception of the historical subject). The discrepancy between existential subjectivity and authorially mediated textual subjectivity is not our concern here, since its dimensions are almost always beyond the reader's ability to assess. The authorial subject position is, however, often accessible to readers through cues in the text or title of a poem; this position may be implicitly gendered.

The product of the authorial subject's negotiation is a poem or prose work in which "someone" speaks (in fiction and some poems, of course, there may be several speaking voices). This chosen voice belongs to the textual subject, the "I" who speaks in the text. The "I" speaks a "self" that may be seen to occupy a certain discursive position (as when a masculine textual subject speaks with the rhetoric and values of "failed intentions," *shiyi*). This "I" speaks interest and desire that arc read as its own but that are tacitly understood to, in some sense, "speak for" the existential subject in a multiply mediated way. Textual subjects can be presented as masculine or feminine, regardless of the gendered position of the authorial subject or the biologic sex and social gendering of the existential subject. Both men and women can choose to represent, persuasively or not, what they believe to be the interests and preoccupations of their gender opposites. If they do so, they may or may not assume the authorial subject position of the gender opposite. Of course, both men and women may also retain their gendered position as authorial subjects to produce a same-gender textual subject. Or, again, both men and women may speak their own gendered interests through an oppositely gendered textual subject. In poems I have defined elsewhere as speaking in the "literati-feminine" voice, the textual subject is feminine, whereas the authorial subject position is gendered masculine, with the feminine text subject serving as a vehicle for the interest of a male readership.

The array of possibilities I am suggesting here, in identifying junctures at which the positions provided by a strongly gendered social system can be operative in the process of representation, reveals my own position regarding the relation of gender and text. The assumption that there is a "litmus test" for authorship by women, or a "feminine signature" lurking in the text that consistently identifies a text by someone who is biologically female and socially feminine, if only we can locate it, is doomed to frustration. (In most cases, normal reading practice in China would have made the question of the author's sex moot; the sex of authors to whom works are attributed was almost always known, although there were cases of misattribution and, no doubt, concealed authorship.) Based on biologism, this assumption about the relation of gender and language would presuppose an essentialized femininity that "carries through" to inevitably mark a text—even when, as in traditional China, the conventions and language out of which that text must be produced evolved historically to represent masculine subjects. The problem for women writers seems, in fact, quite the opposite: how might they manage, despite the odds, to endow texts with signs of their feminine subjectivity?

In practice, Ming and Qing authorial subjects in assuming either gendered position came to have at their disposal (as composition by women increased and diversified) multiple voices belonging to possible textual subjects of both genders that might be learned and produced. There were, of course, certain compositional elements—such as the location of the gaze—that could serve as cues to the genderedness of authorial subjectivity. For women writers of lyric poetry, the practical question was whether to use conventional masculine and feminine textual subjects and voices created from a masculine authorial position; to use feminine subjects from earlier song traditions such as the *yuefu* associated with composition by women; or to use new feminine subjects produced either by reinscribing the subject positions provided by literati writing or by constructing new voices and topics for feminine textual subjects.

Self-representation in Authors' Prefaces

Few descriptions or images of women as legitimate producers of texts appear before the Ming and Qing dynasties. Until the Song dynasty, only the names and words of those protected by very high social status, such as women associated with dynastic courts as learned teachers of women or imperial consorts (and, in rare cases, a daughter or sister of a prominent official or poet), and those occupying, conversely, low social status, such as singers and courtesans with no "respectability" to lose, were very likely to have their names or writings preserved.[10]

Because courtesan writers displayed themselves physically and in written texts to men in public settings, they were not "respectable" in the eyes of polite society and in some periods were not legally eligible for the position of first wife in the household of an elite family. They were not, thus, regarded as bound by the Confucian strictures to seclusion and silence surrounding family women, and their verse was expected to address a readership of men whose interests in them were sentimental; an "air of powder and paint" in their writing was not out of place. Daoist women who socialized in mixed company and produced poetry were regarded as comparable to courtesans in their lack of the propriety characteristic of the wife.

In all periods, but particularly before the Ming dynasty, a woman who learned to write in normative masculine voices, topics, or aesthetic modalities might be praised as an exception to the rule, someone who had transcended the mere prettiness of women's poetry by writing as a man. Gao Zhongwu, editor of the mid-Tang anthology *Zhongxing jianqi ji* (Collected poetry of the restoration period) offers somewhat double-edged praise of Tang poet and Daoist woman Li Ye (*zi*, Jilan, fl. mid-eighth c.) in his characterization of both her personal and literary styles as more masculine than feminine.

> Whereas for gentlemen there are many different kinds of conduct [*bai xing*], for women there are only the four virtues [*si de*: respectful speech, chaste conduct, women's work, and modest demeanor]. This, however, is not so in Jilan's case. In appearance and manner she has a masculine boldness [*xiong*], thus the import of her poetry is, in the same way, reckless [*dang*, "disregarding the usual limits"; also "licentious"].[11]

As a poet, Li Jilan is judged superior for her ability to write in masculine voices; she is the only woman included in Gao's anthology. However, this ability, described as a result of her "masculine" temperament, makes what she says seem uninhibited and "reckless" compared to the norm for women's proper speech. The "masculinity" essential for good poetry is also the source of an implied judgment against Li's character as a woman.

The terms in which Xin Wenfang, author of the twelfth-century *Tang caizi zhuan* (Records of literary geniuses of the Tang dynasty), defends women writers suggest that they were customarily regarded as disruptive and immoral. In this construction, writing women could be represented as guilty of improperly displaying themselves and as expressing excessive and unseemly desires dangerous not only to themselves but to others. Xin responds to those who demonize women writers by addressing some of their objections in his sympathetic representation of women as legitimate writers of poetry.[12]

> Alas! It is certainly true that pen and ink are not the proper occupation of women. However, granted that, what are we to say about it when even so they do employ them? Now, if they are allowed to evade [the way of] heaven/nature, and if their deportment is not strictly correct, then their poetry becomes a device for self-

advertisement, or else one may find pieces full of envious feelings among their compositions, or poems describing clothes, wine, foods, wild behavior, and rich ornaments. These would not be fitting, to be sure. Such poems encourage what is wrong among the people at large. How could they represent the "Guanju" principle?

In his argument, Xin situates woman's voice in poetry in the "Guo-feng" (Airs of the states) section of the *Book of Odes*, quoting the Mao commentary to the first song, "Guanju" (The waterfowl) to show that women's speech in poetry may indeed be considered virtuous.[13] He goes on to rebut criticism of women writers by describing early exemplars in positive terms and inviting a reconsideration of the negative view.

> In periods subsequent to the *Book of Odes*, Ban Jieyu grieved over an autumn fan because the favor shown to her was so short-lived; Xie E sang in praise of willow floss and snow for their sharing the same whiteness. Those who follow the "seven commandments" [by Ban Zhao] will reform their moral character; those who hear Cai Yan's *Tartar Flutesong* feel their hearts are breaking.[14] All these women, with unsullied integrity and admirable sincerity, wishing to let their thoughts and feelings be known abroad, made use of literary composition in order to express themselves. Moistening the brush at their lips, they revealed the resolve in their hearts. How can we say that in such cases uncontrolled profligacy has caused people to strike a blow at virtue and restraint and to run to excesses of corruption? Think about it for just a moment! Can women's writing really be described like that?

As this textual subject speaks in the interests of literary women, the representation of them opposes the strictest construction of a gender ideology that could silence women, yet Xin's own gendered authorial subjectivity is not entirely without its effects upon the woman in the text. There is a point at which another representational discourse, that of woman's body, breaks through the representation of woman as writer.

> In this book, I note in turn each of the refined and honorable gentlemen of Tang, and likewise I shall scatter abroad the fragrance of those bright blossoms of the inner apartments. With their tapestried hearts and silk-embroidered mouths, their sweet marsh-orchid sentiments and refined lily-orchid temperaments, they are truly worthy of admiration!

The conflation of the appeal of her poetry with her desirability as a woman results in a romanticized and ambiguous representation of the woman as a writer. Furthermore, in a long lyrical concluding passage, Xin characterizes the subject matter of women's poetry exclusively as their feelings of grief and suffering at the absence or loss of husbands and lovers. Thus, a restrictively "feminine" representation of the woman writer, one with a certain drift toward the body, emerges from this text, the product of a sympathetic reader of women's poetry whose masculine authorial position shapes representation.

When women began to be more audible as speakers on their own behalf from the late Ming on, they provided evidence through their self-representations in prefaces to their collected works that many educated women desired to regard themselves as legitimate participants in literary culture. They also show that earlier representations of the woman writer could undergo a sometimes dramatic refiguration as women spoke of their own relation to writing and study. The wide-ranging conception of possible subject matter and the passion for poetry and learning expressed in the following lines excerpted from authors' prefaces displace the notion that women had a single poetic topic and reveal that they might actively seek opportunities for study and intellectual development, although they might do so only after performing their domestic duties.

> From the time I was a small child, I have been perversely single-minded about poetry. I studied Cai Yan's lines written on northern yew bark, and I borrowed Empress Zhen's brush and inkstone.[15] Pale writing silk has tethered my heart, and the red and yellow [colors used for punctuation and emendation in texts] have been in my hand for more than twenty years. On winter nights or summer days, whether happy and carefree or melancholy and ill, there is nothing I have not expressed in my poetry.[16]

> The "family treasures" in my husband's household amounted to no more than the books in a small library. I would remove my hairpins and earrings and read by the window until roosters crowed the dawn. And though unable to set my hopes on the examination hall, I became so absorbed in study that even when it threatened to ruin my health, I was unable to stop.[17]

The preface is by convention spoken in the voice of "authorial subject" (that is, it is spoken by a textual subject presented as the author of the poems to follow). Thus the one who speaks in a preface is customarily read as intentionally speaking in a more directly auto-biographical manner, more confidentially disclosing the existential self, than those who speak through the voices of verse. In their constructions of feminine textual subjectivity, a few of the extant prefaces reveal an unconcern on the part of the author with the implications of representing the self as a literary woman; especially after the mid-eighteenth century prefaces sometimes contain quite explicit attempts to rationalize and legitimate an active participation in literary culture. But for many women of gentry families the desire for such participation could conflict with a concern for disapproval or a reluctance to disclose the private self to an unknown reader's eye, should their writing be circulated or published. Their most immediate readers would be family members, most of whom would be keen judges of their propriety, on behalf of the family name. Because the conventions of the preface required an account of how the poems to follow came to be written, the preface invites the representation of woman as writer, as someone with thoughts and feelings and the desire to speak them out. But many women attempted to minimize or avoid such a representation in their prefaces, preferring to use the discourse of women's virtue, which is based upon a rhetoric of duty and obedience.[18]

Since gender ideology made the language that produced the broad concept of "women's virtue," *nü de*, and that of the discourse of literature, *wen*, incompatible without appropriate mediation, such a conflict of discourses could lead to an incoherent or inappropriate representation of self. The convergence of the desire to recognize the self in representations as literary and the desire to retain the image and status of an exemplary daughter, wife, or mother could express itself in prefaces where the illusion of a unitary self is disrupted by a blurring or shifting of the subject between two different discourses. Under the stress of competing imperatives, desires, and the demands of address, the coherence of self-representation may be disrupted by breaks, fragmentation, or contradiction. To resolve this problem, many women attempted to create self-representations in which writing could be assimilated to women's virtue.

The following preface by Zha Changyuan of the early Qing provides an example of how women attempted, not always with complete success, to observe the conventions of the preface by speaking of their literary pursuits while foregrounding "women's virtue," and how this double agenda could create strains and contradictions.

> Starting from the time my hair was tied in tufts, I was ordered by my mother to accompany my elder brother, Jieyan, in receiving instruction. First studying the *Shi jing*, the *Nü xiao jing* [Classic of filial piety

for girls], and the two works *Nei ze* [Guidelines for the inner chambers] and *Nü jie* (Instructions for women), I completed my basic studies with the works of the four [Confucian] masters [*Lunyu* (Analects), *Daxue* (Great learning), *Zhongyong* (Doctrine of the mean), and *Mengzi* (Mencius)]. Next I went on to learn to recite several hundred Tang poems, chanting them under my breath but not having time to learn how to explicate them. From the time that I put up my hair with a hairpin [age fifteen, marriageable age], I stopped my reciting and studying and took up women's work. In leisure time left from needlework, I took the poems I had previously learned to recite and carefully studied them on my own, coming to understand the general meaning of most of them. Sometimes I went to my elder brother in Shimen to ask about points I was not sure of. As for the study of tonal prosody [learning to compose tonally regulated verse, *lü shi*], it was always a case of "I see the hunt and my heart feels glad."[19] However, since I was not very bright, I had never been able to compose poetry; moreover, because it is not the business of women, I did not dare presume to do it. If, inadvertently, there was a small song, I would promptly destroy it by burning it, not even keeping a draft. Then when I married my husband, Jingxuan, we enjoyed the rare [achievements in poetry] and resolved the doubtful behind the doors of our own apartment. I sang along with my husband for sixteen years before, unluckily, I was suddenly designated a widow [*wei wang*, literally, "not yet deceased," one who has not yet joined her husband in death only because of remaining obligations].

Zha goes on to say that, as a widow with duties to her husband's parents and to her children, "my desire to chant poetry left me." However, after the marriages of her children were accomplished, she was able to "read and interpret the poetry of famous masters through the ages, as well as the many poems by ladies, my mind so taken up with them that I have often gone without food and sleep." Describing how she has collected poems by women, edited them, and organized them into an anthology, *Mingyuan shixuan* (Poems by notable ladies), she concludes,

> I hid it away in a bamboo case so that I have had easy access to it for chanting the poems, and by this means I have been able to allay that "I see the hunt and my heart feels glad" sickness of my youth. If the gifted ladies of the land would send me some of their precious writings to supplement this compilation with what has not yet been collected in order to make it a more comprehensive work, it would indeed be my great good fortune! (Preface to *Mingyuan shixuan*, quoted in Hu Wenkai, 426–27)

Viewed as a site of negotiation, this preface illustrates the tension between two forms of self-representation. Foregrounding her dutifulness and obedience, the "author" as textual subject assigns much of the responsibility for her literary activity to others: her mother "ordered" (*ming*) her to study; her brother solved puzzles in reading; after she married, poetry was a pastime of her husband's when at home, and she accompanied him. Although admitting a strong desire to write, she counters this by saying that she was not learned or talented enough and that in any case literature is not an occupation for women. Contradicting herself, she tells how she continued to study on her own and even "inadvertently" produced an occasional "small song." (She avoids the explicitness of "I wrote" and "poems," *shi*, in favor of "there was" [*you*] and a more general word for verse, *yong*.) But, virtuous again, she burns her poems and does not keep copies. As a widow, she does not even allow herself the desire to take pleasure in poetry, but she is able to represent herself as self-indulgent later in life, when her household duties are fewer and her obligations as a mother are fulfilled. At this point she invokes a trope of the discourse of literature: she has often "gone without food and sleep" in her enthusiasm. Yet even here, she still refers to her devotion to poetry as a "sickness," an excess on her part or a guilty pleasure. At this moment, the discourse of women's virtue and the discourse of literature at last collapse into each other. Reference to an enthusiasm for poetry bordering on madness or sickness is part of the discourse of literature, but in the context of a woman's preface such a reference can also signify as part of the discourse of virtue, in which the "author" implies that a truly virtuous woman would wish to be "cured" of too much fondness for what is, after all, not her proper occupation. Zha's is a self-representation at odds with itself; fragments of a different discourse that have their source in an alternative subject position break through the dominant "self" and remain in the text as witnesses to tensions that the "author" has been either unwilling or unable to reconcile.

In comparing this self-representation with what can be known about Zha, we should note that she did not, in fact, burn all her poems. In addition to the *Mingyuan shixuan* and another anthology, *Mingyuan cixuan* (Song lyrics by notable ladies), the existence of Zha's own collected poems, *Xuexiulou yin gao* (Poems from Learning Embroidery Tower) is attested in two gazetteers (Hu Wenkai, 426). Moreover, during a period of some 150 years, from the late seventeenth century to the early nineteenth century, seven women surnamed Zha from

Haining in Zhejiang province (the location of Zha Changyuan's family home) are noted in bibliographical and biographical sources as poets who have left collections.[20] Zha clearly belonged to an extended family or clan that encouraged learning and literary ability in its women, and she herself may have served as a literary mentor and model for younger women of her natal and marital families. In cases such as this, a woman's sincere desire to face posterity as a "woman of virtue," and the realities of domestic and gender politics could make the discourse of virtue necessary to varying degrees. The choices made by the authorial subject in constructing a text "author" are determined by the degree to which local conditions and her own sense of propriety make it possible for her to comfortably assume the normatively male position of author.

A self-representation that successfully assimilates learning and literature to women's virtue in a more apparently seamless way is found in prefaces written by Gu Ruopu (1592–1680's), gentry wife, intellectual, poet, and essayist. At her death in her nineties, she had been a widow in her husband's family for all but thirteen years of her married life. She did not, she says, follow her husband in death only because of her obligation to prepare their sons for future success. Thus, her own studies are represented as a part of her duty to her deceased husband and his family, and her poetry is explained as a means of venting her sorrow over her husband's death.

> At this time my husband's father had just been appointed Superintendent of Schools for the Xi-Jiang area, and since I was far away from parents, brother, and sisters, I had enough time to devote myself to a thorough reading of the classics and the histories, so as to drill the poor orphans and help them toward future success. Every day I felt anxious and worried, fearing that I might not accomplish my life's mission and be therefore unable to follow my husband to the grave. Thus it was that in the spare time from my domestic duties, I would get out all of the books in the library . . . [she names classical and historical works], day after day spreading them out and poring over them as though I could never get enough. When my two boys came into our rooms from their instruction outside, I made a point of calling them to bring the bamboo lantern over and to sit in the corner so that I could explain what I had learned, for their benefit. We would not stop until the third watch.

As for Gu's purpose in writing poetry,

Keeping the *sao, ya, ci,* and *fu* by my side, I found release in them, and took my ease in them, hoping to write, after their model, of my own melancholy thoughts and to express my own frustration and dismay.
. . . .

I inscribe this collection with the title *Woyuan xuan gao* (Poems from the Sleeping in Moonlight Gallery). The Sleeping in Moonlight Gallery is where my husband used to rest and consider his plans for future accomplishments. Late spring, 1626, recorded by the widow Huang Gu Ruopu of Wulin. (Hu Wenkai, 208–9)

In this self-representation, Gu, who in 1626 had already been a widow for seven years, subsumes what her biographical information tells us was a remarkable intellectual and literary ability, as well as personal qualities that commanded great respect, to the image of a widow thinking only of fulfilling her responsibilities to her deceased husband before she joins him in death. Even the title she gives to her collected poems directs attention back to her husband. Almost all of the extensive literary activity undertaken by Gu in her lifetime, at least that for which evidence remains in the record, is assimilated to her textual self-presentation as widow and virtuous wife. Yet she knew clearly that literature was "an undertaking for the ages" (*qiangu shi*). In her preface to the collected works of her deceased sister-in-law Huang Hong (her husband's sister had married Gu's brother, Gu Ruoqun), she says, "Poetry is truly difficult to discuss, and for a woman to discuss poetry is even less an easy thing to do." However, she has agreed to write this preface, she explains, "First, because of my sorrow that the Lady is not alive, and second, because of my joy that the Lady has this immortality [*bu xiu*]" (Hu Wenkai, 181). The consistency with which Gu was able to represent her own intellectual and literary activity as extensions of her duty and faithfulness (numerous poems in her collection refer to her life with her husband and to her ongoing sense of loss after his death) was no doubt a major factor in her success as a writing woman and as the founding figure of a lineage of literary women that was still considered to have its source in Gu some five generations later.[21]

Courtesan writers were unlikely to be caught in the snare of the double discourse. The ease with which they might represent themselves as writers is exemplified in the following preface by Liang Xiaoyu to her late sixteenth-century collection of poems on historical people and events, *Yongshi lu* (Poems on history).

> My favorite material for reading and study is history. For gathering
> all things of this world into one's own breast and playing with a
> thousand ages in the palm of the hand, nothing is better than this
> kind of writing. Taking up matters both delightful and horrible, both
> fearsome and endearing, that are contained in the histories, I have
> hastily put together poems in the "long song" style to recite them.
> Borrowing pages from the works of scholars, I have described the
> dark and the bright in the depths of the human heart. The decom-
> posing bones of treacherous sycophants I have treated severely, and I
> have summoned back the pure souls of the loyal and upright. . . .
> One by one I have revealed the unseen spirit and feeling and have
> passed judgment on character. In this, all I have wished to do is to use
> my heart/mind to inquire into the heart/mind. I would not dare to
> [merely] use my ears [what I have overheard] to speak to the ears [of
> others].

Liang presents herself as a writer with a serious purpose, one who believes her work can have a beneficial effect on society.

> This work does not only overturn verdicts [of the past]; the more
> general intent is to provide an evidential basis for future actions. . . .
> Perhaps this work will also gradually spread [among its readers] a
> more extensive grasp of antiquity and encourage the appreciation of
> poetry. (Hu Wenkai, 161–62)

It is likely that Liang wrote her poems on Chinese history for a
commercial publisher. She appears to address a general reading public and to appeal to a desire for self-improvement on the part of potential middle-class, urban readers who might prefer a more accessible format than the dynastic histories. As someone offering credentials for and advertising her version of history, Liang's self-representation opens with an image of power through texts; the subject that
commands this power is not marked explicitly as feminine. After her
first dramatic announcement, Liang pragmatically dispenses with the
autobiographical and focuses on a description of the work itself, evidently feeling no need to justify her position as the producer of the
text. Her social status renders the issue of "women's virtue" irrelevant; moreover, Liang's address to readers is evidently conditioned
more by her desire to be read than by a desire to recognize herself in
the text as a literary woman. Thus, while the instrumentality of texts is
clearly articulated, neither the discourse of virtue nor the discourse of
literature is foregrounded in this self-presentation.

As various arguments for the legitimacy of literary pursuits for women gained currency, and as more women's writings began to circulate outside family compounds, some women began to examine the obstacles they faced in their efforts to write well. When their reflections on these matters began to appear in their prefaces, we can detect the beginnings of a more polemical tone, of a move toward agency; at the same time, the terms of self-representation shift toward the discourse of literature. Shen Shanbao, in her 1846 preface to her critical remarks on the poetry of individual women, *Mingyuan shihua* (Remarks on the poetry of notable ladies), reviews the gender inequities in the scope and quality of education and in the support of study by family members, and concludes that women face great obstacles in their efforts to write poetry.

> Therefore, if she is not someone whose intelligence is truly exceptional, chances are that a woman will never be able to compose poetry well. For those who come from prominent families and have father, elder brothers, and teachers who understand poetry, it will be relatively easier for them to transmit their writings widely. But if they are born into poorer families and marry village commoners, then they will fall into obscurity, and no one will ever know that they existed. Because I have a deep sympathy for them, I do not hesitate to write this book. Although I am inept with language, and my experience is not broad, since my aim is to preserve their fragments of lines and scattered verses, it does not matter whether my own language is skillful or clumsy. (Hu Wenkai, 367)

While she preserves a modesty appropriate to the preface as a genre, this textual subject dispenses with the rhetoric that would validate her writing as part of the duty of a virtuous wife; instead, she represents herself as someone with a duty to literature, specifically women's literature.

Self-representation in "Shi"

Self-representations mediated with the rhetoric and topics associated with women's virtues and social roles were not limited to prefaces. Poems with text subjects who speak of the importance of women's virtues and their devotion and duty as mothers and wives, or of instructing daughters in womanly virtue (but sons in history and literature), may be found in most anthologies. It is difficult to assess the quantity of such verse without greater access to complete collections, but evidence from anthologies suggests that although woman's virtue was a safe and even attractive topic for some writers, most women seized the opportunity for release from speaking "autobiographically" as "author" and freely adopted the wide variety of voices and topics that the poetic tradition offered them. Still, one finds poems concerned with the proper conduct of women and with their "proper" relation to poetry in anthologies even at the very end of the Qing and into the Republican period, when they co-exist with highly polemical verse on the subject of gender inequalities in traditional society.

Women who write poetry about women's virtue cannot very well disallow literary skills for women. They do, however, often establish the models for women's education and interest in literature in a way that assimilates them to women's virtue. A poem by He Yuying (fl. late seventeenth c.), "Guizhong dushu" (Studying in the inner apartments), illustrates the priorities.

> An elegant literary style
> is not sufficient by itself;
> The teachings transmitted from Ban Zhao
> are something we ought to know about.
> Since ancient times, the reason why many stories
> of exemplary women have been handed down
> is not just to make us knowledgeable,
> it's so we can act on their example.[22]

Directly referring to specific poems in the "Airs of the States" section of the *Book of Odes*, the piece "Yonggu er shou" (On the ancients, two stanzas) by Li Yuqing (fl. late seventeenth–early eighteenth c.) explains how each of the ancient poems teaches women appropriate attitudes and behavior (many of the lyrics in this section of the *Odes* are voiced as women's songs). She names the great queens of antiquity instrumental in the rise of the Zhou and the continuation of its ancestral rites, and she says, "Household and state share a single principle." Her emphasis is on women's conduct, but the entire poem asserts that the civilizing influence of the Zhou is embedded in the *Odes*, particularly in the women's songs. This anthology is thus placed prior to Confucius and conduct books as the "progenitor of women's learning" (*nü xue zong*). Accordingly, the study of poetry is essential for women (Cai Dianqi, 3: 8.2a–3a). Another poem by Li, "Fu jie san shou" (Instructions for wives, three stanzas), is in the mode of Ban Zhao's *Instructions for Women*. It contains quite specific advice on duties and behavior, counsels acceptance of fate ("That I become someone's wife / is because heaven ordains it so"), and, regarding the education of children, says, "If they are girls, then teach them how to spin;

if boys, then teach them the *Odes* and the *History*." This piece evades the issue of women's literacy, study, and writing, even as it demonstrates Li's own ability and appears to require a classical education for mothers (Cai Dianqi, 3: 8.3a–4b).

Jiang Hui (fl. early nineteenth century), in her poem "Du *Zhengshi ji* jicheng Zhenpu taishi mu" (After reading the *Correct Beginnings Collection*, I send this poem, offering it respectfully to Zhenpu, mother of the Grand Instructor), expresses her excitement at reading a new anthology of women's verse.[23] In doing so, she makes it clear that virtue and the enthusiastic practice of a poetry that retains traditional aesthetic modalities are not incompatible, implicitly distinguishing *shi* from newer song forms, such as *qu*. In this piece she sketches a brief history of women's verse, noting that "the combination of [literary] talent [*cai*] and virtue [*de*] was infrequent in ancient times — / Ban Zhao and Noble Consort Xu."[24] Jiang has the highest praise for the *Correct Beginnings*. She commends it as a continuation of the civilizing influence exerted by the *Book of Odes* and the confirmation of dynastic brilliance just as the *Odes* had been. The editor has, she says, "chosen widely from among the fresh and new, the refined and unique talents, / with an intuitive reliance upon the classical principle of sincere generosity [of spirit] and refined gentleness [of feeling] [*dunhou wenrou*]," omitting mean styles and strident voices. Jiang speaks of the popularity of this anthology and of the fame assured to those whose work is collected in it. In closing, she remarks that the ranks of women writers have grown under the "protecting shade" *ci yin* (read also "hereditary privilege," entry into the civil service system accorded to sons of fathers who have achieved a higher ranking or have given exemplary service to the state) of their predecessors, and she modestly jokes, "Even I myself will bequeath something to my poetry disciples; / don't mock the little maids who learn from their mistress!" (Cai Dianqi, 8: 2.2a–b). In this poem, Jiang has claimed both poetry and virtue for women, even welcoming the "fame" (*ming*) that comes with publication in a popular anthology. Jiang believes it is easier in her day than it was in antiquity for women to combine literary talent and virtue. By the nineteenth century, some women, such as Jiang, can confidently reconcile women's virtue and literariness in women, constructing textual subjects who, nourished and "protected" by numerous predecessors like the poets Jiang admires, speak openly of fame for writing women.

Performance as Self-representation in "Shi"

All poems are, in a general sense, performances of a complex of linguistic, cultural, and artistic skills. The word "performance" itself has in recent times, however, acquired more specialized meanings in such contexts as linguistics, literary theory, and cultural studies.[25] In this discussion, I use the word to refer to instances in which women as writers assume authorial positions and interests that are gendered masculine and display their literary competence in reproducing text subjects modeled completely upon those originating in literati poetry. From one point of view, such a practice might be considered worse than useless for the purpose of a woman's self-representation, since no position conventionally identified with feminine voicing is accessible to the reader through the text itself. However, in these cases, the desire of the existential subject for participation in literary culture, the intention to display, as author, her own competence in the skills and forms by which literary ability has been measured, and a personal investment in the issue or affective dimension of the topic could all be represented through the mediation of a performance of this sort. In literary performances of their own, literati poets "imitated," *ni*, or wrote "in the manner of" other literati poets, sometimes using specific poems as models; unlike women writers performing masculine voices, these poets did not have to assume an oppositely gendered authorial position. In performance, women writers, like men, also could increase the challenge by selecting the distinctive styles of specific literati poets or taking specific literati poems as their models. The following poem by Lu Qingzi (fl. 1595) is a performance of the "ancient style," *gushi*, as practiced by a pre-eminent poet of the Tang dynasty.

In the Manner of Li Bo's "Ancient Style"

Heavy gloom blocks the daytime sun,
mild and bright cycles to cold and harsh.
What confusion of mingled snow and sleet!
Leaves fall, scatter from plants and trees.
Ceaseless wind sweeps cruelly through the night,
where can the roosting bird find shelter?
The traveler's fur-lined coat wears thin,
the jobless scholar stores up grains and beans.
So it was, when the old men of Shang mountain
took to the road, bound for a hidden valley.[26]

Lu here reproduces several elements of her model: the dynamic forward movement of Li Bo's personal style, the element of political comment that belongs to his *gufeng* (ancient style), and his interest in the rejection of worldly life by these worthies, expressed in the two poems he wrote about them. That Lu chose to perform the style of such a major poet, a poet whose genius had always been considered elusive for would-be imitators, is itself a claim that she is making about her own ability and her knowledge of Li Bo's work.

The conventional literati topical subgenre "meditation on the past," *huaigu*, evolved as an expression by a masculine subject of feelings about the rise and fall of dynastic fortunes, as a recognition of the pathos in dreams of glory and permanence, and often as a guarded expression of concern for the loss of a more ideal social and political order in the speaker's present. Nostalgia for a past age or a hint of loyalty to a fallen dynasty might inform the "meditation." The *huaigu* is always anchored to a particular site of past human glory; in contemplating this site, the speaker perceives the fundamental transience of human endeavor but also recognizes the momentary splendor such human desires and efforts produce. As a performance, the following poem in *pailü* form[27] by Qian Fenglun (fl. 1680) reproduces the masculine textual subject of the *huaigu*. Its persuasiveness suggests not only that she claims technical command of the form but that topics and emotions traditionally representing the socially gendered concerns and attitudes of men could, as women's literary practice extended to performance of a variety of such topical subgenres, be explored by women writers with an engagement that went beyond performance, expanding the range of interests that women's voices might address.

Meditation on the Past: In Jade Effusion Garden[28]

Running currents of West Lake sing
of ages long in the past;
wind is folding the snowy wave,
water dragons dance.
They say a royal carriage once
held a splendid hunt;
a thousand riders with carved saddles
camped along the water.
Flageolets and songs at dawn
pressed on Phoenix City clouds;[29]
at evening their flags and banners

furled Dragon Mountain rain.
Across the lake now autumn winds
are blowing in the reeds;
red cherry-apple's suspended fruits
are the cuckoo's soul.
The glory and beauty of earlier times
today are truly gone;
from the river village in waning light
washing blocks ring clear.
In the Palace of Renewing Splendor
only moonlight is brilliant;
by the Hall of Virtue and Longevity
only spring grass comes to life.
Events of an age, mere floating clouds,
could they be fixed or secured?
Lake currents, crying and murmuring,
swirl round ruined city walls.
The descending sun strikes dread in my heart
transfixes my distant gaze;
no purple clouds do I see there,
this evening in the southland.[30]
                    (Cai Dianqi, 2: 3b–4a)

Like the Song dynasty, the Ming had made its final stand in the south. Given its closing lines, this poem may be read as a reflection on the loss of Ming imperial power to the Qing. As a performance, it is both a demonstration of skill and a claim that a woman, speaking through a conventionally masculine text subject, may formulate "masculine" attitudes concerning political change through time and the vanity of human aspirations. We may ask: Is Qian "speaking for" men in this poem, exercising her art in the performance of an established form of masculine subjectivity, or is she representing herself, revealing in a mediated way her personal thoughts and feelings about larger questions of history and the dynastic process? Did the involvement of gentry men and gentry women in loyalist resistance to the Manchu conquest in the south offer Qian the possibility of identifying her own subjectivity with that of the masculine speaker of the *huaigu*?

Representing the Feminine Self Through Reinscription

The boundary between performance and reinscription is marked by a shift to a feminine textual subject. In certain cases this shift is signaled by a single detail or is otherwise subtle enough that the reader may remain uncertain about how the voice in the poem is gendered. Literati topics could be performed with the inclusion of a minor detail that reinscribes the textual subject as feminine. The title of the next poem by Lu Qingzi promises a performance of the masculine model, and indeed the poem is very close in style, topic, and language to Tao Qian's poetry, especially to his "He Guo Zhubu, Er Shou" (Matching Recorder Guo's poem, two stanzas), which speaks of the tranquil pleasures of private life in the country.[31] However, one phrase that Lu borrows from this poem might ambivalently cue the reader to read for either masculine or feminine subjectivity.

> *In the Manner of Tao Qian*
>
> Living quietly, little to do
> with the busy world,
> it is my nature
> to forget elaborate hairpins.
> Green waters brim
> in flower-scented pools,
> cool winds are stored
> in leafy woods.
> Minnows play
> in wavelets and ripples,
> wild birds sing out
> their pleasing notes.
> At evening comes
> a timely rain,
> white clouds deepen
> on the highest peaks.
> Plants in the yard are bathed
> in nourishing moisture,
> above mountain meadows
> clouds send showers flying down.
> Completely relaxed
> I give thoughts free rein
> to range far, far —
> and when I like
> pour for myself
> some homemade wine.
>   (Zhong Xing, *Ming-*
>   *yuan shigui*, 32.1a)

The phrase "forget elaborate hairpins" (*wang huazan*) is borrowed from Tao's poem. But "elaborate [or ornamental] hairpins" (*huazan*) is ambiguous: women, as well as men serving as officials, pinned up their hair, but a man in retirement (or a woman living a rustic life in the mountains, as Lu did) could adopt a more relaxed hairstyle. To "forget" or discard the hairpin would be the attitude of a man who wishes to disengage himself from career and politics, a man such as Tao Qian himself. Because the adjective *hua*, however, is equally appropriate for describing a woman's hairpin, Lu has used Tao's diction and scenario in a performance that produces a textual subject resembling a double-exposure print. Recognizing a textual subjectivity that belongs to Tao's verse, readers aware of Lu's authorship may also find themselves cued by the strategically placed *huazan* to hear a feminine voice.

A more unambiguous reinscription of a specific poem by a major poet is a treatment of Du Fu's "Qianyuan zhong yu ju Tonggu xian zuo ge qi shou" (Song in seven stanzas, written in the Qianyuan period [758–59] when I found myself staying in Tonggu district) by Shen Huiyu (fl. mid-eighteenth c.). Du's poem was written soon after the traumatic events surrounding the An Lushan rebellion and the occupation of the capital Chang'an, where he may have been detained by rebel troops for a time before he could make his way back through the war-ravaged countryside to find his family. The text subject in his poem speaks as an old man half-demented with loss and sorrow. He mentions in turn various family members, all scattered and inaccessible, whom he is helpless to care for or console. The elements, animals, birds, and simple people express their pity for the speaker. In an aggrieved voice, he begins the sequence:

> There's a wanderer, a wanderer,
> his name is Zimei;
> on his white head the matted hair
> is hanging past his ears.
> Yearlong he gathers chestnuts
> like the monkey's keeper Zu,
> spends evenings under a cold sky
> in the mountain valley.
> No letters from the central plain;
> he's not able to return.
> His hands and feet are frozen stiff,
> skin and flesh feel dead.
>
> Woe! ah, woe! my first song, oh —
> a song already forlorn;

a doleful wind on my behalf
comes down from the sky.[32]

The two stanzas still extant of Shen Huiyu's "Ni Shaoling qi ge" (In the manner of Shaoling's "Seven Songs") are based closely on the original in form, diction, and mood. However, a change of textual subject to feminine and a concern specifically for female relatives distinguish Shen's version.

I

There's a mother, a mother,
living in the mountains;
red maples and bitter bamboo
mesh across her gate.
Gibbons cry out in the mist,
mountain bogeys howl;
she sends me letters year after year
telling of all her hardships.
I want to go to care for her
but obstacles block the road,
winds blow apart cloud chariots.

Woe! ah, woe! my third song, oh —
a song to break the heart!
Better if you bear a girl
to abandon her by the road.[33]

II

There's a little sister, a little sister,
I grieve that she's fallen to ruin;
her years are not yet thirty
and long has she gone astray.
Orphans play around the bed
asking for chestnuts and pears;
winds blow hard through thin curtains,
lamplight flickers and gutters.
Her white-haired mother worries,
wondering when she'll return;
on the overgrown stream that small boat
has never come back again.

Woe! ah, woe! my fourth song, oh —
a song to double one's fears.
Gaze out to the west, along the stream,
see the sinister look of the waves.

(Cai Dianqi, 4: 7.4a)

Zhu Jingsu (early nineteenth c.) produced a reinscription of the same Du Fu poem, but emphasized the speaker's lament for his own fate present in her model. In eight successive stanzas, the feminine speaker tells of her unhappiness as a married woman. This version, "Dong ri zuo duange ba shou, fang Shaoling ti" (On a winter day I compose eight 'short songs,' copying Shaoling's style) achieves an intensity comparable to that in Du Fu's poem.

> It wouldn't be hard to conceal a sword
> and with it take my life,
> but regret for this sweet child
> would tear my heart with grief.
> Right, left, you've learned to walk
> but your feet are still so tender.
> Already you can understand
> more than a hundred Tang poems;
> but now you are in your third year
> and weaning is never easy.
> Let me see you through these early years,
> then I'm determined to say farewell.
>
> Woe! ah, woe! my sixth song, oh —
> my vitals and heart are burning.
> Ghosts and spirits weep for me
> out in the weedgrown suburbs.[34]
> (Cai Dianqi, 10: 4.2b–4b)

Du Fu's series of poems, as a medium for the expression of anguish, provides an affective basis, as well as a formal model, for Zhu's gendered reinscription of anguish in the context of a woman's life.

Like literati poets, women made use of intertextual references in the form of partial quotation from, or allusion to lines in, well-known poems by major literati poets. In a poem with a feminine text subject, the effect is not only to enhance or complicate meaning and give the well-read reader the pleasure of recognition but also to appropriate the masculine voice and referent for feminine self-representation. Several anthologized poems by women, for instance, reinscribe the lines from Du Fu's poem "Yue ye" (Moonlit night, or Night of the Mid-Autumn moon). In Chang'an, separated from his wife and children and missing them, he is touched by the thought that the children are too young to understand the pain of separation: "Across the miles I feel such tenderness for my little son and daughter; / they don't yet know what it is to think longingly of Chang'an" (Du Fu, 9/14b). Zhu

Rouzi (fl. mid-seventeenth c.) restaged this moment from the perspective of a wife missing her absent husband: "Our foolish boy comes crying to me; / last night he dreamed of Chang'an."[35] It is she who must comfort the boy; as she reminds her husband, the children are not too young to be affected by his absence.

In the following poem a memorable image in a line from a poem by Du Fu expressing his feeling for the poet Li Bo is reinscribed for the feminine voice. After Li Bo appeared to him in a dream, Du Fu worried about the welfare of his friend; he wrote two poems of counsel and consolation for Li, addressing him directly. One poem represents the dream presence of Li as still strong, and the text subject, still in bed, looks up: "Light of the setting moon fills the rafters; / I still seem to see your face there where it shines" (Du Fu, 3.4a) Poet Lin Yining (1655–after 1730) composed the following in memory of her friend and mentor in poetry and painting, Chai Jingyi (*zi*, Jixian).

Lament for Chai Jixian

The painting of Mahakasyapa on the wall
is a relic of your work, still beautiful and vivid;[36]
in the cool of night, it gives off such a shimmering light,
I glance at it sidelong, not daring to look directly.
I recall seeing you lower your brush to begin,
living energy full, your spirit whole.
The way you painted was not demure and dainty;
rather, you drew spontaneously, green sleeves flying.
Often I longed to throw off the duties of worldly life
and follow you in service to cinnabar and white lead.
How could I know you would not be here to guide me?
Suddenly, in death you abandon me forever.
I am moved to the depths, my sorrow is like the clouds —
your beauty and grace I keep like a treasure concealed
in moonlight shining on the beams of my room.[37]

In addition to regendering the lines of major poets, women writers also reinscribed various topical subgenres historically used for men's complaints of lack of recognition despite their worth and talents and of the alienation suffered by the man of integrity because of slander or corruption. The examples below show how two of the most often exercised of these topics, "the lone wildgoose" and "the withered tree," could be converted to the representation of women's problems; here both goose and tree allegorize the condition of women who are isolated or unappreciated, mediating feminine subjectivity.

In such reinscriptions it is gendered interests that are represented, but the ease with which the "masculine" topics of alienation and lack of recognition were reinscribed for women makes clear that the conditions these complaint topoi addressed were perceived to be present in the experience of both men and women.

The Lone Wildgoose

It resolves not to fly with the flock in formation,
soaring aloft, alone and apart in integrity.
In the reed-grown river, its shadow is an illusory mate,
in rushes on the bank, it is used to having no companion.
Through endless night, it shares solitude with the moon,
until with dawn it breaks through clouds, alone.
Calling, calling, its voice is choked with sorrow;
if there is a widow, just don't let her hear.[38]

The Withered Tree

Long has it stood alone by the empty hall;
morning after morning it looks toward the sun.
Who will be able, with his own hands,
to transplant it, making it into
the "fragrance in the back courtyard"?

(Wang Yu, 168.7a)

In the latter poem, Zhang Wanyu (dates unknown; before 1821) has combined the feminine image of the tree in the back courtyard with the masculine image of the withered tree, reinscribing the latter for the representation of a woman's complaint.[39]

Numerous scenarios of literati poetry were available for reinscription into spaces of self-representation for women writers. Chief among those that underwent change at their hands was the "boudoir" scenario. In the literati versions of the boudoir, women are alone and sad, or they are entertaining or dreaming of men. Women writers reclaim the boudoir as their own domestic space; although they sometimes write of their loneliness within the household and of the absence of the men they love, the majority of their poems show the boudoir as the "women's apartments," a de-eroticized place of work, leisure, and companionship with other women. Poems set in the women's rooms display a range of activities including sewing, study, chess, writing, playing and listening to music, teaching (children and other women), conversing, religious activities (meditating, chanting sutras, reading religious works), painting, dinner parties, resting, and sleeping. It is a

place where, late at night, there is even time for the solitary pleasures
of contemplation, reminiscence, and quiet walks alone in the courtyard and garden. Dreaming, in women's poems, does not always
produce a meeting with husband or lover; there are many poems in
which the dreamer meets her mother, a sister, a woman friend, or exotic immortal (*xian*) women. The women's courtyards are places, too,
of holiday preparations, of games and other entertainments, such as
playing in the snow (see "Xue meiren" [The snowwoman], by Guo
Peilan, in Cai Dianqi, 8: 4.3b–4a). The following poem by Qian Fenglun (above) is a product of a convivial gathering of women. The text
subject speaks as one of a company with mutual interests in poetry
and music.

> *Banquet on a Winter's Day*
> *at the Residence of Chai Jixian*

Come full cycle, the stars tell
the year is almost gone;
the sky is cold
the winter bleak and gloomy.
Plants all wither
under severe frost;
scattered dews dry
in early morning sun.
Happily I meet with
these good and modest people,
and we sit down together
in a house of iris and orchid.
As we laugh and talk,
spring breezes rise;
in friendly accord
we busy ourselves with our writings.
Pictures and books
are strewn about the room;
on the table of yew wood
we set out zithers and lyres.
Since the birds have left
the courtyard is even quieter;
when clouds hang low,
shadows on blinds grow dim.
Living a secluded life
keeps noise and dust distant;
thoughts transcend,
range wide and far away.

Time's flowing light goes
swift as a thrown shuttle;
such good times together
are I fear too easily lost.
And so, inspired by wine,
we raise our voices in song;
from beginning to end
enjoying to the fullest
the bounty of this good hostess!
(Cai Dianqi, 2: 4.2a)

Qian Fenglun's poem celebrates the occasion of a dinner at the home of a senior member of the Banana Garden Poetry Club, a group of women (most of them related to each other in some degree) from prominent Hangzhou gentry families.[40] Chai Jingyi (zi Jixian) and her sister Chai Zhenyi, were known as painters as well as poets.[41] (The poem by Lin Yining translated above refers to one of Chai Jingyi's paintings.) In this occasional poem, Qian politely represents Chai as a "goddess" by referring to her apartment, called Ningxiang shi (Lodge of Condensed Fragrances), in the family compound in language borrowed from the ancient poem "Xiang furen" (Lady of the Xiang River), one of the "Jiu ge" (Nine songs) of the Chu ci (Songs of the south). In that piece, the speaker promises to provide the goddess with a fabulous home beneath the waters, constructed with aromatic woods and decorated with fragrant flowers; Qian refers to Chai's apartment as "a house of iris and orchid." With its emphasis on harmony, tranquil seclusion, and an unworldly attitude, this scene illustrates the adaptation of motifs of self-presentation found in literati poetry of "retirement" to the purposes of women writers. The text subject activates the literati rhetoric of the reclusive private life, but positions herself and her companions in the place of the feminine other, the inner rooms of the elusive river goddess of Chu.

Scenes of women waking from sleep or unable to sleep are staples of literati verse, beginning at least with the ballad lyric "Yu suosi" (Longing for someone) and the Gushi shijiu shou (The nineteen old poems) of the Han dynasty. Suffering from the absence of a loved one, this text subject or text image is easily read as one corresponding to the interests of a masculine authorial subject. The masculine subject of an "up at night" scene in literati poetry is, by contrast, typically anguished over his failure to realize personal goals, the decline of the times, or the future of the state. In the following poem, one of three addressed to a friend, Lu Qingzi opens with a classic literati boudoir scene.

To Lady Gu (Second of two)

Moonlight illumines an empty court,
half the double door is shut.
A sweet aroma emanates
from silk bedcurtains —
you've just awakened from dreams.
Petals from the trees
have finished falling,
restless birds have settled.
Not raising pearl blinds
you chant sutras in the night.

(Zhong Xing, *Ming-
yuan shigui*, 32/13a)

Establishing the boudoir setting and positioning a gaze that operates from within the room, Lu initiates the "up at night" motif, only to deny expectations with a shift to a calm exterior night scene recalling Wang Wei's "Niaoming jian" (Birdsong creek).[42] Then, as though she has opened these two possible routes of development for the poem only to play with the conventions and the differing expectations they raise, she rejects the conventional scenario for a completely different representation of the woman up at night. Here the gendered interests of the authorial subject and of the woman who is addressee determine representation. The final lines refer again to the chamber, but the figure of the woman in the inner rooms is blocked, unavailable to the gaze, which now appears to originate from outside the blinds. The dramatized Lady Gu herself is an absence, first behind the silk bedcurtain and next behind the pearl blinds, finally absorbed in a religious exercise that is the antithesis of love-longing. Her presence is signified only by a voice.

The women's rooms are used for study, and women often chose to represent themselves studying and writing. The following two poems express a desire to associate the self with books. In the second piece, the subject falls asleep with her book and dreams of immortals. A distinct change from the more eroticized sleeping and dreaming of women in literati poetry, such a self-presentation would seem more in keeping with the experience and attitudes of an unmarried girl or wife in a gentry family.

Cold at the West Window
Qian Fenglong

A rainstorm passes through,
sweet blossoms are drenched;
when the wind comes,
green leaves yield to it.
With inkstone and red paste
I study the *Changes* of Zhou,
more aware than ever
how remote from the world
is my little window.
             (Cai Dianqi, 2: 4/5a)

Early Summer Night
Tang Qingyun (fl. 1814)

I sit at night outside my room,
thoughts very calm;
the seasonal weather is clear and mild,
it's a late-evening sky.
The breeze through shoots
of young bamboo is supple;
a rising moon beneath new leaves
on the plane tree is round.
I search for a good line of poetry,
 pick one out and write it down;
when eyes get tired from reading,
I fall asleep embracing the book.
Suddenly a complete dream, somewhere
that's like a realm of immortals;
After I wake, the scent of incense
still clings to the hem of my sleeve.
             (in Hongmeige zhuren and
             Qinghuilou zhuren, 5.17b)

The paradisiacal feminine world of the immortals is another literati scenario that women writers could reinscribe with their own interests. In standard literati versions of the *youxian* (wandering with immortals) poem, a man travels to a sky or mountain world where he sees and describes beautiful immortal women. Sylphs entertain him with rare foods, long-life cocktails, music, and dancing; he seems to be the only masculine presence. Like men, women might long for release from the trouble and boredom of daily life, imagine flying to a skyscape or cavern world of rarefied beauty and pleasure. However, in women's versions of this scene, the relation between the text subject and the immortal women is more likely to be one of companionship, with the subject joining the troop of immortals. There is no eroticizing, through description or innuendo, of the band of immortals. The following poem by Xu Quan (fl. eighteenth c.) illustrates this popular form of reinscription.

A Dream of Heaven

Summoned, I go
to a hideaway of immortals,
remote, among islands.
I am carried off
in a car pulled by Cinnabar Phoenix,
a carriage drawn by Red Dragon.[43]
Below we pass over the five sacred mountains[44]
and bow to pure emptiness;
above we touch the sun and moon,
coursing the highways of heaven.
I turn, look back at the human world —
it is utterly lost in the distance;
on level terrain, all is effaced,
shrouded in haze and dim.
Cloudy mountains make several dots
like islands in a sea.
I want to leave it all behind,
to freely soar on high.
Suddenly I hear, out of the void,
music of flutes and drums;
beautiful women, reserved and modest,
come riding the cloudy ethers.
It seems as though we've met before
somewhere in a far blue sky;
I go with them to Jasper Pool[45]
as one of the immortal pages.
Star maidens, moon sisters,
rank after rank they come;
while here I see no spirits
.with tiger tails and leopard teeth.[46]
My only care is to eat delicacies,
drink wine of liquid colored clouds;
with a single cup my heart feels clean,
my bones are light and tingling.[47]
But soaked with sweat, the covers grow cold
and soon I wake from my dream.

Lonely lamp, lonely pillow —
what a dull place!
The west wind sighs and whistles
through the plane tree in the court.
(Cai Dianqi, 4: 1/3a–b)

In speaking through *shi* lyrics, women regularly took opportunities to reinscribe literati practice. In poems on historical events and people, *yongshi*, for instance, they wrote about women in history, often about several women in a series of stanzas, sometimes implying that historians were at fault for neglecting to represent them adequately, as in the following piece by Wu Yonghe (fl. 1700).

Lady Yu

King Xiang was truly a hero;
his lady, too, was a rare woman.
What a pity the Grand Historian
said nothing for the record
of that beautiful person's death.[48]
(Shen Deqian, 31.12b)

The pleasures of solitude and withdrawal from political life were expressed in literati verse in the rhetoric of seclusion, as noted above. For gentry women, seclusion and withdrawal might be constructed somewhat differently, since such women did not have the opportunity to choose between public and private life. Staying exclusively "within the gates," all but a very small number of educated women lived their entire lives in relative "seclusion." A few gentry women, such as Lu Qingzi, might live in homes that were apart from centers of social and political activity. Lu and her husband lived a private life on Cold Mountain, and although the couple maintained social relations with many friends and officials, Lu represents her own life as remote from village and town. In the following poem, she invokes both Tao Qian and Li Bo; the closure reinscribes lines from Li Bo's famous poem "Da suren wen" (Replying to the question of an ordinary fellow), also known as "Shanzhong wenda" (Question and answer in the mountains).

Living the Quiet Life

Closing the gate,
I am free to do as I please;
my humble lane
is overgrown with vines.

The color of willows
excites birds' noisy chatter;
the glitter of waves
makes shades of evening calm.
Quietly, falling petals
blanket the ground;
clouds in the void, serene,
lean upon forest.
You ask why I roost here,
hidden away —
beside my bed I have
a stringless zither.
(Zhong Xing, *Ming-
yuan shigui*, 32.9a)

Although the zither (*qin*) is a companion of the gentleman in "retire-ment," it is also coded feminine in poetry, in certain contexts referring to women. The simple, unornamented, or unpainted (*su*) zither is mentioned in the ancient *Li ji* (Ritual) as essential for the performance of the rites; it connotes purity. In literati poetry, the plain zither, closed gate, and untraveled lane signify an unostentatious, "uncontami-nated" private life. A *suqin* (referred to by Lu in her final line) is not by definition stringless, but the phrase is associated with Tao Qian, who liked to strum a stringless, undecorated zither when he was happily in his cups.[49] Thus the undecorated zither, which may be understood to be "stringless" in a context such as this that invokes motifs of retire-ment and uses the rhetoric of Tao Qian, is doubly coded — for the pu-rity and integrity of private life, and for femininity. Lu uses a closure which, like that of Li Bo, does not offer the questioner an explicit an-swer but makes its point through imagery. Compared with Li's image of peach blossoms drifting on a stream, Lu's "answer" has the effect of bringing the subject indoors and carrying the meanings of seclusion and femininity in the same image.

Former officials in the retirement of old age also speak of the joys of leisure and solitude. The following poem by Cai Wan, written in the mid-eighteenth century, reproduces this mode with a subject who is free from duties and able to enjoy leisure in her old age; only the refer-ences to chess, music, and opium cue for the feminine.

Sitting at Ease Among the Pines

In the leisure of old age, indolence from opium
has made me even more muddled;

> new chessboard or old music score, I have
>   trouble figuring it out.
> For nourishing life, at last I know
>   an idled heart is best;
> withdrawing from the workaday world
>   is good for aches and pains.
> On a small path in the breeze of evening
>   I return walking slowly;
> by the sand dike a bright moon
>   gradually rises.
> Completely rinsed clean of longings
>   for worldly life,
> I've nothing to do but lean on a solitary pine
>   singing a poem.
>   (Cai Dianqi, 2: 1.6b)

Landscape and friendship are two important topical areas in Chinese lyric poetry; reinscription in these topics brings special problems that cannot be addressed in the present format. Landscapes represented in poetry may signify as a "natural" space of self-definition, an "otherness" that can reflect back the speaker's subjectivity. In addition to the descriptions of mountains and "uncultivated spaces" frequent in literati poetry, the artificially "natural" landscapes constituted by the enclosed spaces of garden and courtyard often represented in poems by women can be considered in this light. For gentry women who were not traveling or living in the country, the gaze on the world was usually from inside to outside, with window or porch railing as a containing frame. This gaze reverses literati representations of women looking out, where the woman at the window is seen from the outside.[50] There are, of course, also treatments by women of landscapes beyond the family walls. Friendship poetry, too, deserves a separate discussion, one that addresses its reliance upon and re-coding of the elements of the literati lover's discourse.[51]

Invention: Beyond Reinscription

Ming and Qing women revealed their inventiveness as poets through the ways in which they defined speaking positions for themselves by regendering established subgeneric voices and reinscribing conventional scenarios, image codes, and lines from literati poems of the past. In addition to altering in these ways the traditionally masculine voices in poetry, they introduced new topical subgenres to treat matters important in women's experiences. The autobiographical narrative poem or poem series as a subgenre in women's poetry during the Ming and Qing, for instance, does not derive from a literati model. Women writers found resources for the form in textualized folk poetry in feminine voices and in the poetry of the inner life as exemplified by that of Ruan Ji (210–63 C.E.) and Tao Qian, but as a form, the verse autobiography had no established precedent. Gentry women brought not only a cultivated literary taste to the writing of verse autobiography but also their own classed and gendered interests. Many of the autobiographical poems were written for ritual occasions, often the sixtieth birthday of the author, or in the same year the author fulfilled her responsibilities as a mother in arranging for the marriages of her children. Xu Yunhui's (fl. late 18th c.) "Fang huai" (Casting off my cares), written at the age of 56, and Bao Zhilan's (fl. late eighteenth c.) "Wushi ganhuai" (At 50: my innermost feelings) are representative examples.[52] In such poems, one finds the subject representing a life course and assessing the success or failure of her life as a daughter-in-law, wife, and mother in terms of ideals associated with these roles. Women writers also drew new boundaries for already established subgenres. The poetry of friendship, a literati staple, expanded to encompass literary treatment of friendship between and among women, and the ancient ballad complaints about loss of love, spoken in feminine voices, were infused with new vitality by authors prepared to introduce a wider range of desire and complaint under the old ballad captions.

Distinct from inventiveness (though perhaps only in degree), invention — as I wish to use the word here — involves a different process of self-representation for women. Neither a "performance" nor a reinscription of a literati model, nor a simple re-presentation of attitudes generally considered correct for gentry women in their roles in Ming and Qing society, invention draws upon the coded images of literati poetry (although they may signify differently) and may for its purposes "perform" segments of established topical genres or *yuefu* models or mark a normally masculine-voiced genre with feminine voicing. But the author here welds her materials to a purpose different from that of any of her sources, seeming to articulate a new aspect of feminine subjectivity. Self-presentation in such poems may be covert or direct, may veil itself in irony or openly cross boundaries of propriety. The occurrence, and preservation, of such poems is a sign of a changing consciousness among women who wrote; especially from the mid-eighteenth century on, some writers become distinctly more inventive, calling upon literary resources and exploring their creative possibilities more freely than before. They go beyond the models that either literati poetry or poetry by women has offered them. Such voices might reveal something that had always been present in women's experience, remaining inaccessible through the literary discourses available to women; or, it might point to something newly important in women's experiences that can find expression only through the constructive work of invention. What is new to the poetry of gentry women writers who were inventive in the sense intended here lies both in what is being said by a feminine textual subject and in how it is expressed in verse.

Discussion in this section is limited to selected instances of invention in poems featuring voices of complaint in poetry by Qing women. The English word "complaint" is inadequate to represent the several established poetic subgenres in which literati poets could complain, sometimes in feminine voices. The *sao* (courtier's complaint derived from a style in the *Chu ci*), the *yuan* (plaint, grievance), and the *yong-huai* (disclosing in verse one's troubled innermost feelings and thoughts, sometimes with indirection) are major modes, but there are also conventional titles that begin "In Misery Over . . . " (*ku*), "Lamenting . . . " (*bei*), and the like. In verse characterized by invention, the authorial subject asserts itself over the strict demands of both literary convention and the proprieties of women's speech, creating a text subject that challenges conventional textuality (which accepts the authority of the literary model and works from it, maintaining generic stylistic features) and questions the norms of social custom and gender proprieties. The complaints expressed are not merely local and personal; often they are generalized to suggest that a certain problem affects the lives of all women.

The following poem by Zhuang Tao (fl. mid-eighteenth c.) is titled with the *yuefu* caption "Xinglu nan" (Hardships of the road).[53] Zhuang uses the conventional opening phrase for this ballad, "Haven't you noticed . . . ," but quickly diverges from the many earlier models under the caption. The traditional subject matter of this ballad—primarily the hardships of travel, separation from loved ones, the hard life of the military campaigner, the loss of youth and promise—has most often invited the use of a masculine speaker, but Zhuang Tao intends to take this caption and enlarge its frame of reference to include the hardships of women's lives within the household.

> Haven't you noticed
> how hard traveling on the road of life
> has nothing to do with distance
> (hundreds or thousands of miles)
> or with number (how many times
> you leave or enter your gate)?[54]
> Oh, it's the danger!
> Where every step is a stumble!
> Where thorns spring up!
> Don't call Taihang dangerous,
> don't call Meng Pass trail steep.
> Doesn't anyone realize, within courtyard and door
> how traps and snares oppress us every day?
>
> Eat a plum, you'll know for yourself
> how sour it is;
> taste malt, you'll know for yourself
> it is bitter.
> To the left there are wild dogs!
> To the right, leopards and tigers!
> In front, they draw longbows!
> Behind, mighty crossbows!
> I want to keep going
> but I make no headway —
> where to find help for this woe?
> The mountain demon's grotesque antics!
> The raging of dark winds!
>
> I look up and envy the lone swan
> coming over the sea,
> it flies with the wind
> far off and high —
> who will dare to insult it?
> (Wang Yu, 170.16a)

Developing the theme of hardship, Zhuang asks what it is that makes "traveling" through life so difficult. For earlier poems under this caption, hardship and danger are often found on a journey, or in the ups and downs of public life. But these dangers, figured as perilous mountain paths, are not worse, the speaker claims, than the dangers to women of staying at home, inside the gates. Traps, snares, wild carnivorous animals, deadly weapons, monsters, and violent weather are the metaphors for threats she faces within the household.

Zhuang incorporates coded images from Tang poets Li Bo's "Shu dao nan" (The road to Shu is hard) and Li He's "Gong wu chu men" (Sir, don't go out the gate!), as well as the mountain demon, *shan gui*, from one of the "Jiu ge" (Nine songs) of the *Chu ci* and echoes the directional threats from the ritual survey of spaces found in the two "summoning the soul" songs in the same early anthology. Drawing on another early source, Zhuang has evoked the dark, *yin*, winds (connoting the violence and anger to which the speaker is subject) of the feminine-voiced marriage complaints in the *Book of Odes*. The sometimes lurid imagery and strong voices of Li Bo and Li He seem to mark a limit for the idiosyncratic masculine voice of complaint. The intertextual link to specific poems by these poets gains Zhuang similar qualities of vividness and power for her own voice of protest; because her speaker is feminine, however, she exceeds the conservative limit for feminine voices in a way that seems intended to shock.[55] This is not a protest that submits to the Confucian injunction that literary voices, even in complaint, should be indirect and gentle, nor does it reflect the injunctions to circumspection and forbearance seen in the conduct books for women. Adhering to no single model, Zhuang orchestrates a forceful woman's voice of complaint. It has an intensity and urgency new to lyric poetry by women, even if we include *yuefu*, which permits more freedom from decorum in the construction of textual subject. This is evident if one compares the subject in this poem with the older model of the suffering wife in ballad-style lyrics written under the caption "Boming fu" (The ill-fated wife) frequently used by women writers. The final lines of Zhuang's poem, modulating suddenly to the calm and solitary image of the bird in free flight, shows the speaker reflecting on the difficulty, for the feminine subject, of assuming the position of the noble-minded but often misunderstood figure (symbolized in literati poetry by the high-flying swan), solitary but recognized by the like-minded as a superior being. This position has been reserved by literary tradition and by society for the masculine speaker. The feminine speaker, beset within the gates, cannot gain such a position and will continue to bear insult with no recourse. For men, "entering the gate" and staying at home are equivalent, at the very least, to being safe; but for women, the speaker claims, the place of greatest danger is within the home, and not going out is no guarantee of safety. In this poem, Zhuang has redefined the conventional understanding of "inside" and "outside," with reference to the household, from a woman's point of view. Hers is a voice that claims

authority in the matter ("eat a plum and you'll know for yourself")
and appears to speak as much about the situation of women generally
as about the speaker's personal problem.

Fan Huzhen (fl. 1800) wrote the following poem as a response to
the death of a young woman of the Yang family, a girl as yet unmarried who had ended her life after the death of her betrothed, thus becoming a *zhen nü*, a girl whose chastity was guaranteed. The language
of this poem, on the surface univocal in its celebration of the suicide of
a *zhen nü*, contains certain features that alert the reader to the possibility of an underlying irony and a subjectivity that maintains a critical
distance from its topic.

Chaste Girl Yang

> Once the spring flows out,
> water won't go back to the mountaintop;
> once the bowstring's released,
> no arrow returns to the bow.
> On the day one's name is promised,
> one's life is pledged as well;
> Daughter Yang's unbending courage
> was equal to this charge.
> She studied, but not so much
> as to learn too many words;
> since ancient days, how many boys
> have ever learned to read?
> This girl lives, but is not alive —
> she fills a five-foot coffin.
> This girl died, but isn't dead —
> her name is on everyone's lips.
> We could say it's because she doesn't live
> that she hasn't really died.
> Oh, woe and alas!
> At her throat was a white silk sash
> like a "white rainbow suspended";
> it lifted up those "dark and mothlike brows"
> onto the pages of history.
>   (Hongmeige zhuren and
>   Qinghuilou zhuren, 4.11a)

The opening lines have the diction and sense of folk homily and oral
wisdom; they refer to the finality with which a marriage agreement
places a woman in the role of a wife (there's no going back). For the
most correctly virtuous, like chaste girl Yang, that commitment may

lead to an early death in the name of virtue. After a middle section in which the language of paradox raises the possibility of irony (although it cannot yet be confirmed), the closing lines effect a sudden shift to the highly poetic language of verse that idealizes and objectifies women. This shift, and the contrast it entails with the preceding language, calls attention to the level of language itself, and a gap opens between language and referent that encourages the reader to sense an irony, a discrepancy between the aestheticized representation of the death of a woman and the actual physical death of the suicide (the silk sash that strangles her is depicted in the language used in poetry for the flowing waters of a mountain waterfall, and the dead body is elided, reduced to a poetic pair of beautiful eyebrows). With the "help" of the beautiful sash, the "eyebrows" are "raised" to a fame that lives on in the pages of (local) histories (*qing shi*), where the many names of chaste girls and widows are honored by being entered into the historical record. If this poem falls short of constituting an attack on the custom of chastity-related suicide (some of which, in the case of widows, especially, were prompted by the family of the husband), it is nevertheless very close to what Mikhail Bakhtin, in his discussion of narrative, called a "double-voiced" utterance, in which a textual subject speaks in terms at odds with the position of the authorial consciousness. The authorial consciousness leaves its imprint upon the language of the text, however, in the form of unexplained contradictions or incongruities.[56] Fan Huzhen's poem brings a new approach to the commemoration of a chaste suicide; few gentry women of her day would write or could expect to have published a poem that openly criticized such a practice, and, aware of this, Fan has used the expedient of irony, in this reading. Earlier lines of the poem contain echoes of the injunctions in women's conduct books, but the univocal effect is undercut by the play with paradox in the middle section. In the translation the final poetic phrases have been enclosed in quotation marks in order to emphasize the break with the more vernacular diction of the preceding lines.

The sixth-century ballad "Mulan ci" (Song of Mulan) narrates the story of a filial daughter who, disguised as a man, offers herself as a conscript in place of her aged father. She fulfills her duty heroically and chastely, is commended by the Khan, and returns home to resume her women's work without a backward glance. She is not interested in material rewards or honors for her accomplishments (in fact, it would be difficult for her, as a real woman, to receive titles and property without revealing her deception). Reworking this material, Wang Caiwei (fl. late eighteenth century) places it within a polemical frame in which the speaker is able to comment critically upon the social attitudes that devalue daughters and the gendered roles that make it impossible for women to win recognition and economic rewards. Rather, women are dependent upon family status and marriage for their own status and economic well-being. The speaker's commentary constitutes a direct criticism of the gender hierarchy.

Song of Mulan

When a boy is born, don't feel such joy!
When a girl is born, don't be so annoyed!
When a girl is born, just "hang a bow"[57]
and don't use cloth strips to bind girls' feet.

Haven't you heard of Mulan?
She stood in for her father
and campaigned for the Khan.
. . . .
[Describes Mulan leaving home.]

In the women's rooms, how can we be noble?
Armor, brocade caparisons, saddles of gold
are beyond our reach.
In the women's rooms, how can we be heroic?
We don't get to "Forge through frost, over snow,
and hear the raging waters."
. . . .
[Describes Mulan in the north desert, her audience
with the Khan after victory, her return to her parents,
and her changing back into women's clothes.]

Now the east neighbor's daughter
is a good-looking girl;
poor in the morning, she plies her needle,
poor in the evening, she weaves.
The west neighbor's daughter
has trunks full of clothes;
she brags that she'll marry
a lad with the golden tortoise.[58]

A man is enfeoffed as a marquis,
but what does a woman have?
If she wants to get the yellow gold
she must wrack her brains for a plan!
(Cai Dianqi, 5: 2.3a)

The speaker in this poem uses an informal, critical, transgressively assertive voice that rejects differential treatment of children based on their sex, the practice of footbinding, the restriction of (gentry) women's arena of action to the boudoir, and their economic dependency on family status and marriage. She critiques social practices and the gendered roles that make it impossible for women to win recognition and economic rewards, reserving heroism and its material benefits for men. The older "Song of Mulan" is not a literary model for Wang; rather, it becomes a vehicle and support for the speaker's real concern, her criticism of inequities in the gendered roles of men and women. It is not Mulan's chastity or filiality that Wang foregrounds; for her it is Mulan's achievement of heroic stature, recognition, and the possibility of material reward that is exemplary. The compositional technique that allows the speaker to cut into and out of the narrative frame for the purpose of commentary is one that nicely serves Wang's purpose of reading the Mulan story for new values. Like Zhuang Tao and Fan Huzhen, Wang Caiwei constructs a textual subject that assumes a critical stance toward normative practices within the gender system. As mediated self-representations, the poems of these writers not only place themselves at a certain distance from existing models and compositional norms; they also clearly reveal the emergence of a critical attitude on the part of authors toward their own experience, an assumption that women constitute a solidarity group on the basis of shared experiences, and a willingness to assert the value of women's lives.

The examples offered above of Ming and Qing dynasty women's self-representations in prefaces and *shi* poetry constitute only a minuscule portion of the rich body of material still available as sources for historical and/or literary inquiry and pleasure. As scholars and other readers achieve a more thorough familiarity with these writings, we will gain a substantial basis for a more informed and subtle understanding of late imperial women's literary practice and the lives implied by the self-representations in their writings.

One aspect of self-representation, touched upon in passing above, deserves further consideration as we try to grasp the significance for women of literacy and self-representation in texts in a traditional, patriarchal gender system. For Ming and Qing women writers, the representation of self in literary texts involved engagements with literati models and the challenge of proving literary competence. But the assimilation of women writers to a tradition defined by literati practice is only part of the story. The development of women's poetry in these times was rapid and complex. Learning a set of skills derived from literati literary culture, women writers began in various ways to adjust and refashion the scripted voices and conventional scenarios of tradition in order to express their own lives and interests. Self-inscription, however, is not merely self-expression; it also produces constructions that represent an experiment with identity or desire, constructions that writers may confront in a moment of self-recognition or self-knowledge. The achieved statement or self-construct, contingent as it may be, may come as a revelation to a writer, to be accepted with a genuine sense of discovery. The exploration of thought and feeling through language is a part of the process of self-discovery, and this enhanced self-knowledge — really a process of growth — is one of the writer's greatest rewards. Moreover, represented selves, constructed through textual subjects and accepted as aspects of their own subjectivity by the writers themselves, may then circulate to women readers, offering them a variety of "feminized" subject positions to occupy in the process of reading. Thus, these new literary models of self create, reflexively, an effect upon life for both writers and readers. They continue, through the ways in which they explore discursive possibilities and through the new subject positions they make available, to produce new forms of consciousness, affecting self-conceptions and social behavior on a larger scale. In this dimension, too, beyond their strictly literary implications, the processes by which women writers "changed the subject" were pregnant with consequences for literate women of Ming and Qing.

Part III

Poems in Contexts

8

Writing Her Way Out of Trouble: Li Yuying in History and Fiction

ANN WALTNER

Female literacy in Ming China was a double-edged sword, and nothing illustrates this more clearly than the story of Li Yuying, who lived in the early sixteenth century in Shuntian prefecture (that is, Beijing). Yuying was arrested and sentenced to death for fornication and unfilial behavior because she wrote two poems her stepmother judged to be lewd. From her prison cell she wrote a memorial (*shu*) to the emperor that vindicated her and gained her release. The poems and the memorial earned her fame: her poems have been repeatedly anthologized, and versions of the memorial are preserved in a variety of Ming and Qing dynasty sources. Yuying became the subject of a popular vernacular story, anthologized in the *San yan* (Three words) collection edited by Feng Menglong (1574–1646). Her story resonates with a literary trope discussed elsewhere in this volume, that of the young poet who dies an early and tragic death. Yuying is saved from an untimely death only through the emperor's intervention. A benevolent emperor saving a doomed poet from an evil stepmother — is it any wonder that the story was told and retold?

At least a dozen texts of the memorial have been preserved. They are not identical, although they closely resemble one another. The earliest version that I have located is contained in Li Xu's (1505–93) *Jie'an laoren manbi* (Miscellaneous jottings of the old man from Jie'an), a miscellany published posthumously in 1597 by Li Xu's grandson. Li Xu was from Jiangyin, and the text was published there. It is thought that the miscellany was finished rather late in his life.[1] Essentially the same version of the memorial is reproduced in the *Falin zhaotianzhu* (Forest of laws: a candle to illuminate the heavens), a Ming legal casebook. Another version of the memorial is included in the *Gujin nüshu* (History of women, ancient and modern), edited by Zhao Shijie (fl. 1638).[2] Other early versions of the memorial are imbedded in collections of biographies of exemplary women: one in an edition of the *Lienü zhuan* (Biographies of exemplary women) dated 1591; another in the *Nü fan bian* (Rules for women; preface dated 1602), edited by Feng Ruzong; and yet another in the *Gui fan* (Rules for the inner chambers), by Huang Shangwen. The texts of the biographies and even the illustrations in the last two texts are identical: the only difference is that the *Gui fan* is packaged together with a number of other instructional texts for women, which underlines the didactic nature of the text.[3] The story also appears in a Japanese edition of the *Lienü zhuan*, dated 1763.[4] These five versions resemble one another quite closely: there are occasional variations in wording, but the texts are fundamentally the same, and the order in which the story is related is identical.

There are other versions of the story, most of which include Yuying's memorial or excerpts from it. One version is contained in the *Guose tianxiang* (National beauties and heavenly fragrance), a compilation by a man of the Ming dynasty named Wu Jingso, a text that juxtaposes tales of vice and those of virtue on separate registers of the same page.[5] The early Qing author Zhu Yizun (1629–1709) includes both the memorial and the poetry in his *Jingzhiju shihua* (Tranquil intentions: Talks on poetry).[6] Other accounts reproduce neither the memorial nor the poetry. For example, a very short (63-character) version is contained in Tan Qian's (1594–1657) *Zaolin zazu* (Miscellaneous treats from the forest of jujubes): it preserves the text of neither the poems nor the memorial, though it mentions both.[7] Qing dynasty local gazetteers of Yuying's native place tell the story as well, as does a collection of anecdotes about Beijing, the *Rixia jiuwen kao* (An examination of old texts from under the sun). Short versions of Li Yuying's biography appear in collections of biographies of poets, such as Qian Qianyi's (1582–1664) *Liechao shiji xiaozhuan* (A collection of poems from the various dynasties, with short biographies).[8] The *Liechao shiji* biography and the poems are reproduced in the mammoth eighteenth-century encyclopedia, the *Gujin tushu jicheng* (Books and illustrations, ancient and modern).[9] And finally, the poems themselves are repeatedly anthologized, in places like the *Mingshi zong* (Collected

Ming poetry) (where the entire story, including excerpts from the memorial, is reproduced from the *Shihua*)[10] and in collections of poetry by women, such as *Mingyuan shigui* (Poems by famous beauties) and the *Cuilou ji* (Kingfisher tower collection).[11]

Perhaps the most famous version is the vernacular *San yan* story "Li Yuying yuzhong songyuan" (Li Yuying, imprisoned, pleads injustice) published in the 1620's.[12] In this version, Li Yuying's story becomes subordinated to a family melodrama, and the plot of the melodrama revolves relentlessly around her evil stepmother.

Part of the subordination of Li Yuying is simply the sea of words: even by the rather luxurious standards of the *San yan*, this is a long story, 33 pages in a modern typeset edition. But the *San yan* author elaborates some parts of the story in greater detail than others, to fashion the story into a cautionary tale rather than a celebration of a heroic young woman who writes.

The story does not have a proper *ruhua*;[13] rather, it is introduced by several pages that warn of the problems caused by stepmothers who neglect or abuse the children of a previous wife in order to promote the interests of their own children. The narrator cites a poem on evil stepmothers that concludes:

> It's not because women's hearts are so poisonous,
> But because men have not taken the long view.[14]

That is, a man must take some responsibility if the children of his first wife are abused by his second wife. Thus the story can be read in part as a warning of the dangers of widower remarriage.[15]

The narrative then moves to the particulars of this domestic catastrophe. Li Xiong, a chiliarch in the Embroidered Uniform Guard, has recently been widowed. The death of his wife, the Lady He, left him in charge of four small children, three girls and a boy. When he performed well at work, his children suffered, and when he did an adequate job in the domestic realm, his work suffered. "Truly," the narrator tells us, "it was a case of his not being able to fulfill both public and private."

But Li Xiong knows how to resolve the dilemma: he marries again, so that his wife can take responsibility for the private realm. The match with the Lady Jiao that ends so disastrously for his children is made for their benefit: they need a mother. Lady Jiao is jealous and scheming, even when Li Xiong is alive. Indeed, her misbehavior causes Li Xiong to send her back to her family. But Jiao Rong, her brother, counsels strategic patience, and she returns to her husband and his children. Lady Jiao bears a son of her own, Li Yanu. She continues to treat the children of Lady He so badly that Li Xiong sends them to school to escape her malevolent attention. From what we know about women and education in sixteenth-century China, it would have been extraordinary to send girls out to school. Nonetheless, that is the solution imagined by the *San yan* narrator.

When Li Xiong is killed in battle in 1519, Lady Jiao immediately begins plotting on behalf of her own son. She sends the ten-year-old Li Chengzu to search for his father's bones. About a third of the narrative is occupied by this search. He does not set out alone, as the other versions of the story imply, but rather goes with a servant who is working in tandem with Lady Jiao. When the boy becomes ill, the servant abandons him to die. But the child encounters a kindly old woman who nurses him back to health and a resourceful monk who helps him find his father's bones. When he returns with the bones, the astonished Lady Jiao poisons and then dismembers him. This tragedy is immediately followed by the sale of his sister Taoying.[16] Lady Jiao prepares to move the diminished family to a smaller dwelling, and Yuying considers the possibility of moving in with her paternal grandparents. According to the *San yan* author, it was this conjunction of circumstances that led Yuying to write "Parting Swallows." She observes some swallows repairing an old wall, which is near a new nest, and says: "These swallows are just wild animals. They leave in the fall and return in the spring, yet there is a day on which they do return. I, Li Yuying, will leave this room today, and have no plans to return" (567). Thereupon she composes a poem. The storyteller has given us an explicit context for the poem: Li Yuying is unhappy about moving. Her meditation on the swallows' nest is in this reading a desire not for a future nest with a man but for a secure and stable place to live now. It is the lament of a sad child, not that of an erotically aroused young woman.

The second poem is, according to the *San yan* author, composed somewhat later. Yueying, the youngest child, has been turned out on the streets to beg. Lady Jiao and her son have gone to celebrate the fiftieth birthday of Jiao Rong. Yuying, left at home alone, becomes despondent and considers suicide. Given the fate of her siblings, she has no realistic hope of finding a husband, and she has already reached the advanced age of sixteen. She looks into the garden and sees bright colors, reds and greens, and hears the chattering of swallows. She notices that there are elm seeds scattered on the ground, round like coins. She then composes "Sending off Spring." Still alone, she finds the Lady Jiao's invitation to Jiao Rong's birthday party, and on the reverse side, she writes down both poems.

Upon her return, Lady Jiao notices writing implements on a table. She suspects that Yuying has been writing about her and demands to see what she has written. Yuying says that she was just writing some poetry — there was nothing special about it. Lady Jiao immediately suspects a lover: she does not need to read the poems to know what has happened. The accusation makes Yuying blush, which is taken as further proof of her lack of virtue. Lady Jiao and her brother beat the girl until she is bloody. The noise attracts the attention of the neighbors, who are unable to intervene, but whose musings on the girl's innocence provide the reader with even more confirmation that the poetry was innocent.

Yuying is driven in her desperation to attempt suicide. She hangs herself with the strips of cloth used to bind her feet. But because her stepmother has neglected to look after her properly, her clothes are ragged and her bindings years old. The bindings break, and Yuying falls to the ground, in a scene both tragic and comic. Bindings, simultaneously symbolic of female eroticism and containment, are the weapon with which she attempts suicide. Ironically, her stepmother's neglect has saved her life.

Fearing scandal, Lady Jiao decides to submit the case to the Embroidered Uniform Guard. The narrative is quite cynical: if she herself hounded the girl to death, there would be scandal. It would be much more convenient if she could arrange to have the girl sentenced to death by the authorities. Jiao Rong takes the girl to the yamen, which is staffed by men who owe him favors. She is sentenced to death. The short-story writer provides one more indignity: one of the wardens in charge of her plies her with kindness in the attempt to seduce her. But she sees through the ploy and fends him off.

Her final rescue comes at the instigation of the emperor, who requests that prisoners who had been unjustly sentenced send memorials outlining the particulars of their cases. Li Yuying thus writes her story. (The *San yan*'s version of the memorial is only half as long as versions transmitted in other sources.) The emperor investigates and finds that Li Yuying is telling the truth. The sentences for the various villains are given: Lady Jiao's sentence is made one degree heavier because she is the stepmother (rather than the birth mother) of the child she killed. Jiao Rong's property is confiscated, and Yueying is ransomed. The emperor wants to punish Lady Jiao's child, but Yuying persuades him to show the child mercy, both because of his youth and because he is her father's heir. But he is forbidden to inherit the father's title. And to make the happy ending complete, the storyteller informs us that all three daughters marry literati.

The story ends by citing two poems, the first quoted from the *Lienü zhuan* version of the story (see discussion below):

> Li Yuying,
> Her father died, her family crumbled.
> "Envoi to Spring," "Farewell to Swallows":
> Her mother suspected a lover,
> And she was sentenced to heavy punishment.
> In danger and in sorrow: but she was not punished!
> She told her story in a memorial,
> And then the accumulated wrongs were made right.

The second reads:

> A blind-hearted stepmother is crooked as a hook
> Only on account of her son did she hatch the
>   poison plan.
> If we forgive her, blood will turn into the Western River
> It would be hard to wash the shame in the
>   Yellow Springs.

"Envoi to Spring" and "Farewell to Swallows" are the titles of Yuying's poems. The Western River refers to a cosmic river in the *Zhuangzi*, and paired with the Yellow Springs, a conventional reference to the underworld, it refers to the permanence of the stain that would ensue from forgiving the cruel stepmother.

The focus of the storyteller thus returns to the cruel stepmother, where he began. The last words of the story are given not to details of the narrative, but to a poem that returns us to the universals of the story. The theme of the cruel stepmother is an important one, and the problems of the politics of multiple motherhood were played out both in real life and in fictional arenas. By framing his story in terms of the cruel stepmother, the *San yan* editor has removed our gaze from Yuying.

Let us attempt to return our gaze to Yuying, by a close examination of the memorial she herself wrote. In order to do this, we need to turn from fiction to other kinds of sources. The earliest versions of the memorial I have found come from the Jiangnan area in the waning years of the sixteenth century. The story itself took place in the capital in 1524. The distance in both time and space between the events and the texts purporting to record them creates a serious problem for the historian. What happened to the story in the seventy years and hundreds of miles between the events and the first record we have of them? The events of this episode place it as a northern story from the early sixteenth century: the documents that describe it (with the exception of two Qing dynasty gazetteers from Shuntian prefecture and the legal casebook, about whose publication we know almost nothing) are products of southern culture in the late sixteenth and early seventeenth centuries. Genres that preserve the Li Yuying story in the richest detail derive from a particular Jiangnan culture: the gossipy *suibi* miscellanies, the lavishly illustrated *Lienü zhuan* biographies of exemplary women, and the vernacular story of the *San yan* are a product of a specific historical (and geographical) moment. They were produced by a society with wealth and leisure, a society that fetishized both the book and female virtue, a society where increasing literacy among upper-class women had sharpened the debate over the relationship between a woman's virtue and her education. The story of Li Yuying is a northern story appropriated by southern literati. The world of the Embroidered Uniform Guard is a far cry from the world of the southern literatus: the men who inhabited both worlds were powerful, but whereas the power of the former depended on military might and proximity to the emperor, the power of the latter depended to a large degree on literary skills. The southern fascination with the Li Yuying story might well represent a fascination with the alien northern world, seen through the eyes of a young girl who writes.

Li Xu, who recorded the earliest version of the memorial, provided some clues as to how the text made its way south. A local scholar copied (*chao*) the memorial in the fourth year of the Jiajing reign (1525),[17] and Li Xu had personally seen the memorial and recorded it.[18] Li positioned himself as an eyewitness, not to the events he recounted but to a copy of the text that recounts them. The voyeuristic old scholar is the mechanism whereby the memorial becomes public: the communication meant for the emperor thus becomes anthologized and in the public realm. The text in which Li anthologized the memorial is a genuine miscellany with 574 entries on a wide variety of subjects: he did not seem more interested in women, virtue, or poetry than he is in anything else. The entry on Li Yuying is entitled "A memorial in which a girl charges her stepmother with falsely accusing her."[19] The version cited by Li Xu is, at 1,044 characters, among the longest of extant versions of the memorial. It is also the most immediate: it is present in a miscellany, which is less ideologically oriented than some of the other texts we shall examine, and Li Xu claimed that he personally saw a copy of the memorial.

The memorial is a carefully constructed and crafted document. It was occasioned by a specific act, in which the emperor invoked ancient notions of correlations between the human and the cosmic realm and of his role as an intermediary between them. Because the weather in the summer of 1525 was unseasonably hot, the emperor prepared to issue a limited amnesty. He solicited memorials from prisoners who believed that they had been unjustly sentenced. His clemency would move the cosmos, and the weather would improve. Releasing prisoners in hot weather had a long tradition in China. The tradition of Hot Weather Assizes (*reshen*) was begun in the Ming dynasty by the Yongle emperor (r. 1403–25) and was continued regularly (though not annually) until the fall of the dynasty.[20] The particular order soliciting memorials in 1525 has been preserved in the *Shilu* (Veritable records), a meticulous accounting of court events.[21] Thus Yuying had a specific audience — the emperor — and a particular purpose — clemency. She wrote her story as if her life depended on it: indeed it did.

The summer of 1525 was to continue to be a hot one for the Jiajing emperor: official opposition to his reluctance to be named the adopted heir of his uncle and predecessor, the Zhengde emperor, would finally erupt in public demonstrations in the seventh month. As a result of the demonstrations, a number of officials were flogged or demoted. Sixteen of those flogged died as a result. An emperor embroiled in such a controversy might well want to take advantage of an opportunity to get the cosmos back in order.[22] And since one of the rhetorical positions that the emperor and his partisans adopted in the argument concerned the "natural" feelings existing between parent and child, he might have taken particular interest in a case of a young girl claiming abuse at the hands of her stepmother. Thus we should remember that from its inception the memorial played a role in imperial discourse about clemency and cosmic harmony, as well as about family tensions and political legitimacy.

The story embedded in the memorial runs as follows. Li Yuying was from Shuntian prefecture (that is to say, Beijing) and lived in the late Zhengde (1506–21) and Jiajing (1522–67) reign periods. When

Yuying, the oldest of four children of Li Xiong, an official in the Embroidered Uniform Guard, was six, her mother, a woman of the He family, died. Her father, pitying his motherless children, remarried. His new wife, a woman surnamed Jiao, was young: she was only ten years older than Yuying, and she was ambitious. In due time, Lady Jiao gave birth to a son, Li Yanu. In the fourteenth year of the Zhengde period (1519), Li Xiong was killed while accompanying the emperor fighting "bandits" in Shaanxi. Local histories confirm that the emperor was personally involved in battles with the Mongols in Shaanxi in 1519, although no mention is made of Li Xiong.[23] Tan Qian, in his authoritative annalistic history, the *Guoque*, gives the following brief account for the fourteenth year of the Zhengde reign period: "The Chiliarch of the Embroidered Uniform Guard Li Xiong accompanied the emperor to fight bandits in Shaanxi, and died there. The affair does not appear in histories. But it does appear in his daughter Yuying's memorial, written early in Jiajing. It is certainly not false."[24] Tan Qian thus accepted the memorial as a historical document, as grist for his annalistic mill. But his acceptance of its veracity is not matter-of-fact: his assertion that there is no doubt as to the truthfulness of his source is one he rarely feels constrained to make and indicates that he is perhaps anticipating a skeptical reaction.

The death of Li Xiong precipitated a family crisis of epic proportions. Lady Jiao, greedy and ambitious for her own son, sent the ten-year-old Li Chengzu to Shaanxi to search for his father's corpse, assuming that the rigors of the journey would kill the child. The boy, aided by heaven and the spirit of his dead father, miraculously returned with his father's bones. His stepmother, undissuaded by her first failure, poisoned him and dismembered his body.

Li Chengzu was the main obstacle to the future of Li Yanu, but he was not the only one. There were still the three daughters, and Lady Jiao dealt with them expeditiously and cruelly. Guiying (called Taoying in the *San yan* version) she sold as a servant to a well-to-do household; Yueying she turned out on the street to earn her keep as a beggar. But the cruelest fate awaited Yuying. When Yuying was sixteen years old, she wrote two poems, subtly yet unmistakably erotic. The poems express her loneliness and her fears that time is passing her by. The first poem is entitled "Envoi to Spring":

> The cottage is desolate — as I pass what's left of spring
> Elm-coins cover the ground — they're no cure for
>   poverty.

Cloud-like hair, auroral robes, a companion to
mud and dirt.[25]
A flower in the wilds — why does it resemble a
melancholy person?

The second poem, called "Farewell to Swallows" (or in some versions, the characters are inverted: "The Swallows' Farewell") is as follows:

The new nest is plastered with mud; the old one has
tilted to one side.
Door drapes made of dust; I'd like to draw them,
but I'm too late.
Sadly facing one another, murmuring softly, their
final farewell.
The painted chamber is as before; only the master is
not there.

A modern reader is hard pressed to find what in these poems could lead to charges of immoral behavior. And yet the eroticism of these poems is unmistakable, if muted. In the first poem, the desolation and poverty of her life are contrasted with an eroticized description of her-self — her cloud-like hair and her robes the color of dawn mingle with the dirt of this world. The elm-coins are the pods of the elm, which are simultaneously an image of fertility (they are seeds) and futility (they are not real coins). In the final line, she contrasts herself (the melan-choly person) with a flower growing in the wilderness. Several ver-sions of the poem have a different, and more provocative, ending: "A flower in the wilds: why do you tease me so?"[26] The editor of the *Mingyuan shigui* comments on this line: "There was no actual affair here, but there was real passion."[27] The eroticized description, the self-identification with the flower, and the silent rooms where spring no longer lingers could easily (though perhaps not necessarily) be read as laments for the passing of life without an erotic partner.

The second poem likens a human domestic situation to a swal-low's nest. The poet imagines swallows in a new nest, facing one an-other, in sad farewell conversations. The final line brings the reader back to the human world: we are now in a painted chamber, a cham-ber where the "master" (*zhuren*) no longer lingers. One can imagine how a suspicious stepmother might conclude that the lament of the solitary room came from the imagination of a young woman who had experienced rooms where men did indeed linger. This poem recalls "Swallow Parted from her Nest" by the Tang dynasty courtesan Xue Tao. If indeed Yuying is referring to that poem, the charges of the eroticism of the poem are heightened.[28] We see here in the imagination of Lady Jiao echoes of all the fears we have seen elsewhere in this volume about the dangers of women and writing, of women and poetry. A girl who can write can write love poetry to a man: the dangers education poses to virtue are clear. Lady Jiao may be the villain of the piece, but she is not alone in making these assumptions about poetry and virtue.

Yuying tells us (and the emperor) that her stepmother did not investigate the case, but simply concluded she had a lover. She had her brother accuse Yuying of the crime of "fornication and unfilial behavior" (*jianyin bu xiao*). The accusation was lodged with the Embroidered Uniform Guard. The Embroidered Uniform Guard was a fearsome and often powerful secret police unit in the Ming; they were not to be trifled with. The presiding official was blind to the truth of the case and sentenced Yuying to death by slow slicing. The poems were proof enough for him. Yuying tells us that because she was a woman she was unskilled at defending herself, and so she was convicted. Both the penalty inflicted on Yuying and the procedures that led to the penalty were irregular. But the irregularity is not particularly surprising: the Embroidered Uniform Guard in the Ming was frequently criticized for acting in an arbitrary and capricious manner.

A child falsely charged by her parent with unfilial behavior is in a tricky situation—contesting a charge of unfiliality is itself an unfilial act. As Yuying wrote, "I did not dare contravene my stepmother's desires and thereby compound the crime of unfiliality." But now that the emperor has solicited her story, she protests her innocence. She cites as evidence the neighbors: if she had in fact behaved improperly (*bu cai*), the neighbors would surely have known about it. She concludes by telling the reader that she sent the memorial to the emperor with her sister Taoying, the sister who was a beggar. Her sister's misfortune has proved fortuitous: the young beggar's mobility is an important resource for the imprisoned poet. The emperor is moved by Yuying's story and orders that the case be re-examined. Justice is done: Yuying is pardoned, the cruel stepmother is sentenced to death, and the emperor finds Yuying a husband from among the good men (*cai* again) of the Embroidered Uniform Guard. The maidenly eroticism her poetry expressed has been contained by marriage, and the emperor is the hero of the story. He rights all wrongs and finds a man for the maiden.

Those are the bare bones of the story. But Yuying frames her memorial with allusions that position it carefully in discourses about both virtue and poetry. She begins by mentioning that she has heard the ancient kings had a saying that of all crimes unfiliality was the worst. Lodging a criminal charge against a parent, even a guilty parent, was generally forbidden in Ming China.[29] The emperor has provided the occasion where Yuying can speak against her stepmother and clear her name, but she is aware of the gravity of her deed.

In the next sentences, Yuying invokes the *Lienü zhuan*, a staple of women's education since the Han dynasty: "I have also heard that in the *Lienü zhuan* it says: 'When in your life, you continue the serious matters of ethical behavior [*gangchang*], that is called virtue [*de*]. When with your death, you rectify the serious matters of ethical behavior, that is called benevolence [*ren*].'" At the end of the memorial, she says that although her death would not be a matter of great regret, she worries that if her name is not cleared, she will in the future be regarded as having "with my life, polluted customs, and with my body, profaned *gangchang*." Thus clearing her name is an ethical imperative. It is not just her life she is seeking from the emperor, it is her reputation as well. *Gangchang* refers to the *san'gang* and the *wuchang*—the three bonds (ruler-minister, father-son, and husband-wife) and the five constant virtues (*ren, yi, li, zhi, xin*, which might loosely be rendered into English as benevolence, righteousness, adherence to ritual, wisdom, and trustworthiness). The phrase encodes the principles of hierarchy in the Confucian social order. The virtues invoked are not particular domestic virtues of docility and obedience. They are public, exterior, political virtues. Thus the phrase *gangchang* encapsulates hierarchy and public virtue. By using it at the beginning and the end of the memorial, Li Yuying invokes a consciousness of morality and social order and implies that the meaning of her story centers on political order, or, more precisely, at the intersection of political and domestic order. Li Yuying is an upholder of the social order, one who is able to use the norms of that social order in order to obtain justice for herself.

Having invoked the conceptual vocabulary of the *Lienü zhuan*, Yuying goes on to allude to a story, from the *Lienü zhuan*, of the Tang dynasty Dou sisters who threw themselves off a cliff to avoid being raped by bandits, and the story of Yunhua who threw herself into a well.[30] Reference to these extravagant stories of women who chose virtue over life itself places her within the lineage of the virtuous. It is true she has nothing to lose; she has already been sentenced to death. But she positions herself with other women whose virtue has been threatened, who took acts far more radical than writing a complaint about their stepmother to the emperor. In referring to the *Lienü zhuan*, she makes specific reference to a long tradition of texts (many known by that somewhat generic title first used by Liu Xiang in the Han dynasty) and places herself in the tradition of heroines of that genre. It is a placement later editors of the text share; her own story becomes anthologized in the textual tradition she invokes.

But virtue is not the only issue here: poetry is at the core of the story. Yuying defends her poems and her virtue by making specific reference to the *Shi jing* (Poetry classic), which lay at the heart of the Confucian canon. In so doing, she is asserting not only her innocence (indeed, the *Shi jing* poems may well not be innocent) but also her legitimate position in a poetic tradition. As Kang-i Sun Chang has noted, male editors and anthologists often compared their project of collecting women's writings to Confucius' work in collecting the poems that constitute the *Shi jing*. The later anthologists pointed out that many *Shi jing* poems were thought to have been written by women.[31] Here a woman poet herself makes the analogy explicit. The first poem Li Yuying refers to, "Kai feng" (Genial wind), is a lament about the pain suffered by a good mother and the inability of her offspring (in the poem, seven sons) either to comfort or to be worthy of her.[32] Yuying cites "Kai feng" when she is discussing the necessity of telling her story to remove the stain from the reputation of her own good dead mother.

Later in the memorial she compares her poems to "Xing lu" (Walking on dew). She says that her poem "avoids the dampness" of that ode. The preface to the poem in the authoritative Mao edition says that the poem recounts a lawsuit heard by the Duke of Shao. The Duke of Shao was a crucial participant in the founding of the Zhou dynasty, by some accounts the son of King Wen by a concubine.[33] Commentary to the poem adds that in the waning days of Shang, customs were corrupt, and proper marriage rituals were not followed. A Tang dynasty commentary identifies the lawsuit discussed in the poem as one that took place in the first year of the rule of the Duke of Shao, involving a quarrel over which man the beautiful sister of Xu Wufan would marry.[34] The poem ends, in the translation of James Legge, with these lines:

But though you have forced me to trial,
I will still not follow you.[35]

This poem raises the analogy of a woman who uses the legal system to protect her reputation. By invoking this poem, Li Yuying places herself in a tradition of wronged virtuous poets who seek legal recourse from a benevolent sovereign.

The final poem invoked is "Qing ying" (Blueflies), which counsels the sovereign not to believe slander.[36] The significance of this is not obscure: the whole purport of Li Yuying's memorial is to counsel her sovereign not to believe the slander about her. She is able to use the poetic canon of the *Shi jing* as a weapon to assert her innocence and to place herself in a poetic tradition. She is a skilled reader of the poetic canon. The references are not random: they further the narrative of the memorial.

Five other texts reproduce the text of the memorial essentially as Li Xu records it: one is a legal casebook that we cannot date precisely, and the other four are collections of biographies of exemplary women, three dating from late sixteenth- and early seventeenth-century China and one from eighteenth-century Japan. The legal casebook is the *Falin zhaotian zhu*, compiled and published in the Ming dynasty.[37] The title page of the text notes a pseudonym: Jianghu cuizhonglang sou, which can be rendered loosely into English as "old man in the drunken waves of rivers and lakes." Nothing is known of him.[38] The version in the casebook follows the version in the miscellany phrase for phrase, with some differences. The references to the *Shi jing* do not appear in the casebook, although those to the *Lienü zhuan* are retained. In the miscellany, Yuying explains that her father, although a military man, was well-versed in the classics and taught her, despite the fact that she was a girl. The casebook omits these details, as well as the story of Lady Jiao poisoning and dismembering Li Chengzu.[39] Instead of beginning her memorial by saying that she has heard that of all crimes unfiliality is the greatest, Yuying gets more directly to the point and says, "I have heard that a filial child will not expose her parents' evil." The memorial in the casebook also closes a bit differently from the one in the miscellany. In the casebook, Yuying says: "If after you have investigated the affair you find that my crime cannot be pardoned, then execute me, in order to maintain correct legal procedures." In the miscellany, the reader is told the disposition of the case (including the emperor's role as matchmaker); the reader of the casebook is not told how the story ends. But in all the differences between Li Xu and the *Falin zhaotian zhu* are minor. The two texts reinforce and corroborate one another to a remarkable degree. Li Xu's version of the memorial is gathered in a miscellany: it is for the edification of the curious ordinary reader. The legal casebook is for the use of people who administered the law: magistrates as well as the ordinary curious. The rhetorical position of both of these texts is that the memorial is true, that Li Yuying is real, that the story really happened, that the emperor really saved her.

The memorial is also included in the *Gujin nüshi*, which was compiled by Zhao Shijie (fl. 1628). The memorial is included in a section of memorials written to the emperor by women: all the supplicants except for Yuying are writing to plead for their husband's life. She alone is writing for herself. Again, though, the rhetorical position of the collection is that the text is a genuine memorial and the events it recounts actually transpired.

The rhetorical position of the next two texts we will consider—those appearing in editions of biographies of exemplary women—is somewhat different, although the body of the memorial is consistent with what we have seen in the miscellany and the casebook. Not only does Yuying cite the *Lienü zhuan*, but in a wonderful instance of intertextuality, she appears in three Ming Chinese and one Japanese revision of the *Lienü zhuan*: the *Chuanxiang gujin lienü zhizhuan*, a lavishly illustrated and updated edition of the classic *Biographies of Virtuous Women*, attributed to Mao Kun and published in 1591;[40] the *Nü fan bian*, an equally lavish text by Feng Ruzong with a preface dated 1602;[41] the *Gui fan* of Huang Shangwen, which is another edition of the *Nü fan bian*; and the *Ryū Kyō Retsujoden*, published in Osaka in 1763. These texts are concerned not with the literal truth or the falsity of the story (the legendary mothers of sage heroes are mixed in with historical heroines) but rather with its exemplary nature. What matters about Yuying in these texts is that she can serve as an example; that from the story of her suffering there are lessons ordinary Ming women can learn.

The only significant difference between the versions of the stories in these texts lies in the choice of illustration, which I discuss at some length below. In all these texts the biography begins with a short synopsis of the story, which, among other things, tells the reader that Yuying was both beautiful and talented. These texts categorize virtue minutely, and the category assigned Yuying's virtue is *tongbian*, which

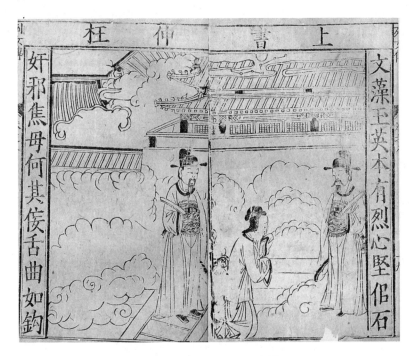

Fig. 8.1 "Sending up a memorial to right a wrong." The line of characters at the right of the illustration reads: "Eloquent Yuying always had a heroic heart, firm as a stone"; the one to the left: "Depraved Mother Jiao, how was her glib tongue crooked as a hook!" Source: *Chuanxiang gujin Lienü zhichuan* (attributed to Mao Kun, 1591), *juan* 8 (reproduced by permission of the Harvard-Yenching Library).

translates to something like "successful at argument." The text in the *Lienü zhuan* ends with the poem, cited above, used in the *San yan* version of the story; that poem is absent from the Japanese version.

Both of these texts are lavishly illustrated, the *Lienü zhuan* with a double-page illustration for each of the biographies (see Fig. 8.1), and the *Nü fan bian* and *Gui fan* with identical single-page illustrations (see Fig. 8.2).[42] Frequently in the *Lienü zhuan* the illustration takes up more space than the text it illustrates. The illustrations can be regarded as instructions for the reader, the editor's commentary on what aspects of the story are most worthy of the reader's attention and imagination. The illustrations become even more significant if we regard them as guides for the semi-literate, integral parts of the text that extend its readership beyond that of the classically literate, a category including many women.

Fig. 8.2 Yuying pleading for her half-brother's life.
Source: Feng Ruzong (reproduced by permission of the
National Central Library, Taiwan).

The *Lienü zhuan* illustration for the Li Yuying story (Fig. 8.1)
shows Yuying presenting the memorial to officials who will transmit
it to the emperor. Lest there be any doubt as to what the scene is about,
it is entitled "Sending up a memorial to right a wrong." The scene is
flanked by a couplet that reads:

> Eloquent Yuying always had a heroic heart [*liexin*],
>   firm as a stone;
> Depraved mother Jiao, how was her glib tongue
>   crooked like a hook!

Yuying kneels on a flight of stairs, flanked by two nearly identically
dressed officials. The Forbidden City looms in the background: it—
indeed the whole scene—is enveloped in scroll-swirled clouds. A
constellation, probably the dipper, which represents the emperor, is
located at the top of the drawing, just beneath the character *shu*. The
selection of this scene to represent the essence of the story in the *Lienü
zhuan* is telling: it represents the restoration of order, and those who

restore that order are government officials. It is a political order, the picture and the story tell us, that intervenes on behalf of sixteen-year-old girls when their families fail them. That the illustration for the story is of Yuying presenting the memorial to the emperor (and not any of the more dramatic scenes in the story) reiterates the centrality of her memorial to her virtue in this telling of the tale. It is not just her suffering that renders her virtuous; she is able to take action that redeems not only her own sufferings but those of her siblings. And the action she takes is literary.

Although the editors of the *Nü fan bian* selected another scene to illustrate the story, their choice also represents the restoration of order (Fig. 8.2). This version of the story adds a new detail. In some versions of the narrative, the emperor wishes to execute the infant son of the Lady Jiao. But Yuying intervenes, saving the life of the baby, who is her half-brother and her father's heir. It is this scene the editors have chosen to represent the story. A man and woman (Lady Jiao and her evil brother) stand with their hands bound behind their backs. On the ground, in front of them, is a small child, the child of Lady Jiao and Li Xiong. Yuying stands, looking at them, smiling indulgently at the child. The whole scene is played out in front of an official in martial garb, perhaps an official of the Embroidered Uniform Guard. This illustration, too, frames the story in a way that emphasizes the restoration of order, but it is a slightly different order. Yuying's wit has brought about the capture of the villains, and her virtue (or her grace) has saved the baby. She is centrally placed here as a daughter saving the ancestral line of her father. Her role as daughter, rather than as memorial-writer, is stressed in this illustration.

According to many (though not all) versions of the memorial, this episode is not the first time that Yuying attracted imperial attention. When she was twelve (or according to some versions of the memorial, fourteen), officials were commanded to present remarkable people (*rencai*; here the term refers to comely young women and men, but the word *cai* can also simply mean talent) to the new emperor on the occasion of his ascending the throne. This would have been the accession of the thirteen-year-old Jiajing emperor in 1521. And under Jiajing, the families of officers in the Embroidered Uniform Guard were a main source of imperial consorts.[43] Thus it is entirely plausible that Yuying attracted the attention of the emperor's agents. The memorial tells us that local officials presented Yuying as a likely candidate for the imperial pleasure, but an official in the Ministry of Rites pitied her because she was a young orphan and had no knowledge of the skills necessary for a palace woman. She was thus allowed to remain at home.[44]

Recruitment as a palace woman, always a chancy prospect, was probably grimmer than usual in 1521. The Zhengde emperor had recruited so many women for the palace that in 1520 court officials complained that there was no room left for all of them and that since supplies were running low, some of the women had already died of starvation.[45] I have not been able to verify that women were rounded up in large numbers at the accession of the Jiajing emperor, although it is well known that on several occasions he ordered that young girls be recruited as consorts.[46] His attraction to prepubescent girls was perhaps enhanced by his search for longevity: Ming ideas about sexual hygiene posited that sexual intercourse with young virgins would prolong life.[47]

Later fictional accounts report that at the Jiajing emperor's accession to the throne, there were widespread rumors—which proved to be false—that young girls would be rounded up as consorts for the young emperor.[48] Jiajing had a problematic relationship with palace women: in 1542 a group of concubines and serving maids made an attempt on his life.[49] Several versions of Li Yuying's memorial omit Jiajing's rounding up of comely youths, perhaps because the practice was disconsonant with the image of the emperor as benefactor of the people.[50] On the other hand, other versions, such as that cited in the *Jingzhiju shihua*, begin with Yuying telling the story of her near-recruitment into the entourage of imperial women. This version of the memorial proceeds directly to a discussion of the loneliness that the sixteen-year-old Yuying felt, a loneliness that she could not help but articulate in her poems.[51] The implication in this version of the memorial is that she was sexually awakened by the thwarted recruitment attempt: the emperor bears some responsibility for the fate that befell her. This version of the story ends with the emperor ordering that a suitably talented (*cai*, again) husband be found for Yuying from among the Embroidered Uniform Guard. The emperor is implicated in her sexual awakening, and he is the agent for her sexual containment in marriage. He is the hero of her story.

The narrations in the versions we have talked about thus far tell the story largely in Yuying's "own" words: that is to say, some version of the memorial is the center of the text. But in other versions, her own words are subsumed within a text framed more explicitly by the agenda of the compiler. One such example is the version of the story incorporated into the "Biographies of Exemplary Women" sections of local gazetteers. In the two gazetteers I have seen, the memorial itself (not even the entire memorial; it is radically excerpted and is so labeled) is attached to the biography as an appendix: it is reproduced in double-columned print, like that used for interlinear commentary. It serves as a reference for the authority and authenticity of the editor's voice. Li Yuying has not been silenced, but she has been subordinated to other purposes. I have not seen any Ming gazetteers that tell the story, but the story is reproduced in two Qing gazetteers. In the *Jifu tongzhi* edited by the nineteenth-century reformers Li Hongzhang and Zhang Zhidong, the story is framed in a way that contains it, in spite of the inclusion of the offending poems. The narrative begins by telling us that Yuying is the orphaned daughter of Li Xiong. We are then told of his five children, who are named, as are their mothers. We are told that because Lady Jiao wanted her son to inherit Li Xiong's position, she sent Li Chengzu to get his father's bones. As in other versions, he does, and she poisons and then dismembers him. We are then told that Guiying is sold as a servant, and that Yuying was lonely. This is the context in which the offending poems are set. A child (she was but sixteen) who had lost both parents and had seen her stepmother murder her brother and sell her sister might well lament the emptiness of her rooms. Context has sanitized the poem of any erotic content. And there is another kind of containment at work as well. The narrative that begins with her losing a father ends with her finding a husband: the story of the smart and assertive young girl has been assimilated to a model of virtue, contained by marriage and domesticity.[52]

The tale of Li Yuying resonates with the sixteenth-century French pardoner's tales that Natalie Davis has studied in *Fiction in the Archives*. In the French tales, the petitioner must first admit his or her guilt and then ask for a remission of the sentence. In the course of requesting the pardon, the petitioner narrates the story of his or her crime. The tale of Yuying is not precisely a pardoner's tale: Yuying is asking for justice (literally, an investigation, *shen*), not mercy. She admits to nothing, save for having written poetry. But she does need to argue that her poems are innocent. Davis writes about ways in which the pardoner's tales are a storehouse from which people could draw various lessons, "a village scolding, a sermon, a moral lesson, a literary tale."[53] The tale of Yuying is a similar kind of storehouse, subject to retelling and reinterpretation. Collectors of miscellanies like Li Xu are interested in the story because they are interested in everything. The texts that collect the lives of exemplary women find in the case of Li Yuying a heroic story of a young girl wronged who through her skill in argumentation gains justice for herself and for her siblings. The Shuntian local histories commemorate her as a local worthy. The poetry collections give excerpts of the memorial as a background for the poems; the information that these poems put their author in mortal danger no doubt gives the reader an extra frisson of appreciation as he or she reads the short and simple texts. The legal casebook anthologizes the memorial as an example of a rather extraordinary case of a young woman charging her stepmother, and the *Gujin nüshi* includes it as an example of a female supplicant to the emperor. Tan Qian uses the memorial as a source for information about battles in which the Embroidered Uniform Guard took part and asserted its historicity in one of the most authoritative annalistic histories of the Ming dynasty. And the *San yan* author takes the plot and weaves a tale of a vicious stepmother, the tragic death of young boy, and, almost incidentally, a young girl who writes a memorial telling her story.

But in conclusion, let us return to the memorial, the construction of the story in Li Yuying's own words, which is central to most versions of the story. With the exception of the *San yan* version, what makes Yuying have a story is that she told her story. Her tale is a perfect embodiment of the double-edged sword that literary skill could be for a young woman in sixteenth-century China: her writing is what put her in mortal peril, and her writing is what saved her life.

9

Embodying the Disembodied: Representations of Ghosts and the Feminine

JUDITH T. ZEITLIN

Ghosts in Chinese culture have predominantly been subjects of religious, anthropological, and folkloric studies, whose authors are anxious to recoup popular beliefs about the afterlife or unravel the meaning of Chinese death ritual. But ghosts in literature are artistic and cultural representations with their own history; they do not passively reflect some social or religious reality but are actively involved in shaping it.[1] The figural richness of ghosts with regard to gender becomes abundantly clear when we consider the prominence of the female revenant in late imperial literature, not only in the ghost *story* but also in theater and poetry.[2] This chapter concentrates on three tales from Pu Songling's (1640–1715) famous collection *Liaozhai's Records of the Strange* (*Liaozhai zhiyi*; hereafter cited as *LZ*), but it will attempt to situate the problem of ghosts and gender in a wider cultural and literary context.

The pronounced taste for female ghosts in late imperial literature is part of the widespread fascination with the death of beautiful, talented women in the sentimental culture of this period, epitomized by the phenomenal success of Tang Xianzu's (1550–1616) southern drama *The Peony Pavilion or The Soul's Return* (*Mudan ting huanhun ji*), completed in 1598. As the play was performed and reprinted throughout the seventeenth and eighteenth centuries, accounts multiplied linking the deaths of young women of talent and their fatal sensitivity to the emotional power of *The Peony Pavilion*.[3] Death was the ultimate female response to the play, and it was contagious. Although male readers were deeply moved by *The Peony Pavilion*, not a single account links *male* death with the play. Instead, men of sentiment (and surviving women of sentiment) assume the role of mourners. C. T. Hsia ("Time and the Human Condition," 275–76) has justly complained that the considerable comic component of *The Peony Pavilion* was largely ignored even in its own time. It was the first half of the play, with its protracted, lyrical enactment of the love-struck heroine's illness and untimely death, her funeral and ghostly return, that prevailed, turning the spectator into a mourner and the dead woman into a specter of melancholy and loss.

The finale of *The Peony Pavilion*, which sanctions both the ghost-heroine's resurrection from the dead and her marriage to her mortal lover, describes these extraordinary events in cosmic terms: "All obeyed the logic proper to the union of yin and yang" (my trans.; Tang Xianzu, *Mudan ting*, scene 55, 286). The interaction between female ghost and human male, especially when it results in rebirth or resurrection, inevitably suggests broader processes of cosmic decay and regeneration. In fact, from a certain perspective, the phrase "female ghost" is something of a tautology. To put it crudely, within the terms of yin-yang complementary opposites, a ghost is "super-yin," an intensification of the qualities or phases associated with yin as opposed to yang. Thus a ghost occupies virtually all points along the symbolic axis of yin (associated with cold, dark, earth, lower, death, femininity, etc.) as defined against the symbolic axis of yang (associated with warmth, light, heaven, upper, life, masculinity). As a story in the early Ming collection *New Tales Under the Lamplight* (*Jiandeng xinhua*) warns: "Man is the fullest flowering of pure yang; a ghost is the noxious filth of deathly yin."[4]

Analogy affords another way to conceptualize the relationship between the two: ghost is to human as female is to male. The analogy emerges most neatly in Pu Songling's clever reworking of a line from a poem by Tao Yuanming (365–427) in the *Liaozhai* tale "Xiangchun." When the story's mortal protagonist hears the news that his young nephew, a child born in the Shades, will somehow be resurrected and join him in the world of the living, he reflects: "A ghost is not human, of course, but as a comfort better than nothing at all" (Pu Songling, *Liaozhai zhiyi*, 10.1324). The line in the original Tao Yuanming poem reads: "A little daughter is not a boy, of course, but as a comfort better than none at all."[5] As both these lines suggest, although on one level yin and yang are complementary and equally important, in a hierarchical culture and society yang tends to be prized at the expense of yin: ghosts are inferior to human beings in the natural and moral order of things, just as daughters are less valuable than sons.

A ghost is essentially invisible, inchoate, and absent. The first part of this chapter examines the idea of the ghost's carnal body, the sexual and medical nexus that makes the ghost visible and tangible; the second part explores the articulation of the ghost's voice, primarily through poetry. The corporeal and poetic modes of materializing the ghost are intimately linked because physical beauty and literary talent are the primary means of arousing desire in the Chinese romantic tradition. In the case of the ghost, imagining her body and inventing her voice in poetry and song frequently lead to the fantasy of her resurrection or rebirth. The final part considers a tale in this vein that deliberately thwarts expectations of resurrection, in which the failure of resurrection is tantamount to political tragedy.

The Ghost's Body and Medical Images of Women

The symbolic reciprocity between woman and ghost makes the ghost the perfect site for imagining a purely aestheticized female ideal; consequently, the ghost comes to function in certain literary texts as a sign for something like hyperfemininity. A brilliant writer such as Pu Songling enjoyed breaking down simple dualities such as yin/yang and ghost/man, particularly through the mechanics of the love triangle. One of the clearest expressions of the ghost's exaggerated yin function in his work emerges when it is defined not against a human male but against a female fox-spirit. In the tale "Lotus-scent" ("Lianxiang"), a young scholar enters separately into clandestine love affairs with two beautiful women, willfully ignorant that one is a fox-spirit and the other a ghost. Even after each woman has secretly revealed the true identity of her rival, the scholar chalks up their charges to jealousy and refuses to believe them. Finally, after the scholar has failed to heed the fox-spirit's warnings (whose name is Lotus-scent) to moderate his sexual conduct and falls deathly ill from overindulgence with the ghost (whose name is Li), both women appear together at his sickbed and launch into a heated and hilarious debate on ghost and fox lore.

"I've heard that ghosts profit from a man's death because after he dies they can be together for eternity," said Lotus-scent. "Is that true?"

"No," replied Li. "There's no pleasure at all when two ghosts meet. If it were pleasurable, do we lack for young men in the Shades?"

"You fool!" said Lotus-scent. "To engage in the sexual act night after night is harmful with a living person, let alone a ghost!"

"Fox-spirits can kill men. Through what art do you alone avoid this?" asked Li.

"There is a type of fox that sucks away human breath, but I am not of that species," said Lotus-scent. "So you see, harmless foxes *do* exist in this world, but harmless ghosts do not because their *yin* (*qi* [yin stuff or essence] is so abundant." As the scholar overheard them talking, he realized for the first time it was true that one was a fox-spirit and the other a ghost. (*LZ*, 2.225)

This story pivots on the contrast between ghost and fox-spirit as intimated in their debate. Each woman is clearly marked as other, just as the male protagonist is marked as normative, but as is often the case in *Liaozhai*, ghost and fox-spirit are not interchangeable. Lotus-scent is decidedly yang to the ghost's yin. The fox-spirit is associated with healing, laughter, warmth, and wisdom; the ghost with disease, melancholy, coldness, and infatuation (*chi*) a close correlative of *qing*). The story owes much of its humor to the fact that it is clearly a twist on the typical "demon story," in which an unmarried man unknowingly becomes involved with a demonic woman. Her dangerous identity is detected and eventually exorcised thanks to the ministrations of a Daoist practitioner (Hanan, *Chinese Vernacular Story*, 44).

In "Lotus-scent," the fox-spirit, ordinarily just such a demonic creature, herself assumes the exorcist role, here (partly to enhance the comedy) recast as a mainstream medical specialist.[6] It is the fox-spirit, then, who observes with alarm her lover's haggard appearance and who diagnoses his condition: "You are in danger! . . . Surely you haven't taken up with somebody else? . . . Your pulse is erratic and disordered like tangled threads. This is a ghostly symptom [*guizheng*]!" (*LZ*, 2.223). Medical cases included in works such as *Classified Case Histories of Famous Physicians* (*Mingyi lei'an*), first published in 1591, confirm that doctors might indeed diagnose sudden fluctuations in pulse as a symptom of a "ghost attack" (*guiji*) or "haunting" (*sui*).[7] Like the medical authorities cited in these case histories, the fox-spirit in Pu Songling's story heals the patient through drug therapy rather than ritual exorcism, expertly doctoring her lover with rare herbal medicines to eliminate the ghost-induced "yin poison" (*yin du*) from his system (*LZ*, 2.223).

Again, the humor in this story derives from the ordinarily insatiable fox-spirit herself mouthing the platitudes about sexual moderation and health common in Ming and Qing medical writings. Doctors, as Charlotte Furth has described them, were "suspicious of erotic passion" and blamed "indulgence in the bedchamber for a variety of debilitating illnesses in both sexes" (Furth, "Blood, Body, and Gender," 58). At the same time, Lotus-scent's medical discourse of moderation, which exculpates foxes from inevitably bringing disease and death to their mortal lovers as ghosts do, helps erase any difference between foxes and human females. As she explains to the scholar: "For someone of your years, if you desist for three days after making love, your essence and vitality [*jingqi*] will be restored—in this case, even if your partner is a fox-spirit, what harm would there be? But if you enter the fray night after night, a human lover will be worse for you than a fox!" (*LZ*, 2.222).

Casting the fox spirit in the benign role of doctor correspondingly shifts the brunt of the story's erotic weight onto the ghost. This division of labor between the two women is inscribed in the final healing scene at the scholar's bedside. The fox-doctor prescribes an unorthodox cure that requires the ghost's intimate cooperation: to activate the medicine's potential, the blushing ghost must press her "cherry mouth" against the scholar's and supply drops of "fragrant saliva" to wash the pill down his gullet (*LZ*, 2.226). (The result, of course, is also to eroticize medicine, but in this story at least, it is the fox who supervises the cure, the ghost who enacts it.)[8]

From the beginning, Lotus-scent is introduced simply as a beauty, but Li is described in detail, an ethereal but insatiable virgin with exceptionally tiny feet and a seductive floating walk, prone to feminine displays of tears and jealousy. She gives her lover one of her tiny slippers as a token; whenever he caresses it and thinks of her, she materializes in response, the manifestation of pure desire.[9] The ghost's physical fragility and emotional weakness, however, are clearly meant to contribute to her allure. The fox-spirit herself later confirms the attraction of this ghostly beauty: "Seeing such loveliness, even *I* have tender feelings; how much the more so would a man!" (*LZ*, 2.227).

In Li and a number of other virgin ghosts in *Liaozhai*, we find a powerful convergence between traditional literary representations of the ghost as a weightless, evanescent, mournful being and new ideals of feminine attractiveness that emphasized qualities such as slenderness, sickliness, and melancholy, often in conjunction with literary or artistic talent and untimely death.[10] Gulik charts a change in visual representations of the physical beauty of both sexes from fleshy and robust to emaciated and frail, a change which he maintains is discernible in the late Ming but really took hold in the Qing (Gulik, 189).[11] As an example, he cites "the ephemeral figure" of Dong Xiaowan, the talented, tubercular courtesan who became the concubine of Mao Xiang at the fall of the Ming: "Often ill and subject to attacks of fever at the slightest emotion, [she] foreshadows the type of very young, fragile and delicate women that during the Ch'ing period would become the ideal of feminine beauty" (Gulik, 294).

The aestheticization of physical weakness and sickliness as a specifically ghostly style of female beauty is most explicit in the *Liaozhai* tale "Autumn Moon" ("Wu Qiuyue"). After the ghost-heroine in this story has been prematurely resurrected, she is exactly the same as an ordinary woman, except for her inability to take more than ten steps unassisted without swaying in the breeze, as though she were about to topple over. "This physical infirmity" (*shen you ci bing*), we are told, however, "actually added to her charms in the eyes of her beholders" (*LZ*, 5.671–72), in part, no doubt, because this fantastic difficulty in walking, here a residue of ghostliness, is also clearly an exaggeration of the eroticized crippled gait that bound feet produced.

This intensification of the physical weakness of female ghosts is related to the striking lack of interest in horror evinced in the Chinese literary tradition of ghost stories from the Tang onward, a trend that becomes increasingly pronounced during the late Ming and early Qing.[12] (This is not to say ghosts are never used for horror, but the proportion of such ghosts is extremely low, especially in comparison with other national traditions of ghost stories, such as Britain or Japan, or the cinema.) The timidity of female ghosts, already evident in Yuan plays, becomes a theatrical convention in Ming and Qing drama: for instance, the stage directions in *The Peony Pavilion* instruct Du Liniang's ghost to "start at the offstage barking of a dog" and at "the sound of chimes in the wind." As she sings, "My heart suddenly catches in fear" (Birch, scene 27, 151–52; Tang Xianzu, *Mudan ting*, 134–35).[13]

The hyperfemininity of the female ghost also has repercussions on representations of masculinity. In the *Liaozhai* tale "Liansuo," the shy and refined ghost-heroine is eventually coaxed into revealing herself to a gentle young scholar with poetic talent but apologetically refuses to exhibit herself to a second mortal admirer, even after he has vanquished her enemies in the underworld, because his fierce, martial style of manliness frightens her too much (LZ, 3.336). The nonthreatening young scholar therefore occupies a somewhat ambiguous middle position in which he mediates between extremes of femininity and masculinity; the overall effect, however, is to push him further toward the feminine pole (like the *xiaosheng*, or young male lead in the theater) and to reinforce the shifting, relational aspect of gender roles.

As the medical terminology and the association of ghosts with illness in "Lotus-scent" and other *Liaozhai* stories indicate, Ming and Qing medical writings provide important concepts linking gender and ghosts. (Pu Songling, like many scholars, was interested in the medical literature of his time and even compiled a pharmacopoeia whose prescriptions were adapted from Li Shizhen's [1518–93] authoritative *Classified Materia Medica* [*Bencao gangmu*].) Drawing on Furth's work on medical images of women in late imperial China, we do find strong connections between literary representations of ghosts and symbolizations of the feminine in Ming and Qing medical texts.

Women were apt to succumb to "static congestion" (*yujie*), which Furth describes as "a kind of melancholy syndrome of congealed blood associated with spleen system dysfunction . . . experienced as feelings of oppression and suffocation, pressure or tightness in the chest, languor and loss of appetite, all linked to pent-up resentments and repressed desires" (60–61).[14] If this condition went unchecked or untreated, the sufferer could waste away and die. *Yu*, an ancient medical term listed in *The Inner Classic* (*Neijing*) as a congestive disorder linked to the seasons and the Five Phases, has a basic meaning of blockage or obstruction (Guo Aichun, 438), but it also has a long history as a broad term for any emotional distress caused by suppressed grief, resentment, or longing and, as such, is often translated "melancholy" or "depression." The pressure resulting from these unvented feelings could eventually cause *qi* to knot up or congeal (*jie*) in various internal organ systems. *Yujie*, albeit in a non-medical sense, is the very phrase the historian Sima Qian employed in his important formulation of literature as the crystallization of pent-up frustration and indignation (Sima Qian, 10: 130.330). The concept of *yujie* also provides a symbolic key to the etiology of ghosts: ordinarily the spirits of the dead dissolve or disperse (*san*); what prevents this dissolution and causes a ghost to materialize is something knotted up or congealed inside it.[15] A ghost is a symptom of fatal blockage and congestion, a pathological return of something incomplete and unresolved.

Paradoxically, static congestion could result from an excess of sexual activity as well as a repression of sexual activity, but cases of melancholy virgins in the medical literature display a close affinity to ghostlore.[16] Bottled-up grievances and unfulfilled desire are precisely what compel a ghost to return as a revenant to the living. A young woman who dies unwed has ample cause for resentment; her death is by definition untimely and tragic: she has no proper place in the ancestral line and no descendants to look after her posthumous ritual. And since she dies a virgin, she inevitably takes unfulfilled sexual desire to the grave; the force of this repressed desire can be measured inversely by the sexual insatiability imputed to her ghost.[17]

The threat such a revenant potentially poses to male health, however, is diffused or domesticated in sentimental treatments of the scholar–virgin ghost romance, such as *The Peony Pavilion*, "Lotus-scent," or "Autumn Moon." This suggests that the most important convergence between Ming and Qing medical images of women and literary representations of ghosts is the struggle to redefine and master the dangerous pollution assigned to both women and ghosts in folk belief. As Furth contends:

> Biology had tamed the powers of pollution associated with the borders between life and death, replacing them by a set of naturalistic symptoms controlled within a system of healing. . . . Threatening symbols of female sexual power were replaced by benign symbols of female generativity and weakness that moderated pollution taboos and permitted an interpretation of gender based on paternalism, pity, and protection. (p. 64)

This process parallels the transformation the female ghost repeatedly undergoes in the Chinese literary tradition (particularly at the hands of Tang Xianzu, Pu Songling, and other late Ming and early Qing writers)—from frightening, malignant, sexually predatory agents of disease and death to timid, vulnerable, fragile creatures in need of male sympathy, protection, and life-giving powers. Standing in for the figure of the doctor, the fox Lotus-scent's changing attitude toward her rival Li perfectly illustrates this shift in point of view: at first condemned as a dangerous, pathogenic carrier of yin-poison, the ghost becomes an object of pity who can be cured and rehabilitated.

The concept of pollution is reinscribed in a moral framework and internalized by the ghost herself. Thus Li relates how, overcome with depression and guilt at having almost caused the scholar's death, she crept off in shame and despair at her body's "otherness" and "filth" (*LZ*, 2.229). This realization marks her repentance and is the precondition for her eventual reincarnation and reunion with the scholar.

The ghost's moral internalization of pollution is also at work in "Liansuo," a resurrection story as melancholy as "Lotus-scent" is comic. The lonely ghost-heroine Liansuo scrupulously refrains from responding to the sexual advances of the scholar she meets, for fear of doing him physical injury: "These moldering bones from the grave are no match for the living. A liaison with a ghost only hastens a man's death; I could not bear to harm you" (*LZ*, 3.332). She agrees to sit beside him, however, and haltingly reveals she has been dead for twenty years, having died of a sudden illness at the age of sixteen. "Slender and chilled, she shrank back as though she could not bear the weight of her clothes" (*LZ*, 3.331–32). Her physical fragility elicits one of the most explicit descriptions of the female body in *Liaozhai*. The scholar, accepting that he cannot fully consummate his physical desire for the ghost, "playfully put his hand inside her bodice; the tips of her breasts were as tender as freshly shelled nutmeats; clearly she was a virgin" (*LZ*, 3.332).[18] In a parallel but more oblique move, he then peeks beneath her skirt to inspect her tiny embroidered shoes and stockings, the fetishized, displaced locus of the female genitals in this period.

The association of chastity with coldness and death makes the virgin ghost the ghostliest figure of all, but the image also contains within it the fantasy that she can be revived through the generative power of male sexuality. This theme is voiced most famously in *The Peony Pavilion*, when the heroine Du Liniang reveals to her lover that she is really a ghost and seeks his help in resurrecting her: "How cold you must have been!" he exclaims. She replies: "Frozen body and soul in coldest chastity . . . [but] my cold flesh already / you have caressed to warmth" (Birch, scene 32, 189; Tang Xianzu, *Mudan ting*, 162).[19] Thanking him after her revival, she declares: "Having returned me to life, you are dearer to me than mother and father" (my trans.; Tang Xianzu, *Mudan ting*, scene 36, 175).

Far more literal-minded than Tang Xianzu, Pu Songling medicalizes the fantasy in "Liansuo." At the end of the story, the ghost-heroine comes to the scholar and seeks his aid in reviving her, but warns him that to do so will cause him to fall seriously ill for a period of time. In accordance with the medical model of procreation, to be reborn she requires not only his semen but his blood. Here the scholar completely takes over the generative function, supplying both male essence and female blood. The act of intercourse through which Lian-suo loses her virginity and receives his semen is narrated in a single perfunctory phrase. It is the transfusion of blood as the masculine counterpart to her defloration that is described in detail: "'I still require a drop of blood from the living,' she said. 'Are you willing to suffer pain for the sake of our love?' The scholar took a sharp blade and stabbed his upper arm until the blood flowed; the girl lay on the couch as he let the blood drip into her navel" (*LZ*, 3.336). After instructing him where to find her burial spot, she vanishes.

The medicalized fantasy of male conception here is reinforced by its aftermath: the scholar falls ill with pregnancy-like symptoms and is cured only by going through a process analogous to childbirth: "Over ten days later, his belly swelled up so painfully he wanted to die. After taking a remedy prescribed by the doctor, he excreted a foul substance something like mud. Within twelve days he had recovered" (*LZ*, 3.337). His experience resembles accounts in the medical literature of a female disorder known as "phantom pregnancy" (*guitai*), in which a woman, often a maiden, exhibits symptoms of false pregnancy: cessation of menses and an expanding belly. Explanations of the disorder vary, depending upon how literally or figuratively the "phantom" is understood. In Chen Ziming's (1190–1270) often-quoted *Complete Good Prescriptions for Women* (*Furen daquan liangfang*), the causes are weakened bodily defenses and psychic decline, which enable demonic forces to penetrate the internal organ systems (Chen Ziming, 48: 14.742–655, 656). Certain later medical writers, such as Fu Shan (1607–84), attributed this disorder to actual dreams of intercourse with gods or ghosts provoked by illicit desires, often ensuing after an excursion to a temple or to the mountains (Fu Shan, 4589–91).[20] The government-sponsored medical encyclopedia *The Golden Mirror of Medicine* (*Yizong jinjian*; published 1742) vehemently attacked this view, rationalizing the cause exclusively as the repression of immoral desires, which congests the blood and qi within the body.[21] Although varying combinations of drugs are prescribed as treatment in these medical cases, the desired result is uniformly to purge the body of the filth that ails it. "Excreting a foul substance" (*xia ewu*), the phrase Pu Songling employed, is the exact wording commonly found in such accounts.[22]

After the scholar's convalescence, he goes to the appointed place and exhumes the grave. "He saw that the coffin had completely rotted away, but the girl looked as though she were alive and seemed slightly warm to his touch" (*LZ*, 3.336). He takes her still unconscious body home, and she revives at midnight. Despite the conventional circumstances of the actual resurrection and the implied happy ending, the story concludes on an elegiac note: "She would always tell him: 'These past twenty years seem just like a dream'" (*LZ*, 3.336). This last line points backward rather than forward, recalling the intensely melancholy and poetic flavor of the story's opening.

The Poetics of Ghosts

The emergence of Liansuo's poetic voice is a precondition for the materialization of her body. The story begins with a description of the scholar's lodgings. "His studio looked out onto a vast expanse of wasteland, and outside his window were many ancient graves. At night he could hear the wind soughing in the white poplar trees, the sound like stormy waves. Sitting up past midnight, with candle in hand, he was overcome with desolation" (*LZ*, 3.331). Suddenly outside his window a voice chants two lines of verse:

> In darkest night, a dismal wind blows queerly
> backward,
> Flitting fireflies tickle the grass, then stick to
> my skirt.[23]

As he listens the lines are repeated over and over; the mournful voice is faint and delicate like a woman's. The next morning he looks outside his window, but of course finds no trace of a human footprint.

It is as though the place itself has produced the couplet. The disembodied lines are both a projection of the loneliness and desolation the scene arouses in him and a response to those emotions. In this context, the opening description functions as a preface to the couplet, which becomes a perfect fusion of scene and emotion, an important aesthetic effect in Chinese poetics. The prose opening seemingly describes an actual scene, for poplar trees, like evergreens, were typically planted in graveyards. But above all the sound of the wind soughing in the white poplars is coded as ghostly because it is a naturalized allusion to a famous sequence of pallbearers' songs by Tao Yuanming. In these dirges, the poet imagines his funeral's ritual process narrated from the macabre perspective of his dead self. The opening of the third song reads:

> How desolate the moorland lies,
> The white poplars sough in the wind.
> There is sharp frost in the ninth month
> When they escort me to the far suburbs.
> There where no one dwells at all
> The high grave mounds rear their heads.
>   (Hightower, 249; Tao Qian,
>   *Tao Yuanming ji*, 142)[24]

The "dismal wind" blowing "queerly backward" in the lines the scholar hears alone in the darkness produces a somewhat similar effect of dislocation, the uncanniness aided by the disquieting sound of the couplet's compulsive repetition. The wind blowing backward probably describes the sudden gust of a whirlwind, a sign that conventionally heralds a ghostly apparition. In the second line, the eerie glow of the flitting fireflies suggests the will-o'-the-wisps or phantom phosphorescence (*guihuo*) that typically marks a ghostly landscape. But the image is also coded as sexual, the nocturnal fireflies who flit through the grass replacing the customary diurnal butterflies and bees of Chinese poetry who frolic amid the flowers. In conjunction with a lady's skirt, which covers the lower body, the verbs "tickle" (*re*) and "stick to" (*zhan*) also give the line a distinct erotic tinge. Taken together, the lines suggest pent-up emotion and unsatisfied desire, especially because there is no progression; the poem is stuck on the first two lines.

Night after night the scholar listens to the same disembodied lines chanted mournfully outside his window. His heart goes out to their author, although he realizes she is a ghost. She proves elusive, however, until one night, waiting for her outside, he recites a couplet of his own to continue the poem:

> What mortal glimpses this hidden desire and inner
>   sadness?
> Kingfisher sleeves are thin against the cold at
>   moonrise.

When he returns to his studio, the ghost Liansuo materializes, and the story proper begins. Here Pu Songling has adapted a device from conventional romances, in which an exchange of matching poems initiates a love affair. The scholar's couplet, which articulates what the

ghost wants to utter yet is too shy to say,[25] is both an expression of his
sympathy for her loneliness and an invitation: he will lend her his
warmth in the cold moonlight. On a symbolic level, the completion of
the poem also foreshadows the union of the two lovers and the ghost's
successful resurrection.

This poetic exchange does not merely play a key role in the plot,
however; the quatrain is important because it exemplifies the concept
of the "ghostly" as a stylistic attribute of writings about ghosts. Just as
the ghost becomes aestheticized as a particular style of feminine
beauty, so too ghostliness becomes aestheticized as a particular poetic
mood with its own repertoire of images. As Feng Zhenluan, one of
Liaozhai's nineteenth-century commentators, remarked approvingly
after Liansuo's couplet: "The verse is ghostly" (*shi you guiqi*) (*LZ*,
3.331). The term *guiqi*, or ghostliness, is employed in the late seventeenth century as an aesthetic evaluation associated with melancholy
and foreboding. As the Three Wives' commentary on *The Peony Pavilion*, published in 1694, observes of an aria the heroine sings on her
deathbed: "The mournful chants of birds and bugs, the soughing of
the rain-lashed wind: the ghostliness one feels in the words and between the lines is overwhelming. Reading this alone on an overcast
night would be frightening" (Wu Wushan and Qian Yi, scene 20,
1.59a.)[26] In Hong Sheng's (1645–1705) play *Palace of Lasting Life*
(*Changsheng dian*), the stage effect of a whirlwind announcing the
sudden entrance of a baleful ghost is likewise pronounced "ghostly."[27] And in the margins of the posthumous collection of a close
friend, who died young, the poet and playwright You Tong (1618–
1704) wrote: "Entirely in the Li He style. The ghostliness of this poem
is overwhelming."[28]

As You Tong indicates, the conscious creation of a ghostly aesthetic in poetry originated with Li He, the late Tang poet, who was
posthumously hailed as the Ghostly Talent (*guicai*) because of his
premature death and the macabre quality of his verse. By the seventeenth century, a circumscribed set of images, phrases, and literary effects, largely derived from or inspired by Li He, had become instantly
recognizable generic markers of ghostliness. Indeed, the second line of
Liansuo's couplet bears a strong resemblance to a line in "Mawei
Slope" ("Mawei po"), a poem Pu Songling wrote in explicit imitation
of Li He's masterpiece, "The Grave of Little Su" ("Su Xiaoxiao mu").[29]
Both the original and its imitation conjure up the glamorous ghosts of
historical beauties, with Li He's Six Dynasties courtesan, Little Su, re-

cast as the Tang imperial concubine Lady Yang (Yang Guifei) in Pu Songling's rendition. The heptasyllabic line of Liansuo's couplet "Flitting fireflies tickle the grass, then stick to my skirt" simply expands the pentasyllabic line "Wet fireflies stick to the dark grass" from "Mawei Slope." Other elements in Liansuo's couplet, such as the "dismal wind" (a phrase that suggests Li He but does not appear in his work) also crop up in two other poems chanted by ghosts in *Liaozhai* and suggest the almost formulaic character of such verse.[30]

An anecdote in Qian Qianyi's (1582–1664) influential *Anthology of Ming Poetry* (*Liechao shiji*) suggests how tempting it was to correlate the poetic effect of the ghostly with the idea that the author of such poetry might actually be a ghost. As two men are strolling together after dark, the anecdote goes, one of them happens to think up this couplet:

> Rain stops in the tall bamboo,
> Flitting fireflies come out after midnight.

The man's initial pleasure swiftly turns to dismay: "These lines are too eerie [*you*]; they're probably the type a ghost would compose."[31] (We find the same flitting fireflies and nocturnal setting as in Liansuo's couplet; here, however, unnatural stillness coupled with dampness, rather than the disquieting sound of the wind, seem to contribute to the ghostly effect.) This anecdote is, in fact, offered as a comment on another poem actually reputed to be the work of a ghost.

Pu Songling's refinement of a ghostly aesthetic needs to be seen in the context of the long-standing interest in the phenomenon of "ghost poetry" — verse attributed to ghost authors in poetry anthologies. Both accounts of the strange (*zhiguai*) and tales of the marvelous (*chuanqi*), the staple genres of the classical tale, were a major source for such poetry, and women figure prominently in the ranks of ghost poets. As early as the Southern Song, Hong Mai (1123–1202), the indefatigable compiler of *Records of the Listener* (*Yijian zhi*), the massive *zhiguai* collection, was combing the anecdotal literature for poems composed by ghosts and immortals to augment his *Ten Thousand Tang Quatrains* (*Wanshou Tangren jueju*), which he presented to the throne in 1192.[32] Specimens of ghost verse continued to be scattered in collections such as Ji Yougong's *Anecdotes About Tang Poetry* (*Tangshi jishi*; earliest published edition 1224), but the first poetry anthology I have found to append ghosts as a separate category is Xin Wenfang's *Biographies of Tang Poets* (*Tang caizi zhuan*; completed in 1304). Whether because the compiler characterized such verse as the "absurd" product of "reflection and echo" or simply because the last pages of a book are particularly vulnerable to loss, no ghost poets are actually listed, however, and this section remains appropriately a blank (Xin Wenfang, *Tang caizi zhuan jiaozhu*, 961–62).[33]

When comprehensive anthologies of women's poetry began to be published in the sixteenth century, it was clear that their male compilers had inherited ghost poetry as a pre-existing category, although they betray some uneasiness about it.[34] As Tian Yiheng explained in his preface to *A History of Women Poets* (*Shinü shi*; published in the Jiajing era): "Poems by female immortals and ghost women certainly abound, but there are also quite a few forgeries, I am just including a few poems to furnish examples of this type" (Hu Wenkai, 877). In his *Remnants from Ladies' Writing Brushes* (*Tongguan yibian*), published in 1567, Li Hu rejected poems composed by the heroines of classical romances popular in his day as "not really being from a woman's hand," but he included some "elegant" and "credible" examples of poetry by supernatural women in a final appendix, at the bottom of his hierarchy of female poets (Hu Wenkai, 879–80).

The growing interest in ghost poetry as a distinct category during the late Ming is most evident in the work of Mei Dingzuo (1549–1615), a bibliophile, playwright, and friend of Tang Xianzu. Mei compiled an exhaustive anthology called *Records of Talented Ghosts* (*Caigui ji*; author's preface dated 1605), expanding a one-chapter work of this title attributed to a Tang author into a sixteen-chapter scholarly tour de force arranged chronologically from the Zhou to the Ming.[35] Like most anthologists before him, Mei included frame stories drawn from a wide range of sources to contextualize the poems as ghostwritten, and women make up a good number of his talented ghosts. Elite interest in automatic spirit writing—a form of divination known as planchette or *fuji*—was certainly another factor that led to the inclusion of ghost poetry in Ming and Qing anthologies, and Mei devoted his last three chapters to talented ghosts of this kind.[36]

Qian Qianyi's *Anthology of Ming Poetry* devotes a specific subsection to supernatural authors, with anecdotes drawn from collections of classical tales and "talks on poetry" (*shihua*) replacing the biographies included for other writers. Qian placed "poems by ghosts and spirits" (*guishen shi*) at the back of the anthology, which was reserved for marginal figures, after monks, women, servants, and anonymous poets, but before Korean and Japanese practitioners of Chinese verse.[37] Inspired by Qian's example and the precedent set by earlier male anthologists of women's poetry, Wang Duanshu (1621–ca. 1706) grouped versifying ghosts, immortals, and other spirits in an "illusion" section ("huan ji") in her *Classic Poetry by Famous Women* (*Mingyuan shiwei;* completed 1667).[38]

Complete Poetry of the Tang (*Quan Tangshi*), one of the enormous scholarly projects commissioned by the Kangxi emperor, completed in 1707, devotes two chapters to poems written by ghosts, sandwiched between chapters of verse attributed to immortals and divinities and chapters devoted to the poetry of demonic spirits (*guai*) and dreams. (This whole section, as in Qian Qianyi's anthology, follows chapters of verse by Buddhist monks, Daoist adepts, and women). Although the subject of this imperial anthology was Tang poetry, the editors' decision to append poetry attributed to supernatural authors as part of a desire for encyclopedic comprehensiveness was clearly in accord with late imperial precedent and taste.[39]

The practice of including ghost poetry in the last section of anthologies classified hierarchically according to the poet's status continued into the Qianlong period. Both Lu Jianzeng's (1690–1768) regional anthology *Shandong Poetry from This Dynasty* (*Guochao Shanzuo shichao;* preface dated 1758) and Wang Qishu's anthology of women poets *A Nosegay of Verse* (*Xiefang ji;* 1773) conclude with poems attributed to ghosts and immortals.[40] By this time, however, Kangxi period accounts of the strange such as *Liaozhai* and Wang Shizhen's (1634–1711) *Occasional Chats North of the Pond* (*Chibei outan*) were supplying anthologists with new source materials to fill this section. Since *Liaozhai* achieved fame only after its first publication in 1766, Pu Songling's talented ghosts, such as Liansuo, are well represented in *A Nosegay of Verse* but not in the somewhat earlier *Shandong Poetry from This Dynasty*.[41] In the anthologies of women's poetry with supernatural subsections, poems attributed to ghosts constitute a relatively large proportion in relation to the anthology as a whole; in the mixed-gender poetry anthologies I have mentioned, proportionately speaking, female poets tend to figure far more prominently in the supernatural subsections than they do in the anthology as a whole.[42] Is there some sense in which women's writing in China, segregated in specialized collections or relegated to the back of anthologies as a curiosity, can be said to occupy the status of ghostwriting in Marjorie Garber's sense of the term—marginal writing that is simultaneously visible and invisible, powerful and powerless (Garber, 25)?

In contrast to early Ming collections of classical tales such as *New Tales Under the Lamplight* in which prose narration is frequently used simply to showcase sequences of poems, Pu Songling used verse sparingly and only for very deliberate effect in *Liaozhai*. Out of the nearly 500 stories in the collection, only twenty-odd tales include verse.[43] About a quarter of these feature poetry composed by female ghosts; I believe we can go so far as to say that poetic talent in women (and its close correlate, musical talent) is, at least symbolically, a ghostly attribute in *Liaozhai* and a number of other late imperial works.[44]

This leads to several possible explanations for the association of female poetic talent and ghostliness during this period. First, the exchange of poetry is a generic feature of the "scholar-beauty romance" (*caizi jiaren*) popular at this time; as a variation on this type of story, the scholar-ghost romance simply retains the heroine's composition of verse characteristic of the genre. Second, the female ghost can be understood as an imaginative transposition of the glamorous figure of the courtesan, who was expected to be an entertainer skilled in poetry and music. To a northerner such as Pu Songling, the exotic allure of southern courtesan culture might well have been translatable into the "otherworldliness" of the ghost.[45] The problem with these explanations is that fox-spirits, who tend to be more closely associated with courtesans and prostitutes than are ghosts, rarely compose verse, except as a joke, either in *Liaozhai* or in the many other treatments of the scholar–fox-spirit romance.

I would propose a third explanation. During the late Ming and early Qing, the always influential theory of poetry and music as the involuntary outlet for the author's suppressed emotion and pent-up resentment seems to become even more important. A poem attributed to an anonymous ghost in Qian Qianyi's *Anthology of Ming Poetry* implies that death, rather than silencing pain and desire, intensifies them; as in Liansuo's case, the drive to express these pent-up feelings in poetry could compel the spirit of the dead to materialize as a ghost:

> Above the grave, autumn winds howl through
>   ancient trees,
> Beneath the grave, the dead relinquish their myriad
>   thoughts.
> Only the versifying soul cannot dissolve. . . .

I am reminded here of Han Yu's (768–824) famous dictum, "All things not at peace will cry out," which likened the human need to express feelings in writing to the natural force that impels plants to rustle in the wind or metal to ring when struck.[46] As Maureen Robertson has demonstrated, to justify women's composition of poetry as a natural and irrepressible act, Ming and Qing women writers not infrequently invoked Han Yu.[47] In his 1677 biography of a beautiful girl who drowned herself, You Tong did indeed borrow Han Yu to help account for the posthumous poetry written by her spirit.[48] If in the medical and literary tradition women were imagined to be especially vulnerable to strong emotions such as melancholy and anger, and if, as I have argued, ghosts represent a symbolic intensification of the feminine, then female ghost poetry has the potential to be the most involuntary and the most moving of all writing. As Liansuo explained to the scholar in *Liaozhai*, she was so lonely in the desolate wastes of the underworld that she composed the couplet "to express her hidden anguish" (*ji youhen*).[49] Her poem is a transposition of the ghostly wail, the pure articulation of emotion.

The Failure of Resurrection

Unlike almost any other story by Pu Songling or his contemporaries, "Gongsun Jiuniang" acknowledges the impossibility of fully suppressing the hostile power of the female ghost and the tragic finality of death. This tale recombines to great effect the twin motifs of poetry and blood—respective synecdoches for the ghost's voice and body—which formed the central subjects of my discussion in the preceding sections. "Gongsun Jiuniang" can be read to a large degree as a recontextualization of the plot and mood of "Liansuo" in response to the terrible violence surrounding the fall of the Ming dynasty and the Manchu conquest. Allan Barr (115–19) offers a sensitive reading of "Gongsun Jiuniang" as Pu Songling's striking commemoration of the many innocent victims slaughtered in the Qing government's 1663 suppression of the Yu Qi rebellion, a local Shandong tragedy that occurred when Pu Songling was in his early twenties, and in which many members of the local gentry were implicated and executed.[50]

The tale is prefaced with a chilling description of the mass executions: in their wake, "The earth ran with the 'jasper blood' of the martyred and stacks of bones stretched to the heavens" (*LZ*, 4.477). The allusion is to a loyal statesman of the fifth century B.C. who was unjustly murdered, and whose blood was said to have crystallized into jasper upon spilling to the ground, as a sign of his martyrdom. This opening figure of blood resurfaces at the end of the story in the form of will-o'-the-wisps, ghostly emanations that natural histories such as *Classified Materia Medica* explained as transmutations of human blood that had long mixed with earth.[51]

In contrast to both "Liansuo" and "Lotus-scent," where the ghost appears to a young man and enters his world, in this tale the hero sets the events of the story into motion by making a libation to a few friends and relatives who perished in the rebellion's aftermath. The year is 1674, eleven years after the executions, when the collective memory of the massacre must already have begun to fade. The ghost of one such friend returns to seek help in arranging a marriage with the hero's dead niece and leads him into the underworld, to a newly established village populated solely by ghosts of the rebellion's victims. There he falls in love with Gongsun Jiuniang, yet another talented and beautiful virgin ghost. On their wedding night, after the consummation of the marriage, he learns the tragic circumstances of his bride's death: she and her mother had been arrested after the rebellion and were being sent to the capital, Beijing. When they reached the city of Ji'nan, the prefectural seat, her mother died of distress. Jiuniang then slit her own throat. "Recalling the events of the past as she lay beside him on the pillow, she was choked with sobs and could not sleep. So she recited two quatrains of her own composition":

I

My silk gown of days past has turned to dust;
In vain I behold my previous karma and resent my
    former life.
After ten years of dew chilling moonlit maples,
Tonight I first encounter spring in this painted chamber.

II

By the white poplar, wind and rain swirl round
    my lonely grave,
Who could anticipate a further rendezvous on
    Sunny Terrace?
Suddenly I open the gold-thread case and look inside,
The reek of blood still stains my old silk dress.

(*LZ*, 4.481)[52]

The first quatrain ends with a beginning: after ten years of despair frozen in ghostly limbo, she has finally encountered the fecund thaw of spring.[53] Her physical initiation into love holds out the prospect of rebirth, a suggestion also implied in the opening of the second quatrain. There we find the same ghostly juxtaposition of white poplar, wind, and grave as in the prose opening of "Liansuo," but with the added element "rain" (another ghostly marker), which in conjunction with the next line's "cloud-making" rendezvous on Sunny Terrace is a common poetic euphemism for sexual intercourse. Read against the phrase "lonely grave," "Sunny Terrace" (literally Yang Terrace) also connotes the cosmic union of ghostly woman and mortal man. Up to this point, the lines Jiuniang chants are a pastiche of common ghost poetry elements that clearly spell resurrection.

But the final couplet of the second quatrain unexpectedly takes a violent turn. The "reek of blood" staining her old silk dress instantly turns the nuptial image of the gold-thread dowry case back into a coffin, shattering any promise of future rebirth. The refined melancholy of a ghostly beauty in the timelessness of the afterlife has reverted to the morbidity of a corpse recalling the past trauma of her suicide. The horror of history has reclaimed the pleasure of fantasy. As part of a verse chanted on the occasion of Jiuniang's wedding night, however, the "reek of blood" staining her dress takes on a double meaning, superimposing defloration and suicide, linking blood not to birth and resurrection, as in "Liansuo," but to decay and death. I am reminded of Chinese wedding laments in which the bride likens her impending marriage to death.[54] Elsewhere in *Liaozhai* necrophiliac desire is overtly displayed toward the dead body of another virgin suicide; there, however, the corpse is reanimated to strike her would-be rapist dead and preserves her posthumous chastity.[55]

In contrast to the straightforward physicality of the ghost's body in "Liansuo," Jiuniang's body is shrouded, evoked only indirectly through the ephemeral material of her clothes. Anticipating the last line of the second quatrain, the opening line of the first quatrain also begins with a textile image: "My silk gown of days past has turned to dust." And when the scholar must leave the village of the dead and she mournfully asks him to rebury her bones by his ancestral tombs so she may have "a place to rest safely for eternity, and though dead . . . not wholly perish,"[56] she gives him one of her silk stockings as a parting keepsake. An intimate piece of female apparel, the stocking, like the shoe, is a frequent lover's token in *Liaozhai*, but in this tale it registers additional meaning.

. Stricken with grief, the scholar promises to do as she requests, but once he has returned to the world of the living, he discovers he has forgotten to ask for the inscription on her gravestone. When he returns that night to the southern outskirts of Ji'nan, where the victims of the Yu Qi rebellion are buried, he finds more than a thousand graves; try as he may, without more specific indications, he cannot locate her grave and fulfill his promise. "He took out the stocking she had given him. The moment the fabric caught in the wind, it rotted into ashes" (*LZ*, 4.482).[57] The image echoes the opening of the first quatrain, lending the poem in retrospect a predictive force, intimating the irrevocability of her body's decay and the obliteration of her name. The stocking's disintegration also signals the rupture of any possible lingering attachment between ghost and man, the end of any hope even for ritual amends.

The scholar moves away to another place, but still cannot repress her memory. About half a year later he revisits the area, longing to find her again. As night falls, he rides once more through the burial ground. This time, however, the atmosphere has changed: "The myriad graves stretched endlessly before him, their desolate wastes blurring his sight, the ghostly will-o'-the-wisps and howling foxes striking terror into the human heart"(*LZ*, 4.482). At this moment, finally the prelude to a horror tale, he sees a girl who looks remarkably like Jiuniang walking alone amid the tombs. As in a dream, he tries to speak to her, but she flees "as though she doesn't recognize him." When he tries to approach her again, "a look of rage convulsed her features. She raised her sleeve to screen her face. As he called out her name, she vanished like smoke" (*LZ*, 4.482).

A ghost also covers her face with her sleeve before disappearing forever in other classical tales, but in these instances, the gesture is part of an amicable farewell and has the effect of a gentle fadeout.[58] Only in "Gongsun Jiuniang" is raising the sleeve a violent act. The abruptness and theatricality of the gesture here suggest that the stage may have offered Pu Songling a more immediate inspiration. When Du Liniang appears midway through *The Peony Pavilion* for the first time after her death, the stage directions read: "She enters wailing as a ghost, and hiding her face with her sleeve." And when she exits, the stage directions indicate that she do so also "wailing as a ghost" (Birch, scene 27, 151, 154, and scene 32, 191; Tang Xianzu, *Mudan ting*, 134, 136, 163).

In the *Liaozhai* tale's final scene, however, Jiuniang is mute and cannot even vent her bitter feelings in a ghostly wail. Communication between man and ghost is no longer possible; there is only the void, as she vanishes like smoke. It matters not that the hero's intentions were good; his failure to discharge his obligation to the dead rouses implacable ire. Forgetting to ask for the gravestone inscription was only a pretense, however; the barren outcome of this union was always predestined, and Jiuniang's rage was provoked by a grievance more serious than the hero's trivial offense.[59] Within the story's historical context, Pu Songling conveys the survivor's feelings of guilt and anguish at the memory of his impotence to save the Yu Qi rebellion's innocent victims.

In conjunction with the look of rage that convulses Jiuniang's features, blocking her face with her sleeve is also a hostile gesture, a veiled threat: Leave me alone, or I'll avenge myself on you. Despite all efforts to diffuse the terrifying power of the ghost by remaking her into a fragile, timid, poetic beauty, the menace of this power always lurks close beneath the surface. Even in *The Peony Pavilion*, Du Liniang's ghost lets the facade crack for a moment as a warning to her mortal lover: "Do not make me hate you from the yellow springs below while you / revile me as an importunate ghost!" (Birch, scene 32, 191; Tang Xianzu, *Mudan ting*, 163).

Jiuniang's veiling herself with her sleeve just before vanishing into smoke also recalls the unstable textile images—the silk gown crumbling into dust, the silk stocking rotting into ashes—used earlier to shroud her body and adumbrate its decay. In this sense, the disembodiment of Jiuniang's presence throughout the story reminds us, in Garber's words, that "the ghost—itself traditionally often veiled, sheeted, or shadowy in form—is a cultural marker of absence, a reminder of loss" (130). In other tales, ghosts of palace ladies or famous courtesans from former dynasties evoke bittersweet nostalgia for a vanished glory; the mortal men who exchange poems with such ladies and bed them are granted the pleasure of possessing this past, if only fleetingly.[60] Unlike these ghosts, however, Jiuniang figures the violent, inexorable disjunction of the past, the victory of absence and loss. She cannot be reburied or resurrected, just as history cannot be corrected or undone.

10

De/Constructing a Feminine
Ideal in the Eighteenth Century:
"Random Records of West-Green"
and the Story of Shuangqing

GRACE S. FONG

Women's biographies and writings from traditional China, when they are preserved at all, typically survive in several forms: in tomb inscriptions and commemorative essays written by male relatives or literati commissioned by them, in local histories that put some premium on recognizing the moral and literary achievements of women, and in publications of their writings, whether as independent works or in anthologies; such publications became more common in the late imperial period.

The poetry of He Shuangqing (fl. 1730's) is a case in point. Most of us encounter her poetry in anthologies and histories of women's poetry, song lyrics (*ci*) in particular, for her song lyrics are a ubiquitous presence in anthologies of women poets compiled between the late Qing and the present.[1] Although a meager corpus of a dozen songs, they read with an intensity and individuality uncommon for the song lyric genre; yet at the same time they embody a language that is a remarkable realization of the feminine poetics of the song lyric. We are drawn to the subject of these poems. Who was she?

As with many women poets in traditional China, the facts about He Shuangqing's life are rather obscure. But unlike many whose works were published and circulated independently, albeit with the help of male relatives or patrons, the record of He Shuangqing's life and poetry can be traced to an unusual source—a male writer's personal travelogue and diary, the *Random Records of West-Green* (*Xiqing sanji*) by Shi Zhenlin (1693–ca. 1779).[2] In the original context, Shuangqing appears without a surname. Apparently it was not until some time later that she mysteriously acquired the surname "He" in anthologies of poetry.[3] When her poems appear in anthologized form, they are read out of context, so to speak, deracinated from Shi Zhenlin's narrative. Does this deracination change the way the poems are read? How important is the context or original source for reading and interpreting the poems?

Shi Zhenlin's obscure *Random Records of West-Green*, with its embedded tale of He Shuangqing, was admired by a small circle of readers during the Qing, and in the twentieth century it caught the attention of well-known scholars such as Hu Shi, Lin Yutang, and Gu Jiegang.[4] Recently a second wave of interest has been generated among scholars in China and in the West. In an earlier paper I discussed in some detail the gendered poetics of the song lyric and analyzed the interplay between *qing*—feeling, passion, love—and the feminine poetics of the song lyric in several of Shuangqing's works.[5] Paul Ropp has also translated and interpreted extensive passages relating to the life of He Shuangqing from the *Random Records* in a conference paper he presented in 1992.[6] The panel at which the ideas in the present chapter were originally presented testified to a continuing interest on the subject on both sides of the Pacific.[7] My intention here is to investigate in greater detail the issues I had to omit in my previous essay, whose critical focus was genre. Here my problematic relocates He Shuangqing within the textual and cultural context of *Random Records*. My analysis will thus focus not on a critical reading of the poetry of Shuangqing but on the cultural representation of woman and desire problematized by her story in *Random Records*.

In reading Shuangqing's story in the *Random Records*, we are examining a woman's life and poetry unquestionably constructed and framed as an ideal in a male vision. In my reading of this record within a record, I want to address several questions: Is there a female subject outside that narrative that we can recover; and if there is, how can we do so? Or is the female subject so much a male construct that it is positioned only within the text; that is, is it only a textual effect? What significance does her recorded poetry hold for understanding women's writing in late imperial China? The issues connected to these basic questions are complex, situated as they are in the gender ideology, aesthetics, and poetics of late Ming and Qing culture. As I show

below, in the highly self-reflexive *Random Records*, concepts of fictionality and historicity in representation are already self-consciously deployed and implicated in the processes of reading and writing, which
thus complicate our own interpretation.

To attempt to answer some of these questions, we need to untan-
gle the labyrinthine web of *Random Records*, to articulate the ideology
that subtends the narrative of Shuangqing. Since Shuangqing's story
dominates certain sections of the book and even becomes inextricably
bound up with its identity or raison d'être, we need to deconstruct the
uniquely male vision of ethics and aesthetics that it is nonetheless
made to serve. Lastly, I want to examine the relationship of the textualization and de-textualization of Shuangqing's life and poetry to
more general questions concerning readership and voice.

The Frame

Random Records of West-Green—the text which (re)produces
Shuangqing—is itself a curious product by a relatively unknown literatus, Shi Zhenlin. It contains a short preface by the author in which
he deliberately obfuscates the boundary between dream and reality.
Toward the end of the preface, Shi explains the origin of the book's
title:

> [When a child] I was crawling along a wall. I found something I
> thought was a piece of candy. I held it in my hand and sucked it. My
> family told me I was an idiot, that it was a piece of rock. On this rock
> were characters—one was "West," the other was "Green." I was
> made to learn them. This was how I began to read. The rock was hol-
> low like a mortar. I still sit facing it today. Hence I made the *Random
> Records*.

This childhood incident marks the subject's point of entry into the
written language, into knowledge and discrimination; it also marks
the arbitrariness of signification and the genesis of the book. However, Shi ends the preface with "On the twelfth day of the twelfth
month, in the second year of Qianlong (1738).[8] Composed in a
dream." Shi Zhenlin was then 45 years old and had earlier that year
passed the highest civil service examination and became a *jinshi* (presented scholar). By stating that the preface was written in a dream, Shi
may be denying the reality and implication of what he has just written
and what may follow, or conversely he may be implying that the
dream world and experiences akin to the insubstantiality of dreams

are equally, if not more, real than our everyday world, suggesting the classic epistemological aporia of Zhuangzi and his dream of the butterfly. In yet another light, read as a Buddhist metaphor, the phenomenal world we live in is a dream, ultimately unreal from the perspective of enlightened transcendence. With this convoluted introduction, we enter into a liminal text that mediates commonsense mundane reality and what common sense presumes to be unreality — supernatural and oneiric experiences. Shi's actions and compositions alternate between submitting to the demands of society and retreating into a private world of dreams and poetry. The representation of Shuangqing is also caught in both worlds.

The textual history of the book, too, is complicated. According to Zhang Gongliang (5–6), some scholars claim that the original printing blocks of *Random Records* were burned shortly after the book's initial publication in 1738 and Shi Zhenlin in his old age produced a much revised and reduced text that contains only about a fifth of the original. Is the revised edition what we have today? Does this account for the elliptical style of the work, the fragmentations and disjunctions in the narrative? Could Shuangqing have lost her surname in the revision rather than gained one later? Unfortunately these textual problems cannot be resolved without conducting archival research into the printing history of *Random Records*, for which there may or may not be sufficient evidence.

Structurally, as we have it today in the popular edition, the *Random Records of West-Green* could not be truer to its name. The four chapters (*juan*) consist of an assortment of seemingly disparate materials haphazardly arranged that fall into several generic categories: the informal essay, personal journal, autobiographical memoir, diary, and records of dreams, travel, and other miscellaneous jottings. In other words, Shi Zhenlin put into this desultory collection records of events and people — in particular a circle of close friends, descriptions of places and journeys, discussions and discourses on various topics, and other odds and ends. And in no small quantity, Shi recorded poems and other types of writing by his friends and others, including a large number by fairy immortals obtained through planchette séances. Although the chapters follow a vague chronology of the years 1723 to 1736, the sense of narrative temporal sequence is disrupted by sudden shifts, insertions, overlaps, and flashbacks in passages dispersed throughout all four chapters. The overall effect is narrative fragmentation. The whimsical and erratic entries of these years, some recorded at the time, others obviously recalled, give no apparent design or organization to the work.

However, from early on in the text, there are numerous instances of self-referentiality that make it clear the text was being read and discussed by various people even as it was being produced. One is reminded of the *Dream of the Red Chamber* by Cao Xueqin (1715?–63), a contemporary text that became much more famous, which has a self-reflexive framing chapter at the beginning and which was simultaneously written, circulated, and commented on by close friends of the author. The self-reflexivity aims at defining the nature of the text: it discloses certain goals, purposes, and functions that the *Random Records* is conceived to serve. It is seen as a *yishu* (2.22), an unusual book aimed at reporting extraordinary persons, events, and situations. To explain the content and moral tone of the *Random Records*, for instance, Shi Zhenlin records the disquisition on writing by one of several immortal fairy maidens who communicate to his hermetic circle of friends through a Chinese form of spirit writing (*fuji*):

> In making the *Random Records*, do not criticize unfairly, do not include the common and vulgar, or make friends on the basis of greed. In all cases of writings by literati, the God of Literature commands ghosts and spirits to examine their fairness and correctness. Those whose writings have just intentions and correct rhetoric will be blessed. Those whose writings are selfish and harmful will be punished. (2.62)

In the *Random Records*, then, it is suggested that the reader will encounter the elevated, the elegant, and the sublime, in fair, objective representations and correct language—or so s/he is led to expect. As noted above, *Random Records* contains an astonishing amount and variety of recorded materials. One of Shi's friends praised Shi's social and literary catholicity and suggests his role as historian, disseminator, and transmitter:

> [For Shi] any phenomenon in the world could be put into writing; and anyone possessing one of the marvelous skills of philosophy, government, poetry, prose, painting, calligraphy, medicine, playing the lute, or the art of the recluse, Gongdu (Shi Zhenlin) would befriend them. Moreover, he would put it into writing for transmission. Thus, all those who are without friends could obtain friends at a distance. (3.35)

Within *Random Records*, Shi Zhenlin referred to another large collection of his writings called the *Separate Records of Wugang* (*Wugang bieji*), which he named after one of his cognomens and lost in 1730 (3.33–34, 4.11). Later on in life he was to write another collection, still extant, entitled the *Random Essays of Huayang* (*Huayang sangao*), named after the most famous grotto on Mao Shan, a center of Daoist religious activity since the Six Dynasties. So it appears that he was justified in representing himself in the *Random Records* as having acquired a reputation as a recorder during the years he was composing it. Indeed, time and again Shi reported being asked by so-and-so to write a biography of this or that person. Filial sons and daughters, chaste widows, virtuous and talented wives, strong self-sacrificing mothers fill the pages of *Random Records*, sometimes in brief sketches and other times in more extended accounts. The thematic emphases of these biographies share much in their Confucian orientation with those gathered in the local gazetteers of late imperial China. The people whose lives are commemorated are meant to be read as exemplary didactic models. As Shi Zhenlin reiterated, he saw the *Random Records* as a vehicle for the preservation and dissemination of such models. A friend who asked to have his father's biography recorded even after it had been engraved on stone said, "Even stones would split in time. It is far better to entrust it to the immortality of the *Random Records*" (3.71). An authored work is considered even more indestructible than an inscription on stone and, we should add, can circulate and reach a larger audience. In quoting incidents such as this, clearly Shi wanted to emphasize the power of his book to confer posthumous recognition and even fame on the people who appear in its pages. We can say, on the one hand, that at least in this respect, Shi's work has performed its professed mission in gaining readers for Shuangqing by preserving her poetry. On the other hand, we can equally argue the opposite case: that more than anything else, it is the poetry and story of Shuangqing that have called attention and given recognition to Shi Zhenlin's *Random Records*.

Although Shi Zhenlin is not known to have participated in any local history project, he was very much a part of the educated scholar class that produced these regional records and was obviously familiar with the codes and conventions of the genre.[9] The self-contained biographical form is not, however, the frame in which the story of Shuangqing is told. Her story is fragmented and, like bits of brilliant colors, woven into the complex fabric of the *Random Records*. It is through an apparent fascination or obsession with the ideal "beautiful woman" (*jiaren*) by "talented men" (*caizi*) that Shuangqing comes to occupy so much space in the *Random Records*. Here, the talented scholar and beauty are not the happy pair of popular romance. Shi and his friends used these terms with a twist by introducing a tragic dimension to the definition of a "beautiful woman."[10]

The Story

I have summarized Shuangqing's story previously but will elaborate its beginning here in more detail according to the layout of *Random Records*.[11] The reader does not encounter the Shuangqing narrative until almost halfway through the second chapter. She is introduced in a standard biographic formula—"Shuangqing is a young woman of Xiaoshan. Her family had been peasants for generations" (2.33). Her narrative starts casually, and the insertion of her biography at this point in *Random Records* appears to promise nothing more unusual or distinctive than other sketches Shi included. However, there is a logic of placement at work in *Random Records*: at the very beginning of this chapter Shi records that in 1733 Mr. Zhang Xiuyuan, father of Shi's good friend Zhang Mengzhan, had invited him to study in Xiaoshan (2.1). This brought Shi into the same locale as Shuangqing. Geographical and physical contiguity is an important factor for her presence in the text. As we shall see, in the case of Shuangqing, Shi is often recording not merely hearsay but apparently personal knowledge gained through direct contact.

The passage on Shuangqing continues with more basic biographical and personal information, with a distinct emphasis on her literary talent. It tells of her native intelligence and interest in poetry from a young age, how she learned by listening from an adjacent room to her maternal uncle who was a village teacher, how she had exchanged her exquisite embroidery for poems to study, and how she learned to do skillful calligraphy and could write the *Heart Sutra* on a leaf. In short, Shuangqing is shown to possess upper-class feminine skills, both literary and domestic, skills rarely encountered in a woman from a lowly background such as hers. An analogously talented peasant boy theoretically could have sought social and perhaps official recognition and reward by passing the examination; the story would have had the potential to become a tale of success and social elevation. However, Shuangqing's gender precluded escape from her material and social conditions through her literary abilities. Indeed, the only chance for change in circumstances would have been through an upward marriage.

Her story captured Shi Zhenlin's attention (and imagination) because fate was against her. He noted that no one in these rural mountains recognized her talent, they only gawked at her beauty. In 1732, when Shuangqing was eighteen, the year before Shi Zhenlin came to Xiaoshan, her family married her to an illiterate farmer surnamed Zhou more than ten years her senior. Farmer Zhou's mother had been Zhang Mengzhan's wet nurse. The Zhous now rented a hut by his villa and were his tenant farmers.

After this biographical preamble, the narrative takes an unexpected turn:

> In the fourth month I was taking a summer holiday at the Hall of Plowing in Xiaoshan. [My friend] Master Embracing Fragrance Duan Yuhan came, and we went to look at the evening hills. Shuangqing was holding a basket outside her house. She was once again carrying a bamboo basket to plant gourds on the bank west of the bridge. Her eyes were lovely and bright, but they also looked sad. The next day we obtained her song lyrics: "Huanxisha" written in powder on a peony leaf [lyric quoted], and "Wang Jiangnan" on a tuberose leaf [lyric quoted]. (2.34)

The narrative turns from an objective, formulaic, and prosaic account to a purported record of Shi Zhenlin's own direct or, more specifically, visual contact with Shuangqing and an indication of the easy access Shi and his friends have to possessing her poems, a point to which we will return.

From this point on, the story of Shuangqing is not a continuous, uninterrupted narrative with a clear plot. In the form of isolated incidents, it meanders through the remaining chapters of the book, transforming Shuangqing into the apotheosis of femininity according to two sets of values that often conflict—ethical and aesthetic—as they converge in the same woman. On the one hand, Shi emphasizes her feminine domestic virtues as wife and daughter-in-law with her capacity for suffering, accepting verbal and physical abuse from her crude husband and cruel mother-in-law without complaint while enduring recurrent bouts of malaria. Incidents accumulate that show her capacity for hard work, filial conduct, obedience, and loyalty to her husband, varying in the degree of pain and abuse she has to bear. The following is the most physically violent:

One day when Shuangqing was out of breath from husking grain, she stood leaning on the pounding pole. Her husband suspected her of being lazy and pushed her. She fell face down by the mortar, and the pole crashed onto her waist. She swallowed the pain, got up, and continued pounding. Her husband shot her an angry look. Smiling, she apologized, "The grain can be taken out now." When the rice gruel was half cooked, her malaria acted up. The fire got too strong, and the gruel boiled over. In a panic Shuangqing poured water on it. Her mother-in-law cursed her violently, grabbed her by her earring and shouted, "Get out!" Her earlobe was ripped as the earring was torn off. Blood flowed down to her shoulders. She covered her ear and sobbed. Raising the ladle, her mother-in-law goaded her, "Cry!" She wiped the blood and finished cooking. Her husband would not allow her any lunch because she had spilled the gruel. Smiling, Shuangqing continued to pound grain at the side. (3.6)

Such graphic descriptions of violence are rare in *Random Records*, but they seem to draw upon a long tradition of violence inscribed on the body in Chinese culture. In early times mutilation of the body was mainly a form of punishment and social ostracism. The *Classic of Filial Piety* of early Han date elaborates upon the prescription that one's body belonged to one's parents and lineage ascendants and therefore it was essential to return it whole to them upon death. This symbolic code of the body was, however, manipulated and developed in later times into a new ideology of conduct, and by the time of *Random Records* acceptance by a junior, most often a female, of physical abuse came to be interpreted as a form of repayment. The most extreme form of this was self-inflicted: the practice of *gegu* — cutting off a portion of flesh to nourish a sick parent. It was not infrequently practiced by the daughter or daughter-in-law, and sometimes by a young son or grandson. Mutilation of the young female body came to be a source of life for the parent and a reinforcement and the most potent sign of the ethical norm of filial piety, frequently recorded in local histories.[12] Shi makes a particular point of recording instances of such devoted behavior by young women.[13] Here and elsewhere in *Random Records* Shuangqing is represented as joyfully and passively accepting brutal abuse — both physical and emotional — by her husband and mother-in-law. Her apparent willing acceptance operates as a functional equivalent of *gegu* for the elite voyeurs — Shi and his friends. Describing the abusive incidents in such "loving" detail is one way of incorporating her within the structure and values of the Confucian ethical system and establishing her credentials as a paragon of virtue.

The recording of Shuangqing's story — her suffering — continues to be punctuated by demonstrations of her virtue, accompanied by statements such as "she fulfills to the utmost the wifely way" (2.74), and "she serves her mother-in-law ever more attentively" (4.46). However, as Shi intimated, Shuangqing's model womanhood is suspect, since her virtue is allied most uncomfortably with her poetic talent and the effects of that talent.

The Imaginary Ideal

If there is a recurring theme or topic in *Random Records*, it is the obsession with the ideal embodied in the *jiaren*, an ideal discussed at length in the long prefaces written by Shi's friends and throughout the text and sought for among the women they encountered. Literally meaning "beautiful woman," *jiaren* to Shi's circle connotes other attributes such as talent, sensibility, and virtue. To them, an ill-fortune and its concomitant suffering are essential components of the *jiaren* as an ideal that could be held up for veneration. Two concerns seem to preoccupy Shi and his friends in their discussions: one is the danger and consequences of such an exquisite feminine ideal falling into the mires of vulgarity, and the other is the fear of her losing her virtue. They could countenance the first, since it would not necessarily change the nature of the *jiaren*. In fact, perhaps they would desire to be witness and spectator to an actualization of ill-fortune that would enhance by contrast the wonderful qualities of the ideal woman. But should the second fear come true, a woman who had lost her virtue would no longer qualify as a *jiaren* and so no longer be of interest to them.

Shortly before Shuangqing is brought into the book, Shi recorded the opinion of his friend Zhao Fengqi regarding the ideal beautiful woman:

Heaven has endowed the ideal woman [*jiaren*] with a spiritual heart and beautiful form. She should cherish and protect herself well. If she, because of a moment's pleasure, forever becomes stained, what endless remorse would there be! It would be better to endure and endure in order to keep oneself pure and whole. If she is ill-fated and suffers in this life, she might be reborn in the Heaven of No Sorrow or in paradise. One never knows. Qingmou [Tang Xianzu] would cry bitterly for not having met an ideal woman,[14] I on the other hand would cry bitterly for an ideal woman who has lost her purity. (2.29)

The message is clear: the *jiaren* who loses her purity (i.e., chastity) would cease to be an ideal, a standard of perfection. However, if she keeps her purity and suffers ill-fortune, the possibility remains for a reward after death. As *Random Records* goes on to show in the case of Shuangqing, a woman could become the object of veneration in this life as a result of being a *jiaren* who not only has a spiritual heart, beautiful form, ill-fortune, and purity but also literary talent. This vision of the feminine ideal finally locates its object in the person and story of Shuangqing.

After the episode of the torn earlobe, when Shuangqing was punished by her husband and had to go on working without any lunch, she was ridiculed by a neighbor woman. Shuangqing broke down and made this proclamation: "Oh Heaven! Please let Shuangqing with her body take the boundless suffering for all the world's incomparable beautiful women [*jiaren*], so that after eons of time, those who are beautiful women would not have to suffer as I, Shuangqing, have" (3.7). In my view, whether these words were actually uttered by Shuangqing is immaterial. This is a point where the text attempts blatant ideological manipulation. No matter how we read it, this avowal to the divine embodies the ideal woman as envisioned by Shi and his circle. If Shuangqing did utter these words, she had internalized their values; if she did not, Shi is projecting their ideal onto her by putting these words in her mouth. The use of the term *jiaren*, discussed earlier, appears to signify the projection of male fantasy. Thus this speech is a function of her role as the ideal woman in the text. Shi Zhenlin and his friends would like to hear it from her, would like other readers to hear it from her. Here, where the text is inscribed strongly with male desire, the diegesis robs or dispossesses woman of her own voice.

Both virtue and talent are necessary to qualify her as the ideal, but what makes Shuangqing uniquely appealing to the literati imagination is the abject misery, the mire of vulgarity, to which she is bound and to which she binds herself while maintaining her purity: she is the true lotus flower growing in a dirty pond. But whereas virtue is supposed to shield her from contact with men, her class, beauty, and talent expose her to their desire, which transforms her and fetishizes her poetry into objects for consumption, possession, and worship.

Shuangqing's visibility must at some point strike any reader familiar with traditional Chinese culture as being at odds with the taboo on women being seen. Proper young women of elite families, whether unmarried or newly married, were supposed to be hidden away in the inner quarters of the home, where ideally they were segregated from contact even with male relatives. Other than special occasions, such as certain festivals and in designated sites such as temples, women of good family did not venture into public spaces. Such strict rules of propriety, however, would not have applied to the lower social classes, such as peasants in rural areas, where women helped by working in the open. However, women of peasant families were almost never the subject of the literatus's brush. Shuangqing belonged to a peasant family. Her exposure in public space is in a way a necessary fact of her social class and not a transgression, and her marital status should make her appearance in public even less inappropriate: she washes clothes in the stream, threshes grain in the open, and often works in the fields. From a social or economic point of view, her behavior is not in any way remarkable.

What is transgressive, however, are these literati eyes spying on her everywhere she goes, waiting for an opportunity to see her, to gaze upon her beauty. In the world of refined sensibilities of *Random Records,* such desire cannot be recognized or expressed as explicit voyeuristic behavior but must be clothed in some more "culturally approved form."[15] Thus, early on in the Shuangqing narrative, male desire is displaced into fetishistic worship, transforming her poetry and painted image into objects of their idolatry. But even that becomes problematic.

The Problem of Her Poetry

Although Shuangqing possesses beauty, ill-fortune, and purity, attributes of the ideal woman sought by Shi Zhenlin and his friends, it is her poetic talent that is the driving force behind the literati's obsessive interest in her. Their passionate pursuit of her poetry and her reciprocation turn her poetry into a mark of transgression. As her poetry becomes a symbolic extension of her own body and own person, desire is displaced onto it, making it the object of male longing — the poetry is possessed, adored, shared, and circulated.

As recorded in Shi Zhenlin's narrative, Shuangqing's frequent exposure, her visibility, makes for easy contact. As mentioned above, at the beginning of her story, after briefly introducing her family background and personal characteristics, Shi Zhenlin immediately turned to a description of Shuangqing going to plant gourds west of the bridge, observed by him and his friend Duan Yuhan, who were supposed to be watching the sunset. The next day they effortlessly obtained two of her song lyrics. The first lyric contains an idyllic description of rural life and speaks of the anger and pain she has to endure in her life. It resonates with the story of Shuangqing the talented and long-suffering peasant girl.

"Tune: Huanxisha" (Washing-brook sand)

A warm rain without feeling drizzles out a few threads.
A cowherd sticks a young flower twig in awry:
The time when the small fields' new wheat is brought
    to the threshing floor.

I draw water to plant the melons: they rage at me for
    being early;
I endure smoke cooking millet: they're angry at me for
    being late.
Through the long day pain stabs through the small of
    my tender back.   (2.34)

The second lyric reads:

"Tune: Wang Jiangnan" (Gazing at Jiangnan)

Spring can't be seen —
Look for it out west past the country bridge.
Dyeing dreams, pale pinks dupe the powdered
    butterflies;
Sealing sadness, dense greens cheat the yellow
    orioles.
Don't mention suppressed sorrows again.

The person can't be seen —
A tryst would turn right into wrong.
Incense for moon-worship teases sleeves in vain,
Grief for flowers, but no tears that could dampen
    a robe.
Over distant hills the evening sun dips.   (2.34)

Even though the significations of this lyric seem obscure, the images are replete with erotic connotations for the reader familiar with conventions of the song lyric: spring is the season of love and romance, dreamlike, sensual, and elusive, with flowers luring eager butterflies and thick foliage attracting orioles. But an empty center behind the surface fullness conceals disappointment and frustration. Something troubling is at play here as images of nature turn into tropes of deception. Both stanzas also begin with negations: "Spring can't be seen,"

"The person can't be seen." Something (emotion, feeling, love?) and someone (the lover?) are missed, misconstrued, or denied. The lyric plays suggestively on a poetics of negation and ambiguity.

After quoting this lyric, Shi states that Shuangqing wrote it to mock Master Embracing Fragrance (Duan Yuhan). This comment acts to contain the apparent erotic sentiments of the lyric, which are at odds with her supposed virtuous conduct, and in doing so, it provides guidance for the readers' "correct" interpretation of its meaning. Presumably we are to understand that Shuangqing is mocking the infatuation of Duan Yuhan, who, as the bits and pieces of the Shuangqing narrative gradually reveal, is a married man in his fifties extremely enamored of her beauty and talent. This lyric starts the strand in the narrative of Shuangqing that runs parallel with and counter to the icon of a chaste and virtuous wife. Like spring and its creatures, she is provocative, alluring, and captivating to old and young literati alike with her unusual song lyrics and poems. They beg for her poetry and shed tears of adoration at its power and beauty, and they dutifully copy, circulate, and chant it. They exchange poems with her and ask her to write poems to match their own rhymes. They have several portraits of her done by a painter-friend, who takes pains to look at her frontally and in profile while she is working outside. These scrolls are then carried around and worshipped with incense and prostrations.

Not so surprisingly, the narrative also takes pains to suppress the powerful fascination and displace the eruption of desire for this idealized woman into more acceptable forms. There is every indication that the free disclosure of her poetry to men has breached the taboo against a woman being seen. Her interaction with men through her poetry arouses great suspicion. In the narrative, when pedantic Confucian moral sticklers object to the exchange of poetry between the sexes as improper intercourse, the friends rise up to defend the act of poetic exchange by arguing that when it comes to cherishing genius and talent, gender should not be a matter of concern (3.67). Shuangqing is also seen coming to her own defense in conversation with a woman neighbor and in several letters, one of which is written to, ironically, Duan Yuhan, her admirer, declaring her honor (3.49–50). These recurring criticisms and countercriticisms become quite muddled and even self-contradictory, as though no one position is ultimately convincing, and the text remains ambivalent about the cultural signification of woman's writing.[16] The text, too, may be embodying the contested nature of changing gender boundaries that have begun in the seventeenth century.[17]

The identification of Shuangqing's poetry with her person derives from the rather orthodox conception of poetry as an extension of the self, enshrined in the endlessly repeated dictum: "Poetry expresses the self's intent" (*shi yan zhi*). Truly understanding readers can know the poet through his or her poetry. Shi recorded how his friends Wu Zhenshan and Cao Zhenting recognized each other as true friends from reading the other's poetry before meeting (1.70–71). He also recounted how in 1729 before they had met each other, Cao Zhenting, having read one of Shi's poems, commented that Shi was not a vulgar man of the world and was able to recognize him physically in their first encounter (4.2). All is well when men exchange and read each other's poetry. When women poets and readers cross the boundaries and enter the male literary scene, the taboo against seeing and being seen, a function of their gender, can bring complication and tension to this conception of poetry. When their gendered selves are unveiled to male readers through their poetry, the potential for fetishization is present. One of Shuangqing's admirers speaks of having seen Shuangqing with his own eyes, but it turns out that he has seen only her poems (3.67). From this critical perspective, if Shuangqing's poetry is identified with her person, its circulation is tantamount to promiscuity on her part.

Indeed, many of the poems are self-expressive: they concern her domestic and farm work, her feelings about herself, her perceptions of nature. Although some integrate with the narrative context, others do not quite fit. The extra-textual background for most poetry in the Chinese tradition is limited to general facts about the personality and life of the poet, and many critics and commentators have spent much energy on historicizing the poetry, giving each poem a specific context as a mode of interpretation. In *Random Records*, Shi Zhenlin seemed to have anticipated the process, or to put it differently, he wanted to control and shape interpretations of Shuangqing's poems by embedding them in diegetic specificities. He tried to mold them to fit the feminine ideal of his narrative. Although we can never arrive at final "proof" for the author-identity of these poems, because any language is constructed and cannot be essentialized by the gender of the author, I believe that the attempts to contextualize or naturalize them—not always successful—betray the "otherness" of their origin.[18]

Yet in spite of being made to serve Shi Zhenlin's teleological narrative, these poems have proved that they can stand on their own. Since early on, Shuangqing's poetry has been anthologized, and it is most often encountered in that form. Liberated from *Random Records*, this voice can be heard differently, by women and men, without always being subjected to the stifling mold of an imaginary ideal that in any case fissures and self-de(con)structs.

Endings

Despite the appearance of randomness and non-intentionality, much artifice underlies the *Random Records of West-Green*. Its sensibility derives to a considerable extent from the aesthetics of the casual *xiaopin* essay that became so popular in the late Ming, one of whose characteristics, brilliantly captured by Gong Pengcheng, is "to take life's real experiences and change them into objects that can be enjoyed and intellectualized" and to imbue them with a tragic dimension essential to the beauty and depth of life transmogrified into art.[19] This process of aestheticization is manifest in a textualization of life. It entails a distancing from the objects for cool, detached contemplation and appreciation best realized in writing.

I believe Shi Zhenlin can be regarded as a master of this kind of aestheticization in the *Random Records*, particularly in textualizing the woman Shuangqing. Ostensibly, Shi stood somewhat removed from the *Random Records*. He seldom expressed his own views directly, except in his preference for the friendship of Daoist recluses — that group of men "detached" from vulgar values. I suspect that when Shi recorded his friends' opinions on things, he was often in accord with them and thus indirectly expressing his own. In spite of his claims of a lack of intentionality in writing the *Random Records*, he often tried to shape the readers' perception and response by incorporating third-person judgments and evaluations, as I have pointed out. In a way he was trying to give "objectivity" to the views he espoused by divorcing them from his own utterance, by distancing himself from the discourse. This was also a part of his whole aesthetic approach to life.

If we compare Shi's record of Shuangqing with memoirs by male writers of women who are intimate partners in their lives, such as Mao Xiang's (1611–93) *Yingmei an yiyu* and Shen Fu's (1762–after 1803) *Fusheng liuji*,[20] we cannot help but question Shi's relationship to Shuangqing and his reasons, overtly stated or otherwise, for recording her story and poetry. If her story could not be manipulated to serve as some kind of signifier in both elite and popular culture, what significance could she have for him? Although an intellectualized exploitation may underlie his undertaking, the conflicting representation also points to Shi's irresolution and ambivalence toward the real woman and his feminine ideal. But logical clarity and unity of thought were not strong points of the aestheticized text in late imperial China.

As the fragmented story of Shuangqing is narrated, it gradually becomes one with the nature and functions of the *Random Records*: it serves as a didactic text as well as an aesthetic one—a most "unusual" book. Toward the end of the volume, one of Shi's friends, Bi Keshan, volunteers to go north (to the capital) to raise funds to print *Random Records* so that it can encourage ill-fated women with the example of Shuangqing (4.40). This same friend also said that by obtaining *Random Records of West-Green*, he had put into his bag both the ideal woman (*jiaren*), that is, Shuangqing, and the talented genius (*caizi*), or Shi Zhenlin (4.42).

Once the desired elements (her poems, her beauty, her suffering) had been procured and transformed, however, Shi eliminated the real woman from his text, both metaphorically and literally. The last record of Shuangqing was made in the spring of 1735, when Shi was visiting in the area again. It includes two more song lyrics by her and more accounts of the domestic violence she has to endure as she turns more and more Buddhist in her acceptance of suffering. Her last recorded words are to her neighbor friend, the young woman Han Xi: "Why is it that my tongue tastes bitter and when I eat sweets I get nauseous?" (4.46–48).

After these words, her voice disappears from the meandering narrative except for one last mention in which Shuangqing is transformed into a cautionary emblem at the core of the *Random Records of West-Green*. This occurs in a story with lesbian overtones about two young sisters—one a natural daughter, the other a concubine-to-be who was co-opted by the daughter to be her sister, forcing the father to adopt the girl he had purchased to be his concubine. The sisters' extreme intimacy, especially after the father's death, aroused malignant gossip. At the end of this account, Shi mentioned that when the *Random Records* was completed, it would be sent to these two sisters so that they could be warned by Shuangqing's example and avoid being ruined by slander (4.68–71). Regardless of the incompatibility of circumstances between these women and Shuangqing, the implication is that Shuangqing has come to a bad end because of the gossip that has arisen around her poetic exchanges with men. If that "end" is the end of her poetic production, the rest of her life — whether or how she lived on or died — becomes insignificant to Shi. Her story is foreclosed.

In 1736 candidate Shi Zhenlin traveled to Beijing to participate in the metropolitan examination the following year, at which he was finally to gain success. *Random Records* ends with a series of astonishingly beautiful prose descriptions of the mountains and landscapes "experienced" during outings Shi took with his bosom friends Wu Zhenshan and Cao Zhenting in the western suburbs of Beijing. Not a trace of Shuangqing can be found in this topography. Shi Zhenlin had "known" her in their native Jiangsu during the two years between 1733 and 1735. She has been the object of his gaze, idealized, exploited, fetishized, and then forgotten.

In a different ending, not only is Shuangqing remembered, but her poetic voice has broken out of the male confines of Shi Zhenlin's narrative to hold its own among other voices, male and female. Ironically, *Random Records of West-Green* in fact owes much of its fame and the critical attention it has received to readers' interest in Shuangqing's poetry. She now speaks to readers across cultural and temporal boundaries.[21]

Part IV

"Hong lou meng"

11

Women's Writing
Before and Within
the "Hong lou meng"

HAUN SAUSSY

> It is a greater joy to see the author's author, than himself.
> — Emerson, "Nominalist and Realist"

> ... the subtilest of authors, and only just within the
> possibility of authorship.
> — Emerson, "Shakspeare; or, the Poet"

Educated women who compose poetry are prominent in Cao
Xueqin's novel *Hong lou meng* (Dream of the red chamber; ca. 1750) —
so prominent, in fact, that Yuan Mei thought the book must have been
inspired by himself and his poetry-writing coterie of women.[1] But
historians of women's literature in China are unlikely to approach
Cao's novel with Yuan Mei's confident realism. The poems composed
by Lin Daiyu, Xue Baochai, Li Wan, and other female characters in the
novel are not raw data to be transcribed directly into the history of
women's writing; rather, they need to be interpreted in light of character, context, plot, topoi, allusion, thematic statements about women,
and so forth. When due allowance has been made for the mediations
of Cao's literary technique, I think we can find in the *Hong lou meng* a
sustained reflection on the place and chances of women in Chinese literary history — and see in this reflection not merely an incidental
theme but one of the master tropes of that complex book.
The poems themselves are not particularly difficult, but learning

how to read them in context is — as this chapter will show — no simple matter. The novel's structure provides some guidance. Twice in the novel a young girl's writing of poetry is associated with the motif of "lantern-riddles" (*dengmi*), the festive compositions presented in social gatherings on the fifteenth night of the first lunar month, and both times the expected trickiness of the riddle hides a deeper irony. The recurrence of similar events in different circumstances or with different personnel is a mainstay of Cao Xueqin's fictional technique, a form of hermeneutic algebra through which the reader is invited to evaluate the constant motifs in terms of variable ones and vice versa.[2] Just as in life outside the novel, the return of the new year provides an opportunity of measuring progress and change.

Gardens, Categories, and Anthologies

The topic of women's writing opens with a bang in chapter 18. The first woman to take up brush and inkstone in the book is, strikingly, the highest-ranking woman and the one least available for male inspection: the Jia family's daughter Yuanchun, who, on a visit from the palace where she is an imperial concubine, wishes to leave behind a verse record of the event.[3] After composing a few decorous lines, she commands her younger male and female kin to extemporize poems on the subject of the garden, specially constructed for her visit and subsequently known as the Daguan (Grand purview) Garden. This command is jokingly cast as an examination theme and leads into some timeworn test folklore.[4] The episode suggests a polarity characteristic of many of the *Hong lou meng*'s themes: taking exams, that most serious occupation of the real outside world of adult gentry men, is reproduced in miniature as an amusement for a society of small girls and boys. In the same way, of course, the garden reproduces the world outside it (with Jia Baoyu its freedom-loving emperor), and Jia Xichun's painting reproduces the garden: each time the simulacrum is (or briefly seems to be) a perfected and purified version of the real thing, with day-to-day interests and conflicts removed.[5] Women's writing, on the evidence of this episode, simply mimics the male literary life, but in the mode of non-purposive fantasy. Jia Tanchun and Lin Daiyu express precisely this view in the course of the poetry lesson of chapter 48 (*HLM*, 2: 667).

And such was, in fact, the view expressed by many writers who, in the previous century or so, had remarked on the relatively new phenomenon of published women. When the famous poet and former courtesan Liu Rushi compiled, around 1650, the notices on women poets in her husband Qian Qianyi's anthology of Ming verse *Liechao shiji*, her women writers entered literary history alongside monks, Japanese, Koreans, Daoists, eccentrics, spirits, nameless persons, stelae, and servants. This seemingly ramshackle collection of groups is unified by their common cultural marginality. The organization of the anthology as a whole is patterned on that of the dynastic histories, starting with poems by members of the Ming imperial lineage and moving progressively downward and outward from nobles to officials to commoners. Monks, Japanese princes, dead people, stone pillars, and women poets were alike in standing far from the magnetic "center" so clearly defined by birth, rank, and office. And, what is more significant for seventeenth-century modes of literary evaluation, no author in these groups would normally have sat the examinations. Hence Liu and Qian's decision to collect them into an "intercalary" or "supplementary" section.[6]

Uncanonical persons live on in the subcanonical sections of Liu and Qian's book; and it was with a kindred gesture of simultaneous rivalry and concession that Wang Duanshu entitled her anthology of female poets *Mingyuan shiwei* (The weft-canon of poems by renowned women; 1667). *Jing*, the term for a Confucian classic and, most relevantly, the *Shi jing* or *Canon of Poetry*, suggests verticality, permanence, and the warp of a fabric; *wei*, Wang's term, refers not only to the horizontal linking threads of a weaving but also to the extracanonical, unrecognized, or apocryphal texts that fill in the gaps of the official record.[7]

The most conspicuous defining trait of women's writing was, for these observers and apparently for the Cao Xueqin of chapter 18, its position outside serious masculine pursuits. The late Ming publisher Zhao Shijie introduced a volume of women's verse with comparisons drawn from the realm of leisured delight:

> This book is like an immense shop where pearls, ornaments, clothes, and every kind of curiosity are spread out. Open the book: left and right you encounter fresh springs, is it not delightful? There is no need [for women poets] to "carve feathers and tree-leaves" [i.e., become specialist scholars] or to "harness the winds and ride the clouds" [i.e., achieve success in the examinations] in order to create a grand literary purview [*shiwen daguan*].[8]

A minority view (predating the consensus of opinions just cited) is given by Yu Xian's preface to the anthology *Shu xiu zongji* (Collected poems by women of purity and beauty; ca. 1570).

> Among the ancients, the verse of women was found both in royal palaces and in common lanes and alleys, because it was held to have a direct relation to morals and government. After the Three Great Dynasties, teaching of and by women fell into disuse. Only under the Tang, when officials were selected on the basis of their *ci* and *fu* compositions, did the wind of literary inspiration return to move the beauties of the inner courtyard. (quoted in Hu Wenkai, 881)

If the notion of the ladies of the Jia family constituting a miniature literary academy reinforces the major theme of the artistically ordered world in Cao's novel, ideas about women's literary talent in general, especially in the form they had taken by the early Qing, may well have helped define that theme.

Unwitting Yongwu

Poems occurring in novels are always framed by character and event; taking them out of context makes for a partial interpretation at best. The poems of X are brought to our attention as examples of the kind of poetry X would write, an indication of the sort of person she is.[9] But when, as so often in the *Hong lou meng*, X's words mean something other than what they say, they become oddly hollow in the immediate context and point to the remoter purposes of X's author, the author of the plot. Between these two frames of reference — what the writing character knows and expresses, and what the narrator and the careful reader find expressed in the character's writing — lies the possibility of adequately formulating what authorship (women's authorship included) means in the *Hong lou meng*.

Some chapters after Yuanchun's visit on the Lantern Festival of the first month, a letter arrives from the palace requesting versified riddles from the Concubine's younger sisters, brothers, and cousins. Once again, the command parodies the official exams in a domestic and coeducational setting, with a female "emperor" as examiner. If the mimicry of the examination system — an anticipation, in the minor key of play, of the all-important examination that concludes the novel — shows Cao's awareness of discussions of women's authorship over the previous century and a half, the verse-riddles composed in response to Yuanchun's second command can be read as a critical backward glance on the history of women in Chinese literature ("in" it as authors and as subject matter). The riddles unfold during the famous party scene of chapter 22. For her opening riddle, the Imperial Concubine writes (in Hawkes's translation):

> At my coming the devils turn pallid with wonder.
> My body's all folds and my voice is like thunder.
> When, alarmed by the sound of my thunderous crash,
> You look round, I have already turned into ash.
>   — An object of amusement.

One of Yuanchun's younger, unmarried sisters, Tanchun, contributes the following:

> In spring the little boys look up and stare
> To see me ride so proudly in the air.
> My strength all goes once the bond is parted,
> And on the wind I drift off broken-hearted.
>   — An object of amusement.[10]

The answers to the riddles are "firecracker" and "kite": festive objects due to their association with the New Year and Qingming festivals and so suitable topics for festive *vers de société*. But Jia Zheng, father of both women and here the master of ceremonies, is unable to dismiss the suggestions of early death and abandonment hidden in every verse and, after hearing a few more riddles in the same mournful vein, goes off to be alone with his melancholy.

Readers have long seen the episode as ironic: feast turning to funeral, gladness turning to misfortune. "Against all expectation, lantern riddles conceal words of foreboding."[11] This irony would seem to be firmly in the service of the novel's plot, a machinery of ends and means in which no fictional character counts for much (for such is the meta-dramatic force of the word *qiao*, "against all expectation" but also "as if by design"). Irony of this type comes admittedly rather cheap, for knowledge of the future is as rare among fictional characters as it is among the rest of us. But there is more than one kind of irony at work. As one of the novel's nineteenth-century readers put it, "Each riddle is nothing but its author's self-portrait."[12] If the authors of these riddles are able to compose self-portraits unwittingly, that sounds like a more potent irony — since we like to think the inability to know what will happen to one in the future is more widespread than the inability to recognize one's "self-portrait," especially a portrait one has painted oneself.

The history of women in Chinese literature helps to explain the irony at all its levels, showing both why the versifiers are able to compose self-portraits without knowing what they are doing, as well as why the composition of such verse should turn a lively festival into an anticipation of loss. To understand the language of the Jia daughters' riddles, one has to look back to the tradition of descriptive palace-style poetry (*gongti shi*), a genre whose specificities are closely intertwined with the question of the representation of women. In the formative early collection of palace-style poetry, the *Yu tai xin yong* (New songs from a jade terrace; ca. 545), a "feminine" voice ("feminine" by convention, and probably sometimes in the body too) often speaks with exemplary decorum in an allegorizing mode. The subgenre that classifies such poetry is called *yongwu shi*, or "poems in praise of objects." Now, in a trivial sense the lantern-riddles are "about objects," but the generic properties of *yongwu shi* are more exacting. A few examples will show how a coded femaleness works together with the technique of descriptive allegory to produce a "praise of objects" that is about anything but "objects" per se.

Fu Yuan: "Song of the Autumn Orchid"

Autumn orchids hang over a pool of jade.
The pool's water is pure and fragrant.
Hibiscus flowers open with the wind,
And on the pool float a pair of mandarin ducks.
Fish-pairs leap and thrash;
Bird-couples now and again rise and return.
Sir, you promised after nine autumns
To share a quilt with your lowly concubine.[13]

This is not strictly speaking a *yongwu* poem, but the allegorical purpose of the description is clear enough. Every element of the landscape translates into an emblem of sexual desire: to read the poem correctly, one would have to suspend the literal meanings of each word in favor of the acquired associational meanings. Now for some more obvious examples of the genre.

Gao Shuang: "Praise of the Mirror"

When first it ascended the Phoenix Courtyard,
this mirror shone on moth-like eyebrows.
It says: I shine on lasting trust,
not on eternal longing.
Having no hidden motives, it does not choose
    its meetings;

pure and brilliant, it is incapable of deceiving.
And so this wordless object
will observe (as always) my next rendezvous.[14]

*Xie Tiao: "Five Poems in Praise
of Things, Number 4"*

As elegant as the Vermilion Railings;
As proudly rising as the Yuan Gatetower.
Paired phoenixes hold it in midair, pure and cold;
From suspended dragons it dangles as a bright moon.
In it are reflected the patting and rubbing-on of rouge,
The insertion of flowers deep in cloudy hair.
In vain do I observe this jade-like beauty;
I always fear your feelings, sir, may come to an end.[15]

Liu Xiaoyi: "In Praise of Stone Lotus"

My name is "Lotus": it is capable of a million deeds,
My surname is "Stone": it is worth a thousand
    ounces of gold.
If you haven't understood this unfeeling thing,
How can you claim a human heart?[16]

The poems cited above—and there are hundreds more like them—have in common with the poems of chapter 22 of the *Hong lou meng* a riddling evocation of an object and the secondary evocation, through that object, of another object. All these poems are double allegories—that is, when you get past the first layer of allegory, you still have a second layer to deal with. In *yongwu* poetry the object sung is always double: the poem is about a mirror, a candle, a mat, a painted fan, a pen, a flute, a dance, but also about that object as a rebus for another object, the object par excellence of this kind of poetry, namely, woman. One would hardly bother to enumerate the properties of an object in a *yongwu* poem if those properties could not be somehow applied to an erotic plot. (As for that erotic plot itself, it is a matter of record that many of these "feminine" poems were written by men.)

Gongti shi is inseparably associated with the name and tastes of Emperor Jianwen of the Liang (r. 550–51), a noted aesthete and admirer of female beauty. From its origins in the courts of the Liang and Tang periods, palace-style verse restricted itself largely to the evocation of beautiful women in states of languor and longing. With its set themes and studiedly unadventurous evocation of pleasing surfaces, such verse went well with a palace environment, it has been suggested, because there was little in it that could be found offensive or partisan. The theme of longing could, at the utmost limit of interpretation, be paraphrased as an expression of the official's desire to serve his lord. This form of poetry has been denounced as decadent many times through the ages. Courtier poetry is minor poetry: it runs counter to that strand of literati values that prizes moral seriousness and dignifies the poet as the maker of admonishments, not amusements, for his ruler. The accusations drawn up by the modern poet and essayist Wen Yiduo strike me as particularly thought-provoking, for they get at the rhetorical foundations of the *yongwu* style:

> One form of the perversity [of *gongti shi*] is its tendency to seek satisfaction in things, not in people. Thus embroidered collars, cummerbunds, wooden clogs, headrests, mats, bedroom furniture, etc., all take on a life of their own and indeed become infected [by the poet's emotions]. Then comes the turn of lamps and candles, jade steps, dust in the rafters, to step forward and abet the poets in their efforts to concentrate their ideas and reach the burning point of absurdity. . . . As we observe these tendencies, we must wonder whether such writing counts as poetry, or should be termed a kind of artificial and shameless pursuit of satisfaction. Under such conditions, how can one hope for good poetry? Once expressed in the faded platitudes and set formulas of the palace style, poems themselves can hardly have been more impressive or interesting than their themes. To tell the truth, oftentimes these poets' art consists, not in writing poetry, but in devising themes. . . . Poems became the servants of their titles.[17]

The art of poetry an ancilla to the art of making up themes, humans in thrall to insentient props and things—Wen Yiduo diagnoses palace-style poetry with a variant of the satiric topos "the world turned upside down." But the reader of *yongwu* poetry, if he is to be a good reader ("if you can't understand this unfeeling thing . . ."), automatically turns the poem right side up. The generic expectation of *yongwu* poetry is that, by describing a thing, one will describe oneself—whereby, of course, one describes oneself as thing.[18] That is, of course, exactly what the amateur poets of *Hong lou meng*, chapter 22, are doing: they are writing perfectly accurate and conventional *yongwu* poetry, although without being aware of doing so. Only Jia Zheng, whom one would expect to be a stern critic of the palace style, discovers the generic switch and applies the right model to obtain the appropriate reading of the poems.

As a reflection on women's poetry, this is not entirely unmixed praise. Women can write about any subject, or, rather, they can convince themselves they can write about any subject, but the knowing reader will transform their writing into *yongwu* poetry, a poetry of objects and of the transformation of selves into objects. Praise of women poets in such terms inescapably trivializes them and equips the reader with the spectacles of what cinema specialists would call a "male gaze," or, to do honor to the present context, an emperor's harem-surveying gaze.[19] To write, all unawares, in a variant of the *yongwu* mode is to reproduce the history and structure of "women's literature"—literature that, even when it is said to have been produced by women, inevitably returns, as to its source, to the topos "woman." Literature about women surrounds, frames, is the decisive context for, literature by women; writing by women merely instantiates what has already been said about women. If this is so, then Cao's generalization of the *yongwu* formula suggests that the masculine appropriation of women's literature is not to be distinguished from the possibilities of women's literature itself—a highly suspicious conclusion, especially coming from a man who produces counterfeits of women's writing.

For Fan, Read Author

The meaning of the episode may be that there is no women's literature—yet. Maybe women's literature will happen when women who write come to understand the genre they are (always already) writing in. Or it may be that women's literature needs to be recovered from the imposing scrap heap of literature about women, and this still lies in the future. Jia Zheng's reading of the lantern-riddles does, after all, redirect our attention from the poems' subject matter to their authors, which is a first step toward undoing the objectification endemic to the palace style. But that reading is itself required by the erotic plot of the *yongwu* subgenre. "I might as well be a candle, or a fan, or a stone lotus, for all the difference it makes," says the conventional speaker of a *yongwu* poem, but underneath the descriptive language of palace-style poetry, there is a hidden woman whom the right reading will set free—perhaps with a kiss as in the fairy tales. Such poetry in the "feminine" voice requires a male reader. If, as Wen Yiduo suggests, the *yongwu* poetry of objects isa displaced or alienated poetry of persons, it now appears to us as a gendered poetry that, for complex stylistic and historical reasons, can only bring its male writers and readers "satisfaction" if it is given voice through a fictional woman.

Scratch an object, and you will uncover a woman; scratch the woman, and you will discover a man. "Women's literature" does not seem to be getting closer to existence through the efforts of Cao Xueqin. I think, however, that if we scratch the man, we will uncover another woman, the real author of the *yongwu shi*'s plot of erotic indirection. The founding reference for this kind of poem is Ban Jieyu's (born ca. 48 B.C.) "Yuan xing" (Song of reproach), a short poem reprinted in every anthology of court poetry, in which this lady-in-waiting narrates the making of a round silk fan and concludes:

> Yet always it fears the coming of autumn,
> When cold winds snatch away blazing heat;
> Negligently dropped into a basket,
> It sees favor and passion cut off in mid-course.[20]

Ban Jieyu's little poem is not, I think, a *yongwu* poem but the necessary condition for *yongwu* poetry: the generic qualities of the later "poems in praise of objects" derive from this poem by inversion and rotation. The main difference between Ban Jieyu's poem and the poems that descend from it has to do with the purpose of talking in a language of objects in the first place. Ban Jieyu's poem is about having been treated unjustly (it expresses *yuan*, reproach); everyone would have known that she was an imperial concubine sent into retirement after the deaths of her children. Her choice to let the fan speak for her is an ethical one, expressive of an exemplary (feminine or gentlemanly) restraint.[21] (We also have her narrative treatment of the same themes in *fu* form, but it is far more rarely anthologized or imitated.)[22] In contrast, the language repudiated by Wen Yiduo and so many others is a language of coyness. In Ban Jieyu's poem, the fact that a fan's career could be treated as equivalent to a human's was a powerful means of ethical condemnation, whereas the palace-style poetry of objects avoids the ethical register altogether. To go from Ban Jieyu's short poem to the later poetry in praise of objects is to move from reproach (*yuan*) to praise (*yong*), from allegory to fetishism. *Yongwu* poetry reads or misreads Ban Jieyu's complaint as a renewed erotic invitation, and it turns the specific personal reproach of her poem into the stance of a generalized and indefinitely adaptable poetic persona.

Poems in praise of objects are, if this hypothesis is correct, in a certain sense unreadable unless we understand them as deliberate transformations of this particular poem. *Yongwu* poetry, we discover, is founded on the reversal of the meanings of a women's literature, insofar as we take Ban Jieyu's poem to be the precedent-setting "woman's poem." Jia Zheng's reading of his daughters' lantern-riddles performs this rite of return, too. He detects the subtext of complaint in their descriptive language of celebration. He reads their poems as variants on the *yongwu* genre *and* as laments by the cast-off woman who might as well be a silk fan in autumn. The two meanings of the phrase "women in literature" are connected here by an irony — not just the dramatic irony that stems from a speaker's ignorance of the future, but a stylistic irony proceeding from the misrecognition of one genre as another. The Jia girls thought they were writing in imitation of the palace mode, the male trope on the original female poem, but the alert reader sees them, to his grief, as Ban Jieyu's unwilling companions.

A Female Historian

A second example — one called to our attention by the novelist himself, through its parallels to chapter 22 — is the set of ten "Poems Remembering the Past" composed by Xue Baoqin in preparation for another New Year's celebration.[23] First, however, a word about Baoqin's role in the novel. At this point in the story, the main amusement of the young inhabitants of the Grand Purview Garden is their poetry club. Baoqin, a new arrival, has lost no time in announcing herself as a competitor in the garden's unending contest of wits — "not just a poetry-writing contest," as Shi Xiangyun puts it, "but a fight to the death!" (*HLM* 50; 2: 693). (The exaggeration is characteristic of Xiangyun, but jokes and fictions in this book have a way of turning serious.) The struggle among the women for intellectual leadership is also, unmistakably, a contest for the attentions of Baoyu, the pleasure-loving heir of the Jia family. Baoqin's star is on the rise. In chapter 50, her verses on plum flowers are the most admired, despite the fact that she is the youngest poet in the group. (I shall return to this poem below.) Spying her on a plum-branch-collecting expedition with Baoyu, Grandmother Jia has called her even prettier than the woman in one of her treasured Qiu Ying pictures (*HLM* 50; 2: 697, 700). Such a comparison, though made by a third person, virtually guarantees Baoyu's erotic interest in Baoqin; and sure enough, before the end of the chapter the matriarch has begun to examine her as a possible marriage partner for her grandson.[24]

Baoqin's family story closely resembles that of her chief competitor, Lin Daiyu: both are orphans, both have seen a lot of the world, and both have benefited from an education normally reserved for boys. The momentary highlighting of Xue Baoqin thus yields information that a careful reader will apply to the "case," as it were, of the more important Lin Daiyu, and more specifically to Daiyu's chances of marriage with Baoyu. We know from the novel's occasional harkings back to the supernatural realm that Daiyu's earthly career follows from her earlier existence as a fairy flower: watered in that realm by the sentimental Stone, she now owes a "debt of tears" to the Stone's incarnation, the boy Baoyu. Baoqin's flowering-plum poem recalls fairyland, too, suggesting a complicity between the two talented girls:

> Surely in a former life you grew on the Jasper
>   Terrace!
> No more will your appearance cast me into doubt.[25]

The greatest difference between the two cases—the fact that Baoqin has already been promised to the son of Mr. Mei of the Hanlin Academy whereas Daiyu's marital fate remains undecided—refers back to Baoqin's plum-blossom poetry, giving it, and the whole episode, a new meaning: for the surname Mei is written with the character "plum." The plum tree bears ancient and familiar sexual connotations. The poem "Biao you mei" (*Mao shi* 20) characterizes a late-marrying woman as a plum tree loaded with overripe fruit.[26] The plum is the first tree to flower but the last to bear fruit.[27] Baoqin's precocity identifies her with the plum flower, but her future is that of the late-bearing tree. Her poetry is thus doubly plum poetry and perfectly reproduces the rules of the *yongwu* mode: poetry about plum branches by a personified plum tree. Like the objects encrypted in the riddle poems of chapter 22, the plum tree with its associations furnishes a bridge between poetry and prose, between the limited knowledge expressed by the character and the more extensive knowledge of the narrator. The ancient emblem allows Cao to imprint a seemingly inescapable pathos on the depiction of this character: it is *because* of her early flowering that Baoqin is doomed to a late or impossible marriage, the confluence of motifs seems to suggest, and the ample literature on ill-fated girls of genius would make the conclusion hard for a contemporary reader to avoid.[28]

The parallels between chapters 22 and 50 seem to point to the *yongwu* mode as Cao's decisive model for the recognition of women as poets. Or perhaps it shows that the readers of the novel have adopted that model and insist on reading women's poetry according to its rules. In fact, we do not know enough about Baoqin in later years to say whether her story really is that of a late-bearing plum and so to pronounce her poem in praise of that object an unrecognized autobiography. Cao's manuscript leaves off after chapter 80 with her marriage to Academician Mei's son still in suspense. It is once again mentioned as a future event in chapter 110 of Gao E's continuation. By chapter 118 she is, according to Gao, finally installed with the Meis, as Wang *furen* tells Baoyu in an aside (*HLM* 118; 3: 1610). But some late Qing readers seem to have found this ordinary happy ending unworthy of her, preferring to take the words of her plum poem more strictly as the program for her own future. "Xue Baoqin, this flower of the world of appearances . . . can never find her match, for [loosely paraphrasing Baoqin's plum-flower poem] in the human world her kind is not found. What sort of creature is this young Mei, that he should have the enjoyment of her?"[29] Other readers, equally indebted to the pattern of *yongwu* poetry and its erotic subplot, find the wedding motif the only reason for including the poetry — and perhaps its authoress — at all. "The point of making Baoqin shine [in the poetry contest] is to anticipate the possibility of a marriage with Baoyu. Such magically indirect technique! One cannot fail to recognize it" (Yu Pingbo, 457). Baoqin is an author, but an authored author, limited and framed by another author's purposes, and the authority the narrator and his readers exercise over her poetic speech derives immediately from the topical organization of *yongwu* poetry.

Oblivious to all this critical signaling over her head and stimulated by her success in the plum-flower session, Baoqin opens chapter 51 with a series of ten poems on historical themes, *huaigu shi*. Each quatrain describes a site made famous by figures from the past, a site that Baoqin has seen for herself at some point in her exceptionally broad travels. (The "history" of her historical poems is amusingly romantic in a touristic or schoolroom way: the great events of the past are pre-eminently those about which famous writers have penned affecting anthology pieces — Su Shi's Red Cliff, Bo Juyi's Mawei Post.) Further, each description contains a riddle, the hidden description of an object the reader must guess. Three from the series (here translated with plodding literalism) will suffice to give the tone:

6. "Peach Leaf Ford"

When withered grasses and dormant flowers are
    reflected in the shallow pool,
Peach branches and peach leaves must separate for ever.
The grand officials of the Six Dynasties all come to this:
A little portrait vainly hung high up on the wall.

(The favorite concubine of the famous calligrapher Wang Xianzhi of the
Jin dynasty was named Taoye, "Peach Leaf." The site of their parting, on
the Qinhuai River near Nanjing, was later called "Peach Leaf Ford.")

7. "Green Mound"

The Black River overflows and sobs, not wishing to
    roll on;
A touch of the icy strings brings forth all the sadness
    of a song.
The Han sovereign's policy is indeed unbearably harsh:
Let that "wood unfit for use" suffer eternal shame.

 (Green Mound, a hill near the city of Hohhot in present-day Inner Mon-
golia, was said to be the tomb of Wang Zhaojun, a palace lady sent by the
Han emperor Yuandi to serve the king of the barbarian Xiongnu as wife
and political hostage. For her story, see *Han shu* 94b, "Xiongnu zhuan,"
and *Hou Han shu* 119, "Nan Xiongnu zhuan." "Wood unfit for use" is
proverbial for a scoundrel, in this case the court painter Mao Yanshou,
whose disappointment at not receiving a bribe was the reason for Zhaojun's exile.)

8. "Mawei"

A still face blotted over with cosmetic and dyed
    with shining sweat—
Her gentleness has now faded into the eastern sea.
But the memory of her beauty ensures
That her grave clothes even today give off perfume.

(Yang Guifei, the favorite concubine of Emperor Ming of the Tang, was
held to be responsible for his neglect of government. When, in the wake of
a rebellion in 755, the court was forced to flee to Sichuan, the imperial
guard mutinied at Mawei and refused to go on until Yang Guifei and her
brother had been executed.)[30]

In striking contrast to most of the poetry in the novel, Baoqin's ten
poems have attracted little critical commentary. The reader (or readers) from Cao's circle of intimates known to us from the so-called Zhiyanzhai annotations said nothing about them, a cause for regret not
only in itself but also because Zhiyanzhai's observations so often
spurred subsequent readers to study and discuss a passage. The anon-

ymous nineteenth-century *Du Hong lou meng suibi* passes over the poems in favor of the conversation that follows them; likewise, the editors of the standard modern edition of the novel limit themselves to saying, "Perhaps the author of the narrative had some other allegorical meaning in mind" (*HLM* 51; 2: 706n1). Of the older commentators, only Wang Mengruan gave a key for each poem. For him, the ten taken together narrate (sometimes in the vaguest of terms) the Manchu conquest of China — just as Cao Xueqin's purpose in writing the whole book, according to Wang, was "to set down in veiled terms a history of the beginnings of the Qing dynasty." "He created an imaginary family and put words in the mouths of boys and girls, pretending to talk of feelings in order to record historical facts."[31]

More recently, Liu Genglu has offered an interpretation of the poems that echoes Wang Mengruan's in focus if not in import. The first poem, a meditation on the river battle at Red Cliff, "with its chilly and tragic tone may very well be an indirect allusion to the Jia family, this seemingly indestructible feudal family that is doomed to pull its own house down in internal conflicts." The poem on Peach Leaf, mournful and full of regret, "has much in common with the Rong [branch of the Jia family] in its coming decay, marked by death and separation of every kind." The poem on Green Mound dared to accuse the Han emperor of harsh policies: "So, too, the tragic fates of the beauties of the Grand Purview Garden derive from the corruption of the men of the Jia household." The depiction of Yang Guifei "is like a shadow cast by the depravities of the Ning and Rong branches [of the Jia family]."[32] Once again, the analogies may be strained, but the point of interpreting is the same. As did Wang Mengruan's, Liu's exegesis leaps over the poems' putative author, Baoqin, and settles on the author's author — Cao Xueqin — whose purposes in writing them crowd hers right out of the reader's field of vision.

The pattern of readings that forms around the lantern-riddles of chapter 22, the plum poems of chapter 50, and the poems on history of chapter 51 suggests a tacit poetics of the fictive "female voice" in the *Hong lou meng*. Women authors write *yongwu*, poems on objects that are given meaning by their reference to the self (a self predominantly defined by marriage). If a poem written by a female character is not interpretable according to the conventions of *yongwu*, it is to be read not in light of the woman author and her motivations but in light of those of the narrator. Baoqin's poems form a perfect test case of the second possibility: since she is only lightly worked into the novel's plot, her poems are of necessity freestanding in a way that Lin Daiyu's, for example, are not. Her role in the novel is thus almost exclusively defined by her femininity and her literary talent. And her poems, for that reason, go unread or nearly so.

The one reader whom I see as forming an exception to this pattern, the modern critic Cai Yijiang, helps define the limits of the *yongwu* mode and suggests a broader vision on Cao Xueqin's part. Cai gives Baoqin herself credit for poems whose melancholy tone "reflects, in an indirect way, her own family, which [since her father's death] is on the way downhill." And Cai points out one crucial difference between the lantern-riddles of chapter 22 and those of chapter 51. Each of Baoqin's "Poems on the Past" contains the name of a common object. "Everyone tried to guess what they were, but no one guessed right," says the narrator (*HLM* 51; 2: 710). Possible answers suggested by the commentators Zhou Chun, Xu Fengyi, and Wang Xilian include meat, a trumpet, a rabbit, a flute, a fan, a chamber pot, a toothpick, willow catkins, and a plumb line. But how, asks Cai, can the solutions to these unanswerable poems be such simple everyday objects, when in earlier chapters riddles on similar themes had given the children of the Jia family no trouble at all? The unusual unperceptiveness of Baoqin's immediate audience suggests that both the characters and the critics may have taken a wrong turn, and that the model for these riddles must not be the easily decoded poems in the *yongwu* mode of chapter 22 but the rebuses and punning verses Baoyu found so incomprehensible on his visit to fairyland in chapter 5. If those riddles were beyond Baoyu's ability, it was for a good reason: for to decipher them is to uncover the fates of all the women in the garden. Baoqin's poems on the past, Cai concludes, are best read as laments for the present and future: the "Peach Leaf" poem with its theme of separation anticipates Yingchun's departure in chapter 99, the "Green Mound" poem refers to Xiangling (Yinglian), sold into captivity, and so forth.[33] Some of Cai's readings are contestable, but their structure announces something new: through them, Baoqin's poems no longer reveal an exteriorized self but tell the fates of others; and instead of revealing the gap separating a character's consciousness from the narrator's consciousness, they present the character's awareness as equivalent to the author's.[34] Such poems would invert the hierarchies, both of gender and of genre, on which the composition of *yongwu* poetry depends. If Cai is right, Baoqin's degree of authorship—her literary originality, as well as her author-like insight into the developing plot of the novel she inhabits—is, I think, unequaled by any other character in the *Hong lou meng*. Not bad for an imaginary woman! But there is a further dimension to the revisionary poetics of her language, this time a generic one.

Female Histories

Perhaps the *Hong lou meng* spoils its readers for wonders. Next to stones that transmute into little boys, magical mirrors, ghostly visitations, and the exquisite workings of intermundial karma, the fact that a young girl chooses to write in a genre so conventionally masculine as the heroic meditation on the past does not strain credulity. The concerns of the "poems on history" genre, however, repeat and reverse some of the distinguishing characteristics of the tacitly gendered poem on objects; writing a poem on history might be the most direct way for a woman poet to step out of the special hermeneutic circle that for readers of the seventeenth and eighteenth centuries constructed "women's literature" as an annex to the existing literature about women.

Poems on objects are courtly amusements, but the poem on the past is as serious a genre as Chinese poetry possesses. If the poem on objects turns on a riddling depiction of its (implicitly female) speaker, the poem on history is by definition a writing about others. What others could be more definitively "other" than the dead? Moreover, these others are people, not objects that substitutively emblematize the self: anyone who scrutinizes a *huaigu* (cherishing the past) poem for traces of self-portraiture (an expectation enshrined in the phrase *huai gu shang jin*, "cherishing the past and bemoaning the present") will find it in the speaker's expressions of verbal sociability (praise, pity, condemnation, and so forth). The speaker takes shape before the reader as an ethical center from which relations to historical figures emerge. That center is generically masculine; a serious genre would not require the Ming or Qing poet to put on a disguise, and most poets were after all men. Not infrequently, poems in the *huaigu* mode take women characters from history as their subject, whether because the helplessness of the most-often described women—Xi Shi, Wang Zhaojun, the Beauty Yu—excites pity, or because faded beauties exemplify mutability, or for other reasons involving the complex relations of authorship, political disappointment, and femininity in traditional China.

Statistics are, of course, hard to come by, since the poem on history is not an easily delimited category, but a glance through several major authors confirms a persistent mutual implication, thematic or affective, between the genre narrating a moment from history and the theme of the unfortunate palace beauty. Wang Wei's poem on the heroic silence of Lady Xi (who, forced to enter the harem of the king of Chu after her country's defeat, bore the king two sons but refused ever to speak to him) is followed by a series of three commemorating the loneliness of Ban Jieyu.[35] Li Bai's poetic interests were far from those normally expressed in this genre, but when he did write a rare *shi* poem on historical themes the story of Ban Jieyu or Wang Zhaojun was likeliest to engage his attention.[36] Du Fu's five "Poems in Reminiscence of Ancient Sites" include one on Wang Zhaojun. These three poets were by no means specialists in the *huaigu* mode, but for that very reason they may give exceptionally clear evidence of what they thought the mode required.

The "poems on history" genre thus offered a rich context of precedents and implications for the women poets ambitious enough to try it. (One might suppose that a genre so often devoted to the depiction of women would automatically interest women writers, but the choice of subject raises different questions of gender rivalry and decorum for every female poet.) Anthologies reveal a surprisingly long tradition of women writing in this mode. A few examples should help to locate Baoqin among these female appropriators of the historical imagination.

Empress Yi De of the Liao (1040–76):
"Poem on History"

In the palace, only the two Zhaos count as wearers
    of cosmetic;
Corrupt rains and cruel clouds have stolen the
    Han king's senses.
Only the slender moon knows what is going on—
It peeped as Feiyan entered the Zhaoyang palace.[37]

(Zhao Feiyan, or Flying Swallow, was the concubine who replaced Ban Jieyu in the Han emperor Cheng's affections, later attaining the status of imperial consort. Her sister was also an imperial concubine. To say "the Han king" shows less respect than to say "emperor of the Han.")

Zhu Jing'an (fl. 1450): "The Concubine Yu"

His feats of strength exhausted, the double-pupiled
    hegemon's might seeps away.

Your remorse at the sound of Chu songs fades
and fades,
And your pure soul transforms itself into a grass
of the plain,
Lest the East Wind sweep it into the suburbs of Han.[38]

(The Beauty Yu was the concubine of Xiang Yu, hegemon of Chu and one
of the rivals of Liu Bang for control of the Chinese world in the period of
disorder following the First Emperor's death. Liu Bang's army surrounded Xiang Yu's at Gaixia, and at nightfall sang the songs of Chu in
order to make Xiang and his men believe Chu had already fallen to Liu.
The Beauty Yu addressed Xiang Yu in a song: "The soldiers of Han have
invaded from the north, and from all four sides we hear the songs of Chu.
Great king, your plans and strength are at an end; how shall your unworthy concubine live from now on?" Her song over, she killed herself.)[39]

Xu Yuan (fl. 1596):
"Renewed Mourning for Lady Sun"
The oriole's cry breaks the traveler's heart.
Look back to the Yong An Palace — the road
indefinitely long.
Strings and pipes of the Brocade City vanish
like a dream,
All one sees is the spring wind sweeping across
green willows.[40]

(In the time of disunion after the breakup of the Han dynasty, the general
Zhou Yu of the state of Wu offered Liu Bei, the ruler of Shu, the younger
sister of Sun Quan, the ruler of Wu, in marriage; Zhou planned to have
Liu ambushed when he visited Wu for the ceremonies. Zhou's scheme
failed, and Lady Sun accompanied Liu to Shu. Later Sun Quan brought
her back to Wu by trickery. Lady Sun finally drowned herself from shame
at the way she had been used.)

Xu Can (1622–77): "Six Poems on
Historical Figures, Number 4"

When a scholar fails to realize his ambition
He can achieve renown by traveling to far-off places.
Ban Chao, in arms, went to the far west;
Wang Zhaojun dwelt in the northern kingdoms.
With a sigh she got up from the dais,
A hundred thoughts compact in her mind.
How many years had she lived in the palace,
And her exceptional beauty was only now recognized!
Now, the Lord of Men, sighing in distress,
Immediately ordered the portraitist's death.
With jade pendants hanging across her carved saddle,

With pearl studs sparkling on her horse's golden bit,
She crossed a thousand, ten thousand, miles of yellow sand
And abruptly reached the felt tents.
Painstakingly she drew mournful sounds from her
    four-stringed lute,
Sounds that inspire sorrow in a thousand generations—
While those who in the Han palace had shone like clouds
Have faded away like fireflies in the grass.[41]

(Ban Chao, brother of the historians Ban Gu [male] and Ban Zhao [female], was unable to find civil employment suited to his talents and entered the army, serving for thirty years as general-in-chief of the Western frontier. On Wang Zhaojun's story, see above, p. 298. Xu Can's narration develops the *Hou Han shu*'s hint that dissatisfaction with her rank in the palace may have spurred Wang Zhaojun to go north. Line 10 refers to the later story that the palace ladies bribed the court painter Mao Yanshou to make beautiful likenesses of them and thus gain them the emperor's attention; Zhaojun refused to pay him a bribe, and the painter accordingly made her portrait ugly. When the emperor needed a "Chinese princess" to marry off to the ruler of the Huns, he chose Zhaojun as the most expendable woman in his palace, on the strength of the portrait. On discovering the beauty of the real Zhaojun, he had the painter killed.)

It is quite extraordinary in the history of the Wang Zhaojun theme to see her Hunnish exile figured as a career move parallel to Ban Chao's entering the army. Baoqin's poem, like most Zhaojun poems, follows the tragic version of the story, the one that makes her an unwilling exile—so unwilling indeed that, in a famous early *yuefu* poem on the subject, even Zhaojun's horses join in the lamentation.[42] With this last poem in this tiny selection of poems on historical figures by women, an important fact about their authors has crept into the depiction of their subjects. If *yongwu* poetry was reminiscent of the boudoir and the world of courtesans or (at the most) palace ladies, what of women who chose to write on history? The examples given above (taken from modern anthologies and unadorned by any claim to statistical representativity) show their authors as quick to take up the imaginative authority of men, perhaps because they benefited from a measure of independent social standing.[43] Xu Can, the daughter and wife of high officials, experienced exile to the remote north alongside her husband, and it is probably reasonable to see an element of bravado, as well as of self-dramatization, in her depiction of Wang Zhaojun as no longer the pitiable victim of cruel policies but rather a willing exile with an abundant sense of her own merit. Similarly,

when the Liao empress Yi De wrote her short poem about the mis-
tresses of that long-ago emperor, her elevated position may have
given a serious edge to a rather frivolous subject.

As we saw earlier, readers of the *Hong lou meng* have usually side-
stepped Xue Baoqin's somewhat mannish poetry or read it as the utterance of her (masculine) creator. Baoqin's poems do stick out from
the rest of the poetry in the book. By reconstructing the context of
writing by women in which Baoqin's poems seem to fit most naturally, we may be able not only to give them verisimilitude but also to
show what their eccentricity means. Like her historical predecessors,
Baoqin uses the *yongshi* mode as a foil to the *yongwu* mode. If *yongwu*
poetry centers on self-description, making its feminine authorial persona the element that is most truly read, *yongshi* poetry allows Baoqin
to adopt the posture of the historian, the person whose role is to observe, record, and judge the actions of others. And although it would
be an exaggeration to claim that all women writers of poems on history establish female agency and the writers of poems on objects systematically deny it, nonetheless the broader range of opportunities for
historical pathos and revisionary retellings of familiar legends in
yongshi poetry corresponds to the ambition that distinguishes Baoqin's poetry from that of her cousins. Perhaps her poems are meant to
be examples of the standard pitch against which the predominant female poetry in the *yongwu* mode rings as insidiously, temptingly, and
dangerously false. It may be that her marriage to the son of Academician Mei is intended to be a happy one, perhaps even a model of
"companionate marriage," and that Gao E, merely filling out what he
saw to be Cao Xueqin's pattern, found nothing to say about such a
union. But it is possible, as Zhi Ruzeng put it, for a woman to be
"fortunate, virtuous, and talented."[44] There were doubtless a few
happy women in eighteenth-century China, and Cao Xueqin, if he
really is an author of Shakespearean roundedness that many of us
think him to be, could have found no reason for shrinking from portraying such a woman. But a full presentation of this idea needs to
take into account the writing of all the women of the novel—and their
fates.

12

Beyond Stereotypes: The Twelve Beauties in Qing Court Art and the "Dream of the Red Chamber"

WU HUNG

A handsome poster attracted people to the conference Women and Literature in Ming-Qing China, which led to the publication of this volume (Fig. 12.1). Its reproduction of three portraits of women, instead of revealing real literary women in their historical setting, reflects a current attempt to identify such women in traditional painting. The three pictures, though centuries apart in date, are juxtaposed because each depicts a woman or women engaged in the act of reading. Together they offer a pictorial translation of the conference's title ("Women *and* Literature") and therefore become emblematic of the scholarly gathering. But this modern synthesis is supported by and attests to a historical generalization: created by different artists and representing different subjects, the three pictures nevertheless show striking similarities in theme, iconography, and pictorial style. Without consulting their titles and inscriptions, no viewer, not even a specialist on Chinese painting, could know immediately that the top picture portrays the Tang dynasty courtesan poet Yu Xuanji, the figures in the middle picture are two anonymous Han dynasty palace ladies, and the bottom painting simply depicts an idealized Beauty (*meiren*).

Such a thematic, stylistic, and iconographic generalization in art and literature is often termed a "stereotype." But this description, or rather qualification, is essentially meaningless and counterproductive, because it dismisses a complex historical process in which a uniform pattern of imagination and representation gradually prevails to control not only the construction of fictional characters and historical personages but also the self-imaging of author, reader, and viewer. Moreover, the notion of a "stereotype" is largely based on formal resemblance and ignores how similar (and even identical) images assume different meaning in different contexts. It also overlooks the dialectical relationship between convention and invention. True, a dominant model in literary and artistic production is essentially conservative, but deliberate variations on an existing model also serve to measure creativity. A literary or pictorial formula is thus necessarily adopted and manipulated by artists with creative intention.

This deconstruction of the "stereotype" as a historical concept underlies my discussion of "the twelve beauties," a set of female images known in Chinese as *shier meiren* or *shier jinchai*. (The first term means literally "the twelve beauties"; the second, "the twelve golden hairpins," a synechdotal designation for such figures.) These images interest me, first, for the difficulty of classifying and evaluating them: they do not lend themselves to the traditional divisions of court, popular, and literati culture; neither can they be easily identified as portraits, narratives, or genre scenes. Pin-ups of Qing court painting and popular New Year prints, the "twelve beauties" seem to conform to a standard, impersonal female imagery in late imperial China. But a similar grouping of female figures also dominates Cao Xueqin's (d. 1763) *Dream of the Red Chamber* (*Hong lou meng*), undoubtedly the most creative literary work of the period. My analysis here of the "twelve beauties" is therefore necessarily double-edged. On the one hand, by linking sets of "twelve beauties" in early Qing literature and art into a single interpretation, it explores common patterns of literary and artistic expressions and attempts to decipher their shared meaning. On the other hand, it also recognizes, as Judith Mayne put it, that "structures and codes are always provisional, and that a reading of what falls through the cracks of dominant structures is ultimately more productive" (Mayne, 17). I hope through such an investigation to show how the standard grouping of the "twelve beauties" lends itself to specific forms of imagination and desire.

The Architecture of the Imagination: "The Twelve Beauties" in Cao Xueqin's Land of Illusion

When Cao Xueqin introduces himself at the beginning of the *Dream of the Red Chamber* as its transmitter and editor rather than its

Fig. 12.1 Poster for Women and Literature in Ming-Qing China conference, held at Yale University, 1993

author, among the contributions he claims to have made is "renaming" the book *The Twelve Golden Hairpins of Jinling* (*Jinling shier chai*, often translated as *The Twelve Beauties of Jinling*).[1] All the commentators, starting from the one known as Red Inkstone (Zhiyanzhai), caution against a straightforward reading of Cao Xueqin's alternative title: "According to this title the story must be about twelve Jinling girls; but readers find many more girls of various ranks in the novel. If it means twelve specific girls among many, Xueqin never identifies them here. Only in a later chapter, 'The Dream in the Red Chamber,' does the hero Jia Baoyu . . . discover the files of 'the twelve beauties of Jinling,' who are further referred to in twelve songs in that chapter" (Zhiyanzhai 1.2b).

Here Red Inkstone explores the double significance of the "twelve beauties" in the *Dream of the Red Chamber* as a group of individual characters *and* as a collective epitome of numerous girls. Cao Xueqin himself must be held responsible for this conceptual ambiguity. Red Inkstone's comment was inspired by Baoyu's question, which he voices upon first discovering the files of the "twelve beauties of Jinling" during his dream journey to the Land of Illusion: "People all say what a big place Jinling is. Surely there should be more than just twelve names?" His guide, the goddess Disenchantment (Jinghuan), answers him: "Certainly there are a great many girls in the whole province, but only those most crucial [*jinyao*] ones deserve recording" (Hawkes and Minford, 1: 132). Why are these twelve characters considered "most crucial" by the goddess, who is actually the mistress of the Land of Illusion? The answer must be sought in their fictional (or illusory) status as personifications of typical images, characteristics, situations, and values. Red Inkstone therefore commented on the "Twelve Songs of the Dream of the Red Chamber" ("Hong lou meng shier qu"): "Although only these twelve beauties are stated here, all girls are alluded to and all situations are included." The twelve beauties are therefore a literary device that allows both generalization and individualization. It is at this juncture that these figures are linked to a fictional *feminine space*, which also generalizes female qualities while providing a specific environment. An effective way to explicate this linkage, I propose, is to reread the novel's fifth chapter — "Baoyu Visits the Land of Illusion; Disenchantment Stages the 'Dream of Golden Days'" — which introduces the twelve beauties in an imaginative dream world.

A well-known episode in this chapter is Baoyu's discovery of a se-

ries of cryptic poems in the files of "the twelve beauties of Jinling."
Literary analysts agree that these poems contain the key to the novel's
basic plot. Great efforts have been made to decipher these riddles, but
the significance of the files as a physical property of an imaginary
place has remained virtually unexplored. This neglect is understandable: scholars of literature are sensitive to text; the relationship between the cryptic poems and the novel's overall narrative naturally
arouses and dominates their interest. This emphasis on textuality nevertheless overlooks other important signifiers of meaning, such as the
files' format and manner of storage, their painted images, and especially their architectural setting. The implications of these tangible
features cannot be fully uncovered by a close analysis of the files
alone, but must be detected through two stages of a contextual reading, first by situating the files in the physical context described in the
novel and then by situating this textual context in the material world
that produced it. Indeed, Cao Xueqin himself never reduced the files
of the twelve beauties to isolated cryptic passages. In his story these
files are concrete objects inside an architectural complex. To discover
them one has to travel into these complex, penetrating layers of barriers to reach the secrets they conceal. Even finding the files does not
end this imaginary journey: the Land of Illusion must be inexhausti-
ble; more about the twelve beauties will be told in other locations inside this imaginary realm.

Since this is essentially the story of Baoyu's journey to the Land of
Illusion, his discovery of the files is a single episode in the dream narrative, and this narrative gradually unfolds as the reader follows
Baoyu's travels through a series of imaginary spaces. It is important to
realize that the twelve beauties are not merely referred to in the files;
they are introduced in several places in the Land of Illusion with
shifting emphases and increasing complexity. After Baoyu has read
the files in their solemn official/ceremonial storage space, the twelve
beauties are introduced again in a garden setting by twelve singing
girls and, finally, represented by a single girl who is waiting for Baoyu
in an inner bed chamber. The reader's changing perception of these
illusory characters is therefore framed by the Land of Illusion as an architectural construction. This, in turn, means that the author Cao Xueqin's literary imagining of the twelve beauties is guided by an architectural imagery, whose spatial structure has the potential to be
transformed into a temporal sequence of events and experiences. I call
such architectural imagery "the architecture of the imagination," not

only because it provides a narrative with a physical environment but, more important, because it determines the structure of the storytelling. My investigation of this architecture of imagination thus differs fundamentally in intention from much previous detective work that tried to track down definitive models for the places described in the novel. Studies in this tradition fall into the category of biographical research, which aims to establish links between Cao Xueqin's life (especially, places he had been or known) and his writing. My interest, on the other hand, is not limited to identifying specific locations that Cao Xueqin may have been familiar with and could have used as his models. Instead, my foci are the sources, materials, and logic of his imagination and his construction of places and characters, and my method of exploring these is to study his architectural imagery and its relationship — both parallels and paradoxes — with certain established architectural types in eighteenth-century China.

In his dream, Baoyu first arrives at a place with "marble terraces and vermilion balustrades" — a set phrase to describe palaces. A huge stone archway leads into this place; four large characters above the entrance identify it as Taixu huanjing or the Land of Illusion (Fig. 12.2). A couplet inscribed on the sides of the archway (which has become all too familiar to students of Chinese literature) declares:

> Truth becomes fiction when the fiction's true;
> Real turns into not-real when the unreal's real.

The archway thus symbolizes a liminal space, where reality and illusion lose their definitions, since they can transform into each other.[2] Having passed through it, the goddess Disenchantment guides Baoyu to another gate, this time a *gongmen*, the front gate of a palatial compound. It too bears a couplet, but the central theme is now *qing* — passion or love:

> Ancient earth and sky, marvel that love's passion
>   should outlast all time.
> Star-crossed men and maids, groan that love's debts
>   should be so hard to pay.

Located within the archway, however, this gate as well as the palatial compound behind it must belong to a space where *qing* transcends real and unreal, truth and fiction.

Following Disenchantment, Baoyu enters this gate and then another gate, until he finds himself enclosed by palatial halls on all sides.

Fig. 12.2 Jia Baoyu's dream journey to the Land of Illusion. Woodblock print.

The halls to his left and right are rows of offices; an inscribed board above the doorway to each proclaims its official function: Department of Fond Infatuation, Department of Cruel Rejection, Department of Early Morning Weeping, Department of Late Night Sobbing, Department of Spring Fever, Department of Autumn Grief, and so on. Disenchantment explains that registers in these departments record the past, present, and future of girls from all over the world, and that no earthly eyes are allowed to see the secrets they contain. But her explanation only arouses Baoyu's curiosity the more, and he begs and pleads till the goddess lets him glance inside the Department of Star-crossed Love. What he sees are "a dozen or more large cupboards with paper strips pasted on their doors on which are written the names of different provinces." Three cupboards labeled with his own birthplace catch his eye: "Jinling, Twelve Beauties of, Main Register," "Jinling, Twelve Beauties of, Supplementary Register No. 1," and "Jinling, Twelve Beauties of, Supplementary Register No. 2."

> Stretching out his hand he opened the door of the second one, took out "Supplementary Register No. 2," which was like a large album, and opened it at the first page.
> It was a picture, but not of a person or a view. The whole page was covered with dark ink washes representing storm-clouds or fog, followed on the next page by a few lines of verse:

> Seldom the moon shines in a cloudless sky,
> And days of brightness all too soon pass by.
> A noble and aspiring mind
> In a base-born frame confined,
> Your charm and wit did only hatred gain,
> And in the end you were by slanders slain,
> Your gentle lord's solicitude in vain.

> (Hawkes and Minford, 1: 132–33)

Readers familiar with the novel can easily solve this riddle: the poem's first two lines play on the name of Baoyu's maid Qingwen (Skybright); the subsequent lines predict her untimely death. But as I proposed earlier, such literary identification is not the purpose of my discussion. I cite this page of the files because it is the *first page* that Baoyu encounters in his dream. Once he opens this page, he enters a new stage of experience: before this moment he has been discovering an unfamiliar place; now he pauses to engage in an act of reading. These two stages of dream experience, however, are related in a continuous narrative framed by a coherent architectural imagery. There is little doubt that this imagery is inspired by a type of palatial architecture. We realize this connection not only because Cao Xueqin consistently referred to structures in the Land of Illusion with terms for palatial buildings — *gong* (palace), *gongmen* (palatial gate), *dian* (palatial hall), and *si* (government department) — but, more important, because the configuration of these structures coincides with the spatial and symbolic plan of this architectural type.

A prominent feature of the Land of Illusion is a series of gates, which transform an undifferentiated void into a number of distinguished yet interconnected places, each with its definite physical boundary and specified symbolism. Elsewhere I have argued that an obsession with repeated gates along a central axis — an architectural device that simultaneously creates spatial enclosures and a temporal continuum — emerged when the ancient Chinese began to construct their first royal palaces. The culmination of this tradition was the Forbidden City of the Ming and Qing dynasties, a labyrinth of broken rectangles linked by what seemed an endless chain of gates — archways, gate houses, and large and small *gongmen*.[3] During a grand audience, a minister undertook a prolonged ritual journey, passing through layers of gates to reach the emperor's throne; his silent experience was voiced by an early twentieth-century visitor to the Forbidden City: "He passed through one blank wall and beneath one brooding gate-house after another, to find beyond it only a featureless avenue leading to yet another wall and gate. Reality was softening into a dream. His mind, so long attentive to a distant goal somewhere ahead in this labyrinth of straight lines, so long expecting a climax that never seemed to come" (Willetts, 678–79).

The writer of this passage hints at an important factor that helps induce the dream-like feeling of such a journey: the architecture of the imperial palace, or any structure modeled on this building type, dissolves the sense of reality. As a visitor passes through one gate after another, he enters deeper and deeper into a system of consecutive enclosures. Reality softens into a dream because all the architectural elements framing his journey exaggerate the speed and effect of dislocation: although only a few gates from the outside world, he finds himself part of a silent realm of artificiality, an enclosed architectural space that produces its own standards of perception. We are reminded of Baoyu's journey to the Land of Illusion; to enter this land he must first pass under the stone archway bearing the couplet "Truth becomes fiction when the fiction's true; / Real turns into not-real when the unreal's real." With this proclamation the archway marks the true beginning of Baoyu's dream (i.e., a state of non-differentiation between real and unreal), which then takes a structural form in accordance with a codified architectural plan.

As I have briefly summarized, the first major event in Baoyu's dream — the discovery of the files of the twelve beauties of Jinling — takes place within a palatial compound. Several features of this compound demand attention: first, it is a place of absolute authority, where the fates of "girls from all over the world" are determined and recorded. Second, it has imperial status, since the girls' files and registers are classified by province, in the same way that civil registrations are kept by the government. Third, it is an anonymous place without people or activity. Even the offices are not active departments of administration but archives where stocks of files are stored in coffin-like cupboards. Fourth, the girls registered here no longer possess proper names and physical forms but are represented by secret verbal and visual codes. The form of their files — albums containing twelve leaves — was a standard format in Ming and Qing painting (see Figs. 12.6–7). But instead of portraying the women, these albums allude to them through pictorial riddles. What Baoyu finds pictured on the pages are, for example, "two dead trees with a jade belt hanging in their branches," "a pile of snow in which a golden hairpin lay half-buried," and "a beautiful jade which had fallen into the mud." Red Inkstone comments: "Here the author has borrowed his technique from the divinatory books known as the *Tuibei tu*, in order to hint upon the destiny and fate of the young maidens in the Daguanyuan garden" (Zhiyanzhai, 5.7b–8a).

No less important is the architecture of this place: Cao Xueqin's description of the palatial compound implies a courtyard structure with double *gongmen* and a central audience hall flanked by two rows of offices.[4] With all the indications of its political symbolism explored above, an eighteenth-century reader of the *Dream of the Red Chamber* would hardly miss the parallel between this "heavenly realm" and the most famous palatial compound on earth — the Hall of Supreme Harmony (Taihedian), which was the ceremonial center of the Forbidden City (Fig. 12.3). Although the hall was off-limits to all but top officials attending grand imperial ceremonies, the image of this most solemn place became known to less privileged people through architectural drawings and reports by participants at royal events. It was no secret that two great gates — the Meridian Gate (Wumen) and the Gate of

Fig. 12.3 The compound of the Hall of Supreme Harmony, Forbidden City, Beijing

Supreme Harmony (Taihemen) — guarded the entrance to the compound. During an imperial ceremony, officials of the top nine ranks lined up in the vast courtyard inside the gates, between two rows of offices facing the audience hall. Their positions were designated by bronze markers; they could hardly see the emperor who remained inside the deep throne hall.

This association between the heavenly palace (where the files of the twelve beauties are stored) and the Hall of Supreme Harmony helps reconstruct a historical reading of the *Dream of the Red Chamber*: if this heavenly palace was conceived as a counterpart of the imperial throne hall, its characterization as an impersonal place of absolute authority becomes understandable, and it can be identified as the nexus of male power or a *masculine space*. No woman ever took part in the grand ceremonies staged before the Hall of Supreme Harmony, which were supreme demonstrations of male ruling power. Not coincidentally, when the twelve beauties are addressed in the context of the heavenly palace, they appear not as persons but as coded images and messages in official "registers." The verdict of their fate has been issued by a faceless authority and cannot be reversed. It therefore becomes clear that the nonfigurative, coded images of the twelve beauties represent only a particular view of these girls in a particular place. As Baoyu continues his journey to the next section of the Land of Illusion, the story of the twelve beauties is retold in a *feminine space*.

> Next moment, without quite knowing how it happened, Baoyu found that he had left the place of registers behind him and was following Disenchantment through the rear parts of the palace. Everywhere there were buildings with ornately carved and painted eaves and rafters, their doorways curtained with strings of pearls and their interiors draped with embroidered hangings. The courtyards outside

them were full of deliciously fragrant fairy blooms and rare aromatic herbs.

Gleam of gold pavement flashed on scarlet doors,
And in jade walls jewelled casements snow white shone.

"Hurry, hurry! Come out and welcome the honored guest!" he heard Disenchantment calling to someone inside, and almost at once a bevy of fairy maidens came running from the palace, lotus-sleeves fluttering and feather-skirts billowing, each as enchantingly beautiful as the flowers of spring or the autumn moon. (Hawkes and Minford 1: 136)

This sharp change in the environment and mood of Baoyu's dream journey, coinciding with an abrupt transition in Cao Xueqin's narrative and language (which suddenly becomes extremely ornate), is again inspired by the imagery of a palatial-style structure, which is always divided into two principal sections: *qianchao* (the audience halls in front) and *houting* (the inner court at rear). In the Forbidden City, the *qianchao* is centered on the Hall of Supreme Harmony; the *houting* forms the imperial household and consists of a honeycomb of residences for royal concubines as well as theaters and gardens of various sizes. The designs of these two sections accord with their contrasting yet complementary functions and symbolism: the front halls are impersonal and monumental, without any landscaping to soften the buildings' severe appearance; the rear chambers are intimate and intricate, surrounded by rare flowers, old trees, and strange rocks. The front halls manifest the public image of the master of the imperial city; the rear chambers conceal his private life and his women. After having visited the ceremonial/administrative center of the Land of Illusion, Baoyu has now entered a place equivalent to the inner court. In other words, he has left the locus of male power and finds himself inside a female quarter. (Indeed, one of the fairies complains to Disenchantment for bringing him into this "pure, maidenly precinct.") Once inside, Baoyu looks around the women's room: there are "musical instruments, antique bronzes, paintings by old masters, and poems by new poets" — all hallmarks of the gracious living of a talented beauty (see Fig. 12.7c).

This "inner court" offers a good example for defining *feminine space*, a key concept explored throughout this essay. This term refers to a real or fictional place that is perceived, imagined, and represented as a woman. Conceptually, it must be distinguished from "feminine figures" and "feminine objects," not because these are conflicting notions but because a feminine space takes figures and objects as its constituent elements and thus encompasses them. Unlike the image of a woman or her symbols and belongings (e.g., her mirror, censer, flowers), a feminine space is a spatial entity — an artificial world composed of landscape, vegetation, architecture, atmosphere, climate, color, fragrance, light, and sound as well as selected human occupants and their activities. An analogy for such a spatial entity is a stage with its props, background scenery, sound and lighting effects, and actresses. Just as the effectiveness of the theater relies on all such components, a representation of feminine space synthesizes multiple genres. A painted feminine space, as I will demonstrate in this essay, derives its vocabulary from individual genres such as portraiture, flower-and-bird painting, still life, landscape painting, and architectural drawing. A literary construction of feminine space, such as the one Baoyu finds in the Land of Illusion, not only is a vernacular narrative but also incorporates elements of poetry and drama.

The twelve dancers begin to sing while dancing to a suite of twelve songs entitled "The Dream of the Red Chamber." Scholars agree that these songs, like the files, also predict the fate of the twelve beauties of Jinling (that is, the twelve beauties in the Main Register). This agreement has again inspired countless efforts to relate these songs to the novel's overall narrative, but my initial reservations about this research method remain: once more, the significance of these songs lies not only in their lyrics but also in the form and place of their performance. This alternative focus of inquiry leads to a question: Why should the fate of the twelve beauties be told for a second time in the Land of Illusion?

This seeming repetition is meaningful because it highlights opposing points of view in a representational symmetry. Although the literary message of the files and songs may be identical, the manner of delivering this message must differ according to the place of delivery and the person (or non-person) who delivers it. Unlike the files, which were productions of an anonymous male power that transformed living women into archives sealed in cupboards and offices, the songs are staged by female performers in an inner chamber of women. Instead of translating characters and events into unfeeling homonyms and analogies, these songs turn stories into rhymed verses and show far greater sympathy for their subject. No narrator appears in the files, but the songs are often sung in the first-person voice. One pair of examples will suffice to show the difference. Both the fourth file from the main register and the fourth song from the suite refer to Tanchun, one of Baoyu's sisters.

(file):

A picture, which shows two people flying a kite and a weeping girl on a boat over a great expanse of sea, is followed by a quatrain:

> Blessed with a shrewd mind and a noble heart,
> Yet born in time of twilight and decay,
> In spring through tears at river's bank you gaze,
> Borne by the wind a thousand miles away.

(Hawkes and Minford, 1: 134).

(song):

> Sail, boat, a thousand miles through rain and wind,
> Leaving my home and dear ones far behind.
> I fear that my remaining years
> Will waste away in homesick tears.
> Father dear and mother dear,
> Be not troubled for your child!
> From of old our rising, falling
> Was ordained; so now this parting.
> Each in another land must be;
> Each for himself must fend as best he may;
> Now I am gone, oh do not weep for me.

(Hawkes and Minford, 1: 141).

We may equate this and other songs with arias sung by heroines in Ming and Qing drama (see Xu Fuming, "*Hong lou meng*," 139–40). Cao Xueqin's decision to have twelve girls perform these songs must have been intentional. The intention seems transparent: in their performance, these girls embody the voices and feelings of the twelve beauties of Jinling and are therefore playing dramatic roles. What is being staged in this inner chamber are not individual songs but a "play" that generates dramatic illusions.

If in the earlier palatial compound the twelve beauties were represented through the medium of the law (i.e., through the files containing the verdict of their fate), they are now associated with the staging and illusionism of a play in the rear section of the Land of Illusion. Again, we find a perfect parallel to this second space in the Forbidden City. Between 1771 and 1776, the Qianlong emperor (r. 1736–95) spent more than 1,430,000 taels of silver to rebuild the complex of Peaceful Longevity (Ningshougong) for his use after abdicating the throne. Occupying the northeastern quarter of the Forbidden City, it is both an integral part and a miniaturization of the imperial palace. Imitating the main palace, it has its own front ceremonial center, the Hall of Absolute Sovereignty (Huangjidian), and an inner court; the latter includes a fantastically beautiful garden called the Garden of Peaceful Longevity (Ningshou huayuan). At the northern end of this garden stands the last building in the entire complex, the Lodge of Retiring from Hard Work (Juanqinzhai).

A visitor recognizes the lodge's unique status even before entering it: instead of imperial yellow, its glazed roof is blue and reflects the color of the sky. The hall is at least sixty feet long, but its interior is surprisingly cramped and dark, a result of a curious decision to divide the main section into small compartments on two levels in an irregular fashion. Following a tunnel-like hallway, the visitor turns left and right, passes doors of different shapes and sizes, and finally reaches the innermost room. His eyes suddenly open and seem dazzled by light, not only because of the dramatic change in the room's size and proportion — it is now a large, single-level hall with a twenty-foot-high ceiling — but also because of the illusionistic murals that transform solid walls into transparent windows open to outdoor scenes (Fig. 12.4). The artists, possibly the famous Italian painter Giuseppe Castiglione (1688–1766) and his Chinese assistants, ingeniously painted an enormous wisteria trellis over the entire ceiling; they also heavily shaded each of the numerous clusters of purple flowers to create the visual illusion that they are three-dimensional objects hanging down from the trellis.[5] A bamboo fence is depicted on the walls to surround the room; beyond the intricate windows and moon door is a great expanse of space. There are a series of palatial halls, whose diminishing size testifies to the artists' familiarity with the "linear drawing method." Cranes, also depicted in a typical Western realistic style, are walking in the open courtyard among rare flowers and herbs. Farther away, a range of rocky mountains is painted against the blue sky.

No people are depicted in the murals. The reason is simple: these visual images were not meant to be appreciated independently, but to provide a backdrop for dramatic performances. Amazingly, a small theater stands in the middle of the hall, surrounded by the flowering trellis, palaces, animals, birds, rivers, and mountains. The stage and the murals must have been designed and conceived as parts of a larger illusionistic entity: a bamboo fence, exactly like the painted fence in the mural, encloses the back stage. We may well imagine that during a performance, characters in a drama would emerge on the

Fig. 12.4 The stage and illusionistic murals in the Lodge of Retiring from Hard Work,
Forbidden City, Beijing

stage as though from the illusory world inside the painting. It would
be difficult to find a better illustration of Cao Xueqin's conception of
the Land of Illusion, a place where fiction *is* truth and the unreal *is*
real.

Still, unreal becomes real only in the perception of a spectator.
Two couches, arranged one above the other on two stories of a
wooden structure, were designed as seats for the emperor to watch
performances. A small room next to the couch on the second floor is
again decorated with trompe d'oeil murals, but this time a beautiful
lady is represented. Lifting a curtain, she seems about to enter the
chamber, where the emperor rests after watching a play (Fig. 12.5).
This image brings us back to the final episode of Baoyu's dream journey. When the songs of "The Dream of the Red Chamber" fail to en-
lighten him about the tragic fate of the twelve beauties, Disenchantment takes him into a dainty bedroom—no longer a general *feminine
space* with its paintings and antiques but a private, erotic realm. "The
furnishings and hangings of the bed were more sumptuous and beautiful than anything he has ever seen. To his intense surprise there was
a fairy girl sitting in the middle of it. Her rose-fresh beauty reminded

Fig. 12.5 A beautiful woman portrayed on the second level in the Lodge of Retiring from Hard Work

him strongly of Baochai, but there was also something about her of Daiyu's delicate charm" (Hawkes and Minford, 1: 146–47). This girl thus unites Baochai and Daiyu (and more generally, the twelve beauties) in one person, and she is called Beauty Combined (Jianmei) or the Pleasant One (Keqing). Disenchantment marries her to Baoyu, but the couple's intimate love-making leads only to a nightmare: Baoyu falls into the Ford of Error and no one, not even Disenchantment, can help him. This dream-within-a-dream cancels the previous dream and brings Baoyu back to reality: he has lost his last chance to transcend illusion, and Cao Xueqin's story of *The Twelve Golden Hairpins* begins in earnest.

The Iconography of the Twelve Beauties: Figure, Prop, Grouping, Activity, Spectatorship, Illusionism

An early Qing reader of the *Dream of the Red Chamber* would have been familiar with the grouping of twelve girls as the "twelve golden hairpins" (see Feng Qiyong and Li Xifan, 5; *Hanyu dacidian* 1: 806). The term can be traced to pre-Tang times. During and after the Tang, it increasingly referred to a group of concubines in a household. Although this usage continued in Ming and Qing literature and appeared in poems by Cao Yin (1658–1712) and Yuan Mei (1716–98), the term also became associated with beautiful and talented courtesans. In late Ming Jinling, for example, twelve courtesans famous for their poetic compositions were grouped together as the "twelve golden hairpins" (see Wang Shunu, 230). During the early Qing, the term was further related to the new vogue for paintings of twelve women. The poet Yin Jishan (1696–1771), a contemporary of Cao Xueqin, once visited the mansion of the Duke of Loyalty and Bravery and composed these lines: "Where are the twelve golden hairpins? / Lined up in the hall and dressed in new clothes are merely paintings" (see Feng Qiyong and Li Xifan, 5). Like Cao Xueqin's heroines, these images were also products of an eighteenth-century conception of feminine space, which, as proposed in this essay, is closely related to many contemporary visual phenomena—architecture, the garden, representations of women and their activities, and visual illusionism. But Cao Xueqin refashioned these conventions in his masterpiece so ingeniously that these conventions were transformed into characters with feeling and life. To understand Cao Xueqin's novel historically, therefore, we must reconstruct these conventions—an "iconography" of *meiren*—against which the *Dream of the Red Chamber* was read and appreciated at the time.

To my knowledge, systematic accounts of *meiren* did not come into existence till the late Ming and early Qing. One of the earliest such writings was Wei Yong's (fl. 1643–54) "Delight in Adornment" ("Yuerong bian"), in which an anonymous *meiren* became the sole focus of the author's attention. We know little about Wei Yong, except that he was from Suzhou and his other works included compilations of contemporary and ancient essays.[6] In his preface to "Delight in Adornment," he introduced himself as a (typical) Ming scholar who failed to pursue a successful official career and sought solace in women. Although most of his works did not survive, "Delight in Adornment" became a popular text during the Qing after Zhang Chao (fl. 1676–1700), an important literary figure of the late seventeenth century, included this essay in his influential *Collectanea of Contemporary Writings* (*Zhaodai congshu*).

Wei Yong divided his essay into thirteen sections, beginning with a general discussion of "following one's affinity" (*suiyuan*) to meet a

beauty. The remaining twelve sections focus on various criteria for a
meiren, such as age, gesture and expression, adornment, dwelling,
furniture and interior decoration, activities, and maidservants. The
author gradually moves from exterior to interior and from the physical environment to intimate human relationships. Readers are first offered a bipartite description of the beauty's dwelling; appended to the
main text in the first paragraph is Wei Yong's account of his own
imaginary garden.

> The place where a beauty lives is like a flower bed or vase. Located
> north of the Pavilion of Garu-wood, encircled by the Railing of a
> Hundred Treasures—it must have been the former home of the
> Heavenly Flower Bud. Although a Confucian scholar or a humble
> gentleman may not have a golden room to house a beauty, he must
> nevertheless provide her with a boudoir so she can adorn herself.
> Whether in a storied gallery or in an intricate mansion, either in his
> second household or in his country villa, it must be a clean room un-
> polluted by vulgar things. Inside, there should be exquisite and taste-
> ful utensils and objects, as well as calligraphy and painting suitable
> for a lady's chamber. Outside, one should find winding balustrades
> along crooked paths and rare flowers that reflect one another, filling
> up all the space. The place can never be complete if potted flowers
> and miniature landscapes are absent. [Such arrangements are neces-
> sary] because a beauty is a flower's "true self" [*zhenshen*] and a flower
> captures a beauty's momentary image. They understand each other's
> language, seek each other's laughter, and care for each other with
> mutual affection. Flowers not only please a beauty's eyes, but also
> enhance her appearance.

>> *I intend to construct a compound of modest scale. Entering the gate one
>> would find water under a zigzag bridge of nineteen turns, which would
>> lead to a bamboo grove on an acre of land. At the other end of the forest,
>> a row of five thatched halls would be flanked by five chambers on each
>> side. Three layers of storied galleries would stand behind the central
>> hall. Each layer would consist of nine rooms in the middle and six
>> rooms on each side, and all the rooms would be connected by winding
>> corridors. I want to surround these galleries with rare flowers, strange
>> rocks, gnarled trees, and twisted vines – the more crowded the better. A
>> large garden would be opened up behind the galleries; inside it I would
>> create hills and ponds, build a wineshop, a nunnery, a studio, and a
>> round thatched hut, and would arrange high cliffs, winding streams,
>> villages, and rural cottages – all scattered in the garden in an irregular
>> but complementary fashion. During the day I would dispatch my beau-
>> ties to visit the garden's scenic spots. At night I would gather them on
>> an upper floor, either discoursing on Buddhist scriptures or comment-*

ing on ancient history, either composing poems with assigned rhymes or guessing riddles and comparing the flowers they collected during the day. [The beauties] should write, and their writings should be circulated in the contemporary world. In this way, they would become known but would not actually have to meet gentlemen of the realm.
(*Xiangyang congshu,* 1: 69)

This particular section of the essay sets up a general context for the other aspects of a *meiren*, which Wei Yong goes on to explain. Two kinds of things make up the place of a beauty and thus transform an ordinary space into a site of femininity. The first are individual items; the second is the architectural layout. The individual items offer static "features" of a feminine space; the architectural layout provides this space with a dynamic spatial/temporal structure and points of view. The features defined in "Delight in Adornment" include environmental elements (e.g., particular kinds of buildings, paths, railings, trees, flowers, plants, rocks, decorative objects, painting and calligraphy), personal attributes (clothes and ornaments, makeup, standardized facial and bodily features), and tableaus of female activities. The first half of the section cited above is basically an itemized list of such features. The second half, on the other hand, shifts focus to an imaginary architectural complex and introduces a narrative sequence. The reader is guided through the compound, crossing the crooked bridge and penetrating the bamboo grove. He finally discovers a large garden behind layers of halls and galleries. In this hidden place, he encounters Wei's beauties. Some late Ming and early Qing paintings are based on similar concepts of feminine space. In Huang Juan's 1639 painting "Playing in Spring" ("Xichun tu"), clusters of beautiful women are engaged in various leisure activities inside a garden. The work's handscroll format supplies the sense of a journey through the painted scenes. In Yang Jin's "Amusement in a Rich Household" ("Haojia yile tu"), dated to 1688, a similar garden with its female residents are enclosed by walls, awaiting the master of the household who is returning home with his male associates.[7]

Having observed the spatial/temporal structure of the inner court in the Land of Illusion, here I will concentrate on the features of feminine space as described by Wei Yong and other authors. It is significant that in an essay defining the hundreds of attributes characterizing a beautiful woman and her place, Wei Yong said not a single word about her individual character and physique. When her body and face become subjects of consideration, they dissolve into the fragments of a blazon: star-bright eyes, willow-leaf eyebrows, cloud-like hair, and snow-white bosom. The question of her personal nature may indeed be irrelevant: a beauty is by definition idealized and must therefore surpass individuation. But the problem of her iconography remains: if her character and physique are never documented, how can one envision a *meiren*? The answer is found in the concept of feminine space as a totalizing entity. Reading through Wei's text, we gradually realize that a beauty is essentially the *sum* of all the visible forms one expects to find in her place — all the pre-arranged components of her place are, in fact, features of herself. She (a constructed persona) is therefore identical to her domain (an artificial space). We identify her as a *meiren* not by recognizing her face but by surveying her courtyard, room, clothes, and her frozen expression and gesture. In other words, what we find in her and her place are numerous signifiers without a focus of signification.

It is therefore not surprising that after describing the beauty's house and room, Wei Yong immediately moved on to specify her clothes and adornment in the following section, which continues to deal with her external appearance or "surface." To qualify as a beautiful woman, "Adornment should not be excessive and yet should not be omitted altogether. . . . Casually wearing a few ornaments of pearl, gold, and jade here and there — she should possess what is called the 'feeling of a painting' [*huayi*]" (*Xiangyan congshu*, 1: 69). In the next section, even maidservants are considered a kind of ornamentation for a *meiren*: "A beauty cannot be without maids, just as a flower cannot be without leaves. If a flower stood on a bare branch, even the most famous species of peony would fail to attract my eye" (*Xiangyan congshu*, 1: 70). The interior of a boudoir is the subject of a section called "An Elegant Display" ("Yagong"); the author simply reduces his job to listing some thirty items necessary for a beauty's private room. Books, paintings, and antiques are excluded here, however: these are reserved to highlight a beauty's "scholarly style" (*rufeng*), the subject of the following section (*Xiangyan congshu*, 1: 71).

The tendency to itemize the iconographical features of a beauty and her place achieved more extreme forms in the early Qing. Two types of "manuals" appeared. One, represented by Li Suiqiu's "Gleaning Beneath the Flowers" ("Huadi shiyi"), catalogued individual female activities.[8] Li began with a short introduction:

Like flashing colors on a butterfly's fluttering wings, "flower events" [female activities] are too numerous to be recorded. Enchanted by those fragrant, tender beings, and also enchanted by the beauty and style of their deep courtyards and intricate chambers, I have nevertheless gone forth to compile this manual [*pu*] as a pastime. Please do not pay too much attention to the writing style, just consider [the items listed here] bare bones to be fleshed out in poetry [*shigu*]. (*Xiangyan congshu*, 1: 8)

Li's "bare bones" consist of some 150 individual poetic themes summarized in pithy sentences; each has the potential to be developed into a full poetic text (or to inspire a painting). Here are a few examples: "Teaching the parrot to recite poems on a hundred flowers," "Secretly praying before a blossoming cassia tree," "While she sleeps under spring flowers, a reckless butterfly rushes into her red blouse," "Commenting on a book from her lover with [paint made from] fallen petals," "Watching flowers falling and thinking about life's emptiness," "Studying painting by copying the shadow of orchard and bamboo," "Swinging in the rain of falling flowers." Li's composition was greatly admired by Zhang Chao, who not only offered additional poetic topics in "A Supplement to 'Gleaning Beneath Flowers'" ("Bu huadi shiyi"; *Xiangyan congshu*, 1: 23–24) but also wrote a preface to Li's text. He seems to have realized the narrowness of the world of Li's beautiful women but tried to defend Li against any possible criticism: "Those who may communicate with a beauty include only three kinds of human beings—her lover, her maids, and the ladies next door—and five kinds of non-humans—the butterfly, the bee, the oriole, paired mandarin ducks, and the parrot. Anyone or anything else is dusty and vulgar and should never be allowed to enter a *meiren*'s place" (*Xiangyan congshu*, 1: 15). (These words seem to be echoed in the *Dream of the Red Chamber*: in the eyes of Cao Xueqin's hero Baoyu, only the Prospect Garden [Daguan Yuan] of his beloved young girls is pure; "anyone or anything else is dusty and vulgar.")

The second type of itemized *meiren* description is exemplified by Xu Zhen's (fl. 1659–1711) "Manual of Beautiful Women" ("Meiren pu"), which aimed to provide a more comprehensive "iconography" by listing not only a beauty's charming activities but also her appearance, style, skill, dwelling, utensils, and proper nourishment. Xu (styled Qiutao or Qiutaozi, also known as Yanshui sanren) was from Xiushui in present-day Zhejiang province and lived his adult life in the early Qing. Like Wei Yong, he seemed never to have held a government office, and some bibliographers describe him as "a poor, miserable failure" (see Liu Shide, 368). The "Manual of Beautiful Women" first appeared as the introduction to his collection of short stories called *A Book of Talented Women* (*Nücaizi shu*). This book, whose original title may have been *A Book of Beautiful Women* (*Meiren shu*), was completed around 1659 and published in the following decades.[9] The "Manual of Beautiful Women" gained an independent life and greater popularity after it was included in the *Sandalwood Desk Collectanea* (*Tanji congshu*), which Wang Zhuo (b. 1636) and Zhang Chao co-published in 1695. Xu Zhen opened his essay with an explanation of the purpose of his work:

> I have been suffering from love-foolishness; romantic dreams make me drunk. Although my sad financial situation forbids me to dress in silk, and although I have never had the fortune to win the devotion of a beautiful singing girl, I have been able to rank "golden hairpins," describing them in ornate language as though flowers grew on the tip of my brush. I have collected the paragons of beauty and compiled a manual of taste in that "tender realm" [*rouxiang*]. Now, gentlemen of style and culture who long for voluptuous and literary women can finally identify a beauty and pursue happiness based on this guide; they can investigate hidden mysteries and be forever appeased. (*Tanji congshu*, 140)

Following this proclamation, he classifies his "paragons" into three groups — courtesans, concubines, and the rest — who exemplify a ten-part iconography of a beautiful and talented woman:

1. *Physical appearance*: Cicada forehead; apricot lips; rhinoceros-horn teeth; creamy breasts; eyebrows like faraway mountains; glances like waves of autumn water; lotus-petal face; cloud-like hairdo; feet like bamboo shoots carved in jade; fingers like white shoots of grass; willow waist; delicate steps as though walking on lotus blossoms; neither fat nor thin; appropriate height.

2. *Style:* Casting her shadow on a half-drawn curtain; leaving her footsteps on green moss; leaning against a railing while waiting for moonrise; holding a *pipa*-guitar at an angle; glancing back before departure; throwing out an artful, captivating smile; having just finished singing and becoming fatigued from dancing.

3. *Skills:* Playing the lute; chanting poetry; playing *weiqi*-chess; playing kickball; copying ancient calligraphy before a pond; embroidering; weaving brocade; playing the vertical flute; playing dominoes; comprehending musical pitches and rhymes; swinging; playing the "double-six" game.

4. *Activities:* Taking care of orchids; preparing tea; burning incense; looking at the reflection of the moon in a gold basin; watching flowers on a spring morning; composing poems about willow cat-

kins; catching butterflies; fashioning clothes; harmonizing the five
tastes [fine cooking]; painting her fingernails with red paint; teaching
a mynah to recite poems; comparing posies collected on Duanwu
day.

5. *Dwelling:* A gold room; a jade-storied gallery; a pearled door
curtain; a screen inlaid with mother-of-pearl; an ivory bed; a lotus-
blossom pink bed-net; a curtain of kingfisher feathers for the inner
chamber.

6. *Seasons and moments:* Flowers blossoming in the Golden Valley
Garden; bright moon over a painted pleasure-boat; snow reflected on
a pearled curtain; silver candles above a tortoise-shell banquet table;
fragrant plants in the setting sun; raindrops pelting banana leaves.

7. *Adornment:* A pearl shirt; an eight-piece embroidered skirt; a
raw silk sleeveless dress; a pair of "phoenix-head" shoes; rhinoceros-
horn hairpins; hairpins made of "cold-preventive" rhinoceros horns;
jade pendants; a "love birds" belt; pearl and gem earrings; head ornaments made of kingfisher feathers; gold "phoenix" head ornaments; embroidered tap pants.

8. *Auxiliary objects:* An ivory comb; a "water-chestnut flower"
mirror; a jade mirror stand; a rabbit fur writing brush; patterned let-
ter-paper; an inkstone from Duanxi; a "green silk" *qin*-lute; a jade
vertical flute; a pure silk fan; rare flowers; a volume of the *Odes with
Master Mao's Commentaries* [*Maoshi*]; a rhyming book; collections of
love poetry including the *New Songs from the Jade Terrace* [*Yutai
xinyong*] and the *Fragrant Dressing Case* [*Xianglian ji*]; witty maidservants; a gold incense burner; ancient vases; jade boxes; rare perfume.

9. *Food:* Seasonal fruits; fresh lichee; dried fish; "kid" wine; various kinds of delicious wine; delicacies from hills and seas; famous tea
from Songluo, Jingshan, and Yangxian; various kinds of pickles in
clever shapes.

10. *Special interests:* Leaning drunkenly on her lover's shoulder;
taking a noon bath in fragrant water; laughing seductively beside the
pillow; secretly exchanging glances; picking up a pellet to shoot a
yellow bird; showing slight jealousy. (*Tanji congshu,* 141–42).

Students of Chinese pictorial art will be familiar with many of the
scenes and images specified here, for they form the basic motif repertoire of a type of female image in Chinese painting. Works belonging
to this type, often termed *meiren hua* or "beautiful woman" paintings,
proliferated steadily from Tang times onward but deliberately maintained a limited and repetitive vocabulary. The rigidity of the painting
genre both led to and in turn was reinforced by a written "iconography" of beautiful women as exemplified by the writings we have examined. As suggested by the background of their authors, this type of

writing perhaps originated from the southern cities, such as Suzhou and Hangzhou, where a courtesan culture flourished and where they lived. But curiously, the standardized *meiren* image they advocated was welcomed by Qing rulers with great enthusiasm and strongly influenced Qing court art. Its impact on court art can be understood in terms of the changing format of painting, the changing style of representation, and the changing implication of *meiren*. In terms of format, sets of twelve compositions illustrating beautiful women and/or female activities became common; in terms of style, these paintings testified to a strong interest in illusionistic effects in physical settings; in terms of *meiren* themselves, these images gained new significance when they were transported from their original Chinese cultural context into the court of non-Chinese rulers.

The iconography of the beauty synthesized existing conventions in depicting beautiful women into neat sets of images that, as I have proposed above, were scattered signifiers without a focus of signification. Xu Zhen claimed that his manual would provide a guide for "gentlemen of style and culture who long for voluptuous and literary women." But an early Qing gentleman who tried to follow his guide would not have found an actual woman, but only the manifestations of an ideal beauty perceivable through predetermined images framed in prefabricated situations. She would be either planting orchids, preparing tea, burning incense, practicing calligraphy, playing chess, watching flowers, composing poems, catching butterflies, weaving brocade, talking to a parrot, swinging, or enjoying painting and antiques. She would appear inside an elegant boudoir, in willows' green shade, among beautiful flowers, under the full moon, in a pleasure-boat, or half-hidden behind a curtain. This iconography opened a door for a synthetic representation of the Beauty, which aimed to comprehend her multiple images in a single work.

It was around this time that writers and painters — indeed self-styled "connoisseurs" of beautiful and talented women — began to collect and represent twelve women in a set. A pioneer of this trend was Xu Zhen himself: his *Book of Talented Women* consists of twelve chapters, each centered on a paragon of beauty and literary talent. It is important to note that the number of chapters (and hence the number of paragons) was predetermined: he told his readers in chapter 8 that for a while he could only identify eleven beauties, until he heard the story of Hao Xiang'e and determined to include her to complete the set (Xu Zhen, *Nücaizi shu*, 101). In the end, he was able to locate seventeen women who qualified to enter his book, but the magic number "twelve" forced him to attach five of them as "supplements" to selected chapters.[10]

Xu Zhen's book exemplifies the trend of compiling sets of twelve identifiable, historical women. Whereas he selected his exemplars from recent periods, other writers and painters found their subjects in ancient history. The famous seventeenth-century poet Wu Weiye (1607–71), for example, wrote a series of poems about twelve paintings of gentlewomen ("Ti shinü tu shier shou"); the set mixes famous beauties (such as Xishi), literary women (such as Cai Wenji), and martial women (such as Hongxian; Wu Weiye, 2: 520–22). A surviving example of such a painting is Tao Hong's *meiren* album dated to 1710, in which each page bears a historical beauty reading a book, composing poems, singing, or watching herself in the mirror.[11] Another album by the court painter Jiao Bingzhen (active 1689–after 1726) again contains twelve leaves, each illustrating a virtuous empress of the past.[12] Although the twelve empresses lived in dynasties from the Zhou to the Ming, they appear as a single slender young lady in different dresses and settings. Ironically, these didactic pictures seem to follow the conventions of seductive "beautiful woman" painting.

Differing from these "historical" images, a second type of twelve beauties painting focuses on group activities of beautiful and literary women. (In fact, since it does not necessarily depict twelve different women, a more appropriate title for this type of painting may be "twelve activities of beautiful women.") In a series of twelve tableaus, these women appear and reappear in a variety of formations and settings. An early example of such works is an album, again by Jiao Bingzhen, datable to the Yongzheng period (1723–35) because each of its twelve painted leaves is followed by a poem by Prince Bao or the future Qianlong emperor (Fig. 12.6).[13] Before creating this work, Jiao Bingzhen had depicted images of beautiful women in individual compositions (see Rosenzweig, 157–63). Now he was able to integrate these scenes into a portable, book-like form. In so doing, he seems to have assumed the same role as Wei Yong, Li Suiqiu, and Xu Zhen in synthesizing dispersed codes of *meiren* into an orderly whole. Not coincidentally, most of his compositions accord with the iconography of *meiren* these writers specified: elegant ladies swinging under spring willows (Fig. 12.6a), boating in a summer lotus pond (Fig. 12.6f); composing poems on a rainy day (Fig. 12.6j), and preparing an offering on Mid-Autumn night (Fig. 12.6l). There are other familiar images and

Fig. 12.6a

Fig. 12.6b

Fig. 12.6c

Fig. 12.6d

Figs. 12.6a–l Jiao Bingzhen, "Pictures of Gentlewomen" ("Shinü tu"). Yongsheng period. Twelve leaves of an album. Ink and color on silk. 30 cm (H) × 21 cm (W). Palace Museum, Beijing.

Fig. 12.6e

Fig. 12.6f

Fig. 12.6g

Fig. 12.6h

Fig. 12.6i

Fig. 12.6j

Fig. 12.6k

Fig. 12.6l

scenes: in addition to buildings and objects, we find female figures playing *weiqi*-chess (Fig. 12.6h), holding a *pipa*-guitar at an angle (Fig. 12.6i), sitting behind a half-drawn curtain (Fig. 12.6b), and attending a literary gathering (Fig. 12.6k). Being an excellent artist, however, Jiao Bingzhen was able to supply a mild sense of drama to these otherwise conventional images. In one scene, for example, three ladies are peeping at a daydreaming friend, who is portrayed in the typical "beauty in spring longing" mode (Fig. 12.6b).

The content of these pictures does not surprise us, but their drawing style does. Jiao Bingzhen's work differs markedly from pre-Qing "beautiful woman" paintings for his extensive use of the "linear method" (*xianfa*—a Chinese term for the Western linear perspective drawing technique), which he probably learned from European astronomers when he served as an official in the imperial observatory.[14] The borrowing of this foreign method was not simply a technical advance; rather, it added an entirely new visual dimension and semiotic field to "beautiful woman" painting. Most important, Jiao Bingzhen reinterpreted the traditional representation of feminine space. To him, this space not only was a symbolic sphere but also had to convey visual believability; it could not simply be the *sum* of individual features but had to be organized according to certain overarching structural principles. This reinterpretation, however, only reinforced the original intention of "beautiful woman" painting, since what Jiao Bingzhen contributed to this art was a deepening mystery and fictionality, not reality. The women's quarter remained a constructed space; only now this space became even more intriguing and mesmerizing. The chess-playing scene (Fig. 12.6h), for example, offers the viewer seductive figures *and* a seductive space. Following a receding path, the viewer's gaze travels from the foreground to the middle ground, where a group of beautiful ladies are playing or watching a game of chess. Additional receding lines and oblique shapes—a table, trellises, and paving stones, as well as figures of diminishing sizes—encourage and sustain the visual penetration. But the inner quarter of palace ladies should never be exhausted: a door, overlapping the supposed vanishing point, stops the viewer's eye but triggers his imagination.

Both this illusionistic style and the album format were inherited by the court painter Chen Mei (active 1720–40). Jiao Bingzhen painted his album a little after 1733. A few years later, in 1738, Chen created an album for the Qianlong emperor, which introduced a new formula in depicting the group activities of beautiful women.[15] The activities il-

Figs. 12.7a–c Chen Mei, "The Pursuit of Pleasure in the Courses of
the Seasons" ("Yueman qingyou"). Dated 1738. Album leaves. Ink
and color on silk. Each 37 cm (H) × 31 cm (W). Palace Museum, Beijing. (*above*) Fig.12.7a The fourth month: enjoying flowers in the
courtyard.

lustrated on the album's twelve pages now followed a strict monthly
order. Images and scenes, which in Jiao's album were still largely dis-
connected episodes of women's life, became integral components of a
"calendar" of female activities — indeed a narrative consisting of
twelve events:

The first month: Visiting flowering plum trees on a chilly night
The second month: Playing chess in a pleasure pavilion
The third month: Swinging under the willow trees
The fourth month: Enjoying flowers in the courtyard (Fig. 12.7a)
The fifth month: Dressing oneself in a water pavilion
The sixth month: Picking lotus flowers in a jade pond (Fig. 12.7b)

Fig. 12.7b The sixth month: picking lotus flowers in a jade pond

The seventh month: Making an offering on the Double Seventh day
The eighth month: Watching the full moon from the Jade Terrace
The ninth month: Enjoying chrysanthemums on the Double Ninth
    day
The tenth month: Embroidering inside patterned windows
The eleventh month: Admiring antiques on a winter day (Fig. 12.7c)
The twelfth month: Looking for plum blossoms in the snow

The third and last representational mode of the twelve beauties
focuses on neither famous historical paragons nor female activities.
Instead, it continues a traditional "portrait" style; only now the subject
of portrayal is no longer a single person, but twelve women (or twelve
variations on a single woman) depicted or described one after another
in a series of compositions. A literary work that falls into this category
is Su Zhikun's (1613–87) "The Enjoyment of Twelve Leisurely Feelings" ("Xianqing shier wu").[16] In extremely ornate language he ex-

Fig. 12.7c The eleventh month: admiring antiques on a winter day

pressed his appreciation for a beauty's transcendence (*xian*), understanding (*da*), and literary talent (*cai*), as well as for her charming
manners on private occasions (*Xiangyan congshu*, 1: 31–36). The best
pictorial example of this mode is a set of twelve female images commissioned by the Yongzheng emperor (r. 1723–35) before he ascended
the throne. A study of these images, as well as their architectural setting and relationship with Yongzheng's writing, will allow us explore
more deeply the meaning of twelve beauties in Qing court art.

Imperial Feminine Space: Yongzheng's Screen of Twelve Beauties and His "Twelve Songs on the Yuanming Yuan's Scenic Spots"

A set of twelve anonymous paintings, each representing an individual woman inside or outside her dwelling (Figs. 12.8a-l), was

found in the early 1950's during the process of inventorying the holdings of the Forbidden City (now the Palace Museum).[17] Three unusual features of these works were noted at once. First, they are uncommonly large for silk paintings. Close to one meter wide and two meters tall, each canvas provided the artist with enough space to depict a life-sized female image in a vertical composition. Second, unlike a traditional Chinese handscroll or hanging scroll, which has a roller attached to one end, these paintings are flat pieces, each loosely rolled around a wooden stick when they were found.[18] Third, although the paintings do not bear the artist's signature, a piece of calligraphy decorating a woman's chamber (Fig. 12.8c) is signed with three sobriquets, including the written signature "A Retired Gentleman Who Breaks Away from the Dusty World" (Pochen jushi) and two seal impressions: "Heaven Inside a Bottle" (Huzhongtian) and "The Master of the Yuanming Garden" (Yuanming zhuren). All three sobriquets were used by Yinzhen or the Yongzheng emperor, but only before 1723 while he was still a prince.

These features contributed to the paintings' initial identification and classification. Their physical attributes, particularly their size and mounting style, led the museum's curators to classify them as *tieluo* (meaning literally "gluing on and taking off") — silk or paper paintings mounted on walls. Unlike a mural, which is a permanent architectural feature, a *tieluo* picture could easily be removed whenever it was found undesirable or too precious to remain a wall decoration. *Tieluo* pictures of the precious variety became part of the imperial art collection and were preserved in the painting storage rooms in the palace; it was believed that the twelve painted ladies fell into this category. Other factors, including the women's life-size images, Yongzheng's calligraphy inside the boudoir, the paintings' striking "realistic" pictorial style, and the great attention paid to detail, further aroused speculation that the painted figures must be "portraits" of real women intimately connected to the prince. This possibility was so enticing that before further investigation or proof, the set of paintings became known as the "Twelve Consorts of Prince Yinzhen" or even the "Twelve Concubines of the Yongzheng Emperor"; such titles were then adopted in exhibitions, catalogues, and research papers (see Huan Miaozi; Palace Museum, *Gugong bowuyuan*, 267).

Both opinions about the paintings' function and subject were imprecise and potentially misleading, however. In 1986, Zhu Jiajin, a senior research fellow in the Palace Museum, discovered a short file in

Fig. 12.8 Anonymous, "Yongzheng's Twelve Beauties." Before 1723. Hanging scrolls (originally mounted on the twelve panels of a screen). Ink and color on silk. Each 184 cm (H) × 98 cm (W). Palace Museum, Beijing. (*above*) Figs. 12.8a (*l.*) and 12.8b (*r.*)

the vast archives of the Internal Affairs Department (Neiwufu) of the Qing court. Written by the official in charge of the Woodwork Division (Muzuo), the file records a special edict made by the Yongzheng emperor in 1732:

> A memoir from the Yuanming Garden states that the garden's treasurer kept twelve silk paintings of beautiful women [*meiren*], which were removed from an "enclosing screen" [*weiping*] in the Reading Hall Deep Inside Weeping Willows [Shenliu dushu tang]. The emperor issued the following order through Eunuch Cangzhou: "Each painting should be kept between pieces of plain paper. A wood stick should be made specially for each painting [so that the painting can be rolled onto it for better preservation]." Twelve sticks of fir wood, each three *chi* and three *cun* long, have been completed today. (Cited in Zhu Jiajin, 45)

Since this document clearly refers to the twelve painted ladies later found in the Palace Museum (which were preserved exactly as

Fig. 12.8c   Fig. 12.8d

the emperor demanded), the paintings' classification and identification must be reconsidered. Most important, the file partially explains the paintings' early history. We now know that the painted ladies, instead of decorating the walls of a palace hall, originally appeared on the twelve panels of a screen; the term *weiping* further suggests that this screen, like many multi-panel screens that still stand *in situ* in the Palace Museum, "enclosed" (*wei*) a throne or a couch. The screen must have been created after 1709: in that year, Yongzheng, then known as Prince Yong (Yong qinwang), received the Yuanming Garden, formerly an imperial garden, from his father, the Kangxi emperor (r. 1662–1722), as a personal gift. The garden's layout and components at that time are unclear; records of this most famous Chinese garden usually describe its appearance following the enormous expansions conducted by Yongzheng's successor, Qianlong. Judging from Yongzheng's writings, the Yuanming Garden before 1725 had fewer buildings scattered throughout a broad area dotted with ponds and lakes of various sizes. It was the private summer resort of the prince,

Fig. 12.8e   Fig. 12.8f

who maintained his office inside the walled capital city, some ten miles away.

One important clue to the screen's significance is its original location: the Reading Hall Deep Inside Weeping Willows in the Yuanming Garden. Interestingly, this building seems to have held a special significance for Yongzheng, but it was seldom noted after his reign. (For some unknown reason, Qianlong seems to have deliberately ignored this site. Although all Qianlong-period illustrations of the Yuanming Garden depicted this building, it was not listed among the garden's "famous scenes" [*jing*] and was rarely mentioned by the emperor in his numerous poems on the garden.) Qianlong's indifference becomes especially suspicious because his father, Yongzheng, passionately favored this place both before and after ascending the throne. Indeed, the Reading Hall Deep Inside Weeping Willows is the most frequent topic of Yongzheng's poetic writings on the Yuanming Garden.[19] Among these works, a series of "Twelve Songs on the Garden's Scenic Spots" ("Yuanjing shier yong") was composed before he became em-

Fig. 12.8g   Fig. 12.8h

peror; the first song is about the Reading Hall (*Qingshizong yuzhi wenji, juan* 26):

> *The Reading Hall Deep Inside Weeping Willows*
>
> How elegant and fine are the thousand weeping willows,
>   Embracing this thatched hall in their cool shade.
> Their floating strands gently brush against an inkstone;
>   Their catkins leave dotted marks on a lute-stand.
> The oriole's song warms up their spring branches;
>   The cicada's cry chills their autumn leaves.
> In moonlight they cast their shadows on the hall's windows,
>   Concealing yet enhancing the fragrance of ancient books.

The images employed here—silky willow strands, fluttering catkins, singing orioles and cicadas, cool shade and shadows, and fragrant ancient books—induce a sense of intimacy and privacy that Yongzheng seemed to associate with this site. Located on the west shore of an enormous lake (later known as Fuhai, or Sea of Happiness)

Fig. 12.8i   Fig. 12.8j

and surrounded by low hills on three other sides, the Reading Hall was hidden from outside; the "thousand weeping willows" must have further concealed it behind their leafy branches. The design of the building — actually an architectural complex consisting of a number of structures — did not aim at a grand public image but stressed changing viewpoints, temporal movement, and spatial intricacy. The existing drawings show three or four single-level buildings of moderate scale, connected by roofed corridors to form a zigzag pattern, stretching from the waterfront into a wooded valley (Fig. 12.9).

But the intimacy and privacy inherent in the Reading Hall must be conceived on a deeper level, beyond architecture and environment: Yongzheng described this spot as if he were writing about one of his favorite concubines. He bestowed on the site overtly feminine qualities; many of his poetic images have a double function, describing a landscape feature and anthropomorphizing it at the same time. The chief image of this sort, of course, is the weeping willow (*liu*), which

Fig. 12.8k   Fig. 12.8l

had become a commonplace metaphor in both elite and popular cultures for beautiful women. Thus, words like *liuyao* (willow-branch waist) and *liumei* (willow-leaf eyebrows) describe fine female features; *liuyao* (tender as willow) and *liuruo* (fragile as willow) characterize exaggerated femininity; *liusi* (willow strands) is a pun on *xiangsi*, a woman's lovesickness; and *liuxu* (willow catkins) sometimes alludes to an intellectual lady. Within this literary and linguistic tradition, the ambiguity in Yongzheng's poem must have been deliberate. The poem's real subject is neither willows nor women, but the feminization of place. Thus the subtle movement of willow branches seems to belong to the one who gently lays her brush on an inkstone and plays her lute; the willows' nocturnal shadow conceals the fragrance of her books. The woman is unidentified; what matters is that her images and sensibility characterize the site.

Other poems in the series encourage such a reading. Following the verses on the Reading Hall, the second poem is subtitled "The Bamboo Cloister" ("Zhuzi yuan").

漁盧朗鑒

Fig. 12.9 Anonymous, Reading Hall Deep Inside Willow Trees (the topmost group of buildings), in the Yuanming Garden. 18th century. Woodcut print. Reprinted from *Yuzhi yuanmingyuan tuyong* (Pictures of the Yuanming Garden with poems by Emperor Yongzheng [Shijiazhuang: Hebei meishu chubanshe, 1979]).

> A stream winds into a deep courtyard.
> A corridor turns into a bamboo-flanked path.
> Their jade girdles give forth a tinkling sound;
> Gracefully they play with the clear breeze.
> Their fragrance penetrates book covers;
> Their cool shade protects patterned window
>   gratings.
> So elegant, fine, and beautiful—
> Yet they determine to flourish only in harsh winter.

Significantly, here the bamboo—a traditional symbol for loyal ministers and pure literati—is likened to a secluded woman who is at once beautiful, faithful, and well read (again, books are mentioned). It seems that in being anthropomorphized, the prince's private garden had to reject any association with masculinity and to transfer conventional male symbols into a female domain.[20]

A number of factors link Yongzheng's screen and the poetry series into a single historical context. In terms of place, both were directly associated with the Yuanming Garden. In terms of time, both were created when Yongzheng was still a prince. In terms of authorship, Yongzheng not only wrote the poems but also took part in the paintings' creation. Although the women and other pictorial images on the screen must have been done by a skilled court painter, Yongzheng inscribed almost all the calligraphy appearing inside the women's painted rooms, including two poetry scrolls signed with his own sobriquets (Figs. 12.8c, k) and perhaps also copies of masterpieces by Mi Fu and Dong Qichang in the boudoir (Figs. 12.8f, i).[21] He thus assumed the roles of both patron and co-artist. As patron, he commissioned the screen and installed it in one of his rooms. As co-artist, he integrated his calligraphy into the paintings' overall design. By cleverly inscribing wall spaces in the boudoir and by deliberately leaving part of an inscription outside the picture frame, his writing contributed to the coherence of the pictorial composition rather than challenging it.

The most convincing evidence for the interrelationship between the poetry series and the painted screen, however, is found in their shared subject and imagery. Although Yongzheng titled his poetry series "Twelve Songs on the Garden's Scenic Spots" and specified the subject of each poem, he offered few physical clues to the actual sites he claimed to describe. Instead, he was motivated by a strong desire to feminize these places in two complementary ways. His first method was to substitute a particular plant for the site and to describe the plant *as if* it were a woman. Thus, the willow trees surrounding the Reading Hall have "floating strands gently brushing against an inkstone," and the bamboo in the garden's Bamboo Cloister wears "jade girdles [that] give forth a tinkling sound." The second method was to center the poetic imagination on an elusive female figure, who seems to occupy the site and whose appearance, activity, and mood seem to give the site a distinctive personality. Thus, a woman seems to be sitting in "The Wutong Cloister" ("Wutong yuan") and waiting for moonrise; another woman (or the same woman?) in "The Peach Blossom Dock" ("Taohua wu") is brightened by peach flowers after an early spring snow.

Both methods were used to create Yongzheng's painted screen as well: each composition is centered on an anonymous lady, and her femininity is enhanced by the physical environment. In some cases, individual poems and paintings even form interreferential "pairs." I have cited "The Bamboo Cloister," in which the evergreen bamboo alludes to an elegant and secluded woman. On one of the screen's twelve panels (Fig. 12.8g), a cluster of lush bamboo half-blocks the entrance to a deep courtyard, and a woman is emerging from behind the doorway. The tall bamboo stems frame the picture on the right; the slender female figure holds the door frame to the left. Their symmetrical placement and echoing relationship imply semantic interchangeability. A similar equation between a plant and a female figure also characterizes other painted panels of the screen. In one case, a lady is sitting beside a large *wutong* tree, whose broad leaves form a canopy for her. Through the moon-gate behind the woman, we see piles of books and a rectangular gate in the distance; both gates have unique bluish frames not seen in other panels (Fig. 12.8l). With these features, this scene seems to be related to the third poem in the series. Titled "The Wutong Cloister," the poem includes these lines: "Chanting in the wind, the sound of leaves passes the turquoise chamber. / Waiting for moonrise, she is seated in a *wutong* pavilion." On another screen panel (Fig. 12.8b), a woman sewing in her room gazes at two lotus blossoms on a single stem outside her window. Called *bingdi lian* in Chinese, this anomaly is a famous symbol for romantic love. The theme of love (conveyed also by other pictorial images such as the two goldfish swimming under lotus leaves) is the topic of Yongzheng's poem, "The Lotus Pond" ("Lianhua chi"):

> Casting their double reflections on deep or shallow
>   water;
> Their joint fragrance is so enchanting . . .
> Please do not break the lotus leaves when collecting
>   flowers,
> Save them to shade the pair of love birds.

Strong parallels again link other poems and paintings. In his verses on "The Peach Blossom Dock," Yongzheng described peach flowers as "crimson snow" that covers a lady's chamber and brightens her clothes. A screen panel (Fig. 12.8j) depicts a chilly day after a light snow. Bamboo leaves have turned white, and a woman in a fur hat is warming herself by a charcoal stove. Only a blossoming peach branch discloses spring's arrival. Hanging down from the eaves, its abundant pink and white flowers indeed invoke the image of "crimson snow." In contrast to this winter picture, another screen panel offers a summer scene (Fig. 12.8a): a large hexagonal window on a rose trellis separates a beautiful woman from us, the onlookers. She leans against layered ornamental rocks and looks out the window. Following her gaze, we find beautiful peony flowers in the foreground. Coupled with layered rocks, their white, pink, and purple petals echo the colors of the lady's face and dress. The whole picture seems to be illustrating Yongzheng's poem "The Peony Chamber" ("Mudan shi"):

> Layered clouds pile up these elegant rocks.
> A winding stream surrounds and passes the Peony
>   Chamber.
> Without equal under Heaven,
> Surely you are the world's supreme flower.
> So voluptuous Shi Chong should have favored you.
> So world-famous that you should have dominated
>   Luoyang.
> Who can stand next to you, the National Beauty?
> Five-colored clouds make up your immortal garments.

Such comparisons do more than just demonstrate a common subject matter and imagery. They reveal a shared intention in forging a feminine space in both the "Twelve Songs on the Garden's Scenic Spots" and the screen of twelve beauties. In both cases, not only is a woman presented as the subject of the male gaze, but she belongs to (and dissolves into) a feminized landscape, in which flowers and plants reflect her radiance and luxury, and mirrors and screens reveal her loneliness and sorrow. This relationship between art and literature was not new, of course. In fact, we can trace this relationship back to the beginning of both literary and artistic representations of *meiren*. We also find that two principal persona of *meiren* provided the foci of imagining and constructing feminine space in art and literature. The earlier persona is a palace lady (sometimes also identified as a goddess), whose desolate boudoir is tirelessly described in the *New Songs from a Jade Terrace*, a poem collection compiled by Xu Ling (507–83) in 545 A.D. The most important feature of this boudoir is its perceptual isolation. In Anne Birrell's words, it is always presented "as a closed erotic world. The normal elements of a lady's daily life, such as servants, children, friends, family, and, most important, her husband or lover, are pruned away from the scenario. In the full flowering of the love poetry of this era woman becomes confined to symbolic isolation in her luxury boudoir" (Birrell, 11–12). Nevertheless, the poet's roving eye could peep into this sealed place, surveying with minute attention all the bodily features and material belongings of a nameless palace lady.

This enclosed inner palace became the subject of numerous paintings from the Tang onward. Ellen Johnston Laing has concluded that, like palace-style poetry, these pictures focus on a lovesick woman whose one-sided love affair leaves her "eternally pining or waiting for an absent, never-to-return lover" (Laing, 287). Although such palace ladies would continue to fascinate Chinese audiences throughout the country's long history, the second "beautiful woman" persona—the courtesan/concubine (again sometimes identified as a goddess)—began to dominate pictorial representations of feminine space from the middle and late Ming dynasty. Courtesans and concubines can be grouped together because, as James Cahill has observed, they could move smoothly from the one role to the other and back again—"Like fish and dragon as a category of painting subjects, since each transforms into the other."[22]

The iconography of the palace lady and her boudoir was fully utilized in depicting idealized courtesans and concubines, but new visual codes were also invented to express a different kind of sensibility. Like a palace lady, the woman in a "courtesan-concubine" painting is nameless and often appears in an opulent interior or a garden setting. She may be engaged in leisurely activities, but more frequently she is alone, either looking at her own reflection in a mirror or gazing at a pair of cats, birds, or butterflies. In both cases, the subtext is that she, as an "amorous beauty," is thinking about an absent lover and suffering from "spring longing" (chunsi). Differing from a portrayal of a palace lady, however, a "courtesan-concubine" picture often delivers a bolder erotic message. Although the painted woman rarely exhibits her sexuality openly, her sexual allure and accessibility are represented through certain gestures (such as touching her cheek and toying with her belt) and sexual symbols (such as particular kinds of flowers, fruits, and objects) that a Ming or Qing spectator would have had no difficulty understanding. Laing first brought people's attention to such images in her paper "Amorous Beauty or Aloof Nymph: A Study of Qiu Ying's Beauty in Spring Thought."[23] Cahill has identified more "coded" images and further linked, convincingly in my opinion, these images (and their creators and viewers) to the "courtesan culture" that flourished in the cities in the Yangzi Delta region during the middle and late Ming; he thus extended existing scholarship on this culture to include its artistic production.[24] Among the several important consequences of this southern courtesan culture is a particular brand of romance between "genius and beauty" (*caizi jiaren*), exemplified by the legendary love affairs between Qian Qianyi and Liu Rushi in real life, and between Hou Fangyu and Li Xiangjun in the famous drama *The Peach Blossom Fan*, completed by Kong Shangren in 1699 (see Ko, *Teachers of the Inner Chambers*, 252–56; Wakeman, "Romantics, Stoics, and Martyrs," 632–39; Kang-i Sun Chang, *Ch'en Tzu-lung*, 9–40).

Yongzheng's "Screen of Twelve Beauties" (Figs. 12.8a-l) clearly continues this tradition of beautiful woman painting. In fact, it combines portrayals of lonely palace ladies and glamorous courtesans. There are enough details, such as the opulent interior and frequent pairs of animals, insects, and birds, to indicate the screen's debt to courtesan-concubine painting. (Indeed, according to Cahill, the screen may have been painted by Zhang Zhen, who began his career as a professional painter in Suzhou, a major center of southern courtesan culture.)[25] On the other hand, we should also remember that this screen belonged to an imperial garden; it thus naturally associated itself with well-known palace lady themes such as "Spring Morning in the Han Palace" ("Han gong chunxiao"). These connections with traditional "beautiful woman" paintings, however, only raise questions about the screen's real meaning. Why did the images of Chinese ladies so strongly attract the Manchu lord? Why were so many similar pictures of beautiful Chinese women also created in the Qing court under imperial patronage?[26] After all, who were these lovesick women in the eyes of the Manchu patrons? Zhu Jiajin's discovery of the archive disproves the old assumption that these are portraits of Yongzheng's twelve consorts, since a consort's portrait in the Qing court was always labeled an "auspicious visage" (*xirong*) or a "place of a mistress" (*zhuwei*); it was never called *meiren*, a term that refers to an ideal and often fictional beauty. But can we then conclude that these images represented idealized courtesans or royal concubines, as they had been represented in traditional Chinese painting?

In my opinion, it would be too simplistic to consider images on Yongzheng's screen a natural outgrowth of the traditional beautiful woman genre and to equate this screen created in the Qing court with works produced in a native Chinese context. This is not only because the southern courtesan culture declined during the early Qing: the famous pleasure district in Nanjing was completely destroyed at the beginning of the dynasty, and by 1673 the Qing court had formally ended the century-long system of official prostitutes throughout the country.[27] More important, once the art of beautiful woman painting was transposed from its original cultural context into the Forbidden City, now occupied by rulers of a non-Chinese origin, it was appreciated for different reasons and given additional significance. To better understand Yongzheng's "Screen of Twelve Beauties," therefore, we must situate it in the context of Qing court art and compare it with other female images created in the Forbidden City.

Based on his study of the Qing archives, Yang Boda has proposed that the Qianlong emperor exercised tight control over court painters, especially when they were assigned the responsibility of portraying members of the imperial household, including female members such as the empress dowager, the empress, royal consorts, and princesses. A court artist had to follow a set of strict codes, and "only after inspection and approval of a preliminary version was the painter permitted to officially undertake the full painting" (Yang Boda, "Development," 335). Earlier rulers must have exercised similar control, since royal portraits from the courts of Kangxi and Yongzheng demonstrate a consistently rigid formula. Anyone comparing such an official portrait (Fig. 12.10) and the women on Yongzheng's "Screen of Twelve Beauties" (Figs. 12.8a-l) would be startled by their radical differences. The portrait, called *rong* or "visage," was official in status and ceremonial in function. Works of this type uniformly employ a pictorial style that rejects any depiction of physical environment, bodily movement, or facial expression. It is true that some of the royal portraits convey a greater sense of personality whereas others reveal a stronger impact of European modeling techniques, but none of them violates the basic codes of the genre: as a formal portrait, a "visage" picture must present an empress or royal consort in a perfect frontal view against an empty background. The women are reduced to nearly identical puppets, whose major role is to display their Manchu-style fur hats and jackets with embroidered imperial dragons as symbols of their ethnic and political identity.

The heavy emphasis on official costumes in these visage portraits attests to the Qing emperors' strong concern with their identity. From the beginning of the dynasty, these non-Chinese rulers attached great importance to their native costumes, rejecting all suggestions that they

Fig. 12.10 Anonymous, "Portrait of Empress Xiaocheng." 17th century. Hanging scroll. Ink and color on silk. 307 cm (H) × 219.8 cm (W). Palace Museum, Beijing.

should now dress in Chinese-style clothes in order to demonstrate their mandate to rule China (Chen Juanjuan, 83–84). The reason for this insistence was simple: the Manchu costumes identified their origin and ethnic superiority. In fact, if Qing rulers were willing to borrow anything from Chinese culture (and they indeed borrowed quite a lot), three things — surname, hairstyle, and clothes — must be exceptions. Beijing's Palace Museum now houses numerous clothes worn by Qing court ladies from the seventeenth century onward, but to my knowledge no Chinese-style dresses have been found. This absence is understandable: beginning with the dynasty's founder, Huangtaiji, each ruler issued threatening documents prohibiting all Banner members — whether Manchu, Mongol, or Chinese — from wearing Chinese clothes.[28] The following passage is from an edict issued by the Jiaqing emperor in 1804, more than one and a half centuries after the founding of the dynasty:

> [Costume] is an important matter related to the tradition of the state and the mind of citizens. I therefore order you, the Commander-in-chiefs and Vice Commander-in-chiefs of both Manchu armies and Han armies in all Eight Banners, to pay great attention, finding out whether there are girls who wear clothes with freely expanded wide sleeves, and whether there are girls who even follow the Chinese costume of having their feet bound. Once you locate such unlawful youths, you must immediately impeach their parents, punishing them according to the legal codes for criminals who disobey government regulations. If after education they still cannot practice the right way and regain their old habit, once I find out this or receive letters of appeal, I will definitely punish them severely, together with the Commander-in-chief and Secretary of their Banner. I will never relent! (Tuojin 1813, *juan* 400)

We thus come to realize a profound irony in Yongzheng's Twelve Beauties and other Qing court depictions of beautiful women: what was presented was actually forbidden, since all the painted ladies are dressed in traditional Chinese costumes and surround themselves with rich symbols and visual allusions from traditional Chinese culture. It seems that the stern official regulation only stimulated the policymakers' private interest in the things they were publicly prohibiting. It is this private interest in the "Chineseness" and exoticism of beautiful women and their world, I would propose, that was responsible for the popularity and proliferation of their images in the Qing court. Only because of this interest and support from the highest patrons could beautiful woman painting develop into a powerful subgenre in court art and could the fantasy of an alien Chinese feminine space be sustained for close to a century.

The original connections between this artistic genre and the glamorous southern culture were not forgotten; but it nourished a different sort of imagination. The feminine space represented on Yongzheng's screen (as well as in other beautiful woman paintings from the Qing court) was given a broad symbolic significance, pertaining to an imaginary south (i.e., China) with all its charm and exoticism, its literature and art, its famous beauties and legendary gardens, and its vulnerability as the consequence of its excessive refinement. In the eyes of the Manchu conquerors, who came from the north and maintained their headquarters in the north, all the attractions of Chinese culture — its exquisiteness as well as its submissiveness — made it an extended, allegorical feminine space that stirred up fantasy and invited conquest. Yongzheng's "Screen of Twelve Beauties" was not the first work that represented Chinese culture as a feminine space. His father, the Kangxi emperor, had already established this symbolic connection: a screen created under his patronage, now in Beijing's Palace Museum, portrays a group of Chinese ladies in a dream-like southern landscape; on the back of the screen the emperor himself inscribed Zhang Xie's (fl. 295 A.D.) "Rhapsody on the Spring Festival at the Luo River" — a prose-poem on an ancient Chinese capital in the south (Fig. 12.11).

Yongzheng was also not the last Qing ruler to imbue images of Chinese *meiren* with political meaning; on this matter he was obediently followed by his son and heir, the Qianlong emperor. In one of Qianlong's portraits titled "Emperor Qianlong Merrymaking" ("Qianlong xingle tu"), the Manchu ruler had himself portrayed in a pavilion, looking down at five young women dressed in traditional Chinese clothes, who are crossing a bridge escorted by a royal procession (Fig. 12.12).[29] Qianlong's inscription on the painting contains these two stanzas:

> Relaxing in the pavilion over a clear stream,
> I hear my alert attendants pass on a message:
> "New royal consorts are arriving!"
> — Isn't this scene better than the picture of Lady Zhaojun
>   leaving China for the north?
>
> Having frequented immortal realms,

Fig. 12.11a, b Anonymous, "Painted Screen." Kangxi period (1662–1722). 128.5 cm (H) × 326 cm (W). Palace Museum, Beijing. (a, *top*) *front*: "Ladies Under Wutong Trees," oil painting on canvas. (b, *bottom*) *back*: calligraphy by Emperor Kangxi.

> Now I just lean against the railing, quiet and relaxed.
> Although people's caps and robes follow the Han style,
> What you see are images of deep meaning in a painting.

To my knowledge, this is the only statement by a Qing ruler about the fictional and symbolic nature of the beautiful-women images in Qing court art: these are not real persons, but are "images of deep meaning." Qianlong revealed their meaning by comparing these painted Chinese beauties to Wang Zhaojun, a famous palace lady of the Han dynasty who was sent as a gift to a Xiongnu king north of the

Fig. 12.12 Jin Tingbiao, "Emperor Qianlong Merrymaking." Dated 1763. Hanging scroll. Ink and color on silk. 167.4 cm (H) x 320 cm (W). Palace Museum, Beijing.

Great Wall. Although this allusion implies China's submission to an alien ruler, Qianlong was more satisfied with himself ("Isn't this scene better than the picture of Lady Zhaojun leaving China for the north?"): he, though non-Chinese in origin and also from the north, had conquered China and become its master.

The beautiful-women painting in the Qing court, therefore, also reinvented the genius-and-beauty romance, which, as mentioned above, was a by-product of Ming courtesan culture. During the Qing, when such romances had become a common theme of novels and plays, a story about an alleged love affair between the Shunzhi emperor (r. 1644–61) and the courtesan Dong Xiaoyuan circulated (Wang Shunu, 211–15). Although this and similar stories resulted from transporting genius-and-beauty romance into the Manchu court, paintings such as "Emperor Qianlong Merrymaking" and Yongzheng's "Screen of Twelve Beauties" prove that Manchu lords may have encouraged this development or may even have invented a "love affair" with Chinese beauties themselves.

In the "Screen of Twelve Beauties," none of the Chinese women smiles; their melancholy expressions reflect their inner suffering from "spring longing" for an absent lover. This supposed lover must be the future emperor Yongzheng. We know this for a number of reasons. Most obvious, although Yongzheng is not depicted in the paintings, his calligraphy and signatures stand for him. That his writing and seals decorate the ladies' boudoirs implies that he is the master of this imaginary, illusionistic feminine space and its twelve exotic and love-sick women. These women were originally painted on the twelve panels of a *weiping* screen that "surrounded" Yongzheng's seat or couch. The women's longing thus had a shared focus and a concrete aim: the empty seat or couch is a constant and crude reminder of their lover's absence. Among these beauties, one woman is lost in deep thought reading a book (Fig. 12.8i). When I began my research on the screen I was eager to know the content of the book, but no reproduction of the picture was clear enough to reveal the passages on the open page. Thanks to the curators in the Palace Museum, I was able to study the original painting in the summer of 1993. Printed on the page is a love song (Fig. 12.13):

> Sir, please don't treasure too much your gold-thread
>   gown;
> Please cling to the moment when you are young.
> Cut the flowers when they are blooming and offering
>   themselves to you;
> Don't wait to cut a branch till all the flowers are gone.

Significantly, this is a Tang courtesan's song for her lover.[30] Yong-zheng is therefore restaging a typical genius-and-beauty drama between a courtesan and a scholar: *his* genius is indicated by his handsome calligraphy; *her* talent and beauty are clinched by her charming image and the book in her hand. *She* is waiting for *him*. But it is also clear that in this case neither is he merely a young calligrapher nor is she simply a beautiful courtesan. He is not only a lover (of the beauty, her space, and her culture) but also conqueror and master (of the beauty, her space, and her culture). On the other hand, concealed in the imperial garden and contrasted with the stiff portraits of Manchu ladies, she was, above all, a "Chinese" beauty: an alien or Other. All her passivity, subordination, and suffering thus gained overt political significance: the possession of her and her space fulfilled not only a private fantasy but also a desire to exercise power over a defeated culture and nation.

This chapter began by questioning the concept of "stereotype" in art and literature: Can a highly formulated image such as the twelve beauties imply anything momentary and personal—anything beyond shared conventions—to signify a particular subjectivity? This question, of course, dwells on a paradox: How can individualism and in-

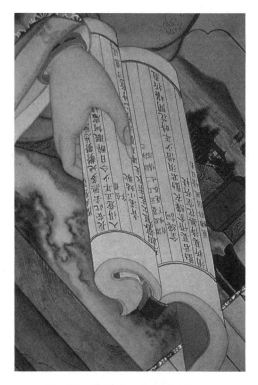

Fig. 12.13 Detail of Fig. 8i

vention be demonstrated (or recognized) *except* against collectiveness
and convention? My investigation of the twelve beauties thus follows
two parallel processes — standardization and reinvention — in a single
historical movement. A number of late Ming and early Qing texts, including Wei Yong's "Delight in Adornment," Li Suiqiu's "Gleaning
Beneath Flowers," and Xu Zhen's "Manual of Beautiful Women," reveal a collective effort to compile a written iconography of a typical
Beauty. As a consequence, women's world (as well as women themselves) dissolves into fragmented features — dwellings, furnishings,
adornment, physique, gestures and movements, maidservants, style,
literacy, activities, and so on — all catalogued in the manner of a (male)
connoisseur's handbook. It was hoped that this iconography would
not only provide a guide to "gentlemen of style and culture who long
for voluptuous and literary women" (*Tanji congshu*, 140) but also
serve as a kind of literary and artistic manual. It condenses persons

and events into "bare bones" themes (*gu*), only to be fleshed out again in poetry, novel, and painting (*Xiangyan congshu*, 1: 8).

The intimate connections between such manuals of stereotypical beauties and representations of women in contemporary literature and art are therefore not surprising. The act of fleshing out the former into the latter — to create female characters based on the standardized features of a beauty, to connect itemized female activities into a continuous narrative, and to install isolated figures into specific environments — is a matter of artistic reinvention. The images or stories resulting from this process no longer just index collective ideals. Although still following the general iconography of beautiful women, their links with the artist or the patron are often private and circumstantial. In this sense, both Cao Xueqin's Twelve Golden Hairpins of Jinling and Yongzheng's Twelve Beauties in the Yuanming Garden rely on a stereotypical conception of feminine space, but both also go beyond stereotypes. The difference between these two sets of twelve beauties is that they transcend conventions in different and even opposite ways. I have tried to capture their semiotic symmetry by analyzing them in the first and third sections of this chapter, around the "core" of the standardized formulation of beautiful women.

Readers familiar with the *Dream of the Red Chamber* can hardly miss its many parallels with the contemporary *meiren* manuals, even though only a tiny portion of these manuals is introduced in this essay. It is impossible to investigate here how Cao Xueqin fleshed out bare-bones themes (e.g., "Watching flowers falling and thinking about life's emptiness," "Commenting on a book from her lover with [colors of] fallen petals," and so on) into events and episodes in his novel. But we may briefly review his several feminine spaces, which echo one another and transform into one another, blurring the boundaries between myth, dream, and reality. In this way they constitute a fictional universe as the subject of imagination and storytelling. Cao Xueqin's perception of this universe owes much to the iconography of *meiren*, but this universe belongs to only one man — his alter ego, Baoyu (Precious Stone).

The novel begins with a fable about a (platonic) love affair between Stone (the former incarnation of Baoyu) and a heavenly flower. It tells that long ago Heaven fell and the Goddess Nüwa made five-colored stones from ordinary rocks to repair the damage. One of these stones was left unused. Having been transformed by the goddess, he assumed human form and even possessed *qing* or passion. He wandered around; "most of his time he spent west of Sunset Glow exploring the banks of the Magic River. There, by the Rock of Rebirth, he found the beautiful Crimson Pearl Flower, for which he conceived such a fancy that he took to watering her every day with sweet dew, thereby conferring on her the gift of life." Deeply grateful, Crimson Pearl decided to be reborn in the mortal world (as Daiyu) to repay Stone with the tears she would shed in her lifetime. "Because of this strange affair," it is told, "Disenchantment has got together a group of amorous young souls, of which Crimson Pearl is one, and intends to send them down into the world to take part in the great illusion of human life" (Hawkes and Minford, 1: 53). These "young souls" are the Twelve Golden Hairpins.

(Had Cao Xueqin read Wei Yong's "Following One's Affinity," published by Zhang Chao in his influential *Collectanea of Contemporary Writings*? In the opening section of this essay, entitled "Delight in Adornment," Wei told his readers that a true gentleman must be extremely dedicated to his *meiren*. "A beauty is a flower's 'true self,'" he claims. Again, "the place where a beauty lives is like a flower bed or vase. Located north of the Pavilion of Garu-wood, encircled by the Railing of a Hundred Treasures — it must have been the former home of the Heavenly Flower Bud" [*Xiangyang congshu*, 1: 69].)

The Twelve Golden Hairpins reappear in Baoyu's dream in chapter 5. As I recount above, when they are found in the female inner court of the Land of Illusion, their garden is filled with "deliciously fragrant fairy blooms and rare aromatic herbs"; their buildings have "ornately carved and painted eaves and rafters, their doorways [are] curtained with strings of pearls"; and their rooms are furnished with "musical instruments, antique bronzes, paintings by old masters, and poems by new poets." (One finds all these images in *meiren* manuals as well as in contemporary beautiful woman paintings [Figs. 12.6–8].) Again, Baoyu is the only male visitor to this "pure, maidenly precinct."

But, mainly, the story of Cao Xueqin's twelve beauties takes place in the Prospect Garden, which is itself an enormously enlarged version of the inner court in the Land of Illusion. The garden is built for the homecoming of Yuanchun, a daughter of the Jia family who has become an imperial consort. Since she does not want to see this beautiful garden wasted after she returns to the palace (which she refers to as "that no-man's land"), she orders it be the home of her talented sisters and cousins. But, "if the girls, why not Baoyu? He had grown up in their midst. He was different from other boys" (Hawkes and Minford, 1: 5). Happily, Baoyu also moves into the garden: "Every day was spent in the company of his maids and cousins in the most amiable and delightful occupations, such as reading, practicing calligraphy, strumming on the *qin*, playing Go, painting, composing verses, embroidering in colored silks, competitive flower-collecting, making flower-sprays, singing, word games and guess-fingers. In a word, he was blissfully happy" (Hawkes and Minford, 1: 460). In other words, Baoyu now devotes himself to all the sorts of female activities ascribed in a *meiren* manual (some of these activities are later developed into sections and chapters in the novel). He commits himself to a feminine space, divorced from the outside world in which a man normally finds his place.

Of course, the Prospect Garden is a hundred times richer than Wei Yong's or Xu Zhen's female quarter. It is no longer a hypothetical model of feminine space, and its residents are convincing characters with personality and feeling. Whereas a typical *meiren* in a *meiren* manual remains anonymous and impassionate, readers of the *Dream of the Red Chamber* feel personal connections with its hero and heroines, often finding themselves drawn helplessly into the novel's fictional world. Also unlike the author of a *meiren* manual, which isolates *feminine space* from rest of the world, Cao Xueqin constantly contrasts it with *masculine space*, on which he bestows negative images. Thus, the tomb-like offices in the Land of Illusion store the files of the Twelve Beauties; in Baoyu's mind, the most fearful place is his father's study outside the Prospect Garden. Shadowy and unfeeling, these masculine spaces set off the purity and liveliness of the feminine spaces. (We are reminded of Baoyu's remark: "Girls are made of water and boys are made of mud. When I am with girls I feel fresh and clean, but when I am with boys I feel stupid and nasty" [Hawkes and Minford, 1: 76].) An eighteenth-century reader must have recognized at once the difference between the *Dream of the Red Chamber* and the numerous beautiful woman catalogues and paintings. Only because of this recognition of the novel's reinvention of standardized cultural conventions could it become an instant masterpiece.

Who, then, are Cao Xueqin's Twelve Beauties? We often have a picture of him living in poverty in Beijing; the happy childhood he spent in Nanjing (before the confiscation of his family estates) must have recurred in his dreams and inspired his writing. Many authors have thus devoted themselves to discovering Cao Xueqin's autobiography in his novel. Many of these discoveries are important, but they should not blur the basic understanding that his Twelve Beauties, so much praised for their "realistic" qualities, mix conventions and fantasies with intimate familiarity. For one thing, they are all dressed in traditional Chinese costume; but as Manchu Bannermen with the status of bondservant (Manchu *bôi*), the Caos must have worn Manchu clothes according to the dynasty's regulations. The Twelve Beauties thus both confirm a stereotype and transcend it. When Cao Xueqin's friends were reading his manuscript, they talked about his "dream of the south." Indeed, the south is also a stereotype. In the eighteenth century, it denoted everything related to an old Chinese culture. But it was also Cao Xueqin's former home.

Dressed in Chinese clothes and surrounded by Chinese symbols, Yongzheng's Twelve Beauties also pertained to the south and the Chinese cultural tradition. But these portraits were commissioned by a Manchu prince; what they symbolized, as I have tried to prove, was a defeated nation that was given an image of an extended feminine space with all its charm, exoticism, and vulnerability. Consequently, the conventional *meiren* image was further exaggerated: she was multiplied and her passivity was stressed. The reinvention of *meiren* was also realized by installing standardized female images into a specific context: the Twelve Beauties were painted on a screen that once belonged to the Yuanming yuan. The changing significance of the garden thus determined the fate of the Twelve Beauties.

The three sobriquets that Yongzheng signed within these images reveal his frame of mind at the time of the paintings' creation. One of these, Master of the Yuanming Yuan, identifies the garden (as well as its belongings including the painted screen) as his private property. Another, Heaven Inside a Bottle, is borrowed from Daoist vocabulary and refers to a transcendent paradise within a tight physical enclosure. This second name actually designated one of the Yuanming Garden's buildings; but in a broad sense Heaven Inside a Bottle pertained to the whole garden—from ancient times, Chinese rulers were accustomed to construct their gardens as paradise on earth.[31] Yongzheng's third sobriquet most explicitly indicates the place of the screen's creation: in calling himself A Retired Gentleman Who Breaks

Away From the Dusty World, he must have been inscribing the screen away from his office and worldly duties.

These three sobriquets, therefore, imply a fundamental dualism in the self-identity of the future emperor: his status as the Master of the Yuanming Garden opposed (and was supported by) his role as the head of the Palace of Prince Yong (Yong wangfu), a huge residential and administrative compound inside the walled city of Beijing.[32] If the garden was compared to a transcendent paradise (i.e., Heaven Inside a Bottle), the palace had to be identified with solid "earth." And, of course, this ambitious prince never "broke away from the dusty world"; in fact, when the screen was made and set up in the Yuanming yuan, he was busily scheming to take over the throne. Yongzheng's dualistic self-identity determined the symbolism of the garden: the Yuanming yuan was imagined to be a place of privacy, relaxation, reclusion, and immortality only because it had a worldly counterpart that stood for public life, social engagement, and political undertaking. Once this dualism was cast in the light of gender (which functioned as a powerful conceptual category in ordering natural and human phenomena, and as a prominent trope to be deployed in any kind of rhetoric), the Yuanming yuan was logically identified with a conceptual feminine space and had to be transformed into a concrete feminine space. This transformation was realized in art — in architecture and landscaping, as well as in literature and interior decoration. This is how we are left with Yongzheng's "Twelve Songs on the Garden's Scenic Spots" and the twelve painted beauties from his screen.

This symbolism of the Yuanming yuan, however, altered somewhat after Yongzheng became emperor. In 1725, three years after he ascended the throne, he constructed a series of official buildings — an audience hall, magnificent palatial gates, and offices — inside the Yuanming yuan, where he was to hold court most of the year. The garden was no longer an entirely private feminine space but came to be characterized by an internal dualism. The emperor still periodically (re)visited the Reading Hall Deep Inside Weeping Willows and wrote more poems there, but the central theme of these writings had become a pursuit for idle relaxation.[33] His earlier fantasy involving some imaginary exotic "Chinese" beauties gradually faded; most portraits he commissioned after he became the emperor represent himself in various disguises (see Wu "Emperor's Masquerade"). Ten years after he became the Son of Heaven, he learned that the twelve painted beauties had been removed from the screen in the Reading Hall. He did not order them restored, but demanded only they be preserved in a dark storage room.

Interestingly and ironically, Yongzheng was the man who crushed the Cao family. The year his Twelve Beauties were sent into storage, Cao Xueqin reached adulthood and probably began to dream about his own Twelve Beauties and their garden.[34]

13

Ming Loyalism and the
Women's Voice in Fiction
After "Hong lou meng"

ELLEN WIDMER

The salacious and violent content of much of Chinese vernacular fiction underlies the common assumption that the genre as a whole was authored by men. These characteristics would, in theory, have put it off limits for the typical *guixiu* (gentlewoman) reader, whom decorum confined to quieter literary pastures, and apart from such high-class women, few others knew how to read. Between the illiterate and the irreproachable, there was no woman left to author fiction, despite ample evidence that their literary abilities were sufficient for this purpose by at least the end of the Ming.

This chapter will question these assumptions, with special reference to two sources of inspiration that induced female authors to think along new lines. The first, Ming loyalism, led some of them to take up new genres of writing during the Ming-Qing transition, although the consequences of this are hard to ascertain. The second, *Hong lou meng* (Dream of the red chamber), provides a clear challenge to the assumption about women readers, for at least one edition catered to women as well as men. Moreover, women's poetry of the late eighteenth and nineteenth centuries, as I shall demonstrate, contains numerous references to *Hong lou meng*. Unconnected in any other particular, loyalism and *Hong lou meng* provide two means of attacking the generalizations raised above.

This inquiry confronts formidable obstacles. The first are the many signs of tentativeness among even the most stouthearted of women writers. Because so many of them burned their poetry, one is not surprised to learn that they burned their fiction too. Yet burned fiction can at least be taken as sign that women wrote in this genre. Another is the custom followed by most authors of fiction of using pseudonyms and otherwise veiling their true identities and careers. *Hong lou meng* is a partial case in point, for, although its author's name was never secret, his biography was occluded for nearly 200 years. Only a vast scholarly enterprise in the twentieth century has brought some particulars into view. Because of the niche fiction occupied in traditional China, it makes sense to assume that an anonymous author, or one known only by a cognomen, is a man. Yet as this chapter will demonstrate, anonymous authors could be women, too.

This finding came to light long after my research on this topic had been completed. It was provoked, in part, by questions asked in Nancy Armstrong's chapter, which is keyed to an earlier version of this discussion. I have therefore chosen to set it slightly outside the main body of my argument and develop it in a postscript at the end.

Wang Duanshu (1621–ca. 1706) and Wang Duan (1793–1839) were unusually prominent women writers of the Qing, and their work was significantly inspired by Ming loyalism. This loyalism was of two kinds. Wang Duanshu's was what is usually meant by the term, for it was a part of the wave of pro-Ming activism during the Ming-Qing transition. Wang Duan's came about much later, as part of a retrospective on the Ming, which occurred under the leadership of Chen Wenshu (1775–1845), her father-in-law. Although it took shape as nostalgia for the Ming, it also came out in writings on loyalists to other regimes. In the first part of this chapter, I consider the differing relevance of the term "Ming loyalism" to these women writers' output. Because it inspired certain kinds of innovation in both writers, I am interested, first, in describing these innovations and, second, in asking why they did not go further. In Wang Duanshu's case it is clear that she read popular narratives, and one of her innovations as a woman writer was to write commentary on drama, a closely related genre. Yet when it came to fiction, whatever writing she may have done in the *xiaoshuo* form or about it was not passed down. Additionally, a series of her sketches about loyalists was published, but they are more prominently linked with a male writer's name. For her part, Wang Duan was deeply interested in loyalism and wrote at least one work of fiction in which loyalism figured as a major theme. This was probably in the form of a novel, or perhaps a poetic narrative (*tanci*) — we cannot be quite sure, because she later burned it — entitled *Yuan Ming yishi* (Forgotten history of the Yuan and Ming). The fact that Wang Duan burned this but not others of her writings points to continuing ambivalence toward narrative among women writers of her day.

A separate line of reasoning lends insight into how women viewed *Hong lou meng*, first published in 1792. *Hong lou meng* has nothing to do with Ming loyalism. Politically speaking, it emerged from the opposite side of the spectrum, being authored by a man whose family was close to the Manchu leadership of the Qing. Yet it, too, brought women closer to fiction. The poetry and prose of some of Wang Duan's associates make it clear that it engaged their interest more than other vernacular fiction, or, at least, that it was a more frequent subject in their poems than earlier fictional works. The comments of these associates about this and other novels reveal more about the inhibitions that kept Wang Duan and other women from feeling at home in this genre. Like the first line of evidence, this one culminates in an example of a woman who wrote fiction. Associated with Wang Duan and her circle as a young woman, the Manchu poet Gu Taiqing (1799–1876) has recently been identified as the author of *Hong lou meng ying* (Shadows of *Hong lou meng*), a sequel to *Hong lou meng*.[1] The preface is dated 1861, and the novel was first published in 1877, probably posthumously. Like *Yuan Ming yishi, Hong lou meng ying* attests to residual discomfort on the part of women writers; yet unlike Wang Duanshu's fictionalized history, *Hong lou meng ying* survives.

From Wang Duanshu to Wang Duan

In Wang Duanshu's case, the designation "Ming loyalist" fits quite nicely, especially at the beginning of her career. Wang Duanshu was the daughter of Wang Siren (1575–1646) of Shaoxing, himself a prominent loyalist, who committed suicide at the beginning of the Qing. She established herself as both active and brilliant at an early age. Her activism came out in her youth, as evidenced by a number of episodes in her biography; for example, she drilled her mother and maids as soldiers at six years of age. As for her brilliance, she read widely in the classics and history, as well as in popular literature (*bai guan*), which probably means *xiaoshuo* (fiction) as well as popular history. Her brothers may have been among her teachers, and her father seems to have taken an interest in her education, for he is said to have exclaimed that if only she were male, she could have counted on an outstanding career. He also noted that she was a better reader than any of his sons. Duanshu's husband, Ding Shengzhao, was also loyal to the Ming. After the dynasty fell, he left his residence in the Beijing area and moved back to the family home in Shaoxing. From that moment on, he lived the life of a recluse, frequently overdrinking and carrying on with a group of fellow loyalists, which included the historian and essayist Zhang Dai.[2]

Ding's state of mind and behavior are described in a piece by Wang Duanshu entitled "Biography of an Idle Tippler":

> The identity of the Idle Tippler shall remain anonymous. Since the dynastic change of 1644 he has been living in the eastern corner of my home district, Kuaiji. Although I complete poems with him day and night, drink wine with him, and call him my best friend, I still am not sure where he comes from. As a person, he is proud of his addiction and enjoys his poverty, he is casual and cannot stand to control his drinking; therefore we call him the Idle Tippler. He often says of himself: "I passed the examinations and once held public office. They can cut off my head, but they cannot change my ideas. If I am not dead, it is because I have not yet buried my father properly." So he took his wife and children and moved to the east of the pond. His roof is in a remote location, his walls are crumbling, and his path is grown over. He lives amid disorderly tombs and desiccated trees. Whenever the wind is harsh or it rains violently, tiles and gravel fly everywhere. Strange birds call out in grief; hungry snakes slither around him. The cold of winter penetrates his bones, and no furniture nestles against his walls. Sometimes cold air blasts through the windows; sometimes he shares his shabby blankets with others. People from the village feel sad when they think about him; passersby look at him and start to cry; relatives are embarrassed by him, and friends feel compassion, but the Idle Tippler is not concerned. He considers that wealth and status are transient things and thinks back to the coldness of people [who liked him only when he was successful]. Daily, he pawns his clothes to buy wine. At night he holds his *qin* and sings drunkenly. When his clothes run out and he has nothing more to sell, he substitutes tea for wine and goes on singing without stopping. . . . Anyone in or outside the walls of Yue who has a modicum of talent flocks to him. . . . The Idle Tippler is good natured and sincere. In matters however trifling, he avoids immorality and never says what ought not to be said. He increasingly enjoys entertaining, to the point that his wife and children have insufficient food and clothing, but he still keeps up his good spirits. He has many friends and relatives at court,

and it would be easy for him to abandon his principles and [ride the political tide]. If he did so, he could soon become well known. Moreover, the Idle Tippler's land is in the Beijing area. His houses are comparable in magnificence to those of a prince. For him to have relinquished all this and brought only a few close relatives and a few shabby books to this dilapidated house and these shabby walls, can anyone say this is not a political statement?[3]

As the prefaces to Wang Duanshu's various writings indicate, Ding Shengzhao's opposition to the Qing was a major reason for his consistent support of his wife's writing career. In fact, her writing was regarded as her husband's salvation, for it kept him from drinking himself to oblivion. Her first celebrated publication was a collection of poems and prose, which included the biography just quoted, as well as other overtly loyalist prose pieces, some of which were later republished, with the author's permission, under Zhang Dai's name.[4] Like the biography of the Idle Tippler, these reveal a gift for characterization, lending support to the view that Wang Duanshu would have had little trouble adjusting to writing fiction.

The collection in which these pieces appear is entitled *Yinhong ji* (Collected writings about the fall). Its publication, in 1651, was paid for by Ding Shengzhao, Zhang Dai, and 47 other members of their poetry group in Shaoxing. Prefaces to this collection exclaim that Wang Duanshu's use of loyalist material brought a new seriousness to the growing body of poetry by women writers, which had hitherto taken up less "important" themes, like willow catkins and flowers. They also suggest that it was artistically liberating for her to suffer the dislocations brought about by the dynastic transfer, since they allowed her to see beyond familiar walls. Without endorsing the pejorative view of other writings by women implied in such comments, we can nonetheless understand that the Ming loyalist emphases in Wang Duanshu's writings established her as a less narrowly domestic writer than many women of her generation and of the two or three generations of women writers who had published their work before her time.

Of course, Wang Duanshu was not the only Ming loyalist among the prominent women writers of the mid-seventeenth century. Liu Rushi's loyalism is documented in Kang-i Sun Chang's recent study of Chen Zilong; and loyalism marked the work of several women closer to Wang Duanshu's elevated social status, such as Shang Jinglan of Shaoxing, Huang Yuanjie of Jiaxing, and Wu Shan of Dangtu in Anhui, all of whom were or had once been first wives rather than courtesans. Just as Wang Duanshu was forced to travel outside her normal habitat, some of these women grew as artists and writers in connection with the dislocations of war. Thus, Shang Jinglan's widowhood after the righteous suicide of her husband, Huang Yuanjie's work as a tutor for women, and Wu Shan's selling of her paintings and poems as a source of income became subjects in their writing and lifted writing to a more visible place in their lives. Thanks to the efforts of such male loyalists as Wu Weiye (1609–72), as well as to their own efforts, these women reached out to one another, through painting, writing and in other ways. Huang Yuanjie, Wu Shan, and Wang Duanshu led particularly unconventional lives for gentry women in the loyalist community of Hangzhou after the fall of the Ming. Whether abandoned, widowed, or unconventionally married, these poets documented their habit of taking boat trips together on the West Lake and drinking as they exchanged verses. This style of life, and the memory of it long after it had ended, lent momentum to what might be called women's literary culture as it had developed earlier in the century, when women writers began to publish in increasing numbers. Unlike Shang Jinglan, who, though widowed and extremely talented, never strayed far from her wifely persona (or from her Shaoxing home), these three were in demand as tutors to women students, prefacers, and editors of women's writings. In this sense as well as geographically, their literary talent took them to new places, and their celebrity continued until the end of the Qing.[5]

Even amid the lively company of Hangzhou, Wang Duanshu made a strong impression. According to Qian Qianyi, she was very beautiful, and others note the combination of erudition and quickwittedness, which allowed her to excel at repartee.[6] Not all of her friends were loyalists during this period, for she was evidently acquainted with the apolitical Li Yu, and she wrote a preface to one of his dramas, *Bimu yu* (Sole mates), in 1661.[7] Yet despite such signs of exuberance and perhaps even bohemianism, Wang Duanshu never lost her reputation for exceptional filial piety, as well as for devotion to family, which included her husband's concubines as well as her husband and children.

Wang Duanshu's visibility as a Ming loyalist was curtailed perforce with the accession of the Kangxi emperor in 1661 and the executions of loyalists that began shortly thereafter. This change, which also eliminated the male loyalist networks that had contributed to her celebrity as a poet, may have accelerated work on what would become her most enduring project, an edited collection of writings by women, published in 1667. Prefaces to this collection, entitled *Mingyuan shiwei* (Classic poetry by famous women), establish that she had begun work on it some 27 years earlier. In 42 *juan*, it is one of the largest collections of poetry by women writers of the seventeenth century; and the prefaces by Qian Qianyi and Ding Shengzhao among others contributed to its visibility among men as well as women writers of the day. Its publication was financed by her natal family and carried out by a commercial bookshop in Hangzhou. By the time the collection was published, Ding Shengzhao and Wang Duanshu were again resident in Beijing.

Particularly in the 1640's when she started work on this project, it was unusual to find a woman editor in the field of women's poetry; by the time *Mingyuan shiwei* was published, however, several women editors had published collections. After *Mingyuan shiwei*'s publication, more women editors entered this field. Influential on later generations of Chinese poets and anthologists, *Mingyuan shiwei* survives in Chinese libraries and remains a critical source for research on women poets to this day.[8]

The prefaces to this collection make it obvious how important it was to Wang Duanshu. One by her husband good-naturedly mentions that his wife's work on this project kept her from paying attention to household management. Another by Wang herself speaks of her desire to become an editor and gives evidence of her sense that editing poems by women, not men, was the most appropriate outlet for this urge. Nowhere is the connection to Ming loyalism mentioned, but Wang had begun work on the collection before the Ming ended, and it must have provided an outlet for the literary energies behind her voicing of loyalist concerns. The celebrity Wang achieved during the overtly loyalist phase of her life probably made it easier for her to collect writings from other women. Although the earliest entries in the collection date from the late sixteenth century, the vast majority of writers represented were Wang's contemporaries. She acquired their work from a variety of sources—anthologies, published collections of individual writers, solicitations, and submissions of unpublished writings to the editor herself or to a bookshop in Hangzhou.[9]

Mingyuan shiwei, despite its focus on poetry, is not completely without relevance to the question of women and fiction. Its *juan* 31 is particularly interesting, in that it purports to be about fiction but contains no entries. All the table of contents says about it is "This *juan* reprints stories by many authors." No entries are supplied in the main body of the text, which moves directly from *juan* 30 to *juan* 32. What to make of this lacuna is a mystery. Because we do not know why it exists, it cannot be used to support the hypothesis that women held back from writing fiction. On the contrary, it seems to mean that women wrote fiction. Thus we might tentatively propose it as evidence that although women wrote fiction, there was some inhibition against their publishing it. Maureen Robertson suggests that this may have been the case, and the situation presented by *Mingyuan shiwei* lends prima facie support to such a view.

After 1667 and *Mingyuan shiwei*'s publication, Wang Duanshu's life becomes much harder to document. Assorted commentaries on Zhu He's drama *Qinlou yue* (Moon at Qin tower) of about 1700 include one by Wang Duanshu, and the poems printed at the end of this work set some of her works alongside those of other women.[10] Other collections and anthologies are attributed to Wang Duanshu, but since they cannot currently be read or dated, it is impossible to know when they were written, and they contribute nothing to our knowledge of her life after *Mingyuan shiwei*.

To sum up the relationship between Wang Duanshu's loyalism and her writing, it is clear that for a time her literary reputation benefited from an association with the loyalist community. Loyalism may even have been the principal reason she began to publish and edit poetry. But Wang Duanshu's willingness to break barriers had its limits. Her decision to edit works by women writers, pathbreaking though it was, is explained as a compromise between her desire to edit something and her sense that for a women to edit anything other than writings by women was taboo. And despite her forcefulness as a loyalist writer, she did not venture with equal energy into every genre. Thus, although she commented on drama, she appears not to have written any, unlike some of her female acquaintances; and although she read fiction and history, she stayed away from narrative, except for the aforementioned loyalist sketches, which were publicly identified with Zhang Dai. Or, if she did write fiction, she felt ambivalent, even negative, about associating her name with it. Perhaps she intended to suggest that fiction was not a genre for ladies. These negatives may be inferred both from the fate of her loyalist sketches and from the empty fiction section in *Mingyuan shiwei*. If Wang Duanshu's case is any example, Ming loyalism was an important theme for talented woman writers, but it did not erase all barriers to women's writing. The frontiers of poetry and commentary were expanded by their efforts, but only a few women ventured into drama, and fiction attracted fewer still.

I shall not comment on the long interval between *Mingyuan shiwei*'s publication in 1667 and Wang Duan's birth in 1793 except to note a few similarities and contrasts between women's literary culture in the early nineteenth century and that of the late Ming and early Qing. Wang Duan's era offers several features reminiscent of seventeenth-century ways. The phenomenon of women selling paintings and poems to support themselves is once again in evidence, apparently after a long hiatus; sometimes "companionate" couples, whose unconventionality recollects Ming loyalist pairs like Wang Duanshu and Ding Shengzhao, had recourse to this means of making a living. Wang Duan came from a prominent family. Perhaps for this reason, she probably never sold her work, although her relationship with her husband, Chen Peizhi, was companionate in style. Moreover, her associates included many whose lives followed familiar lines. Among these, Qian Shoupu and Zhou Qi are discussed below.

The resurgence of women editors and prefacers is another way in which this era returned to mid-seventeenth-century trends. During this era, anthologies of women's poetry edited by women began to reappear, most notably Yun Zhu's (1771–1833) *Guochao guixiu zhengshi ji* (Collected correct beginnings for gentlewomen of this dynasty) of 1831, which mentions several antecedents, among which Wang Duanshu's anthology is the only one edited by a woman.[11] If it is fair to see *Mingyuan shiwei* as a breakthrough for all writing women, its power to inspire must have lapsed after the 1670's; only in the 1830's did it induce another woman to take on a project of comparable visibility and size.

As for prefaces, both Wang Duan and a number of her friends—Gui Maoyi being one example—were active in their composition. Initially one of Yuan Mei's students, Gui entered Chen Wenshu's orbit after Yuan's death, going on to become Wang Duan's sworn sister, although she was a generation older. And, although she never edited a collection of women's writings, Gui was one of many women friends of Yuan Mei and Chen Wenshu who lent their services as proofreaders on Wang Duan's editing projects.[12] Not since the days of Wang Duanshu, Huang Yuanjie, and Wu Shan had women come out so visibly in support of other women's literary goals.

The third way in which this era takes up where the early Qing left off concerns the reprinting in 1804 of the *tanci* known as *Tian yu hua* (Heaven rains flowers) and the publication during the early nineteenth century of four other *tanci* under the editorial direction of Hou Zhi, a woman tangentially linked to Wang Duan.[13] *Tian yu hua* was written in the early Qing, and its preface is dated 1651. Purportedly authored by a woman, Tao Zhenhuai, it is the first in a long line of "women's *tanci*," a special branch of the *tanci* genre. This work's publishing history—its long dormancy in particular—is a striking example of the way in which Wang Duan's era looked back to and revived mid-seventeenth-century themes.[14] Whatever the reason *tanci* were so seldom published before Hou Zhi came along, after her time *tanci* began to be put out by commercial publishers, such as Ai ri tang, a well-known firm whose history dates back to at least the early eighteenth century.[15] I cannot now answer several interesting questions suggested by these data—what prompted Hou Zhi to take up this form, how her writing related to the work of her women poet friends, and how she managed to get her work published in the face of normal familial taboos. It would also be interesting to know what difference, if any, *Tian yu hua*'s Ming loyalism made in its preservation and republication and how such sentiments were received by non-Han Chinese. In any event, hints of a newly commercialized relationship between women editors, *tanci*, and their female readership both extended late Ming developments and advanced them to a whole new stage.

Alongside such similarities, a number of contrasts can be observed. First, by Wang Duan's time, the Qing government had been firmly in power for a century and a half. This meant that men interested in women's writing were no longer active Ming loyalists in the traditional sense. Although they might take an interest in late Ming culture, they were not anti-Manchu, and many had Bannerman friends. Not surprisingly, women who wrote during this period also had ties to Bannermen. Yun Zhu's case is the most striking. A Chinese descendant of the painter Yun Shouping, Yun married a Jurchen, and she became the mother of Linqing, one of the most prominent Bannermen of his day.[16] A marriage such as this would have been impossible for a Jiangnan gentlewoman in the days of Wang Duanshu.

Second, male mentoring had undergone a shift in form. In contrast to late-Ming mentors like Wu Weiye, who were often quite peripatetic, mentors like Chen Wenshu or Yuan Mei received female pupils at their residences or corresponded with them from home. When a mentor died, his female pupils might link up with another mentor, but women often associated with one teacher over long periods of time. In contrast to Wang Duanshu, who is linked with a variety of male intellectuals but not with any one mentor, much of women's literary activity of the late eighteenth and early nineteenth centuries occurred between women who identified themselves as disciples of Yuan Mei, Chen Wenshu, or other males. In any event, taboos against women's creative efforts were at least as strong as they had been at the end of the Ming, and male mentors provided crucial support to women willing to brave this tide. Comments by Yuan Mei's pupils show how much his disciples depended on his emotional support, as well as on his instruction in poetry, painting, and other fields.[17]

Wang Duan's biography provides resources to elaborate on these developments in more detail. Born almost a century after Wang Duanshu's death, Wang Duan lived a life that resembled Duanshu's in many important ways. Like Duanshu, she came from an exceptionally prominent lineage, in this case from Hangzhou, not Shaoxing. Her father was not as distinguished as her two grandfathers, but she nevertheless belonged to the highest level of society. Her mother died young, and she was brought up by her aunt, Liang Desheng, who took great pride in her niece's talent and saw to its development, as did Liang's husband, the historian Xu Zongyan. Wang Duan's early displays of brilliance are said to have lain in the area of writing, whereas Duanshu's took the form of precocious reading skills, but the early onset of literacy is described in similarly glowing terms. Wang Duan's marriage, similarly, contributed to her writing career. Both her husband, Chen Peizhi, and her father-in-law, Chen Wenshu, were exceptionally supportive of female talent. Chen Wenshu, in particular, had women students and maintained a household full of literary women. Wang Duan's relations with her family were no less successful than Wang Duanshu's, in that she, too, was known for her filial piety, and she behaved in exemplary fashion toward her husband, as well as toward one of his concubines, for whom she wrote a moving eulogy when that concubine died at an early age. Like Wang Duanshu, as well, she was said to be somewhat deficient in domestic skills.[18]

Wang Duan's later years were marred by the early death of her husband in about 1825 and the consequent deterioration of her son's state of mind. These two developments led her to turn to Daoism during the thirteen years between her husband's death and her own, at age 44. Over these later years, she edited a collection of her husband's writings and continued writing poetry of her own. Her col-

lected poems were published just after her death in 1839 under the title *Ziran haoxue zhai ji* (Collected works of Natural Love of Learning
Studio). This publication was paid for by her father-in-law, who contributed a long and admiring biography as a preface.[19]

Like Wang Duanshu, Wang Duan's literary reputation was based
on a combination of original writings and edited volumes. Yet despite
her many poems about women writers, living and dead, Wang Duan
never edited women's writings. Her most famous and innovative editing project was a collection of writings by 30 male writers of the
Ming dynasty. Entitled *Ming sanshi jia shixuan* (Selected poems of 30
Ming poets), it was published in sixteen *juan* in 1822, three years before the death of her husband. Publication was paid for by her family,
and the collection, in its original edition, had prefaces by her aunt,
Liang Desheng, among others. Each *juan* was proofread by a female
friend or family member of the editor, including some names already
famous for their association with Yuan Mei. Wang Duan's work on
this editing project is said to have taken her five or six years; she had
spent ten years reading before she took up her editorial pen.[20]

Psychologically speaking, *Ming sanshi jia shixuan* occupied approximately the same place in Wang Duan's life that *Mingyuan shiwei*
occupied in Wang Duanshu's, although they were quite different
types of project. It was *Ming sanshi jia shixuan* more than any other
work that established Wang Duan's literary celebrity, for it displayed
her fine taste, as well as the iconoclastic spirit that led her to question
the literary judgment of such notables as Qian Qianyi and Shen Deqian.[21] Wang Duan's motivation for this project is generally traced to
her wide reading in poetry, in particular to her high valuation of the
late Yuan and early Ming poet Gao Qi. In fact, she regarded herself as
a latter-day incarnation of one of Gao's disciples.[22] Gao had been put
to death during the early Ming; moreover, his poetry was not as
highly valued as Wang Duan thought it ought to be. One aim of *Ming
sanshi jia shixuan* was to set the historical record straight on Gao; another was to reassess the canon, whose partiality Wang Duan saw revealed in its undervaluation of Gao.

These twin goals are encapsulated in Wang Duan's long account
of a dream, which is described in the opening few pages, a dream
supposedly experienced just after the collection was completed. The
central figure is the spirit of Song Lian, a man historians had criticized
for serving both the Yuan and the Ming. The dream is presented as
Song's protest at the omission of his poetry from the anthology. After

rehashing some of Song's complaints about his poor treatment by bi-
ographers, Wang Duan expresses her faith in his innocence. However,
she stands by her initial judgment that Song's poetry, being less good
than his prose, does not belong in the collection. The account ends
with Wang wondering whether her dream about Song—and about
the others represented in the anthology—could have been a reward
for her attempts to set the record straight. Like Wang Duanshu's piece
"The Idle Tippler," this account demonstrates Wang Duan's facility at
characterization and other narrative skills.

Wang Duan's sense of outrage at the vagaries of Yuan and Ming
historical accounting motivated her to undertake a second project, the
fictional *Yuan Ming yishi*. This was a revisionist effort to retell the story
of Zhang Shicheng, a rival of the first Ming emperor as successor to
the Yuan. Wang Duan's interest in Zhang developed out of her interest in Gao Qi, to whom Zhang was sympathetic. However, the remnants of this work preserved in *Ziran haoxue zhai ji* concern only Zhang
and his immediate associates, not Gao. Wang Duan liked to compare
her hero to the defeated general Han Yu, who lost out to Liu Bang at
the beginning of the Han. Similarly, Zhang's defeat by the Ming is the
main focus of her attention, although she also had a section on figures
not associated with Zhang who were loyal to the Yuan. In *Yuan Ming
yishi*, Wang Duan takes an interest in Zhang's women associates, particularly the many wives and concubines who committed suicide at
the time of Zhang's defeat. The work also featured women capable of
contributing their talents to the hero's military campaign. The most
extensively presented character in the surviving remnants is a female
strategist and prognosticator named Miss Jin (Jin ji). According to
these excerpts, Miss Jin played a key role in encouraging Zhang
Shicheng's benevolent leadership. Comments about *Yuan Ming yishi*
in *biji* and other sources have prompted some scholars to suppose that
it was written in novel form. However, Sun Kaidi is undecided as to
whether it was a novel (*xiaoshuo*) or a *tanci*, a point to which I shall return.[23]

Wang Duan's interest in Gao Qi does not qualify as *Ming* loyalism, since Zhang Shicheng was Ming founder Zhu Yuanzhang's rival
for control of the Wu region, and since Gao himself was executed by
the Ming.[24] However, loyalism broadly defined is very much at the
heart of this project. This is most evident in the surviving biographies
of Yuan loyalists, the main point of which is to celebrate their subjects'
unwillingness to collaborate with the Ming, but it is also clear in Wang

Duan's work on Gao Qi and Song Lian. Ming loyalism specifically comes up for comment at the end of *Ming sanshi jia shixuan* in the biographies of Gu Yanwu and others. Elsewhere in her writings are a number of reflections on Ming loyalist women, such as Huang Yuanjie and Liu Rushi, as well as on the loyalist icon Feng Xiaoqing. In addition, Wang Duan wrote on such male heroes of the late Ming as the military leader Zhang Huangyan.[25]

Given Wang Duan's friendships with Mongols and Manchus, *Yuan Ming yishi*'s commemoration of loyalists who had fought on behalf of a Mongol dynasty is less surprising than it might otherwise seem. Although she is hardly against Ming loyalists, it is loyalty to whatever regime one was born in, not Ming loyalism per se, that moves Wang Duan. As long as one's loyalty is sincere, it elicits her sympathy, whether it be to a "barbarian" dynasty like the Yuan, a would-be founder of a dynasty like Zhang Shicheng, or a Chinese dynasty like the Ming. Thus, loyalism is no less closely connected to Wang Duan's most innovative projects than it had been to Wang Duanshu's. The surviving data establish its importance for both *Ming sanshi jia shixuan* and *Yuan Ming yishi*; as well, it is a theme in much of her poetry. Yet Wang Duan's fluid definition of loyalism would not have appealed to Wang Duanshu.

The surviving poetry of Wang Duan's female acquaintances indicates that they shared her interest in late Ming women writers. Gui Maoyi, for example, saw herself — or at least was seen by Wang Duan — as an incarnation of Huang Yuanjie; others of her friends wrote poems about Liu Rushi, Li Yin, Wu Shan, and Xiaoqing.[26] Their collective preoccupation is attributable to Chen Wenshu's devotion to these women, an interest that led him to repair some graves in both Changshu and Hangzhou, as well as to collect writings by and about women in the Hangzhou area on a retreat from official duties during the 1820's.[27] Some of Wang Duan's writings about late Ming heroines took place explicitly in connection with the grave repair project, although she also wrote about them at other times. Among the works on which Chen Wenshu relied in his reconstruction of Hangzhou and other loyalist women was Wang Duanshu's *Mingyuan shiwei*; however, Wang Duanshu's own life story seems not to have captured contemporary imagination.[28]

After Chen Wenshu, the most important supporter of Wang Duan's literary efforts was her aunt, Liang Desheng, who became a surrogate mother after Wang's mother (Liang's sister) died. Biographies in *Ziran haoxue zhai ji*, as well as a number of poems, demonstrate that Liang contributed significantly to Wang Duan's educational development, and several sources attribute Wang's love of history to Liang. The most authoritative of these is the biography of Liang by the scholar and official Ruan Yuan (1764–1849).[29] Ruan was Chen Wenshu's most important teacher. Since he knew both Liang and Chen, his emphasis on Liang's guidance must be taken seriously. However, Liang Desheng's surviving poetry displays far less interest in history than that of her niece. Ruan's point should probably be taken as evidence that Liang encouraged Wang Duan to develop her own innate interests, not that she was directly responsible for Wang Duan's interest in history, in Gao Qi, or in the Ming.

Liang Desheng's connection to Wang Duan's work is particularly interesting in view of her links to *tanci*. More than for her poetry, Liang is famous today for her work on Chen Duansheng's *Zai sheng yuan* (Love destiny reborn). After Chen's premature death in 1797, Liang supplemented the text with three chapters (out of a total of twenty); in most critics' estimation, these additions markedly dilute the feminist tone of the original. Zheng Zhenduo, for example, asserts that one reason for this *tanci*'s disappointingly happy ending lies in Liang's general state of contentment—she and her husband were a famous companionate couple—which contrasts with Chen Duansheng's many years of single living brought on by her husband's trouble with the law. In particular, Liang's decision to marry this *tanci*'s heroine off after she is about to become prime minister strikes Zheng as farfetched, the implication being that Liang and her husband wrote their own likes and dislikes into the action, superimposing them onto the heroine created by Chen Duansheng.[30]

Zai sheng yuan was not without impact on other female members of Chen Wenshu's circle, inspiring what seems to have been a prefatory poem to Liang Desheng's completed version, in six stanzas, by Gui Maoyi.[31] However, Wang Duan's own literary responses to Liang say nothing about *Zai sheng yuan*, nor have I found any mention of *tanci* elsewhere in Wang's writing. Thus, although Wang Duan may have known Liang's *Zai sheng yuan* when she began work on *Yuan Ming yishi*, Sun Kaidi's question about the genre of *Yuan Ming yishi* cannot be answered on the basis of Liang's interest in this genre.

Unlike Sun Kaidi, Tan Zhengbi unhesitatingly assumes that *Yuan Ming yishi* was a novel, most likely a historical novel or *pinghua*.[32] My reading of the evidence leads me to agree with Tan. The most important proof is that Chen Wenshu referred to the text as a *bai guan* (novel or historical fiction). Elsewhere in his work, when Chen talks about *tanci* – in a discussion of *Zai sheng yuan*, for example – he calls them *nanci*, an alternative name for *tanci*.[33] If *Yuan Ming yishi* had been a *tanci*, he should have described it in like terms. Moreover, although the relationship between the surviving remnants of *Yuan Ming yishi* and the original is not altogether clear, these remnants, too, lead me to believe that the original was some kind of fictionalized history. Apparently neither Sun nor Tan had access to these entries in *Ziran haoxue zhai ji*.

Chen Wenshu's preface to *Ziran haoxue zhai ji* states that when Wang Duan burned her work, which by then was at least eighteen *juan* long, "she preserved poems on men of the Yuan and on Zhang Shicheng from among her writings, from which she made poetical histories."[34] These poetical histories are entitled "Zhang Wu ji shi shi" (Poems commemorating the deeds of Mr. Zhang of Wu) and "Yuan yichen shi" (Poems about Yuan loyalists). They consist of short biographies, followed by poetic encomiums, each in two stanzas, eight lines long, of seven-word verse. The one exception is the section on Miss Jin in "Zhang Wu jishi shi," previously mentioned, which is a much longer biography followed by three sets of encomiums. *Ziran haoxue zhai ji* gives certain clues about the relationship between these poetical histories and the original narrative. It presents a set of 30 poems celebrating the 30 major Ming poets in *Ming sanshi jia shixuan* as a separate composition from that work.[35] By analogy, it is likely that Wang's encomiums about Zhang Shicheng and company were constructed independently and were not part of the original *Yuan Ming yishi*. In any case, they are not narrative poetry of the type associated with *tanci*. As for the biographies, they, too, are not verbatim quotations from *Yuan Ming yishi*, for they summarize rather than narrate the lives of the principals concerned. Thus they are close in tone and language to the biographies found in *Ming sanshi jia shixuan*. The one exception is the section on Miss Jin, which narrates her story in a lively manner, using dialogue, dreams, and other devices common to popular history. Along with Chen Wenshu's assertion that the original *Yuan Ming yishi* was based on unofficial histories, it encourages the view that *Yuan Ming yishi* itself was a *pinghua*, or historical novel, as Tan Zhengbi presumes.

In terms of my overall question about women and narrative, what is particularly interesting about Wang Duan's substitution – of two "poetical histories" for the burned work—is that what was preserved under her name for posterity is no longer narrative. Chen Wenshu's version of his daughter-in-law's motives in burning this document before it was finished is that after her conversion to Daoism she preferred to spend her time in religious contemplation rather than disputing the facts of ancient people's lives. However, the fragments that survive are themselves quite disputatious, attacking versions of Zhang Shicheng's story that do not present him in a favorable light. Lack of disputatiousness alone, then, cannot have been what distinguished the two poetical histories from *Yuan Ming yishi*. What is really different about them is that they no longer constitute a coherent story. Rather, they are still-lifes in poetry and prose. And because these still-lifes appear in two discrete sets, the connection between sets—which is to say, between loyalists to the Yuan and to Zhang Shicheng's renegade regime—is never made.

Chen's preface makes another interesting observation: when she burned her work, Wang Duan felt it to be redundant, since the truth about Zhang Shicheng had already come out in other accounts by family members. Conceivably, certain of these accounts were actually the work of Wang Duan.[36] In any event, not one of the family members to whom they are attributed is a woman. Further, it appears that even when she was writing *Yuan Ming yishi*, Wang Duan was defensive about it. Chen's preface mentions that she drew on her status as a reincarnated disciple—presumably masculine—of Gao Qi's when asked about her interest in the subject and her authority to write about it. By inference, narrating Zhang's exploits put Wang Duan in an uncomfortable position. As for her poetical histories, it is tempting to propose that they aroused less authorial ambivalence than *Yuan Ming yishi* because of their radically diluted narrative power. Like *Ming sanshi jia shixuan*, they were contentious, but because they were poetry they were more acceptable, by the standards of Wang Duan's day.

The Woman's Voice in Fiction After "Hong lou meng"

Another way of posing these questions is to ask how literate women responded to *Hong lou meng*. To know what *Hong lou meng* meant in Wang Duan's world, one has to look at the works of Wang Duan's associates, since Wang did not write about *Hong lou meng*. Victorian literature provides an analogy through which to focus the question at hand. As one learns from Nancy Armstrong's *Desire and Domestic Fiction*, the appearance of Samuel Richardson's *Pamela* in 1740—at about the time *Hong lou meng* was being written—led to a flurry of "domestic fictions" by such women writers as Jane Austen, the Brontës, and George Eliot. Armstrong's highly nuanced presentation raises the question of how *Pamela*, though authored by a man, "assumed the distinctive features of a specialized language for women" and eventually gave rise to fictions by women writers. She is ultimately concerned with how the "feminine authority" conveyed by this language and the "work" performed by domestic fiction extend the mentality of the "female conduct book" to fiction. Yet her vision of the transition from male to female authorship via "feminine authority" is of interest here. Feminine authority is conveyed by several means—a woman narrator or author, a focus on women's experience, an intended audience of women, or perhaps critical commentary by women. Adopting the outlook of the proper "domestic woman," Victorian narrative of this type aligns the novel with the values and interests of a newly emerging middle class.[37]

A number of problems make it difficult to transplant Armstrong's analysis to a Chinese setting. To name just a few, there was in the Qing no emerging middle class in need of asserting its rhetoric, and the polygamous nature of the Chinese family makes it far more complicated than in England to define a proper "domestic woman." The nearest Chinese analogue is probably the first wife, who differed from her English counterpart in having to preside over other wives and concubines in the wealthiest of homes. Armstrong's term "companionate marriage" also needs refiguring before it works for China. As it has recently come to be used in China studies, this term describes the relationship between women writers and supportive husbands. These husbands, for all their companionship, still expected to have concubines, whom the good first wife would praise in poems; moreover, wives who wrote were sometimes allowed to dislike household chores. In Armstrong's study, by contrast, "companionate marriage" refers to a division of labor between wife and husband, or at least the fiction thereof, in which the housewife managed household matters, and the husband turned his attention to the public sphere. These fictional divisions ended up granting "feminine authority" broad powers to define proper domesticity and other cultural norms.

Unlike *Pamela*, the *Hong lou meng* is not really feminine in its authority. Although this fiction is deeply interested in its principal women characters, most of whom were literate enough to narrate their own predicaments, it creates a sense that these women depend on the male narrator/author to elucidate their concerns. One might also argue that they depend on the hero Bao Yu's appreciation to bring out their best features. Despite the sustained focus on women's experience, the narrative authority is best defined as that of the male connoisseur of female talent, not the talented female's.[38] Yet no other Chinese work of vernacular fiction can match *Hong lou meng*'s sustained attempt to present household life from a feminine point of view. China's historical, social, and literary circumstances may not have experienced the transition Armstrong analyzes in her study, but the reactions of women readers show that in their minds *Hong lou meng* created meaningful imaginary worlds. On this basis, it seems to me that if any work of fiction might have encouraged Chinese women to begin writing novels, that work would be *Hong lou meng*.

The impact of *Hong lou meng* on members of Wang Duan's circle shows that it brought several of them closer to vernacular fiction than they had been before, although it left them on the margins of that form. In demonstrating this point, what I propose to do is detail the ramifications of *Hong lou meng* in genres traditionally used by women writers, such as editing, poetry, and drama, insofar as these can be demonstrated through women connected to Wang Duan.[39]

The most striking link between *Hong lou meng* and a woman writer is the preface by Gao E, *Hong lou meng*'s second author, to a collection of poetry by Wang Duan's acquaintance Yun Zhu, the editor of *Guochao guixiu zhengshi ji*. Entitled *Hongxiang guan shici cao* (Draft poetry and lyrics of Red Fragrance Hall), Yun's collection was published in 1814, the date of Gao's preface.[40] According to this preface, Gao was a friend of Yun's celebrated son Linqing, although he was older by as much as 50 years. It was Linqing who asked Gao to write the preface. Gao's preface mentions that the women of his own wife's family praised Yun Zhu for her virtue, her many successes in writing and painting, and for her accomplished son, who held the *jinshi* degree. Yun Zhu's work also shows other signs of *Hong lou meng*'s influence. Among the poems in *Hongxiang guan shici cao* are several clearly written in response to *Hong lou meng*. These appear in two sets, both of which follow rhymes used by members of the Crab Flower Club in the novel.[41] This collection leaves no doubt that *Hong lou meng* inspired the poetic games of Yun Zhu and her associates.

Yun Zhu's literary work took the form of editing as well as poetry writing. As previously noted, her *Guochao guixiu zhengshi ji* of 1831 was the most ambitious collection of women's poetry edited by a woman since Wang Duanshu's *Mingyuan shiwei*, a work to which it refers. This collection shows no sign that *Hong lou meng* was in any way a factor behind its publication. However, it reveals that the novel was an influence on drama by women, for one of the women whose work it preserves, a Miss Yao, co-authored a drama with her husband inspired by *Hong lou meng*.[42] Noteworthy, too, is Gao E's daughter's inclusion in this collection. Additionally she is one of a small number of friends and relatives who contributed a prefatory poem, an act that suggests that she was a special friend of Yun Zhu.[43]

Other links between *Hong lou meng* and Wang Duan's circle of acquaintances can be drawn. Jin Yi, a disciple of Yuan Mei, left an earlier example of a poetic reaction to *Hong lou meng*. Her poem, written as she lay dying in 1794 (when Wang Duan was just one year old) is about her discovery that the subject matter of *Hong lou meng* exactly fit her case. Jin's poem reads as follows:

> *Written on a Cold Night Waiting for*
> *Zhushi [Jin's husband], Who Does Not Return,*
> *and Reading "Hong lou meng chuanqi"*
> Cloudiness pervades the snow with a
>   penetrating chill.
> Twisting and turning incense disappears on
>   an agate plate.
> I wait for you who've not yet returned, then
>   abandoning my daydream, I get up.
> Might as well borrow a book to read.
>
> Their feelings run extraordinarily deep.
> Their souls can hardly stand such exertion;
>   they risk their lives.
> Even the toll of tears seems not quite enough.
> On second thought, what has this to do with me?[44]

Wang Duan's connection to Jin, whom she was too young to know directly, is established by a poem in her collected works. It is an inscription to a painting by Jin Yi's husband, Chen Jizhi, a relative of Wang's husband and father in law. The painting in question was done for Jin.

A younger contemporary of Wang Duan, Qian Shoupu is the third woman poet who wrote on *Hong lou meng*. Qian's poetry appears in a collection edited by Chen Wenshu, among other places; and she achieved sufficient distinction as an artist to study under the painter

Gai Qi (1774–1829). Like Wang Duan's, Qian's poems look back to Yuan Mei's circle, but they also relate to more modern developments, particularly in their evocation of the Opium War, from which she was forced to flee. Wang Duan's own poetry yields no direct mention of Qian or her husband, but there are many links between their work, and Qian's collected writings contain one poem honoring Wang Duan. It also contains four verses under the rubric "*Hong lou* qu" (Songs of *Hong lou*) and two other pairs of poems whose main subject is *Hong lou meng*. Two of these eight pieces are reactions to specific characters, Ping'er and Lin Daiyu. The one on Daiyu is rather typical of Qian's work, which frequently laments the plight of the intelligent woman, for whom talent is a source of trouble, not satisfaction.

> *On Reading "Shitou ji" ["Hong lou meng"], I Praise*
> *the Lady of the Xiao and Xiang Rivers (Daiyu)*

A fairy form, an immortal banished to an earthly
    home of wealth.
With poor fate and great talent, it is difficult to
    protect oneself.
A flower endowed with feeling, she often provokes
    resentment.
Women find literacy is the root of their undoing.

In vain did the Lady of the Xiang's tears speckle
    the bamboo.
Who will cherish her delicate soul?
When she returns to the Land of Illusion, she will
    surely reach enlightenment.
There, the spells of passion and intelligence will
    prevail no more.[45]

Qian Shoupu's work yields the fullest evidence to date on *Hong lou meng*'s influence among Wang Duan's immediate circle of friends.

One of the most interesting examples of *Hong lou meng*'s impact in a slightly expanded circle lies in the work of Zhou Qi. Zhou may not have known Wang Duan directly — she was certainly much younger — but both had companionate marriages, both had ties to descendants of Yuan Mei, and both worked closely with Chen Wenshu.[46] Further, like Qian Shoupu, both had links to the painter Gai Qi, albeit in different ways. Unlike Qian, who knew Gai and studied with him, Zhou and Gai may not have been directly acquainted. However, she and her companionate husband, Wang Xilian, were among those who added poems to one of Gai's most famous works, his *Hong lou meng tu yong*

(Pictures on *Hong lou meng,* with Encomiums). The couple signed their encomiums in 1839, ten years after Gai's death — incidentally the year Wang Duan died. Zhou's three encomiums are the only ones by a woman to this set of Gao's paintings. They are to the images of Yuan Chun, Shi Xiangyun, and Bao Qin. Compared to Jin Yi's and Qian Shoupu's poems about *Hong lou meng,* Zhou's can seem rather playful, as in this encomium about Shi Xiangyun:

> Leaving the table, the lady is overcome by
>   drunkenness,
> The power of wine is hard to overcome as
>   evening approaches.
> She sleeps on in the endless spring breeze as
>   spring erupts around her.
> Ceaselessly, falling blossoms cover the
>   beautiful face.
>
> Were it not for her frail constitution, she would
>   be warm enough.
> Fortunately her cold skin is not bothered by
>   the chill.
> Her dedicated romanticism is perhaps more
>   like delicate shyness —
> It takes great effort for a poet to capture this scene.[47]

Yet despite a certain playfulness, it is clear from other writings of Zhou's that she, too, was moved by the tragedy of certain characters in the novel, such as Daiyu. This is apparent in a second set of Zhou's writings on *Hong lou meng* entitled "*Hong lou meng* ti ci" in an edition of the novel with her husband's commentary, which first appeared in 1832, seven years before the encomiums were set down. The interrelatedness of the two projects is established by the fact that the poem about Shi Xiangyun is identical in both, although that is the extent of overlap. Zhou's sense of Daiyu's life as tragedy is obvious both in a poem on this heroine's burning of her poems and in another entitled "The Goddess of Frost and the Lady of the Moon: Li Wan Mourns Daiyu." The latter poem reads:

> In the moonlight, in the frost, she planned to take
>   flight freely.
> The outstanding sister took the lead in literary
>   talents.
> She must have invited jealousy because of her
>   pure genius.

> How is it right for a young girl's life to end
>   while she is young?
>
> If there is a purpose for passion, let it be
>   profound.
> When illness falls on the innocent, it is most
>   pathetic.
> Bamboo welcomes people; she is gone and
>   quiet.
> Alas, only I am filled with tears.[48]

Zhou Qi's response to Daiyu's life and death is emotionally consistent with Qian Shoupu's. Incidentally, both convey a much more detailed familiarity with the novel than Jin Yi's poem does.

The fact that Zhou Qi's poems are included in an edition of *Hong lou meng* is especially interesting for our purposes. Zhou's preface to these poems, numbering ten in all, explains how she came to write them and the negative reaction their writing may have provoked.

> I happened to be beset by petty illnesses and was sitting in our small tower with time on my hands, when I spied my husband Xuexiang's critical edition of *Hong lou meng*. I read through several *juan* and couldn't help being moved to laughter. Its comments put women's experiences at the center of human feeling. Compared to *Shuihu* and *Xixiang*, it was much more satisfying. Had Cao Xueqin known Xuexiang's comments, he would have taken him for a like-minded friend. Among the book's emotional subjects, many are discussed in detail, but there are still some whose implications have yet to be exhausted. I playfully composed ten *lüshi* poems to expand on these subtleties. This is like adding feet to a snake, but I don't think I have turned truth into falsehood. When I finished these poems, my spirit was tired and I felt empty inside. Taking time out for a nap, I dreamed of a person wearing old-fashioned clothes and hat, who bowed to me and said, "You are a woman. Writing poetry goes against what your governess taught you, all the more when you write poems on *Hong lou meng*. Aren't you afraid my generation will make fun of you?" I answered him saying, "Your point is well taken, but 'happiness without licentiousness' and 'sorrow without harm' were the incentive for the 'Guofeng' section of the *Classic of Poetry*. If you insist on taking issue with these poems, compare them with despicable actions that are covered up by refined speech. The difference between [my writing and false speech] is as great as that between Heaven and Earth." I hadn't finished speaking when the person suddenly disappeared, and I woke up. But I could smell cassia fragrance through the curtains, and I heard *wutong* leaves blowing in the wind.

Only the quiet moon atop the tower glanced down at my painted eyebrows.[49]

Like Wang Duan's dream after editing *Ming sanshi jia shixuan*, this dream airs and challenges doubts provoked by the author's writing. Here the *bête noire* is the man in the old-fashioned clothes and hat, whose ideas are resisted by Zhou Qi, as well as by her husband. Not only did he include these writings in his published version of the novel, he must also have encouraged his wife to add the Shi Xiangyun poem and two others to *Hong lou meng tu yong*. In both senses, he was responsible for attaching women's writings to the novel in ways not seen before. Wang's 1832 edition was the first, to my knowledge, to include reactions identifiable as those of a woman among the prefatory materials.

Nevertheless, even this edition cannot quite be said to encourage "feminine authority" in narrative, as Armstrong would define it. Although *Hong lou meng* may have struck Zhou Qi as putting "women's experiences at the center of human feeling," she gives the distinct impression that she came across the text by accident, having picked it up only because her husband left it lying around at home. In this respect, her preface recalls Jin Yi's poem. Further, it conveys some ambivalence about whether she should have written the poems at all, and it is clear that her writings were published alongside Wang Xilian's commentary only because her husband was the editor. Thus, Wang Xilian's 1832 edition follows the implicit rhetoric of the novel and showcases talented women but gives "narrative authority" to a man.

In 1828, four years before Wang Xilian's edition, and again in 1832, another novel, *Jinghua yuan*, was published with congratulatory poems, four of them by women. *Jinghua yuan* was clearly influenced by *Hong lou meng*, and because some of the congratulatory poems by women draw comparisons between the two novels, they have a bearing on the question at hand.[50] Among these, one is of particular interest since it comes from Wang Duan's circle. This is again by Qian Shoupu, whose reactions to *Hong lou meng* have already been cited. Entitled "A Prefatory Poem to Li Shaozi's *chuanqi Jinghua yuan*," it reads:

> Romantic poems are composed in the World of Beauties.
> They are all equally talented but endowed with
>   different feeling.
> You name and tell of those women in the Pavilion
>   of Mourning Beauty.

They are often ill-fated because of their great intelligence.

The young women's writings are freshly transmitted
    on yellow silk.
These women are lucky to live in an auspicious time.
I laugh that they have not yet awakened from the
    Red Chamber Dream.
They are still bound by the passions of ordinary youngsters.

How could there be a little Fairyland on this earth?
Bright thoughts, strange ruminations, are brought to
    life by their pens.
108 fates are drawn together by a thread of nirvana,
Not a word is tainted by dust.

Now let me honor you, as a banished immortal, with
    incense and a solemn salute.
In my last life I too was an autumn lotus.
I'd like to borrow your brush to convey my story.
Please enter me into the flower roster of *Jinghua yuan*.[51]

Unlike Zhou Qi's comments on *Hong lou meng*, Qian's poem is reprinted without reference to her husband, who, as it happens, was also a close companion. As one among several readers' reactions, it gives the impression that *Jinghua yuan* reached out to people of both sexes, whether or not the women among them were married to literate men. Here it advances beyond the companionate model that frames Zhou Qi's poems in Wang Xilian's edition of *Hong lou meng*. Qian's way of connecting *Jinghua yuan* and *Hong lou meng* is another point of interest. Like one other among the congratulatory poems by women, hers expresses the view that *Jinghua yuan* answered the needs of readers who had long awaited a successor to *Hong lou meng*. This poem thus supports the view that at least some women readers took a new interest in fiction after *Hong lou meng* was written and eagerly awaited other fiction on similar themes. This reaction may surprise modern readers, few of whom would put *Jinghua yuan* and *Hong lou meng* in the same category;[52] but it is obvious that for Qian and others, *Jinghua yuan* answered readerly desires to which *Hong lou meng* had given rise.

Qian's request, in the last stanza, that Li Ruzhen's brush write her story for her, and her wish to be entered into the flower roster of *Jinghua yuan* are also of interest. This part of the poem was not reprinted in Qian's poetry collection, and the poem as a whole is somewhat hyperbolic in tone. Yet despite signs that Qian's words were not meant seriously in every particular, they reproduce the cliché that novel writing was better done by men. Alongside Zhou Qi's dialogue with her dream interlocutor, Qian's wish that Li Ruzhen transpose her life story into fiction reinforces the view that whatever satisfaction she derived from *Hong lou meng*'s innovative focus on women and its demonstrable appeal to women readers, women still had difficulty imagining themselves as authors in this genre.

The evidence adduced here provides a basis on which to propose that *Hong lou meng* did change women's relation to vernacular fiction. That influence may have stopped short of producing novels by or narrated by women, but it drew in women readers, such as Zhou Qi, who had not enjoyed fiction much before. A change is also perceptible in the minds of certain editors, who at least by 1828 were including reactions by women as part of the prefatory materials to *Hong lou meng* and its "successor" *Jinghua yuan*. Especially in the latter case, because the poems of these women writers were unmediated by companionate husbands or male mentors, one can infer that they welcomed women readers more directly than Wang Xilian's *Hong lou meng* had done. Yet in no sense do they invite women to take up the authorial pen.

What these combined reactions demonstrate is that despite *Hong lou meng*'s interest in women characters and its stimulating effect on women writers, novel writing was little more conceivable for women after *Hong lou meng* than before. *Yuan Ming yishi* may be a partial exception to this generalization, although to make the point persuasively, one would need to know much more than can currently be known: whether *Hong lou meng* was relevant or irrelevant to Wang's enterprise, whether she would have identified herself as a woman had she published, whether her narrative voice was feminine in any way.[53] At least, however, her family were willing to admit that she had once authored a work of narrative, later destroyed. In this small particular, *Yuan Ming yishi* encourages the view that something—whether loyalism, social change, or a change in literary attitudes after *Hong lou meng*—had begun to erode the taboo against female-authored fiction by Wang Duan's time. Yet the many ambiguities in this case, not to mention Wang Duan's decision to burn her work, make *Yuan Ming yishi* an exception that proves the rule.

These findings for vernacular fiction contrast with the case in "women's *tanci*," where a pattern closer to Armstrong's model can be found. There, but not in fiction, one finds a presumption of female authorship, even when specific *tanci* may have been authored by companionate couples or by men. This is so, in part, because of the feminine-sounding autobiographical commentary in prefaces and head-of-chapter comments that presumes a female author behind the scenes.[54] The possibility that *Tian yu hua*, the seminal work in this branch of literature, had a male author creates a second congruency with the patterns Armstrong analyzes. *Tian yu hua's* republication in the early nineteenth century eventually led to *tanci* written by women, as well as for them, just as Richardson's *Pamela* encouraged Victorian women to write novels. To be sure, women's *tanci* are hardly domestic fictions, in that their subject matter is adventurous. Only obliquely and irregularly do they take up domestic concerns. Yet the evidence suggests that it was here, more than in the novel, that women found a narrative style with which they could feel at home.

The value of the analogy to Victorian England turns out, then, to be suggestive, but in a limited way. What it does is call attention to something that *Hong lou meng* did not inspire. For all of its interest in women and home life, this novel's narrative authority came across as one step removed from that of the literate female, being lodged in the masculine connoisseur of talented women but not in women themselves. Although not only for that reason, it failed to inspire writing women to identify themselves as such—if and when they became authors in this genre. And despite the implicit invitation to women as readers, neither Wang Xilian's *Hong lou meng* nor the 1828 and 1832 editions of *Jinghua yuan* defied the prevailing ethos—that women not become authors in this genre.

What exactly put novel writing off limits for women writers is impossible to say with certainty at present. Evidently, narrative was easier for women to write in their own names when it took place in a separate women's genre, namely *tanci*. Alternatively, *tanci's* heavy use of poetry may have made it seem more properly "feminine" than narratives predominantly in prose. Finally, women's *tanci's* very fancifulness left their narrators freer to advance a fictional world. As imaginary stories, not histories, their main raison d'être was that they helped readers fill long, boring hours. Thus they did not challenge received wisdom, as *Yuan Ming yishi* would have done; still less did they embarrass families by exposing their internal strains.[55] Yet Wang Duanshu's and Wang Duan's work also indicates how women might appropriate male literary voices in other narrative and expository genres. Whatever kept women from identifying themselves as the authors of vernacular fiction, it was not the weight of literary tradition alone. Something specific to fiction's history or its purposes set it off limits for most women, competent though they may have been to read and write in this genre.

If we cannot fully account for this inhibition, we can at least take note of its persistence and power. According to Tan Zhengbi, except for *Yuan Ming yishi* and one other work from the end of the nineteenth century, no woman wrote novels before the end of the Qing.[56] This would mean that throughout the centuries-long duration of the vernacular novel in China, only two women associated their names with this form as authors; and neither one of their works survives. In the closely related genre of drama, by contrast, at least twenty women are identified as authors;[57] and a number of their works are preserved in family collections—beginning in the mid-seventeenth century and continuing until well after *Hong lou meng*. This would again suggest that among all the roles assumed by literate women, that of female novelist was particularly fraught with conflict—not only for individual women but for the families that gave them status, published their work, and otherwise controlled their lives.

Postscript: Hong lou meng Sequels and the Woman Writer: The Case of Gu Taiqing

As mentioned at the beginning, anonymous authors abound in Chinese vernacular fiction, and it is common to assume that they are men. *Hong lou meng* sequels have, of late, proved a fruitful subfield in which to test this generalization. Nanyang shi's *Hong lou fumeng* (*Hong lou meng* resumed) of 1799, which announces a female editor, raises suspicions of female involvement in its composition, and other promising cases may emerge.[58]

For now, Gu Taiqing's all but certain composition of the *Hong lou meng ying* provides the only known example of a female author among the 30-some sequels to *Hong lou meng*. Fascinating in its own right, Gu's biography will be reduced here to a few key particulars— her Manchu background, her long residence in Beijing, and her talent at writing *ci*. In more than one evaluation, she is rated among the best woman *ci* poets of the Qing.[59]

Conveniently for my purposes, Gu was closely linked to Wang Duan's literary associates during a period of residence in Jiangnan. Among other ties to Wang, she was the sworn sister of Shen Shanbao, who knew both Wang Duan and Yun Zhu and was a leading literary figure in her own right. Shen's *Mingyuan shihua* (Poetry talks on famous women, 1846) chronicles many of the women Wang Duan knew.[60] Additionally, Gu had long-standing emotional and literary links to the daughters of Wang's aunt, Liang Desheng.[61] These relationships appear to have solidified around the time of Wang's death and hence did not involve Wang directly, yet there is proof that Gu and Wang were aware of each other's existence and shared a number of friends.[62]

The identification of Gu as *Hong lou meng ying*'s author has been facilitated of late by materials long preserved in Japan. These establish that the pseudonym used in the novel, Yuncha waishi (Cloud raft immortal), and the sobriquet on one of Gu's poetry collections are the same. Adding depth to this identification is the newly increased store of Gu's extant poems, which include one of mourning for Shen Shanbao. This poem reads in part as follows:

> *Hong lou*'s illusory landscape has no basis in reality
> Occasionally I take up my writing brush and add a
>   few chapters.
> [Shen's] long preface brought honor to my work
> Frequent letters from her splendid pen demanded
>   [that I complete the project].

Gu's note to this poem observes:

> I have worked intermittently on a sequel to *Hong lou meng* several chapters long, to which Shen [Shanbao] wrote a preface. She asked to see it without waiting for the completed manuscript. She often blamed me for my lazy nature and would tease me, saying, "You are almost 70 years old. If you don't finish this book quickly, I fear you will never realize its potential."[63]

In fact, Gu was only 63 *sui* in 1861, the year the preface was written. The next year, Shen died. Some of the urgency Shen felt about reading this text and writing its preface may have derived from her own advancing age.[64] Written under the sobriquet Xihu sanren (Prose writer of West Lake), for Shen was a Hangzhou native, the preface is rather perceptive about "the art of the novel."[65] Particularly interesting for my purposes, like the novel itself, it gives no clue as to the gender of novelist or prefacer. Eventually the work was published commercially, by Juzhen tang in Beijing. The publication date, 1877, is thought to follow Gu's own death by approximately one year.[66]

These data shed light on two facets of questions raised above. The first concerns the ambivalence of women writers of fiction. Gu's tardiness and tentativeness about her own fictional endeavor are quite familiar from Wang Duan's example. Coming as late as it does, her work's posthumous publication may owe something to encroaching "modernity," but it can also be explained as an extension of earlier attitudes that had brought women closer to fiction's door.[67] More immediately to the point, her work's completion was the result of Shen Shanbao's prodding. The tug-of-war between Gu and Shen reveals Shen as one of the strongest female advocates of fiction written by women during the Qing. Yet for all of Shen's entreaties and Gu's compliance, *Hong lou meng ying* probably does not quite do justice to Gu's talents. In the mind of at least two critics, its occasional verses are skillful but curiously devoid of emotional content, and the novel reaches no clear resolution.[68] This is hardly what one would expect from an outstanding writer fully engaged with the task at hand.

The other facet has to do with feminine narrative authority, or rather, with its lack in *Hong lou meng ying*. In other words, by adhering to the narrative style of the original work, the sequel provides no clue that its author is not a man, like Cao Xueqin. Without an accidental scholarly discovery, Gu Taiqing's connection to the work would never have been known. Now that we know who the author is, the use of the Beijing vernacular and the familiarity with Manchu customs take on new meaning—as reflections of Gu's personal experience—and they set *Hong lou meng ying* apart from other sequels;[69] perhaps eventually, signs of a nascent "literati-feminine" will also be discerned.[70] Even so, nothing about this novel's narrative stance overtly reveals the woman writer behind the scenes. Being essentially invisible, then, the revolutionary fact of female authorship does nothing to break down long-standing mores. From her extensive study of women writers, Shen would have been well aware that *Hong lou meng ying*'s female authorship was unusual, probably pathbreaking. Yet her preface keeps Gu's secret, and the text presents no other signals that it emerged from women's literary culture or reached out to female readers in a special way.[71]

Gu's motives in undertaking this work and for obscuring her involvement with it demand a fuller treatment on another occasion. What seems obvious even at this juncture, however, is that neither she nor Shen saw any advantage in dropping *Hong lou meng*'s securely masculine narrative mode. To use Armstrong's terminology, Gu does not write "as a woman"; therefore she could not be accused of writing "like a man."[72] By keeping its authorship a secret, her sequel would not be sidelined (or praised) as "women's literature," so long as its true authorship was unknown to all but Gu's best friends. In the shape Gu left it, it would have seemed unexceptionable to readers of its day. Judging from this example, *Hong lou meng* may have piqued women's interest and drawn them in as readers — even as writers — but it did so on terms that excluded "female authors," disallowed female narrators, and eschewed the parochial authority of the women's world.

The absence of full-fledged feminine authority in *Hong lou meng*, *Hong lou meng ying*, and other fiction might be explained in terms of lack — of social and other changes that had not yet made China modern, of formal features that refused to change. Armstrong cautions against such overdetermined readings, a caution that makes sense in view of the evidence at hand. The links from Wang Duanshu to Wang Duan and from Wang Duan to Gu Taiqing give ample reason to propose that fiction, like other genres, was not incapable of admitting women as authors, even before the end of the Qing. In contrast to Wang Duanshu, Wang Duan wrote eighteen *juan* of fiction, albeit eventually destroyed; in contrast to Wang Duan, Gu Taiqing brought *Hong lou meng ying* to completion and published it, albeit posthumously, under a name identifiable as her own. In the intervening period, writers like Qian Shoupu, Zhou Qi, and others laid claim to fiction as readers, a claim acknowledged by publishers, when they prefaced works of fiction with women's critiques and poems. Whether these developments would have led over time to frankly female authorship or full-fledged "feminine" narration, they demonstrate real change. Barely visible on the surface, the lines they describe cast doubt on old clichés.

Postface

Chinese Women in a
Comparative Perspective:
A Response

NANCY ARMSTRONG

To compare two cultures on the basis of how each represents women is to question the validity of comparative analysis itself. How do those of us who acquired identities as women and literate subjects within one culture learn to describe women from quite a different culture, without transforming them into positive or negative versions of ourselves? More specifically, how can we avoid the twin ethnographic sins of universalizing what is peculiar to one of the Western imperial nations and then producing an absolute difference between, say, an Anglophone or Francophone culture and one such as China's, despite the fact there have been centuries of interpenetration between "us" and "them"? Even though it is impossible to remain completely innocent on either count, especially when women provide the basis for comparison, it is still instructive to perform such analyses. They

This essay began with the response I delivered at the Yale Conference "Women and Literature in Ming-Qing China" in June 1993. To that event I brought little more than my research on England and the experience of watching feminism take hold and change a number of fields, among them English and Comparative Literature. I had the opportunity to read papers prepared for the conference, to hear many of the talks delivered there, to take part in the animated discussions during and surrounding the event, and to receive some generously insightful responses to my response. Finally, Ellen Widmer's engagement with *Desire and Domestic Fiction* in the paper she prepared for this volume guided me through the final argument. The references cited below thus represent only a fraction of the help and inspiration I received from people whom I met at the conference.

reveal a great deal about how our disciplines construct their respective objects of knowledge — not only where those disciplines have set boundaries by establishing differences, but also what notions about human nature they must share in order to do so.

I was both surprised and pleased to recognize many of the lines of argument shaping the papers presented at the conference on Women and Literature in Ming-Qing China, held at Yale University in June 1993. There can only be one reason for this: such similarities in critical methods arise, I believe, because feminism has its own way of interrogating the reigning methods and materials of a discipline wherever it first gains a foothold. Any new group of scholars invariably reproduces the sequence of moves and countermoves by which feminism has already engaged and altered the models, methods, and materials dominating other academic disciplines. At the same time, however, since each new venture learns from feminism's gains and losses elsewhere in the academy, feminist scholarship never makes the same sequence of moves and countermoves twice. With this in mind, let me first identify what struck me as familiar in the new work on women in Chinese literature.

A peculiarly self-conscious exuberance colored the way in which the presenters at the Yale conference went about turning over new cultural-historical ground. Each paper took steps to generate a classification system capable of containing the new material, to challenge what had suddenly revealed themselves as masculine criteria for literary value, to map a more adequate sociohistorical context for women's cultural production, and to define more self-consciously gendered positions from which to speak as literary scholars. The various attempts to introduce and interpret writing by, for, and about women lent new complexity and importance to literary works and cultural practices that were, I gather, hitherto considered rather peripheral to Chinese literary studies. There was no doubt in my mind that future scholarship that did not at least acknowledge this material would risk instant irrelevance by demonstrating insensitivity to gender issues.

This transformation of the terms for conducting scholarship was one I had already experienced in English and Comparative Literature, as feminism changed the way we read Western literature and, ultimately, what we thought Western literature was. Along with the introduction of what might be called feminine writing came pressure to rethink masculine standards for literature and literary scholarship. Indeed, in a number of disciplines, the addition of distinctively "feminine" materials created unprecedented opportunities for revising the existing rules, and after a period of intense critical activity, each discipline that had fallen under the influence of feminism emerged significantly changed. In describing what happened to my own discipline, I am inviting my counterparts who study Chinese literature and culture to consider how Western feminism might also be changing theirs.

My professed kinship with other feminist scholars at the Yale conference does not, however, imply that our primary materials have anything in common, just because both of us deal with women. Quite the contrary, my purpose in describing what we share as feminists who think and write in Western universities is to discover where Ming and Qing materials challenge certain assumptions, models, and methods derived from modern European and American culture, especially those we bring to the study of women. Thus the second half of this chapter explains both what I found unfamiliar about the Chinese women's writing that provided the occasion for so much innovative scholarship and why such writing could not have flourished in Europe.

The Historical Problematic of Academic Feminism

During the medieval and early modern periods in Europe, books telling women how to be women played second fiddle in number and political importance to similar books written for men. In the late seventeenth and early eighteenth centuries, however, female conduct books underwent a startling increase in number and consistency, as they spelled out new rules for becoming a marriageable woman and being a good wife. We have no evidence that these rules described what men already desired, much less what women actually thought they should prefer to the allurements of wealth and position. But there is a great deal of evidence to suggest that both these things came to pass and that, by the end of the eighteenth century, literate men and women had been induced in rather large numbers to think that they should want or be wanted for certain qualities of heart and mind called "sensibility" — a precise bundle of psychological capabilities that made a woman "feminine" according to what is still very much the operative definition of the term (Armstrong, *Desire and Domestic Fiction*).

These early rule books telling women how to be women may be

read as proto-feminist in that they urged women to become literate in ways that were specifically suited to women and gave the authority to write as women to those who could demonstrate how to observe and even bend the new rules. Such authors as Jane Austen, the Brontës, and George Eliot subsequently expanded the limits of what was acceptable for women in the way of a rhetorical position, subject matter, and writing style. Their fiction expanded the category "female" to include much more than the traditional notion of "femininity." In doing so, that fiction made room both for women authors and for women's fiction within the category of respectable literature. From the beginning, however, some women wrote in opposition to the rules for feminine discourse and were systematically excluded from the sphere of respectable reading. As late as the 1880's, Annie Bésant was thrown in jail simply for translating Thomas Malthus's well-known principles of population into a handbook on birth control that was sufficiently simple and forthright in its anatomical descriptions to be read and practiced by working-class women. Because she usurped the authority of political economist and doctor and did so in prose addressed by one woman to others of her sex about their own sexuality, her pamphlet was classified as pornographic and banned from bookstalls.

It is fair to say that Bésant walked into the same double bind that Mary Wollstonecraft felt closing around her during the last decade of the eighteenth century (Poovey). The trap was set as writing, spearheaded by domestic fiction and conduct books for women, designated certain areas of an earlier tradition of letters as feminine and made such material promote a new, distinctively modern and middle-class way of life. To participate in this new tradition of writing and receive authority from it, a woman had to accept not only the distinction among various sources of authority but also her own detachment from all but the truly feminine source, which manifested itself in selfless emotion. Thus, as Wollstonecraft argued, a woman's authority as a writer amounted to her complete disenfranchisement in other domains. She particularly lamented the fact that intellectual women, women with the learning to engage in the esteemed tradition of letters, would henceforth be discredited as interlopers in a masculine domain. Indeed, Wollstonecraft found herself deprived of the rhetorical means of transcending the limitations that gender ideology had suddenly placed on women's writing.

In her study of early modern women poets, Ann Rosalind Jones describes a similar double bind at work within the aristocratic tradition of letters. Women occasionally wrote in the elite tradition, they might enjoy the company of intellectual men, and they could even contest their political subordination to men (as in the oft-cited example of the *querelle des femmes*), but they had to represent their position, style, and subject matter as distinct and apart from that of their male counterparts. They had to base their authority to write as women on the fact of their exclusion from the masculine tradition of letters. To write as women, in other words, they had to argue that authority resided, however unjustifiably, in the social and symbolic practices associated with men. The scholarship concerned primarily with male-authored courtier poetry helps to complete the picture of how writing was sexually encoded during the early modern period. Those who gave voice in courtly rhetoric, whether male or female, to a lyrical expression of desire that argued against the traditional subordination of wife to husband announced their lack of position at court the moment their verses went into circulation (Marotti; Tennenhouse, 30–36). Although we still know relatively little about the sociology of publication and reception in early modern Europe, there are clear indications that this kind of verse was not intended for public view. We are consequently safe in concluding that masculine authority was not measured by one's access to publication, not in a culture where political matters of any importance were reserved for the ears of the monarch and those closest to him. To write was a sign of disempowerment, even if one were male. Thus publication provides little or no indication of how much freedom women enjoyed, up through the seventeenth century, or what forms of subordination they endured simply because they were women.

The standard is equally untrustworthy after 1700, when men began to measure authority in terms of literacy. Although it is true that since Wollstonecraft women have argued against the boundaries of feminine writing, we cannot take their negative interpretation of such segregation at face value. For the feminization of certain areas of writing also worked in their favor. Wherever writing has divided an entire field of cultural practices, along with writing itself, into masculine and feminine spheres, we find that two other conditions prevail: writing has assumed precedence over other symbolic practices, and women have been authorized to represent those whom the dominant tradition of letters has suppressed. Henceforth, one's class status and ethnic identity are determined by the way he or she observes and/or modifies the dominant (i.e., written) standards of masculinity and femininity. Thus the segregation of women as a kind of readership and authorial sensibility also empowers them. Writing by, for, and about women produces a separate cultural domain where women are empowered in their own terms — as the spokespeople for those who lack domestic sanctuary and are likely to perish without one — rather than those vying for position within the public sphere.

This, according to Denise Riley, was the cultural situation in England during the second half of the nineteenth century when modern feminism first emerged. From the beginning, feminism had a double and implicitly self-contradictory argument to wage: on the one hand, feminism contended that women were simply different from men, not inferior to them, and, on the other, that women should be treated equally with men rather than differently from them. In other words, whenever women advanced the principle that women could remain feminine and exert authority within the home, within the few professions that drew upon their skills as mothers, and within charitable organizations, they were forced to confront the limitations of such authority. To expand the boundaries of feminine authority, women had to feminize whatever social role they successfully occupied. For a woman to violate the sexual division of social, cultural, and intellectual labor, on the other hand, was to lose her femininity, and this entailed a loss of the very authority that the culture granted to women. The inappropriateness of her mere presence in a traditionally masculine role reinforced the notion that certain arenas of social, cultural, and intellectual life were meant for men, because men were naturally more masculine than women and therefore both inclined to and fit for traditional forms of authority.

But if women could not appropriate traditionally masculine political prerogatives, men were indeed able to draw on the authority of feminine writing. As in the case of Chinese poetry (Kang-i Sun Chang, *Ch'en Tzu-lung*, 11–18), English poetry often implies a feminine source, even when a man has written it. To adopt this position, a male author would simply present himself to the reader as a self-enclosed individual who existed at some remove from the world populated by businessmen and politicians — as if his revulsion or unsuitability for the workaday masculine world somehow gave him the sensitivity to be a poet. However unintentionally, this detachment became the hallmark of literary work. Such Renaissance authors as Ralegh, Sidney, and Donne wrote poetry only when they were away from court, and Milton formulated the persona that earned him the title of first

great English author only after the collapse of the revolutionary government in which he served as Latin secretary. Whereas the eighteenth-century novelist Samuel Richardson spoke almost exclusively
through his epistolary heroines, nineteenth-century poets and liberal
intellectuals took up positions at an increasing distance from those
men whom Arnold labeled "philistines," and male modernists deliberately went into exile during the early decades of the twentieth century in order to make epic literary statements about their respective
homelands.

This brief genealogy of English authorial identity suggests that
men of letters consistently acknowledged some interrelationship between the authority of writing and a position that a woman normally
would occupy. In early modern England, this position was thrust
upon them, and writing poetry would have been considered a poor
substitute for a position at court (Marotti; Tennenhouse, 30–36). With
the advent of the novel, however, we find that men sought out this position as a way of criticizing the status quo from a position that was
politically inoffensive because it focused on matters personal and
domestic. During the eighteenth century, then, being out of power
suddenly offered a powerful vantage point from which to write
(Williams). But the advantages that thus accrued to writing over traditional political practices had to be denied even—and especially—
after those people who read novels came into dominance. For ages
writing implied the author's removal from power, and so, at some
point in the eighteenth century, historical circumstances conspired to
create the curiously paradoxical form of power I call "feminine
authority," authority that could not reveal itself for what it was without losing power (Armstrong, *Desire and Domestic Fiction*).

So formulated, the natural division between masculinity and
femininity cut across various strata of society and intensified around
violations of gender decorum as England modernized and women
began writing in increasing numbers. That the so-called rise of the
novel was part of this two-pronged process of gendering and mod-
ernizing English culture is suggested by the fact that what might more
accurately be called "the rise of domestic fiction" accompanied modernization and made room for women authors, readers, and subject
matter. As a result of the integral relationship between modernization
and the emergence of gender as the first determinant of political identity, it soon became virtually impossible to find a major controversy in
any cultural arena that did not somehow question and redraw the line

between masculinity and femininity (Scott). This work of changing and establishing gender differences was the main work of the novel. The novel dealt with the question of how far one could tinker with the status quo and still produce a world in which readers recognized the one they actually inhabited; it did so by playing with the gender differences given by the culture. This can be said of any and all novels written by and about women—any novel, that is, considered appropriate for women readers. To reject the natural basis for gender differences was consequently to position oneself outside respectable culture. As Wollstonecraft, Bésant, and others quickly discovered, one wrote as a woman but like a man at the cost of the feminine authority that set the standard for public reception. This standard was set in stone by 1847, it appears, when *Wuthering Heights* was first published and failed to meet that standard.

Beginning with the development of a feminist press in the 1860's, a group of authors who called themselves feminists began to pursue an alternative strategy (Riley; Showalter). This event can be regarded as both the first link and the most telling distinction between our own scholarly and critical stance and the materials from the past that we study. These first self-described feminist authors conscientiously violated the intellectual division of labor established by Victorian culture. To change the sexual distribution of political power, as Riley explains, they developed a feminist polemic that drew on the past. They used women's authority in the domestic and social spheres to lay claim to authority in the arenas of politics, business, and the professions: if mothers were the backbone of the nation, shouldn't they be trusted to vote, own businesses, and practice medicine?

This move on the part of women writers simultaneously exposed and reproduced the contradiction whose historical development I have been sketching. "Exposed," in that feminists argued against limiting female authority to an implicitly subordinated feminine sphere, and "reproduced," in that feminists represented themselves as members of a group suppressed or marginalized because of its gender. In other words, feminism founded its political logic and moral appeal on the claims that (1) women were naturally different from men and (2) women had been culturally subordinated to men because of those natural differences. Ever since, feminism has distinguished the second claim from the first on grounds that the second defines the very condition that feminists seek to overturn in the name of equity between different genders. Thus a feminist polemic characteristically places cultural subordination and natural difference in a relation of actual and ideal, or problem and solution.

In strictly logical terms, challenging the assumption that women are culturally subordinated as feminine because they are naturally different does not necessarily challenge the primary fact of natural difference or femaleness itself. But such indeed proved to be the case. By the early 1980's when feminism had successfully infiltrated a number of the disciplines, the reigning definition of what women are by nature and what they can therefore be culturally authorized to think, say, and do had changed significantly. The fact that feminism could gain a foothold within the academy clearly testifies to a recent change in gender differences. It is safe to say, further, that since the early 1980's feminist scholarship has progressively revised the methods and materials of a number of disciplines. First and perhaps most tellingly, this scholarship challenged the cultural centrality of masculine writing in English and the comprehensiveness of English and American literary history as it had been understood for the previous century (Douglas; Gilbert and Gubar; Ryan; Showalter). Most recently, we have seen feminism spread from literature to the more stubbornly masculine fields of history, the social sciences, biology, medicine, and law, where issues formerly considered "feminine" — for example, domestic production and consumption, issues surrounding sexual reproduction and child-rearing, and the effects of such forms of mass-cultural production as popular romance, soap operas, and talk shows — are changing what experts must say and do if they want to maintain credibility.

By way of a transition to the second part of this response, let me consider what lessons we might learn from this brief history of the feminist assumptions that have made their way into Chinese studies through Western literary and cultural studies. Feminism characteristically begins its assault on any such discipline by representing the natural distinction between male and female (male/female) as the oppressive domination of male over female (male vs. female), which the feminist polemic strives to overturn by assuming a rhetorical position of female vs. male. This assumption depends on another, more basic one: even when its position in relation to "male" is reversed (i.e., "female" vs. "male"), the term "female" cannot be oppressive in opposing and — ideally — overturning "male," because "female" is the subordinated term. Feminism's authority as the opposition and alternative to "male" therefore comes from and depends on the fact of women's traditional subordination to men. Feminism understood the woman's position in any culture as one with a potential to subvert and liberate.

At the point in its development where feminism acquired some credibility as a critique of masculine power, this authority was consequently called into question. The possibility that some women could oppress others, say, on the basis of race, class, or sexual preference effectively eroded feminism's moral claim to speak on behalf of the underdog. There was simply too much evidence suggesting that certain women gained ascendancy over other women on the basis of their privileged relation to the reigning group of men (Hartman). Feminism could not tolerate the opposition between "female" and "female"; many feminists felt that feminism would not remain feminism if stripped of its foundational category, "female." Thereupon began a period of expanding, fracturing, and multiplying the term, actions that undermined both its integrity and the rhetorical power of gender as a category of analysis.

This brings us to the present moment, in which the replacement of both "female" and "woman" by the term "feminine" implies a new understanding of gender as an ensemble of cultural practices and performances for which there is no natural antecedent, agent, referent, or result. As feminism succeeded in gathering more and more power and prestige to itself, its foundational category ("female" or "woman") began to collapse (Butler). What had been natural to women became an important object of research, discussion, debate, and controversy in an ever-widening cultural arena. In thus expanding its domain and prestige, it can be argued, feminism also lost its political edge. At the present moment, feminism neither opposes masculine power per se, since it has possessed and redefined substantial chunks of it, nor unifies the category of "female" by including and otherwise appeasing contending subgroups of "women."

The feminist who works on European or North American women confronts the problem of how to read material that has played an instrumental role in determining who we are, how we think, and what we write — determining, indeed, that we write. The task of scholarship requires us to analyze historically the very categories of gender within which we live and work. This situation understandably blinds us at crucial points in cultural analysis to the rhetorical power we inherit by assuming a feminine position. It becomes quite easy to forget that to write from a position of powerlessness is always a self-contradiction

in modern print cultures. The claim to powerlessness not only autho-
rizes some of our most important kinds of writing but also denies the
fact that political force inheres in writing itself.

Ming and Qing Women in a Feminist Problematic

Feminists who write about Ming and Qing women face a second
and perhaps more difficult problem. Even for those scholars who have
studied Chinese literature and culture for many years, the cultural assumptions that make them feminists will differ more profoundly from
those shaping their primary materials than from the assumptions that
inform the moment in Western history when their feminist methodology was born. Indeed, even during the twentieth century, the sexual
relations shaping and shaped by traditional Chinese culture were obviously responding to a very different moment in the modernization
process and to a significantly different version of that process from
our own. So that writing by, for, and about women in Ming and Qing
culture necessarily means something very different from the feminine
tradition of writing that gave rise to Western feminism, a point expressed with notable clarity by Charlotte Furth in her "Editor's Introduction" to a special issue of *Late Imperial China* devoted to the new
scholarship on women. Presumably, it was not only a very different
thing "to write" in China but also something very different to write
as — or indeed to be — a "woman." Where the feminist scholar of European women faces the problem of how to distinguish between her
categories of analysis and those informing the work of earlier women,
the feminist scholar of women in Ming and Qing culture confronts the
questions of what principle distinguishes "male" from "female" in
that culture and how important gender differences were in determining who a person was and the position from which his or her writing
came.

Best to assume, as Ellen Widmer has suggested, that such terms as
"domestic woman" and "companionate marriage" have no counterpart in Ming and Qing China, because private life there was neither
confined to nor divided among a husband, wife, and their immediate
offspring. A contrastingly polygamous social structure provided the
basis on which that culture distinguished male from female and established the terms for their heterosexual union. Widmer contends
that *Hong lou meng* could not hope to serve as the model and inspiration for Chinese women novelists that its European counterpart, Rich-

ardson's *Pamela* (1740–41), did for English women, because the Chinese novel failed to grant the authority of "female" experience, virtue, and knowledge (Widmer, "Xiaoqing's Literary Legacy"). I would like to suggest that *neither* one of these narratives relies on "female" authority and, further, that "female authority" itself is a contradiction in terms—if we take term "female" to mean a biologically determined role in sexual reproduction.

If, on the other hand, we assume that biology in no way affects our capacity for language or the truth of what we say, then the claim that someone—whether Richardson or Austen—wrote "as a woman" and had his or her words well received has to refer to some quality of the writing itself. We must, in other words, reverse our commonsensical notion of cause and effect and regard writing by, for, or about women as the source of an authority subsequently conferred on those who occupied certain sexual roles within the culture's symbolic economy. As if to acknowledge the possibility of such a reversal, the English language conveniently distinguishes between the "female" (or natural) and the "feminine" (or purely cultural) dimensions of that role and of those who fulfill it. So, we must say that although a sentimental novel such as *Pamela* might have a male author, the novel itself became the source of feminine authority, which it conferred both on Richardson and on a substantial number of women who came to be known as "Lady Novelists." At a certain point in modern European history, then, fiction authorized both men and women to write for and about women in a culture and class-specific way. The authority that fiction bestowed on those who seized this opportunity was therefore "feminine" rather than "female." On this basic issue, what is true of English fiction appears to hold true for Chinese poetry as well (Kang-i Sun Chang, *Ch'en Tzu-lung*, 11–17; Robertson, "Voicing the Feminine," 67).

Widmer's comparison of Chinese and English women writers raises another question, namely, the question of genre. Why, she asks us to consider, does the *Hong lou meng* make such an impression on literate women, as exemplified by Wang Duan and her circle, but never move them to write novels? Something formally resembling the genre that brought European and North American women into authorial prominence during the eighteenth century was also there, I gather, to be appropriated both in the *Hong lou meng* and in the *tanci*, which had always been acceptable for women to write although unsuitable for them to publish until the nineteenth century. That Chinese women did not do so had little or nothing to do with the facts that they were by nature women and that men were considered either more inclined or more qualified to author novels in Chinese. If we continue to question the assumption that language comes from a body to whom nature has already given a sexual identity and assume instead that the symbolic economy of a culture confers identity upon those who participate in it, we have to say that the *Hong lou meng* is *not* a novel in the European sense of the term precisely because it does not confer femininity upon its author.

Certain of its formal features may resemble narratives written in the European vernaculars and distributed on a mass basis during the seventeenth and eighteenth centuries, but such resemblances invariably introduce an element of confusion into any debate over the origin of the novel. In the European version of this debate, I am on the side that argues against classifying Cervantes's *Don Quixote*, Sidney's *Arcadia*, Johnson's *Rasselas*, or any number of such *sui generis* narratives as novels. To do so is much like saying that cake is gravy simply because both contain a certain quantity of flour. Perhaps the most important point of Widmer's study for purposes of comparative analysis is the attention she calls to the fact that works of prose fiction cannot be classified as novels on the basis of formal features alone, any more than women can. I would simply add that they have to operate as novels and women in their respective contexts in order to be recognized as such. It is not some quality of the prose, then, that lends feminine authority to its putative source, but rather what that prose does within the larger system of symbolic practices we call a culture.

The difference between and among cultures is not only a matter of territory and tradition but also one of time. The beginning of the modern period in Europe was marked by a change in what writing meant and what it could do (Armstrong and Tennenhouse). This was especially true of those cultures that were simultaneously undergoing colonial expansion and experiencing the emergence of a modern bourgeoisie or middle class (Anderson). The sudden proliferation of conduct books for women and concomitant appearance of domestic fiction evidently offered a means of creating and reproducing a new ruling class in Europe and a new kind of nationalism in the colonies (Sommer). Counterintuitive though it may seem, writing that conferred feminine authority upon its source created with one stroke a method of colonization (i.e., literature devoted to personal improvement and entertainment), the territory to be colonized (i.e., private life and imaginary relationships), and a characteristic means of resistance (by way of feminisms *avant la lettre*).

Widmer's work has demonstrated that women's writing played an equally vital but very different role in preserving certain traditions of the Ming where it might have proved lethal for their husbands to do so. She suggests, as did a number of scholars at the Yale conference, that these women of a banished ruling elite could celebrate the Ming in writing because Chinese culture had a well-established tradition of love poetry that implied a feminine source, though feminine in ways that contradict English norms of femininity. Much like the so-called Lady Novelists who stepped into the rhetorical shoes created by Richardson, who had himself appropriated the position of a woman letter-writer, these wives of an ousted Ming gentry found themselves thrust by history into a writing position that was apparently not available to their counterparts of generations before. As in early modern Europe, there was a place for the intellectual woman in traditional Chinese culture, but it was a place reserved for the protégées and courtesans of prominent men, not for their first wives (Kang-i Sun Chang, *Ch'en Tzu-lung*, 11, 19; Robertson, "Voicing the Feminine," 73). There were, as Widmer reminds us, at once sharp cultural distinctions between these positions and certain rules for crossing or softening those boundaries:

> Male intellectuals could have students who were of the same class as first wives. Usually they were young women, and the practice was not encouraged. The first wife was closer to the protégée than the courtesan; indeed, wives could be their husband's protégées. The concubine or second wife is another distinct but somewhat fluid position. Though of a high class, they are not beyond courtesan-like behavior; some courtesans eventually became concubines and lived within gentry families. (Widmer, editorial comments)

Such potential fluidity implies a classification system that identifies women in relation to one another on the basis of rank, position in family, and their observation of clear standards of behavior. This is very different from the identity politics of a culture undergoing modernization, where a woman tends to be either a good woman or a whore and there is no access to a socially acceptable position if one is poor or has done something to forfeit it.

In contrast with the kind of monogamy characterizing European culture, polygamous cultures do not necessarily pit one woman against another—either first wife against second, or wives against courtesans—not only because there is more than one legitimate position in the family for a sexually mature woman to occupy, but also because that position carries more cultural authority with it the higher the family's rank and the more obedient in other respects is that woman. Thus it was possible for a Wang Duanshu to write the kind of verse associated with courtesans without renouncing her claims to filial piety (Ko, "Pursuing Talent and Virtue"; Robertson, "Voicing the Feminine," 99–100). If this was indeed the position from which Wang Duanshu wielded her considerable literary influence, then Widmer is accurately ironic in calling this relationship among Wang Duanshu, her father, and her husband a "companionate" one. The companionate relationships that developed among certain members of the English and French gentry near the end of the early modern period made it possible for women's writing to participate in an implicit dialogue between two self-enclosed and gendered sensibilities who exchanged personally nuanced forms of feeling by means of writing (Stone). The epistolary novel of the mid-eighteenth century (as exemplified by Richardson and Pierre Choderlos de Laclos) clearly appropriated this tradition of personal letter-writing.

I agree with Widmer that we cannot think of Wang Duanshu's place as a woman in a masculine tradition of letters as anything like the one that European women took up as personal letter-writers at the onset of the modern period (Chartier). If the first wives of Ming gentry could not reveal their most private thoughts in print without diminishing their cultural authority as women, Wang Duanshu could remain a good wife and still publish poetry only because history had significantly modified that position by removing her family from power (Widmer, "Xiaoqing's Literary Legacy"). Under European monogamy, any such elision between the obligations of wife or daughter and those associated with the "other woman" would automatically condemn the woman who dared to make that move. She took up the role of intellectual at the risk of losing respectability and on rare occasions even her life. During the period leading up to the French Revolution, for example, salon women who tried to occupy both these roles were considered seditious, and Mme. de Roland's literary activity provided grounds for capital punishment (Hunt).

By modifying a feminine tradition of verse to serve political objectives specific to the late Ming period, Wang Duanshu did something to the tradition in which she worked. When she used verse that, as Widmer explains, had "hitherto taken up 'less important' themes, like willow catkins and flowers," as an expression of Ming loyalism, she "brought a new seriousness" to this tradition and significantly changed the kinds of issues that feminine poetry could address. Not only was she actively involved in keeping Ming tradition alive within a historical framework hostile to it, she also became the center of a group of women who made writing central to their lives during a period of social upheaval. "This style of life, and the memory of it long after it had ended," according to Widmer, "lent momentum to what could be called women's literary culture, as it had developed since earlier in the century, when women writers began to publish in increasing numbers" (Widmer, pers. comm.). This "women's literary culture" bore conspicuous fruit in the publication in 1667 of *Mingyuan shiwei*, an edited collection of writings by women that remains a critical source for research on women poets to this day.

There is no doubt important evidence to suggest that women's education flourished during the eighteenth century and that it probably did so within the confines of the family (Furth, "Poetry and Women's Culture," 5; Ko, "Pursuing Talent and Virtue"). It was not until the late eighteenth and early nineteenth centuries, however, that, as Widmer tells the story, Chinese culture saw a resurgence of women's literary culture, with Wang Duan, Wang Duanshu's counterpart, at its center. It made sense, as Widmer suggests, for this new literary culture to adopt the themes of Ming loyalism identified with the work of their female predecessors. They undertook an editing project designed both to revise the relative position of certain male writers in the literary canon and to stimulate new interest in women writers of the late Ming period. It is hard to imagine European women attempting revisionary work of this magnitude until a century later, and even then such a prominent woman of letters as Virginia Woolf simply protested the exclusion of women from the literary canon. She could not see her way clear to describe the poetic tradition, and specifically its use of the past, as part of a larger political struggle. A project comparable to Wang Duan's *Yuan Ming yishi* (1822) was not something that would earn a European woman intellectual prominence, not even if she were Virginia Woolf. Although Wang Duan eventually decided to burn her masterwork, enough apparently remains to tell us that this extended narrative reassessment of Ming loyalism was written as a fictionalized history whose form comes close, in Widmer's estimation, to that of the historical novel.

Widmer has explained how certain materials by, for, and about women burst into mainstream Chinese culture, first in the late seventeenth century and then again in the early nineteenth century. She demonstrates that the migration of these materials into the cultural spotlight, contrary to the British pattern, preserved an aristocratic tradition of writing by feminizing it. Indeed, because an environment congenial to women authors, editors, and critics failed to inaugurate a Chinese tradition of domestic fiction, we must regard the lack of such a tradition until very recently as overdetermined. We know that the advent of novel production on a mass basis marks the onset of modernization when it happens to Western nations or their colonies. We also know that with the novel comes the formation both of a new ruling class and of a new national culture (Anderson; Armstrong and Tennenhouse; Sommer). Historians of European culture tend to assume that what happens before modernization happens in preparation for it, as if history always intended to make the world we now inhabit. Widmer's study suggests that all the conditions for the production of novelistic narratives were right (the novelistic model of *Hong lou meng*, the feminine narrative tradition *tanci*, and the fictionalized history *Yuan Ming yishi*), and yet something like the European domestic novel simply refused to emerge. In the present version of her chapter, Widmer offers what I take to be the exception that proves this rule—that the kind of femininity we (in the imperial West) can identify with modernity awaits and finds expression in telling its story in fiction. A sequel to the *Hong lou meng* was indeed written and written by a woman, but "nothing about her novel's narrative stance overtly reveals the woman writer behind the scenes. . . . Further, nothing elsewhere in the text subverts the illusion that the author was a man" (see Chapter 13 in this volume). The novel, we must conclude, is not something that can happen on the terrain of literature alone. Other cultural-historical conditions are necessary.

Thus Widmer's research supports my own claim that domestic fiction is specific to what she calls "modern times," not only because the formal features of domestic fiction were directly responsible for modifying the culture's marriage rules around gender differences, but also because that change in rules was in turn responsible for the rise of the modern middle class. In Ming and Qing culture, as compared with both Catholic and Protestant Europe, the formation of domestic space, private property, and an exclusionary intimacy within monogamous pairs would have entailed a far more radical displacement of the marriage rules ensuring the reproduction of the traditional ruling class. Such a displacement would attribute a very different sexuality to both writing subject and reader and thus elicit a very different affect from that reader. If, as both Widmer's research and my own suggest, modernization entails a revision of kinship practices such as the one performed by domestic fiction, then modernization must have taken an alternative route in Chinese culture, presuming it had to happen at all.

To answer the question why publishing fiction might not enhance the authority of Chinese women, we cannot simply fall back on the old feminist assumption that men have something to gain by suppressing women's writing. We should assume instead that Chinese women would have written novels centuries ago had their doing so enhanced their position as women in that culture. We should assume, further, that English women would not have begun to write domestic fiction in such numbers had certain men not felt it furthered male interests as well. Adopting these assumptions requires that we abandon the assumption that Asian women acquire identity in the same way modern Western women do. We must agree instead that, in order to last, cultures have to ensure the means of their reproduction. These assumptions do not demand that we take anything for granted about men and women, except that they are creatures of culture, not of nature. Proceeding on these assumptions, together with the insight so far gleaned from comparative analysis, we can say a number of things. First, modernization could not have occurred in China in the same way it did in Europe, because it had to confront and remodel very different definitions of male and female. Second, there is good reason to think that in Ming and Qing culture women's writing maintained the sexual and social hierarchy of male over female without insisting, as Western feminism does, that their respective desires and sensibilities exist in opposition to each other, that, in other words, desire is masculine, and its object inherently feminine.

During the century and a half of Chinese women's writing discussed in Widmer's chapter in this volume, women's literary culture apparently flourished twice without yielding either domestic fiction or the kind of feminism that informs our scholarship, both of which assume that cultural identity derives first and foremost from gender differences. As a rule, it seems, Chinese narratives did not produce this same world of differences. Widmer's account of the historical fictions that managed to survive in narrative form when the *Yuan Ming yishi* was dismantled into its component parts provides a beautiful demonstration of how relations among and within established family lines, rather than the formation of a totally gendered world that measures each individual according to the quality of his or her domestic life, govern the Chinese sense of narrative space and temporality. If, as I am suggesting, Chinese culture cannot be understood in terms of the modern opposition between "male" and "female," does this mean that it is inherently antagonistic to feminist analysis?

To the contrary, it can be argued that "feminine authority" in Chinese literature offers more solid historical ground for mounting a feminist critique of that culture and the scholarship that overvalues its masculine traditions than does the English brand of feminine authority, to which modern feminism owes much of its logic and rhetorical force. Writing in a tradition that was outside and potentially hostile to bourgeois domestic ideology, "courtesan" poets established a position from which a later generation of intellectual women could pay otherwise subversive homage to the former political regime. The circumstances that Widmer describes suggest that a Wang Duanshu could assume a position previously off-limits to a woman of her status, not only because the dynasty that would have fixed her position within a hierarchy of women was passing out of power, but also because the positions of wife and courtesan did not exist in such sharp opposition to one another as they did within English culture. Indeed, given the right historical circumstances, Wang Duanshu was evidently able to take up the position of an intellectual woman without compromising her authority as wife and daughter, despite the fact that tradition linked such a position with that of the courtesan. This option was not available in England until the beginning of the twentieth century and only then at the price of marginalization — as we see, for instance, in the cases of Jean Rhys and Olive Schreiner. It could be argued further that historical circumstances allowed her to represent a form of political authority in verse that her husband and father could no longer exercise in fact. Nor could their nostalgia be called conservative, given the fact that the loyalist theme drove a wedge into the tight link between literary training and political authority.

A century later, according to Widmer, Wang Duan reworked the themes of Ming loyalism into a more generalized expression of nostalgia and so succeeded in formulating the aesthetic core around which a new women's literary culture coalesced. These women evidently found in the tradition, as it had been transformed by Wang Duanshu and her circle, a platform for expressing their own nineteenth-century viewpoint, one bearing certain formal resemblances to the European Romantic tradition (Kang-i Sun Chang, *Ch'en Tzu-lung*; Robertson, "Voicing the Feminine"; Widmer, "Xiaoqing's Literary Legacy"). European Romanticism remained strictly a masculine preserve, however, even though the tradition celebrated women, and despite the hundreds of women who wrote poetry in this mode. Particularly fascinating in Widmer's account is the fact that the women of Wang Duan's circle were inspired to comment on the *Hong lou meng* but not compelled to reproduce it. Nor did they participate in any narrative tradition other than the fanciful adventure stories that tradition had reserved for women authors. It was in poetry, not prose, that Wang Duan's era went about reclaiming the lives of the women writers of Wang Duanshu's time. The early nineteenth century thus presents us with a situation where women writers were involved in a project structurally resembling the imperialist activities that Eric Hobsbawm and Terence Ranger call "the invention of tradition." A whole constellation of intellectual movements, best exemplified perhaps by Wordsworth's and Coleridge's collection of lyrical ballads, Walter Scott's celebration of a chivalric past, and the publications of the British Folklore Society, operated in concert to generate a sense of longing for the more authentic England that existed prior to the onset of modernization. This was of course the very England that writing destined for the new urban readership, the very England that writing such as theirs was rapidly consigning to the past.

The commentaries accompanying the publication of an edition of the *Hong lou meng* and *Jinghua yuan* in 1832 suggest that the Chinese way of dividing intellectual labor according to gender was not simply different but in certain respects quite the reverse of that characterizing English culture, though perhaps just as fixed. Where it was for a John Keats and not an Emily Brontë to transform the cultural past into the components of a nineteenth-century literary imagination and the basis for a new elite tradition, the members of Wang Duan's circle—led by the family patriarch, Chen Wenshu—were the ones to mold Ming loyalism into nostalgic verse forms that completed the transformation of certain aspects of Chinese political history into an elite art form. The congratulatory and critical poetry commenting on the novelistic narratives of 1832 preserve this distinction. At least the poetry on which Widmer focuses our attention indicates that of all the historical material composing the *Hong lou meng* and *Jinghua yuan*, the thing that seemed to catch the female commentators' attention most often was the tendency for intellectual women to perish in the ideological milieu created by those texts.

If on the level of plot a woman's fate is likely to be as poor as her intelligence is great, then on the level of genre, one might say, the feminine tradition of verse that thrived within Chinese culture is in some profound way at risk in a culture dominated by the novel. And to this generic antagonism we can indeed find an appropriate counterpart in England. If nothing else, Brontë's *Wuthering Heights* demonstrates that Romantic displays of patriarchal power and unmarried love, however tragic, have no place in a progressively domesticated future; the novel confines such excesses to the categories of archaic poetry, a dying woman's fancy, and the unconscious regions of the modern individual. Throughout her career, furthermore, and especially in the early novel *Mill on the Floss*, George Eliot demonstrated that the very position from which she wrote and formulated her authorial identity had no place within the narrative tradition in which she wrote; that tradition systematically destroyed the intellectual woman. There, hyperdeveloped forms of subjectivity were radically at odds with the same sense of national destiny that the masculine egoism of Romanticism seemed to support.

The Chinese Lesson for Feminism

In its willingness to grant a place of some authority to such a woman, her desires, her words, and her view of masculine authority, Chinese women's writing might be considered more congenial to feminism than the work of domestic novelists and bourgeois feminists. Isn't the lack of such a place precisely what intellectual women in the West, beginning perhaps with Mary Wollstonecraft, have found so limiting? At the same time, in that those writing in this tradition do not claim to be promoting the improvement of conditions for all oppressed groups by promoting the improvement of conditions for women, conditions that presumably need improvement because they have been engineered by men, Chinese women's writing can also be considered a less suitable foundation for a feminist agenda than the women's writing indigenous to England and the United States. As I explained in the first half of this essay, such modern middle-class cultures invariably represent themselves in novels that can transform the interiority of a heroine so that a household magically forms around her and seems to leave the political order of things pretty

much as it was before she fell in love and got married. This culture-
and class-specific version of heterosexual monogamy operates in the
manner that Foucault attributes to "discourse" and Derrida calls "the
supplement," as does the mass-culture fiction that simultaneously
disseminates and contests its rules. To the aristocratic manor house
dominated by a *paterfamilias*, domestic fiction added an alternative,
middle-class household with a well-mannered and affectionate
woman at its center. Fiction won the literary battle for heart and home.
By the force of sheer repetition, it invalidated the marriage rules that
had long been aristocratic prerogatives and made the destiny of indi-
viduated emotions serve as the rationale for sexual relationships instead (Armstrong, *Desire and Domestic Fiction*; Douglas). In winning
the struggle for the means of social and cultural reproduction, it can
even be argued, fiction also signed the death warrant for an agrarian
way of life, as it helped to shift control of the means of production to
the new industrial and professional classes (Davidoff and Hall).

Does anything on this order happen in China? According to Rey
Chow, popular novels written for and about women first emerged
during the first three decades of the twentieth century. This Mandarin
Duck and Butterfly fiction, as it was called, played an instrumental
role in the modernization process, and this role in turn determined the
genre's narrative composition. In these stories, she explains, "we often
find a collage of narratives that are split between sensationalism and
didacticism, between sentimental melodrama and the authors'
avowed moral intent. This crude fragmentedness produces the effect
not of balance and control, but rather of a staging of conflicting, if not
mutually exclusive, realities (such as Confucianism and Westerniza-
tion, female chastity and liberation, country and city lives, etc.)" (55).
Chow does not regard these conflicting realities as equivalent, however. Central to her argument is that the gender gap between narrator
and protagonist both creates and conceals an epistemological contradiction within these stories.

On the one hand, the emotional density of the protagonist's experience gives meaning a feminine source, despite the author's male
identity. In this respect, the Chinese use of love stories to stage the
most fundamental cultural conflicts follows a course similar to the
historical trajectory of European domestic fiction. What Chow says of
Mandarin Duck and Butterfly fiction could as easily be said of
Wuthering Heights or *Jane Eyre*: "What used to be unutterable, 'feminine' feelings were now put on a par with the heroic and patriotic, cir-

culated, and made lucidly 'available' for the first time through the mass practices of reading and writing, activities that used to belong exclusively to the highbrow scholarly world. Going hand in hand with the sentimental liberation were increasingly fragmented and commodified processes of production and consumption" (56). By saying this, Chow locates a solid plot of cultural ground where we might be able to transplant Western feminism and watch it grow. Here at last is a narrative genre in which the Chinese woman serves as the site of a new interiority and the embodiment of popular literacy, conjoining the two in an irreversible way. Women become actors in melodramas of moral development in which "the male will be remembered as a stage prop" (Chow, 57). But whereas European narratives that similarly linked the nation's destiny to a woman's fate quickly became repositories from which future feminisms could draw their moral and political tropes, Butterfly fiction could not provide this rhetorical foundation. For, as Chow contends, "the conscious deployment of women as figures of change becomes ambiguous in its implications when we see that change itself is often repudiated in conservative attitudes that embrace traditional values through the agent of the narrative voice" (56).

In that it produces a feminine territory wherein traditional culture encountered and incorporated the themes of modernization, Butterfly fiction does resemble that of Richardson, only to diverge from the English model in what is perhaps its more important aspect. Butterfly fiction failed to produce a position that women could assume and from which they could write with authority. As Chow explains, Butterfly fiction was narrated from a position that "often repudiated" the progressive attitudes incorporated in and deployed through female experience. Thus although it implied a feminine source and writing subject according to the Richardsonian premise that fiction can constitute its own authorial source, Butterfly fiction also contradicted that very set of assumptions: it implied a writing subject that was empowered because that subject was male. This epistemological contradiction has an ideological component. First criticized by the tradition for being too new and too popular, Butterfly fiction was then attacked by May Fourth writers for being too attached to an elite literary tradition. Thus, according to Chow's account, Right and Left entered into an unwitting but successful conspiracy to denounce what appears in hindsight to be a genuinely middlebrow art form, because that form failed to meet either one of the two opposing definitions of literature.

There is, however, another way of reading this fiction: as a genre that defies the labels of both progressive and conservative and challenges the notion of authentic Chineseness on which they both agree. From this perspective, we cannot construe the traditional elements in the genre as a return to the past. Chow shows how the details of narrated experience impede the progressive unfolding of the narrative. By so challenging masculine narration, woman's experience challenges the historical-epistemological framework that presumes to contain her; female adherence to the most traditional sexual rules produces an excess of subjectivity that cannot be accounted for by progressive or conservative readings but remains, as a remainder, after we have attended to their criticisms. Thus it is a mistake to dismiss this body of fiction as degenerate, Chow maintains. It is more accurate to understand its excesses in terms of what the West calls sexuality, a logic of desire that not only resists the literary and ideological categories that cling to nationalism, but also eludes feminist analyses that assign all sexual behavior a place within the binary opposition of "progressive" and "conservative." It is in this respect that fiction for and about women might shed some light on the elite tradition of women's writing exemplified by Wang Duan and Wang Duanshu. Both these women, in Widmer's account, infused the traditions of a bygone era with intense longing and committed their poetry to print, and each of them progressively feminized the past by transforming it into a quality of the poet's mind and testimony to the durability of poetry. Yet because they were writing from and about a woman's experience, their interiorization of traditional culture might well have generated the kind of excess that indicates extra-social and prelinguistic desire — something more essential to human identity than the operative categories of identity. Not having read the poetry first-hand, I cannot say that this is so. But were feminist criticism to locate such a "remainder" or "excess," I would have to regard it as the early traces of a sexuality specific to modernity by virtue of their relationship to print (Foucault).

What are we to conclude from Chow's boldly doubled reading of women and Chinese modernity? First of all, that "femininity" is the primary object of feminist analysis, especially when we want to understand where various representations of women differ or converge. The answer does not lie in real women but in the logic of representation itself, since the culture's definition(s) of femininity will determine what a "woman" really is, that is, the remainder that seems to resist the categories of its moment. Chow suggests as much in dealing with the women's fiction that emerged during the contemporary period. Obviously influenced by the May Fourth movement, the new Chinese women novelists eschewed what the new aesthetic regarded as signs of degeneracy in Butterfly fiction. Yet as Chow observes, the appeal of recalcitrantly "feminine" details nevertheless impedes the narration of a new national subject whenever the narrator dwells on her protagonist's domestic life. Because these novelists write as women, moreover, such lapses into traditional femininity are necessary to their authorial identity. Thus, it is fair to say, a conservative element that resists contemporary nationalism connects the mature work of Ding Ling to the popular fiction she turned against, as well as to the elite forms of woman's literary culture. Second, given that each culture defines "femininity" within its own historical trajectory and in opposition to what is going on elsewhere, it is simply wrong to say that Chinese culture is either more or less "feminist" than those of Europe and the United States. Any careful comparison between Chinese and British women's writing will reveal two different feminisms instead of one. Widmer, Chow, and many others have so eloquently demonstrated that we can see new things in Chinese culture by viewing that culture through the lens of Western feminism. But we also stand to learn something about our own feminism by discovering where and how those methods find — or fail to find — historical analogues in the Chinese tradition of women's writing.

My own research on English cultural history suggests that the feminist methodology practiced in Western universities belongs to a tradition of women's writing that can be traced back to eighteenth-century conduct books for women. If, as Chow suggests, so-called women's writing necessarily contains a conservative element that in turn plays an important part in the modernization process, then we must consider whether feminist scholarship has inherited similar tendencies from the Anglo-American tradition of women's writing. Western feminism rarely acknowledges the conservative undertow that invariably accompanies the repertoire of characters, plots, and moral rhetoric that it transformed into the terms and logic of critique. Nor has feminism paused to examine its intimate relationship with a process of modernization that depends to some degree on converting many symbolic practices to print, especially those surrounding sexual desire and domestic life (Armstrong, "Reclassifying Clarissa"; Chow; Foucault; Sommer). The emancipatory ethos of upwardly mobile

Anglo-American heroines tends to blind us to the ways in which they, not unlike their more melancholy Chinese counterparts, were in fact democratizing and so invigorating traditional categories of male and female by turning them into affective strategies suitable for a mass literary market. We may well have developed theories to challenge the gender essentialism that feminism attributes to other cultures and the limitations of a femininity that it identifies with earlier moments in its own history. But the Chinese example suggests that we do not yet have an adequate way of articulating the history of gender differences to that of modernization. By "adequate," I mean a history capable of explaining the situation today: why feminism thrived under conditions of late capitalism and especially in relation to the Reagan and Thatcher regimes.

We obviously need to understand how feminism can be progressive, because it argues on behalf of oppressed groups, and, at the same time, be conservative because it does so in a way that serves the interests of the dominant group, including many women. Indeed, with the example of Chinese women's writing in mind, how can we safely assume that feminism's political role is inherently emancipatory? In purely historical terms, it is just as likely that we are adapting traditional gender distinctions and the model of the nuclear family for a world in which they no longer serve a progressive purpose. No one can say with any certainty what master narrative will unfold in the new transnational mass cultural arena as a result of this effort. The intellectual conflicts occurring within and around feminism throughout the disciplines and in a number of countries virtually guarantee that the intersecting plot lines I have engaged in writing this response have yet to play themselves out.

Reference Matter

Notes

For complete author names, titles, and publication data for items cited here in short forms, see the Works Cited, pp. 479–501.

Introduction

I am grateful to Charlotte Furth, Patrick Hanan, Dorothy Ko, and Judith Zeitlin for reading and commenting on this introduction.

1. For details about the conference and about a previously published selection of the Chinese papers, see the Acknowledgments.

2. "Letter from the New Editors," from the first issue of *Late Imperial China* (under that title), 6, no. 1 (June 1985).

3. Hu's catalogue is entitled *Lidai funü zhuzuo kao.* The store of poetry by Ming and Qing women available in English will be greatly increased with the appearance of *Chinese Women Poets: An Anthology of Poetry and Criticism from Ancient Times to 1911,* edited by Kang-i Sun Chang and Haun Saussy.

4. She appears in section 23, "Runji," *xia.* Cf. Zou Siyi; on which see Hu Wenkai, 848–49), among other mid-seventeenth-century collections edited by men. Wu was the prefacer to another important collection edited by Zou, entitled *Hong jiao ji* (Red plantain collection). For a list of Wu's writings, see Hu Wenkai, 104–5.

5. *Wu Ruixian shi* (Poetry of Wu [Qi]); cited in Hu Wenkai, 105.

6. See Wang Qi, supplement 3a. Li appears in "Zhengji" 18, a respectable category in Wang Duanshu's anthology. This same anthology puts Wang Wei in "Zheng ji fu," *shang,* and Liu Rushi in "Zheng ji fu," *xia.* Their placements are not appreciably less respectable than Li Yin's.

7. Li appears almost at the beginning of Yun's *juan* 1, and Liu and Wang appear in a part of *juan* 20 that is explicitly reserved for such non-

gentlewomen as *mingji* (famous courtesans) and others. Incidentally, Wu Qi appears in a section on nuns, under the name Shangjian, in *Guochao guixiu zhengshi ji*. Because of the name change, it is almost impossible to locate her in this collection.

8. Huang Zongxi. I am much indebted to Lynn Struve for locating this source for me. I am further indebted to Kang-i Sun Chang for pointing out Li's background to me in the first place. This background is also mentioned in Yan Dichang, 546. But cf. Liang Yizhen, 285–86. In this widely respected source, Li appears in a section on poetry by *guixiu*, or gentlewomen.

Chapter 1

Research on this paper has been conducted intermittently over several years, with assistance from many individuals and institutions. Two Clark University grants, from the Faculty Development Fund and the Higgins School for the Humanities Grants, provided support for two summers. Research in Taiwan in 1990–91 was made possible by grants from the Center for Chinese Studies and the Inter-University Program for Chinese Language Studies, both in Taibei. For indispensable comments and assistance on the above translations, I am indebted to Kang-i Sun Chang, Chen Jia, Liu Chunhua, Hao Zhihang, Charles Kwong, Shi Yaohua, Michael True, and Wen Anping. Sarah Deutsch, Thomas Massey, Jonathan Spence, Ellen Widmer, and many other participants in the Yale conference provided valuable comments on an early draft. Needless to say, I am solely responsible for any errors of fact and interpretation.

The source of the epigraphs following the subheads in this chapter are Zhou Shouchang and Jiang Gongyi, 22.13b; Yu Huai, 3.6a; and Zhou Shouchang and Jiang Gongyi, 22.10a.

1. Useful treatments of Ming and Qing courtesanship that focus more on the social and economic institutions themselves include Wang Shunu, 193–225, 230–317; Chen Dongyuan, 202–6, 292–99; Gronewald, esp. 1–50.

2. Ko, *Teachers of the Inner Chambers*, 253–55.

3. Ropp, "Love, Literacy, and Laments."

4. Zhang Gongchang, 155; and Su Zhecong, *Funü zuopinxuan*, 326.

5. Jing Pianpian, "Qingxi qu" (Song of Qingxi), in Zhou Shouchang and Jiang Gongyi, 16.14b–15a.

6. Jing Pianpian, "Yuan ci," in Zhou Shouchang and Jiang Gongyi, 16.14a–b.

7. For other examples of scolding yet clever and flirtatious poems by Jing Pianpian, see Zhou Shouchang and Jiang Gongyi, 16.14b–15a. I translate and discuss one of these, "Taoye ge" (Peach leaf song), in "Love, Literacy, and Laments," 114, 138.

8. In "Love, Literacy, and Laments" (117–20), I discuss several examples of mildly flirtatious poems written by gentry women to their husbands or lovers.

9. Conversation with Stephen Owen. The practice of weaving palindromes in brocade seems to have begun during the Jin dynasty (265–420) when a woman named Su Hui demonstrated her devotion to her absent husband (who was serving as the governor of Qinzhou) by sending him an entire *juan* of palindromes (840 characters in all) woven in brocade. For this work, *Zhijin huiwenshi*, see Hu Wenkai, 11–12. My thanks to Pauline Yu for bringing Su Hui's work to my attention. Three *juan* (24–26) of Zhou Shouchang and Jiang Gongyi's *Gonggui wenxuan* are devoted entirely to various types of palindromes.

10. Jing Pianpian, "Guisi," in Zhou Shouchang and Jiang Gongyi, 26.4a. Below is a translation of the reversed version (on the left side in Fig. 1.1). Because translation into English often requires changes in word order (and because I am unfortunately not a poet!), much of the cleverness in Jing Pianpian's original is lost in this translation.

> Orioles sing in profusion, making me quietly spellbound;
> As far as the eye can see, dark green mountains everywhere.
> With a flick of my sleeve I disperse a cloud [of incense], red
>   encircles my couch;
> Fine, thin eyebrows like green willows drooping by the bridge.
>
> I tune the *zheng* time and again for songs both long and short;
> A pair of pillows, a pair of stains, tears of solitude.
> The bright sun shines on flower petals floating piece by piece;
> Feeling fills the room at daybreak, quietly blows a flute.

11. Chang, *Ch'en Tzu-lung*; and idem, "Wu Wei-yeh."

12. Chang, *Ch'en Tzu-lung*, 17.

13. Peterson, 143–44.

14. Su Zhecong, *Funü zuopinxuan*, 328.

15. See Ko, *Teachers of the Inner Chambers*, 270–72.

16. Lu Qingzi, "Baizhu ci,"in Zhou Shouchang and Jiang Gongyi, 16.10b.

17. Bryant, 28.

18. Zhang Yingchang, 3. For a discussion of poems in this anthology that deal with women, see Ropp, "Confucian View."

19. Yan Weixu, "Qinhuaihe ge," in Zhang Yingchang, 979–80.

20. On the tradition of "poems written on walls," see Ko, "A Social History of Women," 16–19.

21. Gao Zhixian, *ci* to the tune of "Guo Qin lou" (Passing by Qin pavilion), quoted in Su Zhecong, *Funü zuopinxuan*, 442–43.

22. Another example of this kind of lament is a song lyric to the tune of "Nüguanzi" (quoted in Su Zhecong, *Funü zuopinxuan*, p. 450), by Fang Shixian (dates unknown), a famous Qing courtesan from Wuxing in Zhejiang province. I translate and discuss this song lyric in my original paper for the Yale conference, pp. 14–15.

23. I am grateful to Catherine Swatek for pointing out to me the sources of these allusions.

24. Zou Zaiheng, "Dujiang Su Huai tuzhong suojian," in Zhang Ying-chang, 987.

25. Zhu Peng, "Gusu chuanniang qu," in Zhang Yingchang, 951.

26. Chen Shenghe, "Pipa nü," in Zhang Yingchang, 982–83.

27. I am indebted to Kathy Lowry for explaining some of the musical notations and "padding syllables" in these popular songs.

28. Literally, "Comb, window, guests, crashing sounds," which I take to refer to being combed and displayed in windows for noisy customers.

29. "Jinü beishang," to the tune of "Bajiao gu," in Hua Guangsheng, 3.27b–28a.

30. "Under the balcony" is a euphemism for prostitution.

31. "Fan taohua," literally, "violating the peach blossom."

32. "Tan wugeng," to the tune of "Matou diao," in Hua Guangsheng, 1.43a–b.

33. On *huaxin* as a sexual allusion, see the introduction by Stephen West and Wilt Idema to Wang Shifu, 152.

34. It is significant, I think, that in the eighteenth and early nineteenth centuries, the best-known prose writings that describe courtesan culture in some detail are not by the kinds of prominent literati who patronized and memorialized courtesans in the late Ming. Rather, they tend to be works by such marginalized literati as Wu Jingzi in *The Scholars*, and Shen Fu (1763–after 1809) in his memoir *Six Records of a Floating Life* (*Fusheng liuji*). Both Wu and Shen, though in very different ways, portray courtesans at the lower end of the spectrum, as mirrors of themselves, bound in poverty and hoping against all odds for liberation. I discuss the portrayal of courtesans in these two works, respectively, in *Dissent in Early Modern China*, 135–36, and "Between Two Worlds," 109–18.

35. Chang, *Ch'en Tzu-lung*, 119–20. I have changed Chang's romanization to *pinyin*, substituting Qing for Ch'ing, etc.

36. A 1935 guidebook to Beijing reports triennial examinations for all the courtesans in the demimonde, complete with publicly posted rankings in each category of accomplishment, in precise imitation of the civil-service examination system (Arlington and Lewisohn, 273).

37. Clunas, 118.

Chapter 2

1. The edition used in this essay is *Kong Shangren shi he "Taohua shan"* (hereafter *THS*).

2. The edition used here is *Yingmeian yiyu* (hereafter *YMA*).

3. The edition used here is *Banqiao zaji* (hereafter *BQ*).

4. Chen Yinke, *Liu Rushi biezhuan* (hereafter *LRS*).

5. The Qinhuai River (Qinhuai he) lies within present-day Nanjing. According to one (unfounded) tradition, the Huai River was dug by the First

Emperor of Qin when he went to Kuaiji, hence the name Qinhuai (see *Yudiji*, quoted in *Taiping yulan, juan* 30 of the section on geography).

6. Government prostitutes were banned during the Xuande era (1426–36). Prohibition decrees were issued during the Kangxi period (1662–1723) and, locally by individual governors, in the years 1796, 1812, 1873, and 1910. See Lao Tan, preface to *Qinhuai guangji*, 1a–2a.

7. See Owen for a discussion of Su Kunsheng's song in the context of the cultural memory of Jinling (Nanjing).

8. All translations are my own, unless otherwise indicated.

9. Chen Yinke (*LRS*, 1082–85) suggests Yu Huai was actively involved in plots to restore the Ming dynasty. Qian Qianyi's note to one of his own poems refers to Yu Huai's "labor of collecting poems" (*caishi zhi yi*; *LRS*, 1082), which implies that some of the poems included in the *Miscellaneous Records of the Wooden Bridge* were written by Ming loyalists who congregated in Jinling under the pretext of pursuing pleasure.

10. When Yu Huai failed to win honors in the civil sevice examination, the proposed union came to nought. After the fall of the Ming, Yu Huai met Li Mei again, now the concubine of the prefect of Taizhou. The contrast between past and present in Qinhuai is summarized in an exchange between Yu and Li (*BQ*, 9).

11. In "The Biography of Mao Xiang's Concubine Dong Xiaowan" ("Maoji Dong Xiaowan zhuan"), Zhang Mingbi refers to the same episode: "Tens of thousands of people vied to come close to them, saying that this was the Lady of the River with her mate, stepping on the waves and ascending (to Heaven)" (*YMA*, 3). The Lady of the River alludes to the river goddesses of the *Chuci* tradition.

12. *The Swallow's Letter* (*Yanzi jian*) by Ruan Dacheng (1587–1646) is a classic example of sentimental *chuanqi* drama with a plot built around the romantic vicissitudes of talented scholars and beautiful women. The dubious moral character and unmistakable talent of Ruan Dacheng made him a compelling symbol of late Ming decadence. In scene 5 of *The Peach Blossom Fan*, Ruan Dacheng is chagrined by the news that Mao Xiang, Fang Yizhi (1611–71), and Chen Zhenhui (1605–56) first praised the play and then denounced his character (*THS*, 19–23).

13. Zheng Ruying (*zi* Wumei, alias Tuoniang) was a famous Qinhuai courtesan. Although cast in the role of clown (*chou*) in *The Peach Blossom Fan*, she was in fact a noted poet. Mao Xiang collected the poetry of Zheng Ruying, Ma Xianglan, Zhu Wuxia (*zi* Qinyu), and Zhao Caiji (*zi* Jinyan) in *Poetry of the Four Beauties of Qinhuai* (*Qinhuai si meiren shi*). Cf. Qian Qianyi, *Liechao shiji xiaozhuan*, 2: 766–67; Chen Wenshu, entries on Zheng Ruying in *Muolingji*, appended to Yu Huai's *Miscellaneous Records of the Wooden Bridge*, in *BQ*, 31–32; *Yuan shi*, quoted in *Qinhuai guangji*, 2.13b–18a.

14. I have not been able to find these plays. References to these plays are found in Cai Yi, 4: 2590–92; Mao Guangsheng, 90–98.

15. An allusion to lines from Wu Weiye's "Song of Yuanyuan" ("Yuanyuan qu": "The wailing six armies were all clad in the white of deep mourning, / His headgear was raised in anger — all because of a beautiful woman" (*Wu Meicun quanji* [hereafter *WMC*], 78). Zhang did not live to finish the play, which survives only in fragments.

16. According to "Yu'an huaxiang ji" (Account of the portrait of Yu'an), Yu'an was Chen Yuanyuan's Buddhist name after she began living as a Buddhist nun; see Cai Yi, 4: 2666. In his preface to the play, Jieyu Sheng (a pseudonym meaning "person left behind after the catastrophe") referred to the analogy between Wu Sangui and the traitors in the war against Japan; the play is thus a rallying cry for the war of resistance. See Cai Yi, 4: 2658–62. I have not been able to find the play.

17. Chen started to use the name Gold Brightness Studio in the early 1960's. *Miscellaneous Writings of Gold Brightness Studio (Jinmingguan conggao)* was sent to the publisher in 1962. In 1965, when he began his autobiographical writings, he called it *Records of Dreams at Cold Willow Hall, Unfinalized Manuscript (Hanliu tang jimeng weiding gao)*. See Yu Yingshi, 76–77.

18. See also Liu Mengxi for a discussion of this issue in his essay, "Yishi zhengshi, jiezhuan xiushi, shiyun shixin," in *Zhongguo wenhua* 3, 99–111. I thank Kang-i Sun Chang for bringing Liu's article to my attention.

19. Yu Yingshi, 29.

20. On Qian Qianyi's eightieth birthday, the red bean tree (*Arbus precatorius*) in his Red Bean Estate (Hongdou shanzhuang) flowered after a lull of twenty years. Liu Rushi sent a red bean from that tree to congratulate him, and Qian wrote ten quatrains on it; see *LRS*, 1198–202.

21. Chen Yinke explains his attention to "classical allusions" (*gudian*), both in their locus classicus and in the form as modified and embellished by later usage, and to "contemporary topical allusions" (*benshi, jindian*), both to specific events and to literary expressions from contemporary poets, in *LRS*, 7–15.

22. "Wang Guantang xiansheng wanci," "Yinke xiansheng shicun," 6, in Chen Yinke, *Hanliu tang ji*.

23. According to the account in the *Soushen ji*, "When Emperor Wu was having the Pond of Kunming dug, black ashes were found at a very deep level, and there was no longer any earth. The whole court was puzzled. The Emperor asked Dongfang Shuo. Shuo replied, 'Your minister is too ill-informed to know about this. Let us ask someone from the Western Regions.' During the reign of Emperor Ming of the Latter Han, a Daoist from the West came to Luoyang. At that time someone remembered Shuo's words and ventured to ask him about the black ashes from Emperor Wu's reign. The Daoist said, 'According to the sutras, when heaven and earth come to an end, there will be kalpa ashes. These are remains of kalpa ashes' " (Gan Bao, 13.98).

24. See, e.g., Chen Yinke's attempt to reconstruct a letter from Liu Rushi to Chen Zilong (now lost) from the latter's poem "Eternal Longing" ("Chang xiangsi"), which was probably written for Liu, in *LRS*, 331–33. In his discus-

sion of the motif of picking lotus in the works of Liu Rushi and Chen Zilong, Chen suggests that Chen Zilong's "Poem on a Painting of Picking Lotus, Written a Day After the Beginning of Autumn" ("Liqiu hou yiri ti cailian tu") may be describing Liu Rushi's self-portrait or a portrait by a contemporary, unfortunately long lost (*LRS*, 299–302).

25. The locus classicus of these lines can be found in Zhang Yanyuan's (ca. 815–after 875) *Lidai minghua ji*, 2.35.

26. The Jishe was a local branch of the Fushe (Restoration Society). For the role of Chen Zilong in the Jishe, see Chang, *Ch'en Tzu-lung*, 6–7. For an informative study of the Fushe, see Atwell.

27. *Milou ji*, 1: 42.

28. Qian Qianyi describes another famous courtesan of the period, Wang Wei, with a similar image: "She took her books on her small boat, traveling back and forth in the Wu and Kuaiji area" (*Liechao shiji xiaozhuan*, 760). Zhou Caiquan suggests that Wang Wei and Liu Rushi were probably both "boat courtesans" (*chuanji*) who set up "floating establishments" (14–22).

29. As Chen Yinke observes, Wang Ranming's painted boats in West Lake make up an important chapter in late Ming social history. References to Wang's most famous boat, named *Untied Garden* (*Buxi yuan*, an allusion to the "untied boat," *buxi zhi zhou*, in *Zhuangzi*), before and after the fall of the Ming mark crucial social and cultural changes; see *LRS*, 373–78. At one point Liu Rushi borrowed one of Wang Ranming's boats (second letter in the correspondence compiled by Wang Ranming, *LRS*, 373). The boat suggests tenuous expectations and transitory meetings, as in Liu's twenty-sixth letter to Wang Ranming (*LRS*, 434).

30. Perhaps the ambience of existence on water also informs Chen Zilong's "*Fu* on Picking Lotus" ("Cailian fu") and Liu Rushi's "*Fu* on the Male Spirit of River Luo" ("Nan Luoshen fu"). Zhou Caiquan (19) suggests that even when there is no explicit reference to boats, some of Liu's poems seem inspired by scenes viewed from a boat.

31. The edition used here is Qian Qianyi, *Zhuben Qian Zeng Muzhai shizhu* (hereafter *MZ*), 1283.

32. When Fan Li left office, he changed his name to Zhiyi Zipi, see "Hereditary Family of the Goujian, King of Yue," in Sima Qian, *juan* 41.

33. The gift of the jade pendant (*pei*) as a pledge of love from a goddess or a mortal in quest of the goddess is a standard topos in classical poetry, beginning with the *Chuci*. Here Liu alludes to the story of Zheng Jiaofu's encounter with two beautiful women along the Han River who give him their girdle jades in response to his gifts of oranges. As he walks on, both they and their girdle jades vanish (*Hanshi neichuan*, comments on the song "Hanguang"; *Taiping guangji*, 59.364–65).

34. Here Liu uses an uncharacteristic self-deprecatory term, "your humble concubine" (*jianqie*). According to Chen Yinke, this indicates an exceptionally contented mood rather than deference to Qian Qianyi's wife, Lady Chen (*LRS*, 654).

35. The name of the chamber combines with Liu Rushi's name to form the phrase *rushi wowen*, "thus have I heard," a standard phrase at the beginning of Buddhist sutras. The disciples of Buddha, most notably Ananda, used the phrase to refer to what they have heard from Buddha. Liu Rushi seemed to have used the name Wowen jushi (I Have Heard Recluse) before she met Qian Qianyi; see *LRS*, 36.

36. Song Yu is a nebulous figure whose existence, date, and writings are widely debated. He is supposed to have been active in the court of Chu in the third century B.C. The "*Fu* on Gaotang" and "*Fu* on the Goddess" are probably from a later period, between the second century B.C. and first century A.D.

37. Cf. Xu Jiu, 190–91.

38. "As for Hedong jun, who excelled in poetry and wit and was elusive and unpredictable in coming and going, she certainly shared common traits with the spirits described in the tales of Pu Songling" (*LRS*, 75). "Hedong jun," another of Liu Rushi's courtesy names, alludes to the Tang poet with the same surname, Liu Zongyuan (773–819), who was from Hedong [present-day Shanxi]. The name Hedong jun began to gain currency after Liu Rushi and Qian Qianyi met in 1641 (*LRS*, 218).

39. The word *wen* means colors and patterns in clouds. According to Chen Yinke, Yinwen is probably an allusion to the speech of Tao Dazi's wife from *The Biographies of Women* (*Lienü zhuan*): "In the Southern Mountain there was a dark leopard that did not come down [the mountain] for food during seven days of mist and rain. Why is that so? It wished to enhance the beauty of its hair, so that patterns [*wenzhang*] will be formed. Thus did it hide and remove itself from danger" (*Lienü zhuan*, Sibu beiyao ed. [Taipei: Zhonghua shuju, 1987], 2.6b). See also the poem by Xie Tiao: "Although I lack the beauty of the dark leopard, / I will yet hide in the mist of the Southern Mountain" (*LRS*, 34). The name Yinwen thus suggests the necessity of inward distance for escaping danger and for allowing literary, spiritual self-cultivation.

40. *The Singing Phoenix* (*Mingfeng ji*), attributed to Wang Shizhen (1526–90), is a forceful indictment of Yan Song's abuse of power.

41. *Quan Song ci*, ed. Tang Guizhang (Beijing: Zhonghua shuju, 1986 reprint of 1965 ed.), 1: 246.

42. Dong Qichang praised the achievement of both Lin and Yang as painters in his preface to Wang Ranming's collection of poetry, *Chunxingtang shiji*. Dong claimed that after Yang Yunyu's death Wang treasured her works like "the jade received [from the goddess] at the Han River"; see *LRS*, 379. Liu Rushi refers to Yang's paintings in her sixth letter to Wang Ranming (*LRS*, 378). The preface to the correspondence between Liu Rushi and Wang Ranming was written by Lin Tiansu (*LRS*, 368–71).

43. Disguise in the other direction is, however, often regarded as pernicious. See Zeitlin, *Historian of the Strange*, 98–132.

44. Xue Susu was a noted painter, poet, and horsewoman. See Qian Qianyi, *Liechao shiji xiaozhuan*, 770.

45. Chen Qinian, 1: 123.
46. Qian Qianyi, *Liechao shiji xiaozhuan*, 773–74.
47. Yuan shih, quoted in *Qinhuai guangji*, 2.II.2b.
48. Qian Qianyi, *Liechao shiji xiaozhuan*, 765. For other descriptions of Ma Xianglan as *nüxia*, see Yao Lu's poem "On Passing the Old Abode of Ma Xianglan" ("Guo Ma Xianglan guju), in Xu Jiu, 155; and Xu Dianfa's comments on Chen Xuyin's poem "Mourning the Ruins of Ma Xianglan's Abode" ("Diao Ma Xianglan feiju"), in ibid., 155.
49. See "The Biographies of Ji Bu and Luan Bu" and "The Collected Biographies of Wandering Knights" in Sima Qian, *juan* 100, 124.
50. Allusions to Cao Zhi's (192–232) "*Fu* on the Goddess of the River Luo" ("Luoshen fu") and Song Yu's "*Fu* on Gaotang" and "*Fu* on the Goddess."
51. *Qinhuai guangji*, 2.II.3b.
52. See Zhou Caiquan, 45–56; *LRS*, 345, 450.
53. For a discussion and translation of parts of "Male Spirit of the River Lo," see Chang, *Ch'en Tzu-lung*, 24–26. Chang also translates and discusses Chen Zilong's "*Fu* on Picking Lotus" ("Cailian fu"), which was probably inspired by or written in response to Liu's *fu* (ibid., 27–37; cf. *LRS*, 301–4).
54. See Wai-yee Li, 3–46.
55. Chen Zilong had written a "*Fu* on the Goddess of River Xiang" ("Xiang'e fu"); see *LRS*, 137–38.
56. For a discussion of this preface, see Kang-i Sun Chang, *Ch'en Tzu-lung*, 22–23.
57. For possible origins of the term *qinglou*, see Tao Muning, 1–6.
58. Chen Zilong, 445; poems by Chen Zilong are quoted from *Chen Zilong shiji* (hereafter *CZL*).
59. Liu Rushi herself shows great familiarity with poetic references to willows; see *LRS*, 336–41, 435. Cf. Kang-i Sun Chang, *Ch'en Tzu-lung*, 59–63.
60. See Lu Qinli, 334.
61. The phrase *taochan* sometimes has the opposite connotation of "seeking escape in the teachings of Chan."
62. See Wang Pijiang, 178–84.
63. Lin Tiansu, in her preface to the correspondence between Wang Ranming and Liu Rushi, also described Wang as "wandering freely in the mountains and rivers, a veritable 'heroic friend in a yellow cloak' [*huangshan haoke*]"; see LRS, 369.
64. See also Zhang Mingbi, "Maoji Dong Xiaowan zhuan," 3, in *YMA*.
65. Wang Zhong's elegy is quoted in *Qinhuai guangji*, 2.II.5b–6b.
66. An allusion to Du Guangting's "The Story of Curly-Beard" ("Qiuran-ke zhuan"). For a collated edition of the story, see Wang Pujiang, 178–84. Red Duster is the name of Yang Su's concubine. Seeing through Yang's mediocrity, she offers her love to Li Jing.
67. *Headgear-Raising Anger*, scenes 11, 29. Chen's lament echoes Huo Xiaoyu's accusation of Li Yi on her deathbed: "I, a woman, am yet ever so ill-

fated, while you, a man, betray your intention in this manner." See Jiang Fang's "Huo Xiaoyu zhuan" in Wang Pijiang, 81.

68. See "Biography of Liji" ("Liji zhuan"), in Hou Fangyu, 130–31. In "Reply to Tian zhongsheng (Tian Yang)," Hou dexterously denied having advised Li Xiang to refuse Tian's "invitation" made with 300 pieces of gold. Here Hou referred to Li Xiang half-disparagingly as *ji* (courtesan), but also covertly expressed his admiration. See ibid., 52–53.

69. I have been unable to find this play. The author's preface is included in Cai Yi, 4: 2595.

70. Kang-i Sun Chang discusses this problem in "The Idea of the Mask in Wu Wei-yeh."

71. Qian Qianyi, *Liechao shiji xiaozhuan*, 2: 760–61. To preserve the coherence of this image of detachment from worldly entanglements, Qian does not mention Wang's marriage to Mao Yuanyi or the fact that her union with Xu Yuqing did not last (*LRS*, 432). Elsewhere Qian refers to Wang Wei's poetry as "close to [the mood of] knight-errants" (*jin yu xia*); see "Preface to the Writings of the Gentlewoman Huang Jieling" ("Huang Yuanjie's zi") in *Youxue ji*; quoted in *LRS*, 483.

72. *LRS*, 767–70.

73. The historical Hou Fangyu took the examination under the Qing (in the play he becomes a Daoist) and thus invites sarcastic lines such as the following: "How can Master Hou, who took the examination under two dynasties, / Face Li Xiang in the Underworld?" (quoted in *LRS*, 715).

74. For examples of a critical and ironic attitude toward Qian Qianyi, see *LRS*, 668, 701, 1025.

75. Cf. Chen Yinke's theory that given the vague details surrounding the supposed death of Dong Bai, she may actually have been taken away by some member of the new nobility from the north (*LRS*, 776–78).

76. *Yubian jilüe*, quoted in *Qinhuai guangji*, 2.14b–15a.

77. An allusion to the celestial maiden who scatters flowers on the bodhisattvas and occasions a discussion with Sariputra on the meaning of phenomenal existence in the Vimalakirti Sutra. Here Chen Yinke is referring to Liu Rushi's conversion to Buddhism. The comparison of Liu Rushi to the celestial maiden also appears in the poems Cheng Mengyang and Qian Qianyi addressed to her; see *LRS*, 174, 549–50.

78. An allusion to a story from *The Biographies of Immortals* (*Shenxian zhuan*): the goddess Magu tells Wang Fangping that she has seen the Eastern Sea change thrice into mulberry fields. Chen is referring to the cataclysmic changes in modern Chinese history, especially under the Communist regime. Cf. *LRS*, 982.

79. Cui Hui was a Tang courtesan who died pining for her lover and left him her portrait; see Yuan Zhen's notes to his "Song of Cui Hui" ("Cui Hui ge").

Chapter 3

I thank Gail Hershatter, Marilyn Young, and participants in the conference for their comments on an earlier, albeit quite different, draft of this essay.
Ellen Widmer, Katherine Carlitz, Maureen Robertson, and Sophie Volpp
provided help toward revision.

1. Susan Mann (*Women in Eighteenth-Century China*, chap. 5) has illuminated the decline of the courtesan's cultural status and the rise of a commercial sex market in the high Qing period due to demographic pressure, state
policies, and the rise of classical learning. For the destruction of the Nanjing
quarters, its revival in the late Qianlong period, and the early Qing monarchs'
efforts to end official prostitution, see Wang Shunu, 261–69.

2. Peng Huasheng, 4965.

3. Ibid., 4963, 4988–89. The first volume, *Qinhuai huafanglu*, was published in 1817. It is anthologized in *Xiangyan congshu*, 3917–4056.

4. China's first major illustrated newspaper, the *Dianshizhai huabao*, was
first published by lithography in 1884. For the relationship between litho-
graphic technology and a "pre-history" of mass culture, see Kahn.

5. The connection between merchants and the pleasure industry was
particularly evident in Shanghai. The brothels in Shanghai thrived in the
1860's, when the Taiping rebellion drove many merchants to sojourn in the
city. A decade later, when the rebellion was quelled and many of the merchants returned to their native places, the pleasure quarters suffered heavily
(Songbei yuchen sheng, 5706).

6. One example of an educated courtesan in the nineteenth century is
Wang Zilan (1803–24), who became one of the concubines of Chen Peizhi
(1794–1826), a minor scholar-official. Chen's reminiscences of Wang can be
found in Xiangwanlou yiyu. I thank Ellen Widmer for bringing this example
to my attention.

7. Ebrey, 37–38.

8. Chen Peizhi's *Xiangwanlou yiyu* provides a fitting example of this
crossover. Not only did Chen refer to and cite from several works of the blue-
building genre in his reminiscences (126–27), a nineteenth-century critic also
compared this work to Yu Huai's *Banqiao zaji*, a noted example of blue-
building literature (159).

9. Goldman (12–14, *et passim*) describes the *huapu* genre and the social
world in which it thrived as a "borrowed discourse" and an "appropriation"
of an existing tradition of writing about courtesans.

10. Historian Victor Xiong (6) estimates that Sun Qi completed *Beili zhi*
around 885.

11. Courtesans appeared in local gazetteers in the nineteenth century. In
the sub-county-level gazetteer *Shenghu zhi* (edited 1874; published 1925), for
example, biographies of courtesans (*mingji*) appeared as a subsection in the

"Biographies of Women" (*lienü*) section (*juan* 10). Shenghu, a district in Suzhou prefecture, was a late-Ming center of pleasure, where the famous courtesan Liu Rushi received her training. However, I have not found any late Ming gazetteers that gave courtesans such prominent play.

12. Weidner et al., *Views from Jade Terrace*, 95–96. Three of Lin's landscapes painted on fans are reproduced there.

13. Cited in Tang Shuyu, 5.78. Dong's praise was also cited in the works of Wang Ranming, a Hangzhou patron of art, where "Wang Youyun" became Yang Yunyou, another courtesan painter (Chen Yinke, *Liu Rushi beizhuan*, 379).

14. A further support for this conflation of categories of domestic and public women can be found in gentry poet Shen Yixiu's usage of *linxia zhifeng* to refer to her daughter, Ye Xiaoluan (Ko, *Teachers of the Inner Chambers*, 167).

15. Wang Ranming referred to all courtesans as *nüshi*, and reserved *guige* for talented women who were not courtesans. His rigid usage, however, apparently was not widely shared. Both Lin's usage and Wang's are cited in Chen Yinke, *Liu Rushi biezhuan*, 368–70.

16. Tan Youxia, 159.

17. Chen Yinke, *Liu Rushi biezhuan*, 431–32.

18. Ostensibly, fame is not a Confucian virtue. The gentleman was not supposed to promote himself or to seek profits from his name. Yet as the pace of publishing and traveling quickened in the late Ming, scholars and officials often became quite famous beyond their native places. By dint of fame, they became arbiters of artistic taste.

19. Wang Shunu, 78–83, 138–44. Victor Xiong has calculated that "of the forty clients recorded in the *Beili zhi*, twenty were *jinshi* or advanced degree candidates, eighteen were government officials, and two were rich merchants" (10).

20. Peterson, *Bitter Gourd*, 26; see also pp. 141–44.

21. One transmitter of the story, the historian Zhao Yi (1727–1814), erroneously attributed it to Yu Huai's *Banqiao zaji* (Zhao Yi, 397–98). There are many variations to this story of Ma and the White Silk Skirt. See, e.g., the early Qing account by Chu Jiaxuan, 4686–87, 5144. According to a late Ming work, Shen Defu's *Yehuo bian* (26.34a–35a), Zheng's drama *Bailian qun* ridiculed the aging Ma's frolicks with her old lover, Wang Baigu, then approaching seventy. There is no mentioning of Zheng's being rejected by Ma. For another legend of Ma rejecting a failed candidate who eventually became an official, see Weidner et al., *Views from Jade Terrace*, 72. For the Siamese envoy's interest in Ma's fans, see Tang Shuyu, 5.72.

22. Cao Dazhang, "Liantai xianhui pin," 44. See also Wang Shunu, 223. For Cao's deeds, see Zhang Huijian, 172, 221, 223, 240, 258, 261, 307.

23. The Chinese population was around 65 million at the beginning of the Ming dynasty. By 1600 it had doubled, and by 1800 it grew to 300 million (Ho Ping-ti, 219). The crunch was felt most keenly by candidates from com-

moner families. For changes in the quotas for the lower and metropolitan degrees, see ibid., 172–90.

24. Cao Dazhang, "Liantai xianhui pin," 3b.

25. Cao Dazhang, "Qinhuai shinü biao," 2a, in *Shuofu xu*, 44.

26. Yu Huai, 3674. An earlier contest was held in Beijing in 1597. In 1656, barely twelve years after the fall of the Ming dynasty, another flower register contest was reportedly held in Suzhou. For records of Northern Song contests, see Liu Dalin, 621–22. Wang Shunu (223) was wrong in stating that flower registers were a Ming invention.

27. Li Yu, *Fuyun lou*, 130.

28. Privately organized flower contests were also held in Canton in 1904 and 1925 (V. Ho, 128–29).

29. Chang, *Ch'en Tzu-lung*, 18.

30. Robertson, "Voicing the Feminine," 99.

31. Chang, "Anthologies of Female Poetry," 137.

32. Hu Wenkai, 81–82.

33. "Liyan," in Yun Zhu, *Guochao guixiu zhengshi ji* (1831–36). See Mann, *Women in Eighteenth-Century China*, for the contests over the place of the female poetic voice in the public sphere in the eighteenth century.

34. Zhong Xing, *Mingyuan shigui*, Ming ed. Kang-i Sun Chang ("Anthologies of Female Poetry," 123) has dated this anthology ca. 1620. The other three poets who occupied an entire chapter are Xu Yuan, Lu Qingzi, and Bo Xiaojun, all gentry wives whose poems are unusually candid in expressing emotions.

35. Watt, 7.

36. For a brief biography of Xiang, see Qian Qianyi, *Liechao shiji, runji* 4.45a–46a. Xiang was also a friend of Lu Qingzi, who contributed a preface to one of her poetry collections, *Caiyun cao*. This preface is anthologized in Zhao Shijie, *juan* 4; also reprinted in Hu Wenkai, 176. For a poem Lu wrote for Xiang, see Lu Qingzi, *Xuanzhi ji* 2.14a–15a. For a poem Xiang sent to Lu, see Qian Qianyi, *Liechao shiji, runji* 4.46a. It is not clear, however, if Lu and Xiang ever met.

37. Cited in Qian Qianyi, *Liechao shiji, runji* 4.45b.

38. Wang Wei, "Ku Huang funren Mengwan," in Qian Qianyi, *Liechao shiji, runji* 4.58b–59a. For her earlier poem in response to one sent by Xiang, see ibid., 4.58b. I am grateful to Kang-i Sun Chang and her graduate student Chi-hung Yim for suggesting the translation of the last two lines of this poem.

39. For details of these activities of Fan Yunlin, see Zhang Huijian, 363, 372, 406, 457, 473. Xu Yuan's upbringing and education are mentioned in prefaces to her poetry collection; see, e.g., "Xujie Fan furen shi xu," 2a–b, and "Fan furen Luowei yin xu," 4a, in Xu Yuan.

40. For Xue Susu's paintings, see Weidner et al., *Views from Jade Terrace*, 82–88. Xue Susu used a seal with the name "Nü jiaoshu" (Female Collator) on one of her paintings, a name first used by Xue Tao. This suggests that Susu identified herself with Xue Tao with pride (ibid., 86).

41. "Zeng Xue Susu wu shou," in Xu Yuan, 8.22a–23b.

42. Fan Yunlin also inscribed the title of the painting. For this colophon, translated by Irving Lo, and a reproduction of the painting, see Weidner et al., *Views from Jade Terrace*, 84–85.

43. "Zeng geji Anqing," in Xu Yuan, 3.31b–32a.

44. Xu, "Xizeng geji Sanli wushou," *Luowei yin*, 8.4a–5a.

45. Xu Yuan, 8.45b–46a, 50a–b. The term *meiren* was used in the *Book of Songs* (no. 94). Most critics, except those who insist on the most allegorical reading of these poems, agree that it refers to a beautiful woman or even man, but not to an upright official.

46. The different representations of Xu Yuan in these anthologies is interesting. Qian Qianyi and Liu Rushi, for example, were extremely terse, including only two conventional poems using the voice of a palace woman in the *Liechao shiji*. At the opposite end is Zhong Xing, who, in his *Mingyuan shigui*, devoted an entire chapter to Xu, and another to her friend Lu Qingzi (*juan* 32, 33). Several pieces of Xu's prose can be found in a popular anthology by a commercial printer: Zhao Shijie, 8.42a–b, 9.14a.

47. That scholar-officials (*shidafu*) took the lead in popularizing Xu's works was disclosed by Qian Qianyi and Liu Rushi in their entry on Xu (see Qian Qianyi, *Liechao shiji, runji* 4.44b). They found Xu's verse wanting in literary merit. Lu Qingzi fared slightly better (see ibid., 4.43b). For an example of Xu's inclusion in local gazetteers, see the "Literature" (*yiwen*) section in *Suzhou fuzhi* (1883), 139.1b.

48. Both Carlitz and I use "feminization" in a way different from Ann Douglas in her *Feminization of American Culture*. I use the term to refer to the heightened visibility of women (courtesan and wife) and valorization of attributes construed as feminine (sensuality, sentimentality, purity) in late imperial Chinese cultural life.

49. Zhang Huijian, 259, 378, 398, 440, 444, 457, 460, 474. See also the gazetteer *Wuxian zhi* (1933), 79.52b, 54a, for other titles of Zhao's works.

50. Lu Qingzi, *Xuanzhi ji*, 3.5a, 9a.

51. Lu Qingzi, *Kaopan ji*, 2.2a–b, 6b–7a; 4.10b–12a; 5.8a, 15a–b.

52. "Ji Fan furen Wuhu," in Lu Qingzi, *Kaopan ji*, 2.5a. Only the middle half of the poem is translated here.

53. Lu, "Song Fan furen cong Yi you Diannan," in Lu Qingzi, *Xuanzhi ji*, 1 *shang*.4b.

54. Robertson, pers. comm., Feb. 27, 1994.

55. Huang Xuesuo, 1326.

56. Yu Huai, 3665–66.

57. "Building of Enchantment" (Mi Lou), a legendary quarter of pleasures and illusions built by Sui Yangti, is a pun on Gu Mei's name. Cf. Wai-yee Li.

58. Yu Huai, 3665–66.

59. Ibid., 3672–73.

60. McMahon, 127–28, 133. The only veiled reference to the completely naked bound foot is a scene in the mid-Qing novel *Lin Lan Xiang*, in which Xiang'er, one of the six wives of a man, strips another wife naked "not leaving her even the footbindings" (ibid., 215).

61. *Rouputuan*, 2.3a–b.

62. Ibid., 1.12b.

63. Ibid., 1.26b–27a.

64. *Zhuquan jushi*, 5346.

65. The same complaint against ridiculously small feet is frequent in Yao Lingxi; see, e.g., 263, 278.

66. *Fenli tahengzhe*, 3373. For Yang Tieya, see Shen Defu, 23.28a.

67. Laurel Bossen, pers. comm., Mar. 26, 1994.

Chapter 4

I am grateful to Dorothy Ko and Maureen Robertson for extremely helpful comments on an earlier draft of this paper. A grant from the Committee for Scholarly Communication with China enabled me to examine the 1620's Ming text of *Hui tu Lienü zhuan* at the Beijing Library in Oct. 1991.

1. For a biography of Chen Yujiao, see Carrington and Fang, 1: 188–90. All of Chen's plays were probably written between 1592 and 1605.

2. See, e.g., *Zhong qing li ji* (A graceful account of profound love), discussed in Chu Hung-lam.

3. Du Liniang, the heroine of *Peony Pavilion*, discussed below.

4. Ko, *Teachers of the Inner Chambers*, 166–67, 265.

5. Ko, "Pursuing Talent and Virtue."

6. There is a burgeoning literature on the Ming and Qing cult of women's fidelity. For a historical overview, see Mark Elvin. For a content analysis of Ming representations of Confucian virtue for women, see Carlitz, "Desire, Danger, and the Body." See also works by Jerry Dennerline, Jennifer Holmgren, Susan Mann, and T'ien Ju-k'ang cited in Carlitz, "Desire, Danger, and the Body."

7. "Jia zhou He E," in 1779 *Hui tu lienü zhuan*, 12.23b–24b, with commentary in Zhen cheng tang edition only, 12.39b–40a. See "Works Cited" for editions of *Hui tu lienü zhuan*.

8. See *Guifan*, 1.82b. For a discussion of this edition, see Carlitz, "The Social Uses of Female Virtue."

9. Tang dynasty daughters: *Guifan*, "Shang xing guan shi," 2.52a–53b. Madame Song: *Guifan*, "Qin xuan wen jun," 3.111a–12a.

10. See the representative quote by Zhou Quan in Kang-i Sun Chang, *Ch'en Tzu-lung*, 9–10.

11. Li Zhen, "Tianshu yu Xue Tao lian ju ji," 179–88; also included in Zhang Pengzhou, 96–118.

12. "Jian ji ren lin zhuang kan jing zhong la mei hua," in Zhong Xing, *Yin xiu xuan ji*, 64.

13. "Xin ji shou zhi pen lan yin," in ibid., 65.

14. See p. 21 in this volume.

15. Elman.

16. "De xing" (Virtuous conduct), in He Liangjun, *juan* 1–3.

17. For representative stories, see Carlitz, "Desire, Danger, and the Body," 113.

18. Desire, law, and ritual: Lü Kun, *Shen yin yu*, all of *juan* 5, but especially p. 235. Unregulated sexual desire: Lü Kun, *Guifan*, 3.30a. Establishments of singing-girls and actors: *Guifan* 1.3b.

19. Gui Youguang, *Zhen chuan xian sheng ji*, 728 *et passim.*

20. For an excellent discussion of the late Ming literati search for "the genuine," see Lowry, 97.

21. Kang-i Sun Chang's chapter in this volume quotes Zhong Xing as counterposing women's genuine *qing* to men's "false" (*jiao*) self-interested self-expression (see p. 152).

22. Wai-yee Li, 30.

23. Li Kaixian, 524–25.

24. Lü Kun, *Shen yin yu*, "Wen xue" (The pursuit of knowledge), 2.116.

25. See Swatek, "Feng Menglong's Romantic Dream," for contemporary reaction to the plays of Tang Xianzu.

26. *Zaju* are the short four-act plays characteristic of the Yuan dynasty but still a popular form during the Ming. *Chuanqi* are the long plays of variable length, derived from southern Chinese dramatic traditions, that were the dominant dramatic form during the Ming. Chen Yujiao's four *chuanqi* plays are reproduced in facsimile in *Gu ben xiqu congkan*, 2d series.

27. R. Huang, 202.

28. For Wang Daokun's biography, see Goodrich and Fang, 2:1427–30. For Wang Daokun and gender conventions, see Carlitz, "Desire, Danger, and the Body," 119.

29. For biographies of Wang Tingna, see Berliner; Xu Shuofang, 3: 505–46; and Zhuang Yifu, 453.

30. R. Huang, 221.

31. The Beijing Library Rare Book Room has a copy of Wang Tingna's *Qi pu.*

32. See Zhuang Yifu, 439–42 and 858–60, for capsule summaries of Chen Yujiao's plays, and 852–56 for summaries of Tang Xianzu's plays.

33. "Wei Gao," *Taiping guangji*, 2159–61. A biography of the historical Wei Gao can be found in the *Jiu Tang shu* (Old Tang history), *juan* 140.

34. This lore is collected and evaluated in Zhang Pengzhou.

35. Larsen (xx) suggests the actual reasons Xue Tao may have chosen Daoist reclusion: it offered her the life of cultivated retirement typical of major male poets. See also Wai-yee Li, 39, 85–86. But in *Parrot Island*, Xue Tao's main motive is unambiguously reduced to jealousy, and as we will see below, this was part of Chen Yujiao's strategy of containment.

36. For the *Nü xun* (preface dated 1508) and similar conduct books from Han through Qing, see Tienchi Martin-Liao, "Traditional Handbooks of Women's Education," in Gerstlacher, 165–90.

37. The exact relationship between *Parrot Island* and the nearly contemporaneous *Peony Pavilion* must await further research. Revivifying passion was a trope so popular in the Ming that both authors may have taken it up independently.

38. See Zhang Pengzhou, 63–64.

39. See Wai-yee Li, 25–28.

40. When attendants arrive in Scene 31 to speed the bashful Yuxiao to her reunion with Wei Gao, they sing that "the parrot is being released from her cage." This evokes "The Parrot Parted from her Cage," one of the poems in Xue Tao's celebrated suite "Shi li" (Ten partings), translated in Larson, 51–60. Our attention has already been drawn to the "Ten Partings" in Scenes 25, 27, and 30. In *Parrot Island*, Xue Tao bestows these poems on Wei Gao, whereas in much of the lore collected by Zhang Pengzhou, she writes them to win back the love of Yuan Zhen.

41. Hu Ying has shown how Diao Chan, a "jia ji" in the seventeenth-century Mao Zonggang commentary edition of the novel, is ethicized and given the liang attributes (that is to say, the class-marker attributes of shidafu self-representation) that justify the hero's interest in her.

42. Idema, 111–17.

43. The pivotal midpoint scenes of a Ming *chuanqi* play bring to a head the conflicts that will be resolved in the second half.

44. "Yuxiao nü zai shi yu huan yuan," in Tian ran chi sou (pseud., fl. ca. 1620), *Shi dian tou*. This collection and its author are discussed in Hanan, *Chinese Vernacular Story*, 120–39.

45. This is the major argument of Kang-i Sun Chang in *Chen Tzu-lung*.

46. See note 2 to this chapter.

47. For editions of *Yu huan ji*, see Zhuang Yifu, p. 932. For scene-by-scene summaries of the extant editions, see Carlitz, "The Role of Drama in the *Chin p'ing mei*," 460–78.

48. See Carlitz, *The Rhetoric of "Chin p'ing mei*," 115–16.

49. Widmer, "Xiaoqing's Literary Legacy."

50. Ko, *Teachers of the Inner Chambers*, Part III ("Women's Culture"), 177–293; and Widmer, "Epistolary World."

51. Ropp, "Love, Literacy, and Laments," 109.

52. Gui Youguang, 519.

53. For the *Illustrated Biographies*, see Carlitz, "Social Uses of Female Virtue." All citations below are to the Taiwan reprint of the 1779 edition, hereafter abbreviated as *IB*, except where noted.

54. *IB*, 9.22b–24a.

55. *IB*, 15.35a. For Zou Saizhen, see Ko, *Teachers of the Inner Chambers*, 138–39.

56. See Carlitz, "Social Uses of Female Virtue," 126n26.
57. Ko, *Teachers of the Inner Chambers*, 197.
58. Tanaka Issei, 152.
59. Widmer, "Xiaoqing's Literary Legacy."
60. Ko, *Teachers of the Inner Chambers*, 82; Zeitlin, 129.
61. Carlitz, "Social Uses of Female Virtue," 121.
62. Carlitz, "Desire, Danger, and the Body," 117.
63. Commentary to the entry on *Wang shi fu* (The wives of the Wang family), in Wang Tingna, *Ren jing yang qiu*, 16.47b–48a.
64. 1620's Zhen cheng tang ed. only, 9.43a.
65. For women addressing each other with the trope of "beauty," see the letter from Huang Dezhen quoted by Ellen Widmer in "Epistolary World," 19–20. Widmer points out that male literati anthologists dealt with this issue by keeping their courtesans beautiful, but describing their gentry women authors as losing some of their physical attractiveness when they wrote; see ibid., 29. On the other hand, Dorothy Ko (*Teachers of the Inner Chambers*, 166–69) notes the ways late Ming governing-class women were able to participate in the surrounding sensuous culture by conflating talent, virtue, and beauty.
66. Central to Maureen Robertson's seminal essay "Voicing the Feminine" are the construction and effects of the "literati-feminine voice" created by male writers for the feminine persona to which they so often resorted. On p. 75 of "Voicing the Feminine," Robertson gives an example of the Tang woman poet Li Jilan writing in the "literati-masculine" voice.
67. *IB*, 15.46a–48a.
68. Ropp, "Love, Literacy, and Laments," 117–23.
69. Widmer, "Epistolary World," 10.
70. Ibid., 16.
71. Ye Changhai is a teacher at the Shanghai Drama Institute.
72. Ko, *Teachers of the Inner Chambers*, 256, 266–74.
73. Ibid., 125–29.
74. Widmer, "Epistolary World," 23.
75. Ibid., 13.
76. Songs performed by entertainers for the women of the Ximen household in the novel *Jin ping mei* are frequently on this theme. But *Jin ping mei* bears such a complex relation to late Ming society that care must be exercised in reading the text as a straightforward record of social practice. See Carlitz, *The Rhetoric of "Chin p'ing mei."*
77. "Gu Lienü," 1538 *Kunshan xianzhi*, 16.17a–b.
78. Widmer, "Xiaoqing's Literary Legacy," 134.
79. Widmer, "Epistolary World," 23.

Chapter 5

1. In 1934 the original published version of *Mountain Songs* was discovered in She county, Huizhou prefecture, Anhui province. Huizhou was the

birthplace of many merchants in the Ming, and quite possibly this book, published in Suzhou, had been purchased there and brought back by a Huizhou merchant. This text was edited by Gu Jiegang and was published in 1935 by the Chuanjingtang Bookstore in Shanghai. It was republished in 1962, edited by Guan Dedong, as a volume in the *Ming Qing min'ge shidiao congshu* series published by Zhonghua shuju. The original edition is now in the collection of the Beijing Library.

2. For the language of the work, see McCoy; Hu Mingyang; Shi Rujie and Chen Liujing; and Zhang Huiying.

3. The only monograph about *Mountain Songs* published to date is Töpelmann; it contains a full translation. For articles, see the prefaces and essays by various scholars printed in the 1935 and 1962 editions mentioned in note 1. Notable articles published in China in the past few decades include Li Ping; Wu Zhangsheng; Li Ning; You Youji; and Lu Yilu. Japanese essays include Takeda; Adachibara; Ōki, "Fū Muryū *Sanka* no kenkyū"; idem, "Zokkyokushū *Kashiji* ni tsuite"; and idem, "Fū Muryū Jo *Sanka* kō."

4. *The Record of the Western Chamber*, the story of a girl from a good family who secretly has a relationship with a student, was popular in the late Ming and was often proscribed as a lewd book.

5. Liu Ke, 144.

6. Cf. Ōki, "Fū Muryū *Sanka* no kenkyū." Song festivals in the Tang, Song, and later dynasties in the Middle and Lower Yangzi regions took place at Hangzhou, Suzhou, Nanjing, Chuzhou, Zhangling, Jiujiang, Huangzhou, Yueyang, Jiangling, and Sanxia.

7. Shenghu zhi, *juan* 3, "Fengsu" (published in the Shunzhi era, 1644–61).

8. Song Moucheng reported in "Ting wuge ji" (Listening to Wu songs) in his *Jiuyao qianji* that he had heard servants sing 500–600 Wu dialect songs in 1595.

9. Males who limited their extramarital relations to courtesans and prostitutes were not criticized. The urban entertainment quarters were often the sites where their works were created and appreciated (Ōki, "Fū Muryū to gijo").

10. Only the woman in the longest song, "Pilgrimage of a Lady," in *juan* 9, is active and vigorous. In my opinion, this song must come from the common people.

Chapter 6

An earlier version of this paper appeared in *The Gest Library Journal*, 5, no. 2 (1992): 119–60. I especially appreciate the help of F. W. Mote, Haun Saussy, Zhen-ping Wang, and Ellen Widmer, who offered useful comments and suggestions on this paper. I am also indebted to Wen-k'ai Kung and Ch'iu-ti Judy Liu for locating and providing valuable source materials. In addition, I wish to express my thanks to many other friends, teachers, and colleagues who gave me important information, among them Zhengguo Kang, Shuen-fu Lin, Susan Mann, Tai-loi Ma, Paul Ropp, Chun Shum, Shi Zhicun, Yü-lin Wang, and Xu Shuofang. Finally, grateful acknowledgment should be made to Eugene Wu of Harvard-Yenching Library for permission to photocopy rare editions of anthologies.

1. See Hu Wenkai.

2. There is an original copy of *Shi nüshi* in the Beijing Library. The University of Chicago has a microfilm made from the original. It should be noted that long before the Ming, the Song dynasty poet Ouyang Xiu already expressed views similar to Tian Yiheng's. In his foreword to Xie Ximeng's collected works, Ouyang wrote: "In the past, works of Zhuang Jiang of Wei and Lady Xumu were recorded by Confucius and ranked among the "Guofeng" [of the *Shijing*]. If there were today a heroic person who could evaluate contemporary poets and inspire confidence in later generations, people would rank her [Ximeng] highly and her name would not be lost to memory" (Hu Wenkai, 66). Such views did not, however, become prevalent until the late Ming.

3. See Shen Yixiu's preface to *Yiren si*, 1, in Ye Shaoyuan, vol. 2.

4. Robertson, "Voicing the Feminine," 64.

5. See Shi Zhicun, *Tang shi baihua*, 769.

6. Ibid., 775.

7. Hongshulou, "Fanli," in Lu Chang, 2b.

8. See Ko, *Teachers of the Inner Chambers*, 4.

9. Ko, "Social History," 2n4.

10. For "contextual poetics," see Fraistat, 3–17. I owe this specific citation to Pauline Yu ("Poems in Their Place," 195).

11. Widmer, "Epistolary World," 22.

12. On the canon as a means of "providing models, ideals, and inspiration," see Harris, 111.

13. Kang Zhengguo, *Fengsao yu yanqing*, 345.

14. I am indebted to Shuen-fu Lin for enlightening me on this point.

15. Ji Yun, 193: 4301.

16. Ibid., 193: 4318.

17. Trans. by Haun Saussy, "Female Scribes, Ancient and Modern."

18. Ibid.

19. I am grateful to Xu Shoufang for calling my attention to the particular entries that were clearly done by Liu Shi herself and to those obviously prepared by Qian Qianyi (pers. comm., July 8, 1993).

20. The *Wuyin cao* and *Hushang cao* are now in the Zhejiang Provincial Library in Hangzhou. It should be noted that Chen Yinko, author of the highly acclaimed biography of Liu Shi, did not have access to these two collections while writing his *Liu Rushi biezhuan* (see Huang Chang, 167).

21. According to reliable sources, the project of *Liechao shiji* was started in 1646 and completed in 1649. (See the foreword by the Publishing Committee of Shanghai Guji chubanshe. In Qian Qianyi, *Liechao shiji xiaozhuan*, 1: 1).

22. See my *Ch'en Tzu-lung*, 19.

23. See also Widmer, "Epistolary World," 20.

24. Qian Qianyi, *Liechao shiji xiaozhuan*, 2: 752.

25. Ibid., 751.

26. Ibid, 752.

27. Ibid., 760.

28. Chen Yinke, *Liu Rushi biezhuan*, 3: 827–1224.

29. Ji Yun, 190: 4229.

30. Ibid.

31. See Zhu Yizun, *juan* 98, 2: 712.

32. Wang Shilu's *Ranzhi ji* exists only in manuscript form. The Shanghai Library has the original of the anthology, though *juan* 16 to *juan* 20 are missing (Hu Wenkai, 906).

33. For example, Zou Siyi placed her at the beginning of his anthology *Eight Famous Women Poets* (see discussion above). And in 1661 the dramatist Li Yu asked Wang to write a foreword to his play, *Bimu yu* ("Sole" mates); see also Widmer, "Epistolary World," 11.

34. The Naikaku Bunko in Japan has the original of *Yinhong ji*.

35. For some reason, Qian Qianyi's important preface is missing from the Central Library copy. The Yale microfilm, which was acquired by Wen-k'ai Kung from the Beijing Library, does contain Qian's preface.

36. Wang Duanshu, 3b. For the idea of *neiyan buchu* in Zhang Xuechang, see Mann, " 'Fuxue,' " 50.

37. Wang Duanshu never mentioned the historical Weishu. But it might be significant that the original Weishu is a lost book which gave unorthodox interpretations of the classic (see *Sui shu*, "Jing ji zhi").

38. Qian Qianyi, Foreword (dated 1661) to Wang Duanshu, 3a.

39. See my *Ch'en Tzu-lung*, 9–18.

40. Incidentally, Wang Duanshu once wrote a poem (see Wang Duanshu, 42.2b) about doing a painting for Liu Shi at the request of Liu conveyed through Qian Qianyi. But this does not rule out the possibility of biases or feelings of rivalry on Wang Duanshu's part—for although Zou Siyi placed Wang Duanshu at the beginning of his anthology, he also judged Liu Shi first among famous women poets.

41. As mentioned above, Liu Shi included only two poems by Xu Yuan in the *Liechao shiji*.

42. Harris, 116.

43. For information of this anthology, see Widmer, "Epistolary World," 41.

44. See the modern punctuated ed. by Shi Zhicun, *Tang shi baihua*, 1.

45. See Zong Yuanding's foreword to the anthology (Hu Wenkai, 903–4).

46. See also my "Liu Shih and Hsü Ts'an: Feminine or Feminist?"

47. See my *Ch'en Tzu-lung*, 41–68.

48. *Linxia cixuan* selects works of women *ci* poets from the Song to the early Qing. The Ming-Qing works are in *juan* 6–13.

49. Trans. Haun Saussy, "Poetic Flowers."

50. For example, Xu Can is the only woman poet included in Long Muxun's highly acclaimed anthology of late imperial song lyrics, *Jin sanbai nian mingjia cixuan;* see pp. 24–26.

51. See Shi Zhicun, "Lidai ci xuanji xulu," 247–48.

52. See Jiang Jingqi.

53. For Zhang Xuecheng's criticism against Yuan Mei and his female disciples, see my "Ming-Qing Women Poets."

54. Here Wang Gu copied verbatim from Yuan Mei's epitaph for Jin Yi, "Jin xianxian nüshi muzhiming" (see Yuan Mei, *Xiao cang shan fang wenji, juan* 32, in *Suiyuan san shi ba zhong,* 4.8a).

55. Ibid. See also "The Image" under Hexagrams no. 58 and 30, respectively (Wilhelm and Baynes, 224, 119).

56. In his "Fuxue," Zhang summed up his position on this issue: "Ignorant people have supposed that the poem "The Zhen and Wei Rivers" and others like it were written by lovers themselves, and so they claim that the young women of ancient times simply opened their mouths and poured out complete verses that are superior to those of later male writers. Such people do not know that this belief is utterly without foundation" (Mann, " 'Fuxue,' " 52).

57. Borer, 3.

58. For details, see my "Ming-Qing Women Poets."

59. For an English translation of the *Wenxuan,* see Knechtges.

60. For an English translation of the *Yutai xinyong,* see Birrell.

61. See Xu Ling's preface to *Yutai xinyong,* 1: 11–13.

62. For names of these ten poets, see Hu Wenkai, 851.

63. For names of these three women, see ibid., 865.

64. See Cai Dianqi's preface to *Guochao guige shichao,* in Hu Wenkai, 861.

65. See Schultz's note on Wang Pengyun, in Lo and Schultz, 343.

66. For the "women's script," see Gao Yinxian and Yi Nianhua. Unfortunately, few pre-Qing works written in the women's script seem to have survived, although we may assume that the numerous folksongs available in the *nüshu* reflect a long-standing oral tradition. It was customary for country women to burn their songs written in the women's script, because they believed that poems could thus be carried to the underworld after the woman's death.

67. See also Chiang. Chiang thinks that the genre of folksongs and folktales "merits particular notice because it may have influenced the format and literary style of all other genres" in the *nüshu* (p. 197). Village women often sang the songs and stories recorded in the women's script while they gathered for needlework. According to Chiang, there are still no data on the origins of the women's script, although there exist several legends that reflect *nüshu's* social function—allowing women to vent personal griefs and the like. One legend, for example, has it that a Song dynasty woman named Hu Yuxiu invented the women's script in order to communicate her secret, lonely thoughts after becoming a royal concubine of the emperor Song Zhezong (ibid., 313). I feel that what is important to us is not when the script originated, but rather the fact that

women have been actively involved in an oral tradition since ancient times, even if the script might not have been invented until later.

68. See Mann, " 'Fuxue,' " 52.

69. As cited in Liang Yizhen, 204.

70. Widmer, "Xiaoqing's Literary Legacy," 40.

71. Even Shen Shanbao (1796–1862?), one of the most liberated women critics during the Qing, often judged women poets according to moral considerations in her *Mingyuan shihua*. I am grateful to Kang Zhenggu for calling my attention to this point (pers. comm., Oct. 1993).

72. I am indebted to Ellen Widmer for this point.

73. See my "Ming-Qing Women Poets."

74. Pauline Yu, "Poems in Their Place," 196.

75. Shi Shuyi, 5.

76. See my *Ch'en Tzu-lung*, xiii.

77. Bloom, 63–80.

Chapter 7

I am grateful to the editors of this volume and to the participants in the conference "Women and Literature in Ming-Qing China" for their many helpful corrections and suggestions.

1. For a detailed discussion of the social and gender relations among members of this group and between group members and Ren Zhaolin, see Dorothy Ko, "Lady Scholars at the Door."

2. An even broader, cross-cultural contextualizing would reveal some striking similarities, despite cultural differences, in seventeenth-century Chinese and Anglo-European women's heightened visibility as writers, in some of their literary practices, and in difficulties experienced. In both groups women formed same-sex and informal, largely familial coteries; circulated unpublished manuscripts among relatives and friends; faced printed criticism from men who publicly questioned their virtue; prompted with their writings debates about women's psychology, intellect, and social roles and whether there was a feminine "signature" that marked women's writings; sometimes burned their writings; and in various ways attempted to reconcile their desire to write with the anxiety they felt about circulating their words in texts. For examples of discussions of these matters in studies of seventeenth-century Anglo-European women's writing, see Grundy and Wiseman; and Brant and Purkiss.

3. This emphasis upon a defining characteristic of governing-class culture, its literariness, shows that women with literary abilities could be felt to contribute evidence of a family's authentic class membership, in a period characterized by "the blurring of status distinctions" among differing segments of society; see Wakeman, *The Great Enterprise*, 1: 98.

4. References to Tao Qian, to peach tree retreats, and to the "three paths"

and other motifs associated with Tao's work and life occur frequently in women's poetry. Tao's validation of the private life makes him an especially attractive model for the woman writer. *Xianju* (living the quiet life), an ideal for Tao, can be read by women to suggest their own condition, idealized as a life spent quietly and with integrity, remote from worldly affairs.

5. Given the ephemeral nature of women's writings in China before the twentieth century, shown clearly by the disappearance of so many collections and parts of collections (most often the sections containing prose writings), anthologies are indispensable to our work on Chinese women's poetry and literary history today, and I do not intend to suggest that they are not valuable sources, if used carefully. We can only be deeply grateful for the work of editors in preserving what would otherwise, in the majority of cases, have vanished entirely. On anthologies of women's writings, see Kang-i Sun Chang, "Guide"; and her chapter (pp. 147–70) in this volume.

6. See Robertson, "Voicing the Feminine."

7. The word "ambivalence," used here to refer to the attitude of many women writers of the Ming and Qing toward their own writings, especially the circulation of those writings, is employed with caution. It can too easily reflect a modern desire to map out the positions of women of earlier times into categories derived from our own social experience or from contemporary feminist theory. I wish to avoid the implication that these women felt they had to make a principled choice between compliance with gender norms and resistance or contestation, although I believe that the latter postures may be found in some of the textual subjects produced by women writers of the Ming and Qing. The ambivalence referred to here is that of a woman in a patriarchal society whose horizon of expectation does not yet include the notion of a reform in the gender system. It is the mark of conflicting desires for active participation in an officially masculine literary culture that speaks and supports "self" and for a feminine social identity, with approval for the proper performance of the "self"-effacing role of gentry daughter or wife. For discussions of a similar form of ambivalence in earlier women's writings in England, see Poovey.

8. Smith, xxvii. Most of the working concepts outlined briefly here are consistent with Smith's interpretation and critique of Marxist, Lacanian, and feminist concepts of the subject. I have not, however, followed his elaboration upon the Lacanian unconscious or his theorizing of the unconscious as the source of agency. I prefer simply to grant that the subject has the capacity for negotiation, in the Gramscian sense, without arguing the issue of the unconscious. The definition of three subject "functions," for discussion of gendered writing, is mine.

9. The traditional Chinese concept of the expressive process, described in the "Da xu" (Major preface) to the *Shijing* (Book of odes) implies such an unproblematic, transparent textual subject. Educated readers did, however, certainly expect to "read through" or "read from" the conventional literary codes in a sophisticated way, in their pursuit of the historical subject. The

present analysis complicates the relationship of the one who speaks as historical or existential subject and the one who speaks in texts.

10. Liang dynasty critic Zhong Hong (*ming* also pronounced Rong, fl. 505), in his *Shipin* (Classification of poets), includes four women among the total of 122 poets. Ban Jieyu (B.C.E. 48?–6?), a consort of Emperor Cheng of the Han, and Han Lanying (fl. 460 C.E.), a learned teacher of palace women under emperors Xiaowu of the Liu Song dynasty and Wu of the Qi dynasty, were associated with the court. Bao Linghui (fl. 464 C.E.) was a younger sister of the major poet Bao Zhao; she was received into the court of the Song emperor Xiaowu. The exception, Xu Shu (fl. 147 C.E.), was praised by Zhong Hong for the moving expression of devotion and sorrow in parting poems she and her husband exchanged.

11. *Tangren xuan Tang shi*, 292.

12. Xin Wenfang, *Tang caizi zhuan*, 27–28.

13. The "Guanju" is described in the commentary to the *Book of Odes* as a song celebrating the virtue of the queen. Understood as representing the queen's voice or sentiments, the song is praised because she "does not give way to unruly passions" (*bu yin qi se*) and "does not wish to do injury to what is good" (*wu shang shan zhi xin*), as she unselfishly seeks and finds suitable consorts for her lord, putting the interest of her husband's lineage before personal feelings; see Kong Yingda, 1.1a–3a.

14. Ban Jieyu, consort of the Han emperor Cheng (B.C.E 33–7), was known for her refusal to encourage the ruler's frivolous behavior, her devotion to the empress, and her ability as a poet. In her most famous poem, the autumn fan laid aside when cool weather comes represents her fear that the emperor's affections will cool. Xie E was Xie Daoyun (fl. 376 C.E.), niece of the Chen dynasty statesman Xie An. She bested all the younger members of her family, male and female, when her uncle challenged them to write a verse couplet describing snow. "Seven commandments" refers to the Han dynasty conduct book for women, *Nü jie* (Instructions for women), written in seven sections by scholar, poet, and historiographer Ban Zhao (?–116 C.E.). Cai Yan (fl. 200 C.E.), well-educated daughter of eminent Han dynasty scholar-official Cai Yong, was kidnapped by invading Xiongnu troops in 194 and forced to marry a Xiongnu leader. Ransomed by Cao Cao, she was forced to leave her two children behind when she returned. Her poem cycle "Eighteen Songs for a Transverse Flute of Hu" narrates her experiences.

15. Empress Zhen (182–221 C.E.) from childhood loved to study and became known as an erudite woman. After the death of her husband at Cao Cao's hands, she was claimed in marriage by Cao Cao's son Cao Pi, who became Emperor Wen (r. 220–26) of the Wei dynasty (220–65 C.E.).

16. Wu Xiao, *Xiaoxue'an shigao* (Poems from Whispering Snow Retreat), 1695 ed. of a late Ming collection; quoted in Hu Wenkai, 106.

17. Gu Ruopu, 1626 preface to *Woyue xuan gao* (Poems from Sleeping in Moonlight Gallery), in Ding Bing, ed., *Wulin wangzhe yizhu* (The written legacy of Wulin sages of the past). Gu's preface is also quoted in Hu Wenkai, 208.

18. The discourse of women's virtue, exemplified in the tradition of conduct books beginning with the Han dynasty *Lienü zhuan* (Biographies of exemplary women), positions woman in a relation of obedience and self-sacrifice with respect to parents, husband, and children. Her domain is the household, and ideally she is never seen by anyone outside the family. Her speech is analogous to the chastity of her physical person and must not be promiscuous, i.e., must not be displayed abroad. Representing the self as a virtuous woman involves employing the rhetoric of duty and obedience. The discourse of literature is derived from the central importance of writing and textuality in governing-class men's careers and reputations. As a property of the literati-officials, literature and its pursuit produced a cult that contributed themes and tropes to the discourse of *wen*, literature. Among these are a devotion to texts and study (at times bordering on enthrallment); belief in immortality through texts; a desire for continuity and communion with scholars/poets of the past; a sense of mission regarding the preservation of texts, leading to editing, anthologizing and archival work, annotation, and commentary; use of literary models and imitation of styles; the practice of literary criticism; the mentoring of younger writers; and participation in group activities such as poetry games, poetry excursions, literary correspondence, and literary friendships. Evidence from their poetry and prefaces shows that literary women of the Ming and Qing engaged in all of these practices and enjoyed using references to them thematically in their writings.

19. Zha has borrowed an expression that the Neo-Confucian philosopher Cheng Hao (1032–85) used in his teachings on desire and self-regulation. As a youth of sixteen, Cheng had loved to hunt. Later, as part of a serious effort at self-cultivation, he declared he would give up hunting. Chou Dunyi (1017–73) chided him for assuming that desires could be eradicated from the heart so easily. Desire may lie hidden deep in the heart, like a sickness one believes to have been cured, but will re-emerge, strong as ever, given the right occasion. This was confirmed for Cheng when some years later he returned to his family home for a visit and happened to see a hunt in progress. Spontaneously, he felt happy at heart (Zhu Xi, 5.176). Through the allusion to Cheng Hao, Zha identifies her desire to write poetry as an obstacle to the serious performance of moral duty, a "sickness" of her youth. In her middle age, however, this obsession seems to be re-situated within the discourse of literature, since it can be allayed when the desire is indulged. I am grateful to Tu Wei-ming for suggesting the source of Zha's reference to the hunt.

20. Biographical entries for Zha women from Haining can be found in Shi Shuyi, *juan* 3– 5. Information on the literary works of eight Zha women from Haining is given in Hu Wenkai, 426–29.

21. See Hu Wenkai, 543, for a description of a work by Gu's fifth-generation granddaughter by marriage, Liang Ying. An accompanying preface by Banana Garden Club poet Lin Yining emphasizes the family connec-

tion and reminisces about her own earlier years as a member of the large group of interrelated literary women linked with Gu's household. Lin was the sister-in-law of the poet Qian Fenglun, Gu's grand-niece.

22. Cai Dianqi, 2: 9.4b–5a.

23. For a discussion of *The Correct Beginnings Collection: Poetry by Refined Ladies of Our Dynasty*, see the chapter by Kang-i Sun Chang in this volume, pp. 147–70. The phrase "mother of the Grand Instructor" in Jiang's title refers to the fact that editor Zhu Yun's son, Wanyan Linqing (*jinshi* 1809), was a secretary in the Supervisorate of Imperial Instruction from 1814 to 1821. This raises a problem in dating, however. Yun Zhu's anthology was published in 1831, by which time Linqing was serving as provincial judge of Henan province (1829–32; see Hummel, 506–7). Yun Zhu died in 1833. It seems that Jiang either had read a manuscript copy of *The Correct Beginnings Collection* prior to its publication, and early enough to write her poem during Linqing's tenure in the Supervisorate, or she wrote at some time after the anthology's publication, unaware of Linqing's rise in official rank. It is also possible that Jiang wrote the poem after 1833, before learning of the death of Yun Zhu.

24. Ban Zhao is paired with another exemplar, Xu (?–961 C.E.), who was a prolific writer of palace-style lyrics and the consort of Meng Chang, the king of the Five Dynasties state of Shu. She is known best by her title, Huarui furen, Lady Flower Pistil. When Meng Chang died during the Song conquest of Shu and Xu was taken to the Song court, she remained faithful, refusing to enter the ranks of the first Song emperor's women. In recognition of her moral position, she was permitted to commit suicide.

25. The linguist J. L. Austin used this term in his exposition of speech act theory to refer to an oral event, "the performance of an 'illocutionary' act, i.e., the performance of an act in saying something as opposed to the performance of an act of saying something" (p. 99). Literary critics such as J. Hillis Miller have claimed that all literary works are illocutionary acts in Austin's sense; Miller speaks of literary texts as "performatives." Cultural critic Judith Butler (24–25) uses the term in a discussion of gender as performative.

26. Zhong Xing, *Mingyuan shigui*, 32.1a–b. The four white-haired and venerable old men of the Shang mountains (*shangshan sihao*) had fled social disorders at the end of the Qin dynasty (B.C.E. 249–206), retreating deeply into the Shang Mountains. They refused to come out after the establishment of the Han dynasty and the restoration of peace, even though their wise counsel was sought by the Han emperor. Li Bo's admiration was expressed in two poems, "Shangshan sihao" (The four white-haired old men of the Shang Mountains) and "Guo sihao mu" (Visiting the tombs of the four white-haired old men); see Li Bo, 2: 22.11b–13a.

27. In *pailü*, the base eight-line stanza of the tonally regulated lyric poem, *lüshi*, is expanded to produce a longer stanza by means of repetitions of the middle part of the tripartite stanza structure.

28. In the mid-tenth century B.C.E., a Jade Effusion Garden was said to have been constructed under imperial Zhou dynasty auspices. In 1147, dur-

ing the Southern Song dynasty (1127–1279), another garden with the same name was built north of Dragon Mountain in the West Lake area of Hangzhou, in Zhejiang province. In 1185, Emperor Xiao (1163–90) held a great hunting party there, and visited the garden several times thereafter. "Jade effusion" (*yujin*) is a term originating textually in the early work *Han Wudi gushi* (Tales of Emperor Wu of the Han); there the divinity Queen Mother of the West refers to it as a substance that confers immortality. In Daoist health and meditation practices, it was the name given to saliva.

29. Phoenix City, a name normally used for the imperial capital, also designated any temporary residence of the emperor.

30. Purple clouds connote imperial authority, the aura of an emperor, suggesting his spiritual as well as temporal power.

31. Tao Qian, *Tao Jingjie jizhu*, 2: 23.

32. Du Fu, 3.12a–13a.

33. Shen here uses an adage that appears also in another Du Fu poem, "Xinhun bie" (Farewell of the newlyweds), in which a wife says goodbye to her conscript husband: "Rather than marry your daughter to a border soldier / better to have abandoned her by the road" (Du Fu, 2.14b).

34. Graveyards were situated out beyond the city walls.

35. "Ji yuan" (Sent far away), in Shen Deqian, 31.17a.

36. The painting represents a brahmin of Magadha, who became one of the principal disciples of Sakyamuni; after the latter's death, Mahakasyapa became leader of the disciples, the first of the 28 Patriarchs and first compiler of the Buddhist canon.

37. Yun Zhu, *Guochao guige zhengshi ji*, 2: 4.2a.

38. Qian Zhen (fl. 1800), in Wang Yu, 166.10a.

39. The last line refers generally to a beautiful woman's presence in the women's apartments at the back of a large residence. The phrase alludes to song lyrics written by the last ruler of the southern Chen dynasty (557–89), Chen Houzhu. The poem, a *yuefu* under the caption "Flower on a Jade Tree in the Back Courtyard," figures a beautiful and seductive woman's face as a flower on a tree of jade (her body); see Guo Maoqian, 47.1b–2a. The speaker in Zhang's poem implies that, were she not so ignored, she could provide the pleasure and feminine beauty associated with Chen Houzhu's back courtyard soirees. The phrase "morning after morning" is borrowed from an earlier, anonymous, *yuefu* titled "Flower on a Jade Tree in the Back Courtyard: Music for the Beginning of Spring."

40. For an excellent discussion of the social, familial, and intellectual relations in this important group of literary women and of the group as a "public" women's community, see Ko, *Teachers of the Inner Chambers*, 234–42.

41. See Weidner and Indianapolis Museum of Art, 108–9.

42. Cao Yin, 2: 1302.

43. The speaker dreams of being taken on a skyride far over the ocean to the mythical islands inhabited by immortals; the most often specified of these

was called Penglai. The cloud chariots of the immortals were drawn by fabulous animals.

44. The major five sacred mountains of China are Taishan (east), Huashan (west), Hengshan (north), a different Hengshan (south), and Songshan (central).

45. The reference to Jasper Pool evokes the unearthly elegance of the gardens of the mythical Queen Mother of the West, since ancient times thought to be on the summit of the Kunlun mountains to the west of China.

46. An early description of the Queen Mother of the West in the mythical geography *Shanhai jing* (Classic of mountains and seas) represented her as half-human and half-animal. In later descriptions she became a beautiful woman.

47. Those who sought Daoist immortality believed that the exquisite food and drink of the immortals had a transmuting effect upon mortal bodies.

48. King Xiang was Xiang Yu of the former Zhou kingdom of Chu, who led an army in an attempt to overthrow the Qin dynasty and found its successor; he was defeated by his rival Liu Bang, who founded the Han dynasty. The biography of Xiang Yu in Sima Qian's *Shiji* (The historical record) describes Xiang Yu's farewell to his companion, the beauty Yu, in his field tent and his subsequent heroic death, but Yu's fate is not recorded. From their poems, we can see that women writers understood the beauty Yu to have acted heroically as well; she is believed to have committed suicide rather than allow herself to fall into the hands of Xiang Yu's enemy. See Qian Fenglun's description of Yu's suicide in "Yu meiren" (The beauty Yu), *Guxianglou ci*, 3b.

49. Shen Yue, ed., *Song shu*, Bona ed. (reprinted — Taibei: Shangwu yinshuguan, n.d.), "Lie zhuan," no. 53, 14.17a.

50. As in "Qingqing heban cao" (Green, green, the grass on the riverbanks), one of the *Gushi shijiu shou*.

51. Topics such as the poetry of women's friendship, gender, and landscape, and the development by women writers of preferred verse subgenres are included in my book in progress, a study of poetry by Ming and Qing women.

52. For Xu Yunhui, see Hongmeige zhuren and Qinghuilou zhuren, 5.20b–21a. Bao Zhilan, 3.11a–12b. I am indebted to Cathy Silber for bringing Bao's poem to my attention and providing a copy of the text.

53. One biographical source quotes interestingly from a preface to Zhuang's collected poems, *Jianshui shanfang shichao* (Poems from Cleave the Waters Mountain Lodge): "Madame married very late; therefore, able to extend the leisure time [at her natal home], she used it to perfect her learning" (Shi Shuyi, 6.26b–27a). The earliest examples of lyrics under the ballad caption *Xinglu nan*, as well as later versions up through the thirteenth century, are collected in Guo Maoqian, *juan* 70 and 71. Most early lyrics under this caption, such as the touchstone series of nineteen by (Liu) Song dynasty poet Bao Zhao, contain melancholy reflections by a masculine speaker. The motif

of the lonely or abandoned wife occurs featuring a feminine speaker in three of the seventeen; in one of these the woman's speech is quoted. Use of the opening phrase, "Haven't you noticed . . . " is a standard feature of "Hardships of the Road," as well as of several other ancient ballad lyrics and ballad-style poems. This phrase cues the reader to enter imaginatively into an oral context of reception in which the speaker addresses a single or collective listener as "you."

54. The ups and downs of public life for men may be charted by the number of times they leave for office and later — due to career difficulties — re-enter their gate and take up private life.

55. In "The Road to Shu Is Hard," Li Bo opens with exclamations of awe and horror, contemplating the journey over dangerous mountain terrain. He goes on to describe further dangers: "Mornings one runs from fierce tigers, / Evenings one runs from long snakes. / They gnash their fangs, suck human blood / and maul people down like hemp" (Liu Wu-chi and I. Lo, 106; Li Bo, 3.3b–7b). In Li He's "Sir, Don't Go out the Gate!," a bitter and despairing speaker claims that the good are doomed to early death; to go into public service is to invite injury and defeat. He speaks of dangers in dramatic images: "The nine-headed monster eats our souls, / Frost and snows snap our bones. / Dogs are set on us, snarl and sniff around us . . ." (Graham 117–18; Li He, *Sanjia pingzhu*, 149–50). *Nie*, "malt, fermented grain" (Read, 243, 252), is homophonous with *nie*, "slander, make false accusation." Likewise, *mei*, "plum," might cue a homophone, *mei*, "anxiety, depression." It is also visually linked to the word *wu*, "insult," in the last line of the poem. Among relevant marriage complaints in the *Book of Odes* are nos. 30 ("Zhongfeng"), 35 ("Gufeng"), and 26 ("Bozhou"). The first two describe fierce storms, winds, and darkness as correlatives for angry feelings that the speaker in no. 30 says have led her husband to take a new wife, rejecting her despite her many contributions to his household. The third poem speaks of insults and of the desire to fly up and away from trouble.

56. See "Discourse in Dostoevsky," in Bakhtin, 181–269.

57. Hanging a bow on the door was in ancient times a way to announce the birth of a son. The expression was used later in offering congratulations to the new parents of a boy.

58. Used here to signify the high status and wealth of the husband-to-be, the golden tortoise was a Han dynasty insignia of rank worn by those rewarded with the aristocratic title of marquis (*hou*). In the Tang dynasty, officials of the third rank (*pin*) and above wore the golden tortoise.

Chapter 8

I would like to acknowledge the various contributions made by the following people to this chapter: Katherine Carlitz, Valerie Hansen, Peter Ditmanson, Jiang Yonglin, Hsu Pi-ching, Lisa Norling, Edward Farmer, and Li Rongqing.

1. Li Xu. The biographical material on Li is gleaned from the preface by the modern editor, Wei Lianko, in Li Xu, 1–9.

2. *Gujin nüshi*, Ming ed. held at Harvard-Yenching library.

3. This text is substantially the same as the *Nü fan bian*. The biographies are identical, as are the illustrations. The difference is that the *Guifan* is packaged with a number of other didactic texts for women.

4. *Ryū Kyō Retsujoden*, 1.27a–30a.

5. This account is reproduced in Tan Zhengbi, *Sanyan Erpai ziliao*, 513–57.

6. This text is included in Tan Zhengbi, *Sanyan Erpai ziliao*.

7. "Yi ji," 11a–b, in Tan Qian, *Zaolin zazu*, 79. The context is a list of women poets.

8. Qian Qianyi, *Liechao shiji xiaozhuan*, 742.

9. *Gujin tushu jicheng*, "Ming lun hui pien"; "Guiyuan dian," *juan* 336, p. 42.

10. *Mingshi zong*, 86.7b–8a.

11. Quoted in Tan Zhengbi, *Sanyan Erpai ziliao*, 513–14; Zhong Xing, *Mingyuan shigui*, 28.2a–3b. The *Mingyuan shigui* devotes more space (two double-columned pages) to the story of Li Yuying than it does to her poems.

12. *Xingshi hengyan*, no. 27. See the discussion in Lévy, pt. I, 1: 722–27. The best authority on the sources of the story remains Tan Zhengbi, *Sanyan Erpai ziliao*. See also the discussion in Hanan, *Chinese Short Story, passim*. Hanan believes that this story is one of those edited by "Langxian."

13. Most of the stories in the *Sanyan* have a *ruhua*, a short introductory story that serves as a contrast or counterpoint to the main story.

14. *Xingshi hengyan*, 548.

15. For an explicit discussion of the problems of male remarriage, see the views of Wang Huizu (1731–1807) as discussed in Susan Mann, "Grooming a Daughter," 216–19.

16. Other versions of the story call her Guiying.

17. The Chinese term is *xuejiu*, which Hucker says "in later dynasties became a common, somewhat derisive reference to elderly scholars and teachers of only local reputation" (252).

18. *Jie'an laoren manbi, juan* 3, p. 122.

19. Ibid., 120–22.

20. McKnight, 101–2. All capital cases were personally reviewed by the emperor at the assizes.

21. *Ming Shizong shilu*, 1269.

22. On the ritual controversy, see Fisher.

23. See, e.g., *Yansui zhenzhi*, 110.

24. Tan Qian, *Guoque, juan* 51, p. 3182.

25. In some versions, the line reads "half in mud and dirt."

26. The *Lienü zhuan* and the *Sanyan* versions of the poem contain this version.

27. Zhong Xing, *Mingyuan shigui*, 28.3b.

28. Xue Tao's poem reads,

In and out through crimson gates:
she never was put off.
Her master always loving,
she twittered
mate-sweet-mate.

But a beakful of mud
stained the coral pillow
and she no longer builds
her nest
up among his rafters.

The translation is from Larsen, 55.

29. *Da Ming lü jijie fuli*, 22.30a–31b, 5: 1711–14, states the general principle that a junior may not file accusations against a senior and lists the few exceptions to the rule. Of course, Yuying is not actually filing a criminal complaint against her stepmother: she is merely accusing her in a letter to the emperor.

30. The story of Dou shi can be found in *Lienü zhuan*, 9.27b. The edition I cite is a reprint of a 1779 edition, which is purportedly a reprint of a late Ming edition with illustrations by Qiu Ying. I have not located the story of Yunhua. For a discussion of the Dou sisters, see Carlitz, "Desire, Danger and the Body," 115. Carlitz points out that because the Dou sisters had been eulogized by Zhu Xi, they attained a prominent place in neo-Confucian mythology.

31. Kang-i Sun Chang, "Guide," 1–2.

32. Legge, 4: 50–51; Waley, 73. Waley no. 78; Mao no. 32. Legge's translation reads as follows:

The genial wind from the south
Blows on the heart of the jujube tree,
Till that heart looks tender and beautiful.
What toil and pain did our mother endure!
The genial wind from the south
Blows on the branches of that jujube tree,
Our mother is wise and good;
But among us there is none good.
There is the cool spring below [the city of] Tseun.
We are seven sons,
And our mother is full of pain and suffering.
The beautiful yellow birds
Give forth their pleasant notes.
We are seven sons,
And cannot compose our mother's heart.

33. *Mao shi*, 1.6b. For the Duke of Shao, see Legge, 3: 420. For more on the Duke of Shao, see Sima Qian, *juan* 34, 1549–62. Legge says that the story is from a *Lienü zhuan* biography of a woman of "Shin" who was promised in marriage to a man of Feng. His family did not provide adequate betrothal gifts, and so

she called off the wedding. They then brought a legal suit, but she refused to marry him anyway (Legge, 3: 27–28.) I still have not located the *Lienü zhuan* story. For an extended discussion of this poem, see Granet, 243–53. Granet does not accept the interpretation of traditional commentators that an actual trial is being described. However, it is very clear that that is the traditional interpretation and that is how Yuying probably read the poem.

34. The identification of this poem and the trial in the first year of the Duke of Shao is made in the *Shisan jing* edition of the Mao commentary on the poems, 4.12a. The relevant passage is in Legge, 5: 571 (Chinese text) and 578 (English trans.). The story does involve a lawsuit involving a marriage brought to the Duke of Shao, but the details of the case make it hard to see how a compelling case for its relevance to this poem could be made. The sister of Xu Wufan was betrothed to Gongsun Chu when Gongsun Hei insisted on leaving a goose at her house. The goose was a betrothal gift, and accepting it implied that the betrothal had been accepted. The young woman's brother was alarmed by the dual betrothal and consulted with Zichan, who said that the woman herself should be allowed to choose which man to marry. She chose Gongsun Chu, because she had been properly betrothed to him.

35. Waley, 65 (no. 68); Legge, 4: 27–28. Legge's translation reads:

> Wet lay the dew on the path: —
> Might I not [have walked there] in the early dawn?
> But I said there was [too] much dew on the path.
> Who can say the sparrow has no horn?
> How else could it bore through my house?
> Who can say that you did not get me betrothed?
> How else could you have urged me on this trial?
> But though you have forced me to trial,
> Your ceremonies for betrothal were not sufficient.
> Who can say that the rat has no molar teeth?
> How else could it bore through my wall?
> Who can say that you did not get me betrothed?
> How else could you have urged on this trial?
> But though you have forced me to trial,
> I will still not follow you.

36. Legge, 4: 394–95. Legge's translation of the poem is as follows:

> They buzz about, the blue flies,
> Lighting on the fences.
> O happy and courteous sovereign,
> Do not believe the slanderous speeches.
> They buzz about, the blue flies,
> Lighting on the jujube trees.
> The slanderers observe no limits,
> And throw the whole kingdom into confusion,
> They buzz about, the blue flies,

> Lighting on the hazel trees.
> The slanderers observe no limits,
> And set us two at variance.

37. *Falin zhaotianzhu*, 5.23a–25a. I am grateful to Dorothy Ko for leading me to this text.

38. Zhang Weiren, 320, says nothing is known of the author or the publisher.

39. Other minor details differ. Jiao Rong's name is written with a different character; the text of the emperor's edict soliciting the memorial is omitted; there is more careful labeling of Lady Jiao as a stepmother (*jimu*) in the casebook—in the miscellany she is often referred to simply as *mu*.

40. This edition is described in Carlitz, "Social Uses," 125.

41. I am grateful to Dorothy Ko for sharing this citation with me.

42. On illustrated editions of *Biographies of Exemplary Women*, see Carlitz, "Social Uses"; and Edgren.

43. *Libu zhigao*, 6.27a–b; cited in Soullière, 268.

44. *Guose tianxiang*, cited in Tan Zhengbi, *Sanyan Erpai ziliao*, 515.

45. Geiss, 433.

46. See Goodrich and Fang, 318; Shen Bang's *Wanshu zaji* (74) describes an episode in 1534 in which girls from the ages of 11 to 17 *sui* were recruited (cited in Soullière, 264). Shen Defu also reports that in 1550 three hundred girls age eight *sui* to fourteen *sui* were recruited, and in 1553, another 160 girls under than the age of ten were recruited (see the discussion in Xu Daling and Wang Tianyu, 232).

47. See the discussions in Wile; and Gulik.

48. "Han Xiucai cheng luan pin jiaoqi; Wu Taishou lian cai zhu yinbu," in Ling Mengchu, 1: 191–208. The panic that ensued in Zhejiang when rumors of the emperor's search spread there caused people to arrange marriages for both young girls and boys. The panic enabled the main character of the story, a penniless scholar, to marry a young woman from a well-to-do family. When the rumors were discovered to be false, the girl's family regretted the hasty marriage. Clearly Ling Mengchu is not an authoritative source on events in the Jiajing reign, although he can testify on how those events are constructed in later imaginations. It is well documented that later in the sixteenth century, rumors that agents of the emperor were searching for consorts caused panic among the populace and precipitated marriages. See the discussion by Hu Fan, 8–9.

49. See the discussion by Lienche Tu Fang in Goodrich and Fang, 318; *Ming Shizong shilu*, 27.5b–6a, 5824–25; Xu Daling and Wang Tianyu, 231–32.

50. Zhong Xing, *Mingyuan shigui*, cited in Tan Zhengbi, *Sanyan Erpai ziliao*, 514.

51. Cited in Tan Zhengbi, *Sanyan Erpai ziliao*, 517.

52. *Guangxu Shuntian fuzhi*, 8186–87. See also the account in the *Jifu tongzhi*, 7707.

53. Davis, 64.

Chapter 9

The title is inspired by Marjorie Garber's contention: "A ghost is an embodiment of the disembodied, a remembering of the dismembered, an articulation of the disarticulated and inarticulate" (15). I am deeply grateful to Stephen Owen and Charlotte Furth for advice on sources relating to this paper.

1. For instance, Anthony C. Yu observes that amorous ghosts in Chinese stories are virtually always female, just as their mortal lovers are virtually always male. He contrasts this literary imbalance in the gender of ghosts and those they encounter with modern ethnographic accounts, which report cases of women possessed by amorous male ghosts as well as the reverse (Yu, 429).

2. The Chinese term *gui* covers a wider span of meanings than the English concept "ghost" and can also mean demon or monster. This paper treats revenants (*huanhun*), the returned spirits of the dead, the most important type of *gui*.

3. See Xu Fuming, *Yuan Ming Qing xiqu tansuo*, 104–18; and idem, *Mudan ting*; Ko, *Teachers of the Inner Chambers*; Widmer, "Xiaoqing's Literary Legacy"; and Zeitlin, "Shared Dreams."

4. "The Peony Lantern" ("Mudan deng ji") in Qu You, 50.

5. "To Match a Poem by Liu, Prefect of Chai-sang" ("Chou Liu Chai-sang"), in Tao Qian, *Tao Yuanming ji*, 159; trans. Hightower, 76.

6. On the association between fox-spirits as healers in Qing popular religion and the representation of foxes as doctors in literary accounts of the period, see Rania Huntington's 1996 Harvard Ph.D. dissertation on fox-spirits in Ming and Qing literature.

7. In the first case, a man is struck by a woman in a dream and falls ill; the doctor who examines him explains: "Your pulse suddenly becomes stronger and weaker and suddenly becomes longer and shorter. This means your *qi*-vitality and blood are unequal and a heteropath *qi* is harming your proper [health]." See first entry under "Guizhu" ("Ghost affliction") in Jiang Guan, 8.242. In the second case, a virgin dreams of intercourse with a god after having seen his statue in a temple and she displays the symptoms of a false pregnancy. The doctor who examines her explains: "The girl suddenly blushes and blanches, this is a sign of shame; her pulse suddenly grows stronger and weaker: this is a sign of being haunted." See the seventh entry under "Jingshui" ("Menstruation") in Jiang Guan, 10.311. For a similar diagnosis, see Fu Shan, 4590.

8. Admittedly, the fox ends up giving the scholar mouth-to-mouth resuscitation to disseminate her revitalizing *qi* through his body. See "Jiaona" (*LZ*, 1.60) for an account of surgery performed by a female fox-doctor, which is experienced by the male patient as erotic pleasure.

9. On desire in *Liaozhai*, see Wai-yee Li, 89–151.

10. In "Xiang Yu," the ghost of a flower spirit contrasts her former state as a goddess with her present state as a ghost: "Before I was a goddess, so my

body was dense [*ning*]; now I am a ghost, so my body is diffuse [*san*]." When the mortal hero embraces her, "she feels insubstantial, as though his hand were clasping himself" (*LZ*, 11.1553).

11. The Chinese visual arts did not develop a special iconography for revenants. Occasionally, revenants are depicted in a bubble, the convention for illustrating dreams, or stepping on clouds, a common means of portraying a divinity. In most woodblock illustrations, however, a female revenant is indistinguishable from a mortal woman. See the anonymous late Ming illustrations to *The Peony Pavilion* reprinted in Tang Xianzu, *Xiqu ji*, vol. 1, for such examples.

12. Tian Pu and Cha Hongde argue that in pre-Tang accounts ghosts with grievances are forceful and inspire awe and submission; after the Tang, such ghosts are meek and evoke human sympathy. See their introduction to Mei Dingzuo, *Caigui ji*, 6.

13. For a Yuan example, see Zheng Guangzu, *Qiannü lihun*, in Gu Zhaocang, 367. For a Qing example, see Hong Sheng, *Changsheng dian*, scene 37, 190).

14. Blood is said to be "the ruling aspect in women" and becomes symbolized as female, especially when paired with male essence or vitality (*jingqi*) in models of procreation. Furth argues that Ming and Qing medical writers defined a blood-dominated female biology around symbolic poles of vitality and loss, however, rather than in terms of power and pollution, as anthropological interpretations of folk taboos surrounding female blood would suggest. Instead, Ming and Qing medical texts developed "a model of female generativity seen as a biological exchange economy that condemned women to bodily depletion and loss. . . . In the course of elaborating this model, Chinese medical experts developed stereotypes of female sickliness and emotionality" ("Blood, Body, and Gender," 44).

15. See the comment in *Qing shi*, 1: 8.224: "Thoughts of longing and yet more thoughts of longing, and one may commune with gods [*shen*] and spirits [*gui*]. For thoughts of longing arise from love and gods and spirits are but love crystallized" (trans. Wai-yee Li, 89–90).

16. *Mingyi lei'an* offers several cases classified under melancholy (*yu*) of maidens or young women who suffer from fatigue and digestive disorders, which are attributed to bottled-up grievances and thwarted desires. In one case, a betrothed maiden is unable to eat and takes to her bed after her fiancé, a merchant, postpones their marriage by staying abroad for several years. The doctor consulted on the case diagnoses her illness as "the congestion of qi due to longing. . . . Excess longing will cause qi to congest in the spleen and prevent the patient from eating" (Jiang Guan, 2.74–75). He advises trying to make her angry, but the patient only fully recovers after her fiancé's return. In another case, a maiden who has had something "go against her wishes" develops static congestion in the spleen and is unable to eat for half a year. The doctor prescribes medicine, and she recovers (ibid., 2.74). Since the case histo

ries in these books are usually meant to be examples of successful cures, all the melancholic sufferers recover.

17. On spirit marriage in Taiwan and the insatiability attributed to female ghosts, see Wolf, 148–52; and Jordan, 144–55.

18. The metaphor was originally applied to Yang Guifei emerging from the bath (*LZ*, 3.332).

19. Catherine Swatek ("Plum and Portrait," 137–38) sensitively argues that the imagery in this passage suggests the creative force of human sexual love, one of Tang's major themes in the play.

20. Fu prescribes a "ghost-pacifying tonic" (*danggui tang*) for the relief of women afflicted with these symptoms (Fu Shan, 4598).

21. *Fuke xinfa yaojue* in Wu Qian et al., 3.63. For an earlier, extended version of this argument made by a sixteenth-century physician, see de Groot, 5: 789–90.

22. As Fu Shan puts it, "Expelling the filth is of chief importance" (Fu Shan, 4589). See also under *guitai* in Wu Zhiwang, 9.349–50. The verb *xia* (excrete) is occasionally replaced by *chu* (to discharge) or *xie* (to have diarrhea).

23. My thanks to Karl Kao for his suggestion that *wei* should be translated as the "front panel of a skirt," rather than the more common "bed-curtains."

24. "Bearers' Songs" ("Wan ge"), no. 3. The funereal sound of the wind soughing in the poplar trees first appears in the *Nineteen Old Poems* (*Gushi shijiu shou*), no. 14. Prior to Tao, the poet Lu Ji wrote a funerary dirge in the voice of the deceased. On the fascination with imagining the self on the other side of death during the Six Dynasties, see Wu Hung, *Monumentality*, chap. 5.

25. This is commentator Dan Minglun's point (*LZ*, 3.331).

26. The comment is by the third wife, Qian Yi. On this edition, see Zeitlin, "Shared Dreams"; and Ko, *Teachers of the Inner Chambers*.

27. Hong Sheng, *Changsheng dian* (1919), scene 272, 6a. The commentator is Wu Wushan, a close friend of the playwright and the husband involved in the Three Wives' edition of *The Peony Pavilion*.

28. The poem is entitled "O, sadness!" ("Bei zai xing"). You Tong was responsible for preserving and publishing this friend's work, which he appended to his own literary collection. See Tang Qingmou, *Xiangzhong cao*, 2a, in You Tong.

29. The poem's complete title is "Mawei po, ni Li Changji"; see Pu Songling, *Ji*, 1: 499. For an analysis of this poem and Li He's influence on Pu Songling's poetry, see Yagi. Yagi curiously overlooks the poems in *Liaozhai* itself, although many of the ghost poems bear obvious marks of Li He's influence.

30. In "Tian Zicheng," a ghost chants this line: "A river full of wind and moon, cold and dismal" (*LZ*, 12.1628). Compare this with the line another ghost chants in "Jiaping gongzi": "Dismal wind and cold rain fill the river town" (*LZ*, 11.1588–89).

31. "Wancui ting shi," in Qian Qianyi, *Liechao shiji, runji,* 6. 7b.

32. Aside from separating heptasyllabic and pentasyllabic quatrains, Hong Mai had no obvious mode of classification or organization. Nonetheless, ghost poems are concentrated in heptasyllabic *juan* 66 and pentasyllabic *juan* 2, which both include many poems by women. Hong gives only the poem itself and not the anecdotal source that would explicitly identify the poem as ghost-written. Hiraoka et al. relied on Hong's anthology as the main source for ghost poems in *Quan Tangshi.*

33. Given the complicated textual history of this book, it is possible that a few entries were originally provided and subsequently lost. On the history of this anthology's transmission, see Sun Yingkui's introduction to Xin Wenfang, *Tang caizi zhuan jiaozhu.*

34. Not all Ming anthologies of women's verse included ghost poetry; Zhong Xing's *Poetic Retrospective of Famous Ladies* (*Mingyuan shigui*) is a prominent example of an anthology that omitted ghost poetry entirely.

35. For editions of the original *Caigui ji,* attributed to Zheng Fen of the Tang, see *Zhongguo congshu zonglu,* 2: 1110. For the microfilm of the preface to Mei, see *Guoli Beiping tushuguan,* 172. The 1989 edition of *Caigui ji* provides annotations, a useful introduction, and appendix of works Mei consulted. *Caigui ji* was intended to be part of a trilogy of poetry anthologies by supernatural authors, but the other volumes are not extant or were never compiled.

36. For the interest in spirit writing among Ming and Qing literati, see Xu Dishan; and Goyama.

37. The biographical format of *Liechao shiji* was based on Yuan Haowen's (1190–1257) anthology of Jin dynasty poets, *Zhongzhou ji,* although Yuan included neither women nor ghosts. The earliest poetry anthology to place women and monks at the end is Wei Zhuang's *Youxuan ji* (preface dated 900). But this book was lost early in China and was unknown in Ming and Qing times (see Shi Zhicun, 769). Gao Bing's early Ming anthology of Tang poetry, *Tangshi pinhui* (completed 1393), likewise incorporated women and monks at the back, but ignored supernatural authors. *Huacao cuibian* (compiled by Chen Yaowen), a late Ming compendium of song-lyrics (*ci*) with a preface dated 1583, includes women and ghost poets (along with fictional characters) but does not segregate them in separate subsections as do the biographically organized anthologies. On *Huacao cuibian,* see Hanan, *Chinese Short Story,* 166–67.

38. I am grateful to Ellen Widmer for lending me her photocopy of the edition in the Beijing University Rare Book Library. Qian Qianyi wrote a preface for *Mingyuan shiwei* and Wang Duanshu cites *Liechao shiji* as a source several times in the illusion section. On Wang Duanshu, see Widmer, "Xiaoqing's Literary Legacy"; and other chapters in this volume.

39. *Complete Poetry of the Tang* was based on two earlier collections, Hu Zhenheng's (1569–ca. 1644) *Tangyin tongqian* and a manuscript compiled by Qian Qianyi and augmented by Ji Zhenyi (*jinshi* 1647); see Nienhauser, 364–

65. Qian's manuscript included poetry by supernatural authors but did not segregate them in separate chapters; see Liu Zhaoyou, 126.

40. Lu preface dated 1758; see also Hu Wenkai, 913.

41. Wang Shizhen's account of the ghost Lin Siniang, not Pu Songling's version, is reprinted in the spirit section of *Guochao Shanzuo shichao.*

42. According to my rough calculations, the ghost chapters (*juan* 866–87) of *Quan Tangshi* break down as follows: 42 entries attributed to male ghosts or ghosts of unspecified gender and 25 attributed to female ghosts, mainly clustered at the end of the second chapter. Women are also well represented in the other supernatural subsections, and an entire chapter is devoted to female immortals.

43. See Barr, 232–33. This figure covers only stories that provide the texts of poems, not stories that cite poems by title. According to my calculations, the breakdown is six by female ghosts, four by other sorts of supernatural women, one by a courtesan, one composed jointly by a palace lady and her lover; five by mortal men, one by a male ghost, one by a thaumaturgic Daoist, and one by a planchette immortal.

44. For example, the ghost chapter of *Qing shi* (*juan* 20) has one of the heaviest concentrations of verse of any chapter in the collection. All the stories concern female revenants, most of whom compose poems, which are usually exchanged with a mortal lover.

45. Barr (189–91) suggests that the figure of Liansuo might have been modeled on the talented concubine of an official for whom Pu Songling worked for a year as a clerk in the south. Pu wrote several poems to her that touch on her gift for poetry and music. He even wrote a poem mourning her death that alludes to *The Peony Pavilion.*

46. Han Yu, "Song Meng Dongye xu," in Guo Shaoyu, 1: 443.

47. Robertson (unpublished) argues that women used such claims to portray writing as a distinctly human rather than masculine field of action, but the same argument could have also been extended to justify or explain writing by any marginal group.

48. See "A Brief Biography of the Beautiful Immortal of the Mudu River" ("Mudu xianji xiaozhuan") in *Xitang zazu*, third collection, 6.16b in You Tong.

49. A Tang poem attributed to a female ghost is entitled "Poem of Hidden Anguish" ("Youhen shi"; Cao Yin, 866.9805); another such poem is entitled "Telling Hidden Grievances" ("Shu youyuan"; ibid., 865.9782). The constellation of meanings surrounding the character *you* (hidden) is crucial throughout "Liansuo." *You* refers to darkness and the underworld, but it also connotes melancholy, loneliness, refinement, and suppressed emotion. The phrase *youqing* in the scholar's poem means the sad, concealed feelings of being a ghost, but in parallel to *youhuan* (carnal pleasure with a ghost), a phrase Liansuo herself employs, or *youhun* (spirit marriage), it also strongly suggests sexual desire.

50. See also Nie Shiqiao and Deng Kuiying, 36–41. On Pu Songling and the historical background of the Yu Qi rebellion, see Xie Guozhen, 268–72.

51. Li Shizhen (4: 52.100) cited both this legend of the statesman Chang Hong and the etiology of will-o'-the-wisps as evidence of the transformative properties of blood.

52. The first quatrain is my translation. The translation of the second quatrain is from Barr, 118.

53. For spring as a metaphor for resurrection in ghost poetry, see "Zhang Yunrong" (Cao Yin, 863.9754). In the frame story, a man makes love to three female ghosts, only one of whom is fated to become immortal. "He makes a sprig of spring bloom in the dark valley," chants the one who will revive. "Tonight's bright spring will merely turn to fall," chants one who will remain dead.

54. On the similarity between women's funeral and wedding laments in Hong Kong, see Blake; and Johnson, 136–37.

55. The story is "Shang Sanguan" (*LZ*, 3.373–75). For a discussion of this story, see Zeitlin, *Historian of the Strange*, 122–25.

56. Trans. Barr, 119.

57. Disintegration is a common motif in ghost stories, but the meaning differs. In "Wu Qiuyue," when the hero inters the ghost's corpse prior to resurrection, the corpse looks as though it were alive, but "her graveclothes disintegrate with the wind" (*LZ*, 5.671), signifying the triumph of life over death. In the Tang anecdote "Jiewei gui" (Cao Yin, 865.9778), the paper a poem is written on disintegrates as soon as the reader touches it, convincing him that the author must have been a ghost.

58. For an early Ming example, see "Visit to the Mandolin Pavilion on an Autumn Night" ("Qiuxi fang Pipating ji") in Li Zhen, *Jiandeng yuhua*, 189. This story circulated widely and was included as an example of ghost poetry in anthologies such as *Caigui ji* and *Liechao shiji*. For another example in Liaozhai, see "Lin Siniang" (*LZ*, 2.288). Early instances of a ghost vanishing like smoke appear in *Soushen ji* (Gan Bao, 16.200, no. 394) and "Pang'e" (*Taiping guangji*, 358, 2830). Du Liniang's ghost expresses a fear of vanishing like smoke; see Tang Xianzu, *Mudan ting*, scene 36, 174.

59. This point is brought out in the author's bitter comment to the story under his pseudonym Historian of the Strange (*LZ*, 4.483).

60. Mei Dingzuo's *Caigui ji* includes ten stories about the ghosts of palace ladies; the ghost section of *Qing shi* begins with a subsection entitled "Famous Ghosts of the Palace."

Chapter 10

1. But, as befitting the circumstances surrounding the record of her life, my own discovery of her poetry is also more complicated than it appears on the surface: I would like to thank Professor Chia-Ying Yeh for first calling my attention to He Shuangqing's song lyrics in Chen Tingzhuo's *Baiyuzhai cihua*, 4: 3895–97, when I was working on my paper "Engendering the Lyric: Her Image and Voice in Song" for the International Conference on Ci Poetry, June

1990, Breckinridge Center, Bowdoin College, York, Maine. For a revised version of that paper, see Yu, *Voices of the Song Lyric*, 107–44.

2. Standard modern editions of *Xiqing sanji* are the *Guoxue jiben congshu* edition (Shanghai, 1935; 2d printing, 1936); and the edition recently published by Beijing Zhongguo shudian (1987), with individual pagination for each of the four chapters (*juan*). The latter is the edition used in this paper.

3. The 1831 anthology of women poets *Guixiu zhengshi ji* by the woman compiler Yun Zhu already referred to Shuangqing by the surname "He." Yun Zhu apparently claimed *Xiqing sanji* as her source. See Zhang Gongliang, 7–8. We cannot say now whether the edition of the *Xiqing sanji* from which Yun Zhu selected the poems recorded Shuangqing's surname.

4. See Gu Jiegang, 6; Hu Shi, 3.8.683–85; and Lin Yutang, 86–90, 107–111, 328.

5. Fong, 125–33.

6. Paul Ropp, "Shi Zhenlin."

7. Including my own paper, three out of the four papers on the panel "The Female Image as Masculine Self-Reflection" concerned He Shuangqing. The other two were by scholars from China. Su Zhecong took a Chinese social-realist approach to the life of He Shuangqing and her poetry, reading them as products of feudal oppression. Kang Zhengguo considered the issue of the fictional creation of talented women as a reflection of "self" by marginalized literati, using Shi Zhenlin's *Random Records* as an example.

8. The twelfth lunar month of the second year of Qianlong corresponds to the beginning of 1738 in Western reckoning.

9. For a study of the biographies of women in local gazetteers as they relate to the social construction and application of female chastity in Southeast China, see Tien, as well as the thoughtful review by Susan Mann in the *Harvard Journal of Asiatic Studies* 52, no. 1 (1992), 362–69, which discusses and raises questions about some of the central issues of the book, such as agency and the role of Confucian and Buddhist teachings in female suicide.

10. The term *caizi jiaren* gained currency as a popular genre of sentimental romance in the sixteenth and seventeenth centuries. Shi Zhenlin certainly dispensed with the usual theme of a happy match between a beautiful young lady and a talented young scholar of the elite class. See McMahon's illuminated study of this genre from the perspective of sexuality in eighteenth-century fiction, 99–125.

11. Fong, 130–31.

12. For a discussion of *gegu* in Chinese history, see T'ien, 149–61. See also Chou Wan-yao's (Zhou Wanyao's) detailed study of women's extreme practices in moral conduct—*gegu*, widow suicide, and virginal widow chastity—in Tongcheng, Anhui, and their relationship to the influence of the moral philosophy of the Tongcheng School in the Qing.

13. See, e.g., the story of the filial daughter Hu Fangkui, who performed *gegu* three times in place of her father to cure her grandmother's illness. She died in the end (1.74–75). See also the anonymous daughter-in-law who was

asked by her husband to perform *gegu* for his father; she also died as a result (1.75).

14. This is a reference to Ming playwright Tang Xianzu's (1550–1616) famous exaltation of *qing* (love, passion) in his preface to the *Mudan ting*. For a translation and discussion, see Wai-yee Li, 50–64; see also Ko, *Teachers of the Inner Chambers*, 68–112.

15. The term is Nancy Armstrong's; see Armstrong and Tennenhouse, 1.

16. Ann Waltner's chapter on Li Yuying in this volume (see pp. 221–41) also touches on the perception in Chinese culture of danger in women's writing, especially poetry. That poetic writing is potentially damaging to feminine virtue lies in the medium's potential for self-expressiveness/exposure; thus it can act as a conduit for romantic communication. Cf. the erotic interpretation given to Li Yuying's two poems by her stepmother.

17. See Ko, *Teachers of the Inner Chambers*, for a rich and insightful examination of the contested and negotiated nature of gendered spaces in this period.

18. The question of the historicity or fictionality of Shuangqing commands continuing interest among scholars and generates considerable speculation. See the review article by Chou Wan-yao (Zhou Wanyao) on Shuangqing studies, "Xiaoshan chuanqi: He Shuangqing yanjiu zhi jiantao yu zhanwan" (*Xinshixue*, forthcoming). I wish to acknowledge Professor Chou's generosity in sharing her forthcoming article with me during my stay at the Academica Sinica. My own position regarding this question is similar to that arrived at by Professor Chou. That is, I believe there was a real rural woman with poetic talent behind the representation in the *Random Records*. But her image and story are aestheticized and subjugated to the overall design and tone of the work. We may call this process fictionalization. It is probable that Shi Zhenlin "edited" her poems in the process.

19, Gong Pengcheng, "Daodu," in Zhou Zuoren, 10. See also Liu Dajie, 3: 125–32.

20. For translations of these two works, see, respectively, Tze-yen Pan, trans., *The Reminiscences of Tung Hsiao-wan* (Shanghai: Commercial Press, 1931); and Leonard Pratt and Chiang Su-hui, trans., *Six Records of a Floating Life* (Harmondsworth, Eng.: Penguin, 1983).

21. See translations of her poetry by Paul Ropp and myself in Kang-i Sun Chang and Haun Saussy.

Chapter 11

I am grateful to Chang P'ei-tz'u, Jennifer MacFarlane, Lucia Re, Sam Weber, Yim Chi-hong, Anthony Yu, and the editors of this volume for comments and suggestions. This work was supported by a Research Fellowship in the Humanities from the Office of the President, University of California, in 1993–94.

Epigraph: Emerson, *Essays and Lectures*, 579, 722.

1. Apparently Yuan's Sui Garden was located on part of the original site of Cao's grandfather's house; see Yuan Mei, *Suiyuan shihua*, cited in Yi Su, 1: 12–13.

2. See Yee.

3. Cao Xueqin, chap. 18, 1: 250 (henceforth cited as *HLM* followed by chapter and page references). For an English translation, see Hawkes and Minford.

4. The Concubine's command to Baoyu: "Ru jin zai ge fu wuyan lü yi shou, shi wo dangmian shiguo" ("Compose a poem in five-character regulated verse on each of these four themes: I want to examine you here and now"). When Baoyu is unable to finish his second series of poems, his cousin Lin Daiyu (being a girl and not a close relative, she has not been favored with such a request) scribbles down an elegant answer, balls it up, and throws it at him. A similar story is told of Wen Tingyun (812?–70), who, having finished his essays, proceeded to write papers for several other candidates but did not pass the exam himself.

5. On this theme, see Plaks, 162–66, 187; and Stewart, esp. 20, 69.

6. For Liu's notices, see Qian Qianyi, *Liechao shiji xiaozhuan, runji*, 665–817. See Hu Wenkai, 433, for a bibliographical description and a common misprint (*guiji*, "gynecaeum collection," for *runji*, "extra collection"). See Kang-i Sun Chang's chapter in this volume, pp. 147–70, for a discussion of the extent of Liu Rushi's contributions.

7. Wang Duanshu, *Mingyuan shiwei*, 1b: "The *wei* [apocryphal texts] of antiquity were composed on the pattern of the *jing* [canonical texts], and when the canonical texts had been lost, scholars were able to restore the *jing* with the help of the *wei*." For a complete translation of this preface, see Chang and Saussy. On Wang's activities and on women's chances for publication generally, see Widmer, "Epistolary World."

8. Zhao Shijie, ed. and pref., *Gujin nüshi* (Female scribes, ancient and modern; 1628), preface in Hu Wenkai, 888–89. For a translation of the whole preface, see Chang and Saussy. Educated leisure would have been the right vocabulary to describe Zhao's product: although it merely reprinted work that had been collected earlier, the anthology was available in a fancy edition of ten *juan* and a plain one of eight (see Wang Chongmin, 453–54). On Ming leisure pursuits, see Clunas. On the enforced idleness of most late-Ming degree seekers, see the statistics in Ho, 32–34, 107–11, 184.

9. The speaking Stone, in chap. 1, castigates the authors of generically indistinguishable "scholar and beauty" novels who, "merely wanting to copy out their own two or three little love poems, fabricate names for the male and female leads" and insert them into a story (*HLM*, 1: 5).

10. Hawkes and Minford, 1: 448; *HLM* 22, 1: 313–14.

11. Zhiyanzhai, general comment to chap. 22. My translation somewhat overstates the original: "deng mi qiao yin chen yan." See Yu Pingbo, 306, and also 320–21.

12. Yuanwei mingjingshi zhuren, "Shitou ji fen ping," in *Xiangyan congshu,* series 14, 2.41a.

13. Fu Yuan, "Qiu lan pian," in Xu Ling, 2.13a. "Your lowly concubine" is confusing unless annotated: *qie* often occurs as a polite term of self-reference used by a proper wife.

14. Gao Shuang, "Yong jing," in Xu Ling, 5.15b.

15. In praise of a mirror stand: Xie Tiao, "Za yong wu shou: jing tai," in Xu Ling, 4.16a–b. The phrasing of that poem alludes to descriptions of palaces in *fu* poetry of the Han period, thus permitting a courtly levity in the description of this small and intimate object.

16. Liu Xiaoyi, "Yong shilian," in Xu Ling, 10.22b. "Stone" is a surname and, with a different pronunciation, a measure of weight. A "stone lotus" is an edible lotus seed, dark outside and white inside, that survives frost; see Li Shizhen, 3: 622–33. As an epithet for things related to the Buddha, "lotus" connotes supernatural power, in particular power over death; *lian* also puns on another word meaning "infatuation." A "stone *lian*" is then a rebus for "enduring love."

17. "Gongting shi de zishu" (The redemption of palace-style poetry; 1940), in Wen Yiduo, 3: 12–13. I have somewhat condensed the last sentence. Wen's condemnation of palace-style poetry for its "perversity" seems to me to draw on Marx's theory of commodity fetishism and Freud's account of hysteria, both well known to Wen.

18. On the semantic polarity "person"–"thing" as a major structural principle of the *Hong lou meng,* see Haun Saussy, "Reading and Folly in *Dream of the Red Chamber,*" CLEAR 9 (1987): 38–39.

19. The locus classicus for this idea is Laura Mulvey's "Visual Pleasure and Narrative Cinema."

20. Ban Jieyu, "Yuan xing," in Xu Ling, 1.14b–15a (also included under her name in Xuan Tong, 27.17a). "I always fear," in Xie Tiao's poem cited above, directly quotes from Ban Jieyu.

21. On the poetics of restraint and "indirect admonition" (*jue jian*), see the "Great Preface" to the *Mao shi* (*The Book of Odes* as edited by Master Mao). The "Preface" in its present form may postdate Ban Jieyu, but much of its content is traditional. See also *Xunzi,* "Zheng ming" (Wang Xianqian, 283): "The noble man is reserved yet visible, subtle but plain. He demurs and yields, but conquers."

22. See Ban Jieyu's biography in *Han shu* (History of the Former Han dynasty), 97b, "Wai qi zhuan," where this *fu* is reproduced in its entirety (Ban Gu, 3985–87).

23. HLM 51; 2: 706–10. On the development of the subgenre of "Poems Remembering the Past" (*huaigu shi*), see Owen.

24. HLM 50; 2: 701. On the motif of desire for a pictured woman, see chap. 5 (1: 71).

25. HLM 50, 2: 697.

26. Ruan Yuan, ed., *Mao shi zhushu*, in *Shisanjing zhushu*, 1: 5.2a–b. The text of the *Shijing* preferred by the Han school wrote *mei* differently, making the character for "plum" closely resemble that for "marriage broker" (also *mei*).

27. Common knowledge; but see also Hui Zhouti, *Shi shuo* (Explanations of the *Odes*), in Ruan Yuan, *Huang Qing jingjie*, 191.2a–b.

28. An oft-cited example is that of Feng Xiaoqing, hounded to an early death by the jealous main wife of the man who had taken her as a concubine. "When Xiaoqing was but ten years old, she met an old nun who wanted to teach her the Heart Sutra. Xiaoqing read it several times through and then recited it from beginning to end without dropping a word. The old nun said: 'This child is sensitive and brilliant, but I am sorry to say her luck will be poor'" (Yanshui sanren, 2). On Xiaoqing's story in its many fictional, dramatic, and poetic versions, see Widmer, "Xiaoqing's Literary Legacy."

29. Tu Ying, "*Hong lou meng* lun zan," in Yi Su, 1: 128.

30. Compare Hawkes's translations, *Stone* 2: 512–14, and his annotations, 588–94.

31. Wang Mengruan, 745–46, "Liyan," i, "Tiyao," 1.

32. Liu Genglu, 273, 275, 278–80.

33. Cai Yijiang, 259–65.

34. How can a character be the author's equal in knowledge? For many readers, Baoqin lives on a different plane from the other characters of the novel: see, e.g., Jie'an jushi, "Shitou yishuo" (in Yi Su, 1: 196), Qingshan shannong, "*Hong lou meng* guang yi" (ibid., 212), Hong Qiufan, "*Hong lou meng* jue yin" (ibid., 240).

35. "Xi furen," "Ban Jieyu san shou," in Wang Wei, 252–53.

36. Li Bai, "Ju chan" (Beware of flatterers), in Cao Yin, 3: 1876; "Chang xin gong" (The Palace of Lasting Trust), in ibid., 3: 1880.

37. [Liao] Yi De huanghou, "Huai gu," in Su Zhecong, 243. On the unfortunate Yi De, forced to commit suicide on suspicion of adultery, see Chen Yan, 2.4a–6b. A later Liao dynasty imperial concubine, Wenji, also left a poem on history (ibid., 2.7a).

38. Zhu Jing'an, "Yu Ji," in Su Zhecong, 289.

39. Sima Qian, *Shiji*, 7.

40. Xu Yuan, "Chong diao Sun furen," in Zheng Guangyi, 1310.

41. "Yongshi," 4, in Xu Can, 1.2a–b.

42. Shi Chong, "Wang Zhaojun," in Guo Maoqian, 2: 426.

43. For an example of a courtesan writing poems on history, see Maureen Robertson's chapter in this volume, pp. 171–217.

44. Zhi Ruzeng, *Nü zhong caizi lanke er ji* (The second Orchid Slope anthology: seven talented woman scholars; early 17th c.), preface; reprinted in Hu Wenkai, 845–46. For a translation of the whole preface, see Chang and Saussy.

Chapter 12

1. "[Vanitas] changed the title of the book from *The Story of the Stone* to *The Tale of Brother Amor*. Old Kong Meixi from the homeland of Confucius called the book *A Mirror for the Romantic*. Wu Yufeng called it *A Dream of Golden Days*. Cao Xueqin in his Nostalgia Studio worked on it for ten years in the course of which he rewrote it no less than five times, dividing it into chapters, composing chapter headings, renaming it *The Twelve Beauties of Jinling*, and adding an introductory quatrain" (Hawkes and Minford, 1: 51).

2. For the symbolism of the gate, see Wu, "Transparent Stone."

3. For the origin and the political symbolism of this architectural design, see Wu, "From Temple to Tomb"; and idem, "Tiananmen Square."

4. Cao Xueqin called these offices *peidian* (flanking halls), which certainly implies a central hall.

5. Nie Chongzheng, a scholar in Beijing's Palace Museum and an authority on Qing court painting, believes that some principal images in the murals, such as cranes and animals, must have been by Castiglione himself. Since Castiglione died before Qianlong rebuilt the Complex of the Peaceful Longevities, Nie further suggests that these murals, which were painted on silk mounted on walls, may have been removed from an earlier building. It is known that Castiglione had created some illusionistic wall paintings for Qianlong. It is possible that the emperor, a great supporter of Castiglione's art, would have relocated them to the palace where he spent his last years (Nie, "Architectural Decoration").

6. For Wei Yong's life and publications, see Yong Rong, 1129; Zhang Huijian, 571, 661. One of his compilations is *Secrets in a Pillow* (*Zhenzhong mi*), which includes "Delight in Adornment." I thank Judith Zeitlin and Ma T'ai-lai of the University of Chicago for providing me with these sources.

7. For illustrations, see *Zhongguo gudai shuhua tumu*, vol. 4, Hu 1-2057; vol. 7, Su 24-0707.

8. Li Suiqiu lived during the late Ming and early Qing. Some of his activities are recorded in Zhang Huijian, 550, 571.

9. The book is also known as *A Collection of Talented Women* (*Nücaizi ji*), *Beautiful Stories of Young Maidens* (*Guixiu jiahua*), *A Supplement to "History of Love"* (*Qingshi xuzhuan*). Xu Zhen frequently used the title Meiren shu in the book and also subtitled the book's preface "A Register of Beauties" ("Meiren pu"). For the date of the book, see *Zhongguo tongsu xiaoshuo zongmu tiyao*, 330–31. According to Zhong Fei, this book must have been completed, or nearly completed, by 1659. It was probably first published during the Shunzhi or Kangxi period and was reprinted during the Qianlong and Daoguang periods.

10. These twelve main characters of the book are (1) Xiaoqing, (2) Yang Biqiu, (3) Zhang Xiaolian, (4) Cui Shu, (5) Zhang Wanxiang, (6) Chen Xiaru, (7) Lu Yunqing, (8) Hao Xiang'e, (9) Wang Yan, (10) Xie Cai, (11) Zheng Yuji,

and (12) Song Wan. Five other women, Li Xiu, Zhang Lizhen, Yujuan, Xiaoying, and Shen Bitao, are attached to four individual chapters.

11. This album is in the Shanghai Art Museum; for the illustrations, see *Zhongguo gudai shuhua tumu*, vol. 4, Hu 1-2821.

12. Entitled "Stories of Virtuous Queens of the Successive Dynasties" ("Lidai xianhou gushi tu"), this album is in Beijing's Palace Museum and is reproduced in Palace Museum, *Gugong bowuyuan*, pl. 2.

13. This album is reproduced in Palace Museum, *Gugong bowuyuan*, pl. 1. Hongli or the future Qianlong emperor received the title Prince Bao in 1733. This album, therefore, must have been made after this date. Although most books introduce Jiao Bingzhen as a court painter active in the Kangxi period, he must have continued to serve in theYongzheng emperor's court. In addition to the album, a portrait of Zhang Detian in the Beijing Administration of Cultural Relics (dated to 1726) was made by Jiao Bingzhen during the Yongzheng reign. See Liu Wanlang, 146.

14. For a brief discussion of the "linear method," see Nie Chongzhen, "Xianfahua xiaokao." For a brief introduction to Jiao Binzhen and his activities, see Rosenzweig, 149–67; Yang Boda, *Qingdai yuanhua*.

15. Qianlong must have greatly enjoyed this album. He not only twice stamped its pages with his various seals, but also personally ordered it copied as a set of ivory carvings. See Museum Boymans–van Beuningen Rotterdam, 160-61.

16. For a brief biography of Su Zhikun, see Luo Kehan, 894. I thank Ma Tai-lai for providing me with this and other biographical references.

17. I thank Yang Chengbin and Shi Yuchun, two former colleagues and members of the Palace Museum's Painting and Calligraphy Division, who recalled the 1950 inventory in our private conversations in 1993.

18. After their rediscovery, these paintings were mounted as hanging scrolls.

19. Yongzheng's poetry collection contains some fifty poems related to the Yuanming yuan; three of them are specifically about the Reading Hall Deep Inside Weeping Willows. He wrote on other sites in the garden only once or twice. See Zhu Jiajin and Li Yanqin.

20. We should note, however, that a female figure "matched" with bamboo is not unique to this painting. An earlier example is a Song painting in the collection of Beijing's Palace Museum (Palace Museum, *Lidai shinühua xuanji*, pl. 9).

21. Among the sons of the Kangxi emperor, Yinzhen was well-known for his imitations of ancient calligraphy; see Feng Erkang, 10.

22. James Cahill, lectures on female images in later Chinese painting, delivered at the University of Southem Califomia in 1994. I thank him for providing me not only with his lecture drafts but also with materials he prepared for a course on Chinese paintings of women at U. C. Berkeley.

23. Paper delivered at the symposium Genres in Chinese Painting at the

College Art Association meeting in Houston, Feb. 1988. I thank her for providing me with a copy of this paper.

24. Cahill, lectures on female images in later Chinese painting.

25. I thank Cahill for this suggestion in a private conversation. Cahill discussed Zhang Zhen and one of his portrayals of a beautiful woman in his lecture "Painting in Semi-westernized Styles by Urban-professional Artists of 18th-century China," delivered on Nov. 7, 1994, at Princeton University.

26. Such beautiful-women pictures were created in the Qing court under the patronage of many emperors. For examples, see Palace Museum, *Gugong bowuyuan*.

27. The pleasure industry in some southern cities did not recover fully until the late years of Qianlong, long after the creation of Yinzhen's "Screen of Twelve Beauties"; see Wang Shunu, 256.

28. This policy is asserted in the "Edict of the Ninth Year of Jiaqing," in Qing Jiaqing shilu (Vertitable records of the Jiaqing reign): "In the selection of women for service in the palace, they must dress in Manchu-style clothes. If they dress in opulent and lavish Han attire, this constitutes a serious breach. This prohibition shall be rigorously made clear to all Banner members, in order to eschew lavishness and respect economy"; cited in Shan Guoqiang, 58.

29. For a more detailed discussion of this painting and related examples, see Wu, "Emperor's Masquerade."

30. In a poem describing the courtesan Du Qiuniang, the Tang poet Du Mu wrote: "Qiu is drunk—with a jade wine bottle in her hand. / What can she offer you?—the "Gown of Gold Threads." He then included the song lyrics in a note.

31. A well-known example is Emperor Wu of the Western Han, who built a huge garden near the capital Chang'an to imitate immortal islands and heavenly palaces; see Wu, *Monumentality*, chap. 3, "The Monumental City Chang'an."

32. This princely palace was turned into the Lamaist temple Yonghe Gong after Yinzhen ascended the throne.

33. These poems include "Shenliu dushutang xiaoxia" (Passing the summer in the Reading Hall Deep Inside Weeping Willows) and "Shenliu Dushutang bishu" (Avoiding summer heat in the Reading Hall Deep Inside Weeping Willows), both in "Siyitang ji" (Writings from the Siyi Hall), in *Qingshizong yuzhi wenji, juan* 30. As the titles of these later works suggest, in the poems the Reading Hall is presented straightforwardly as a summer resort.

34. Much debate has been centered on the dates of Cao Xueqin's birth and death. According to one opinion, he died in 1763 when he was "in his forties." This makes it highly probable that he was born in 1714 or 1715. When Yongzheng wrote the edict about the Screen of Twelve Beauties, Cao Xueqin would have therefore been seventeen or eighteen.

Chapter 13

Research for this project was sponsored by grants from the Committee on Scholarly Communication with China, funded by USIA, and from the American Council of Learned Societies. I am grateful to Judith Zeitlin, Haun Saussy, Kang-i Sun Chang, Wai-yee Li, and John Ziemer for reading drafts of the manuscript and providing helpful suggestions. Patrick Hanan and Ting-ting Chi also provided assistance on specific points.

1. See Zhao Botao. For a discussion of Gu's many names, see Hu Wenkai, 800.

2. For biographical information on Wang Duanshu, see Hu Wenkai, 248–50; Zhong Huiling, 278–95; Yu Jianhua, 121; Zou Siyi; and Deng Hanyi.

3. Wang Duanshu, *Yinhong ji*, biography section.

4. See, e.g., Zhang, 315, for a biography of a Nanjing beggar, which appears in the biography section of *Yinhong ji*. A note there expresses Wang's pleasure that Zhang published this and others of her biographies.

5. The drinking with Wu Shan is described in a poem by Wang to Wu; see *Yinhong ji*, seven-word regulated verse, *shang*, 12a–b.

6. The matching of wits is described in Yu Jianhua, 121. For Qian Qianyi's comment, see his preface to Wang Duanshu, *Mingyuan shiwei*. For the comment on wittiness, see Deng Hanyi.

7. Hanan, *Li Yu*, 18.

8. I used the edition in the Beijing University Library.

9. See Wang Duanshu, *Mingyuan shiwei*, "Fanli."

10. For the date 1700, see Zhang Huijian, 924.

11. Contemporary library catalogues list a few other examples in the intervening 163 years, but these works appear not to have circulated far or been widely known. Indeed even the few that can be found were compiled no more than one generation after Wang Duanshu. See, e.g., Gui Shifen's *Gujin mingyuan baihua shiyu* of 1685 (Hu Wenkai, 784).

12. See note 22 below.

13. On Hou, see Hu Wenkai, 411. Hou was considerably older than Wang. She was close to certain of Yuan Mei's disciples, such as Jiang Zhu; Wang was close to others, such as Xi Peilan.

14. Despite *tanci*'s irregular publishing history, they were of great interest to women readers throughout the Qing. Even if, as is sometimes claimed, the early Qing *Tian yu hua*'s author was Xu Zhihe, a man and not a woman, he is said to have written it to entertain his mother (see Xiong Deji). For more on *Tian yu hua*, see Zheng Zhenduo, 370–72; Toyoko Yoshida Chen, 52–177; and Hu Siao-chen.

15. On Ai ri tang, see Wang Chongmin, 9.

16. Among Wang Duan's literary accomplices, Cao Zhenxiu was another who associated with non-Chinese. Her husband, Wang Qisun (1755–1818), was a close acquaintance of a Mongol, Fa-shi-shan (1753–1813), and

she herself wrote a preface to the works of a Manchu woman, Rui-tai-fu-qin (see Hu Wenkai, 817).

17. See, e.g., Luo Qilan's preface to her collection *Ting qiu guan guizhong tongren ji,* cited in Hu Wenkai, 939–40. Luo spoke of being persecuted for her interest in poetry. Only when she found Yuan and other mentors was she reassured about her intent to write. Support by Yuan and others of like mind also took the practical turn of publishing women's writings and engaging them in editorial projects, as with Chen Wenshu's study of Hangzhou women, *Xiling guiyong.* Yuan's and Chen's libraries, further, were important resources for women interested in earlier generations of writers.

18. See Chen Wenshu's biography at the beginning of Wang Duan, *Ziran haoxue zhai ji.*

19. For biographical information on Wang Duan, see Hu Wenkai, 357; Zhong Huiling, 363–89 *et passim;* Chen Wenshu's biography at the beginning of Wang Duan, *Ziran haoxue zhai ji,* as well as in the other prefaces to that collection; and Hummel, 839–40.

20. On the duration of the project, see Chen Wenshu's biography, in Wang Duan, *Ziran haoxue zhai ji,* 2b. The list of proofreaders includes Sun Yunfeng, Xi Peilan, Gui Maoyi, and Qu Bingyun—all disciples of Yuan—as well as a woman named Wang Qiong who once refused to become Yuan's student.

21. Of course, by the 1830's, Qian Qianyi's currency was not high because he had served two dynasties. It should also be noted that Wang Duan's standard of poetical judgment has antecedents in those of Yuan Mei. See Zhong Huiling, 252–78, on Wang Duanshu's close critical connections to Qian Qianyi and Wang Duan's to Yuan Mei.

22. See Chen Wenshu's biography, in Wang Duan, *Ziran haoxue zhai ji,* 5a.

23. Sun Kaidi, 216–17.

24. Mote, 21–25.

25. Wang Duan, *Ziran haoxue zhai ji,* 3.7b, 8b; 4.6a, 7a; 5.1a; 7.12b, 13a, 18a, 19a. This interest in earlier women poets was not always loyalist in nature, since it also attached itself to women like Lu Qingzi and the Korean Xu Jingfan, both of whose work came too early to have been loyalist, strictly speaking. The female loyalist general Qin Liangyu, who was not a writer, was another stimulus for Ming loyalist commentary in Wang Duan's poetry.

26. See Wang Duan, *Ziran haoxue zhai ji,* 3.22a, in which Wang wrote to Gui: "In a former life you were Huang Jieling; nearing old age to express your sorrows you consign them to poetry."

27. Hummel, 103–4.

28. For a reference to Wang's collection, see Chen Wenshu, *Lan yin ji.*

29. It appears at the beginning of Liang's collected works, *Guchun xuan shichao,* 1847. See also Hu Wenkai, 544.

30. See Zheng Zhenduo, 372. See also Chen Yinke, "Lun *Zai sheng yuan.*"

31. See Gui Maoyi, 4.9b–10a. The poem is entitled "On *Zai sheng yuan chuanqi.*" The poem refers to the heroine's marriage, as in the final stanza:

> *Zai sheng yuan* ends up resolving the problems of this life
> And forging a conjugal alliance of gold and stone.
> The moon naturally completes its cycle, two flowers unite in love,
> In reality, can things turn out so well?

Its reference to the marriage is the way one associates it with Liang's revised version of the text.

32. See Tan Zhengbi, *Zhongguo nüxing wenxue*, 374.

33. Cf. the preface to Wang Duan, *Ziran haoxue zhai ji*, 5a; and Tan Zhengbi, *Zhongguo nüxing wenxue*, 388.

34. Chen's biography says *Yuan Ming yishi* was 80 *juan* long, but this is probably a misprint for 18; see Jiang Ruizao, 37.

35. See Wang Duan, *Ziran haoxue zhai ji*, 4.14b–19a. For "Zhang Wu jishi shi" and "Yuan yichen shi," see ibid., 6.12a–18b and 7:5a–12b, respectively.

36. The biography of Miss Jin refers to a work by Chen Wenshu on the same subject, entitled "Jin ji shilüe," which was culled from unofficial histories. It turns out that this work, which appears in Chen's *Yidao tang wenchao* (10.12a–15b), is identical to Wang Duan's work on Miss Jin, except for the addition of a short passage at the end. More work is needed to clarify the relation between these two texts.

37. See, e.g., Armstrong, 30.

38. I have benefited from David Schaberg's comments in an unpublished paper entitled "Bisexuality in *The Dream of the Red Chamber.*"

39. This is certainly not to suggest that members of Wang Duan's circle were the only women to respond to *Hong lou meng*. One early response dates to 1774, almost twenty years before both the publication of the novel and Wang Duan's birth. It is found in the work of one Miss Chen (Chen shi), a Manchu, and appears in her collection *Bingxue tang shi* (Hu Wenkai, 608; Yi Su, 457). An 1842 edition of *Bingxue tang shi* is part of the collection of the Palace Museum Library, Beijing. I am indebted to Wu Hung for helping me gain admission to this library.

40. See Hu Wenkai, 630.

41. See chap. 38 of *Hong lou meng*, and chap. 28 of the pseudonymous Xiao yao zi's *Hou Hong lou meng*.

42. Entitled *Shier chai* (Twelve beauties), it is preserved in a collection of dramas whose subject is *Hong lou meng* (see Xu Fuming, *Yuan Ming Qing*, 280).

43. The daughter is named Gao Yifeng. The notice about her appears in section 20.

44. The poem is referred to but not translated in David Hawkes's article on Xi Peilan, another disciple of Yuan (see his "Hsi P'ei-lan"). It is found in Yuan Mei, *Suiyuan nüdizi shi*, 2.3a. I appreciate Ch'iu-t'i Judy Liu's help with the poetry translations.

45. Qian Shoupu, 39a.

46. Zhou Qi wrote a preface to the works of Yuan Hua, one of Yuan Mei's descendants, on which see Hu Wenkai, 491. Her own work appears in a collection edited by Chen, entitled *Bicheng xianguan nüdizi shi*. Chen edited several editions under this title. The one containing Zhou's work is dated 1842; a copy is held in the Suzhou Library. Qian Shoupu's collected poetry has a preface by Yuan Shou, on whom see Hu Wenkai, 493. Her membership in Chen's circle is well known. Her colophon appears on Chen Peizhi's memoir to his deceased concubine, Miss Wang, "Xiangwan lou yiyu," on which see Hummel, 840.

47. Gai Qi.

48. See Zhou Qi.

49. Ibid.

50. H. C. Chang (415) dates these congratulatory poems to between 1829 and 1830. However, the poems appear in the 1828 edition held in the Beijing Library. Those by women number four, not three, as Chang states. In addition to the three Chang mentions on p. 420, there is one by Jin Ruolan. For more on Jin, see Hu Wenkai, 405.

51. Reprinted in many editions, such as that held in the Academy of Social Sciences Library in Beijing.

52. C. T. Hsia ("Scholar-Novelist," 276 and elsewhere) talks about how old-fashioned *Jinghua yuan* seems to Chinese today.

53. Ironically, the case that her work might have been a *tanci* is undercut by the probability that she was actually serious about revising history. "Women's *tanci*" are not known for their seriousness in this regard.

54. See Hu Siao-chen for trenchant analysis of such commentaries.

55. Hu Siao-chen's dissertation shows how they touched, but only obliquely, on these themes; see, e.g., 168–232.

56. Tan Zhengbi, *Zhongguo nüxing wenxue*, 373–38. His other example is *Zhexian lou*, a novel by Chen Yichen published in 1890, which does not survive.

57. Xu Fuming, *Yuan Ming Qing*, 270–72.

58. Sun Kaidi, 122.

59. Zhao Botao, 245–46; Liang Yizhen, 259.

60. Zhao Botao, 249. See Shen's accounts of Wang and Yun in her *Mingyuan shihua* of 1846; see *juan* 6 (Wang) and 8 (Yun). Yun's granddaughter Wanyan Foyunbao was one of the editors of *Mingyuan shihua*.

61. Liang Yizhen, 259.

62. Wang Duan, *Ziran haoxue zhai ji*, 10.32a; see also Liang Yizhen, 260.

63. Zhao Botao, 247.

64. On Shen's death, see Zhao Botao, 249.

65. It is cited in part in Huang Lin and Han Tongwen, 614–65, with the criticism that the fiction itself does not live up to the principles articulated in the preface. David Rolston (88) also cites it for its use of the term "zhu nao" (key), which derives from Li Yu.

66. Zhao Botao, 248. Zhao argues the date of death on the basis that a woman could not have published a novel with a commercial firm while she was living. But cf. Hou Zhi's publication of the *tanci Zai sheng yuan*, which took place well before she died. Hou's preface to *Jin gui jie* (preface dated 1822), her sequel to *Zai sheng yuan*, makes this clear.

67. I do not yet know whether the publishing house in question had undergone any "Western influence" in 1877.

68. Zhao Botao, 250. See also Huang Lin and Han Tongwen, 614–15.

69. Zhao Botao, 250.

70. For a definition of this term, see Robertson, "Voicing the Feminine."

71. For Shen's *Mingyuan shihua*, see note 62. *Hong lou meng ying*'s posthumous publication and the general tone of secrecy about its authorship would certainly have deterred Gu's friends from adding complimentary comments, one frequent way in which a text's special appeal to women is discerned.

72. See p. 408 of this volume.

Works Cited

Adachibara Yatsuka 足立原八束. "*Sanka to Kashiji*" 山歌と挂枝兒, *Gakuen* (Shōwa joshi daigaku Kōkakai) 15, no. 2 (1953).

Anderson, Benedict. *Imagined Communities: Reflections on the Origin and Spread of Nationalism*. London: Verso, 1991.

Arlington, L. C., and Lewisohn, William. *In Search of Old Peking*. Reprinted — Oxford: Oxford University Press, 1987.

Armstrong, Nancy. *Desire and Domestic Fiction*. New York: Oxford University Press, 1987.

———. "Reclassifying Clarissa: The Making of the Modern Middle Class." In *The Clarissa Project*, vol. 16, *The Critical Controversy — New Commentaries*, ed. Edward Copeland and Carol Houlihan Flynn. New York: AMS, 1996.

Armstrong, Nancy, and Leonard Tennenhouse, eds. *The Ideology of Conduct: Essays on Literature and the History of Sexuality*. New York: Methuen, 1987.

Atwell, William. "From Education to Politics: The Fu She." In *The Unfolding of Neo-Confucianism*, ed. Wm. Theodore De Bary, 333–68. New York: Columbia University Press, 1975.

Austin, J. L. *How to Do Things with Words*. Cambridge, Mass.: Harvard University Press, 1962.

Bakhtin, Mikhail. *Problems of Dostoyevsky's Poetics*. Trans. and ed. Caryl Emerson. Minneapolis: University of Minnesota Press, 1984.

Ban Gu 班固, comp. *Han shu* 漢書. Beijing: Zhonghua shuju, 1962.

Bao Zhilan 鮑之蘭. *Qiyunge shichao* 起雲閣詩鈔. 1798. In *Jingjiang Baoshi san nüshi shichao* 京江鮑氏三女士詩鈔. N.p., 1882. Copy in the Harvard-Yenching Library.

Barr, Allan. "Pu Songling and *Liaozhai zhiyi*: A Study of Textual Transmission, Biographical Background, and Literary Antecedents." Ph.D. diss., Oxford University, 1983.

Berliner, Nancy. "Wang Tingna and Illustrated Book Publishing in Huizhou." *Orientations* 25, no. 1 (1994): 67–75.

Birch, Cyril, trans. *The Peony Pavilion*. Bloomington: Indiana University Press, 1980.

Birrell, Anne, trans. *New Songs from a Jade Terrace*. London: Allen & Unwin, 1982.

Blake, C. Fred. "Death and Abuse in Chinese Marriage Laments: The Curse of Chinese Brides." *Asian Folklore Studies* 37, no. 1 (1978): 3–33.

Bloom, Harold. *A Map of Misreading*. New York: Oxford University Press, 1975.

Borer, Mark. "Yuan Mei and Zhang Xuecheng on the Education of Women." Seminar paper, Yale University, 1991.

Brant, Clare, and Diana Purkiss. *Women, Texts, and Histories, 1575–1760*. London: Routledge & Kegan Paul, 1992.

Bryant, Daniel. "Syntax, Sound, and Sentiment in Old Nanking: Wang Shih-chen's 'Miscellaneous Poems on the Ch'in-huai.'" *Chinese Literature: Essays, Articles, Reviews* 14 (Dec. 1992): 25–50.

Butler, Judith. *Gender Trouble: Feminism and the Subversion of Identity*. New York: Routledge, 1990.

Cai Dianqi 蔡殿齊, comp. *Guochao guige shichao* 國朝閨閣詩鈔. 10 vols. N.p.: Langhuan bieguan cangshu, 1844. Copy in the Harvard-Yenching Library. *Xubian* 續編 in 2 vols., 1874.

Cai Yi 蔡毅, ed. *Zhongguo gudian xiqu xuba huibian* 中國古典戲曲序跋彙編. Ji'nan: Qilu shushe, 1989.

Cai Yijiang 蔡義江. *"Hong lou meng" shiciqufu pingzhu* 紅樓夢詩詞曲賦評注. Beijing: Beijing chubanshe, 1984.

Cao Dazhang 曹大章. "Liantai xianhui pin" 蓮臺仙會品. In *Shuofu xu* 說郛續, comp. Tao Ting 陶珽. Qing ed. Copy in the Naikaku bunko.

———. "Qinhuai shinü biao" 秦淮士女表. In *Shuofu xu* 說郛續, comp. Tao Ting 陶珽. Qing ed. Copy in the Naikaku bunko.

Cao Xueqin 曹雪芹, supplemented by Gao E 高鶚. *Hong lou meng* 紅樓夢. Beijing: Renmin wenxue chubanshe, 1972. 1982.

Cao Yin 曹寅, ed. *Quan Tangshi* 全唐詩. Taibei: Wenshizhe chubanshe, 1985. Beijing: Zhonghua shuju, 1960 (1707).

Carlitz, Katherine. "Desire, Danger, and the Body: Stories of Women's Virtue in Late Ming China." In *Engendering China: Women, Culture, and the State*, ed. Christina K. Gilmartin, Gail Hershatter, Lisa Rofel, and Tyrene White, 101–24. Cambridge, Mass.: Harvard University Press, 1994.

———. *The Rhetoric of "Chin p'ing mei."* Bloomington: Indiana University Press, 1986.

———. "The Role of Drama in the *Chin p'ing mei*." Ph.D. diss., University of Chicago, 1978.

———. "The Social Uses of Female Virtue in Late Ming Editions of *Lienü zhuan*." *Late Imperial China* 12, no. 2 (Dec. 1991): 117–48.

Carrington, Goodrich L., and Fang Chaoyang. *Dictionary of Ming Biography*. 2 vols. New York: Columbia University Press, 1976.

Chang, H. C. *Chinese Literature: Popular Fiction and Drama*. New York: Columbia University Press, 1973.

Chang, Kang-i Sun. "A Guide to Ming Ch'ing Anthologies of Women's Poetry and Their Selection Strategies." *Gest Library Journal* 5, no. 2 (1992): 119–60.

———. "The Idea of the Mask in Wu Wei-yeh (1609–1671)." *Harvard Journal of Asiatic Studies* 48, no. 2 (1988): 289–320.

———. *The Late Ming Poet Ch'en Tzu-lung: Crises of Love and Loyalism*. New Haven: Yale University Press, 1991.

———. "Liu Shih and Hsü Ts'an: Feminine or Feminist?" In *Voice of the Song Lyric in China*, ed. Pauline Yu, 169–87. Berkeley: University of California Press, 1994.

———. "Ming-Qing Women Poets and the Notions of 'Talent' and 'Morality.'" In *Culture and State in Chinese History: Conventions, Conflicts, and Accommodations*, ed. R. Bin Wong, Theodore Huters, and Pauline Yu. Stanford: Stanford University Press, forthcoming.

Chang, Kang-i Sun, and Haun Saussy, eds. *Chinese Women Poets: An Anthology of Poetry and Criticism from Ancient Times to 1911*. Stanford: Stanford University Press, forthcoming.

Chartier, Roger. "The Practical Impact of Writing." In *A History of Private Life*, vol. 3, *Passions of the Renaissance*, ed. Roger Chartier; trans. Arthur Goldhammer, 111–65. Cambridge, Mass.: Harvard University Press, 1989.

Chen Dongyuan 陳東原. *Zhongguo funü shenghuo shi* 中國婦女生活史. Taibei: Shangwu yinshuguan, 1990 (1937).

Chen Duansheng 陳端生; supplemented by Liang Desheng 梁德繩. *Zai sheng yuan* 再生緣. Henan: Zhongzhou shuhua she, 1982.

Chen Juanjuan 陳娟娟. "Qing dai fushi yishu, 1" 清代服飾藝術, 1. *Gugong bowuyuan yuankan* 1994, no. 2 : 81–96.

Chen Peizhi 陳裴之. *Xiangwanlou yiyu* 香畹樓憶語. 1824. In *Guizhong yiyu wuzhong* 閨中憶語五種, comp. Tu Yuanji 涂元濟. Beijing: Zhongguo guangbo dianshi chubanshe, 1993.

Chen Qinian 陳其年. *Furen ji* 婦人集. In *Hongxiu tianxiang shi congshu* 紅袖添香室叢書. Shanghai: Shanghai qunxueshe, 1936.

Chen shi 陳氏 (Guizhen daoren 歸眞道人). *Bingxue tang shi* 冰雪堂詩. 1774. Copy in Palace Museum Library, Beijing.

Chen Tingzhuo 陳廷焯. *Baiyuzhai cihua* 白雨齋詞話. Cihua congbian ed. Beijing: Zhonghua shuju, 1986.

Chen, Toyoko Yoshida. "Women in Confucian Society: A Study of Three T'an-t'zu Narratives." Ph.D. diss., Columbia University, 1974.

Chen Wenshu 陳文述. *Bicheng xianguan nüdizi shi* 碧城仙館女弟子詩. 1842.

———. "Lan yin ji" 蘭因集. In *Wulin Zhanggu congbian* 武林掌故叢編, ed. Ding Bing 丁丙, 4: 2220–45. Reprint of 1882 ed. Taibei: Tailian, n.d.

———. *Xiling guiyong* 西泠閨詠. 1827.

———. *Yidao tang wenchao* 頤道堂文鈔. 1828. Copy in Seikado bunko, Tokyo.

Chen Yan 陳衍. *Liao shi ji shi* 遼詩記事. In *Lidai shishi changbian* 歷代詩史長編, ed. Yang Jialuo 楊家駱, vol. 11. Taibei: Dingwen, 1979.

Chen Yaowen 陳耀文, comp. *Huacao cuibian* 花草粹編. From a draft by Wu Cheng'en 吳承恩. Facsimile of Ming ed. Beijing, 1933 (preface dated 1583).

Chen Yinke 陳寅恪. *Hanliu tang ji* 寒柳堂集. Shanghai: Shanghai guji chubanshe, 1980.

———. *Liu Rushi biezhuan* 柳如是別傳. 3 vols. Shanghai: Shanghai guji chubanshe, 1980.

———. "*Lun Zai sheng yuan*" 論再生緣. In *Guoxue mingzhu zhenben huikan* 國學名著 珍本彙刊, ed. Yang Jialuo 楊家駱, 1-25. Taibei: Tingwen, 1975.

Chen Yujiao 陳與郊. *Ying wu zhou* 鸚鵡洲. In *Gu ben xiqu congkan* 古本戲曲叢刊, 2d series. Shanghai: Shangwu yinshuguan, 1955. Facsimile of Ming dynasty Wanli era (1573-1620) ed. published by Chen Yujiao.

Chen Zilong 陳子龍. *Chen Zilong shiji* 陳子龍詩集. Ed. by Shi Zhicun 施蟄存and Ma Zuxi 馬祖熙. Shanghai: Shanghai guji chubanshe, 1983.

Chen Ziming 陳自明. *Furen daquan liangfang* 婦人大全良方. Taibei: Shangwu yinshuguan, n.d. (photoreprint of Wenyuange siku quanshu ed., vol. 14).

Chiang, William Wei. "'We Two Know the Script: We Have Become Friends.' Linguistic and Social Aspects of the Women's Script Literacy in Southern Hunan, China." Ph.D. diss., Yale University, 1991.

Chow, Rey. *Women and Chinese Modernity: The Politics of Reading Between West and East*. Minneapolis: University of Minnesota Press, 1991.

Chu Hung-lam. "The Authorship of the Story *Chung-ch'ing li-chi*." *Asia Major*, 3d series, 1, no. 1 (Jan. 1988): 71-82.

Chu Jiaxuan 褚稼軒. *Jianhu ji* 堅瓠集. 66 *juan*. In *Biji xiaoshuo daguan* 筆記小說大觀, ser. 2, vol. 23. Reprinted—Taibei: Xinxing shuju, 1978.

Clunas, Craig. *Superfluous Things: Material Culture and Social Status in Early Modern China*. Cambridge, Eng.: Polity Press; Urbana and Chicago: University of Illinois Press, 1991.

Da Ming lü jijie fuli 大明律集解附例. Taibei: Chengwen, 1969.

Davidoff, Leonore, and Catherine Hall. *Family Fortunes: Men and Women of the English Middle Class, 1780-1850*. Chicago: University of Chicago, 1987.

Davis, Natalie Zemon. *Fiction in the Archives: Pardon Tales and Their Tellers in Sixteenth-Century France*. Stanford: Stanford University Press, 1987.

De Groot, J. J. M. *The Religious System of China*. Vol. 5. Reprinted—Taibei: Ch'eng-wen, 1969.

Deng Hanyi 鄧漢儀, comp. *Tianxia mingjia shiguan chuji* 天下名家詩觀初集. Preface dated 1672. Copy in Naikaku bunko, Tokyo.

Derrida, Jacques. *Of Grammatology.* Trans. Gayatri Chakravorty Spivak. Baltimore: Johns Hopkins University Press, 1976.

Douglas, Ann. *The Feminization of American Culture.* New York: Avon, 1977.

Du Fu 杜甫. *Du Gongbu shiji* 杜工部詩集. Sibu beiyao ed. Taibei: Zhonghua shuju, 1976.

Ebrey, Patricia Buckley. *The Inner Quarters: Marriage and the Lives of Chinese Women in the Sung Period.* Berkeley: University of California Press, 1993.

Edgren, Sören. "The *Ching-ying hsiao-shuo* and Traditional Illustrated Biographies of Women." *Gest Library Journal* 5, no. 2 (Winter 1992): 161–74.

Elman, Benjamin. "Political, Social, and Cultural Reproduction in Civil Service Examinations in Late Imperial China." *Journal of Asian Studies* 50, no. 1 (1991): 7–28.

Elvin, Mark. "Female Virtue and the State in China." *Past and Present* 104 (1984): 111–52.

Emerson, Ralph Waldo. *Essay and Lectures.* Ed. Joel Porte. New York: Library of America, 1983.

Falin zhaotianzhu 法林照天燭. Ming ed. held at the Library of Congress.

Feng Erkang 馮爾康. *Yongzheng zhuan* 雍正傳. Beijing: Renmin chubanshe, 1985.

Feng Qiyong 馮其庸 and Li Xifan 李希凡, eds. *Hong lou meng dacidian* 紅樓夢大辭典. Beijing: Wenhua yishu chubanshe, 1990.

Feng Ruzong 馮汝宗. *Nü fan bian* 女范編. Ming ed. held at the National Central Library, Taiwan.

Fenli tahangzhe 芬利他行者. *Zhuxi huashi xiaolu* 竹西花事小錄. In *Xiangyan congshu* 香艷叢書, vol. 12. Shanghai: Guoxue fulun she, 1914.

Fisher, Carney. *The Chosen One: Succession and Adoption in the Court of Ming Shizong.* Boston: Allen & Unwin, 1990.

Fong, Grace S. "Engendering the Lyric: Her Image and Voice in Song." In *Voices of the Song Lyric in China,* ed. Pauline Yu, 107–44. Berkeley: University of California Press, 1994.

Foucault, Michel. *The History of Sexuality: An Introduction.* Trans. Robert Hurley. New York: Vintage, 1978.

Fraistat, Neil. *Poems in Their Place: The Intertexuality and Order of Poetic Collections.* Chapel Hill: University of North Carolina Press, 1986.

Fu Shan 傅山. *(Fu Qingzhu) nüke/nanke/erke* (傅青主) 女科 / 男科 / 兒科. Taiyuan: Shanxi renmin chubanshe, 1992.

Furth, Charlotte. "Blood, Body, and Gender: Medical Images of the Female Condition in China, 1600–1850." *Chinese Science* 7 (1986): 43–66.

———. "Poetry and Women's Culture in Late Imperial China: Editor's Introduction." *Late Imperial China* 13, no. 1 (1992): 1–9.

Gai Qi 改琦. *Hong lou meng tu yong* 紅樓夢圖詠. 1879.

Gan Bao 干寶. *Soushen ji* 搜神記. Ed. Hu Huaichen 胡懷琛. Taibei: Dingwen shuju, 1978. Ed. Wang Shaoying 汪紹楹. Beijing: Zhonghua shuju, 1979.

Gao Yinxian 高銀仙 and Yi Nianhua 義年華. *Nüshu* 女書. Ed. Gong Zhebin 宮哲兵. Taibei: Funü xinzhi jijinhui, 1991.

Garber, Marjorie. *Shakespeare's Ghost Writers*. New York: Methuen, 1987.

Geiss, James. "The Cheng-te Reign." In *The Cambridge History of China*, vol. 7, pt. 1, *The Ming*, ed. Frederick W. Mote and Denis Twitchett, 440–510. New York: Cambrige University Press, 1988.

Gerstlacher, Anna, ed. *Women and Literature in China*. Bochum, Ger.: Brockmeyer, 1988.

Gilbert, Sandra, and Susan Gubar. *The Madwoman in the Attic: The Woman Writer and the Nineteenth-Century Literary Imagination*. New Haven: Yale University Press, 1979.

Goldman, Andrea S. "Gazing at Stamen, Romanticizing Flowers: Towards a Re-evaluation of the Social Construction of Sexuality and Gender as Seen Through Late Eighteenth- and Nineteenth-Century Flower Register Writings on Opera in Beijing." Paper presented at the Annual Meeting of the Association for Asian Studies, Boston, Mar. 23–27, 1994.

Goodrich, L. Carrington, and Chaoying Fang, eds. *Dictionary of Ming Biography*. 2 vols. New York: Columbia University Press, 1976.

Goyama Kiwamu 合山究. "Min-Shin no bunjin to okaruto no shumi" 明清の文人とオカルトの趣味. In *Chūka bunjin no seikatsu* 中華文人の生活, ed. Arai Ken 荒井健. Toyko: Heibonsha, 1994.

Graham, A. C. *Poems of the Late T'ang*. Harmondsworth, Eng.: Penguin, 1965.

Granet, Marcel. *Festivals and Songs of Ancient China*. New York: E. P. Dutton, 1932.

Gronewald, Sue. *Beautiful Merchandise: Prostitution in China, 1860–1936*. New York: Haworth Press, 1982.

Grundy, Isobel, and Susan Wiseman. *Women, Writing, History, 1640–1740*. London: B. T. Batsford, 1992.

Gu ben xiqu congcan 古本戲曲叢刊. 2d series. Shanghai: Shangwu yinshuguan, 1955.

Gu Jiegang 顧頡剛. "Shuangqing (dushu zaji)" 雙卿 (讀書雜記). *Xiaoshuo yuebao* 15, no. 11 (1924): 6.

Gu Ruopu 顧若璞. *Woyue xuan gao* 臥月軒稿. In *Wulin wangzhe yizhu* 武林往哲遺著, comp. Ding Bing 丁丙. Qiantang: Dingshi jiahuitang, 1900 (1887, 1626).

Gu Zhaocang 顧肇倉, ed. *Yuanren zaju xuan* 元人雜劇選. Beijing: Renmin wenxue chubanshe, 1978.

Guangxu Shuntian fuzhi 光緒順天府志. Taibei: Wenhai chubanshe, 1965.

Gui Maoyi 歸懋儀. *Xiuyu xucao* 繡餘續草. 1823. Copy in Harvard-Yenching Library.

Gui Youguang 歸有光 (1507–71). *Zhenchuan xiansheng ji* 震川先生集. Shanghai: Guji chubanshe, 1981.

Gujin tushu jicheng 古今圖書集成. Shanghai: Zhonghua shuju, 1934.

Gulik, Robert Hans van. *Sexual Life in Ancient China*. Leiden: E. J. Brill, 1974 (1961).

Guo Aichun 郭靄春 et al., comps. *Huangdi neijing cidian* 黃帝內經詞典. Tianjin: Tianjin kexue jishu chubanshu, 1991.

Guo Maoqian 郭茂倩, ed. *Yuefu shiji* 樂府詩集. Taibei: Zhonghua shuju, 1961 (1341). Beijing: Zhonghua shuju, 1979.

Guo Shaoyu 郭紹虞, ed. *Zhongguo lidai wenxue lun* 中國歷代文學論. Hong Kong: Zhonghua shuju, 1979.

(*Guoli Beiping tushuguan*) *shanben shumu* (國立北平圖書館)善本書目. Taibei: Guoli zhongyang tushuguan, 1969.

Hanan, Patrick D. *The Chinese Short Story: Studies in Dating, Authorship and Composition.* Cambridge, Mass.: Harvard University Press, 1973.

————. *The Chinese Vernacular Story.* Cambridge, Mass.: Harvard University Press, 1981.

————. *The Invention of Li Yu.* Cambridge, Mass.: Harvard University Press, 1988.

Hanyu dacidian 漢語大辭典. 12 vols. Shanghai: Cishu chubanshe, 1986–94.

Harris, Wendell V. "Canonicity." *PMLA* 106, no. 1 (1991): 110–21.

Hartman, Heidi. "The Unhappy Marriage of Marxism and Feminism: Towards a More Progressive Union." In *The Unhappy Marriage of Marxism and Feminism: A Debate on Class and Patriarchy*, ed. Lydia Sargent, 1–42. London: Pluto, 1981.

Hawkes, David. "Hsi P'ei-lan." *Asia Major* 7, no. 1–2 (1959): 113–21.

Hawkes, David, and John Minford, trans. *The Story of the Stone*, by Cao Xueqin. 5 vols. Harmondsworth, Eng.: Penguin Books, 1973–86.

He Liangjun 何良俊. *Yu lin* 語林. Shanghai: Guji chubanshe, 1982.

Hightower, James R., trans. *The Poetry of T'ao Ch'ien.* London: Oxford University Press, 1970.

Hiraoka Takeo 平岡武夫 et al. *Tōdai no shihen* 唐代の詩篇. Tang Civilization Reference Series, 11–12. Kyoto: Jinbun kagaku kenkyūjo, 1964–65.

Ho Ping-ti. *The Ladder of Success in Imperial China: Aspects of Social Mobility, 1368–1911.* New York: Columbia University Press, 1962.

Ho, Virgil Kit-yiu. "Selling Smiles in Canton: Prostitution in the Early Republic." *East Asian History* 5 (June 1993): 101–32.

Hobsbawm, Eric, and Terence Ranger. *The Invention of Tradition.* Cambridge, Eng.: Cambridge University Press, 1983.

Hong Mai 洪邁. *Wanshou Tangren jueju* 萬首唐人絕句. Beijing: Wenxue guji kanxingshe, 1955 (1192). Photoreprint of Ming ed.

Hong Sheng 洪昇. *Changsheng dian* 長生殿. In *Nuanhong shi huike chuanqi* 暖紅室彙刻傳奇, comp. Liu Shiheng 劉世珩, no. 25. 1919 (1705).

————. *Changsheng dian* 長生殿. Ed. Xu Shuofang 徐朔方. Beijing: Renmin wenxue chubanshe, 1986.

Hongmeige zhuren 紅梅閣主人 and Qinghuilou zhuren 清暉樓主人, comps. *Qingdai guixiu shichao* 清代閨秀詩鈔. Shanghai: Zhonghua xinjiaoyu she, 1922.

Hou Fangyu 侯方域. *Zhuanghui tang ji* 壯悔堂集. Shanghai: Shangwu yinshuguan, 1937.

Hou Zhi 侯芝. *Jin gui jie* 金閨傑. 1822. Copy in Qinghua University Library.

Hsia, C. T. "The Scholar-Novelist and Chinese Culture: A Reappraisal of *Ching-hua Yuan*." In *Chinese Narrative: Critical and Theoretical Essays*, ed. Andrew Plaks, 266–305. Princeton: Princeton University Press, 1977.

———. "Time and the Human Condition in the Plays of T'ang Hsien-tsu." In *Self and Society in Ming Thought*, ed. William de Bary, 249–90. New York: Columbia University Press, 1970.

Hu Fan. "Lun Mingdai de xuan xiunü zhi zhi" 論明代的選秀女之制. Paper presented at the Sixth International Conference on Ming History, Fengyang, Aug. 1995.

Hu Mingyang 胡明揚. "Sanbai wushinian qian Suzhou yidai Wuyu yiban: *Shan'ge* he *Guazhier* suo jian de Wuyu" 三百五十年前蘇州一帶吳語一斑:「山歌」和「掛枝兒」所見的吳語. *Yuwen yanjiu* 1981: 2.

Hu Shi 胡適. *Hu Shi wencun* 胡適文存. Taibei: Yuandong tushu gongsi, 1953.

Hu Siao-chen. "Literary *Tanci*: A Woman's Tradition of Narrative in Verse." Ph.D diss., Harvard University, 1994.

Hu Wenkai 胡文楷. *Lidai funü zhuzuo kao* 歷代婦女著作考. Rev. ed. Shanghai: Guji chubanshe, 1985.

Hu Ying. "Angling with Beauty: Two Stories of Women as Narrative Bait in *Sanguo zhi yanyi*." *Chinese Literature: Essays, Articles, Reviews* 15 (Dec. 1993): 99–112.

Hua Guangsheng 華廣生, comp. and ed. *Baixue yiyin* 白雪遺音. 4 *juan*. Shanghai: Zhonghua shuju, 1959 (1828).

Huang Chang 黃裳. *Fu xuan lu* 負暄錄. Hunan: Renmin chubanshe, 1986.

Huang Lin 黃霖 and Han Tongwen 韓同文, eds. *Zhongguo lidai xiaoshuo lunzhu xuan* 中國歷代小說論著選. Nanchang: Jiangxi renmin chubanshe, 1982.

Huang Miaozi 黃苗子. "Yongzheng fei huaxiang" 雍正妃畫像. *Zijincheng* 1983, no. 4: 28–34.

Huang, Ray. *Taxation in Sixteenth-Century Ming China*. Cambridge, Eng.: Cambridge University Press, 1974.

Huang Shangwen 黃尚文. *Gui fan* 閨範. Microfilm of Ming ed. held at the Library of Congress.

Huang Xuesuo 黃雪簑. *Qinglou ji* 青樓集. In *Xiangyan congshu* 香艷叢書, vol. 5. Shanghai: Guoxue fulun she, 1914.

Huang Zongxi 黃宗羲. "Li Yin zhuan" 李因傳. Nanlei wen'an, zhuan zhang ji 南雷文案撰杖集. Sibu congkan ed., 1.17a–18a.

Hucker, Charles. *A Dictionary of Official Titles in China*. Stanford: Stanford University Press, 1985.

Hui tu Lienü zhuan 繪圖列女傳. N.d., but illustration style places it 1610–20. Beijing Library has *juan* 3–14 of Ming dynasty Zhen cheng tang 貞誠堂 ed. An edition in 16 *juan*, missing some of the Zhen cheng tang commentary, was reprinted by the Zhi bu zu zhai 知不足齋 in 1779. A facsimile of the Zhi bu zu zhai ed. reprinted in Taiwan by Zhengchong shuju in 1971 is widely available in U.S. libraries.

Hummel, Arthur. *Eminent Chinese of the Ch'ing Period*. Taibei: Ch'eng-wen, 1967 (1943).

Hunt, Lynn. "The Unstable Boundaries of the French Revolution." In *The History of Private Life*, vol. 4, *From the Fires of Revolution to the Great War*, ed. Michelle Perrot; trans. Arthur Goldhammer, 13–45. Cambridge, Mass.: Harvard University Press, 1990.

Idema, Wilt. *The Dramatic Oeuvre of Chu You-tun (1379–1439)*. Leiden: E. J. Brill, 1985.

Ji Yougong 計有功. *Tangshi jishi* 唐詩紀事. Taibei: Zhonghua shuju, 1970 (1224).

Ji Yun 紀昀. *Siku quanshu zongmu tiyao* 四庫全書總目提要. 5 vols. Taibei: Shangwu yinshuguan, 1971.

Jiang Guan 江瓘. *Mingyi lei'an* 名醫類案. Taibei: Hongye shuju, 1971 (1591). Reprint of Qianlong ed. redacted by Wei Zhixiu 魏之琇.

Jiang Jingqi 蔣景祁. *Yaohua ji* 瑤華集. Beijing: Zhonghua shuju, 1982. Facsimile reproduction.

Jiang Ruizao 蔣瑞藻. *Xiaoshuo kaozheng xubian* 小說考證續編. Shanghai: Shangwu yinshuguan, 1922.

Jifu tongzhi 畿輔通誌. Taibei: Huawen shuju, 1968 (1910).

Jiu Tang shu 舊唐書. Comp. Liu Xu 劉昫 (887–946).

Johnson, Elizabeth L. "Funeral Laments of Hakka Women." In *Death Ritual in Late Imperial and Modern China*, ed. James L. Watson and Evelyn Rawski, 135–60. Berkeley: University of California Press, 1988.

Jones, Ann Rosalind. *The Currency of Eros: Women's Love Lyrics in Europe, 1540–1620*. Bloomington: University of Indiana Press, 1990.

Jordan, David. *Gods, Ghosts, and Ancestors*. Berkeley: University of California Press, 1972.

Kahn, Harold. "Drawing Conclusions: Illustration and the Pre-history of Mass Culture." In *Excursions in Reading History: Three Studies*. Taibei: Academia Sinica, Institute of Modern History, 1993.

Kang Zhengguo 康正果. "Bianyuan wenren de cainü qingjie ji qi suo chuanda de shiyi: *Xiqing sanji* chutan" 邊緣文人的才女情結及其所傳達的詩意－西青散記初探. Paper presented at the Conference on Women and Literature in Ming-Qing China, Yale University, June 22–26, 1993.

———. *Fengsao yu yanqing* 風騷與艷情. Henan: Renmin chubanshe, 1988.

Knechtges, David R., trans. *Wen xuan, or Selections of Refined Literature*. Princeton: Princeton University Press, 1982.

Ko, Dorothy. "Lady Scholars at the Door: The Practice of Gender Relations in Eighteenth-Century Suzhou." In *Boundaries in China*, ed. John Hay. London: Reaktion Books, 1994.

———. "Pursuing Talent and Virtue: Education and Gentry Women's Culture in Seventeenth and Eighteenth-Century Jiangnan." *Late Imperial China* 13, no. 1 (June 1992): 9–39.

———. *Teachers of the Inner Chambers: Women and Culture in Seventeenth-Century China.* Stanford: Stanford University Press, 1994.

———. "Toward a Social History of Women in Seventeenth-Century China." Ph.D. diss., Stanford University, 1989.

Kong Shangren 孔尚任. *Kong Shangren shi he "Taohua shan"* 孔尚任詩和桃花扇. Ed. Liu Yeqiu 劉業秋. Henan: Zhongzhou shuhuashe, 1982.

Kong Yingda 孔穎達, comm. *Maoshi zhengyi* 毛詩正義. Sibu beiyao ed. Taibei: Zhonghua shuju, 1966.

Laing, Ellen Johnston. "Chinese Palace-Style Poetry and the Depiction of a Palace Lady." *Art Bulletin* 72, no. 2 (June 1990): 284–95.

Larsen, Jeanne. *Brocade River Poems: Selected Works of the Tang Dynasty Courtesan Xue Tao.* Princeton: Princeton University Press, 1987.

Legge, James. *The Chinese Classics*, vol. 3, *The Shoo King*; vol. 4, *The She King*; and vol. 5, *The Ch'un Ts'ew with the Tso Chuen.* Hong Kong: Hong Kong University Press, 1960.

"Letter from the New Editors." *Late Imperial China* 6, no. 1 (June 1985).

Lévy, André. *Inventaire analytique et critique du conte Chinois en langue vulgaire.* Paris: Collège de France, 1978.

Li Bo 李白. *Li Taibo shiji* 李太白詩集. Sibu beiyao ed. Taibei: Zhonghua shuju, 1966.

Li He 李賀. *Li He shiji* 李賀詩集. Ed. Ye Congqi 葉蔥奇. Beijing: Renmin wenxue chubanshe, 1959.

———. *Sanjia pingzhu Li Changji geshi* 三家評注李長吉歌詩. Shanghai: Zhonghua shuju, 1959.

Li Hu 酈琥. *Tongguan yibian* 彤管遺編. Late Ming ed.; in the Beijing Library.

Li Kaixian 李開先. *Li Kaixian ji* 李開先集. Ed. Lu Gong 路工. Beijing: Zhonghua shuju, 1959.

Li Ning 李寧. "Lun Feng Menglong de *Shan'ge*" 論馮夢龍的「山歌」. *Minjian wenyi jikan* 1986, no. 1.

Li Ping 李平. "Feng Menglong yu Mingdai min'ge" 馮夢龍與明代民歌. *Minjian wenyi jikan* 1982, no. 3.

Li Ruzhen 李汝珍. *Xiuxiang Jinghua yuan* 繡像鏡花緣. N.p.: Jiezi yuan, 1828.

Li Shizhen 李時珍. *Bencao gangmu* 本草綱目. Beijing: Zhongguo shuju, 1988 (1593). Reprint of 1930 Shangwu yinshuguan ed.

Li Suiqiu 黎遂球, "Huadi shiyi" 花底拾遺. In *Xiangyan congshu* 香艷叢書, 1: 8.

Li, Wai-yee. *Enchantment and Disenchantment: Love and Illusion in Chinese Literature.* Princeton: Princeton University Press, 1993.

Li Xu 李詡. *Jie'an laoren manbi* 戒庵老人漫筆. In *Yuan Ming shiliao congkan* 元明史料叢刊. Beijing: Zhonghua shuju, 1982.

Li Yu 李漁. *Fuyun lou* 拂雲樓. In *Shier lou* 十二樓. Reprinted—Beijing: Renmin wenxue chubanshe, 1986.

Li Zhen 李禎. *Jiandeng yuhua* 剪燈餘話. In *Jiandeng xinhua wai erzhong* 剪燈新話外二重, ed. Zhou Yi 周夷. Shanghai: Shanghai guji, 1981 (ca. 1420).

————. "Tianshu yu Xue Tao lian ju ji" 田洙與薛濤聯句記. In his *Jian deng yu hua* 剪燈餘話, originally published in 1420. In *Jian deng xin hua wai er zhong* 剪燈新話外二種, ed. Zhou Yi 周夷, 179–88. Shanghai: Gudian wenxue chubanshe, 1957.

Liang Desheng 梁德繩. *Guchun xuan shichao* 古春軒詩鈔. 1847.

Liang Yizhen 梁乙眞. *Qingdai funü wenxue shi* 清代婦女文學史. Taibei: Zhonghua shuju, 1958.

Lienü zhuan 列女傳. Tokyo: Omura Seigai, 1923–26. Reprint of a 1779 ed. that purports to be a reprint of a late Ming ed.

Lin, Yutang. *The Importance of Understanding.* Cleveland and New York: World Publishing, 1960.

Ling Mengchu 凌濛初. *Pai'an jingqi* 拍案驚奇. Hong Kong: Union Press, 1966.

Liu Daijie 劉大杰. *Zhongguo wenxue fazhanshi* 中國文學發展史. Hong Kong: Xuelin youxian gongsi, 1979.

Liu Dalin 劉達臨. *Zhongguo gudai xingwenhua* 中國古代性文化. Ningxia: Ningxia renmin chubanshe, 1993.

Liu Genglu 劉耕路. *"Hong lou meng" shici jiexi* 紅樓夢詩詞解析. Jilin: Wen-shi chubanshe, 1986.

Liu Ke 劉柯. *Guizhou shaoshu minzu fengqing* 貴州少數民族風情. N.p.: Yun-nan minzu chubanshe, 1989.

Liu Mengxi 劉夢溪. "Yishi zhengshi, jiezhuan xiushi, shiyun shixin" 以詩證史借傳修史韻詩心. In *Zhongguo wenhua* 3 (1990): 99–111.

Liu Shi 柳是 and Qian Qianyi 錢謙益, eds. *Juan* 4 of "Runji" 閏集. In Qian Qianyi.

Liu Shide 劉世德, comp. *Zhongguo gudai xiaoshuo baike quanshu* 中國古代小說百科全書. Beijing: Zhongguo dabaike quanshu chubanshe, 1993.

Liu Wanlang 劉萬朗, comp. *Zhongguo shuhua cidian* 中國書畫辭典. Beijing: Huawen chubanshe, 1990.

Liu Wu-chi and Irving Lo, eds. *Sunflower Splendor: Three Thousand Years of Chinese Poetry.* Garden City, N.Y.: Doubleday, 1975.

Liu Xiang 劉向, comp. *Lienü zhuan* 列女傳. Sibu beiyao ed. Taibei: Zhonghua shuju, 1987.

Liu Yunfen 劉雲份, comp. *Cuilou ji* 翠樓集. Shanghai: Zazhi gongsi, 1936 (1673). Modern punctuated ed. by Shi Zhicun 施蟄存.

Liu Zhaoyou 劉兆祐. "Yuding *Quan Tangshi* yu Qian Qianyi Ji Zhenyi diji Tangshi gaoben guanxi tanwei" 御定全唐詩與錢謙益、季振宜遞輯唐詩稿本關係探微. *Youshi xuezhi* 15 (1978): 101–36.

Lo, Irving Yucheng, and William Schultz, eds. *Waiting for the Unicorn: Poems and Lyrics of China's Last Dynasty, 1644–1911.* Bloomington: Indiana University Press, 1986.

Long Muxun 龍沐勛. *Jin sanbai nian mingjia cixuan* 近三百年名家詞選. Hong Kong: Zhonghua shuju, 1979.

Lowry, Kathryn. "Feng Menglong's Prefaces on Currently Popular Songs." *Papers in Chinese History* (Harvard University, Fairbank Center) 2 (Spring 1993): 94–119.

Lu Chang. *Lichao mingyuan shi ci* 歷朝名媛詩詞. 1773.

Lu Jianzeng 盧見曾. *Guochao Shanzuo shichao* 國朝山左詩鈔. Preface dated 1758; Qing ed. in Harvard-Yenching Library.

Lü Kun 呂坤 (1536–1618). *Gui fan* 閨範. 1618 Huizhou ed.

———. *Shen yin yu* 呻吟語. Taibei: Hele tushu chubanshe, 1974.

Lu Qingzi 陸卿子. *Kaopan ji* 考槃集. N.p., 1600.

———. *Xuanzhi ji* 玄芝集. N.p., preface dated 1610.

Lu Qinli 逯欽 立, ed. *Xian-Qin Han Wei Jin Nanbeichao shi* 先秦漢魏晉南北朝詩. Taibei: Muduo chubanshe, 1981.

Lu Yilu, *Feng Menglong suoji min'ge yanjiu* 馮夢龍所集民歌研究. Taibei: Xuehai, 1988.

Luo Kehan 羅克涵. *Shaxian zhi* 沙縣志. Taibei: Chengwen chubanshe, 1975.

Mann, Susan. " 'Fuxue' (Women's Learning) by Zhang Xuecheng (1738–1801): China's First History of Women's Culture." *Late Imperial China* 13, no. 1 (June 1992): 40–62.

———. "Grooming a Daughter for Marriage: Brides and Wives in the Mid-Ch'ing Period." In *Marriage and Inequality in Chinese Society*, ed. Rubie S. Watson and Patricia Buckley Ebrey. Berkeley: University of California Press, 1991.

———. *Women in Eighteenth-Century China: Gender and Culture in the Lower Yangzi Region, 1683–1839*. Stanford: Stanford University Press, 1997.

Mao Guangsheng 冒廣生. *Mao Heting ciqu lunwen ji* 冒鶴亭詞曲論文集. Shanghai: Shanghai guji chubanshe, 1992.

Mao Kun 茅坤, attrib. *Quanxiang gujin Lienü zhuan* 全像古今列女傳. Copy of Ming Zhengde ed. at Harvard-Yenching Library.

Mao shi 毛詩. Sibu beiyao ed.

Mao Xiang 冒襄. *Yingmei an yiyu* 影梅庵憶語. In *Meihua wenxue mingzhu congkan* 美化文學名著叢刊, ed. by Zhu Jianmang 朱劍芒. Shanghai: Shanghai shudian, 1982.

Marotti, Arthur F. " 'Love Is Not Love': Elizabethan Sonnet Sequences and the Social Order." *ELH* 49 (1982): 396–428.

Mayne, Judith. *Cinema and Spectatorship*. London and New York: Routledge, 1993.

McCoy, John. "The Linguistic and Literary Value of the Ming Dynasty 'Mountain Songs.' " *Journal of the Hong Kong Branch of the Royal Asiatic Society* 9 (1969).

McKnight, Brian. *The Quality of Mercy: Amnesties and Traditional Chinese Justice*. Honolulu: University of Hawaii Press, 1981.

McMahon, Keith. *Misers, Shrews, and Polygamists: Sexuality and Male-Female Relations in Eighteenth-Century Chinese Fiction*. Durham, N.C.: Duke University Press, 1995.

Mei Dingzuo 梅鼎祚. *Caigui ji* 才鬼記. Author's preface dated 1605; microfilm of late Ming edition in Harvard-Yenching Library.

———. *Caigui ji* 才鬼記. Edited by Tian Pu 田璞 and Cha Hongde 查洪德. Zhengzhou: Zhengzhou guji chubanshe, 1989.

Mei Yusheng 梅禹生 (Mei Dingzuo 梅鼎祚). *Qingni lianhua ji* 青泥蓮花記. 13 *juan*. Reprinted in *Zhongguo jindai xiaoshuo shiliao huibian* 中國近代小說史料彙編, vol. 12. Taibei: Guangwen shuju, 1981.

Miao Lianbao 妙蓮保, ed. *Guochao guixiu zhengshi ji xuji* 國朝閨秀正始集續集. 1863.

Miller, J. Hillis. "Parable and Performative." In idem, *Tropes, Parables, Performatives: Essays on Twentieth Century Literature.* New York: Harvester Wheatsheaf, 1990.

Milou ji 迷樓記. In *Hongxiu tianxiang shi congshu* 紅袖添香室 叢書. Shanghai: Shanghai qunxue she, 1936.

Mingshi zong 明詩綜. Taibei: Shijie shuju, 1961.

Ming Shizong shilu 明世宗實錄. Taibei: Academia Sinica, 1965.

Mote, F. W. *The Poet Kao Ch'i.* Princeton: Princeton University Press, 1962.

Mulvey, Laura. "Visual Pleasure and Narrative Cinema." *Screen* 16, no. 3 (1975): 6–18.

Museum Boymans–van Beuningen Rotterdam. *De Verboden Stad.* Rotterdam, 1990.

Nie Chongzheng. "Architectural Decoration in the Forbidden City: Trompe-l'oeil Murals in the Lodge of Retiring from Hard Work," *Orientations* 26, no. 7 (July/Aug. 1995): 51–55.

———. 聶崇正. "Xianfahua xiaokao" 線法畫小考. *Gugong bowuyuan yuankan* 1983, no. 3: 85–88.

Nie Shiqiao 聶石樵 and Deng Kuiying 鄧魁英. *Gudai xiaoshuo xiqu luncong* 古代小說戲曲論叢. Beijing: Zhonghua shuju, 1985.

Nienhauser, William, Jr., ed. and comp. *The Indiana Companion to Traditional Chinese Literature.* Bloomington: Indiana University Press, 1986.

Ōki Yasushi 大木康. "Fū Muryū Jo *Sanka* kō: Shikyō gaku to minkan kayō" 馮夢龍「敘山歌」考:詩經學と民間歌謠. *Tōyō bunka* 71 (1990): 121–45.

———. "Fū Muryū *Sanka* no kenkyū" 馮夢龍「山歌」の研究. *Tōyō bunka kenkyūjo kiyō* 105 (1988): 57–241.

———. "Fū Muryū to gijo" 馮夢龍と妓女. *Hiroshima daigaku bungakubu kiyō* 48 (1989): 71–91.

———. "Zokkyokushū *Kashiji* ni tsuite: Fū Muryū *Sanka* no kenkyū hosetsu" 俗曲集「掛枝兒」について:馮夢龍「山歌」の研究補說. *Tōyō bunka kenkyūjo kiyō* 107 (1988).

Owen, Stephen. "Place: Meditation on the Past at Chin-ling." *Harvard Journal of Asiatic Studies* 50, no. 2 (1990): 417–57.

Palace Museum. *Gugong Bowuyuan cang Qing dai gongting huihua* 故宮博物院藏清代宮廷繪畫. Beijing: Wenwu chubanshe, 1993.

———. *Lidai shinühua xuanji* 歷代士女畫選集. Tianjin: Renmin meishu chubanshe, 1981.

Peng Huasheng 捧花生. *Huafang yutan* 畫舫餘談. Preface dated 1818. In *Xiangyan congshu* 香艷叢書, vol. 18. Shanghai: Guoxue fulun she, 1914.

Peterson, Willard J. *Bitter Gourd: Fang I-chih and the Impetus for Intellectual Change.* New Haven: Yale University Press, 1979.

Plaks, Andrew. *Archetype and Allegory in "Dream of the Red Chamber."* Princeton: Princeton University Press, 1976.

Poovey, Mary. *The Proper Lady and the Woman Writer: Ideology as Style in the Works of Mary Wollstonecraft, Mary Shelley and Jane Austen.* Chicago: University of Chicago Press, 1984.

Pu Songling 蒲松齡. *Liaozhai zhiyi (huijiao huizhu huiping ben)* 聊齋誌異 (會校會註　　　). Ed. Zhang Youhe 張友鶴. Shanghai: Shanghai guji chubanshe, 1983 (late 17th c.).

———. *Pu Songling ji* 蒲松齡集. Ed. Lu Dahuang 路大荒. Shanghai: Shanghai guji, 1986 (1962).

Qian Fenglun 錢鳳綸. *Guxianglou ci* 古香樓詞. 1680. In *Xiaotanluanshi huike baijia guixiu ci* 小檀欒室彙刻百家閨秀詞, comp. Xu Naichang 徐乃昌. Nanling, 1896.

Qian Qianyi 錢謙益. *Zuben Qian Zeng Muzhai shizhu* 足本錢曾牧齋詩注. Annot. Qian Zeng 錢曾. Edited by Zhou Fagao 周法高. Hong Kong: n.d.

Qian Qianyi 錢謙益, ed. *Liechao shiji* 列朝詩集. 81 *juan.* 1652. Reprinted—Shanghai: Guoguang yinshuashuo, 1910.

———. *Liechao shiji xiaozhuan* 列朝詩集小傳. Shanghai: Zhonghua shuju, 1961. Rev. ed. in 2 vols. Shanghai: Guji chubanshe, 1983 (1959).

Qian Shoupu 錢守璞. *Xiufo lou shigao* 繡佛樓詩稿. 1869. Copy in Harvard-Yenching Library.

Qing shi 情史. Comp. Zhanzhan waishi 詹詹外史. Attributed to Feng Menglong 馮夢龍. Ed. Zhang Fugao 張福高 et al. Liaoning: Chunfeng wenyi chubanshe, 1986.

Qing Shizong yuzhi wenji 清世宗御製文集.

Qinhuai guangji 秦淮廣記. N.p., 1912.

Qu You 瞿佑. *Jiandeng xinhua* 剪燈新話. In *Jiandeng xinhua wai erzhong* 剪燈新話外二種, edited by Zhou Yi 周夷. Shanghai: Shanghai guji chubanshe, 1981 (author's preface dated 1379).

Read, Bernard E. *Chinese Medicinal Plants from the "Pen Ts'ao Kang Mu," A.D. 1596.* Taibei: Southern Materials Center, 1982 (1936).

Riley, Denise. *"Am I That Name?": Feminism and the Category of "Women" in History.* Minneapolis: University of Minnesota Press, 1988.

Rixia jiuwen kao 日下舊聞考. Sibu congshu ed.

Robertson, Maureen. "Refiguring the Feminine: Self-representation by Literary Women in Late Imperial China." Unpublished paper.

———. "Voicing the Feminine: Constructions of the Gendered Subject in Lyric Poetry by Women of Medieval and Late Imperial China." *Late Imperial China*, 13, no. 1 (June 1992): 63–110.

Rolston, David, ed. *How to Read the Chinese Novel.* Princeton: Princeton University Press, 1990.

Ropp, Paul S. "Between Two Worlds: Women in Shen Fu's *Six Chapters of a*

Floating Life." In *Woman and Literature in China*, ed. Anna Gerstlacher et al., 98–140. Bochum, Ger.: Brockmeyer, 1985.

———. "A Confucian View of Women in the Ch'ing Period: Literati Laments for Women in the *Ch'ing Shih tuo*." *Chinese Studies* (*Han-hsueh yen-chiu*) 10, no. 2 (1992): 399–435.

———. *Dissent in Early Modern China: "Ju-lin wai-shih" and Ch'ing Social Criticism*. Ann Arbor: University of Michigan Press, 1981.

———. "Love, Literacy, and Laments: Themes of Women Writers in Late Imperial China." *Women's History Review* 2, no. 1 (1993): 107–41.

———. "Shi Zhenlin and the Poetess Shuangqing: Gender, Class, and Literary Talent in an Eighteenth-Century Memoir." Paper presented at the Harvard-Wellesley Conference, "Engendering China," Feb. 7–9, 1992.

Rosenzweig, Daphne Lange. "Court Painters of the K'ang-hsi Period." Ph.D. diss., Columbia University, 1973.

Rouputuan 肉蒲團. 1705 Edo ed. Reprinted — Hong Kong: Lianhe chubanshe, n.d.

Ruan Yuan 阮元, ed. *Huang Qing jingjie* 皇清經解. Guangzhou: Xuehai tang, 1860.

———. *Shisanjing zhushu* 十三經注疏. 1815. Reprinted — Taibei: Dahua shuju, 1987.

Ryan, Mary. *The Empire of the Mother: American Writing About Domesticity, 1830–1860*. New York: Haworth, 1982.

Ryū Kyō Retsujoden 劉向列女傳. Osaka, 1763.

Saussy, Haun, trans. "Female Scribes, Ancient and Modern." In *Chinese Women Poets: An Anthology of Poetry and Criticism*, ed. Kang-i Sun Chang and Haun Saussy. Forthcoming.

———. "A Hundred and More Poetic Flowers, by Famed Beauties of Past and Present." In *Chinese Women Poets: An Anthology of Poetry and Criticism*, ed. Kang-i Sun Chang and Haun Saussy. Forthcoming.

Schaberg, David. "Bisexuality in *The Dream of the Red Chamber*." Unpublished ms.

Scott, Joan. "Gender: A Useful Category of Historical Analysis." In idem, *Gender and the Politics of History*, 28–52. New York: Columbia University Press, 1988.

Shan, Guoqiang. "Gentlewomen Paintings of Qing Palace Ateliers." *Orientations* 26, no. 7 (July/Aug. 1995): 56–59.

Shen Defu 沈德符. *Wanli yehuo bian* 萬曆野獲編. Preface dated 1606.

Shen Deqian 沈德潛, comp. *Qing shi biecai ji* 清詩別裁集. Beijing: Zhonghua shuju, 1975 (1760).

Shen Shanbao 沈善寶. *Mingyuan shihua* 名媛詩話. 1846. In *Qing shihua fangyi chubian* 清詩話訪佚初編, ed. Du Songbo, 9: 3–208. Taibei: Xinwenfeng chubanshe, 1987.

Shi Rujie 石汝傑 and Chen Liujing 陳榴競, comps. *Sanka sakuin* 山歌索引. Tokyo: Kōbun shuppan, 1989.

Shi Shuyi 施淑儀. *Qingdai guige shiren zhenglüe* 清代閨閣詩人徵略. Shanghai: Shanghai shudian, 1987 (1922). Taibei: Dingwen shuju, 1974 (1922).

Shi Zhenlin 史震林. *Xiqing sanji* 西青散記. Beijing: Beijing Zhongguo shudian, 1987.

Shi Zhicun 施蟄存 (pseud. Shezhi 舍之). "Lidai ci xuanji xulu" 歷代詞選集續綠. In *Cixue* 4 (1986): 242–55.

———. *Tangshi baihua* 唐詩百話. Shanghai: Shanghai guji, 1987.

Showalter, Elaine. *A Literature of Their Own: British Women Novelists from Brontë to Lessing*. Princeton: Princeton University Press, 1977.

Sima Qian 司馬遷. *Shiji* 史記. Beijing: Zhonghua shuju, 1982 (1959).

Smith, Paul. *Discerning the Subject*. Minneapolis: University of Minnesota Press, 1988.

Sommer, Doris. *Foundational Fictions: The National Romances of Latin America*. Berkeley: University of California Press, 1991.

Songbei yuchen sheng 淞北玉魷生. *Haizou yeyou fulu* 海陬冶遊附錄. In *Xiangyan congshu* 香艷叢書, vol. 20. Shanghai: Guoxue fulun she, 1914.

Soullière, Ellen. "Palace Women in the Ming Dynasty, 1368–1644." Ph.D. diss., Princeton University, 1987.

Stewart, Susan. *On Longing: Narratives of the Miniature, the Gigantic, the Souvenir, the Collection*. Baltimore: Johns Hopkins University Press, 1984.

Stone, Lawrence. *The Family, Sex and Marriage in England, 1500–1800*. New York: Harper & Row, 1977.

Su Zhecong 蘇者聰. "Cong He Shuangqing shici kan Qingdai nongfu de sixiang xingge" 從賀雙卿詩詞看清代農婦的思想性格. Paper presented at the Conference on Women and Literature in Ming-Qing China, Yale University, June 22–26, 1993.

Su Zhecong 蘇者聰, ed. *Zhongguo lidai funü zuopinxuan* 中國歷代婦女作品選. Shanghai: Guji chubanshe, 1987.

Sun Kaidi 孫楷第. *Zhongguo tongsu xiaoshuo shumu* 中國通俗小說書目. Taibei: Fenghuang, 1974 (1957).

Swatek, Catherine. "Feng Menglong's Romantic Dream: Strategies of Containment in His Revision of *Peony Pavilion*." Ph.D. diss., Columbia University, 1990.

———. "Plum and Portrait: Feng Meng-lung's Revision of *The Peony Pavilion*." *Asia Major* 3d series, 6, no. 1 (1993): 127–60.

Taiping guangji 太平廣記. Comp. Li Fang 李昉 et. al. Beijing: Zhonghua shuju, 1981 (1961). 5 vols. Taiwan: Pingping chubanshe, 1975.

Takeda Taijun 武田泰淳. "*Sanka*" 山歌. *Chūgoku bunkaku geppō* 11 (1936).

Tan Qian 談遷. *Guoque* 國榷. Beijing: Zhonghua shuju, 1958.

———. *Zaolin zazu* 棗林雜组. In *Biji xiaoshuo daguan* 筆記小說大觀, vol. 16, *ce* 32, 1–203. Yangzhou: Jiangsu guangling guji keyin chubanshe, 1984.

Tan Youxia 譚友夏 (Yuanchun 元春). *Tan Youxia heji* 譚友夏合集. *Zhongguo wenxue zhenben congshu* 中國文學珍本叢書, vol. 1, no. 8. Shanghai: Shanghai zazhi gongsi, 1935.

Tan Zhengbi 譚正璧. *Sanyan Erpai ziliao* 三言二拍資料. Shanghai: Guji chu-banshe, 1980.

―――. *Zhongguo nüxing wenxue shihua* 中國女性文學詩話. Tianjin: Baihua wenyi chubanshe, 1984.

Tanaka Issei. "The Social and Historical Context of Ming-Ch'ing Local Drama." In *Popular Culture in Late Imperial China*, ed. David Johnson, Andrew J. Nathan, and Evelyn Rawski, 143–60. Berkeley: University of California Press, 1985.

Tang Guizhang 唐圭璋, ed. *Quan Song ci* 全宋詞. Beijing: Zhonghua shuju, 1986 (1965).

Tang Shuyu 湯漱玉. *Yutai huashi* 玉臺畫史. In *Xiangyan congshu* 香艷叢書, vol. 10. Shanghai: Guoxue fulun she, 1914.

Tang Xianzu 湯顯祖. *Mudan ting* 牡丹亭. Ed. Xu Shuofang 徐朔方 and Yang Xiaomei 楊笑梅. Beijing: Renmin wenxue chubanshe, 1978 (1598).

―――. *Tang Xianzu xiqu ji* 湯顯祖戲曲集. Ed. Qian Nanyang 錢南揚. Shanghai: Shanghai guji, 1982.

Tangren xuan Tangshi 唐人選唐詩. Shanghai: Zhonghua shuju, 1958.

Tanji congshu 檀几叢書, comp. by Wang Zhuo 王晫 and Zhang Chao 張潮. Shanghai: Guji chubanshe, 1992.

Tao Muning 陶慕寧. *Qinglou wenxue yu Zhongguo wenhua* 青樓文學與中國文化. Beijing: Dongfang chubanshe, 1993.

Tao Qian 陶潛. *Tao Jingjie jizhu* 陶靖節集注. Hong Kong: Taiping shuju, 1964.

―――. *Tao Yuanming ji* 陶淵明集. Ed. Lu Qinli 逯欽立. Beijing: Zhonghua shuju, 1979.

Tao Zhenhuai 陶貞懷. *Tian yu hua* 天雨花. 1657.

Tennenhouse, Leonard. *Power on Display: The Politics of Shakespeare's Genres.* New York: Routledge, 1986.

T'ien, Ju-kang. *Male Anxiety and Female Chastity: A Comparative Study of Chinese Ethical Values in Ming-Ch'ing Times.* T'oung Pao Monographs 14. Leiden: E. J. Brill, 1988.

Töpelmann, Cornelia. *"Shan-ko" von Feng Meng-lung: Eine Volksliedersammlung aus der Ming-Zeit.* Münchener Ostasiatische Studien, vol. 9. Wiesbaden: Franz Steiner Verlag, 1973.

Tuojin 托津 et al. *Da Qing huidian shili* 大清會典事例. Beijing: Neifu, 1813.

Wakeman, Frederic, Jr.. *The Great Enterprise: Manchu Reconstruction of Imperial Order in Seventeenth-Century China.* 2 vols. Berkeley: University of California Press, 1985.

―――. "Romantics, Stoics, and Martyrs in Seventeenth-Century China." *Journal of Asian Studies* 43, no. 4 (1984): 632–39.

Waley, Arthur. *The Book of Songs.* New York: Grove Press, 1987.

Wang Chongmin 王重民. *Zhongguo shanben shu tiyao* 中國善本書提要. Shanghai: Guji chubanshe, 1983.

Wang Duan 汪端, comp. *Ming sanshi jia shixuan* 明三十家詩選. 1873 (1822).

―――. *Ziran haoxue zhai ji* 自然好學齋集. 1839.

Wang Duanshu 王端淑. *Yinhong ji* 吟紅集. 1651. In Naikaku bunko, Tokyo.

Wang Duanshu 王端淑, ed. *Mingyuan shiwei* 名媛詩緯. 1667. Photocopy of edition in the Beijing University Rare Book Library.

Wang Mengruan 王夢阮. *"Hong lou meng" suoyin* 紅樓夢索引. Preface dated 1913. Reprinted — Tianjin: Guji shudian, 1989.

Wang Pijiang 汪辟疆, ed. *Tangren xiaoshuo* 唐人小說. Taibei: Chunzhen chubanshe, 1983.

Wang Qi 汪淇, ed. *Chidu xinyu guangbian* 尺牘新語廣編. 1668. Copy in the Nanjing Library.

Wang Qishu 汪啓淑, ed. *Xiefang ji* 擷芳集. 1773. Regenstein Library, University of Chicago (photocopy of edition in the Fudan Library).

Wang Shifu. *The Moon and the Zither: The Story of the Western Wing*. Ed. and trans. Stephen West and Wilt Idema. Berkeley: University of California Press, 1991.

Wang Shizhen 王士禎. *Chibei outan* 池北偶談. Beijing: Zhonghua shuju, 1982 (published by 1696).

Wang Shunu 王書奴. *Zhongguo changji shi* 中國娼妓史. Shanghai: Sanlian shudian, 1988 (1935).

Wang Tingna 汪廷訥 (fl. 1573–1620). *Qi pu* 棋譜. Wanli era (1573–1620) ed. in Beijing Library.

———. *Ren jing yang qiu* 人鏡陽秋. Several fragmentary Wanli era eds. in Beijing Library.

Wang Wei 王維. *Wang Youcheng ji jianzhu* 王右承集箋注. Ed. Zhao Diancheng 趙殿成. Shanghai: Guji chubanshe, 1961.

Wang Xianqian 王先謙, ed. *Xunzi jizhu* 荀子集注. Taibei: Shijie shuju, 1978.

Wang Xilian 王希廉. *Xinping xiuxiang Hong lou meng quanzhuan* 新評繡像紅樓夢全傳. 1832. Copy in Beijing University Library.

Wang Yu 王豫, comp. *Jiangsu shizheng* 江蘇詩徵. N.p.: Jiaoshan weige, 1821. Copy in the Harvard-Yenching Library.

Watt, James C. Y. "The Literati Environment." In *The Chinese Scholar's Studio: Artistic Life in the Late Ming Period*, ed. Chu-tsing Li and James Watt. New York: Asia Society Galleries, 1987.

Weidner, Marsha, and the Indianapolis Museum of Art. *Views from Jade Terrace: Chinese Women Artists, 1300–1920*. Exhibition catalogue. Indianapolis: Indianapolis Museum of Art; New York: Rizzoli, 1989.

Wen Yiduo 聞一多. *Wen Yiduo quanji* 聞一多全集. Shanghai: Kaiming, 1948.

Widmer, Ellen. "The Epistolary World of Female Talent in Seventeenth-Century China." *Late Imperial China* 10, no. 2 (1989): 1–43.

———. "Xiaoqing's Literary Legacy and the Place of the Woman Writer in Late Imperial China." *Late Imperial China* 13, no. 1 (1992): 111–55.

———. "Xiaoqing's Literary Legacy and the Place of the Woman Writer in Late Imperial China." Ms., 1992 (ms. version of preceding item).

Wile, Douglas. *Art of the Bedchamber: Chinese Sexual Yoga Classics Including Women's Solo Meditational Texts*. Albany: State University of New York Press, 1992.

Wilhelm, Richard, and Cary E. Baynes, trans. *The I Ching, Or Book of Changes.* Rendered into English by Cary F. Baynes. Princeton: Princeton University Press, 1967.

Willetts, William. *Chinese Art.* New York: George Braziller, 1958.

Williams, Raymond. *The Long Revolution.* New York: Columbia University Press, 1971.

Wolf, Arthur. "Gods, Ghosts, and Ancestors." In *Religion and Ritual in Chinese Society,* ed. Arthur Wolf, 131–82. Stanford: Stanford University Press, 1974.

Wu Hung. "Emperor's Masquerade: 'Costume Portraits' of Yongzheng and Qianlong." *Orientations* 26, no. 7 (July/Aug. 1995): 25–41.

———. "From Temple to Tomb: Ancient Chinese Art and Religion in Transition." *Early China* 13 (1988): 78–116.

———. *Monumentality in Early Chinese Art and Architecture.* Stanford: Stanford University Press, 1996.

———. "Tiananmen Square: A Political History of Monuments." *Representations* 35 (1991): 84–117.

———. "The Transparent Stone: Inverted Vision and Binary Imagery in Medieval Chinese Art." *Representations* 46 (1994): 58–86.

Wu Qian 吳謙 et al., eds. *Yizong jinjian* 醫宗金鑒. Beijing: Renmin weisheng chubanshe, 1977 (1742).

Wu Weiye 吳偉業. *Wu Meicun quanji* 吳梅村全集. Ed. Li Xueying 李學穎. 3 vols. Shanghai: Shanghai guji chubanshe, 1990.

Wu Wushan 吳吳山 and Qian Yi 錢宜, eds. *Wu Wushan sanfu heping "Mudan ting"* 吳吳山三婦合評牡丹亭. 1694. Photocopy of an edition based on 1694 woodblocks in the Tōyō bunka kenkyūjō, Tokyo.

Wu Zhangsheng. "Du Feng Menglong de *Guazhier, Shan'ge*" 讀馮夢龍的「掛枝兒」,「山歌」. *Wenxue pinglun congkan* 22 (1984).

Wu Zhiwang 武之望. *Jiyin gangmu* 濟陰綱目. Ed. Wang Qi 汪淇. Shanghai: Keji weisheng chubanshe, 1958 (1665).

Xiangyan congshu 香艷叢書, comp. Chongtianzi 蟲天子. Shanghai: Zhongguo tushu gongsi, 1914. Reprinted—4 vols. Beijing: Renmin wenxue chubanshe, 1992.

Xiao Tong 蕭統, comp. *Wen xuan* 文選. Annot. Li Shan 李善. Taibei: Hanjing, 1983.

Xiao yao zi 逍遙子. *Hou Hong lou meng* 後紅樓夢. N.p., n.d.

Xie Guozhen 謝國禎. *Mingmo Qingchu de xuefeng* 明末清初的學風. Beijing: Renmin wenxue chubanshe, 1982.

Xin Wenfang 辛文坊. *Tang caizi zhuan* 唐才子傳. Shanghai: Zhonghua shuzhu, 1965 (1302).

———. *Tang caizi zhuan jiaozhu* 唐才子傳校註. Annot. Sun Yingkui 孫映逵. Beijing: Zhongguo kexueyuan chubanshe, 1991 (1304).

Xingshi hengyan 醒世恒言. Hong Kong: Guji, n.d.

Xiong Deji 熊德基. "'Tian yu hua' zuozhe wei Mingmo qinüzi Liu Shuying kao" 「天雨花」作者爲明末奇女子劉淑英考. *Zhonghua wenshi lun-cong* 中華文史論叢 11 (1979): 318–28.

Xiong, Victor. "*Ji* Entertainers in Late Tang Chang'an." Unpublished paper, 1995.

Xu Can 徐燦. *Zhuozheng yuan shiji* 拙政園詩集. In *Baijing lou congshu* 拜經樓叢書, comp. Wu Qian 吳騫. 1803.

Xu Daling 許大齡 and Wang Tianyou 王天有, eds. *Mingchao shiliu di* 明朝十六帝. Beijing: Xinhua shudian, 1991.

Xu Dishan 許地山. *Fuji mixin di yanjiu* 扶乩迷信地研究. Changsha: Shangwu yinshuguan, 1941.

Xu Fuming 徐扶明. "*Hong lou meng*" *yu xiqu bijiao yanjiu* 紅樓夢與戲曲比較研究. Shanghai: Guji chubanshe, 1984.

———. "*Mudan ting*" *yanjiu ziliao kaoshi* 牡丹亭研究資料考釋. Shanghai: Shanghai guji chubanshe, 1987.

———. *Yuan Ming Qing xiqu tansuo* 元明清戲曲探索. Hangzhou: Zhejiang guji chubanshe, 1986. Shanghai: Shanghai guji chubanshe, 1986.

Xu Jiu 徐釚. *Xu benshi shi* 續本事詩. In *Benshi shi, Xu benshi shi, Benshi ci* 本事詩、續本事詩、本事詞. Comp. Meng Qi 孟棨 et al. Edited by Li Xueying 李學穎. Shanghai: Shanghai guji chubanshe, 1988.

Xu Ling 徐陵, ed. *Yu tai xin yong* 玉臺新詠. Annot. Wu Zhaoyi 吳兆宜. Taibei: Guangwen shuju, n.d. *Yutai xinyong [jianzhu]* 玉臺新詠[箋注]. Annotated by Wu Zhaoyi 吳兆宜 and Cheng Yan 程琰. Punctuated by Mu Kehong 穆克宏. Beijing: Zhonghua shuju, 1985.

Xu Naichang 徐乃昌, comp. *Xiaotanluanshi huike baijia guixiu ci* 小檀欒室彙刻百家閨秀詞. 10 *ji*, 1896.

———. *Guixiu cichao* 閨秀詞鈔 in 16 *juan*, 1906.

Xu Shumin 徐樹敏 and Qian Yue 錢岳, comp. *Zhongxiang ci* 衆香詞. Shanghai: Dadong shuju, 1934 (1690).

Xu Shuofang 徐朔方. *Wan Ming qujia nianpu* 晚明曲家年譜. 3 vols. Hangzhou: Zhejiang guji chubanshe, 1993.

Xu Yuan 徐媛. *Luowei yin* 絡緯吟. Qiyuan tang, 1613.

Xu Zhen 徐震. "*Meiren pu*" 美人譜. In *Tanji congshu*, 140–42.

——— (psued., Yanshui sanren 煙水散人). *Nücaizi shu* 女才子書. 1658. Shenyang: Chunfeng wenyi chubanshe, 1983. Shanghai: Guji 1990.

Yagi Akiyoshi 八木章好. "Ho Shōrei to Ri Ga" 蒲松齡と李賀. In *Geibun kenkyū* 54 (1989): 134–51.

Yan Dichang 嚴迪昌. *Qing cishi* 清詞史. Huaiyin: Jiangsu guji, 1990.

Yang Boda. "The Development of the Ch'ien-lung Painting Academy." In *Words and Images: Chinese Poetry, Calligraphy, and Painting*, ed. A. Murck and Wen Fong, 333–56. Princeton: Princeton University Press, 1991.

——— 楊伯達. *Qing dai yuanhua* 清代院畫. Beijing: Zijincheng chubanshe, 1993.

Yansui zhenzhi 延綏鎮志. Taibei: Chengwen chubanshe, 1969 (1673).

Yao Lingxi 姚靈犀. *Caifeilu, sibian* 采菲錄四編. Tianjin: Tianjin shuju, 1938.

Ye Changhai 葉長海. "Ming Qing xiqu nü xing jiao se" 明清戲曲女性角色. Paper presented at the conference Women and Writing in Late Imperial China, Yale University, June 1993.

Ye Shaoyuan 葉紹袁. *Wumengtang quanji* 午夢堂全集. Punctuated ed. Shanghai: Shanghai zazhi gongsi, 1936 (1636).

Yee, Angelina C. "Counterpoise in *Honglou meng*." *Harvard Journal of Asiatic Studies* 50, no. 2 (1992): 613–50.

Yi Su 一粟, ed. *Hong lou meng juan* 紅樓夢卷. Beijing: Zhonghua shuju, 1963.

Yong Rong 永鎔. *Siku quanshu zongmu* 四庫全書總目. 2 vols. Beijing: Zhonghua shuju, 1965.

You Tong 尤侗. *Xitang quanji* 西堂全集. Qing ed. In Regenstein Library, University of Chicago.

You Youji 游友基. "*Guazhier, Shan'ge*, qianlun" 「掛枝兒」「山歌」淺論. *Minjian wenyi jikan* 1986, no. 3.

Yu, Anthony C. "'Rest, Rest, Perturbed Spirit!' Ghosts in Traditional Chinese Prose Fiction." *Harvard Journal of Asiatic Studies* 47, no. 2 (1987): 397–434.

Yu Huai 余懷. *Banqiao zaji* 板橋雜記. Shanghai: Dada tushu gongyingshe, 1934. Changsha: Yemin, 1908 (1697). In *Xiangyan congshu* 香艷叢書, vol. 13. Shanghai: Guoxue fulun she, 1914. Trans. Howard S. Levy as *A Feast of Mist and Flowers*. Yokohama: mimeographed, 1966.

Yu Jianhua 俞劍華. *Zhongguo meishujia renming cidian* 中國美術家人名詞典. Shanghai: Renmin meishu chubanshe, 1981.

Yu, Pauline. "Poems in Their Place: Collections and Canons in Early Chinese Literature." *Harvard Journal of Asiatic Studies* 50, no. 1 (1990): 163–96.

Yu, Pauline, ed. *Voices of the Song Lyric in China*. Berkeley: University of California Press, 1994.

Yu Pingbo 俞平伯, ed. *Zhiyanzhai "Hong lou meng" jiping* 脂硯齋紅樓夢輯評. Hong Kong: Taiping, 1979.

Yu Yingshi 余英時. *Chen Yinke xiansheng wannian shiwen shizheng* 陳寅恪先生晚年詩文釋證. Taibei: Shibao chuban gongsi, 1986.

Yuan Mei 袁枚, comp. *Suiyuan nüdizi shi, Suiyuan quan ji* 隨園女弟子詩、隨園全集. N.p.: Wenming shuju, n.d.

———. *Suiyuan nüdizi shixuan* 隨園女弟子詩選. Shanghai: Dada tushu gongyingshe, 1934 (1796).

———. *Suiyuan san shi ba zhong* 隨園三十八種. 40 vols. 1892.

Yun Zhu 惲珠, comp. *Guochao guixiu zhengshi ji* 國朝閨秀正始集. N.p.: Hongxiang guan, 1831. Copy in the Harvard-Yenching Library.

———. *Hongxiang guan shici cao* 紅香館詩詞草. 1814.

Yuncha waishi 雲槎外史 (Gu Taiqing 顧太清). *Hong lou meng ying* 紅樓夢影. Beijing: Beijing daxue chubanshe, 1988.

Zeitlin, Judith T. *Historian of the Strange: Pu Songling and the Chinese Classical Tale*. Stanford: Stanford University Press, 1993.

———. "Shared Dreams: The Story of the Three Wives' Commentary on *The Peony Pavilion*." *Harvard Journal of Asiatic Studies* 54, no. 1 (1994): 127–79.

Zhang Chao 張潮. "Bu 'Huadi shiyi'" 補花底拾遺. In *Xiangyan congshu*, 1: 23–24.

———. "Huadi shiyi xiaoyin" 花底拾遺小引. In *Xiangyan congshu*, 1: 15.

Zhang Dai 張岱. *Shikui houji* 石匱後集. Beijing: Zhonghua shuju, 1959.

Zhang Gongchang 張弓長. *Zhongguó de jinü yu wenxue* 中國的妓女與文學. Taibei: Changchunshu shufang, 1975.

Zhang Gongliang 張公量. "*Xiqing sanji* cankao ziliao" 西青散記參考資料. In Shi Zhenlin 史震林, *Xiqing sanji* 西青散記, appendix, 1–9. Zhongguo wenxue zhenben congshu ed. Shanghai, 1936. Originally published in the book supplement of the *Tianjin dagongbao*, Feb. 6, 1936.

Zhang Huijian 張慧劍. *Ming Qing Jiangsu wenren nianbiao* 明清江蘇文人年表. Shanghai: Guji chubanshe, 1986.

Zhang Huiying. "Sanka chū." *Kaihen* 10 (1992).

Zhang Pengzhou 張篷舟. *Xue Tao shi jian* 薛濤詩箋. Beijing: Renmin chubanshe, 1983.

Zhang Weiren 張偉人. *Zhongguo fazhishi shumu* 中國法制史書目. Taibei: Academia Sinica, 1976.

Zhang Yanyuan 張彥遠. *Lidai minghua ji* 歷代名畫記. Beijing: Renmin wenxue chubanshe, 1983 (1963).

Zhang Yingchang 張應昌. *Qingshiduo* 清詩鐸 (reprint of *Guochao shiduo* 國朝詩鐸). Beijing: Zhonghua shuju, 1983 (1960).

Zhang Zilan 張滋蘭, comp., and Ren Zhaolin 任兆麟, ed. *Wuzhong nüshi shichao* 吳中女士詩鈔. N.p., 1789. Copy in the Harvard-Yenching Library.

Zhao Botao 趙伯陶. "*Hong lou meng ying* de zuozhe ji qi ta" 紅樓夢影的作者及其他. *Hong lou meng xuekan* 41 (1989): 243–51.

Zhao Shijie 趙世杰, comp. *Gujin nüshi* 古今女史. Shanghai: Saoye sanfang, 1928 (1628). [*Jingke*] *Gujin nüshi* [精刻] 古今女史. 12 *juan*. N.p., 1628. Ming ed. held at Harvard-Yenching library

Zhao Yi 趙翼. *Gaiyu congkao* 陔餘叢考. 1790. Reprinted — Shanghai: Shanghai guji, 1957.

Zheng Guangyi 鄭光儀, ed. *Zhongguo lidai cainü shige jianshang cidian* 中國歷代才女詩歌鑒賞詞典. Beijing: Zhongguo gongren chubanshe, 1991.

Zheng Zhenduo 鄭振鐸. *Zhongguo su wenxue shi* 中國俗文學史. Beijing: Zuojia chubanshe, 1957.

Zhiyanzhai 脂硯齋. *Qianlong jiaxu Zhiyanzhai chongping Shitou ji* 乾隆甲戌脂硯齋重評石頭記, by Cao Xueqin 曹雪芹. 2 vols. Taibei: Shangwu yinshuguan, 1961.

Zhong Hong 鍾嶸. *Shipin* 詩品. Hong Kong: Shangwu yinshuguan, 1959.

Zhong Huiling 鍾慧玲. "Qingdai nü shiren yanjiu" 清代女詩人研究. Ph.D. diss., Zhengzhi daxue, 1981.

Zhong Xing 鍾惺, comp. *Mingyuan shigui* 名媛詩歸. N.p., late Wanli period. Copy in the Harvard-Yenching Library. 36 *juan*.

———. *Yin xiu xuan ji* 隱秀軒集. Shanghai: Guji chubanshe, 1992.

Zhongguo congshu zonglu 中國叢書總錄. Comp. Shanghai Library. Beijing: Zhonghua shuju, 1962.

Zhongguo gudai shuhua tumu 中國古代書畫圖目. 12 vols. Beijing: Wenwu chubanshe, 1983–95.

Zhongguo tongsu xiaoshuo zongmu tiyao 中國通俗小說總目提要. Beijing: Zhongguo wenlian chuban gongsi, 1990.

Zhou Caiquan 周采泉. *Liu Rushi zalun* 柳如是雜論. Huaiyin: Jiangsu guji chubanshe, 1986.

Zhou Qi 周綺. "*Hong lou meng ti ci*" 紅樓夢題詞. Preface to Wang Xilian.

Zhou Shouchang 周壽昌, comp. *Gonggui wenxuan* 宮閨文選. 1843.

Zhou Shouchang 周壽昌 and Jiang Gongyi 蔣恭鎰, eds. *Gonggui wenxuan* 宮閨文選. N.p.: Xiao Penglai shan guan, 1846.

Zhou Wanyao (Chou Wan-yao) 周婉窈. "Qingdai Tongcheng xuezhe yu funü de jiduan daode xingwei"清代桐城學者與婦女的極端道德行爲. In Bao Jialin 鮑家麟, ed., *Zhongguo funü lunji* 中國婦女論集, 4: 185–251. Taibei: Daoxiang, 1995.

Zhou Zuoren 周作人, comp. *Mingren xiaopin ji* 明人小品集. Taibei: Jinfeng chubanshe, 1987.

Zhu He 朱鶴. *Qinlou yue* 秦樓月. Ca. 1700. Guoli zhongyang tushuguan microfilm.

Zhu Jiajin 朱家溍. "Guanyu Yongzheng shiqi shierfu meirenhua de wenti" 關於雍正時期十二幅美人畫的問題. *Zijincheng* 1986, no. 3: 45.

Zhu Jiajin 朱家溍 and Li Yanqin 李艷琴. 1983. "Qing wuchao 'Yuzhiji' zhong de Yuanming yuan shi" 清五朝御製集中的圓明園詩. *Yuanming yuan* 1983, no. 2: 54–57.

Zhu Xi 朱熹, ed. *Jinsi lu jijie* 近思錄集解. Commentary by Zhang Boxing 張伯行. N.p.: Shijie shuju, 1971 (1900).

Zhu Yizun 朱彝尊. *Mingshi zong* 明詩綜. 2 vols. Taibei: Saijie shuju, 1989.

Zhuang Yifu 莊一拂. *Gudian xiqu cun mu hui kao* 古典戲曲存目 會考. Shanghai: Guji chubanshe, 1982.

Zhuquan jushi 珠泉居士. *Xuehong xiaoji* 雪鴻小記. 1787. In *Xiangyan congshu* 香艷叢書, vol. 19. Shanghai: Guoxue fulun she, 1914.

Zou Siyi 鄒斯漪, comp. *Shiyuan ba mingjia ji* 詩媛八名家集. Preface dated 1655.

Character List

Entries are alphabetized letter by letter, ignoring word and syllable breaks.

Ai ri tang 愛日堂
An Lushan 安祿山

bai guan 稗官
Bailian qun 白練裙
bai xing 百行
Baixue yiyin 白雪遺音
Ban Chao 班超
Ban Jieyu 班婕妤
Banqiao zaji 板橋雜記
ba nude huaxin lai rousui 把奴
　的花心來揉碎
Ban Zhao 班昭
Bao Linghui 鮑令暉
Bao Zhao 鮑照
Bao Zhilan 鮑之蘭
bei 悲
Beili zhi 北里志
"Bei zai xing" 悲哉行
benshi 本事
Bian Mengjue 卞夢玨
Bian Sai (Daoist name Yujing dao-
　ren) 卞賽 (玉京道人)

Bian Yujing 卞玉京
Bian Yujing siyi Meicun 卞玉京
　死憶梅村
biji 避跡
Bi Keshan 畢柯山
Bimu yu 比目魚
bingdi lian 并蒂蓮
Bixue hua 碧血花
Bo Juyi 白居易
"Boming fu" 薄命婦
Bo Shaojun 薄少君
"Bozhou" 柏舟
bu cai 不才
"Bu 'Huadi shiyi'" 補花底拾遺
bu xiu 不朽
Buxi yuan 不繫園
buxi zhi zhou 不繫之舟
bu yin qi se 不淫其色

cai 才
Cai Dianqi 蔡殿齊
caiguan 采觀
"Cailian fu" 採蓮賦

cainü 才女
caishi zhi yi 採詩之役
Cai Wan 蔡琬
Cai Wenji 蔡文姬
Cai Yan 蔡琰
Cai Yong 蔡邕
caizi 才子
caizi jiaren 才子佳人
Cangsang yan 滄桑艷
Cangzhou 滄州
Cao Cao 曹操
Cao Dazhang 曹大章
Cao Pi 曹丕
Caotang shiyu 草堂詩餘
Cao Xueqin 曹雪芹
Caoyi daoren 草衣道人
Cao Yin 曹寅
Cao Zhenting 曹震亭
Chai Jingyi 柴靜儀
changji 倡(娼)妓
"Chang xiangsi" 長相思
changyou 倡優
chao 抄
Chaoguo furen 朝國夫人
Chen Duansheng 陳端生
Cheng (emperor, Han dynasty) 成
Cheng Hao 程顥
Cheng Mengyang 程孟陽
Chen Houzhu 陳後主
Chen Huan (*zi* Yuanyuan) 陳浣 (圓圓)
Chen Ji 陳基
Chen Jiru 陳繼儒
Chen Mei 陳枚
Chen Peizhi 陳裴之
Chen Shenghe 陳聲和
Chen Weisong 陳維崧
Chen Wenshu 陳文述
Chen Xiaru 陳霞如
Chen Yinke 陳寅恪
Chen Yujiao 陳與郊
Chen Zilong 陳子龍
chi 癡
Chongguan nu 衝冠怒

"Chongguo shengnü ci" 重過聖女祠
"Chou Liu Chaisang" 酬劉柴桑
"Chou Si'an xizeng" 酬思黯戲贈
chu 出
chuanfang 傳芳
chuanji 船妓
chuanqi 傳奇
Chu ci 楚辭
chuijie 垂戒
chunsi 春思
Chunxing tang shiji 春星堂詩集
"Chuqiu" 初秋
ci 詞
Ci Mulan daifu congjun 雌木蘭代父從軍
"Ciyun fengda" 次韻奉答
Cui Hui 崔徽
Cuilou ji 翠樓集
Cui Shu 崔淑

da 達
Daguanyuan 大觀園
dang 蕩
danggui tang 蕩鬼湯
Dan Minglun 但明倫
"Da suren wen" 答俗人問
"Daxu" 大序
Daxue 大學
de 德
Deng Hanyi 鄧漢儀
deng mi 燈謎
deng mi qiao yin chen yan 燈謎巧引讖言
dian 殿
Ding Changfa 丁長發
Ding Chuanjing 丁傳晴
Ding Shaoyi 丁紹儀
Ding Shengzhao 丁聖肇
Dong Bai (*zi* Xiaowan) 董白 (小宛)
Dong Qichang 董其昌

"Dongri tong Rushi fanzhou youzeng" 冬日同如是泛舟有贈

"Dong ri zuo duange ba shou fang Shaoling ti" 冬日作短歌八首倣少陵體

Dongshan chouhe ji 東山酬和集

Dong Shaoyu 董少玉

Dong Xiaoyuan 董小宛

Duan Shuqing 端淑卿

duanwu 端午

Duan Yuhan 段玉函

Du Fu 杜甫

Du Gongbu shiji 杜工部詩集

Duke of Loyalty and Bravery 忠勇公

Du Lanxiang 杜蘭香

duli 獨立

dunhou wenrou 敦厚溫柔

duobaoge 多寶格

duoqiu duobing 多愁多病

Du Rangshui 杜讓水

"Du 'Zhengshi ji' jicheng Zhenpu taishi mu" 讀正始集寄呈珍浦太師母

E lühua 萼綠華

Emei jianxia 峨眉劍俠

Falin zhaotianzhu 法林照天燭

"Fang huai" 放懷

"Fangmu" 訪墓

Fang Weiyi 方維儀

Fang Yizhi 方以智

Fan Huzhen 范壺貞

Fan Li 范蠡

Fan Yunlin 范允臨

Feng Menglong 馮夢龍

Fengsao yu yanqing 風騷與艷情

Feng Xiaoqing 馮小青

Feng Zhenluan 馮鎮巒

fu 賦

Fuhai 福海

fuji 扶乩

"Fujie san shou" 婦誡三首

Fuke xinfa yaojue 婦科新法要訣

funü 婦女

Furen ji 婦人集

Fuxue 婦學

Fu Yuan 傅元

Gai Qi 改琦

gangchang 綱常

Gao Bing 高棅

gaodi 高弟

Gao E 高鶚

Gao Qi 高啓

Gao Shuang 高爽

"Gaotang fu" 高唐賦

Gao Yinxian 高銀仙

Gao Zhixian 高芝仙

gegu 割股

Ge Nen 葛嫩

"Gengyun" 縆雲

Ge Zhengqi 葛徵奇

gong 宮

Gong Dingzi 龔鼎孳

Gonggui shiji yiwen kaolüe 宮閨氏籍藝文考略

Gonggui wenxuan 宮閨文選

gongmen 宮門

"Gongsun Jiuniang" 公孫九娘

gongti shi 宮體詩

"Gong wu chu men" 公無出門

Gong Zhebing 宮哲兵

Gu (Lady) 顧

guai 怪

guangda fengliu jiaozhu 廣大風流教主

"Guanju" 關雎

Gu Dajiao 顧大腳

gudian 古典

"Gu feng" 谷風

gufeng 古風

"Gugong yuan" 古宮怨

gui 鬼

guicai 鬼才

Guifan 閨範

guifang zhixiu 閨房之秀

guihuo 鬼火
guiji 闈集
guiji 鬼擊
Gui Maoyi 歸懋儀
guimen 閨門
guiqi 鬼氣
guishen shi 鬼神詩
guitai 鬼胎
guixiu 閨秀
Guixiu jiahua 閨秀佳話
guixiu shi ping 閨秀詩評
Guiying 桂英
Gui Youguang 歸有光
guizheng 鬼症
"Guizhong dushu" 闈鍾讀書
"Guizhu" 鬼疰
Gujin mingyuan baihua shiyu 古今
    名媛百花詩餘
Gujin mingyuan shi ci xuan
    古今名媛詩詞選
Gujin nüshi 古今女史
Gujin nüshu 古今女書
gulai meiren 古來美人
Gu Ling 顧苓
Gu Mei 顧媚(眉)
Guochao guige shichao 國朝閨閣
    詩鈔
Guochao guixiu zhengshi ji 國朝
    閨秀正始集
Guochao shiduo 國朝詩鐸
"Guofeng" 國風
"Guo Jinshulin Yujing daoren mu
    bing zhuan" 過錦樹林玉京
    道人墓并傳
Guo Maoqian 郭茂倩
Guo Peilan 郭佩蘭
Guoque 國榷
Guose tianxiang 國色天香
"Guo sihao mu" 過四皓墓
"Guo Zhongyonggong di jishi"
    過忠勇公第即事
Gu Ruopu 顧若璞
Gu Ruoqun 顧若群
gushi 古詩
"Gushi shijiu shou" 古詩十九首

Gu Taiqing 顧太清
Gu Wenwan 顧文婉
Guxianglou ci 古香樓詞
Gu Yanwu 顧炎武

Haining 海寧
Han E 韓娥
"Han gong chunxiao" 漢宮春曉
Han Lanying 韓蘭英
Hanliu tang 寒柳堂
Han Shizhong 韓世忠
Han Wudi gushi 漢武帝故事
Han Xi 韓西
"Hanxi wenyan zaidie qianyun
    shiri Wowen shi luocheng"
    寒夕文讌再疊前韻是日
    我聞室落成
Han Yu 韓愈
hao 號
"Haojia yile tu" 豪家佚樂圖
haoming er wuxue 好名而無學
Hao Xiang'e 郝湘娥
He, Lady 何氏
Hedong 河東
Hedong jun zhuan 河東君傳
"He Guo Zhubu er shou" 和郭
    主簿二首
heji 合集
heke 合刻
He Liangjun 何良俊
He Shuangqing 賀雙卿
He Yuying 何玉英
hongdou 紅豆
Hong lou fumeng 紅樓復夢
Hong lou meng 紅樓夢
"Hong lou meng shier qu" 紅樓
    夢十二曲
"*Hong lou meng* ti ci" 紅樓夢
    題詞
Hong lou meng tu yong 紅樓夢
    圖詠
Hong lou meng ying 紅樓夢影
"*Hong lou qu*" 紅樓曲
Hongmeige zhuren 紅梅閣
    主人

Hongxian 紅線

Hongxiang guan shici cao 紅香館詩詞草

Hou Fangyu 侯方域

houting 後庭

Hou Zhi 侯芝

hua'an 花案

huabang 花榜

huabang xuanju 花榜選舉

"Huadi shiyi" 花底拾遺

Hua Guangsheng 華廣生

huaigu 懷古

huai gu shang jin 懷古傷今

huaigu shi 懷古詩

Huajian ji 花間集

Huang Hong 黃鴻

Huangjidian 皇極殿

Huang Juan 黃卷

Huang Mengwan 黃孟畹

huangshan 黃衫

Huang Shangwen 黃尚文

huangshan haoke 黃衫豪客

Huangtaiji 皇太極

Huang Yuanjie (*zi* Liyin) 黃媛介 (離隱)

Huang Zongxi 黃宗羲

huanhun 還魂

"huan ji" 幻集

"Huanxisha" 浣溪沙

huapu 花譜

Huarui furen 花蕊夫人

Huayang sangao 華陽散稿

huayi 畫意

Hui tu Lienü zhuan 繪圖列女傳

huiwenshi 回文詩

"Hunyou" 魂遊

"Huo Xiaoyu zhuan" 霍小玉傳

Hushang cao 湖上草

Hu Wenkai 胡文楷

Hu Zhenheng 胡震亨

Huzhongtian 壺中天

ji (maiden, concubine) 姬

ji (prostitute) 妓

Jia Baoyu 賈寶玉

Jiajing 嘉靖

jian 賤

Jian deng yu hua 剪燈餘話

Jiang Hui 蔣徽

Jiang Jingqi 蔣景祁

"Jiangluan" 降鸞

Jiangsu shizheng 江蘇詩徵

Jiang Zhu 江珠

Jianmei 兼美

jianqie 賤妾

Jianshui shanfang shichao 剪水山房詩鈔

jianyin bu xiao 奸淫不孝

Jiao, Lady 焦氏

Jiao Bingzhen 焦秉貞

Jiaona 嬌娜

Jiao Rong 焦容

"Jiaping gongzi" 嘉平公子

jiaren 佳人

Jia Tanchun 賈探春

Jia Yuanchun 賈元春

Jia Zheng 賈政

Ji Bu 季布

jie 結

Jie'an laoren manbi 戒庵老人漫筆

"Jiewei gui" 介胄鬼

Jieyan 介弇

Jieyu Sheng 劫餘生

Jifu tongzhi 畿輔通誌

jindian 今典

jing (classic) 經

jing (scenery) 景

Jinghua yuan 鏡花緣

Jingjiang Baoshi san nüshi shichao 京江鮑氏三女士詩鈔

"Jing jiuyuan diao Ma Shouzhen wen" 經舊院弔馬守眞文

"Jing ji zhi" 經籍志

Jing Pianpian (*ming* Yao; *zi* Sanmei) 景翩翩 (搖; 三昧)

jingqi 精氣

Jingshan 徑山

"Jingshui" 經水

Jingzhiju shihua 靜志居詩話

Jin ji 金姬
Jinling 金陵
Jinling shier chai 金陵十二釵
"Jinling zati" 金陵雜題
"Jinming chi yong hanliu ci"
　　金明池詠寒柳詞
Jinming guan 金明館
Jin sanbai nian mingjia cixuan
　　近三百年名家詞選
jinshi 進士
Jinsi lu jijie 近思錄集解
jinü 妓女
jinyao 緊要
Jin Yi 金逸
jin yu xia 近於俠
"Jiu ge" 九歌
"Jiuri zuo" 九日作
Jiuzhai zaju bazhong
　　疚齋雜劇八種
Ji Xian 季嫻
ji youhen 寄幽恨
"Ji yuan" 寄遠
Ji Yun 紀昀
Ji Zhenyi 季振宜
Juanqinzhai 倦勤齋
jue jian 譎諫
junzi 君子
Juzhen tang 聚珍堂

"Kai feng" 凱風
Kangxi 康熙
Kang Zhengguo 康正果
Keqing 可卿
Kong Shangren 孔尚任
Kou Mei (*zi* Baimen) 寇湄 (白門)
ku 苦
kuangcao 狂草
Kuang guli yuyang sannong
　　狂鼓吏漁陽三弄
kunqu 崑曲

li 禮
liang 良
Liang Desheng 梁德繩
Liang Hongyu 梁紅玉

Liang shi yin yuan 兩世姻緣
Liang Xiaoyu 梁小玉
Liang Ying 梁英
Liang Yizhen 梁乙眞
"Lianhua chi" 蓮花池
"Liansuo" 連瑣
"Lianxiang" 蓮香
Liaozhai zhiyi 聊齋誌異
Li Bai/Bo 李白
Li Chengzu 李丞祖
Lidai ci xuanji xulu 歷代詞選集
　　敘錄
Lidai diwang houfei kao 歷代帝
　　王后妃考
Lidai funü zhuzuo kao 歷代婦女
　　著作考
Lidai nüzi shiji 歷代女子詩集
Lidai nüzi wenji 歷代女子文集
"Lidai xianhou gushi tu" 歷代
　　顯后故事圖
Liechao shiji 列朝詩集
Liechao shiji xiaozhuan 列朝詩集
　　小傳
Lienü zhuan 列女傳
liexin 烈心
"Liezhuan" 列傳
Li He 李賀
Li Hu 酈琥
Li ji 禮記
Li Kaixian 李開先
Li Mei 李媚
Li Meiqing 李毓清
Linchun ge 臨春閣
Lin Daiyu 林黛玉
Linqing 麟慶
"Lin Siniang" 林四娘
Lin Tiansu 林天素
Linxia cixuan 林下詞選
Linxia yayin ji 林下雅音集
linxia zhifeng 林下之風
Lin Yining 林以寧
Li Qingzhao 李清照
"Liqiu hou yiri ti cailian tu"
　　立秋後一日題採蓮圖
Li Ruzhen 李汝珍

Li sao 離騷
Li Shangyin 李商隱
Li Shiniang 李十娘
Li Suiqiu 黎遂球
Li Taibo shiji 李太白詩集
liu 柳
Liu Bang 劉邦
Liu Dajie 劉大杰
liuji 流妓
Liu Lüe 劉略
liumei 柳眉
liuruo 柳弱
Liu Rushi 柳如是
"Liu Rushi" 柳儒士
Liu Rushi biezhuan 柳如是別傳
Liu Ruzhi yishi 柳如之軼事
Liu Shi 柳是
Liu shi zhong qu 六十種曲
liusi 柳絲
Liu Xiang 劉向
Liu Xiaoyi 劉孝儀
liuxu 柳絮
liuyao (tender as willow) 柳夭
liuyao (willow-branch waist)
　柳腰
Liu Yong 柳永
Liu Yun 柳惲
Liu Yunfen 劉雲份
Liu Zongyuan 柳宗元
Li Wan 李紈
Li Xiang (or Xiangjun) 李香
　(香君)
Li Xiong 李雄
Li Xiu 李秀
Li Xu 李詡
Li Yanu 李亞奴
Li Ye (*zi* Jilan) 李冶(季蘭)
Li Yin 李因
Li Yu 李漁
Li Yuying 李玉英
"Li Yuying yuzhong songyüan"
　李玉英獄中訟冤
Li Zhenli 李貞麗
Li Zicheng 李自成
Long Muxun 龍沐勛

Long Shi 龍釋
Lü Kun 呂坤
Lunyu 論語
Luowei 絡緯
Luowei yin 絡緯吟
Lu Qingzi (*ming* Fuchang)
　陸卿子 (服常)
lü shi 律詩
Lu Shidao 陸師道
Lu Yunqing 盧雲卿
Lu Yunshi 陸雲士

Mao Guangsheng 冒廣生
Mao Jun 冒俊
Maoshi 毛詩
Maoshi zhengyi 毛詩正義
Mao Xiang 冒襄
Mao Yanshou 毛延壽
Mao Yuanyi 茅元儀
Ma Ruyu 馬如玉
Ma Shiying 馬士英
Ma Shouzhen (*zi* Xianglan)
　馬守眞 (湘蘭)
Mawei 馬嵬
"Mawei po, ni Li Changji"
　馬巍坡擬李長吉
Ma Xianglan 馬湘蘭
Ma Xianglan shengshou Bogu
　馬湘蘭生壽百穀
mei (anxiety) 痗
mei (marriage broker) 媒
mei (plum) 梅
Mei Dingzuo 梅鼎祚
Meilou 眉樓
meiren 美人
meiren hua 美人畫
"Meiren pu" 美人譜
Meiren shu 美人書
Mei Zisou 梅子廋
Meng Chang 孟昶
mengdi 盟弟
Mengzi 孟子
Miao Lianbao 妙蓮保
Mi Fu 米芾
Mi Heng 彌衡

Milou 迷樓
Minchuan guixiu shihua mingjia
    閩川閨秀詩話名家
ming (fame) 名
ming (to order) 命
Mingfeng ji 鳴鳳記
mingji 名妓
Ming sanshi jia shi xuan
    明三十家詩選
Mingshi biecai ji 明詩別裁集
Mingshi zong 明詩綜
Mingyuan cixuan 名媛詞選
Mingyuan shigui 名媛詩歸
Mingyuan shihua 名媛詩話
Mingyuan shiwei 名媛詩緯
Mingyuan shixuan 明媛詩選
Mingyuan wenwei 名媛文緯
miwu 蘼蕪
mo qi 默契
"Mudan deng ji" 牡丹燈記
"Mudan shi" 牡丹室
Mudan ting 牡丹亭
"Mudu xianji xiaozhuan" 木瀆
    仙姬小傳
"Mulan ci" 木蘭詞
Muzhai yishi 牧齋遺事
Muzuo 木作

Nanbeishi 南北史
nanci 南詞
"Nan Luoshen fu" 男洛神賦
Nanyang shi 南陽氏
Neiwufu 內務府
Nei ze 內則
ni 擬
"Niaoming jian" 鳥鳴澗
nie (malt) 糵
nie (slander, accuse) 揑
ning 凝
Ningshougong 寧壽宮
Ningshou huayuan 寧壽花園
Ningxiang shi 凝香室
"Ni Shaoling qi ge" 擬少陵七歌
Nücaizi ji 女才子集
Nücaizi shu 女才子書

nü de 女德
Nü fan bian 女范編
Nüjie 女誡
Nüsao 女騷
nüshi 女史
nüshu 女書
Nüwa 女媧
nüxia 女俠
nü xian 女仙
Nü xiao jing 女孝經
Nüxue zong 女學宗
Nü xun 女訓
nü yingxiong 女英雄
nü zhangfu 女丈夫
nüzhong caizi 女中才子
Nü zhong caizi lanke er ji 女中
    才子蘭咳二集
Nüzhong qi caizi lanke ji 女中
    七才子蘭咳集
Nü zhuangyuan cifeng dehuang
    女狀元辭鳳得凰
nüzi wucai bianshi de 女子
    無才便是德

Ouyang Xiu 歐陽修

pailü 排律
"Pang'e" 龐阿
peidian 配殿
pin 品
ping'an Du shuji 平安杜書記
pinghua 評話
Pinniang 聘娘
Pochen jushi 破塵居士
Prince Bao 寶親王
Prince Yong 雍親王
pu 譜
Pu Songling 蒲松齡
Pu Yinglu 浦映淥

qi 氣
qianchao 前朝
Qian Fenglun 錢鳳綸
qiangu shi 千古事
Qianlong 乾隆

"Qianlong xingle tu" 乾隆行樂圖
"Qiannü lihun" 倩女離魂
Qian Qianyi 錢謙益
Qian Shoupu 錢守璞
"Qianyuan zhong yuju Tonggu
    xian zuo ge qi shou"
    乾元中寓居同谷縣作歌
    七首
Qian Yue 錢岳
Qian Zhao'ao 錢肇鰲
Qian Zhen 錢珍
qiao 巧
Qiao Ji 喬吉
"Qiaoniang" 巧娘
qin 琴
qing (clear) 清
qing (feelings, emotions) 情
Qingci zong bu 清詞綜補
Qingdai funü wenxue shi 清代
    婦女文學史
Qingdai guige shiren zhenglüe 清代
    閨閣詩人徵略
Qingdai guixiu shichao 清代閨秀
    詩鈔
qingguo qingcheng 傾國傾城
Qinghuilou zhuren 清暉樓主人
qinglou 青樓
Qinglou ji 青樓集
Qingni lianhua ji 青泥蓮花記
Qingping cixuan 清平詞選
"Qingqing heban cao" 青青
    河畔草
qing shi 青史
Qingshi biecai ji 清詩別裁集
Qingshiduo 清詩鐸
Qing shi hui 清詩匯
Qing shi lei lüe 情史類略
Qingshi xuzhuan 情史續傳
qingsuo 青鎖
qingtan 清談
Qingwen 晴雯
Qingxi yinshe 清溪吟社
"Qing ying" 青蠅
Qinhuai ganjiu 秦淮感舊
Qinhuai guangji 秦淮廣記

Qinhuai he 秦淮河
Qinhuai siji shi 秦淮四姬詩
Qinhuai xiangyan congshu
    秦淮香艷叢書
Qinlou yue 秦樓月
qiqi 奇氣
"Qiujin wantiao" 秋盡晚眺
"Qiuran ke zhuan" 虬髯客傳
Qiutao(zi) 秋濤(子)
"Qiuxi fang Pipating ji" 秋夕訪
    琵琶亭記
"Qiuxi Yanyu tang huajiu
    yougan" 秋夕燕譽堂話舊
    有感
Qiu Ying 仇英
Qiyunge shichao 起雲閣詩鈔
Quan Tang shi 全唐詩
Quanxiang gujin lienü zhizhuan 全
    像古今列女誌傳
Qu Bingyun 屈秉筠

Ranzhi ji 然脂集
Ranzhi yuyun 然脂餘韻
re 惹
ren (benevolence) 仁
ren (person) 人
rencai 人才
Ren Zhaolin (*zi* Wentian, *hao*
    Linwu shanren) 任兆麟(文田,
    林屋山人)
reshen 熱審
Rixia jiuwen kao 日下舊聞考
rong 容
Rou Pingfeng 肉屏風
rouxiang 柔鄉
Ruan Dacheng 阮大鋮
Ruan Ji 阮籍
Ruan Yuan 阮元
rufeng 儒風
ruhua 入話
ru jin zai ge fu wuyan lü yi shou,
    shi wo dangmian shiguo 如今
    再各賦五言律一首、使我
    當面試過
Rulin waishi 儒林外史

runji 閏集
rushi er jian xianü 儒士而
　兼俠女
rushi wowen 如是我聞
Ryŭ Kyō Retsujoden 劉向列女傳

san 散
san'gang 三綱
Sanjia pingzhu Li Changji geshi
　三家評注李長吉歌詩
San yan 三言
sao 騷
Saoye shanfang 掃葉山房
se 色
Shangjian 上鑒
Shang Jinglan 商景蘭
"Shang Sanguan" 商三官
Shangshan sihao 商山四皓
"Shan gui" 山鬼
"Shangyi xing" 上已行
Shanhai jing 山海經
"Shanzhong wenda" 山中問答
shen 審
Shen Bitao 沈碧桃
Shen Deqian 沈德潛
Shen Fu 沈復
Sheng (life) 生
Sheng (sound) 聲
"Shengsheng ling" 聲聲令
shengyuan 生圓
Shen Huiyu 沈蕙玉
Shenliu dushu tang 深柳讀書堂
"Shennü fu" 神女賦
Shen Shanbao 沈善寶
Shen Yixiu 沈宜修
shen you cibing 身有此病
Shen Yue 沈約
Shezhi 舍之
shi 詩
shidafu 士大夫
Shi dian tou 石點頭
Shier chai 十二釵
shier jinchai 十二金釵
shier meiren 十二美人
shigu 詩骨

shihua 詩話
Shiji 史記
Shijie weiyi di nüxing wenzi
　世界唯一的女性文字
Shi jing 詩經
Shiliu lou 十六樓
Shimen 石門
Shinü shi 詩女史
Shipin 詩品
Shishuo xinyu 世說新語
Shi Shuyi 施淑儀
shiwen daguan 詩文大觀
Shi Xiangyun 史湘雲
shi yan zhi 詩言志
shi you guiqi 詩有鬼氣
Shiyuan 詩媛
Shiyuan ba mingjia ji
　詩媛八名家集
Shiyuan shi mingjia ji
　詩媛十名家集
Shi Yuchun 石雨春
Shi Zhenlin 史震林
Shi Zhicun 施蟄存
shu 疏
"Shudao nan" 蜀道難
Shunzhi 順治
Shuoyuan 說苑
Shuxiu zongji 淑秀總集
"Shu youyuan" 述幽怨
si 司
si de 四德
Sikong Tu 司空圖
Siku quanshu zongmu tiyao
　四庫全書總目提要
Sima Qian 司馬遷
Sisheng yuan 四聲猿
Song Lian 宋濂
Songluo 松蘿
"Song Meng Dongye xu"
　送孟東野序
Song shu 宋書
Song Wan 宋琬
Song Zhengru 宋徵輿
sui 崇
Sui shu 隋書

suiyuan 隨緣
Suiyuan nüdizi shixuan
　隨園女弟子詩選
Su Kunsheng 蘇崑生
Sun Huiyuan 孫惠媛
Sun Kaidi 孫楷第
Sun Lin (zi Kexian) 孫臨 (克咸)
Sun Quan 孫權
Sun Wugong 孫武公
Sun Zuofu 孫左輔
"Su Xiaoxiao mu" 蘇小小墓
Su Zhikun 蘇之琨

Taihedian 太和殿
Taihemen 太和門
Taiping guangji 太平廣記
Tanchun 探春
tanci 彈詞
Tang caizi zhuan 唐才子傳
Tang Qingmou 唐卿謀
Tang Qingyun 唐慶雲
Tangren xuan Tang shi 唐人選
　唐詩
Tangshi baihua 唐詩百話
Tangshi pinhui 唐詩品彙
Tang Xianzu 湯顯祖
Tangyin tongqian 唐音統籤
Tanji congshu 檀幾叢書
Tan Qian 談遷
Tan Youxia 譚友夏
Tan Zhengbi 譚正璧
taochan 逃禪
Tao Hong 陶宏
Taohua shan 桃花扇
"Taohua wu" 桃花塢
Tao Jingjie jizhu 陶靖節
　集注
Tao Qian 陶潛
taoye 桃葉
Taoying 桃英
Tao Zhenhuai 陶貞懷
tian 天
Tianxia mingjia shiguan chuji
　天下名家詩觀初集
Tian Xixiu 天錫秀

Tian Yiheng 田藝蘅
Tian yu hua 天雨花
"Tian Zicheng" 田子成
tibici 題壁詞
tieluo 貼落
"Ting nüdaoshi Yujing tanqin ge"
　聽女道士玉京彈琴歌
"Ti shinü tu shier shou" 題士女
　圖十二首
tongbian 通辯
tongxinjie 同心結
Tuibei tu 推背圖

"Wai qi zhuan" 外戚傳
"Wancui ting shi" 晚翠亭詩
Wang Caiwei 王采薇
Wang Daokun 汪道昆
Wang Duan 汪端
Wang Duanshu 王端淑
"Wan ge" 挽歌
Wang Gu 汪穀
Wang Guowei 王國維
wang huazan 忘華簪
"Wang Jiangnan" 望江南
Wang Pengyun 王鵬運
Wang Ranming 汪然明
Wang Shilu 王士祿
Wang Shizhen 王士禎
Wang Siren 王思任
Wang Tanzhi 王坦之
Wang Tingna 汪廷訥
Wang Wei (female) 王微
Wang Wei (male) 王維
Wang Weibo 王微波
Wang Xianzhi 王獻之
Wang Xilian 王希廉
Wang Youyun 王友雲
Wang Yan 王琰
Wang Yu 王豫
Wang Yunzhang 王允章
Wang Yuzhen 汪玉軫
Wang Zhaojun 王昭君
Wang Zhideng (zi Bogu) 王穉登
　(百穀)
Wang Zhong 汪中

Wang Zhuo 王晫
wanlian 娩戀
Wanyan Linqing 完顏麟慶
wei (screen) 幃
wei (surround) 圍
Wei Gao 韋皋
weiping 圍屏
wei wang 未亡
Wei Yong 衛泳
Wei Zhuang 韋莊
wen 文
Wen (emperor, Wei dynasty) 文
wenhua yimin 文化遺民
wenrou dunhou 溫柔敦厚
Wen Tingyun 溫庭筠
Wenxuan 文選
Wen Zhengming 文徵明
Wode tian yao hai 我的天喲咳
Wowen shi 我聞室
Woyue xuan gao 臥月軒稿
wu (insult) 侮
Wu (emperor, Qi dynasty) 武
wuchang 五常
Wugang bieji 悟岡別集
Wu Jingsuo 吳敬所
Wu Jingzi 吳敬梓
Wulin wangzhe yizhu
　　武林往哲遺著
Wumen 午門
Wumengtang quanji 午夢堂全集
Wu Qi (female) 吳琪
Wu Qi (male) 吳綺
"Wu Qiuyue" 伍秋月
Wu Sangui 吳三桂
Wu Shan 吳山
wu shang shan zhi xin
　　無傷善之心
"Wushi ganhuai" 五十感懷
wutong 梧桐
"Wutong yuan" 梧桐院
Wu Weiye (*zi* Meicun) 吳偉業
　　(梅村)
Wu Wushan 吳吳山
Wu Xiao 吳綃
wuyi 無益

Wuyin cao 戊寅草
Wu Yonghe 吳永和
Wu Zao 吳藻
Wu Zhenshan 吳震山
Wuzhong nüshi shichao
　　吳中女士詩鈔

xia e'wu 下惡物
xian 仙
xianfa 線法
"Xiangchun" 湘春
"Xiang furen" 湘夫人
Xiang Hongzuo 項鴻祚
Xiang Lanzhen 項蘭貞
Xianglian ji 香奩集
Xiangling (Yinglian) 香菱(英蓮)
xiangsi 相思
xiangsi zi 相思子
Xiang yan congshu 香艷叢書
"Xiang Yu" 香玉
Xiang Yu 項羽
Xiangzhen ge 湘眞閣
Xiangzhong cao 湘中草
xianju 閒居
"Xianqing shier wu"
　　閒情十二憮
Xiao Baojuan 蕭寶卷
Xiao Gang 蕭綱
Xiao jing 孝經
xiaopin 小品
Xiaoqing 小青
Xiaoshan 綃山
xiaosheng 小生
xiaoshuo 小說
Xiaotanluanshi huike baijia guixiu ci
　　小檀欒室彙刻百家閨秀詞
Xiao Tong 蕭統
Xiaowu (Song emperor) 孝武
Xiaoxue'an shi gao 嘯雪菴詩稿
xiao yao zi 逍遙子
Xiaoying 小鶯
"Xichun tu" 嬉春圖
xie (depravity) 邪
xie (scatter) 泄

Xie An 謝安
Xie Cai 謝彩
Xie Daoyun 謝道韞
Xie E 謝娥
Xie Tiao 謝朓
Xie Ximeng 謝希孟
Xihu sanren 西湖散人
Xijiang 西江
"Xiling" 西泠
xin (heart-mind) 心
xin (trust) 信
xingling 性靈
"Xing lu" 行露
"Xinglu nan" 行路難
"Xinhun bie" 新婚別
Xin Wenfang 辛文坊
xiong 熊
Xiongnu 匈奴
Xi Peilan 席佩蘭
Xiqing sanji 西青散記
xirong 喜容
Xishi 西施
Xitang zazu 西堂雜俎
Xiushui 秀水
Xu (Noble Consort) 徐賢妃
Xu Can 徐燦
Xue Baochai 薛寶釵
Xue Baoqin 薛寶琴
"Xue meiren" 雪美人
Xue Susu 薛素素
Xue Tao 薛濤
Xuexiulou yin gao 學繡樓吟稿
Xu Fengyi 徐風儀
Xu Fo (*zi* Yunxuan) 徐佛 (雲翾)
"Xu huizhen shi" 續會眞詩
Xu Jingfan 許景樊
Xu Ling 徐陵
Xumu 許穆
Xu Naichang 徐乃昌
Xun Fengqian 荀奉倩
Xu Quan 許權
Xu Shichang 徐世昌
Xu Shu 徐淑
Xu Shumin 徐樹敏

Xu Wufan 徐吾犯
Xu Yuan 徐媛
Xu Yunhui 許韞輝
Xu Zhen 徐震
Xu Zongyan 許宗彥

ya 雅
"Yagong" 雅供
yan 艷
Yang 楊
Yang Biqiu 楊碧秋
Yang Boda 楊伯達
Yang Chengbin 楊成彬
Yang Guifei 楊貴妃
Yang Huilin (*zi* Yunyou) 楊慧林
  (雲友)
Yang Jin 楊晉
Yang Tieya 楊鐵崖
yangu 沿古
Yang Wan (*zi* Wanshu) 楊宛
  (宛叔)
Yang Wencong 楊文聰
Yangxian 陽羨
Yan Jidao 晏幾道
Yanshui sanren 煙水散人
Yan Song 嚴嵩
Yan Weixu 宴維旭
Yanzi jian 燕子箋
Yaohua ji 瑤華集
ye 冶
Ye Shaoyuan 葉紹袁
Ye Wanwan 葉紈紈
Ye Xiaoluan 葉小鸞
Ye Xiaowan 葉小紈
yi 義
Yi De 懿德
yi gui 異軌
Yijian zhi 夷堅志
yin (dark) 陰
yin (polluted) 淫
yin du 陰毒
Yingmei an yiyu 影梅庵憶語
Ying wu zhou 鸚鵡洲
"Yingying zhuan" 鶯鶯傳

Yinhong ji 吟紅集
Yi Nianhua 義年華
Yin Jishan 尹繼善
yin qi 陰氣
Yinwen 隱雯
yinyu Zhangtai liu 隱于章台柳
Yinzhen 胤禎
Yiren si 伊人思
yishu 異書
yi tu 異途
yiyu 憶語
Yiyunci binggao xu
　　憶雲詞丙稿序
"Yiyun fenghe" 依韻奉合
Yizhong yuan 意中緣
yong 詠
"Yonggu er shou" 詠古二首
yonghuai 詠懷
yongshi 詠史
Yongshi lu 詠史錄
Yongwangfu 雍王府
"Yong wanju" 詠晚菊
yongwu 詠物
yongwu shi 詠物詩
Yongzheng 雍正
you (have) 有
you (mysterious) 幽
"Youhen shi" 幽恨詩
youhuan 幽歡
youhun 幽婚
"Youmei shi yibai yun"
　　有美詩一百韻
youqing 幽情
"You suosi" 有所思
You Tong 尤侗
youxian 遊仙
Youxuan ji 又玄集
Youxue ji 有學集
yu (pent up) 鬱
Yu (sage) 虞
yuan 怨
Yuan Haowen 元好問
Yu'an hen chuanqi 玉庵恨
　　傳奇

"Yuanjing shier yong"
　　園景十二詠
Yuan Mei 袁枚
Yuanming yuan 圓明園
Yuanming zhuren 圓明主人
Yuan Ming yishi 元明遺史
Yuan shi yi quan 袁氏義犬
"Yuan xing" 怨行
"Yuan yichen shi" 元遺臣史
"Yuanyuan qu" 圓圓曲
Yuan Zhen 元稹
yueding 閱定
yuefu 樂府
Yuefushi ji 樂府詩集
yueman qingyou 月曼清游
"Yuerong bian" 悅容編
"Yue ye" 月夜
Yueying 月英
Yu Huai 余懷
Yu huan ji 玉環記
yujie 鬱結
yujin 玉津
Yujuan 玉娟
Yuncha waishi 雲槎
　　外史
Yunjian 雲間
Yunjuan 雲娟
Yun Shouping 惲壽平
Yun Zhu 惲珠
Yu Qi 于七
Yutai xinyong 玉臺新詠
Yuxiao 玉簫
Yu Xian 愈憲
Yu Xuanji 魚玄機

Zai sheng yuan 再生緣
zaju 雜劇
Zaolin zazu 棗林雜俎
"Zaomei" 早梅
Zha Changyuan 查長鵷
zhan 沾
Zhang Chao 張潮
Zhang Dai 張岱
Zhang Fengyi 張鳳翼

Zhang Hongbin 章鴻賓
Zhang Hongqiao 張紅橋
Zhang Huangyan 張煌言
Zhang Lihua 張麗華
Zhang Lizhen 張麗貞
Zhang Mengzhan 張夢覘
Zhang Shicheng 張士誠
Zhang Wanxian (*zi* Xiangyin) 張宛仙 (香隱)
Zhang Wanxiang 張畹香
Zhang Wanyu 張宛玉
"Zhang Wu ji shi shi" 張吳紀史詩
Zhang Xiaojiao 張小腳
Zhang Xiaolian 張小蓮
Zhang Xie 張協
Zhang Xiuyuan 張修園
Zhang Xuecheng 張學誠
Zhang Yingchang 張應昌
"Zhang Yunrong" 張雲容
Zhang Yunzi (*zi* Zilan) 張允滋 (滋蘭)
Zhao, Duke of 昭公
Zhaodai congshu 昭代叢書
Zhao Feiyan 趙飛燕
Zhao Fengqi 趙鳳岐
Zhao Yiguang (*zi* Fanfu) 趙宧光 (凡夫)
Zhao Shijie 趙世杰
Zhao Shiyong 趙時用
Zhao Wenhua 趙文華
Zhao Yanru 趙燕如
"Zhaoyun" 朝雲
Zhen (empress) 甄
zhen (genuine) 眞
zhen (purity) 貞
zheng (proper) 正
zheng (strife) 箏
Zheng Fen 鄭蕡
Zheng Guangzu 鄭光祖
Zheng Ruying (*zi* Wumei, alias Tuoniang) 鄭如英 (無美、妥娘)
Zheng Tuoniang zaju 鄭妥娘雜劇

Zheng Xiu 鄭袖
Zheng Yingni (Baoxian) 鄭應尼 (豹先)
Zheng Yuji 鄭玉姬
Zheng Zhenduo 鄭振鐸
zhen nü 貞女
Zhenpu 珍浦
zhenshen 眞身
Zhenzhong mi 枕中秘
zhi 智
zhiguai 志怪
zhi qing 致情
Zhi Ruzeng 支如璔
Zhiyanzhai 脂硯齋
Zhiyi 鴟夷
Zhizhi tan'er 質直談耳
Zhong Fei 鐘斐
"Zhong feng" 終風
Zhong Hong/Rong 鍾嶸
Zhong qing li ji 鍾情麗集
Zhongxiang ci 眾香詞
Zhong Xing 鍾惺
Zhongxingjian qi ji 中興間氣集
Zhongyong 中庸
Zhongzhou ji 中州集
Zhou 周
Zhou Chun 周春
Zhou Daodeng 周道登
Zhou Dunyi 周敦頤
Zhou Ming 周銘
Zhou Qi 周綺
Zhou Shouchang 周壽昌
Zhou Yu 周瑜
Zhou Zhibiao 周之標
Zhuang Jiang 莊姜
Zhuang Tao 莊濤
Zhu Baoguo gong 朱保國公
Zhu He 朱鶴
Zhu Jia 朱家
Zhu Jing'an 朱靜庵
Zhu Jingsu 朱景素
Zhuozheng yuan shiji 拙政園詩集
Zhu Peng 朱彭
zhuren 主人

Zhu Rouzi 朱柔則
zhuwei (principal place) 主位
zhuwei (whisk) 麈尾
Zhu Wuxia 朱無瑕
Zhu Xi 朱熹
Zhu Yizun 朱彝尊
Zhu Youdun 朱有燉
"Zhuzi yuan" 竹子院

Zichai ji 紫釵記
Ziran haoxue zhai ji
    自然好學齋集
zi yin 慈蔭
Zong Yuanding 宗元鼎
Zou Siyi 鄒斯漪
Zou Zaiheng 鄒在衡
zuli 族里

Index

In this index an "f" after a number indicates a separate reference on the next page, and an "ff" indicates separate references on the next two pages. A continuous discussion over two or more pages is indicated by a span of page numbers, e.g., "57–59." *Passim* is used for a cluster of references in close but not consecutive sequence. The entries are alphabetized letter by letter, ignoring word and syllable breaks, with the exception of personal names, which are ordered first under the surname and then under the given name.

He Liangjun, 108

He Shuangqing, 10–11; anthologized song lyrics of, 264, 464–
65n1; as male construct, 264–65,
274, 465nn2–3; problematic
fictionalization of, 265–66, 278,
465n7, 466n18; and *Xiqing sanji*,
268–70; Shi Zhenlin's chronicling
of, 270–73; as *jiaren* ideal, 273–74;
literati's interest in, 275–76, 277;
poetic self-construction of, 276–
78; metaphorical/literal
elimination of, 280–81

He Yuying, 190

Hedong jun zhuan (Gu Ling), 60

Heke (composite compilations), 165–
67. *See also* Anthologies

Heroic action symbolism, 19, 69f

Hobsbawm, Eric, 416

Homeopathic magic, 135

Hong Mai, 255, 462n32

Hong Sheng, 254, 461n27

Hongfu (Ming female warrior), 30

Hong jiao ji (Red plantain
collection), 425n4

Hong lou fumeng (*Hong lou meng*
resumed, Nanyang shi), 393

Hong lou meng (Dream of the red
chamber, Cao Xueqin), 4, 7, 72,
268; feminized spaces of, 11, 316–
18, 323, 360–63; women's interest
in, 12, 366, 368, 391, 416; examination parodies in, 286, 288–89,
467n4; lantern riddles of, 286,
288–90; *yongwu* allegorizing
mode of, 290–95, 296–97; Xue
Baoqin's role in, 295–96, 297;
"Poems on the Past" of, 295–305
passim; plum tree poems of, 296f,
469n28; Qing court art and, 307;
changed title of, 309, 470n1;
architectural imagery of, 310–11,
313–15; and Wang Duan's circle,
384–86, 389–91, 416, 475n39,
475n42; poetic reaction to, 385–

89, 390; lacking feminine
authority, 389, 395–96, 407–8,
409; male narrative authority of,
389, 392; *Jinghua yuan's* link to,
389–90; authorship of sequels to,
393. *See also* Feminine space;
Meiren; Twelve beauties

Hong lou meng tu yong (Pictures on
Hong lou meng, with Encomiums,
Gai Qi), 386–87, 389

Hong lou meng ying (Shadows of
Hong lou meng, Gu Taiqing), 12,
368, 393–96, 476n65, 477n66,
477n71

Hongxiang guan shici cao (Draft
poetry and lyrics of Red
Fragrance Hall, Yun Zhu), 384

Hot Weather Assizes (*reshen*), 228

Hou Fangyu, 26, 57, 69, 71, 351,
434n68, 434n73

Hou Zhi, 375, 473n13, 477n66

Hsia, C. T., 243, 476n52

Hu Fangkui, 465–66n13

Hu Shi, 265

Hu Wenkai, 4f, 153, 425n3

Hu Ying, 441n41

Hua Guangsheng: popular songs
collection of, 35–42

Huacao cuibian (Chen Yaowen),
462n37

"Huadi shiyi" (Gleaning beneath
the flowers, Li Suiqiu), 326–27,
359

Huaigu (cherishing the past) poems,
193–94, 297–305 *passim*

Huang Dezhen, 442n65

Huang Hong, 187

Huang Juan, 325

Huang Shangwen, 235

Huang Yuanjie, 128f, 156, 159, 370f,
379, 474n26

Huang Zongxi, 6

Huangtaiji, 354

Huayang sangao (Random essays of
Huayang, Shi Zhenlin), 269

"Meditation on the Past: In Jade Effusion Garden" (Qian Fenglun), 193–94, 451–52n28, 452nn29–30

Mei Dingzuo, 27, 31, 256, 462n35, 464n60

Mei Zisou, 21

Meiren (beauty): Xu Yuan's usage of, 92f, 438n45; as stereotype, 306–7; constructed feminine space of, 324–25; Qing manuals on, 326–28, 359–60, 361f, 470n9; iconographical features of, 326–29, 330, 359–60; as sets of historical women, 330–31, 337–38, 470–71n10, 471nn11–13; palace lady persona of, 349–50; courtesan/concubine persona of, 350–51; Qing dynasty's portrayal of, 351–52, 354–58, 363, 472n27. *See also* Twelve beauties

Meiren hua ("beautiful-woman" paintings), 329–30. *See also* Paintings

"Meiren pu" (Manual of beautiful women, Xu Zhen), 327–29, 359

Memorials, 228

Meng Chang, 451n24

Mentoring, 20–21, 104–5, 375–76, 474n17

Mi Fu, 347

Mi Heng, 58

Miller, J. Hillis, 451n25

Mill on the Floss (Eliot), 417

Milou (House of labyrinths), 53–54, 97, 438n57

Milton, John, 402–3

Min De'er, 99

Minchuan guixiu shihua, 167

Ming, Tang Emperor, 298

Ming dynasty (1368–1644), 1–2, 9f; eulogized demise of, 19, 25–26, 27–29, 47–48, 67; faded appeal of, 42, 428n34; poetry anthology of, 160, 165. *See also* Late imperial China

Mingfeng ji (Singing phoenix, Wang Shizhen), 57, 432n40

Mingji (famous prostitute), 18. *See also* Courtesans

Ming loyalism: courtesans' ties to, 6–7, 19, 25–26, 69–70, 86, 370; of Yu Huai, 41–42, 49, 429n9; of Liu Rushi, 69–70, 370; of Qian Qianyi, 155–56; of Wang Duan, 168, 367–68, 378–79, 412, 415–16, 474n25; and *huaigu* poems, 193–94; and women's writing innovations, 366, 367–68, 370, 373–74; of Wang Duanshu, 367–74 *passim*, 411–12; of gentry women, 370–71, 410; and revived literary genres, 374–75

Ming sanshi jia shixuan (Selected poems of 30 Ming poets, ed. Wang Duan), 168–69, 377–78, 381, 474n20

Mingshi biecai ji (ed. Shen Deqian), 148

Mingshi zong (Collected Ming poetry, ed. Zhu Yizun), 148, 156, 222–23

Mingyi lei'an (Classified case histories of famous physicians), 245, 460–61n16

Mingyuan cixuan (Song lyrics by notable ladies, ed. Zha Changyuan), 185

Mingyuan shigui (Poems by famous beauties, ed. Zhong Xing), 88, 151–52, 154f, 223, 230, 437n34, 438n46, 455n11, 462n34

Mingyuan shihua (Remarks on the poetry of notable ladies, Shen Shanbao), 189, 394, 476n60

Mingyuan shiwei (Classic poetry by famous women, ed. Wang Duanshu), 5, 379, 412, 462n38; organization of, 87, 158–59, 162,

257, 425n6, 445n40; as comprehensive compilation, 157–58, 169, 287, 467n7; canonical status of, 158, 445n37; personal/literary significance of, 372–73, 374

Mingyuan shixuan (Poems by notable ladies, ed. Zha Changyuan), 184

Mingyuan wenwei (ed. Wang Duanshu), 157

Miscellaneous Records of the Wooden Bridge (Yu Huai), see *Banqiao zaji*

Modernization era: genealogy of authorial identity in, 399–403; gender essentialism and, 403–4, 422; domestic fiction and, 409–10, 413–14, 417–18; Butterfly fiction and, 418–21. *See also* May Fourth era

Mountain Songs, see *Shan'ge*

Mudan ting (Peony pavilion, Tang Xianzu): *Ying wu zhou* and, 102, 113, 115, 120–21, 137, 441n37; female readership of, 124–25, 242–43; female ghosts of, 243, 247, 250, 254, 262, 461n19

"Mulan ci" (Song of Mulan), 214–16, 454nn57–58

Mulvey, Laura, 468n19

Music Bureau tradition, 28

Names: as self-definition, 55–57, 432nn38–39

Name the Candidate (game), 83–84

Nanjing courtesan quarters, 74–75, 77, 82–83, 352, 435n1. *See also* Qinhuai River district

Nan Keji (Story of Nan Ke, Tang Xianzu), 113

Nanyang shi, 393

Nationalism: domestic fiction and, 409–10, 413

Neijing (The inner classic), 248

New Songs from the Jade Terrace, see *Yutai xinyong*

Nie Chongzheng, 470n5

"Ni Shaoling qi ge" (In the manner of Shaoling's "Seven Songs," Shen Huiyu), 197, 452n33

Niu Yuqiao, 68

Nostalgia: literati's expression of, 19, 25–29, 44f; in courtesan poetry, 29–31, 427n22; as fusion of historical/personal past, 47, 48–49, 72; of twentieth-century writers, 50–52; and *huaigu* poems, 193–94, 297–305 *passim*; Ming loyalism and, 415–16

Novel, the, 409. *See also* Domestic fiction

Nücaizi shu (A book of talented women, Xu Zhen), 328, 330–31, 470nn9–10

Nü fan bian (Rules for women, ed. Feng Ruzong), 222, 235f, 238, 455n3

Nü jie (Instructions for women, Ban Zhao), 106, 449n14

Nüsao (Female Sao, ed. Zhao Shiyong), 150

Nüshi (lady scholar), 80, 436n15

Nüshu (women's script), 167–68, 446nn66–67

Nüxia appellation, 60–63

Nü xun (Instructions for women), 114

Nüzhong qi caizi lanke ji (ed. Zhou Zhibiao), 154

Ōki Yasushi, 8–9, 13

Oral tradition, 167–68, 446nn66–67

Ouyang Xiu, 444n2

Owen, Stephen, 427n9

Pailü form, 193, 451n27

Paintings: *meiren* images in, 325, 329–30, 355–57; of historical women, 330–31, 471nn11–12; of

"Twelve Concubines of the Yongzheng Emperor," *see* "Screen of Twelve Beauties"
"Twelve golden hairpins" (*shier jinchai*), 307, 323. See also *Meiren;* Twelve beauties

Unfiliality: crime of, 231f, 234, 456n29
"Up at night" motif, 202–3

Victimhood, *see* Bondage
Virtue: anthologies' rankings of, 5–6, 9, 88, 169, 425–26nn6–8; Confucian hierarchies of, 105–6, 110f, 272, 465nn12–13; discourse of literature and, 183–91 *passim*, 277–78, 450n18, 466n16; and memorial of Li Yuying, 231–38 *passim; gangchang* principle of, 232
"Voicing the Feminine" (Robertson), 442n66

Waltner, Ann, 10, 466n16
Wang Caiwei, 166, 215–16
Wang Daokun, 112
Wang Duan, 166, 396, 420; editing projects of, 168–69, 376–78, 412, 474n20, 474nn20–21; revived loyalist themes of, 367–68, 378–79, 412, 415–16, 474n25; *Yuan Ming yishi,* 368, 378–79, 380–82, 391, 475n34, 476n53; background of, 376; and Liang Desheng, 379–80; poetical histories of, 381–82; and Jin Yi, 385; and Qian Shoupu, 385–86; and Gu Taiqing, 393–94
Wang Duanshu: anthology of, 87, 156, 396, 420; male friendships of, 157, 445n33; Ming loyalism of, 367–74 *passim*, 411–12; "Biography of an Idle Tippler," 369–70; in literary community,

371, 473nn5–6; cultural authority of, 411, 415; and feminine verse, 411–12. See also *Mingyuan shiwei*
Wang Gu, 163
Wang Mengruan, 299
Wang Pengyun, 166–67
Wang Qiong, 474n20
Wang Qishu, 257
Wang Qisun, 473–74n16
Wang Ranming, 54, 60, 66, 431n29, 432n42, 433n63, 436n13, 436n15
Wang Shilu, 156, 445n23
Wang Shizhen, 27–28, 31, 41, 151, 257
Wang Shunu, 426n1
Wang Siren, 157, 368
Wang Tanzhi, 29
Wang Tingna, 112, 125
Wang Wei: rankings of virtue of, 5f, 158–59, 425nn6–7; as recluse, 71, 434n71; as "lady scholar," 80–82; anthologies' inclusion of, 88, 154f, 160; and Xiang Lanzhen, 89–90; "Niaoming jian," 203; *huaigu* poems of, 302; boat imagery of, 431n28
Wang Weibo, 85
Wang Xianzhi, 298
Wang Xilian, 386, 389
Wang Yangming, 110–11
Wang Youyun, 79, 436n13
Wang Yuzhen, 163
Wang Zhaojun, 298, 302, 304, 356–57
Wang Zhideng, 62, 67
Wang Zhong, 66–67
Wang Zhuo, 328
Wang Zilan, 435n6
Wanli era, 137
Wanshou Tangren jueju (Ten thousand Tang quatrains, Hong Mai), 255, 462n32
Wanshu zaji (Shen Bang), 458n46
Wanyan Linqing, 384, 451n23
Weeping willow (*liu*), 344–45, 347

Library of Congress Cataloging-in-Publication Data

Writing women in late imperial China / edited by Ellen Widmer and Kang-i
    Sun Chang.
        p.   cm.
    Includes bibliographical references and index.
    ISBN 0-8047-2871-2 (cl: alk paper)   ISBN 0-8047-2872-0 (pbk: alk. paper)
    1. Chinese literature—History and criticism.   2. Chinese literature—Women
authors—History and criticism.   3. Women and literature—China.   I. Widmer,
Ellen.   II. Chang, Kang-i Sun, 1944–
PL2264.W72   1997
895.1' 099287' 0903 — dc20   96-30597
                                                                                          CIP

♾ This book is printed on acid-free paper

Original printing 1997

Last figure below indicates year of this printing

06   05   04   03   02   01   00   99   98   97